Legal Aspects of
CORRECTIONS MANAGEMENT

FOURTH EDITION

DARYL KOSIAK, JD

Regional Counsel (Retired)
Federal Bureau of Prisons
Adjunct Instructor
Northern State University
Aberdeen, South Dakota

JONES & BARTLETT
LEARNING

World Headquarters
Jones & Bartlett Learning
5 Wall Street
Burlington, MA 01803
978-443-5000
info@jblearning.com
www.jblearning.com

Jones & Bartlett Learning books and products are available through most bookstores and online booksellers. To contact Jones & Bartlett Learning directly, call 800-832-0034, fax 978-443-8000, or visit our website, www.jblearning.com.

48406-9

Production Credits
VP, Product Development: Christine Emerton
Director of Product Management: Laura Pagluica
Product Manager: Sophie Teague
Content Strategist: Tess Sackmann
Content Coordinator: Paula Gregory
Project Manager: Jessica deMartin
Project Specialist: David Wile
Digital Project Specialist: Rachel DiMaggio
Marketing Manager: Suzy Balk
VP, Manufacturing and Inventory Control: Therese Connell

Composition: Exela Technologies
Project Management: Exela Technologies
Cover Design: Kristin E. Parker
Text Design: Kristin E. Parker
Media Development Editor: Faith Brosnan
Rights Specialist: James Fortney
Cover Image (Title Page, Part Opener, Chapter Opener):
  © EJ_Rodriquez/iStock/Getty Images Plus/Getty Images
Printing and Binding: McNaughton & Gunn

Library of Congress Cataloging-in-Publication Data
Library of Congress Cataloging-in-Publication Data unavailable at time of printing.

LCCN: 2020923179

6048

Printed in the United States of America
25 24 23 22 21   10 9 8 7 6 5 4 3 2 1

This 4th Edition of *Legal Aspects of Corrections Management*
is dedicated to Clair A. Cripe, 1935-2020, in recognition of his
contributions to the field of correctional law.

Brief Contents

PART 3   **Statutory and Administrative Law, Jails, Juveniles,
Privatization, and Other Special Issues in Corrections   311**

Contents

PART 3 Statutory and Administrative Law, Jails, Juveniles, Privatization, and Other Special Issues in Corrections   311

Chapter 19   Federal Statutes: Equal Employment, Disabilities, and Tort Claims **327**

Chapter 20   Jails **355**

Preface to the 4th Edition

This is the fourth edition of *Legal Aspects of Corrections Management*, and while the first edition was published over 20 years ago, many of the critical issues related to correctional law remain the same, spanning some 60 years of case law development. This edition is an updated discussion of the law, which most forcefully impacts the operations of corrections. It is a voluminous body of law—court cases, statutes, regulations, and standards. And it is a body of law that continues to evolve, expand, and become more complex.

By far the most important legal influences and constraints on corrections are those coming from the courts. The book presents an introduction to the workings of the courts, with an emphasis on Supreme Court decisions, as these decisions define corrections law throughout the country. First, there is a description of how the legal system works in the United States, the nature of the criminal justice system, and how legal conflicts and issues get into courts. In those organizational respects, there has been little change over recent years. How the courts have ruled upon those legal complaints that are brought to them is the main focus of the book.

The law of the U.S. Constitution is the major thrust of judicial actions in this area. Those constitutional rulings form the central part of the book. The Supreme Court has provided guidelines on most areas where the practices of corrections are impacted by provisions of the Constitution. This fourth edition presents those governing Supreme Court decisions. Plus, it updates the case law with recent court rulings, including applications of the Supreme Court's guidance by courts at lower levels. The updated edition also contains expanded examples of state corrections policy, updates in such areas as interstate compacts and collateral consequences of convictions, and discussions of employee law and standards of conduct.

To some extent in reaction to those court rulings, the legislative branches of federal, state and local government (particularly the U.S. Congress) have enacted statutes that regulate and circumscribe correctional practices, as well as the very basic aspect of going to court. This edition presents that group of recent enactments. Congress has delegated the authority to operate federal correctional facilities to the Attorney General (18 U.S.C 4001). However, Congress still exercises great control over federal prisons by enacting statutes that govern the Bureau of Prisons (BOP), the BOP's budget, and the federal prison population. The great majority of persons under correctional supervision in the United States are supervised by state and local governments, and in some areas, private contractors working with governmental correctional agencies.

In creating this updated edition of the text, I was able to expand on the excellent work of Clair A. Cripe and Michael G. Pearlman, the co-authors of the earlier editions. Clair's contributions to the field of correctional law, with his hands-on experience as a correctional attorney, included significant time as the General Counsel for the Federal Bureau of Prisons. As a practicing correctional lawyer during the beginning of the prisoner rights revolution, Clair had a view of the field of correctional law from its inception. In this respect, his contributions and observations not only helped shape the law but also how at least one correctional agency responded to changes in law. Important aspects of these contributions included an astute understanding of the thinking of judges on the federal bench, and crafting legally sound policies and procedures, which were responsive to correctional needs. As Clair himself noted in the Preface to the First Edition of this text:

> *I was there with those hard-nosed wardens and commissioners of the 1960s when the first cases came down, which required revision of practices that had been assumed to be solidly justified, impervious to outside review.*

Mike Pearlman added additional depth based on his experience working in prisons, his legal training and work, and his teaching in a college and university setting.

Daryl Kosiak

Acknowledgments

We would like to thank the following reviewers for their input in the revision of this text:

Regena Weatherford, Chaffey Community College
Kelly Henderson, Langston University
Gary Kowaluk, Lincoln University
Adrienne C. Watts, County Community College District
Kyle R. Reimann, JD University of Wisconsin—Platteville
Raleem Broadhead-Moses, John Jay College
David C. Cannon, Henry Ford College
Christopher Irwin, Fresno State
Regina Armstrong, Olivet College
Nigel Cohen, Sam Houston State University
Reginald Clemons, Taft Community College
Ryan Maring, Baker College

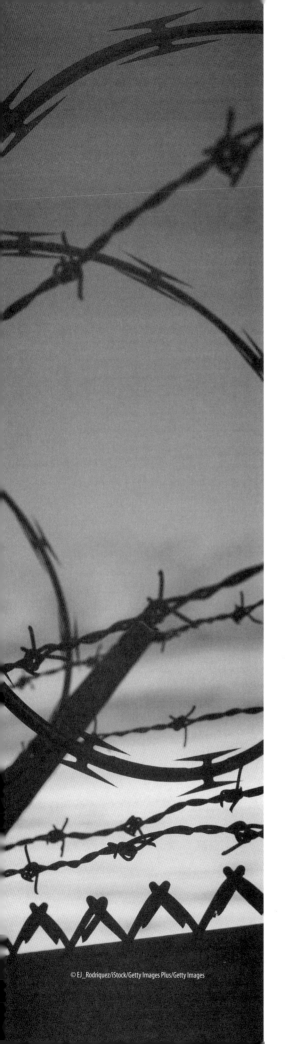

PART 1

Sources of Corrections Law

Part I (Chapters 1 through 4) examines the background of corrections and of the law. Chapter 1 provides a brief introduction, reviews the organization of the text, and looks at a broad and general history of the law and how our legal system in the United States works. In Chapter 2, the focus is on the criminal justice system—looking at the field of corrections and how it fits into the bigger criminal justice picture and the different components that make up the field of corrections. Chapter 3 focuses on the specific legal provisions that are most often encountered in corrections litigation. The chapter also examines the types of legal actions that are most often used by prisoners or other offenders to complain about their conditions and treatment. Chapter 4 discusses, the legal steps that occur in a corrections lawsuit.

Virtually any kind of corrections activity performed in any of the various corrections agencies and facilities may be the subject of a lawsuit. The first part of the text sets the stage for a better understanding of what "corrections law" means, where it comes from, and how it affects the individual corrections worker. These introductory chapters describe the sources of this area of the law. The sources are found in American law itself and in its intersection with the practical workings of corrections agencies, in their huge variety and complexity.

CHAPTER 1

An Introduction to the Law and to the Legal Aspects of Corrections Management

The judicial Power of the United States, shall be vested in one supreme Court, and in such inferior Courts as the Congress may from time to time ordain and establish.

U.S. Constitution, Article III, Section 1

CHAPTER OUTLINE

- Organization of the Text
- The Law
- Historic Origins
- Branches of Government
- The Court System
  - Federal Courts
  - State Courts
- Criminal and Civil Law

The purpose of this text is to acquaint the reader with the legal complexities of the correctional component of the criminal justice system in the United States. While the correctional system is impacted by many factors, the most significant, and the one factor that has changed dramatically, is the impact of the law and judicial opinions on correctional policies and practices. Since the 1960s, the law has had more of an impact on corrections than any other factor or force. More than new programs. More than research. More than studies and developments in criminology, rehabilitation methods, or any theories of punishment and sentencing. The law has also had more of an impact on corrections than management theory and even new technologies.

Court rulings have directly impacted the operations of corrections facilities. They have also changed the way managers have had to think about their decision making, on matters great and small. In setting their priorities in running institutions and community programs, corrections administrators must take legal considerations into account. This means that, from academic study to the day-to-day work of the corrections officer, legal rulings have been absorbed into the corrections field.

It has not been easy for corrections professionals to accommodate the legal "intrusions." Corrections professionals know their business. They know what the problems are and what needs to be done. The last thing they ever wanted was a bunch of uninformed, or ill-informed, outsiders (that is how corrections workers saw the lawyers and the judges) to make their work more complicated and unpredictable.

As the legal "revolution" in corrections occurred, particularly in the 1960s and 1970s, corrections managers resented the intrusion of the law into their work. That resentment was deep-seated and bitter. With time, most of the corrections managers understood that they needed advice that would help them get along with the courts with the least possible confrontation and the least amount of outside intrusion. Inmate litigation became endemic and, for most people working in adult corrections, litigation was accepted as an inevitable part of corrections operations and management.

Those established, hard-nosed administrators and workers of the 1960s and 1970s are now retired from the profession. They have been replaced by managers who, from the time they came to work, had to face the realities of litigation and court involvement. Some current corrections administrators would prefer the simpler task of running prisons and jails without legal intrusions, but they know that this is not possible in the world of corrections in the United States. (I am careful to specify "in the United States," because, to my knowledge, no other country experiences anything close to the level of involvement of the courts in corrections that occurs in this country.)

This brings us to the purpose of writing this text. It is designed to serve as a teaching reference for those who are going to work in corrections or those who want to know more about this part of the criminal justice field. At the same time, it should serve as a reference tool for today's corrections workers who need, and want, to know what they must do to run corrections facilities with minimal legal entanglements.

I began working in corrections in the 1980s with some of the previously mentioned old-line wardens and commissioners who were working in the 1960s when the first "prisoners' rights" cases were decided. The court decisions required corrections administrators to revise practices that had been considered solidly justified and immune to outside review. It was not easy being a corrections lawyer, preaching a new sermon of caution and concern based on a scripture of constitutionality. Corrections lawyers were often disliked, even though they worked for the government and were proposing what was considered to be best for the protection of corrections principles and corrections workers.

In the intervening decades since the prisoners' rights revolution began in the 1960s, thousands of lawsuits and hundreds of court decisions have defined legal constraints on corrections policies and practices. For example, in the twelve-month period ending on March 31, 2018, 26,650 prisoner civil rights and prison conditions lawsuits were filed in the 94 United States District Courts.[1] Most importantly, the U.S. Supreme Court, over time, has produced (at the rate of about one or two decisions per year) the central constitutional guidelines.

There is an expression that "prisons reflect society"; this refers to the view that what a person sees in the "free world" exists in some form or other within the correctional environment. Accordingly, there is no aspect of correctional life and work, to my knowledge, that has not been the subject of litigation. Over time, many areas have been ruled to be outside of the realm of judicial review. This text focuses on those areas that are inside that realm: those areas in which lawyers and judges will insist upon compliance with constitutional or other legal standards.

▶ Organization of the Text

This text presents the accumulated legal developments (limitations) in a format that is created with the corrections practitioner in mind. It begins with general discussions of what the law is and in what areas it interfaces with corrections. Most of the text is a detailed presentation of what the law has said about specific areas of corrections operations and practices.

First, we look at the background of corrections and of the law. Next, we look at constitutional law—those areas of corrections work in which different provisions of the U.S. Constitution have been examined to see whether they define or limit what may be done by corrections officials. In many areas, there are now Supreme Court decisions that provide the authoritative word and interpret the U.S. Constitution on corrections issues. This is one of the most exciting aspects of corrections. The following provisions of the U.S. Constitution will be covered:

- Inmate access to the courts
- The First Amendment: inmate correspondence, inmate association rights, visiting, and religion
- The Fourth Amendment: search and seizure and privacy
- The due process provisions of the Fifth and Fourteenth Amendments, as they apply to such areas as inmate discipline, classification, transfers, personal injuries, and property loss
- The Fourteenth Amendment Equal Protection clause
- The Eighth Amendment as it applies to the death penalty and other sentencing issues, conditions of confinement, cruel and unusual punishment, and health care

Our look at constitutional law also includes a discussion of probation and parole, community corrections, and fines. Finally, we will look at law that governs corrections by means other than the Constitution and at corrections issues that are somewhat outside of the central core of managing prisons.

For each subject covered, there are other resources to assist the reader with understanding the material, along with a general summary and "Thinking About It" questions, which are relevant to the covered material. To help you find important statements of the law as you look through this text, holdings of cases and statements of important legal principles are given in boldface font. On every Supreme Court opinion, you can expect to find a boldface presentation of the important statements of the Court in that case. In the text, use of the word Court refers to the U.S. Supreme Court. If there are such important statements of the law in other cases (or in statutes), these will be presented in boldface font as well.

A glossary of key terms that defines words and terms that are often found in corrections, criminal justice, or the law is located near the end of the text. The glossary is followed by an alphabetical listing of cases. The Table of Cases also provides the page number(s) where the case can be found within the text.

We note that throughout the text, the words *he* and *she* and the words *his* and *her* are used interchangeably. The use of these terms reflects the significant number of women working in the corrections field. During 2005, women accounted for 33% of the employees in correctional facilities under state or federal authority (Stephan, 2005).[2]

My hope is that this text will serve as a handy reference to the corrections professional and as a valuable teaching resource for the criminal justice professor and student. It must be understood that this text is a digest—it distills into a comparatively small volume what has become an overwhelmingly large body of law. The goal has been to make this text an understandable collection of essential and representative court decisions, combined with some background on the various aspects of corrections on which those decisions touch.

▶ The Law

What is the law? Legal scholars do not agree on definitions. A generally accepted definition of the law is the set of principles and rules established to determine the rights and duties of the people of a state (*state* is used here in the sense of any level of autonomous government) and to resolve disputes among those people. The law has binding legal force.

Central to nearly all legal systems, and certainly to ours in the United States, is the judiciary. **Courts** are the voice of legal authority. The courts interpret and administer the laws, and determine the specific rights and duties of persons within the jurisdiction. Note that the courts are central to the legal system of government, not to all of government. There are three branches of government, and each branch is theoretically of equal importance.

▶ Historic Origins

American law mainly comes from English law, which in turn comes historically from Roman law, with some influences from the Normans, the Scandinavians, and church (**canon**) law. After the American Revolution, in the late 1700s, there was a reaction against many things English, including legal decisions and procedures. Generally law in the United States adopted English concepts and legal language. Louisiana is an exception due to its French law tradition, until today. Several southwestern and western states include a Spanish influence, particularly in property matters.

English law relied very heavily on the decrees, orders (sometimes called **writs**), and **decisions** of its judges. Together, these judicial pronouncements constitute the **common law**.[3] In English law, there was equity law alongside common law. **Equity** dealt with matters of "doing the right thing" (keeping the "King's conscience"), particularly in hardship cases. Separate courts, called **chancery courts**, handled equity matters. In equity cases, courts ordered specific performance or injunction rather than money damages, and they developed maxims rather than decisions. Equity was used when common law did not provide an adequate remedy.[4] Equity law was also taken from English law and incorporated into American law. However, in most jurisdictions in the United States, equity and common law have been merged, so that both kinds of cases are heard in the same courts. As part of the revolutionary break from English rule in 1776, the former colonies, now states, adopted written **constitutions** as the prime statement and source of the law. The same was done for the federal government in the "supreme law" of the land, the U.S. Constitution. The reliance on written constitutions was the most significant break from English legal tradition because Britain does not have a codified constitution. Today, it is still the most significant difference between English and American law, which are in most other respects closely related.

▶ Branches of Government

The constitutions of the United States and of each of the individual states establish three branches of government:

1. The legislature, which enacts laws
2. The executive branch, which enforces and carries out the laws
3. The judiciary, which interprets and applies the laws

These very basic descriptions of the functions of the three branches do not take into account some governmental activities that do not fall clearly into one category or another. For the purpose of this text, however, these broad definitions describe the basis for the activities of government and the conflicts that almost inevitably come out of them.

The functions of the three branches of government also give rise to two important principles of our American government. The first is the **separation of powers**, which holds that each branch should perform its own function and should not intrude into the functions of the other two independent branches. The second major principle is one of **checks and balances**, which establishes, by constitutional requirements, procedures whereby each branch has some constraints on each of the other two. An example is the process of appropriating money: Only the legislature (Congress) can impose taxes and raise money for the government to spend. Thus, the executive branch cannot carry out any activity it wishes, unless the money for it is appropriated. But the president must approve, in turn, any appropriation of money, and can veto an appropriation.

Another foundation of the American government is the establishment of a national (**federal**) government, along with the recognition of the political independence of each state. This system leads to certain hierarchical principles: federal law prevails in conflicts with state or local law *Gonzales v. Raich*, 545 U.S. 1 (2005). However, federal laws that encroach upon the historic legislative authority of the states to regulate activities within their borders have been declared unconstitutional. *United States v. Windsor*, 570 U.S. 744 (2013). The U.S. Constitution is the highest source of law, over statutes, treaties, and regulations. Thus, the U.S. Constitution is the highest law in the country.

> **This Constitution, and the Laws of the United States which shall be made in Pursuance thereof; and all Treaties made, or which shall be made, under the Authority of the United States, shall be the supreme Law of the Land; and the Judges in every State shall be bound thereby, any Thing in the Constitution or Laws of any State to the Contrary notwithstanding.**
>
> U.S. Constitution, Article VI, Clause 2

In the same manner, the constitution of a state is, for that state, the supreme source of law. The legislature of each state enacts laws within the framework of its constitution (as does the federal legislature, the Congress).

In the early decades of the United States, laws were principally derived from common law (judicial) decision making. Legislatures were not very active. This changed during the late 1800s (from the Civil War on), and the national Congress and the state legislatures became more and more active in the 20th century. The courts did not back off from their historic role, though, so the American legal system is truly a mixture of the elements of common law development (with its emphasis on judicial decisions), along with **statutes** and **regulations**.

▶ The Court System

Federal Courts

Under the U.S. Constitution, judicial authority is given to "one Supreme Court, and in such inferior Courts as the Congress may from time to time…establish" (Article III, Section 1). Thus, the U.S. Supreme Court is the only court established by the Constitution. The Constitution specifies neither the number of members who will sit on the Supreme Court (it has varied from six to 10), nor the qualifications of Court members or the Court's precise **jurisdiction** (what kinds of **cases** it will review).

The lower federal courts are established by statute. Federal courts may consider civil matters (involving private rights), criminal cases (involving violations of federal criminal law), equity-type cases (involving the spirit of fairness) and commercial matters (involving business and commerce). But unlike state courts of general jurisdiction, "[f]ederal courts are courts of limited jurisdiction," possessing "only that power authorized by Constitution and statute." *Kokkonen v. Guardian Life Ins. Co.*, 511 U.S. 375 (1994).

The first level of federal courts includes the U.S. District Courts. These are the federal courts in which **trials** are held and federal cases are initially filed and disposed of. A case is a dispute or controversy between opposing parties that a court is asked to resolve. Every state has at least one federal district. Larger states may have several district courts. Thus in some states there may be a Northern, Southern, Eastern, Western, Middle, or Central Districts. California, Texas, and New York each have four districts, which is the greatest number of districts in any one state. Each federal judicial district also has a separate U.S. Bankruptcy Court.[5]

There are usually several judges appointed to sit in each district. Cases are heard before a single judge.[6] Assisting the U.S. district judges on many matters, but not with the same wide authority, are U.S. magistrate judges.

The district court's role is to receive **evidence** about the "facts of the case" (establishing who did what). Higher-level courts will not retry a case, but instead serve as a forum for review and **appeal**. This review process is one reason why cases with factual similarities can have different results.

Appeals from the decisions of the federal district courts are taken to U.S. Courts of Appeals. Each **court of appeals** has jurisdiction over several states. Appeals from all of the district courts in those states are taken to the designated court of appeals. The geographic area that a court of appeals covers is called a "circuit." The circuits are numbered, and there are now 11 numbered federal circuits.[7] For example, all federal appeals from Maine, New Hampshire, Massachusetts, and Rhode Island (plus Puerto Rico) are taken to the U.S. Court of Appeals for the First Circuit. Appeals from the U.S. District Courts in Vermont, New York, and Connecticut go to the Second Circuit Court of Appeals. In common usage, these courts are sometimes called "circuit courts." You will hear, as a common abbreviation, something like, "That case was decided in the Eighth Circuit," which means the U.S. Court of Appeals for the Eighth Circuit decided the case. **FIGURE 1-1** is a map showing the breakdown of the United States into federal judicial circuits.

In most cases, when appeals are taken, the lawyers for each side file **briefs**, arguing their cases in writing, and later they argue their cases orally before the court of appeals. There are usually three judges who sit and decide each case at the appellate level. Sometimes, in special matters and because of the importance of the case, it will be heard by all members of that particular court. This is called a hearing **en banc**. Cases are decided by a majority of the judges who sit on the case. One judge is designated to write the **opinion** of the court. If not all of the judges agree, the disagreeing judge or judges will often write a dissenting opinion. In some cases, one or more judges may agree with the outcome but not with the rationale used by other judges. In these cases, that judge may write a concurring opinion. This practice of writing majority and dissenting opinions goes on in the Supreme Court, as well. With nine justices voting, there are many more dissenting opinions in the Supreme Court.

It is the **majority opinion** that prevails for the individual case on which the judges are deciding. That opinion also becomes the prevailing law, or **precedent**, on any legal matter that is decided by that case. It is the governing law for that circuit, and it will be followed by all courts in that circuit when that particular legal question arises in the future. It is not binding in other circuits but may be looked to for guidance by other courts. Through this procedure, you can see that there may be disagreeing opinions or legal conclusions in different circuits. This does happen, and such disagreements are often grounds for taking cases to the Supreme Court. Only the Supreme Court can resolve differences between the lower federal courts of appeals. Sometimes the judges on an appellate court will decide a case without a majority of the judges agreeing on a rationale for the decision. The outcome and rationale gathering the most votes is called a **plurality decision**.

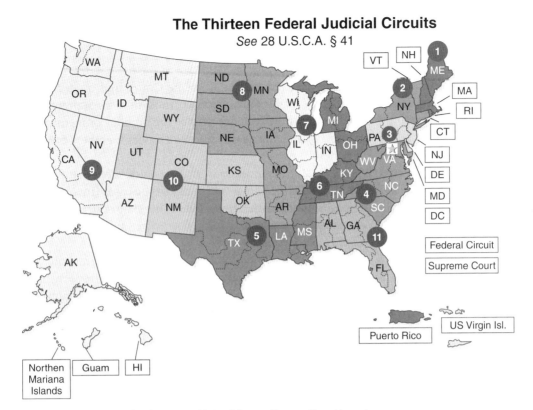

FIGURE 1-1 The Thirteen Federal Judicial Circuits. United States Courts. Court Locator.

United States Courts. Court Locator. Available from https://www.uscourts.gov/sites/default/files/u.s._federal_courts_circuit_map_1.pdf

The U.S. Supreme Court is the highest and final federal appellate court. There is a direct appeal to the Supreme Court on only a few kinds of cases (for example, if a federal law, or a state law of statewide application, is found by a three judge district court to be unconstitutional, that decision can be appealed directly to the Supreme Court).[8] Most cases come to the Supreme Court by means of **certiorari**, which means that the Supreme Court certifies that the legal question raised by the case is of considerable importance and that the Supreme Court should decide that question. As noted, one frequent basis for the Supreme Court to review a case is that it presents a question that has caused a conflict or difference of opinion between two or more courts of appeals.

When a party loses its case in a court of appeals and it wants the Supreme Court to consider and reverse that decision, it files a petition for a writ of certiorari, which is a legal paper asking the Supreme Court to review the lower court's decision. The Supreme Court votes (in chambers—not in public) on whether the case is one that the Supreme Court should consider. If four or more justices vote to review the case, the Court issues an order certifying the case to be heard in the Supreme Court. This is called granting a writ of certiorari. If, as in most cases that are petitioned to the Supreme Court, the justices do not vote to review the case, the writ of certiorari is denied. Each year, several thousand cases are taken by petition to the Supreme Court. The Court votes to accept the appeal or grant certiorari in relatively few cases (73 cases were argued, 69 cases were decided, and 66 signed opinions were issued in the 2018-2019 term).[9]

Cases in the Supreme Court, like the appellate courts, are considered by a process that involves each party submitting written briefs and then arguing the case orally before the Court. All cases in the Supreme Court are considered by all nine justices of the Court unless there are extenuating circumstances such as when a justice disqualifies themselves because of some prior involvement, or a vacancy on the Court that remains unfilled. Thus some cases are decided by eight or fewer justices.

The Supreme Court still sits in a "term of court," as virtually all courts once did. The term of the Supreme Court runs from October through June. Lower federal courts no longer have such terms. Federal judges at all levels (the Supreme Court and district and appeals courts) are appointed by the president, with the advice and consent of the Senate (meaning their appointments must be approved in the Senate by affirmative vote). They serve for life and can be removed only by impeachment. This contrasts with the states, where many judges are elected to their offices.

State Courts

Each state has a similar hierarchy of courts, which is structured much like the federal system. In every state, there are levels of trial courts and appellate courts. That is as far as a general statement can go, because there is a huge difference among states regarding how their court systems are organized and named. You will have to investigate the state of interest to you regarding what the courts at different levels are called.

For example, **trial courts** may be called circuit courts (typically for counties), district courts, superior courts, or municipal courts (in larger cities). There may be courts authorized to handle certain specialized kinds of cases at the first level, such as juvenile courts, probate courts, domestic relations courts, and traffic courts. In some jurisdictions, all of these special matters and all kinds of cases—civil and criminal—are handled in the trial courts, which we then call **Courts of General Jurisdiction**. It is becoming more and more common, especially in counties and cities of larger populations, to reduce the burdens on the trial courts by having more minor matters taken to small-claims courts (for civil matters with limited jurisdiction, such as those involving matters of up to $5,000), police courts, magistrates, or justices of the peace (for criminal matters, with jurisdiction to impose small sentences such as fines or short jail terms of 10 days or fewer). Persons often appear in these small-claims courts or traffic courts without counsel, which tends to save money and speed up the process.

Most states have two levels of appellate courts. The middle level is called a court of appeals, an appellate division, or some similar name. A few states (Delaware, Maine, Montana, New Hampshire, Rhode Island, South Dakota, Vermont, West Virginia, and Wyoming) do not have an intermediate appellate court and have only one level of appeal. Two states, Alabama and Tennessee, have separate intermediate appellate courts for criminal and civil matters but allow appeals from those intermediate courts to the state supreme court.[10]

The final level of appeal in the state is usually the **supreme court** of that state, with a few exceptions (exceptions include the Court of Appeals in New York, where the supreme court is a first-level court; the Supreme Judicial Court in Massachusetts; the Court of Appeals in Maryland; the Supreme Judicial Court Sitting as Law Court in Maine; and the Supreme Court of Appeals in West Virginia). These appellate-level courts handle appeals in all kinds of cases, both civil and criminal. Only Texas and Oklahoma have supreme appellate courts that are divided—one for civil and one for criminal cases.[11]

As noted previously, state judges at all levels are elected in many states. In some states, judges are appointed by the governor or by legislative election.[12] The means of selecting state judges, particularly by election, has been the subject of criticism and debate. In many states, the judges do not run as nominees of political parties, making them (theoretically) separated from the partisan political process. Upon re-election, many judges may run unopposed, reducing the political effects on their offices.

▶ Criminal and Civil Law

Legal matters are divided, for study and for practical concerns, into divisions or topics. A division is often made between criminal and civil matters of the law. What difference does it make? It is not purely an academic question. In some jurisdictions, certain courts only consider one kind of case or the other, civil or criminal. Some lawyers specialize in **criminal law** and others practice only **civil law**. There are different rules of procedure in federal and in many state courts that govern criminal trials and proceedings, as opposed to civil ones.

Examples of different rules include those for **burden of proof**. For criminal cases, the standard is proof beyond a reasonable doubt; the evidence must be entirely convincing in establishing the defendant's guilt. In civil cases, the usual standard is proof by a preponderance of the evidence; the evidence must show a greater likelihood that the person did, as opposed to did not commit the act as charged. This is also referred to as the "greater weight" of the evidence. The reason for this dual standard and for the higher standard of proof in criminal trials is that, in a criminal case, the defendant is facing the loss of freedom (**liberty**). Different burden of proof standards can lead to different results, even with the same basic facts. Perhaps the best-known example is the O. J. Simpson case, where the former football great was found not guilty of murder in the criminal trial but had a monetary judgment entered against him in the civil trial, which was based on the same set of facts.

Crimes (criminal offenses) are those acts that are described by a state (that is, a government) in its laws or regulations as prohibited activities, for the protection of its citizens. Every citizen has a duty to conform to those standards of conduct. A violation of that duty, or commission of such a prohibited act, is a crime, and the violator (the criminal or the **offender**) is subject to punishment. It is important to note that the description of criminal acts and the punishment authorized for them are matters of legislation and not judicial (common) law. A crime is a violation of a duty owed to the state and all of its citizens. Court actions are thus brought by state officials, called prosecutors (often district or state attorneys), on behalf of all citizens in that state. There are, of course, wide ranges of criminal activities, from the practically trivial (parking and small traffic matters) to violations of the most horrendous nature (homicides, acts of terrorism, and other violent behaviors).

Crimes are often divided into the more serious, called **felonies**, and the less serious, called **misdemeanors**. This is done for procedural reasons (such as the type of punishment upon **conviction** or the kinds of court procedures that apply). The most common dividing line between felonies and misdemeanors is the maximum **penalty** authorized for the particular offense. As a general rule, if a crime carries a penalty of more than one year in prison, it is a **felony**; if it carries a penalty of one year or less, it is a misdemeanor. There are, in some criminal systems, offenses of even lesser importance than misdemeanors, such as **petty offenses** (which may be punishable only by fines or by jail terms of 30 days or less, as examples).

Civil law is the entire body of law that is not criminal—that is, it deals with duties owed by one person to another and not to the state. (This area of noncriminal law is also sometimes called "private law.") The two most common kinds of civil law are contracts and torts. Contract law is the set of rules established to deal with promises made by one person to another. For legal purposes, a "person" may be a corporation, business, or an agency as well as an individual human being. At one time, contract law was governed primarily by court decisions and precedents—that is, by common law. Over time, legislatures have enacted more and more rules with respect to contracts, so that the law today is a large mix of common law and legislation.

Tort law covers other types of duty owed by one person to another (that is, other than duties owed by contracts) and is the means by which an **injury** or harm caused can be remedied through a legal action. In civil law, both for contracts and for torts, the remedy that is most often sought by the injured person are money damages; although in some cases, specific performance (of a contract) or injunctive relief (to force action or to restrain it) may be the remedies sought. All of these are now considered to be civil actions (and almost all of the litigation in the corrections field is civil, not criminal.)

Some actions may be a violation both of criminal law and civil duties owed to others. For example, **assault** may lead to a civil suit, whereby an individual attempts to recover money damages for the harm inflicted by a wrongful action. The same activity, investigated by the police, may be the basis for a prosecutor bringing a criminal prosecution for assault.

Civil actions are usually initiated when an **attorney** files a legal document —a **complaint (civil procedure)**— on behalf of their client, asking for relief, usually in terms of money damages, because of a wrong inflicted or a duty violated by another person. The person bringing the action is the **plaintiff**; the person sued is the **defendant**. By contrast, criminal cases are brought by a **grand jury** (handing up an indictment) or by a prosecutor (filing a bill of information or some other title in lesser cases). A criminal prosecution is brought by the state (or the people of the state) against a defendant, who is charged with wrongdoing. (Of course, there may be multiple defendants involved in criminal activity. In a civil case, there may also be more than one plaintiff and more than one defendant.) Class actions are civil cases in which, for purposes of economy, a plaintiff or a group of plaintiffs who have the same legal complaints against a defendant (or defendants) may be joined together by a court into a single class; one plaintiff or several are allowed to proceed with the lawsuit on behalf of all the others, who are notified of the proceedings. A decision or judgment in a class action suit is entered on behalf of all of the plaintiffs and is binding on all the parties.

While criminal law and civil law are the two major components of the law, the law may be categorized in other ways. Any one, or all of the following may be evident in criminal or civil litigation.

Case law is the common law that was discussed earlier. It refers to written decisions of courts published in law books (called reporters) or available in digital format on court websites and other legal research platforms such as Westlaw, Findlaw or Google Scholar. A significant portion of this text includes a discussion of case law.

Statutory law is the body of law created by the acts of the various legislatures, including Congress. Examples of such laws, discussed later in this text, are the Prison Litigation Reform Act and the Interstate Agreement on Detainers.

Administrative law is a body of law created by administrative agencies (for example, departments of justice and state regulatory agencies). These laws, discussed with statutory law, are seen in the form of rules, regulations, orders, and decisions. Administrative law is often developed to more effectively carry out statutory law.

Procedural law refers to the methods by which a legal right or duty is enforced (for example, entering a plea, presenting evidence, or establishing jurisdiction).

Substantive law is the whole area of the law that creates and defines legal rights and obligations (for example, tort law and criminal law).

Summary

- Law in the United States is principally derived from English law, which in turn was largely based on judicial rulings, collectively called the common law. A major difference between the United States and England is that the supreme law of the land in the United States is the Constitution. Each of the states also has a written constitution, which is the highest law of that state.
- In the federal, state, and local governments, there are three branches: legislative, executive, and judicial. Each of these branches has separate powers, which are spelled out in the respective constitutions.
- Under the Supremacy Clause of the U.S. Constitution, laws of the federal government are the highest laws of the country. The U.S. Supreme Court is the highest court of the country.
- In the federal government, the levels of courts are trial courts, called U.S. District Courts; appellate courts, called U.S. Courts of Appeals (designated primarily by numbered circuits); and the U.S. Supreme Court.
- Cases in the Supreme Court are usually considered when at least four justices of the Court agree to review a case by granting a writ of certiorari (certifying the case's importance to be heard in the Supreme Court). Only a small percentage of cases that are petitioned (appealed) to the Supreme Court are actually reviewed by the Court. In a few cases, there is a right of direct appeal to the Supreme Court.
- Each state has similar levels of courts: trial courts at the county, city, or town level; appeals courts (in most states); and a supreme court, which is the final judicial authority for cases brought under state laws.
- Legal matters are divided into criminal law and civil law. Criminal law is used for the prosecution of offenders who violate statutes that define conduct or activity that is prohibited because it is offensive to the state's citizens. Upon conviction of any such crimes, sanctions (sentences) are imposed, as authorized by the state's criminal statutes. Civil law comprises the rest of the law—that is, all of the law that is not criminal. There are many kinds of civil law, but the most common are contract law (the duties owed by one person to another because of promises made) and tort law (the remedies the law provides for injuries done by one person to another, other than by contract violation). The law may be further categorized into such areas as case, statutory, administrative, procedural, and substantive law. Any of these may appear within the context of criminal and civil litigation.

Thinking About It

Mary, a sentenced inmate in Missouri, tells prison officials the First Amendment requires prisoners to have access to Netflix. To support her demand, the inmate gives officials a copy of a state court opinion from Hawaii, which ruled that prisoners have a constitutional right to access Netflix.

Are prison officials in Missouri obligated to follow decisions of courts from other states? What if the opinion was from a federal district court in another state?

Key Terms

administrative law
appeal
assault
attorney
brief
burden of proof
canon law (church law)
case (legal proceedings)
case law
certiorari
chancery (court of chancery)

checks and balances
civil law
common law
complaint (civil procedure)
constitution
conviction
court
court of appeals
court of general jurisdiction
crime (criminal offense)
criminal law

decision
defendant
en banc (courts)
equity (courts)
evidence
federal
felony
grand jury
injury
jurisdiction
liberty
majority opinion
misdemeanor
offender
opinion (court)

penalty
petty offense
plaintiff
plurality opinion
precedent
procedural law
regulation
statute
statutory law
substantive law
supreme court
trial
trial court
writ

Endnotes

1. Administrative Office of the U.S. Courts. *2019 Annual Report of the Director: Judicial Business of the United States Courts.* Table C-2 U.S. District Courts–Civil Cases Commenced by Basis of Jurisdiction and Nature of the suit. Washington, DC. https://www.uscourts.gov /statistics/table/c-2/statistical-tables-federal-judiciary/2019/06/30

2. Stephan, J. *Census of State and Federal Correctional Facilities, 2005.* (2005). Appendix table 12. Washington, DC: Bureau of Justice Statistics, U.S. Department of Justice, October 2008.

3. Courts and Tribunals Judiciary: History of the Judiciary: When Common Law Failed. https://www.judiciary.uk/about-the-judiciary /history-of-the-judiciary/ There was, in English law, equity law alongside common law. Equity dealt with matters of "doing the right thing" (keeping the "King's conscience"), particularly in hardship cases. Separate courts, called chancery courts, handled equity matters. In equity cases, courts ordered specific performance or injunction rather than money damages, and they developed maxims rather than decisions. Equity was used when common law did not provide an adequate remedy. Equity law was also taken from English law and incorporated into American law. However, in most jurisdictions in the United States, equity and common law have been merged, so that both kinds of cases are heard in the same courts. The equity concept persists in some different legal language, in some differences in philosophical approaches to cases, and in procedural differences, such as the fact that there is a right to a jury trial only in common law cases and not in equity matters, which are decided by the judge alone. (This explains why there is no jury in injunction cases.) An example of a chancery court in the United States is Delaware's Court of Chancery. https://courts.delaware.gov/chancery /jurisdiction.aspx, Tennessee also has retained chancery courts, and the jurisdiction of the chancery court is as follows:
    CHANCERY COURTS
    Chancery Courts are courts of equity that are based on the English system in which the chancellor acted as the "King's conscience." A chancellor, the judge who presides over chancery courts, may modify the application of strict legal rules and adapt relief to the circumstances of individual cases. Chancery Courts handle a variety of issues including lawsuits, contract disputes, application for injunctions and name changes. A number of matters, such as divorces, adoptions, and workers' compensation, can be heard in either chancery or circuit court.
    http://www.tsc.state.tn.us/courts/circuit-criminal-chancery-courts/about

4. See endnote 3.

5. There are also specialized courts in the federal system, such as bankruptcy courts (exclusive jurisdiction over bankruptcies), U.S. Tax Court (jurisdiction over disputes between taxpayers and the Internal Revenue Service), and military tribunals. Administrative Office for U.S. Courts, *Court Role and Structure.* https://www.uscourts.gov/about-federal-courts/court-role-and-structure. There is also a Court of International Trade which hears civil cases relating to customs and international trade law. U.S. court of International Trade, *About the Court.* https://www.cit.uscourts.gov/ and the Court of Appeals for the Armed Services. Which exercises worldwide jurisdiction over persons subject to the Uniform Code of Military Justice. Court of Appeals for the Armed Services. https://www .armfor.uscourts.gov/newcaaf/home.htm toms courts, tax courts, and military courts-martial. These trial-level courts have counterpart appellate courts. These specialized courts are not of concern to us in this study, because they do not deal with corrections matters, with the exception of the military courts—including the Court of Military Appeals—which do deal with sentencing and corrections litigation.

6. 28 U.S. Code Section 2284 requires that a district court consisting of three judges be convened when required by an act of Congress or in cases involving challenges to the apportionment of congressional districts. 28 U.S. Code Section 3626(a)(3)(B) requires release orders made in prison conditions lawsuits be made only by three judge courts pursuant to 28 U.S. Code 2284. This section of the PLRA was one issue addressed by the Supreme Court in *Brown v. Plata*, 563 U.S. 493 (2011) which is discussed in the chapter on health care.

7   Administrative Office for the U.S. Courts. *About the U.S. Courts of Appeal.* https://www.uscourts.gov/about-federal-courts/court-role -and-structure/about-us-courts-appeals. See Figure 1-1: The Thirteen Federal Judicial Circuits. In addition, and as an exception to the numbering rule for circuits, there are two courts of appeals that sit in the District of Columbia. The U.S. Court of Appeals for the District of Columbia Circuit hears appeals from the U.S. District Court for the District of Columbia. The Federal Circuit Court hears appeals from specified federal boards and administrative courts.

8. 28 U.S. Code Section 1253 authorizes any party to "appeal to the Supreme Court from an order granting or denying, after notice and hearing, an interlocutory or permanent injunction in any civil action, suit or proceeding required by any Act of Congress to be heard and determined by a district court of three judges." There is an even smaller number of cases that may, by direction of the Constitution (Article III, Section 2), be brought directly and from the beginning into the Supreme Court. These are cases that involve ambassadors and those in which a state is a party. There have been a few such cases, which involved such matters as disputes between states about their boundaries or the allocation of water from rivers. Because the Supreme Court is not a trial court and has no procedure to take testimony or receive evidence, it has usually appointed a special master to conduct such a trial on its behalf.

9. John G. Roberts, 2019 Year End Report on the Federal Judiciary. The Supreme Court of the United States. https://www.supremecourt.gov/publicinfo/year-end/2019year-endreport.pdf

10. Information on the Alabama Court of Criminal Appeals can be found at: http://judicial.alabama.gov/Appellate/AppellateProcessChart. Information on the Tennessee Court of Criminal Appeals can be found at: http://www.tsc.state.tn.us/courts/court-criminal-appeals/about

11. National Center for State Courts. (2020). *State Court Web sites.* Available at: https://www.ncsc.org/Information-and-Resources/Browse-by-State.aspx. Accessed December 13, 2020. Under the states listed, there is a court structure chart.

12. National Center for State Courts. Methods of Judicial Selection. Available at: http://judicialselection.us/judicial_selection/methods/selection_of_judges.cfm?state=. Accessed February 9, 2020

CHAPTER 2

Corrections and the Criminal Justice System

It is the mission of the Federal Bureau of Prisons to protect society by confining offenders in the controlled environments of prisons and community-based facilities that are safe, humane, cost-efficient, and appropriately secure, and that provide work and other self-improvement opportunities to assist offenders in becoming law-abiding citizens.

Mission Statement of the Federal Bureau of Prisons

CHAPTER OUTLINE

- The Police
- Arrest and Release
- Prosecution
- The Courts
- Sentencing
- Corrections
  - Probation
  - Fines
  - Restitution
  - Electronic Monitoring
  - Community Service and Creative Sentencing

This chapter provides a quick, broad look at the criminal justice system in the United States and how corrections, as a discipline, fit into that system. Because there are many areas in which the different components of criminal justice interrelate, it would be desirable to coordinate planning and working between those components. In practice, unfortunately, and in most jurisdictions, there is very little coordination among the different components. That lack of coordinated planning is also evident in most legislatures, where programs and appropriations are historically pursued in one area, with little attention paid to how legislative action may affect other criminal justice areas.

One example of such lack of attention to coordinated planning is a fairly common one: the enactment of new criminal statutes that increase the penalties for crimes without consideration for the impact that action will have on police, prosecutors' offices, the courts, and corrections. For example, the implementation of determinate sentencing (a sentence with a fixed term, such as five years) and the abolishment of parole have clearly achieved a "get tough on crime" position.

The U.S. prison population grew dramatically after 1970, increasing from just over 200,000 sentenced state and federal prisoners in 1969 to over 300,000 by 1980. See Appendix 2-1, Offender Population Fact Sheet on the Navigate eBook site on jblearning.com.

To illustrate, we can look at Florida. Between 1993 and 2007, the state's inmate population grew from 53,000 to over 97,000. A number of state correctional policies and practices contributed to this growth. In 1995, Florida's legislature abolished **good time** credits and discretionary release by the parole board. The legislation required every inmate to serve 85% of his sentence. A "zero tolerance" policy was also put in place, requiring probation officers to report every offender who violated any condition of supervision and increasing prison time for these "technical violations." From this legislative action, the number of violators in Florida's prisons increased by an estimated 12,000.[1] This report also noted that while crime in Florida did drop during this time, crime also dropped as much or more in other states that had not increased, or had even shrunk, their prison systems. A by-product of this increase is the need for additional expenditures. This impacts the state's budgetary resources, as those newly expended funds can detract from the funds that are available for other programs.

Since 2011, the federal government and many states, including Florida, have taken steps to reduce their correctional populations. In 2018, Congress passed, and the President signed into law, the First Step Act (FSA), P.L. 115-391. The major components of the FSA requires the Federal Bureau of Prisons (BOP) to implement a risk and needs assessment tool for offenders and to develop institutional programs with the goal of reducing recidivism, make changes to federal sentencing procedures for certain offenses, and reauthorize the federal Second Chance Act of 2007.[2]

At the same time, practices such as determinate sentencing and the abolishment of parole have produced the unintended consequence of lessening the motivations for inmates to abide by an institution's regulations and work toward their release. This placed an increased burden on prison administrators to maintain institution security and good order. Some state governments and state legislatures have tried to provide a more comprehensive process by creating criminal justice planning agencies for an entire state or by better organizing committee work and legislative drafting in the legislature. On the federal level, legislation was first introduced in 2009 in the United States Congress proposing the establishment of the National Criminal Justice Commission. The legislation proposed making the commission responsible for a comprehensive review of all areas of the criminal justice system, including criminal justice costs, practices, and policies of federal, state, local, and tribal governments. In 2010 the bill passed in the U.S. House but did not pass in the U.S. Senate. The bill was reintroduced in Congress on August 1, 2019 as the National Criminal Justice Act of 2019.[3]

Criminal law deals with violations of duties that citizens owe to the society at large. By enactments of the legislature, certain conduct is considered prohibited and violates society's standards. By those legislative actions, such conduct is considered criminal. These legislative enactments, taken together, constitute the "criminal law" for a specific jurisdiction. When conduct is declared to be criminal, the statute that defines the crime also sets the punishments (or range of punishments) that accompany that particular crime.

The legislature, whether state or federal (or even local, in cases where counties, towns, or cities have been given limited authority to legislate on criminal matters), also defines the procedure by which crimes are investigated, prosecuted, and punished. In law schools, courses are often taught in these two areas: criminal law, which examines the substantive law of criminal activities, definitions of different crimes, and classification of crimes; and criminal procedure, which is the study of the agencies and actions of criminal law enforcement, prosecution, court proceedings, and criminal sanctions. These procedures, as well as the agencies and individuals that pursue them, make up the criminal justice system.

FIGURE 2-1 shows the main elements in the United States' criminal justice system. There may be variations of this system in individual states, but the major components are the same: police, prosecution, courts, and corrections.

▸ The Police

The role of the police in our criminal justice system is to prevent, detect, and investigate crime and apprehend offenders. This role is sometimes called law enforcement. The police carry out this role within the constraints of constitutional and statutory requirements and with the overriding principle that their work is done for the protection and welfare of the public as a whole.

What is the sequence of events in the criminal justice system?

FIGURE 2-1 The criminal justice system. The above diagram illustrates the sequence of events in the criminal justice system. To link to a description of one of the areas shown, go to http://bjs.ojp.usdoj.gov/content/largechart.cfm and click on the section of interest.

Bureau of Justice Statistics, United States Department of Justice. Available from htttps://www.bjs.gov/content/largechart.cfm

Source: Adapted from *The challenge of crime in a free society.* President's Commission on Law Enforcement and Administration of Justice, 1967. This revision, a result of the Symposium on the 30th Anniversary of the President's Commission, was prepared by the Bureau of Justice Statistics in 1997.

Note: This chart gives a simplified view of caseflow through the criminal justice system. Procedures vary among jurisdictions. The weights of the lines are not intended to show actual size of caseloads.

Crimes may be committed within sight of the police. Most crimes, however, are not observed by the police. Some of these are reported to the police, and some are never reported. The police have the authority to prevent crimes, enforce the criminal law, investigate criminal activities, turn investigative material over to prosecutors for initiating criminal prosecutions, and work with prosecutors in the prosecution of cases.

Police have great discretion in investigative matters. Through training and experience, they learn that certain crimes may be effectively handled informally. Some reported crimes are investigated vigorously and swiftly; others are investigated perfunctorily or not at all. These investigative decisions are based on local law enforcement policy, which, in turn, is derived from a range of sources, including available police resources and the relative seriousness of different crimes as viewed by the police department, prosecutors, and local courts. In theory, the views of the police department, prosecutors, and the courts reflect the opinions and attitudes of the citizenry in that jurisdiction regarding the relative seriousness of different crimes. After all, the criminal justice system is founded on the premise that criminal law should appropriately punish those who violate prescribed standards of conduct.

Because of the volume of crime in most jurisdictions and seriously limited police resources, the discretionary action of police is, in fact, a potent element of law enforcement. Decisions not to investigate or decisions to handle some cases of misconduct that are technically criminal by informal resolution, such as with a discussion and warning, result in a large number of criminal matters that proceed no further into the system. Adding the cases that are never reported and those that are handled "in-house" by the police (that is, the cases that are not referred for prosecution), only a small minority of the total cases of criminal conduct is pursued in the courts. For example, in 2018 in California, there were 215,283 felony arrests. Convictions were obtained in 65.7% of those arrested, 12.6% of cases were dismissed or acquitted after charges were filed, 18.6% were prosecution rejections and resolution and 3% were released by the police without further referral to prosecutorial agencies.[4]

▶ Arrest and Release

Of significant importance, especially to the accused, is the decision to hold the suspect in custody. Taking a person into custody based on suspicion of criminal conduct is called **arrest**. There are precise standards that the police use to decide whether a person may be arrested. These involve such elements as the seriousness of the offense committed, the record of the suspect, actions of the suspect when apprehended, and, certainly, action that has been taken in comparable cases. If taken into custody by the police (by physical restraint, such as placing in handcuffs and placing in a cell), the suspect will be advised of their right to remain silent and to contact and consult with an attorney. The suspect will also be booked, which can include photographing and even taking a DNA specimen. This is where the information about the crime and the suspect is entered into the police records.

At this point, there may be a process for obtaining **release on bail**. An attorney will often move promptly to obtain bail or have the suspect **released upon their own recognizance (ROR)** (that is, without any bail or any **bond** having to be posted). Depending on the crime and local procedures, this may be obtained in some cases without court review. Otherwise, the application for release will be made at the initial court appearance or as soon thereafter as possible.

▶ Prosecution

Another component with great discretionary authority is the prosecution. *Bordenkircher v. Hayes*, 434 U.S. 357 (1978). The title for this agency varies. In federal courts, each federal judicial district has a U.S. Attorney, who has prosecutorial authority. In the states, prosecutions are pursued at the county or city (or town) level. These prosecutors are called state's attorneys, district attorneys, prosecuting attorneys, city attorneys, or other titles, depending on the location.

The police bring to the prosecutor's office their records of investigation, which include the complaint made (by the victim or others); statements of witnesses; other evidence gathered; in some cases, a statement by the accused (confession); the prior record of the accused; and, usually, recommendations for prosecution. The **prosecutor** weighs this information and makes a decision about proceeding. Weak cases may be dropped here or sent back for further investigation. More complex cases may remain under continuing investigation by the police. However, such a case may be referred to the prosecutor for preliminary review regarding the strength of the case or to meet time requirements to bring the accused into court for an initial appearance while they are under arrest.

If the prosecutor decides that there is sufficient evidence to proceed, the prosecutor will initiate the formal steps of prosecution. The steps depend upon the nature of the crime and how serious that crime is. This in turn may vary from one jurisdiction to another. (As with all criminal justice procedures discussed in this text, this discussion is based on the most common practice. The reader should always be aware that circumstances may be different in a particular local jurisdiction.)

If the offense is minor—that is, a petty offense—the prosecutor files a complaint, an **information**, or a criminal charge, and the defendant is taken promptly before a lower court (a magistrate, a commissioner, or a justice of the peace). Note that once **charges** are filed, the person accused of the criminal act has become a defendant—a party in a criminal proceeding. The title of the case will typically read, "*The People of the State*" or "*The State of (name of the state) versus (name of the accused), defendant*" For minor crimes, the proceedings are usually quick; the defendant is advised of their rights and asked for their plea. Even if the defendant denies the charges, the case will usually proceed quickly. If a trial is requested, an early trial date will be set, but sufficient time for attorneys to prepare and to obtain the presence of necessary witnesses must be allowed. If the defendant is found guilty (by plea or by trial), penalties are proportionally smaller (usually limited to fines or short jail terms) for minor offenses.

If the offense is a more serious one, the crime is considered to be either a misdemeanor or a felony. As noted previously, in most jurisdictions, misdemeanors are offenses that carry penalties of up to one year in prison. Most jurisdictions have sub-classes of felonies and misdemeanors, with a corresponding difference in the maximum sentence. An example, North Dakota has two classes of misdemeanors: a Class B misdemeanor which carries a maximum penalty of 30 days in jail and a fine of $1500 or both compared to a Class A misdemeanor which carries a maximum penalty of one year in jail and a fine of $3000 or both. (North Dakota Century Code Section 12.1-32-01.) The state of Missouri has five classes of felonies labeled A-E, with a Class E felony carrying a maximum term of imprisonment of 4 years, and a Class A felony carrying a minimum term of ten years and a maximum term of 30 years or life. (Revised Statutes of Missouri 558.011.) Felonies are offenses that carry penalties of more than one year in prison. For misdemeanors, prosecutors can almost always file the charges by signing an information or similar prosecutive document. For felonies, an **indictment** is one method of charging the accused, and this requires taking the evidence before a grand jury, which decides whether there is sufficient evidence to take the accused to trial, and, if there is, the grand jury hands up an indictment. (Some states have no grand juries. Other jurisdictions seldom use them.) It is common for a defendant who is charged with a felony to be asked to waive indictment and to agree to proceed by information. Thus only a small number of prosecutions nationwide originate with grand jury action. The Fifth Amendment to the U.S. Constitution requires felony prosecutions to be initiated by a grand jury, unless waived by a defendant. Neither the Fifth Amendment nor the Fourteenth Amendment Due Process clause requires the use of grand juries in state prosecutions. *Hurtado v. California*, 110 U.S. 516 (1884) (Fifth Amendment) and *Alexander v. Louisiana*, 405 U.S. 625 (1972) (no right to a grand jury indictment provided by the Fourteenth Amendment.)

Soon after arrest, defendants are brought before the lower (preliminary) judicial authority, where they are advised of their rights, the assignment of **counsel** is discussed (if they have not retained an attorney), and the sufficiency of the charges is preliminarily reviewed by a judicial official, ensuring, for the first time, review of the evidence by someone outside of the prosecution and police offices. Whether by indictment, information, or other official prosecutor's charges, the case is formally and publicly filed in the court system at this time. After an information or indictment is filed, the defendant is taken before the criminal court for arraignment.

At **arraignment**, the accused person is brought before the court and is asked to enter a plea of "guilty" or "not guilty." Arraignment is conducted in open court and consists of reading the indictment or information to the defendant or otherwise providing them with the substance of the charges against them. At arraignment, the court makes certain that indigent defendants (persons without funds) are provided counsel. Here also the defendant elects whether to waive a **trial by jury** or have a **trial by judge** alone (bench trial).

After reviewing the evidence presented at this preliminary stage, the court may order some charges to be dismissed for insufficient evidence or some charges to be reduced to lesser offenses. From these earliest stages, the defense counsel will negotiate with the prosecutor to get charges dropped or reduced, either on the basis of the strength of the case or in return for entering a guilty plea. The defense counsel will file motions with the court, challenging the legality of the prosecution papers, sometimes challenging arrest or other police actions, or challenging the propriety of detention.

▶ The Courts

After the initial papers are filed with the court clerk, the judge assigned to the criminal matter has jurisdiction over the disposition of the case.

In all criminal prosecutions, the accused shall enjoy the right to a speedy and public trial, by an impartial jury of the State and district wherein the crime shall have been committed, which district shall have been previously ascertained by law, and to be informed of the nature and cause of the accusation; to be confronted with the witnesses against him; to have compulsory process for obtaining witnesses in his favor, and to have the Assistance of Counsel for his defence.

U.S. Constitution, Amendment 6

No person shall be ... deprived of life, liberty, or property, without due process of law.

U.S. Constitution, Amendment 5

No State shall make or enforce any law which shall abridge the privileges or immunities of citizens of the United States; nor shall any State deprive any person of life, liberty, or property, without due process of law; nor deny to any person within its jurisdiction the equal protection of the laws.

U.S. Constitution, Amendment 14

Every criminal court must ensure that constitutional standards for **criminal proceedings** and **due process** are met. If the defendant pleads guilty, the court makes sure that the defendant's guilty plea is understood and is voluntarily made. If the defendant pleads not guilty, the case proceeds to trial. If the defendant waives their right to have a trial by jury, the court will consider the evidence presented at trial and make the decision as to the defendant's guilt. During a jury trial the judge supervises all proceedings, makes rulings on evidence and procedural matters, and instructs the jury about the law that applies to their deliberations. A defendant found not guilty is released (unless there are other charges pending on which to hold them). A defendant found guilty is then ready for sentencing.

The corrections component involvement in the criminal justice process can begin as early as the arrest stage if the suspect is detained in jail, and for some, pretrial release may include aspects of correctional supervision. However, for many criminal defendants, the corrections stage of criminal justice becomes involved at sentencing. Sentencing is the legal process that anticipates the correctional function. In many cases, corrections authorities may be involved in the sentencing itself. But sentencing is a judicial function; only courts impose **sentences**, as authorized by the criminal statutes. It is true that, in some jurisdictions, sentencing reforms in recent years have diminished the wide authority of sentencing judges by prescribing mandatory or determinate sentences. In most cases, these procedures reduce the range of sentences that may be imposed by the judges. There is usually a formula, in states that have adopted sentencing, under which elements of criminal conduct are described and assigned values, which are then used (in charts or by other means) to arrive at a narrow range of sentences. Judges may be allowed to go above or below these sentence guides, for reasons that are found in the record and that are based on circumstances that are particularly mitigating or aggravating, compared with the average case. The National Center for State Courts reports that 21 states have some system of sentencing guidelines.[5] In 2008, the National Center for State Courts issued a research report on "Assessing Consistency and Fairness in Sentencing-A comparative Study in Three States."[6] The report indicates at least 20 states and the District of Columbia have sentencing guidelines. These guidelines are described as "a relatively new reform effort to encourage judges to take specific legally relevant elements into account in a fair and consistent way when deciding whether a convicted offender should be imprisoned, and if so, for what length of time." Guidelines may be either advisory (voluntary) or mandatory (more presumptive—stricter requirements for departure from the guidelines, tighter sentencing ranges, more vigorous appellate review). (See endnote 6). Where such sentencing guidelines have not been adopted, judges are typically given (by the legislature, through the criminal statute) a wider range of penalties that may be imposed. While many judges object to the restrictions placed on their wide discretion as a result of sentencing guidelines or **mandatory sentences**, others welcome the attempts to ensure more consistent results in sentencing from case to case across all courts in the jurisdiction.

▶ Sentencing

To assist in their sentencing decisions, it has become common in many jurisdictions for the courts to request sentencing reports regarding individual defendants. The Supreme Court has made it clear that individualizing sentences to fit particular defendants is an approved practice (*Williams v. New York*, 337 U.S. 241 (1949)). In that case, the Court also emphasized that the sentencing procedure is more relaxed than the strict procedural and evidentiary requirements of **due process** at the criminal trial itself:

> **[A] sentencing judge ... exercise[s] a wide discretion in the sources and types of evidence used to assist him in determining the kind and extent of punishment to be imposed within limits fixed by law ... Highly relevant—if not essential—to his selection of an appropriate sentence is the possession of the fullest information possible concerning the defendant's life and characteristics ... [M]odern concepts individualizing punishment have made it all the more necessary that a sentencing judge not be denied an opportunity to obtain pertinent information by a requirement of rigid adherence to restrictive rules of evidence properly applicable to the trial.**

The Court repeatedly emphasized the importance of individualizing sentences in modern sentencing philosophy. The reason for this was also stated by the Court:

> **Retribution is no longer the dominant objective of the criminal law. Reformation and rehabilitation of offenders have become important goals of criminal jurisprudence.**

Note that this was said in a case where the Supreme Court upheld the imposition of the death penalty. However, *Williams* is still good law, and it is often cited to sustain rulings about the relaxed nature of sentencing portions of criminal trials and importance of getting as much information as possible about the defendant in order to fit the sentence to the individual. To assist the courts in this process, the Supreme Court recognized the value of the sentencing report:

> **Under the practice of individualizing punishments, investigational techniques have been given an important role. [The reports of probation workers] have been given a high value by conscientious judges who want to sentence persons on the best available information rather than on guesswork and inadequate information.**

Presentencing reports are often sought, particularly in felony cases. In earlier days, these reports usually came from the prosecutor and possibly from the defense. To obtain a fairer, more balanced, and more consistent report, nowadays, such reports are usually provided by a judicial office, the probation office, or even from the corrections department. Sometimes, these reports are started before the defendant is found guilty. More often, the judge orders a report to be prepared following the defendant's entering a guilty plea or after conviction. This report usually reviews the criminal conduct of the defendant but focuses more on social, educational, psychological, medical, and family background and needs. These, together with the criminal record that is always available from the police and prosecution, are used to enable the court to impose a more informed sentence:

> The aim of the [federal] presentence investigation is to provide a timely, accurate, objective, and comprehensive report to the court. The report should have enough information to assist the court in making a fair sentencing decision and to assist corrections and community corrections officials in managing offenders under their supervision (Administrative Office for the U.S. Courts, 2013).[7]

See Appendix 1, model **presentence report**, on the Navigate eBook site on jblearning.com, which shows the kind of language that would be used in providing a good report to the sentencing judge. This model report is very detailed and involves complicated criminal activity. It shows the range of information a judge needs in order to make an informed sentencing decision.

This inevitably brings us to the question: What is the purpose of sentencing? Although some criminal statutes have attempted to address this ultimate penological question, most legislation is silent, or ambiguous, about the purpose of punishment. The historic and traditional answer to the question is that we sentence criminal offenders for **retribution, incapacitation, deterrence** (general and individual), and **rehabilitation**. When a judge sees rehabilitation as the primary purpose to be achieved in sentencing, the presentence report, with its detailed information about the defendant, is of greatest use. For incapacitation, retribution, or general deterrence, the details of the defendant's psychological or educational background may be viewed as irrelevant, except for possible mitigation or aggravation in exceptional cases.

In any event, the final answers regarding the purposes of sentencing have not yet been made. Criminal justice authorities, and especially legislatures, have not reached an agreement about which of the grand purposes (individually or in combination) are most justified in sentencing. The debate continues, and what is certain is that judges and the public, as well as professors and legislators, hold widely varying views about the proper purposes of punishment. The emphasis on one sentencing goal or another seems to shift from decade to decade. Rehabilitation as a primary goal was widely taught in schools beginning in the 1930s and after. It was finally adopted by many judges and legislatures in the 1950s and 1960s. By the 1980s, serious questions were raised by academicians, correctional practitioners, and judges regarding the goal of rehabilitation as a correctional purpose. These concerns, and those of the public in response to increasing criminal activity led to a swing of the pendulum in the 1980s and 1990s toward retribution and incapacitation as the justifiable (and more clearly achievable) goals of sentencing. In the first part of the 21st century, there was a belief that imprisonment was warranted for persons committing the most serious criminal acts (e.g., violent crimes) but that alternatives should be considered for persons posing a minimal risk to the community. In August 2010, the American Correctional Association (ACA) approved a new public correctional policy that, with respect to criminal sentencing, said:

> The length of a term of incarceration resulting from a criminal conviction should be only as long as necessary to accomplish the objectives of punishment … This will optimize the cost to the taxpayers … minimize any deleterious effects of imprisonment, and maximize the chances for the successful reintegration of offenders into the community after release and also ensure that the public's interest in the long-term incarceration of habitual, violent and predatory sexual offenders is preserved.[8]

Beginning in the second decade of the 21st century, there has been a strong movement to address the large prison U.S. correctional supervision population. In addition to the above noted ACA action, the federal government made changes in federal sentencing law. Examples include The First Step Act noted earlier, and reforms to federal law, such as the Fair Sentencing Act, which reduced the disparity in federal law for possession of crack cocaine from 100/1 to 18/1.[9] States also have taken steps to address sentencing disparities.[10] Nongovernmental organizations have initiated steps to inform the public and policymakers and to suggest changes to federal and state sentencing laws, which impact corrections such as The Urban Institute, The Pew Charitable Trusts, The Marshall Project, The Sentencing Project, the Vera Institute of Justice, and the Prison Policy Initiative.[11]

▶ Corrections

Corrections is the collection of agencies that perform those functions that carry out the sentencing orders of criminal courts. It is the last component in the continuum of criminal justice activities of the criminal justice system. Included in corrections are (1) the probation authority, (2) **jails** (at least to the extent that they carry out short sentences, usually called jail terms), (3) the agencies that perform community corrections functions, (4) prisons, and (5) paroling authorities. Under our definition, those who collect **fines** and **restitution** money (often clerks of the court) and those who assist in supervising offenders in the community (which may include the police) are also part of corrections. But the five authorities listed are the principal, traditional components of corrections.

Sentences in the United States range from fines, restitution, community service, probation supervision, suspended sentences, and terms of imprisonment, to execution in capital cases. Corrections agencies carry out all of these sentences. Fines and restitution are typically paid by the defendant to the clerk's office or another judicial office, so involvement of a corrections agency in such cases is minimal as long as payments are made.

Probation is a type of sentence that allows the defendant to remain in the community, and it usually allows an offender to stay at their home and keep their job. The defendant who is placed on probation is required to report regularly to a probation officer who counsels the probationer and helps in crises. There are always conditions imposed by the court that govern the activities of the defendant. Violations of these may result in a negative report to the court. If these are serious enough, the probationer may be called into court to determine whether the probation should be revoked. Courts rely heavily on the insights and judgment of the probation officers on these matters. In most cases, if probation is revoked, the defendant can be sent to prison at that time.

Nonpayment of fines or restitution may also result in the defendant being called before the court to face possible jail terms as sanctions.

It should be noted that, for all of these components of corrections for **adults**, there are similar components in the **juvenile** justice system. From probation to **incarceration**, specialized juvenile agencies handle delinquency cases in the criminal justice system.

In recent years, there has been much said and written about "alternatives to imprisonment." In truth, there have always been alternatives to imprisonment (probation being the main one), but because of the attention, legislatures and courts have looked to additional ways to sentence. Why? There are many reasons. Because of crackdowns on sentencing (longer sentences for many offenses, especially involving violence), prisons have become more crowded. Prisons are expensive to build and run. For less serious offenders, at least, it seems to make sense to use anything that might work instead of prison. But what will work? Here are descriptions of some of the alternatives that have been tried.

Probation

Probation is a commonly used sanction and is often used for first- or second-time offenders and those involved in less serious crimes. The essence of probation is that the defendant is allowed to remain in the community while under some degree of supervision by a **probation officer**. In some cases, a judge imposes a term of imprisonment upon a defendant and suspends the execution of it as long as the defendant satisfactorily completes a designated period of time under supervision. Some states authorize the suspensions of sentences involving fines or other penalties or the suspension (deferring) of the imposition of a sentence, allowing the judge (upon revocation of probation) to impose any sentence that could have been imposed at initial sentencing.

There are usually general conditions imposed upon the **probationer** that are used in all similar cases. (For example: do not commit any offense, do not use drugs, and maintain steady employment.) In addition, very specific conditions geared to the individual defendant may be used. (For example: do not go to the Main Street Tavern, where there are bad influences; get training in welding to improve your employment opportunities; and pay restitution of $150 per month to the victims from whom you embezzled money.) See Appendix 2- mandatory, standard, special and other conditions of supervised release, on the Navigate eBook site on jblearning.com.

Although many people (in the media, in the public, and even in the judiciary) do not consider probation a sanction, but rather a "slap on the wrist" that allows criminals to get off free, probation is properly viewed as an alternative sanction, carrying varying degrees of restraint on freedom. In many jurisdictions, more than half of the persons who are sentenced receive probation. More persons are on probation supervision in the United States than are in prison. At the end of 2018, 6,410,000 adults were under some form of correctional supervision in the United States. Of that number, 3,540,000 were on probation, 878,000 were on parole, 738,400 were in jails and 1,465 million were in state and federal prisons.[12]

Probation officers have a difficult job. One of the major problems they face is the large numbers of persons whom they are expected to supervise. Sometimes, the numbers run to 200 offenders or more per officer. Some states have actively attempted to lower the number of probationers supervised by probation agents. For example, Georgia has lowered its average probation officer case load from 250 in 2008 to 130 in 2017.[13] This usually means that officers look after the most demanding problem probationers, and many probationers are left unsupervised. At best, many probationers report in every month or so by telephone, which serves as their supervision.

There are many degrees of supervision within the realm of probation. At one extreme is *unsupervised probation*, which is virtually an oxymoron, given that supervision is the essence of probation. Still, with overloads of probationers, many officers do minimal supervision on many cases. Because of the reality of minimal supervision by probation officers, some courts approve probation for some defendants without any supervisory contact at all. Unless the probationer is arrested for a new offense, probation is dormant. At the other extreme is intensive probation, in which a court requires much more frequent contact between probation officer and probationer. This level of contact necessarily requires smaller **caseloads** for the probation officer, and if there are resources for this in the jurisdiction, *intensive probation* is a more meaningful alternative for some defendants who would otherwise go to prison. Some studies indicate that intensive probation results in more violations—which could be explained by the fact that probationers placed on intensive probation are more at risk (more likely to commit violations) or that greater supervision uncovers more technical violations.[14] Many well-trained probation officers in this country, with additional resources, could make probation a strong and viable sentencing alternative. Probation is the most reliable and potentially the most valuable type of community correction.

It is important to distinguish between probation and parole. Probation is a sanction, imposed by a judge at sentencing. **Parole** is release from a term of imprisonment by a paroling authority. They are similar in that both probationers and parolees are released into the community and placed under the supervision of government officers; in some jurisdictions, the same officers supervise both probationers and parolees. But the status of probationers and the status of parolees are very different, both in their initial placement and in their revocation. Both placement and revocation of probationers are done by the sentencing court. The placement into parole and revocation of parole—returning the parolee to prison—are done by the paroling authority, which is usually an independent administrative board or a commission appointed by the executive, typically by the governor of the state. In the federal criminal justice system, offenders frequently receive a judicially imposed term of supervised release following their release from a sentence of imprisonment. During supervised release, the offender is monitored by U.S. Probation Officers. Like probation, a violation of supervised release conditions results in a hearing before the sentencing judge who can revoke the supervised release and return the offender to prison for an additional period of incarceration.

Fines

For many offenses, fines may be used in lieu of, or in addition to jail or prison terms. For crimes at the bottom end of the severity scale (traffic offenses), fines have become the accepted method of punishment. In some other countries, fines are used more often than in the United States. The advantages of fines are that they are punitive; fairly easy to administer; and fairly easy to fit into a sentencing schedule, with ranges of severity. The disadvantages are that fines are seen as being unavailable for many defendants who are indigent, and they are viewed by some as being not punitive enough for high-income defendants (such as drug dealers or wealthy, white-collar defendants). Using fines for the latter types of defendants is often seen as an example of rich people being able to buy their way out of criminal difficulties.

Restitution

Restitution is an attempt in the criminal system to make the injured "whole," to even the balance that has been unjustly tipped by the criminal act. Victims may feel that restitution is a satisfying type of sentence, because they personally receive something for their injuries.

Every state gives courts statutory authority to order restitution. In over one-third of the states, courts are required to order restitution unless there are compelling or extraordinary circumstances. An example is Florida Statutes section 775,089 (2019) which provides that "[i]n addition to any punishment, the court shall order the defendant to make restitution to the victim for: 1) Damage or loss caused directly or indirectly by the defendant's offense; and 2) Damage or loss related to the defendant's criminal episode, unless it finds clear and compelling reasons not to order such restitution."

Restitution sanctions are some of the oldest kinds of sentences used.[15] The concept is one of leveling benefit and loss; the defendant must pay back their ill-gotten gains, either directly to the victim or to some place (such as a victims' fund) where it can be used for the good of those harmed by criminal activity. The U.S. Department of Justice report on ordering restitution[16] identifies an issue that impacts restitution. This is the presence of conflicting directives on restitution within a state; for example, states may give the victim the right to restitution but may fail to require that courts order restitution. Some other identified restitution problems include the victim's failure to request restitution, the difficulty in calculating loss, and the defendant's inability to pay.

As with fines, there are frequent problems in making sure restitution is paid. This is partly because payments are being made over time. In addition, many offenders who were ordered to pay are confined and unable to make significant payments until they are released or placed in a work program; other factors can include limited assets, difficulty in securing and maintaining employment, and the lack of skills to get higher-paying jobs. Efforts are being made by the states to enforce restitution orders, including improved monitoring of restitution payments; the attachment of state payments to the defendant; the revocation of probation or parole for willful failure to pay; and using state entities or private collection agencies to collect restitution (any collection fee can be added to the amount of the debt).[17] An example of a state's efforts to improve a victim's experience with issues related to restitution is the information on the Colorado Judicial Branch website on Victim Restitution.[18]

Electronic Monitoring

All 50 states, the District of Columbia, and the federal government use electronic devices to monitor persons under correctional supervision via parole, probation or pretrial release.[19] The rationale for the use of these devices is that with huge supervision loads and difficulty in keeping track of offenders in the community, electronic monitoring does what a probation/parole officer cannot do—keep constant track of the whereabouts of the offender. This, in theory, helps to enforce the conditions of community release that relate to where the probationer/parolee can be, whether at home or at work, or at limited other places (such as school, church, or social places). There is usually a bracelet, anklet, or other electronic device, including smart phones, that provides real time information on a monitored person's location. Programs go by different names depending on the jurisdiction, including "location monitoring" in the federal system, or "satellite-based monitoring" in North Carolina or "supervised electronic confinement" in California. Although there are some equipment and administrative costs associated with running such programs, they are, of course, far less expensive than the cost of imprisonment. Some argue that, for persons at the lower end of the imprisonment spectrum, electronic monitoring provides public protection and a degree of sanction that justify its use as an alternative to prison. A publication from the International Association of Chiefs of Police (IACP) notes electronic monitoring may also be used for individuals posing a higher risk. The publication states that law enforcement agencies are beginning to get funding from state legislatures to begin Global Positioning Satellite (GPS) sex offender tracking programs.[20] The costs of such programs can be high and can be passed on to the person supervised. In Portage County, Wisconsin, the cost for electronic monitoring includes a $25 risk evaluation fee, $30 for an installation fee, and a daily monitoring fee of $22 plus tax, which must be paid in advance.[21]

Like most innovations in the criminal justice system, as the use of the practice expanded, litigation followed. As the use of electronic monitoring increased (estimates reflect that the practice increased by 140% from 2006 to 2016), legal questions arose related to the burden placed on the individual offender's constitutional rights. In *Grady v. North Carolina*, 575 U.S. 306, (2015), the Supreme Court addressed a Fourth Amendment issue related to electronic monitoring. After defendant Grady had completed a state prison sentence, a state court ordered, pursuant to state law, that Grady be required to wear a GPS tracking bracelet for the rest of his life. Grady argued that under U.S. Supreme Court precedent, such an order constituted a search and violated his Fourth Amendment right to be free from unreasonable searches and seizures. Grady's arguments were unsuccessful in state courts, which ruled that requiring Grady to wear the monitoring bracelet was not a search within the meaning of the Fourth Amendment. In a unanimous *per curiam* opinion, the Court ruled:

> *The State's program is plainly designed to obtain information. And since it does so by physically intruding on a subject's body, it effects a Fourth Amendment Search.*

The judgment of the North Carolina Supreme Court was vacated and the case was returned to the state courts for further proceedings not inconsistent with the Court's opinion. This opinion did not address or resolve all of the new legal issues, which are raised by electronic location monitoring but only established that such practices impact federally protected constitutional rights.

Community Service and Creative Sentencing

To avoid prison as a sanction and to give more clout to the noncustodial sentence, some courts regularly use an order for **community service** or for some type of work or activity that is intended to "teach a lesson." Sometimes, these sanctions are used often enough (such as requiring offenders who have committed less-serious offenses to work in the parks for a certain number of days) that they have become established alternative sanctions. We also read about them in the press, in instances in which a judge is reported to have used a "creative" order to fit the criminality of a particular offender. A slumlord is ordered to live for two weeks in one of his filthy apartments and to clean it up, or an attorney is ordered to give talks to high school classes on the benefits of the American legal system. These examples illustrate an inherent problem in such sentencing: it is eccentric and departs from a system that aims for consistency as a goal to promote fair sentencing. It also tends to be used for the affluent offender.

Creativity probably needs to be encouraged, but creative ideas should be incorporated into sentencing standards to avoid any further disparity in our sentencing structure.

Summary

- The criminal justice system in the United States is divided into four components: police, prosecution, courts, and corrections.

- Police prevent, detect, and investigate crimes and apprehend offenders. Different levels of crimes are handled by the police with different levels of intensity. There is considerable discretion given to the police in carrying out their functions.

- When a suspect is taken into custody, this is called an arrest. An arrested person will be taken before a judicial authority to obtain release on bail or on recognizance.

- Police take their records of investigation to prosecutors. Prosecutors evaluate the investigative material and, if they determine that there is sufficient evidence to proceed, they will take steps to file charges (by indictment from a grand jury, information, or criminal complaint). Felonies, which typically carry penalties of more than one year in prison, may be initiated by indictments. Lesser offenses (misdemeanors or petty offenses) are initiated by information or criminal complaints.

- Once charges are filed, the criminal court is responsible for seeing to it that a speedy and fair trial is conducted. The procedural rules for guaranteeing fair trials (due process) are complex. If the defendant is convicted, which may be by jury trial or by the court alone, he may be sentenced according to the criminal statutes in the jurisdiction.

- Many courts use sentencing reports, from the probation office or another source, to assist in sentencing, especially in higher-penalty cases. The Supreme Court has encouraged the individualization of sentences.

- Corrections agencies carry out the sentences of the criminal courts. The field of corrections includes probation authorities, jails, community corrections agencies, prisons, and parole authorities. (There are also juvenile corrections counterparts to all of these criminal corrections agencies for adults.)

- Fines and restitution orders are other types of sentences, but they are usually enforced by officials within the judicial system (such as clerks of court) and so are not included within traditional "corrections agency" definitions. Electronic monitoring, community service, and other "creative sentencing" alternatives have been employed in recent years. These are typically supervised and enforced by one of the traditional corrections agencies.

- All 50 states and the federal government utilize some type of electronic monitoring of persons under community supervision. The U.S. Supreme Court has ruled that the use of such monitoring on an individual who has completed their sentence constitutes a search under the Fourth Amendment to the U.S. Constitution. *Grady v. North Carolina.*

Thinking About It

How would you decide the following true case? William is 88 years old and fell in his home, causing permanent paralysis from the neck down. He tells his wife of over 60 years, Frances, that he is in constant pain and no longer wants to live. After two weeks of watching her husband's suffering and listening to his pleas for death, Frances brings a gun to the hospital where she shoots and kills William. She then tries to kill herself with the weapon but the gun jams. You are the prosecutor—what would you do? What is the purpose of criminal sanctions in this case?

Key Terms

adult	**counsel**
arraignment	**criminal proceedings**
arrest	**deterrence**
bond (appearance bond)	**due process (due process of law)**
caseload (corrections)	**fine**
charge	**good time**
community service	**incapacitation**
corrections	**incarceration**

indictment	rehabilitation
information	release on bail
jail	released upon their own recognizance (ROR)
juvenile	restitution
parole	retribution
presentence report	sentence (criminal law)
probation	sentence, mandatory
probation officer	trial by judge (court trial)
probationer	trial by jury (jury trial)
prosecutor	

Endnotes

1. Pew Center on the States. (2008). One in 100: Behind Bars in America 2008, Washington, DC: The Pew Charitable Trusts.
2. Nathan James, "The First Step Act of 2018: An Overview" Congressional Research Service March 4, 2019. Available: https://crsreports.congress.gov/product/pdf/R/R45558. Accessed 30 January 2020.
3. The National Criminal Justice Act of 2019. https://www.congress.gov/bill/115th-congress/senate-bill/573/text.
4. Xavier Becerra, (2018). Crime in California. *Crime in California, 2018.* California Department of Justice. Available: https://data-openjustice.doj.ca.gov/sites/default/files/2019-07/Crime%20In%20CA%202018%2020190701.pdf. Accessed 30 January 2020.
5. Neal B. Kauder & Brian J. Ostrom, "State Sentencing Guidelines-Profiles and Continuum" (July 2008). National Center for State Courts. Available: https://www.ncsc.org/__data/assets/pdf_file/0022/25474/state_sentencing_guidelines.pdf. Accessed 30 January 2020.
6. Brian J. Ostrom, Charles W. Ostrom, Roger A. Hanson & Matthew Kleiman, "Assessing Consistency and Fairness in Sentencing-A Comparative Study in Three States". (2008). National Center for State Courts. http://www.njjn.org/uploads/digital-libraryconsistencyfairness.pdf
7. Office of Probation and Pretrial Services. Administrative Office of the United States Courts. *The Presentence Investigation Report (Publication 107.* Appendix A. Available at http://cdn.ca9.uscourts.gov/datastore/library/2013/02/26/Horvath_presentence.pdf
8. American Correctional Association. (2010). Public Correctional Policy on Criminal Sentencing and Early Release from Confinement. *Corrections Today, 72*(5), 86–87.
9. P.L. 111-20 *Fair Sentencing Act of 2010*, enacted August 3, 2010. Available: https://www.congress.gov/111/plaws/publ220/PLAW-111publ220.pdf. Accessed 18 March 2020.
10. National Conference of State Legislatures. (2017). *Statewide Sentencing and Correctional Legislation*, Available: https://www.ncsl.org/research/civil-and-criminal-justice/state-sentencing-and-corrections-legislation.aspx. Accessed February 3, 2020.
11. Pew Research Center. (2020). Available: https://www.pewresearch.org/topics/criminal-justice/. Accessed February 3, 2020; The Urban Institute, Available: https://www.urban.org/features/criminal-justice-reform.
12. Maruschak, L.M. & Minton, T.D. *Correctional Populations in the United States, 2017-2018.* Bureau of Justice Statistics. Table 1. Washington, D.C.: Bureau of Justice Statistics, U.S. Department of Justice, August 2020. Available: https://www.bjs.gov/index.cfm?ty=pbdetail&iid=7026 Accessed 13 December 2020.
13. Council of State Governments Justice Center. (2018). *Changes to Georgia's Probation System Yields Positive Early Results.* The Available at https://csgjusticecenter.org/2018/04/18/changes-to-georgias-probation-system-yield-positive-early-results/. Accessed February 20, 2020.
14. Pew Charitable Trust. *To Safely Cut Incarceration, States Rethink Responses to Supervision Violations*, July 2019. https://www.pewtrusts.org/en/research-and-analysis/issue-briefs/2019/07/to-safely-cut-incarceration-states-rethink-responses-to-supervision-violationsos.
15. The *Code of Hammurabi*, dating from about 1750 B.C., included the following: "Anyone trespassing upon the land of another and cutting wood therefrom, shall pay to the owner thereof one-half 'mine' of gold." Baum, H. M., ed. *Records of the Past*, 2. Philadelphia: Patterson & White, 1903.
16. U.S. Department of Justice, Office for Victims of Crime. "*Ordering Restitution to the Victims of Crime*", Washington, D.C. (November 2002). https://www.ncjrs.gov/ovc_archives/bulletins/legalseries/bulletin6/ncj189189.pdf
17. U.S. Department of Justice, Office of Justice Programs. Office for Victims of Crime, "*Restitution-Making it Work*", Washington, D.C. (November 2002). https://www.courts.state.co.us/Self_Help/Restitution.cfm
18. Colorado Judicial Branch-Victim Restitution. https://www.courts.state.co.us/Self_Help/Restitution.cfm
19. PEW. (2016). Use of Electronic Offender-Tracking Devices Expands Sharply. *Pew Trusts.* Available at https://www.pewtrusts.org/en/research-and-analysis/issue-briefs/2016/09/use-of-electronic-offender-tracking-devices-expands-sharply. Accessed February 3, 2020.
20. IACP. *Tracking Sex Offenders with Electronic Monitoring Technology.* Alexandria, VA: International Association of Chiefs of Police, 2008.
21. *Portage County, Wisconsin, Electronic Monitoring Program.* https://www.co.portage.wi.us/department/sheriff-s-office/corrections-division/home-detention-electronic-monitoring. Accessed February 3, 2020.

CHAPTER 3

Habeas, Torts, and Section 1983

The essence of habeas corpus is an attack by a person in custody upon the legality of that custody. The traditional function of the writ is to secure release from illegal custody.

In 1670, the Chief Justice of England was able to say, in ordering the immediate discharge of a juror who had been jailed by a trial judge for bringing in a verdict of not guilty, that "the writ of habeas corpus is now the most usual remedy by which a man is restored again to his liberty, if he have been against law deprived of it."

U.S. Supreme Court, *Preiser v. Rodriguez*

CHAPTER OUTLINE

- Habeas Corpus
- Torts
- Section 1983

Although corrections is part of the criminal justice system, most of the litigation that affects corrections officials is in the civil area. Remember that within the legal system the law is divided into two main types: criminal and civil. In some jurisdictions, there are different courts that handle criminal and civil matters. Usually, there are different rules that govern criminal cases as opposed to civil cases. There are also different standards of evidence in the two kinds of trials. As you may remember, in a criminal case, the defendant is facing the loss of freedom thus a higher standard of proof is required. There are, especially in larger jurisdictions, different lawyers who specialize in handling the different kinds of cases. The civil law is for adjudication of controversies between individual, private parties. The criminal law is for the administration of criminal laws, the end goal of which is the punishment of wrongs done to the public.

Corrections staff are sometimes involved in criminal cases. Probation officers make sentencing reports to judges at the sentencing stage of criminal trials. When persons under community supervision do not meet the conditions of their community placement, the probation officers, or others, who supervise the offenders will go into court to report on their status. That court is usually the criminal court that originally tried and sentenced the defendant. Jail and corrections officers will also go into court as witnesses in criminal cases, typically in cases in which offenses (such as escape or assault) have been committed in the jail or prison facility.

Except for the comparatively small number of appearances in criminal cases, such as those just mentioned, corrections staff will be seen mostly in civil court cases, not criminal. Most of this text is a review of the kinds of cases that make up corrections litigation. This area of the law is sometimes called "prisoners' rights." The dockets in many jurisdictions in this country, especially in those jurisdictions where a large prison facility is located, are clogged with many lawsuits filed by prisoners or others serving sentences. This examines the major kinds of cases that make up correctional law litigation.

From 1980 to 1996, the number of prisoner petitions filed by federal and state inmates in U.S. district courts rose from 23,287 in 1980 to a high of 68,235 in 1996. In 1996, the Prison Litigation Reform Act (PLRA) was enacted. The PLRA has had an impact in reducing the number of prisoner litigations, as intended (See Appendix 3-1 on the Navigate eBook site on jblearning.com). Prisoner petitions in the U.S. district courts declined by 21% from 1996 to 2019, while the prison population increased by over 30%. These totals do not include prisoner petitions filed in state courts. One of the requirements of the PLRA is for prisoners to exhaust available administrative remedies within the correctional system prior to bringing a prison conditions law suit in federal court. In *Woodford v. Ngo,* 548 U.S. 81 (2006), the Supreme Court held that the PLRA requires the proper exhaustion of administrative remedies for inmate grievances before inmates bring Section 1983 actions into federal courts .Today, there are some who believe that the PLRA has been "too effective," in preventing judicial consideration of meritorious issues.[1]

▶ Habeas Corpus

Habeas corpus is one of the oldest kinds of court actions, going far back into English law. It is recognized, and guaranteed, in the U.S. Constitution:

> **The Privilege of the Writ of Habeas Corpus shall not be suspended, unless when in Cases of Rebellion or Invasion the public Safety may require it.**
>
> U.S. Constitution, Article I, Section 9

Availability of the writ is also assured in state constitutions, where it is sometimes called "the great writ of liberty."

A habeas corpus action is started when a prisoner (or detainee) files a **petition**, asking for relief. The matter complained about must be the legality of imprisonment (or detention). The relief sought is release from illegal confinement. The petition should be filed against the person or authority who is the official custodian. The person filing the paper (for our purposes, a prisoner) is called a **petitioner**; the custodian (in prisoner rights cases, the **warden** or **superintendent**) is called the **respondent** in the case. (This is in contrast to other civil cases, where the action is usually started by filing a paper called a complaint; the parties in such a case are the plaintiff and the defendant. In Appendix 3, (see 1997 complaint on the Navigate eBook site on jblearning.com) there is a copy of a 1997 complaint filed in the United States District Court for the District of Columbia. The complaint states the facts as alleged by the claimant, the violative claims that are being made, and the relief that the plaintiff wishes the court to grant.)

In a habeas action, the court will then order the respondent to show cause why a writ of habeas corpus should not be issued (why the prisoner should not be released). Habeas corpus is regarded as an urgent legal action; the **response** by the custodian is usually required within a very short time (often 10 days or fewer), and all actions by the court are usually taken in a prompt manner. Habeas corpus actions are treated as emergency matters and, as such, go to the top of court dockets, ahead of other types of civil cases. After an attorney for the custodian (the respondent) responds, the court may dismiss the petition, hold a hearing to obtain more information, or grant the request and issue a writ. (Note that only courts can issue writs. In prisons and jails, we often hear of inmates who file writs; they are called writ-writers. This is poor nomenclature, and bad use of language, because only judges— and not inmates—have the legal authority to write writs.)

Habeas corpus is Latin for "have the body." It is an order directed to the person with custody, commanding him to "have," or produce, the body of the person who is in custody before the court. In fact, there are several types of habeas corpus, and all of them have Latin names. The common one is the writ of *habeas corpus ad subjiciendum.* When the term *habeas corpus* is by itself, this is the type that is meant. It is used to review the legality of the **confinement** of the detainee or prisoner. Two other types are encountered occasionally in corrections: *habeas corpus ad prosequendum* is a writ issued by a court ordering the custodian to bring the prisoner before the court for purposes of prosecution; *habeas corpus ad testificandum* is an order to bring a prisoner before the court to give evidence in a court case. Some courts still use these kinds of writs to bring prisoners to court, although, as the decades go by, fewer and fewer courts are using these ancient (and foreign language) styles of orders.

A habeas corpus action will ordinarily be filed in the court where the prisoner is being held—that is, the court with jurisdiction over the custodian (the warden, for example) and the prisoner. (*Braden v. 30th Judicial Circuit Court of Kentucky*, 410 U.S. 484, 1973). Braden was indicted in Kentucky in 1967 on two criminal counts. He escaped from the custody of Kentucky and remained at large until he was later arrested in Alabama. He was convicted in Alabama and confined within that state. Although he was located in Alabama, he filed a habeas corpus action in Kentucky, which was granted by the district court in that state. The court of appeals reversed, holding that the law requires that the prisoner be within the territorial limits of the district court. Stating that the writ is directed to and served on the "jailer," not the prisoner, the Supreme Court reversed, holding that "the language of § 2241(a) requires nothing more than that the court issuing the writ has jurisdiction over the custodian."

Relief in habeas corpus is release from custody. It traditionally meant total release from confinement. In more recent years, it has also been used to achieve release from limited confinement or a particular type of confinement. (For example, a prisoner may use habeas corpus to claim that his placement in **segregation** in an institution was illegal. If he is successful, the court may order his release but only into the regular prison population.)

Habeas corpus is not the proper action to test the guilt or innocence of the person in custody. (That is properly accomplished in the court where the person in custody is prosecuted or in appeals from judgments of that court.) Damages are not awarded in habeas corpus actions. Habeas corpus is, however, one of the tools almost always used by attorneys for persons under death sentence to challenge the propriety of that status.

There are federal statutes that spell out the authority of federal courts to issue writs of habeas corpus. These statutory provisions are contained in Title 28 of the U.S. Code. Federal laws are compiled, for ease of use, in a collection of books called the *U.S. Code*. (The *U.S. Code Annotated* is just another version of this collection, which includes commentary and court decisions printed with each section to show what has been done with each particular section.) The entire body of statutes is divided into titles. Each title deals with a different subject matter. Title 28, which we refer to here, deals with the judiciary and court matters. Within each title, there are chapters and sections. These divisions are also made for ease of use and to make individual subjects easier to find. When referencing federal statutes, we will provide the title number followed by the section number. (For example, 28 U.S.C. § 2241 stands for Title 28, U.S. Code, Section 2241).

There are provisions for federal prisoners to seek habeas corpus relief, which are found under Title 28, U.S. Code, Section 2241. There are also provisions that authorize federal courts to consider applications from state prisoners for release under Title 28, U.S. Code, Section 2254. As a general rule, federal courts are not quick to jump into habeas matters involving state prisoners; they usually defer to the states to take care of such problems in their own courts, as the federal law contemplates.

In an effort to limit a prisoner's ability to file petitions in federal court, Congress, in 1996, passed the Antiterrorism and Effective Death Penalty Act (AEDPA). AEDPA made several amendments to the habeas corpus requirements. For example, an amended Section 2254 provides that federal habeas corpus relief is only available to a state prisoner if the petitioner has exhausted the remedies that are available for such relief in the state where they are confined or detained; if there is no available state exhaustion process; or if there are circumstances that exist to make the process ineffective to protect the rights of the applicant. This section further allows federal courts, upon finding that the application for a writ of habeas corpus has no merit, to dismiss the application even if there has been no **exhaustion** at the state level. Another example of the amendments occurs in Section 2255 and establishes a one-year period of limitation for a federal prisoner to file a motion attacking the legality of his sentence. The section specifies when the limitation period begins to run.

As suggested above, one objective of AEDPA was to promote the finality of criminal convictions and sentences. Contrary to its intent, AEDPA may have resulted, at least initially, in a higher number of petitions filed in U.S. district courts, especially with respect to petitions filed by state inmates using Section 2254. In April 1997, the year following passage of AEDPA, the number of habeas corpus petition filings by state prisoners had increased from 1.1 per 1,000 inmates per month to 3.4 per month—an increase of 2,600 petitions. In the year 2000, four years after the passage of the AEDPA, the number of state prisoner habeas petitions increased to 21,090. The number of such petitions has declined, reaching 14,360 in 2018[2] (see **FIGURE 3-1**).

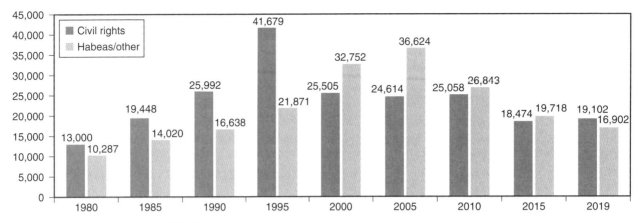

FIGURE 3-1 Prisoner Litigation in U.S. Courts.

Data from 1980 – 2000 Scalia, J. *Prisoner Petitions Filed in U.S. District Courts 2000 with Trends 1980-2000.* (Washington, D.C.: Bureau of Justice Statistics, U.S. Department of Justice, 2002). 2005, 2010, 2015 and 2019 data collected from Administrative Office for U.S. Courts, Caseload Statistics Data Tables, Table C-2, *U.S. District Courts-Civil Cases Commenced, by Bavsis of Jurisdiction and Nature of Suit during the 12 month period ending March 31, 2005-2010-2015 and 2019.* https://www.uscourts.gov/statistics-reports/caseload-statistics-data-tables

Correctional Litigation in Federal Court System Data Bullets

- The number of prisoner petitions filed by federal and state inmates in U.S. district courts rose from 23,287 in 1980 to a high of 68,235 in 1996. This total includes suits by both federal and state prisoners, and includes civil rights actions, prison conditions case, habeas challenges to custody, and sentence modification actions.[i]

- From 1980 to 1996, fewer than 2% of the petitions were adjudicated in favor of the inmate and 62% were dismissed.[ii]

- Prior to 1996, 24% of inmate petitions that were dismissed in the district courts were appealed.[iii]

- In 1996, the Prison Litigation Reform Act (PLRA) was enacted. The PLRA has had an impact in reducing the number of prisoner litigations, as intended. At year-end 1996, there were approximately 1.18 million prisoners under the jurisdiction of federal or state adult prison authorities.[iv]

- By 2000, after enactment of the PLRA, prisoner petitions in district courts had declined by 15% (9,978) to 58,257. This decrease occurred while the prison population had increased by over 2% (272,000) to 1.39 million.[v]

- In 2010, prisoners filed 51,901 petitions in district courts, a 24% decline (16,334) from 1996 while the prison population had increased by 400,000 to 1.6 million.[vi]

- For the computational period of April 1, 2018, to March 31, 2019, 54,066 prisoner petitions were filed in federal district courts.[vii] Prisoner petitions in the federal courts of appeal made up 26% (12,593) of appeals commenced in the 12 months ending March 31, 2019.[viii]

▶ Torts

A **tort** is a private wrong or injury for which a court will provide a remedy in the form of damages. It is also an ancient remedy in English law. A tort always involves a violation of some duty owed to the person injured—other than by agreement of the parties (that is, by contract). These are the two main areas of the civil law: torts and contracts.

---

[i]Scalia, J. *Prisoner Petitions Filed in U.S. District Courts, 2000, with Trends 1980-2000* (Washington, DC: Bureau of Justice Statistics, U.S. Department of Justice, 2002),

[ii]Id.

[iii]Id.

[iv]Id.

[v]Id.

[vi]Administrative Office for U.S. Courts, Caseload Statistics Data Tables, Table C-2, *U.S. District Courts-Civil Cases Commenced, by Basis of Jurisdiction and Nature of Suit during the 12 month period ending March 31, 2005-2010-2015 and 2019.*

[vii]Administrative Office for U.S. Courts, Caseload Statistics Data Tables, Table C-2, *U.S. District Courts-Civil Cases Commenced, by Basis of Jurisdiction and Nature of Suit during the 12 month period ending March 31, 2019.*

[viii]Administrative Office for U.S. Courts, Caseload Statistics Data Tables, Table B-1 , *U.S. Courts of Appeal-Civil Cases Commenced, by Basis of Jurisdiction and Nature of Suit during the 12 month period ending March 31, 2019.*

There are three elements in any tort action: (1) a legal duty owed by the defendant to the plaintiff, (2) a breach of that duty, and (3) injury (damage) as a proximate result of the breach of duty. The duties that are owed have been established by law and go back to principles of the common law. Some are defined (in more recent times) in legislation, but even those are based on, and are interpreted by, court rulings.

Torts may be either intentional or negligent. In intentional torts, the wrong is done by someone who intends to do what the law has declared to be wrong. In negligent torts, the wrong is done by someone who fails to exercise the degree of care that is required by the law in performing acts that are otherwise permissible.

The most common type of tort that we encounter in our everyday lives today is probably the accident that is caused by the negligent operation of an automobile. The injury caused may involve property damage, personal injury, or both. Every driver has a duty to operate a vehicle safely and in accordance with rules of the road, and every driver must learn and adhere to those rules. Failure to use proper or "reasonable" care in the operation of a vehicle is a breach of duty, and, if it causes injury to another person, it is a tort. The injured party may file suit for the injury suffered and, in doing so, becomes a plaintiff against the defendant who has injured him.

There are two types of **damages** that may be recovered in a civil tort suit: compensatory damages and punitive damages (although some states do not allow punitive damages in tort actions). Compensatory damages are awarded to cover the actual monetary loss suffered by the plaintiff. In cases of property damage, these would include the costs of restoring or repairing the property. In cases of personal injury, compensatory damages would include medical bills, lost wages, pain and suffering, and an estimate of future losses in these same categories. Punitive damages are designed to punish the defendant for severely bad conduct. Here, more than simple **negligence** is required; a defendant may have shown gross negligence (acting recklessly) or willful negligence (acting intentionally to cause harm) in order to justify an award of punitive damages. There are also nominal damages, which are damages of small amounts that are awarded when a tort has technically been committed, but the judge or jury deciding on the amount of damages believes that a minimal award is the most just result. Again, the relief given in a tort action is an award of money. There is no injunctive relief in tort suits, and attorney fees are not usually given in common law tort suits.

The most frequently encountered common law torts are assault, **battery, false imprisonment, libel**, and **defamation**. Negligent loss of someone else's property is also a tort, as is medical malpractice. These last two are the kinds most often encountered in corrections facilities, although assault and battery are also the basis of some prisoner suits.

In English law, the **sovereign** (the king or queen) could not be sued in its (his or her) own courts, unless the sovereign gave permission to be sued. The courts were a part of the sovereignty and, as such, could not be used to attack the sovereign. Over the centuries, the courts became more and more independent, but the principle of sovereign immunity continued. It was carried over into the United States, where the legal principle states that the sovereign (the government) cannot be sued without its permission. Most governments have abandoned strict sovereign immunity. Today, the federal government permits tort actions to be brought (with strict statutory restrictions), and most state governments permit some kinds of tort actions against the state. These are usually called tort claim acts. In most cases, they require administrative claims to be made first against the government. If those are not successful, the injured party may be able to go into court to pursue the tort action.

For some time, even though there was a Federal Tort Claims Act, there was some question as to whether federal prisoners could sue the U.S. government for tort injuries. Lower courts had ruled both ways—that they could and that they could not. The Supreme Court finally ruled that federal inmates could use the Tort Claims Act in *United States v. Muniz,* 374 U.S. 150 (1963). Two cases were decided under *Muniz:* one dealing with injuries suffered by an inmate who was assaulted during a prison disturbance (Muniz), and a second case dealing with an inmate who went blind (Winston) as a result of alleged medical malpractice by government doctors. Those two kinds of cases happen to be the most common kinds of tort claims arising out of federal prison operations, except for claims for damaged or lost property.

Prison systems routinely take temporary custody of the personal property of prisoners, including at those times when prisoners are transferred between facilities. During these transfers, some personal property of the prisoner may be lost or damaged while in the possession of prison officials. To compensate prisoners for such losses, if caused by a negligent act or the omission of a prison employee, various administrative procedures have been developed. An example of this type of administrative procedure is Title 31, U.S.C. Section 3723, which permits a prisoner to submit a claim to the Bureau of Prisons for personal property that was lost or damaged as a result of the negligence of a federal employee. Claims may not exceed $1,000 and must be presented within one year of the loss.

In *Ali v. BOP,* 552 U.S. 214 (2008), the U.S. Supreme Court ruled that federal prisoners could not use the Federal Torts Claims Act (FTCA) to seek damages from the United States for the loss or damage to personal property while in the possession of BOP employees as Congress had expressly precluded consideration of these types of claims under the FTCA.

▶ Section 1983

There is another major group of legal actions available to prisoners, sometimes called constitutional torts. These are torts in the sense that they represent injuries or harm suffered by a person because of wrongful actions by another. They are not common law torts, however, because they are not included in the body of torts that have been developed by court rulings (common law) over the centuries. Instead, they are injuries caused by a violation of rights guaranteed by the Constitution. They are recognized and authorized as court suits by a federal statute, which is contained in the Civil Rights Act of 1871. This law is codified in Title 42, U.S. Code, Section 1983:

> **Every person who, under color of any statute, ordinance, regulation, custom, or usage, of any State or Territory or the District of Columbia, subjects, or causes to be subjected, any citizen of the United States or other person within the jurisdiction thereof to the deprivation of any rights, privileges, or immunities secured by the Constitution and laws, shall be liable to the party injured in an action at law, suit in equity, or other proper proceeding for redress.**

As the Supreme Court has stated: "*Section 1983 "is not itself a source of substantive rights," but merely provides "a method for vindicating federal rights elsewhere conferred." Baker v. McCollan,* 443 U.S, 187 (1979). Most states also have provisions in state law that allow suits to be brought for injuries sustained as a result of violations of state constitutional guarantees.

Although it was enacted in 1871, the federal Civil Rights Act was not used much until the civil rights litigation explosion of the 1950s and the prisoner rights litigation explosion of the 1960s. Since then, it has been the most frequently used type of lawsuit in corrections litigation. Lawsuits under Section 1983 allege that state officials have deprived the prisoners of their constitutional rights. Examples include the right to due process in disciplinary hearings (Fifth and Fourteenth Amendments) in *Wolff v. McDonnell,* 418 U.S. 539 (1974); access to law libraries in *Bounds v. Smith,* 430 U.S. 817 (1977); and access to health care (Eighth Amendment) in *Estelle v. Gamble,* 429 U.S. 97 (1976). Thousands of these suits are filed in federal courts each year. Section 1983 actions are the most frequently used type of prisoner litigation. Habeas corpus and torts are limited in scope and the kinds of relief they make available. Section 1983 allows broad relief, in law, equity, or any "other proper proceeding." This has resulted in suits in which both damages and injunctive relief are commonly sought, and often given, in Section 1983 actions.

There are two main kinds of injunctive relief: (1) *restrictive injunctions,* in which defendants are enjoined (that is, they are legally ordered to stop) from doing things they have been wrongfully doing; and (2) *mandatory injunctions,* in which defendants are required to do things they should have been doing. If plaintiffs can show that government authorities have not been following constitutional requirements, it may be most valuable to obtain **injunctions**, either to stop them from doing something (ordering prison officials to stop putting people into a segregation unit that is inadequately heated, for example) or to require them to start doing something (ordering prison officials to adequately heat the segregation unit in winter, for example).

State prisoners also brought suits in federal court using the Civil Rights Act, because the federal courts (at least in the 1960s and 1970s) were seen, in most jurisdictions, as being more liberal, and more likely to rule in favor of prisoners than state courts. Also, the law as it applies to prisons became more established, over time, in federal courts, and prisoners in one jurisdiction could use rulings in other parts of the country as leverage to get favorable rulings in their own situations. As already noted, a state prisoner is barred from bringing a habeas corpus action in a federal court unless the prisoner has already used the state remedies that are available to litigate the same matter. This was confirmed in *Wilwording v. Swenson,* 404 U.S. 249 (1972), and *Preiser v. Rodriguez,* 411 U.S. 475 (1973).

The Supreme Court, in *Heck v. Humphrey,* 512 U.S. 477 (1994), held that a state inmate's claim for damages is not cognizable (capable of being tried or examined) under Section 1983 if a judgment for the plaintiff would imply that the conviction or sentence was invalid, unless the inmate could show that such conviction or sentence had already been invalidated. The question in *Edwards v. Balisok,* 520 U.S. 641 (1997), was whether an inmate's challenge to the procedures used to deprive him of **good time** credits was cognizable under Section 1983. Balisok, a Washington State prison inmate, was charged with and found to have committed four prison rule infractions, for which he was punished by segregated confinement and a loss of 30 days' good time credit. He filed a Section 1983 action requesting, in part, a declaration that the disciplinary hearing procedures used by state officials violated due process and requesting compensatory and punitive damages because they used those procedures. He did not request that his good time be restored, as *Preiser* held that the exclusive remedy in federal court for an inmate seeking this substantive relief is a writ of habeas corpus.

Balisok's main allegation was that he was not allowed to present a defense through specifically identified witnesses who had exculpatory evidence. He further alleged that the action of excluding witnesses was a consequence of the deceit and bias of the hearing officer. The Supreme Court noted the following:

> **The due process requirements for a prison disciplinary hearing are in many respects less demanding than those for criminal prosecution, but they are not so lax as to let stand the decision of a biased hearing officer who dishonestly suppresses evidence of innocence.**

The Supreme Court held that Balisok's claim for declaratory relief and monetary damages, based on allegations of deceit and bias by the decision maker, could invalidate the punishment that was imposed, and it was, therefore, not cognizable under Section 1983. In such instances, habeas corpus would be the appropriate judicial remedy.

In a **per curiam** opinion in *Muhammad v. Close,* 540 U.S. 749 (2004), the Supreme Court held that *Heck* did not apply to prison disciplinary issues where the inmate's complaint poses no challenge to his conviction or to the duration of his sentence. In *Muhammad,* the inmate's amended complaint sought compensatory and punitive damages for his predisciplinary hearing detention. It did not challenge the disciplinary finding of insolence or the action taken because the inmate was found to be insolent.

In *Wilkinson v. Dotson,* 544 U.S. 74 (2005), two state prison inmates challenged their parole status (eligibility for parole in the first case, suitability for parole in the second). The inmates separately sued under 42 U.S.C. § 1983, claiming that Ohio's parole procedures violated the Federal Constitution. The district courts held that relief had to be sought through habeas corpus. On appeal, the Sixth Circuit consolidated the two cases and reversed the lower courts, holding that the actions could occur under Section 1983. In affirming the Sixth Circuit, the Supreme Court held:

> *Heck* specifies that a prisoner cannot use § 1983 to obtain damages where success *would necessarily* imply the unlawfulness of a (not previously invalidated) conviction or sentence. And *Balisok* ... demonstrates that habeas remedies do not displace § 1983 actions where success in the civil rights suit *would not necessarily* [emphasis added] vitiate the legality of (not previously invalidated) state confinement.

The connection between the constitutionality of the inmate's parole proceedings and release from confinement was seen by the Court as too tenuous to require a suit in habeas corpus. Litigation success for either inmate did not mean release but rather at most a new eligibility review or new parole hearing. Since such action does not clearly demonstrate the invalidity of confinement or its duration, the inmates could proceed under 42 U.S.C. § 1983.

In *Skinner v. Switzer,* 562 U.S. 521 (2011), the Supreme Court considered whether "a convicted state prisoner seeking DNA testing of crime scene evidence" could make such a claim under a Section 1983 civil rights action, or whether it must be done in a petition for a writ of habeas corpus. In allowing for a Section 1983 action, the Court, referring to its decisions in *Heck* and in *Wilkinson,* said "[s]uccess in his suit for DNA testing would not 'necessarily imply' the invalidity of his conviction. While test results might prove exculpatory, that outcome is hardly inevitable; ... results might prove inconclusive or they might further incriminate Skinner."

Under 42 U.S.C. § 1983, a suit can be brought by any person who claims their constitutional rights have been abridged by a person acting under color of state law. This person (the plaintiff) can sue an offending person, who can be any state or local government official or corrections staff member. Such actions may not be brought against the state itself or corrections agencies (although municipal corporations have been held to be "persons" and may be sued).[3] The persons sued must be operating under color of state law. Section 1983 defendants are thus always state employees or officials (or, as we will see later, persons functioning just as if they were state employees, such as doctors under contract who provide medical services to state prisoners.)

Can a state divest itself of jurisdiction over Section 1983 suits seeking monetary damages from corrections officers? Believing that damage suits filed by inmates against state corrections officers were largely "frivolous and vexatious," New York enacted Correction Law § 24. The law effectively stripped its courts of jurisdiction over such damage claims, requiring these claims to be brought in the court of claims, with the claim being made against the state. The impact of this change meant the inmate would be suing a different defendant (the state), there would be different relief (no right to attorney fees or to seek punitive damages or injunctive relief), and that there would be different procedural protections (not entitled to a jury trial). The law's focus was narrow in scope, as it did not prevent the trial courts that generally exercise jurisdiction over Section 1983 suits from continuing to do so against other state officials. In *Haywood v. Drown*, 556 U.S. 729 (2009), the question was whether that "exceptional treatment of a limited category of § 1983 claims are consistent with the Supremacy Clause of the United States Constitution."

In *Haywood*, a state prison inmate began Section 1983 actions against several New York state correctional employees, alleging violation of his civil rights relating to inmate disciplinary proceedings and an altercation. The trial court dismissed the action, saying that under Correction Law § 24, the court did not have jurisdiction. Both the intermediate appellate court and the state court of appeals (the state's highest appellate court) affirmed. The court of appeals rejected the inmate's claim that Correction Law § 24's jurisdictional restriction was contrary to the Supremacy Clause. The court held that the law treated state and federal actions against correction officers in the same manner (neither can be brought) and is best characterized as a "neutral state rule."

The Supreme Court reversed.

[A]lthough States retain substantial leeway to establish the contours of their judicial systems, they lack authority to nullify a federal right or cause of action they believe is inconsistent with their local policies. "The suggestion that [an] act of Congress is not in harmony with the policy of the State, and therefore that the courts of the State are free to decline jurisdiction, is quite inadmissible, because it presupposes what in legal contemplation does not exist."

It is principally on this basis that Correction Law § 24 violates the Supremacy Clause. In passing Correction Law § 24, New York made the judgment that correction officers should not be burdened with suits for damages arising out of conduct performed in the scope of their employment. Because it regards these suits as too numerous or too frivolous (or both), the State's longstanding policy has been to shield this narrow class of defendants from liability when sued for damages…The State's policy, whatever its merits, is contrary to Congress' judgment that *all* persons who violate federal rights while acting under color of state law shall be held liable for damages.

In its opinion, the Court also addressed the New York court of appeals' holding that Correction Law § 24 was constitutional because it treated both federal and state claims the same.

Although the absence of discrimination is necessary to our finding a state law neutral, it is not sufficient. A jurisdictional rule cannot be used as a device to undermine federal law, no matter how evenhanded it may appear.

The Court also commented on the fact that the state held inappropriate for its trial courts only certain types of lawsuits—those seeking damage relief against corrections officers.

We therefore hold that, having made the decision to create courts of general jurisdiction that regularly sit to entertain analogous suits, New York is not at liberty to shut the courthouse door to federal claims that it considers at odds with its local policy.

Our holding addresses only the unique scheme adopted by the State of New York—a law designed to shield a particular class of defendants (correction officers) from a particular type of liability (damages) brought by a particular class of plaintiffs (prisoners)…Correction Law § 24 is effectively an immunity statute cloaked in jurisdictional garb.

Section 1983, which covers only persons acting under color of state law (state, county, and municipal officers), cannot be used to sue persons acting under color of federal law (federal employees). However, the Supreme Court ruled that because there was a federal right, there must be a judicial mechanism to enforce the right, even in the absence of express legislative authority. So, the Court created an implied remedy, in the absence of legislation, allowing persons to sue federal officials (not their employer the United States) for money damages for unconstitutional searches and seizures in violation of the Fourth Amendment. *Bivens v. Six Unknown Federal Narcotics Agents,* 403 U.S. 388 (1971). The complaint in that case alleged that on November 26, 1965, agents of the Federal Bureau of Narcotics, acting under claim of federal authority, entered the petitioner's apartment without warrant, searched the apartment, and arrested the petitioner on narcotics charges—all without probable cause. In 1967, the petitioner sued, alleging the arrest was made unlawfully, unreasonably, and contrary to law. He sought monetary damages from each of the agents.

The district and appeals courts ruled for the government, holding that the complaint failed to state a federal cause of action. In reversing, the Supreme Court held that an individual could sue an individual federal agent for an arrest and home search that were alleged to be illegal. The Court further held that the actions of the federal agents in violation of the Fourth Amendment's prohibition against unreasonable search and seizure were a "federally protected interest" and not one better handled under state tort law, as the federal government had argued. This case was interpreted to authorize persons to sue for money damages for the violation of constitutional civil rights committed by federal officials in the same way that Congress had authorized such suits against state officials in Section 1983.

The Supreme Court ruled that federal prisoners housed in a private correctional facility could not bring a Bivens action against employees of the private correctional company for alleged violations of the prisoner's constitutional rights. The Court held that Pollard could not assert a *Bivens* claim, that his "Eighth Amendment claim focuses upon a kind of conduct that typically falls within the scope of traditional state tort law. And in case of a privately employed defendant, state tort law provides an 'alternative, existing process' capable of protecting the constitutional interests at stake." The Court said "the prisoner must seek a remedy under state tort law."[4]

For some time, there was a question about whether the "*Bivens* doctrine," which allowed civil rights suits against federal agents, applied only to violations of the Fourth Amendment, because the *Bivens* case itself dealt with allegations of illegal search and seizure. Initially, the Supreme Court extended the *Bivens* implied cause of action to two other constitutional provisions: for violations of the **due process clause** (Fifth Amendment—gender discrimination), as in *Davis v. Passman,* 442 U.S. 228 (1979). They could also be brought against prison officials for claims of cruel and unusual punishment (Eighth Amendment—denial of medical treatment), *Carlson v. Green,* 446 U.S. 14 (1980). Thus, federal prisoners bring **Bivens actions**, not Section 1983 actions.

Lower federal courts, in many cases, extended the *Bivens* doctrine to other constitutional claims, although the Supreme Court in a number of decisions declined to extend the *Bivens* doctrine to other constitutional rights. Some 45 years after *Bivens* was decided in 1971, the Supreme Court emphatically ruled that a *Bivens* action for money damages against individual federal officers was not authorized in every case of an alleged constitutional violation. *Ziglar v. Abbasi,* 582 U.S. ____. 137 S. Ct. 1843 (2017). Following the terrorist attacks of September 11, 2001, several hundred persons were detained by federal authorities in federal correctional facilities in the United States. After these detainees were released, several initiated a *Bivens* law suit against various federal officials, including former Attorney General John Ashcroft, former FBI Director Robert Mueller, former Immigration and Naturalization Service Commissioner John Ziglar (the Executive Officials), and Bureau of Prisons staff members at the detention facility (the Warden and two Associate Wardens). The detainees alleged that the defendants (1) detained them in harsh conditions of confinement at the federal correctional facility in Brooklyn, New York, for punitive purposes in violation of the detainees' Fifth Amendment right of substantive due process; (2) that the harsh conditions of confinement were imposed on them because of their race, religion, or national origin in violation of the Fifth Amendment; (3) that the detainees were subjected to unconstitutional punitive strip searches in violation of the their Fourth and Fifth Amendment rights; and (4) that the Warden knowingly allowed subordinate staff to abuse the detainees in violation of the Fifth Amendment. After the Second Circuit Court of Appeals reversed a district court's dismissal of claims against some of the defendants and affirmed the district court's decision to allow the lawsuit to proceed, the federal defendants appealed to the U.S. Supreme Court.

The Supreme Court's opinion in *Ziglar* is unusual in that only six of the sitting justices took part in considering the case. Two of the six justices dissented from the plurality ruling, and four justices joined the plurality decision. The first issue addressed by the Court was whether the defendants were subject to suit for money damages under an implied *Bivens* cause of action. The Court noted that the implied cause of action created by *Bivens* in 1971 was premised on the legal assumption **that courts must "adjust their remedies so as to grant the necessary relief" when "federally protected rights have been invaded."** In the years following the *Bivens, Passman,* and *Carlson* trilogy, the Supreme Court adopted a more cautious approach to implying remedies to new constitutional contexts.

The Court first noted that the question about whether to create a cause of action against federal actors was a task better left to the legislative branch. Federal courts should analyze claims for money damages from federal officers using a two-step approach: The court should first determine if the case seeks to extend *Bivens* liability to a new context or presents one of the three claims recognized in *Bivens, Passman,* and *Carlson.* If the claim arises under one of the three recognized *Bivens* contexts, the suit should proceed. Courts may wish to consider any of the illustrative, but not exhaustive, factors in determining if the case arises in a new context:

> *The proper test for determining whether a case presents a new Bivens context is as follows. If the case is different in a meaningful way from previous Bivens cases decided by this Court, then the context is new. Without endeavoring to create an exhaustive list of differences that are meaningful enough to make a given context a new one, some examples might prove instructive. A case might differ in a meaningful way because of the rank of the officers involved; the constitutional right at issue; the generality or specificity of the official action; the extent of judicial guidance as to how an officer should respond to the problem or emergency to be confronted; the statutory or other legal mandate under which the officer was operating; the risk of disruptive intrusion by the Judiciary into the functioning of other branches; or the presence of potential special factors that previous Bivens cases did not consider.*

If the court determines the case creates an extension of *Bivens,* the court must still determine if any "*special factors counsel hesitation before implying a new cause of action.*"

Under this analysis, the Court in *Ziglar* concluded the plaintiffs' claims were a new *Bivens* context, and before implying a *Bivens* remedy, the lower courts needed to perform a "special factors" analysis. The Court concluded that a number of "special factors" existed in this case, including: allowing a *Bivens* claim to proceed would challenge a high level-executive branch policy; that such litigation would distract high-level officials from performing their functions; and the challenge dealt with issues of national security, which are particularly within the authority of the legislative and executive branches of government. The Court also noted that Congress had opportunities to create the remedy sought by the plaintiffs but had chosen not to do so. Finally, the existence of other types of judicial relief is a factor to consider before judicially creating a new cause of action.

The Court also noted plaintiffs' claims against the prison officials were different in context from those previously approved in *Carlson v. Green* because the claims arose under the Fifth Amendment rather than the Eighth Amendment. The court of appeals also failed to conduct any analysis of "special factors counseling hesitation." The holding of the Court reversed the judgment of the court of appeals authorizing a *Bivens* action for money damages against the federal defendants.

A week after *Ziglar v. Abbasi* was decided, the Court issued its opinion in *Hernandez v. Mesa,* 582 U.S. ___, 137 S.Ct. 2003 (2017) a case involving the fatal transnational shooting of a child by a U.S. Border Patrol Officer. The parents had asserted a *Bivens* claim against the officer for violations of the decedent's Fourth and Fifth Amendment rights. The district court dismissed the claims under both amendments and the parents appealed. The court of appeals, sitting en banc, determined that the parents failed to state a claim for a violation of the Fourth Amendment because their child was "a Mexican citizen who had no 'significant voluntary connection' to the United States" and "was on Mexican soil at the time he was shot." *Hernandez v. United States,* 785 F.3d 117, 119 (C.A.5 2015) (*per curiam*) (quoting *United States v. Verdugo-Urquidez,* 494 U.S. 259, (1990)). As to the parents' claim under the Fifth Amendment, the court's judgment was "somewhat divided on the question of whether [the agent's] conduct violated the Fifth Amendment," but was "unanimous" in concluding that [the agent] was entitled to qualified immunity. The Supreme Court vacated the judgment of the court of appeals and remanded the case back to the lower courts to reconsider its rulings in light of *Ziglar.*

The court of appeals reconsidered the case as instructed by the Supreme Court. Sitting *en banc,* the court decided that the claims of the parents were a new context for *Bivens* and there were special factors "including the incident's relationship to foreign affairs and national security, the extraterritorial aspect of the case, and Congress's "repeated refusals" to create a damages remedy for injuries incurred on foreign soil," which counseled hesitation in extending *Bivens* to the parents' claims against the federal officer. The parents again appealed to the Supreme Court and in *Hernandez v. Mesa,* 589__ U.S. ___ 140 S.Ct. 735 (2020) the Court affirmed the judgment of the court of appeals ruling that the parents' claim of excessive use of force and denial of due process arose "in a "new context" or involve[d] a "new category of defendants" and there were special factors counseling hesitation in expanding the implied cause of action. While the parents 'claim did arise under the Fourth and Fifth Amendment like in *Bivens* and *Davis v. Passman,* the parents' claim was "meaningfully different" from those in *Bivens* and *Passman*. Moving to an analysis of the special factors which might counsel hesitation, the Court concluded that the basis of the claim, a fatal cross border shooting of a foreign national, involved *"matters relating 'to the conduct of foreign relations . . . so exclusively entrusted to the political branches of government as to be largely immune from judicial inquiry or interference.'"* National security was also a special factor because *"whether the Judiciary should alter the framework established by the political branches for addressing cases in which it is alleged that lethal force was unlawfully employed by an agent at the border" . . . is the prerogative of the Congress and President."* The Court also noted that Section 1983 actions may be brought only by U.S. citizens or other person within the jurisdiction of the United States. Finally, the Court concluded that Congress could authorize such suits if it chooses to do so. In affirming the judgment of the court of appeals dismissing the parents' claim, the Court stated:

> **When evaluating whether to extend Bivens, the most important question "is 'who should decide' whether to provide for a damages remedy, Congress or the courts?" Abbasi, 582 U. S. at ___ (citation omitted). The correct "answer most often will be Congress."**

Throughout this text, you will often see these lawsuits referred to simply as "Section 1983" or "*Bivens*" suits. This is just shorthand for the entire statutory or case cite because those two kinds of actions are so common in corrections law, and the majority of decisions discussed in this book were decided under one or the other of those two authorities. Until the Court's opinion in *Ziglar,* many of the provisions and court rulings under one kind of suit (Section 1983 or Bivens) were used in the other. In those cases where a *Bivens* cause of action is authorized against federal officers, court rulings under Section 1983 for persons acting under color of state law would be generally applicable to constitutional claims against persons acting under color of federal law. However, in light of the Court's decision in *Ziglar*, a *Bivens* actions may not be available against federal officers for all violations of an individual's constitutional rights.

In practice and in fact, using Section 1983 actions, although limited to suits against individual officials, has been very effective. This is because rulings that defendants have violated constitutional rights and relief in money damages or injunction, or both, carry considerable impact, and they often bring about the correction of what have been unconstitutional actions or conditions. Thus, the impact of a successful Section 1983 lawsuit often is much broader than just the victory for the individual plaintiff.

One significant aspect of a Section 1983 or *Bivens* suit is that a judgment in favor of the prisoner plaintiff may mean that the individual official defendant must pay a monetary award from the defendant's own financial resources. While the employee may receive representation by the government, be held not liable for monetary damages by the court, or, if held liable, receive indemnification from the government, these are not automatic occurrences.

Summary

- There are three types of legal actions that cover nearly all of the lawsuits brought by inmates to complain about the conditions under which they are being held, sue for money damages because of injuries they have suffered, or complain about other matters related to their status as offenders. The three commonly used actions are habeas corpus (petitions by prisoners seeking release from custody because of some illegality in their confinement); torts (tort claims or lawsuits by prisoners seeking money damages for injuries or losses sustained because of wrongful actions by a corrections employee); and Section 1983 (complaints by prisoners alleging violations of constitutional rights and asking for money damages or injunctive relief, pursuant to 42 U.S.C. § 1983).
- Habeas corpus is an ancient remedy, which was taken from English law, and is guaranteed in the U.S. Constitution. Section 1983 (and Bivens lawsuits for federal prisoners) is the most commonly used legal action to challenge prison and jail conditions. Tort Claims Acts are used for common law tort actions in those jurisdictions in which the government has waived its sovereign immunity, allowing suits to be brought against the government. The most frequently encountered tort claims in prisons involve money damages for negligent loss of or damage to an inmate's property, injuries suffered because of assaults caused by the negligence of corrections officers or staff, and medical malpractice claims.
- Recent decisions by the U.S. Supreme Court (*Ziglar v. Abbasi* and *Hernandez v. Mesa*) have raised questions about the general availability of money damage lawsuits against persons acting under color of federal law for violations of constitutional rights. *Bivens* has only been applied in three situations and there may not be a money damages remedy against federal officials in all alleged constitutional violation cases.

Thinking About It

When stepping out of the shower, inmate Smith slips on a bar of soap. He falls, injuring his back. The injury occurs in the presence of Officer Jones. Inmate Smith blames Officer Jones for his injury. If inmate Smith decides to file a lawsuit, he has the best chance of success under which of the three types of inmate lawsuits?

Key Terms

battery

Bivens action

confinement

damages

defamation

due process clause

exhaustion

false imprisonment

good time

habeas corpus

injunction (court order)

libel

negligence

per curiam

petition (legal proceeding)

petitioner

respondent

response

segregation (corrections)

sovereign

superintendent

tort

warden

Endnotes

1. Schlanger, Margo *"Trends in Prisoner Litigation, as the PLRA Approaches 20"*, Criminal Law Reporter Volume XXVIII, no. 5 (February/March 2017): 69. https://www.law.umich.edu/facultyhome/margoschlanger/Documents/Publications/Trends%20in%20Prisoner%20Litigation%20as%20the%20PLRA%20Aproaches%2020.pdf. A criticism of *Woodford* is that the ruling holds that the PLRA prevents the filing of even meritorious claims if an inmate fails to meet the prison's procedural grievance filing requirements.

2. *Annual Report of the Director, Judicial Business of the United States Court.* Prisoner Petitions Filed, by Jurisdiction and Nature of Suit, during the 12-month Periods ending June 30, 1990 and September 30, 1995–2018. Available: https://www.uscourts.gov/federal-judicial-caseload-statistics-2019-tables The website provides access to current and historical caseload statistics from 1990 to present. A researcher can select data tables by table number, reporting period, and reporting period.

3. *Monell v. Department of Social Services,* 436 U.S. 658 (1978).

4. In *Minneci v. Pollard*, 565 U.S. 118 (2012) the Supreme Court ruled that federal prisoners housed in a private correctional facility could not bring a Bivens action against employees of the private correctional company for alleged violations of the prisoner's constitutional rights. Court held that Pollard could not assert a *Bivens* claim, that his "Eighth Amendment claim focuses upon a kind of conduct that typically falls within the scope of traditional state tort law. And in case of a privately employed defendant, state tort law provides an 'alternative, existing process' capable of protecting the constitutional interests at stake." The Court said "the prisoner must seek a remedy under state tort law."

CHAPTER 4

Going to Court

Prison officials must be free to take appropriate action to ensure the safety of inmates and corrections personnel and to prevent escape or unauthorized entry. They should be accorded wide-ranging deference in the adoption and execution of policies and practices that in their judgment are needed to preserve internal order and discipline and to maintain institutional security.

U.S. Supreme Court, *Bell v. Wolfish*

CHAPTER OUTLINE

- You Are Summoned
- Getting Representation
- Step by Step
- Not Going to Trial
- Trial
- Appeal

This chapter involves the serious matter of having to appear in a court proceeding, either as a **witness** or as a party in a case. The reader should consider it a guide for preparing for such a court appearance, whether it is about to happen or even if it may never occur. For a person working in the corrections field, the reality is that a correctional employee may have to go to court. This may occasionally be necessary in criminal cases, for which the employee may be called as a witness. An example is when a staff person responds to serious inmate assault (staff, inmate, or visitor) and that assault is being criminally prosecuted. It is more likely, however, that an employee will be called as a witness for a civil case. An example is where an inmate sues prison officials, claiming that their actions under prison policy are denying adequate medical care. Another example is illustrated in Appendix 3, where the inmate's complaint concerned a denial of access to electric or electronic musical instruments.

Much more serious is when the employee is sued. This is likely to be in a Section 1983 (constitutional tort) case, unless the employee is a warden or otherwise a legal custodian, in which case it may be either a habeas corpus action or a Section 1983 action, depending upon the nature of the complaint and the kind of relief that is requested. Appendix 4 provides an example of an inmate filing a complaint under the Civil Rights Act, 42 U.S.C. § 1983. (Note: this inmate's complaint worked its way through the judicial system, up to and including the United States Supreme Court.)

It is unsettling to be sued. For persons in virtually all other walks of life, it is unusual to be sued. For those working in corrections, an environment where an inmate's actions and choices need to be more controlled to better ensure institution security, discipline, and good order, and the protection of persons, including the public, it has almost become commonplace. Being sued is nothing to be taken lightly, and this chapter attempts to put the corrections lawsuit in to perspective.

▶ You Are Summoned

A person first learns they are being sued when they receive a **summons** or **waiver of summons** (this may go by a different name in some jurisdictions). The summons may be served by an official of the court. (In a federal Section 1983 case, a U.S. Marshal is responsible for serving the summons; in a local state court, it may be someone from the sheriff's office.) A summons may also be served by certified mail.

Attached to the summons is the complaint (or petition or whatever legal document has been filed in court to start the lawsuit). The complaint (see Appendix 4) states who is bringing the action (the plaintiff) and who is being sued (the defendant or, more likely, defendants). It also contains the allegations made by the plaintiff. For the purpose of this discussion, consider the lawsuit to be made by a prison inmate against a correctional officer. (Note: An inmate could also decide to sue more than one person; for example, the inmate could sue several workers at the prison, from the warden down through correctional supervisors and some line corrections staff.) The prisoner, in a Section 1983 action, will state that certain actions have been taken that amount to violations of their constitutional rights. There may be references to specific statutes (showing the jurisdiction of the court to consider this kind of case) and court rulings (showing that there is a constitutional right that has been recognized), but these are not strictly necessary, especially in an inmate suit. The most important component of a complaint is the statement of facts—the allegations by the plaintiff of the things that have violated his rights The importance of the factual statement in a civil rights complaint is shown in *Ashcroft v. Iqbal*, 556 U.S. 662 (2009). In that case, the Supreme Court held that "...[Iqbal's] complaint fails to plead sufficient facts to state a claim for purposeful and unlawful discrimination against petitioners [Attorney General Ashcroft and FBI Director Mueller]."

Courts are more lenient in reviewing the language of papers filed by inmates, because inmates are allowed to do their own research and legal drafting. They are also allowed to file their actions **pro se**—that is, on their own behalf, without the assistance of attorneys. Finally, the complaint will state what kind of **relief** (injunction, declaratory relief, and/or money damages) the plaintiff is seeking.

The summons (issued by the court) will also indicate that the defendant has a specified amount of time in which to answer the complaint. Federal Rule of Civil Procedure directs a defendant to file an answer or other responsive pleading within 21 days of service, if that defendant has not waived the service of summons.[1] If a defendant has waived service of a summons under F.R.Civ.P 4, a defendant has 60 days to file an answer or responsive pleading. When an officer or employee of the United States is named as a defendant in either their individual or official capacity, the federal defendant has sixty days to file and answer or other responsive pleading. This notice of "time to answer" is most important, because it sets a legal deadline for the defendant to be sure that an answer is filed in the court.[1]

▶ Getting Representation

What next? Getting representation is the most basic, and important, step for the defendant. What is *not* done: The defendant must not seek out or talk to the plaintiff. Even if it is someone who is seen at work at the prison or jail every day, the defendant should avoid all confrontations with the plaintiff. The defendant should never discuss the lawsuit with the prisoner–plaintiff. It is possible that the prisoner will try to engage in conversation about the court case, but this should be avoided. If it is too difficult to avoid the prisoner who has sued, the defendant may want to ask for a transfer to another post or shift to avoid the problem. It is also not advisable for the defendant to contact the court, or any official at the courthouse, about the case. The defendant should not attempt to answer the complaint themselves.

If an employee is sued and there are a number of defendants, the employee will undoubtedly know and work with some, or all of them. It is all right for co-workers to talk to other co-defendants about the case; to ask if they have been served with a summons (or whether there was a waiver of summons) and to discuss how to get representation. Even if the suit looks frivolous or ridiculous, or if the employee knows nothing about the facts of the complaint, the only way to get rid of it is to have a lawyer file the necessary papers to get it dismissed. Failure to do this could result in a court judgment against the employee. Doing nothing is the worst thing that the defendant can do. Employees should be advised, during training or elsewhere at work, about how to get a lawyer to represent them. In some agencies, there are lawyers on the staff, and perhaps even assigned to the facility where the employee works, who do this legal work. In many agencies, representation is provided by the attorney general's office (for state corrections workers). For example, Louisiana Revised Statute 13:5108(B)(3) Indemnification of officers and employees of the state; civil rights; representation by the attorney general. And New Jersey Statute Section 59:10A(1): Attorney General's Duty to Defend State Employees: *Except as provided in section 2 hereof, the Attorney General shall, upon a request of an employee or former employee of the State, provide for the defense of any action brought against such State employee or former State employee on account of an act or omission in the scope of his employment.* In counties, it is commonly provided by the county attorney or solicitor. An example is from the El Paso County (Texas) Attorney's Office: Defense Litigation: . . . *Represent the County in civil lawsuits filed against the County and/or its officials and monitor cases in which the County is represented by outside counsel . . . .*[2] Some jurisdictions even provide a way to get representation by private attorneys, who are paid by the government. Due to the importance of this aspect, new correctional employees should always ask during staff training sessions about procedures if they are sued in a work-related matter.

The employee should also notify their supervisor about the lawsuit. Correctional agencies have a formal procedure (such as a form or written report) to do this, or oral reporting may be enough. It is important for a number of reasons that supervisors and prison managers know that an employee has been sued. It may be necessary for the employee to take time from work in order to consult with lawyer or go to court. A lawsuit may affect an employee's working relationship with plaintiff–inmates. If an employee doesn't know, or isn't sure how to get a lawyer, the supervisor should help the employee with the steps necessary to get representation.

The employee should keep all papers, including the envelope (noting the date and time received) in which the papers were mailed or carried and any notes made. When an employee consults with their lawyer, they should take the papers in their possession that relate to the case. Because of the strict time deadlines, the employee should obtain representation as soon as possible after they are served. From then on, it is the responsibility of the lawyer to meet deadlines, take the necessary legal steps to protect their the client's interests, notify the client of any developments in the case, and get necessary information from the client to prepare the case. If at any time the client is not aware of what is happening, they should not hesitate to ask their lawyer. It is the attorney's responsibility to represent the client, and part of that responsibility is answering the client's questions and keeping the client advised of important court dates and rulings. If the case does go to trial, the client's lawyer will represent the client in the courtroom and, if need be, on appeal. But the most important thing is for the lawyer to get actively involved right at the beginning because most prisoner suits are dismissed at an early stage, and only a small number actually go to trial. In the 12 month period ending March 31, 2020, only 1% of prisoner civil rights or conditions of confinement cases that were terminated in U.S. district courts (271 trials out of 23,573 terminations) were terminated by trial.[3]

All of this discussion, of course, assumes that the employee are entitled to representation. Every state has rules about the standards for representing employees. In the vast majority of cases, corrections staff are represented at no expense by government lawyers. In a very few cases, there may be a determination that a defendant is not entitled to representation by the state. This will usually be because the corrections employee acted in a blatantly offensive manner (as shown by investigation and not merely by an inmate's allegations) or acted totally outside the scope of any policies governing his duties. The defendant must be notified of any such determination. Still, the employee must obtain representation. In such a situation, they must find a private attorney to represent them.

In order to determine whether an employee is entitled to representation, there is an important standard used called the **scope of employment** (also known by other names, such as "scope of duties" or "line of duty"). This concept is used to set the boundaries and to determine whether the employee was acting properly and in such a manner that the government will take responsibility for the employee's actions. It is also used to decide other very important questions, such as indemnification in the case of adverse judgment in a lawsuit and the responsibility of the government (in case of tort claims) for the actions of its agents. Plaintiffs may have an interest in scope of employment issues because, should the plaintiff prevail in their suit, the plaintiff can rely on the government employer to indemnify a defendant which should ensure that the judgment is paid. While most of the cases discussed in this text address federal law, "scope of employment" is usually a matter of state law. The circles show different factors that define the responsibilities of each employee. The outer circle defines the boundary of an employee's duties. If the employee goes beyond that boundary, they will be considered to be "outside the scope" of their employment. The employee will then be on their own to obtain counsel and to face any other legal ramifications of his actions. The determining factors (and the elements in the concentric circles that define an employee's duties) may vary from one agency to another. But they are important for each corrections employee to know, at every level, in order to determine what is expected of an employee on the job and to what extent their employer (the government) will defend and support the employee's actions.

Some prison workers carry liability insurance to cover their actions while at work. An insured worker must notify the insurance company, which will likely provide an attorney or give instructions about how the worker is to get representation. As long as the worker's actions are covered by the terms of the policy, the insurance carrier will pay for lawyers' fees and for any judgment that may result in a case. Insurance coverage may present some complications. For example, there may be other defendants in the case who do not have insurance or there may be requests for injunctive relief, which the insurance company may have no responsibility or authority to address. A less apparent concern is the possibility that an insurer may feel it is appropriate to settle the suit by making a nominal payment to the inmate, rather than undergo the time and expense of prolonged litigation. Such a practice can be detrimental to prison administration, as it could serve as an incentive for inmates to file more lawsuits, regardless of merit, or it may undermine sound policy or practice.

▶ Step by Step

A correctional worker's attorney will review the papers that have been filed in court and will decide the best steps to take to protect client's interests. The answer to the complaint is called just that—an **answer**. A defendant may file a motion to dismiss the complaint and/or for summary judgment prior to filing an answer. That paper must be filed by the deadline indicated by the court, unless an extension is obtained. The attorney will obtain from their client (and other persons having knowledge of the incident) information about the incident or actions complained about. This may be done by asking for a written report from the client, having an interview with the client, or both. From these, and any other papers and reports that may have been prepared about the matter, the lawyer will prepare and file an answer with the court. It is also likely that the attorney will file **motions** with the court to dismiss the case because of defects in it. This may be pursued for a wide variety of reasons: because the defendant was not properly served (notified) of the complaint, because the court has no jurisdiction to consider such a case, or (very frequently) because what the inmate alleges does not entitle them to any judicial relief, even if the facts are true. These motions to dismiss are quite technical, but they are very important to protect the defendant. The lawyer should send their client a copy of any such papers filed on the client's behalf. If the client does not get these copies, the client should ask for them.

If the case is not dismissed by the court at this early stage, the litigation will enter a phase of the proceedings called **discovery**. There are four principal kinds of discovery.

1. **Interrogatories:** These are written questions that an attorney for one side submits to the other side. (Interrogatories may also be submitted to possible witnesses who have information about the case.) Attorneys and their clients should review the interrogatories, prepare answers to be filed. The attorney may decide, for strategic purposes, that it would be advantageous to ask the inmate, or witnesses, what the facts are. For this reason, the attorney may then send interrogatories to the plaintiff.

2. **Depositions:** These are questions asked in person and under oath and their responses, with a court reporter taking down all that is said. It is similar to examining a witness in a courtroom, except there is no judge present, so the questions tend to be more freewheeling. The deposition is usually taken in a lawyer's office, not in the courthouse. In a civil case, it is common for a plaintiff to take the deposition of a defendant, and vice versa. (In prisoner suits; however, discovery is not nearly as common as it is in other civil actions.) Depositions of key witnesses in civil cases who are not parties are also usually taken. By taking a deposition or asking interrogatories, an attorney tries to nail down what testimony the other side has to offer. This process gives a good indication of the strengths and weaknesses of the witnesses and of the overall case.

3. **Motions to produce documents:** These entail just what the title says: one party obtains from the other any documents that may be relevant to the case. (What may not be obtained are attorney's papers; these are the lawyer's work product, such as the notes taken at your interview, and are not available to the other side.)

4. **Requests for admissions:** These are also just what the title says: one party asks the other whether it is true that certain facts exist. These requests will refer to specific facts that are relevant to the case. They may be used to confirm that certain vital facts are clearly true and are not contested by either side. They may also be used to see whether certain things can be eliminated from controversy (and possibly from the trial) by getting the other side to agree on what the facts are.

All types of discovery have deadlines. These deadlines must be met; otherwise, assistance will be sought from the court to compel the discovery, or even a default of the entire case may be ordered.

With good discovery, an attorney may obtain virtually the entire factual and evidentiary case that the other side may use. This is done purposely, to encourage parties to find out what kind of case the other side has (strengths and weaknesses) and furthermore, to encourage settlement of cases. If an attorney has accomplished thorough discovery and a case does go to trial, there should be few surprises.

▶ Not Going to Trial

As noted previously an attorney will file motions to dismiss a case, based on the original papers that are filed. If these motions are not successful, and the case goes to trial, other motions will likely be filed. The most common is the motion for **summary judgment**. To support this motion, the attorney will often file affidavits from their client or from witnesses. **Affidavits** are sworn written statements containing information relevant to the case. The attorney will argue that their client is entitled to win the case based on the law governing the case because the facts shown in affidavits (plus depositions or other discovery) are not in dispute and do not require a trial. The opposing side will respond, asserting why summary judgment is not appropriate (and probably asking for summary judgment for their client instead).

The court will rule on the motion for summary judgment, either denying it (usually, denial is on the grounds that there are still disputed facts to be resolved) or granting it. If it is granted to the defendant, the case is dismissed. If it is granted to the plaintiff, the court must decide what relief (such as money damages, injunction, or other relief) is appropriate.

As a result of the preparation of the case and as the trial gets closer, parties (and especially attorneys for the parties) feel pressure to settle cases without going to trial. Many judges will call attorneys in and urge them to try to settle the case. If an attorney has found that their case is weak, their client is not strong on the controlling facts, or the judge is obviously leaning toward the other side, the attorney may discuss with their client about settling the case, usually with a compromise instead of a significant ruling and judgment for the other side. This kind of compromise settlement is probably not as common in prisoner cases, for a number of reasons: inmates may see the issue purely as either a win or a loss, with nothing in between (less than a total win) being acceptable; injunctive relief may require a significant change in agency policy or practice, which management may not be willing to consider; money damages are usually recoverable only from the individual worker's pocket, so that even a comparatively small settlement is seen as unacceptable; or agreement to even a small award may require admission by prison staff of violation of constitutional rights as to certain activities, which may be considered totally unacceptable because of the precedent it sets, both for this defendant and especially for other inmate–plaintiffs. It is only in unusual instances where settlement in prison cases is in the best interests of the defendant(s), such as where the case is factually weak, or the law is unclear.

▶ Trial

If the case is not dismissed or settled, it will proceed to trial, which is very different from what is seen on television or in the movies. A hearing date is set by the judge, at which time the attorneys for both sides will appear in the courtroom, usually with their clients present (although this is not required in a civil case). At the time set, the attorney should ensure that their case is ready, the documentary evidence is available, and the witnesses are prepared to testify. A trial may proceed with or without a jury. A **jury**, **trial jury** (also called a **petit jury**) is a group of citizens who decide what the facts are—they are solely fact finders. Some cases are tried without a jury—that is, by the judge alone (a bench trial). There is never a jury in habeas corpus cases. In torts and Section 1983 cases, the parties are usually entitled to a jury. If both sides waive jury trial (and there may be good tactical reasons for doing this, such as a history of juries not being favorable in locality), the judge will hear the case.

Then the judge becomes the trier of fact and also decides (as they do in all cases) what law applies to the facts of the particular case.

A defendant in the case will likely be called as a witness. Or a person may be called to testify because they have information relevant to the outcome of someone else's case. If a person is "summoned," or called to testify, the person must notify their superiors, who will have to arrange to allow the employee to go to court. And, most importantly, the witness should contact the attorney who is calling the witness to testify and discuss with them their role as a witness. As a matter of good trial preparation, the attorney should be in touch with their client and witnesses and set up an appointment to talk about testimony, but, because of the press of business, this may not happen. If this is the case, a witness or client should get in touch with the attorney.

There are a number of rules and reminders that apply to conduct as a witness in a court case and the party's attorney will go over these with you. Sometimes, because of the time crunch—and corrections trial lawyers tend to be very busy indeed—the attorney will not have time to go over things in detail. A party, or witness should always ask for time to go over their testimony and time to ask questions about the case that may be of special concern to them. A helpful resource for correctional workers going to court is *Correctional Law for the Correctional Officer*.[4] Here are some very basic rules:

- A witness should review any records and reports that are available to them that relate to the facts of the case. Specifically, review any records, reports, written statements, and depositions that the witness may have given. Testimony should not be memorized as such testimony will sound rehearsed and may cause the jury to lose confidence in your testimony.
- A witness should dress and act professionally. A correctional worker should consult with their attorney about the propriety or expectation of wearing their uniform at trial if they wear one at work, especially in criminal trials in which they are a witness. Limit facial gestures to presenting a pleasant but serious focus. There should be no smirks, grimaces, or similar expressions. It is very important that the witness demonstrate they are taking the proceedings seriously.
- A witness should try to remain as calm as possible. Take the amount of time necessary to think about answers to questions. A witness should speak clearly and loudly enough so that all of the jurors can hear the testimony given. Speak directly to the judge or jury as much as possible. A witness should avoid allowing an opposing attorney to get them angry.
- A witness should answer only the question, exactly as it is given to them. Additional information should not be volunteered. A witness does not have the right to object to a question—counsel will do that if the question is objectionable. If a witness does not understand a question, they have the right to ask their attorney or the judge for clarification. Answers should be complete, but brief.
- If a witness does not know the answer, they should say so. There is nothing wrong with this. A witness should not try to come up with information that they are not sure about, just because a question has been asked. The witness must tell the truth, no matter what. If a wrong or misleading answer has been given, the witness should clarify their answer as soon as they realize the error.
- In response to a question, it is permissible for a witness to admit that they have discussed their testimony before trial with their attorney and other appropriate parties.
- Be courteous. If the judge or an attorney interrupts, stop talking and wait for someone to tell the witness to go on. A judge may sometimes ask the witness questions or give the witness some advice or instructions.
- When the witnesses' testimony is over, they should leave the courtroom, unless they are a party to the case. A party to the case may return to the defense table and sit with their attorney.
- A party in a case (plaintiff or defendant) is permitted to be in the courtroom during the trial. If a party wants to leave the courtroom, they should consult with attorney about this. If a witness is not a party but wishes to remain in the courtroom, after (or before) they have testified, ask counsel who called the witness if this is permitted. Sometimes, witnesses are excluded from sitting in the courtroom, except when they are testifying. (The attorney should let a non-party witness know before they go on the witness stand whether there is a local rule that excludes a non-party witness from sitting in on the trial after they have finished testifying.)

At the end of all testimony, the attorneys will argue the case, summarizing the points that are most important and favorable to their clients. If there is a jury, the judge will give **instructions** to the jury. These are the rules that the jury must use to decide the facts of the case. After deliberating, the jury returns a **verdict**. This decides liability in the case—whether the defendant is liable or whether the plaintiff has failed to prove the defendant to be liable. If the defendant wins, the case is dismissed. Judgment is entered for the defendant(s). If the plaintiff wins, the court proceeds to the next stage, which is deciding on the appropriate relief to be given; if the relief requested is money damages, the jury will be used and instructed about how to decide upon appropriate damages. If there is no jury, the judge decides this as well. After the verdict and the damages are decided, the court enters a **judgment** in the case. This is the official court order, which states the outcome and is filed in the court records.

▶ Appeal

The attorney for the losing party will usually file motions in an attempt to set aside the verdict and judgment that have been entered. If these are not successful (and they usually are not), a notice of appeal is filed. There is a strict time limit for this to be done by.

In a civil case, either side may appeal if it is dissatisfied with the outcome. (In a criminal case, as a general rule, only the defendant can appeal a loss.) If a government employee is a defendant, the government will again provide representation for the employee if the plaintiff appeals or to take an appeal if the defendant has lost. Often, certain lawyers specialize in handling appeals, while other attorneys try the cases in the lower courts. Again, the employee should make inquiries about whether their interests are being protected. They should not hesitate to contact the attorney who has been assigned to handle the appeal of their case.

There are many names for the courts that handle appeals. In federal courts and in many states, they are called courts of appeals. The case in appellate court will be handled by filing papers (briefs and motions). The court will set a date for the case to be argued. A court of appeals usually consists of three or more judges. A lawyer for each side will argue the case. Most of these arguments are based solely on the legal merits of what has gone on in the trial court. Appellate courts will review the record to determine if the trial court judge made errors in handling the case or in interpreting the law. Courts of appeals do not ordinarily review the facts of the case with regard to whether the verdict is correct. Only the issue of whether certain facts should *not* have been considered and the issue of whether there is enough evidence in the record to support the verdict will be reviewed.

Although arguments in appellate courts are open to the public, most government employees are not likely appear there. A court of appeals takes no testimony; it only hears legal arguments, and these tend to be technical (and pretty boring). However, if a party wants to hear case when it is argued, they have a right to attend. The party should ask their attorney about the time and place. Most federal appellate courts post the audio portion of oral arguments on the circuit's website. An example is the Eighth Circuit: https://www.ca8.uscourts.gov /oral-arguments.

Judgments that are approved (affirmed) in the appellate courts are returned as final. If the appellate court finds that significant mistakes have been made, it will return the case to the trial judge, along with instructions about how to proceed. Sometimes, the case will have to be tried over. This is called a **reversal** and a **remand** (sending the case back to the trial court for corrections to be made, which may mean trying the case over from the beginning).

All states allow for one level of appeal from trial courts, which is usually an intermediate court of appeals. In those states, the state's highest appellate court usually exercises discretionary authority to hear cases from the intermediate appellate courts of the state. A small number of states provide for direct appeal to the state supreme court. When a decision of a state's appellate court involves a federal question, review may be sought in the United States Supreme Court. An example is the case of *Roper v. Simmons* (concerning the death penalty for juvenile offenders) which was an appeal from the Supreme Court of Missouri. The U.S. Supreme Court exercises discretion to review cases from the U.S. Courts of Appeal. The U.S. Supreme Court will agree to look at a case only if there is a substantial legal question that should be addressed. The Supreme Court usually considers only about 1% of the cases that are asked to be reviewed. While in theory litigants have a right to a first level of appeal, appellate courts do not frequently reverse trial court judgments. Administrative Office of the U.S. Courts. *U.S. Courts of Appeals - Decisions in Cases Terminated on the Merits, by Nature of Proceeding* for the 12-month period ending March 31, 2020. Table B-5 https://www.uscourts.gov/statistics-reports/caseload-statistics-data-tables?tn=&pn=All&t=37&m%5Bvalue %5D%5Bmonth%5D=3&y%5Bvalue%5D%5Byear%5D=2020. There is, in practice, a right of appeal up to the first level of appeal, the appellate court. In the 12- month period ending March 31, 2020, only 11.5% of prisoner petitions terminated on the merits in U.S. courts of appeal resulted in reversal of the district court's judgment.[5]

The decision of that court is, in most cases, the final decision on the case. "I'm going to take this case all the way to the Supreme Court" is more attorney bravado and posturing than a legal certainty.

Summary

- This chapter is presented as a guide to be used by the corrections worker if he or she is sued.
- A corrections lawsuit (most commonly under Section 1983) is commenced when an inmate files a complaint. Each named defendant is served with a summons and the complaint. In the federal courts and some state courts, service of the summons may be waived by the defendant.
- The person being sued (the defendant) should take the summons or waiver, and any relevant records he has in his possession, to the attorney who is responsible for representing staff members in the case. That attorney will provide information about local court procedures, answer questions about the case, and take necessary steps to file the appropriate papers (an answer and motions) in court.
- If the case is not dismissed by the court, the next stage of the case is discovery. Discovery is not as frequently used in prisoner suits as in other civil lawsuits. The purpose of discovery is to find out all of the information one can about the other side's case. Types of discovery are interrogatories, depositions, motions to produce documents, and requests for admissions.
- An attorney will continue to try to avoid trial by the use of pretrial motions. One of the most commonly used at this stage is the motion for summary judgment. This motion argues that there are no facts in dispute that would necessitate a trial and; therefore, the attorney's client should win the case on the basis of the undisputed facts and the law that governs the case.
- If the case goes to trial, it may be before the trial judge alone or with a jury. The jury decides only the facts of the case; the verdict (either in favor of the plaintiff or the defendant); and, if the verdict is for the plaintiff, the amount of damages to be awarded.
- A person called as a witness should go over his prospective testimony with the attorney who is calling him as a witness and should adhere to the rules for being a good witness (some important rules are set out in the chapter).
- A party who loses a case may take an appeal if the attorney who represents that party thinks there is any good argument to be made that there was an error in any part of the trial. No testimony or evidence is taken in an appeals court. That court decides the appeal based on written records (including a transcript of the trial) sent up by the trial court. Attorneys for each side submit written briefs, making their arguments about the case and usually are allowed to argue the case before the judges (most commonly, there are three judges) of the appellate court.

Thinking About It

Officer Smith is a five-year employee of the Department of Corrections. He has earned very good work evaluations and is in line for a promotion. He often works in the cell block and walks down the tiers past each inmate's cell. On May 12, as he walks by inmate Johnson's cell, Johnson throws a piece of feces at Officer Smith, hitting him in the face. Smith yells for Johnson's cell to be opened. When it is, Smith enters the cell and hits Johnson in the face. Smith then leaves the cell, yelling for the door to be closed. Inmate Johnson sues Officer Smith, alleging assault. The officer denies the assault, saying that his actions were appropriate to gain control of Johnson. Officer Smith requests representation. Will the government agree to represent the officer? Why or why not?

Key Terms

affidavit

answer (civil procedure)

deposition

discovery (court procedure)

instructions

interrogatories (court procedure)

judgment

jury, trial jury, petit jury

motion

motion to produce documents (court procedure)

pro se

relief (court procedure)

remand

requests for admissions (court procedure)

reversal

scope of employment

summary judgment

summons

verdict

waiver of summons

witness

Endnotes

1. Federal Rule of Civil Procedure 12(a).
2. El Paso County, Colorado, District Attorney's Office: Available at: https://www.epcounty.com/ca/civilunit.htm. El Paso (Texas) County Attorney's Office. https://www.epcounty.com/ca/civilunit.htm. Accessed 31 July 2020.
3. Administrative Office of the U.S. Courts. *U.S. District Courts - Civil Cases Terminated, by Nature of Suit and Action Taken* for the 12-month period ending March 31, 2020. Table C-4. https://www.uscourts.gov/statistics-reports/caseload-statistics-data-tables
4. Collins, W. *Correctional Law for the Correctional Officer.* 5th ed. (Alexandria, VA: American Correctional Association, 2010), 173–175.
5. Administrative Office of the U.S. Courts. *U.S. Courts of Appeals - Decisions in Cases Terminated on the Merits, by Nature of Proceeding* for the 12-month period ending March 31, 2020. Table B-5 *https://www.uscourts.gov/statistics-reports/caseload -statistics-data-tables?tn=&pn=All&t=37&m%5Bvalue%5D%5Bmonth%5D=3&y%5Bvalue%5D%5Byear%5D=2020*

PART 2

Constitutional Law of Corrections

"The Law of Corrections" begins to take shape with the recognition of prisoners' rights to free exercise of religion. Until the 1960s, the courts generally had a "hands-off" philosophy toward intervening in correctional matters. Perhaps this position is best shown by the statement in the 1871 Virginia case, *Ruffin v. Commonwealth*, 62 Va. 21 Gratt. 790 (1871): "[A]s a consequence of his crime [he] not only forfeited his liberty, but all his personal rights except those which the law in its humanity accords to him. He is for the time being the slave of the State."

In 1967, The President's Commission on Law Enforcement and Administration of Justice, in its *Task Force Report: Corrections*, stated the following:[1]

A variety of rights and privileges are traditionally lost upon conviction of a crime. While before conviction the Government must justify every assertion of authority, after conviction such assertions stand on a different footing ... And virtually all of an offender's activities may be subject to regulation by correctional officials, particularly in institutions. He has no absolute right to see friends or relatives or to do any of a multitude of things that the rest of society takes for granted.

Yet it is inconsistent with our whole system of government to grant such uncontrolled power to any officials, particularly over the lives of persons. The fact that a person has been convicted of a crime should not mean that he has forfeited all rights to demand that he be fairly treated by officials.

This 1967 report correctly noted that there were "increasing signs that the courts are ready to abandon their traditional hands-off attitude." In 1961, the Supreme Court, in *Monroe v. Pape*, 365 U.S. 167 (1961), said that in passing the Civil Rights Act of 1871, Congress intended to provide a remedy to parties deprived of their constitutional rights, privileges, and immunities by an official's abuse of his position. As applied, this Act allowed inmates to sue public officials for monetary damages and injunctive relief, if their clearly established constitutional rights were violated.

Some prison cases during this era clearly showed such violations. Cases arose from "vicious and brutal staff behavior, literal torture of inmates, overcrowded, dark, vermin-infested facilities, and other deprivations of fundamental freedoms."[2] While these conditions certainly did not exist at all correctional institutions, the fact they existed at any of them validated some inmate claims and contributed to court intervention. In *Wolff v. McDonnell*, 418 U.S. 539 (1974), the Supreme Court stated the following:

> **Lawful imprisonment necessarily makes unavailable many rights and privileges of the ordinary citizen ... But though his rights may be diminished by the needs ... of the institutional environment, a prisoner is not wholly stripped of constitutional protections when he is imprisoned for crime. There is no iron curtain drawn between the Constitution and the prisons of this country.**

In Part II (Chapters 5 through 17), we look at constitutional law. This includes a discussion of those areas of corrections work in which different provisions of the Constitution define or limit what may be done by corrections officials. In many areas, there are now Supreme Court decisions, which provide the authoritative word by interpreting the U.S. Constitution on corrections issues. There are also additional court decisions presented from lower courts (mostly federal but also some state), which provides the history of the litigation in the area under discussion, interpret or extend the Supreme Court ruling, or, in some cases, present constitutional interpretation on points on which the Supreme Court has not yet ruled.

Some have called the court rulings on these corrections matters "the law of prisoners' rights." Although prisoners' rights are discussed in Chapter 5 as a generic category, we do not use that phrase here for the discussion of the law for two reasons. First, the field of corrections encompasses more than prisons and prisoners. Even if the area of "prisons and prisoners" is interpreted to include jails and pretrial detainees (and much of the law on prisons does apply to jails, as discussed in Chapter 20), there are also issues of probation and parole, juveniles and young offenders, and community corrections that do not neatly (or properly) fit under the phrase "prisons and prisoners." Second, using the term "prisoners' rights" implies the emphasis on concern for the law as it could be used or interpreted for the benefits or rights of prisoners. The law in this area is more complex. The law of corrections in virtually all areas of concern becomes a balancing of interests: the interests of prisoners on one hand and the interests of corrections managers on the other. Of course, it is natural for prisoners (and their advocates) to seek the greatest benefits and privileges they can obtain in the prison setting. But there are valid concerns that must be weighed on the other side. During the "correctional law revolution" of the 1960's and 1970's many judges accorded greater weight to the individual rights of offenders without careful evaluation of the needs of corrections administration. It took many years of litigation to obtain recognition in the law that individual freedoms in prisons had to be limited, for the good of the prison as a whole—that is, to obtain orderly running, security, and safety in corrections facilities. We try to present faithfully the development of those counterbalancing interests: the interests of prisoners and of their keepers. The interests are not always hostile; in many cases, they coincide or come close to matching. It is fairer though to title this discussion the Law of Corrections, rather than to say it is the Law of Prisoners' Rights.

Supreme Court decisions are presented in this part in some detail. Often, the facts of a case are helpful in the study of how the law in a particular area developed. The reasoning of the Court may also be useful. (Note: the word "Court" used with a capital "C," refers to the U.S. Supreme Court. Lower courts are referred to with a small "c," except when an official name is used, as in "the U.S. Court of Appeals for the Eighth Circuit.") The most important thing of all is the court's holding—what it concludes is the governing legal principle for that area of the law. As already noted, to help you find important statements of the law as you look through the book, holdings of cases and statements of important legal principles are given in **boldface font**. On every Supreme Court opinion, you can expect to find boldface presentation of the important statements of the Court in that case. The few exceptions are instances in which the Supreme Court decision does not contain a ruling or language that is vital to understanding the "law of corrections." If there are such important statements of the law in other cases (or in some chapters, in statutes), they will be presented boldly.

For every case discussed, there will be a citation of the case given; this allows the reader to find the whole judicial opinion in a court reporter or other resource, if reading the whole opinion (or more of it than is presented here) is desired. Contrary to practice in legal writing, the text does not give page numbers for the quotations from opinion and ordinarily do not indicate the vote on court decisions or the discussions contained in dissenting or concurring opinions. Those practices may be helpful in legal writing and discussions that give a fuller picture of the case. The text skips them, however, because they are contrary to the purposes of this text; they would tend to clutter the discussion, and perhaps even cloud the issues, for non-attorney readers who just want to know "the law." In every case, it is the holding of the majority that is presented in boldface font. You can rely on this material to be "the law" of that case.

The sheer volume of "the law" in this area is huge. No book can present all of "the law of corrections." Such a collection would not be a book, but a long shelf of books, because the number of reported opinions on corrections matters now stretches into the many hundreds. Any author or teacher must select the cases that will give the reader the best understanding of the current state of the law. This text attempts to select cases that touch on the wide variety of issues that may be of interest to corrections workers and to students in this field. The text utilizes selected cases in which the law has spoken in some authoritative way (that is, more than just a lonely judicial voice in some isolated court). Besides the leading and controlling Supreme Court opinions, The text includes a smattering of opinions from lower courts to give the reader an idea of the issues that have been considered historically and those that are being considered currently in the courts.

As with all such legal discussions, the reader must remember that only the Supreme Court (or federal law) speaks for the whole country. The holdings of the Supreme Court on corrections matters govern those areas of corrections work, constitutionally and legally. If the Supreme Court has not given a conclusive ruling on a particular question of concern, then an inquiry must be made as to whether a local court (such as a federal circuit court, district court, or state court) has made a ruling on that question. If there is no Supreme Court ruling and no ruling by a court that controls in your jurisdiction, the matter is still open to litigation, and the law is not settled. If a court in another location (such as a court of appeals in another part of the country or a supreme court in another state) has spoken on the issue, that ruling may be informative about how the law may be interpreted, but it is not binding or settled law for your local jurisdiction.

Endnotes

1. President's Commission on Law Enforcement and Administration of Justice. *Task Force Report: Corrections* (Washington, DC: U.S. Government Printing Office, 1967), 82–83.
2. Harris, M. and Spiller Jr., D. *After Decision: Implementation of Judicial Decrees in Correctional Settings*. (Washington, DC: National Institute of Law Enforcement and Criminal Justice, Law Enforcement Assistance Administration, U.S. Department of Justice, 1977), 22.

© EJ_Rodriquez/iStock/Getty Images Plus/Getty Images

CHAPTER 5

A General View of Prisoners' Rights Under the Constitution

The problems of prisons in America are complex and intractable, and, more to the point, they are not readily susceptible of resolution by decree.

U.S. Supreme Court, *Procunier v. Martinez*

This chapter introduces the detailed study of the constitutional law as it applies to corrections management and operations. This is done by looking at prison itself, the structure and the people (inmates and staff) within its walls, and the means that prisoners use to pursue their rights in courts. Most of this pursuit, over the past five decades, has been through the guarantees of rights contained in the U.S. Constitution. Next, the statutory channel (42 U.S.C. § 1983) that is used to assert those constitutional rights and to complain about violations of those rights in federal courts will be examined. The final section of this chapter will focus on prisoners' rights litigation from the viewpoint of corrections workers and the various ways corrections staff can protect themselves from being found responsible for violating the constitutional rights of inmates.

▶ The Nature of Prisons

Here are three statements from prison systems of different sizes:

> [The Florida Department of Corrections' mission is to] "Provide a continuum of services to meet the needs of those entrusted to our care, creating a safe and professional environment with the outcome of

reduced victimization, safer communities and an emphasis on the premium of life"[1] (Florida Department of Corrections). (Florida had 97,538 sentenced prisoners under its jurisdiction as of December 31, 2018.)[1]

[The Virginia Department of Corrections is] . . . in the business of helping people to be better by safely providing effective incarceration, supervision, and evidence-based re-entry services to returning citizens, parolees, and probationers.[2] (Virginia had 36,660 sentenced prisoners under its jurisdiction as of December 31, 2018.)

The mission of the North Dakota Department of Corrections and Rehabilitation is "Transforming lives, influencing change, strengthening community."[3] (North Dakota had 1,695 sentenced prisoners under its jurisdiction as of December 31, 2018.)[4]

These statements are representative of mission statements for most correctional agencies, whether there are 1,000 or 100,000 inmates. Protecting the public, providing a safe and humane environment, and providing inmates with the opportunities for self-improvement are common elements of these statements.

The total number of persons on correctional supervision rose to almost 7.2 million in 2006 before declining to 6.6 million in 2018.[5] The prison population reported is the number of prisoners under the *jurisdiction* or legal authority of state and federal correctional officials. This number includes persons held in prison or jail facilities outside of the state or federal prison system (in local jails, or inmates in transit—for example, going to court). It is worth noting that there is also a prison population count of prisoners under the *custody* of state and federal correctional officials. In 2018, this number was 1,465,200.[6] It represents the number of inmates physically housed in state and federal correctional facilities regardless of which entity has the legal authority, as well as state and federal inmates in privately operated facilities. The number may also include juveniles held in adult facilities in the six states that have combined jail–prison systems. See endnote 4, table 7. See Appendix 5-1 Correctional Population Data on the Navigate eBook site on jblearning.com. From 2006 to 2009, the number of persons confined in state and federal correctional facilities increased to 1.6 million[7] before almost steadily declining in 2018 (1.5 million).[8] In state systems, persons whose most serious crime of conviction was a crime of violence such as murder, rape, and/or assault made up 56% of the inmate population in 2017.[7] In 1990, the percentage of state prisoners serving sentences for violent offenses made up 46% of the state prison population of 708,000- by 1999[10] the percentage of state prisoners serving sentences for violence offenses increased to 48% of the state prison population of 1.2 million. See endnote 7. The growth in the violent offender inmate population may result in more confrontations and behavioral incidents, giving prison officials increased management and litigation concerns.

Inmates are generally housed in one of three types of prisons:

Maximum (Close, High) security is characterized by a perimeter of double fences or a wall and outside patrols or towers (see **FIGURE 5-1**). Inside, there is cell housing, highly controlled movement, direct supervision, and regular searches of inmates and housing areas. These prisons have a high staff-to-inmate ratio. Super maximum-security prisons fall within the maximum-security category and have highly restrictive conditions.

FIGURE 5-1 A guard's tower at Fort Ord Prison.

They ordinarily house those persons who have shown that they are unable to adjust to a maximum-security setting. Examples include extremely assaultive inmates, gang members, and inmates who have killed other inmates or staff.

Medium security is usually characterized by a perimeter of single or double fences and external patrols. Inmate housing may be in cells or secure dormitories. Work and self-improvement programs are available. Internal inmate movement is often unescorted but frequently supervised. Regular searches of inmates and housing areas are conducted.

Minimum security is characterized by a perimeter of a single fence or no fence, and there are no towers and less frequent patrols. Inmates are assigned to room or dormitory housing and are allowed a greater degree of unrestricted movement. These facilities generally have a relatively low staff-to-inmate ratio. Inmates in these facilities may participate in outside work and/or program assignments. These facilities often are called prison camps.

In addition to these **classifications,** there may also be administrative institutions. These facilities have a specific purpose and may house inmates of different security levels. Examples include prison medical centers and detention facilities (see **FIGURE 5-2**). Detention facilities house inmates in various stages of the criminal justice process, including many pretrial inmates.

In determining an inmate's institution placement, the objective of the staff is to assign an inmate to the least restrictive environment that still provides appropriate control. Over the years, efforts have been made to standardize this process—for example, by assigning point totals to various factors (such as age, prior record, and nature of offense) and then designating an institutional placement based on the inmate's total points. Within this context; however, the professional judgment of the staff continues to be a significant component of the designation process.

A prison is a community unto itself, with very specific outer boundaries, such as a fence or wall. The interior components of a prison also resemble a community: there is an organizational control structure (prison administration), along with those living under its guidelines (inmates). There are various work assignments and, usually, educational opportunities. There are those who abide by prison rules and those who don't—and for those who don't, there is an enforcement mechanism (an institution disciplinary system). There is a store (prison commissary), where inmates may purchase selected items, often from their institution earnings. There may be television, movies, and other recreational opportunities. There are visiting and telephone privileges; of course, these are more limited than in the outside world. No matter the "amenities" offered, the one item that is not available is arguably the most important: the freedom to come and go at will.

In discussing confinement, it is important to remember that prison is not a housing of choice. To run effectively, institutions require a high degree of uniformity in rules and control, in such things as lights on and lights out, mealtimes, work schedules, and free-time activity. "Treat people firmly but fairly" is a common expression within a prison environment. To do otherwise is seen as creating a potentially disruptive situation within the

FIGURE 5-2 A corrections building in Chicago, Illinois.
© Benkrut/Dreamstime.com

prison. For example, allowing each inmate to decide what and how much property they can keep would create a situation of "haves" and "have-nots" and encourage the development of an underground marketplace, as well as produce potential safety, sanitation, and fire hazards. This would create dissension among the inmates and make it more difficult to maintain institutional security, discipline, and good order.

Over 60 years ago, Gresham Sykes wrote about the "pains of imprisonment".[11] While his focus was on a maximum security prison, the "pains" identify aspects of prison life that may exist in all prisons:

Deprivation of liberty: The inmate's conviction and subsequent confinement may be seen by the inmate as a deliberate rejection by the community. Within the prison, his movement is further restricted.

Deprivation of goods and services: While the inmate's basic needs are met, this is done within the highly structured confinement of the institution. Gone is his opportunity to choose to buy a hamburger at a fast food restaurant. His is a material impoverishment.

Deprivation of heterosexual relationships: The lack of these opportunities can be frustrating and can affect the inmate's self-image.

Deprivation of autonomy: The nature of an institution, as noted, requires a high degree of uniformity and consistency to operate smoothly. To accomplish this, the inmate is subject to a variety of institution rules that are intended to control his behavior. Dependence, as opposed to independence, is the expected condition.

Deprivation of security: The prison houses the inmate with other convicted criminals, many of whom may have violent histories. This can affect an inmate's feeling of well-being. Physical assaults, or threats of them, may be prevalent.

Each of these deprivations may affect an inmate's self-concept and lead the inmate to develop coping mechanisms. Litigation is one such mechanism. For some inmates, litigation can serve as a means to keep one's mind active or to "get back at the system." Here are four reasons why lawsuits may be filed by prisoners:

Fact: There is a justified reason for the suit. An example is litigation by an inmate who has a serious medical condition and is deprived of their right to medical care.

Frustration: The inmate feels they have no other option available. An example is litigation by an inmate who feels they have a valid issue but is unable to get a response from someone in authority.

Fancy: The inmate thinks litigation might be a "fun" thing to do and feels there is nothing to lose. An example is litigation by an inmate who wants an additional slice of bacon served with their breakfast meal.

Fiction: The inmate asserts an untruth. An example is litigation by an inmate who does not like a staff member and files suit, making false allegations, as a type of harassment.

Regardless of the reason for the litigation, staff must treat all litigation seriously. Failure to do this can result in a suit without merit suddenly receiving credibility.

An inmate often has a propensity to act out or challenge authority. In a position of authority, correctional staff must be trained on how to handle a variety of situations, exercise supervision, and use good interpersonal communication skills. When a staff member lets their guard down, difficulty can arise, and it usually will.

▶ Section 1983 and the Constitution

Title 42 of the U.S. Code, Section 1983, establishes a mechanism for persons to bring suit against government officials, based on alleged violations of constitutional rights. Over the past 50 years, this type of action remains a common type of lawsuit brought by prisoners nationwide. In 1966, the first year the U.S. Courts separately counted section 1983 actions by state prisoners, the courts recorded 266 such suits filed by all prisoners nationwide. By 1992, the number had grown to 26,824.[12] In the 12-month period ending March 31, 2020, the number of prison conditions and civil rights suits filed in U.S. district courts totaled 28,393.[13] (Remember that Section 1983 is unavailable to federal prisoners because Section 1983 refers to constitutional violations by state officials, but federal inmates have a similar remedy in Bivens actions.)

For a number of reasons, Section 1983 suits have become the most prevalent type of legal action against government officials, and they have been used to establish most of the constitutional rights of prisoners that have been defined by the courts—especially by the U.S. Supreme Court—in the past 35–40 years. This is not to say that common law torts and habeas corpus are not important. They provide avenues for court review of prisoner complaints in many hundreds of cases every year, but they provide a much more limited scope of review. In a variety of constitutional claims, Section 1983 actions have provided the means to achieve a wider scope of judicial review of prison activities and programs. Section 1983 also provides broader relief, especially in the way of injunctive relief, monetary relief and the award of attorney's fees to the prevailing party. It can be used for class action lawsuits, which challenge prison policies on a broad scale. It can also be brought before federal courts, where, historically, prisoners have found friendlier forums than in many state courts. Most states have similar provisions in state law, whereby state prisoners can challenge prison conditions under provisions of the state constitution. As federal courts became more conservative in the 1980s and 1990s, and as decisions of the U.S. Supreme Court in that period prescribed more pro-government standards for federal courts to use in handling claims of constitutional violations, and with the Prison Litigation Reform Act, prisoners turned more frequently, at least in some states, to their local courts for relief under the provisions of state law, including the state's constitution.

The most important source of prisoners' rights is still the U.S. Constitution, and the U.S. Supreme Court, as the final arbiter and definer of constitutional provisions, is still the most important source of definitions of prisoners' rights.

For a selection of clauses in the U.S. Constitution that has been used most frequently in prisoner litigation, see **BOX 5-1.** You will note that most of these are from the first 10 amendments of the Constitution, commonly known as the **Bill of Rights.** There are also some other provisions that are used in prisoner litigation (remember

---

BOX 5-1　Articles of Amendment to the Constitution of the United States

Amendment 1

Congress shall make no law respecting an establishment of religion, or prohibiting the free exercise thereof; or abridging the freedom of speech, or of the press; or the right of the people peaceably to assemble, and to petition the Government for a redress of grievances.

Amendment 4

The right of the people to be secure in their persons, houses, papers, and effects, against unreasonable searches and seizures, shall not be violated, and no Warrants shall issue, but upon probable cause, supported by Oath or affirmation, and particularly describing the place to be searched, and the persons or things to be seized.

Amendment 5

No person shall be held to answer for a capital, or otherwise infamous crime, unless on a presentment or indictment of a Grand Jury, except in cases arising in the land or naval forces, or in the Militia, when in actual service in time of War or public danger; nor shall any person be subject for the same offence to be twice put in jeopardy of life or limb; nor shall be compelled in any criminal case to be a witness against himself, nor be deprived of life, liberty, or property, without due process of law; nor shall private property be taken for public use, without just compensation.

Amendment 6

In all criminal prosecutions, the accused shall enjoy the right to a speedy and public trial, by an impartial jury of the State and district wherein the crime shall have been committed, which district shall have been previously ascertained by law, and to be informed of the nature and cause of the accusation; to be confronted with the witnesses against him; to have compulsory process for obtaining witnesses in his favor, and to have the Assistance of Counsel for his defense.

Amendment 8

Excessive bail shall not be required, nor excessive fines imposed, nor cruel and unusual punishments inflicted.

Amendment 14, Section 1

All persons born or naturalized in the United States and subject to the jurisdiction thereof are citizens of the United States and of the State wherein they reside. No State shall make or enforce any law which shall abridge the privileges or immunities of citizens of the United States; nor shall any State deprive any person of life, liberty, or property, without due process of law; nor deny to any person within its jurisdiction the equal protection of the laws.

Articles of Amendment to the Constitution of the United States, U.S. Constitution.

that the right to petition for the writ of habeas corpus is guaranteed in Article I of the Constitution). The provisions in the Bill of Rights, however, are the ones used most often.

▶ Defenses: How Do Correctional Workers Avoid Workplace Liability?

In Section 1983 actions, if the prisoner shows that there has been a violation of their constitutional rights, one form of relief (and this type is almost always sought by the prisoner-plaintiff) is monetary damages. These damages are assessed against the individual defendant who has been found responsible for the constitutional violation. These may involve punitive, as well as compensatory, damages. The amounts awarded (by a jury or judge) may be very small (these are called nominal damages, which demonstrates the person's rights were violated, but the person suffered no substantial harm) but may also be, in some cases, very large. If the worker is not covered by insurance or a state policy of indemnification, the personal judgment against the worker will have to be paid out of their own pocket. This may threaten any of the worker's savings that they have, their future earnings, ability to obtain a loan, and even their home or other assets held in their name.

For this and other reasons, the corrections worker and corrections agencies must be very concerned about prisoner lawsuits. There is no immunity against being sued. What can the worker do to protect their assets?

The first rule for the corrections worker is to follow policies and the instructions of supervisors. Because there are many good reference sources of sound policy today, and because most corrections agencies have legal counsel to advise them and to review policy issuances to be sure that they are constitutionally defensible, a corrections worker may assume that the policies of their agency are good, in accordance with current judicial rulings and statutory provisions. A principal duty of any attorney who is assigned to provide legal advice and assistance to a correctional agency or facility is to make certain that policies are constitutionally and statutorily sound. Also, when a court ruling (any U.S. Supreme Court ruling and lower court ruling that is applicable to the agency's location) is made, it must be immediately reviewed so that any changes to agency policy can be drafted if changes are required in order to bring agency practices into line with the new ruling.

As a practical matter, the staff member should, of course, follow policy to be in step with the professional expectations of the agency's management. As a legal matter, the staff member should follow policy to ensure compliance with legal standards and especially to avoid liability in the event of inmate lawsuits. Furthermore, being able to show that an action taken was strictly according to agency policy is ordinarily a good defense if the staff member is ever sued. This holds true even if the policy is later determined to be inaccurate or wrong. By following policy, the staff member is operating within the scope of employment and according to what prison management says is proper.

A second rule is to obtain, or provide, good training. As the field of corrections has become more complex and more affected by court rulings and other legal factors, it has become more important for corrections managers to provide good training to ensure that staff members will act consistently and in accord with agency policy and constitutional requirements. It is important for supervisors at all levels to be aware of those practices that are constitutionally mandated and to inform staff members, particularly those who are new, about the accepted and expected way to perform their duties.

This is not to say that all staff must receive legal training or instruction by lawyers. At a minimum, staff, including supervisors, must know the areas of performance in which there are the greatest exposures to constitutional liability. Corrections workers at every level must be aware of the importance of acting at all times in a professional manner; these days, this means learning, and passing on to subordinates, the legal requirements of the job.

A third rule is to become familiar with the law in your jurisdiction that directly affects your job. Whatever the specialty—security, casework, education, personnel matters, parole, health care—the corrections worker should know the law that is applicable to that special kind of work. In any agency, the worker should study the statutes that govern the agency as a whole and those statutes that specifically govern the worker's special area. Further, the worker should learn about the court rulings that interpret prisoners' rights and staff responsibilities in any area where the official regularly works. To do this, the worker follows the second and first rules: get good training from someone who knows legal rulings and constraints, and be sure to follow policies, which are written to incorporate legal requirements.

A fourth rule to ensure a good defense when sued is to find a good mentor. The new worker should follow instructions from supervisors at all times and will, with time, learn the accepted ways of performing according to agency standards. It often happens that there is a particular supervisor around, an "old hand," who is particularly good at conveying agency policies and practices and who may also know sufficient legal information to advise the new worker of the best way to do things. A related piece of advice is that, no matter how much education the staff person has or how much they think they may know from other experiences, when a person first goes to work in a correctional environment, watch and listen. There is nothing a correctional worker may have learned from the classroom or from other work experiences that will prepare them thoroughly for work inside a prison. A new correctional worker must learn from good and respected co-workers around them until they have the understanding and credibility to be a respected correction professional, and to then serve as a role model and mentor to others.

A fifth rule is to keep good records. Hopefully, the training for all staff members, whether in classrooms or on the job, will emphasize the need for, and the way to write and to maintain, good records. Whether it is filling out the forms that are routinely required to cover certain staff actions or writing a special report to record what happened in an unusual circumstance, there is nothing more important to the lawyer in defending an action than having good, clear, reliable records of what happened, whatever the nature of the lawsuit. When an employee who is called on later to testify in a trial or to help investigators get all of the facts about an occurrence, the existence of good records are invaluable to refresh memory and to establish a more reliable, factual basis for what transpired some weeks or months earlier.

Having good knowledge of the law, being well trained in the job, keeping good records, and knowing agency policies and adhering to them are the basic lines of defense for the corrections worker. They serve to ensure that staff activity is lawful to start with and then, if there is an inmate suit, they provide the best legal defense to protect the worker against losing the case.

▶ Inmate Grievances

Another method of protection for the worker is the inmate **grievance** system. It serves to protect in a practical way, as well as legally.

> The purpose of the [Florida Department of Corrections] grievance procedure is to provide an inmate with a channel for the administrative settlement of a grievance. In addition to providing the inmate with the opportunity of having a grievance heard and considered, this procedure will assist the department by providing additional means for internal resolution of problems and improving lines of communication. This procedure will also provide a written record in the event of subsequent judicial or administrative review.[14]

> PURPOSE: The purpose of this standard operating procedure (SOP) is to increase the safety and security of Idaho Department of Correction (IDOC) correctional facilities by providing offenders a process to voice complaints about policies, division directives, SOPs, field memorandums, conditions of confinement, employee actions, actions of other offenders, healthcare, and other incidents occurring within the jurisdiction of the IDOC unless otherwise noted in this SOP.[15]

The concept underlying an inmate grievance system is that inmates will have complaints about their treatment and that there is some benefit in providing a means for them to channel those complaints in a uniform manner. It is good for inmates to receive answers to their complaints, even though the answers may not be what they want to hear. The mere fact of providing a response provides the inmate with a sense of being recognized and may reduce feelings of frustration. It also may prevent the development of a new feeling—anger—that may arise when no response to a complaint is received.

Prison grievance policies offer a credible, timely, and effective means of staff–inmate communication with the intent of resolving issues at the lowest possible level.

Corrections agencies have come to accept a grievance system for inmates as a sound correctional tool. In a survey of adult state correctional agencies and the District of Columbia, 28 agencies reported activities in their grievance systems. For 2013, those 28 agencies reported, a total of 500,224 grievances filed.[16] In the past, particularly in the 1970s, there was experimentation with a variety of systems to provide a mechanism for the inmate to raise complaints and achieve an informal resolution of those complaints. In this sense, "informal" means resolution without violence, direct confrontation, and the inmate going to court to file a formal legal complaint.

Such mechanisms included attempts at mediation or arbitration, with rules and procedures that brought them just short of court actions. A few states tried using an ombudsman, a system that, by definition, used an outside party to review and investigate complaints. Such a person has authority only to recommend changes in policy or action. Some corrections facilities turned to hearing panels—a committee of staff members who heard complaints from the inmates and had the authority to recommend, or in some cases to order, corrective action. There were a few instances in which inmates were included on such hearing panels and were even allowed to vote on the outcome. Some states also tried using inmate advisory groups, which are committees composed entirely of inmates who review complaints and recommend action. These groups were also used for other matters, such as reviewing new policy and reviewing disciplinary actions taken. These attempts to incorporate direct inmate involvement in institution activities and problems, although based on enthusiastic ideas about democratic training for the inmates and participatory management, were neither notably successful nor widely adopted.

The system that has been adopted nearly universally (that is, in all of the states, the federal government, and many of the city and county systems), at least in large corrections systems, is the written grievance system. Typically, there are published rules in such a system that provide for: (1) the opportunity for any inmate to file a written grievance; (2) time limits for filing the grievance and for responding to it; (3) a description of the kinds of actions that may be the subject of grievances or those that may not (in many states, disciplinary sanctions are not grievable, for example); (4) emergency handling of certain complaints, such as medical or personal injury complaints or impending loss of property; (5) safeguards against reprisals that might be taken against inmates for using the system; and (6) at least one level of appeal from initial disposition of the complaint—usually an appeal to the headquarters-level of the system. **FIGURE 5-3** contains flow charts diagramming two of the inmate grievance processes used by the Arizona Department of Corrections. https://corrections.az.gov/sites/default/files /policies/800/0802_032519.pdf.

As a practical matter, using such written inmate grievances provides a number of benefits. It alerts staff to problem areas in the institution. It spotlights those matters that are of greatest inmate concern. It may point out an individual officer or an isolated activity where corrective action may be needed. It serves, when run properly, to diffuse inmate resentment and hostility. It often lessens the number of lawsuits that are filed. When lawsuits are filed, it provides a quick record to attorneys and the courts of what has been done already to address the complaint. It may provide a statistical basis, either grossly or precisely, to assess programs, policies, or activities that need more careful review and possible revision. It gives the corrections agency the chance to address its problems of management and operation and to correct them internally, without having the courts step in and order corrective action of the courts' preference.

There are weaknesses in the system. It does not provide all kinds of relief—usually the only relief is corrective action for the aggrieved inmate. Money damages are not necessarily available. Injunctive relief is rare, taken only in those cases mentioned in the preceding paragraph in which management recognizes an ongoing problem that needs correction. Often, it fails to cover some of the greatest complaints of inmates, such as serious disciplinary action or medical malpractice. Inmates may try to undermine the system—by filing great numbers of complaints, for example—to try to clog up the system or exhaust the patience of the staff, or by filing frivolous complaints. Inmates may file complaints that they know are without merit, have no basis in fact, are repetitious of claims that have already been addressed, or are otherwise written in bad faith.

States use various means to maintain the effectiveness of their grievance system. Examples include staff training, limiting the number of filings an inmate may make over a given time period and setting up procedures to address an inmate's abuse of the system. An inmate who abuses the grievance system (for example, an inmate who files emergency grievances that are not emergencies or who files a malicious grievance—intentionally falsifying information with the intent to do harm) may be subject to restrictions on filing grievances. Restrictions may include limiting the number of grievances that the inmate may file over a set period of time and taking disciplinary action against an inmate for a demonstrated pattern of abuse.

Time limits to respond to inmates' grievances may drag on and be discouraging. Inmates may perceive that corrective relief is never given. However, on balance, for a wide range of prison complaints, the written grievance system is recognized as a very useful tool.

Besides the practical benefits, the courts have also generally recognized that an administrative grievance system is a desirable mechanism. Many courts have encouraged corrections agencies to adopt such systems. The primary reason has been a desire to cut down on the large number of prisoner lawsuits that are filed. Trivial matters

ATTACHMENT A
DEPARTMENT ORDER 802

Inmate Grievance - Standard Grievance Process

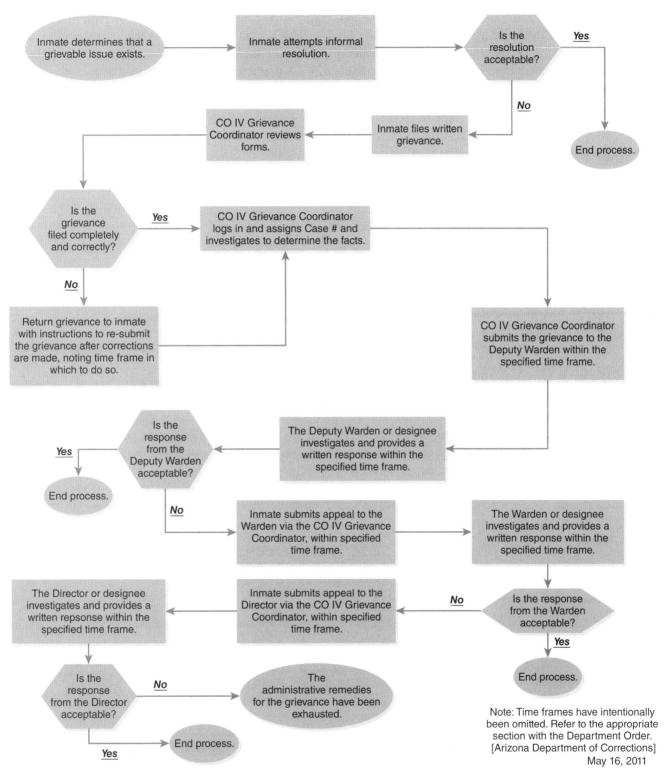

FIGURE 5-3 Inmate Grievance—Standard Grievance Process.

Provided Courtesy of Arizona Department of Corrections.

that can be the subject of lawsuits, which can quickly clog up the courts' time, should be disposed of internally at the prison, and not at the courthouse. A side benefit is that, if and when a case does come to court, there will be a written record already made, which can be attached to the agency's response and may allow for quick resolution of the case on the pleadings.

For these reasons, many courts have required use of the grievance system before the inmate pursues a lawsuit. This is called an exhaustion requirement, which means that, if the agency has a grievance system (and if the subject matter of the lawsuit is covered by the grievance system), the inmate will be required to "exhaust" their administrative grievance remedy before they come into court. As to Section 1983 actions, however, the Supreme Court has held, in *Edwards v. Balisok,* 520 U.S. 641 (1997), "that § 1983 contains no judicially imposed exhaustion requirement … [A]bsent some other bar to the suit, a claim either is cognizable under § 1983 and should immediately go forward, or is not cognizable and should be dismissed." The next section discusses the Prison Litigation Reform Act (PLRA) which established "some other bar," that is, some constraints on using Section 1983 for prisoner lawsuits.

▶ The Prison Litigation Reform Act

In 1980, prior to passage of the PLRA, Congress, in part to recognize the usefulness of prison grievance procedures, enacted amendments to the Civil Rights statute (Section 1983) in the Civil Rights of Institutionalized Persons Act (CRIPA). This statute (42 U.S. Code § 1997e(a) and (b)) provided, in part, that a court could suspend a Section 1983 action if the inmate had not used an available grievance system. There were two strong limitations to the suspension of a case: the action was suspended for a maximum of 90 days, and the grievance system must have been certified by the U.S. Attorney General or by a federal district court. This certification was to be based upon a determination that the system was in compliance with the minimum standards of the act. Essential standards were an advisory role for inmates and staff in formulating, implementing, and operating the system; time limits for staff replies; and safeguards against reprisals. The 1996 passage of the PLRA amended CRIPA. The previous limitation provisions, allowing for up to a 90-day suspension of a Section 1983 action to allow for grievance exhaustion and requiring compliance with the minimum standards for certification, were removed. In the September 27, 1995, Congressional Record (S14413), Senator Dole, in introducing the legislation, said that one purpose of the legislation is "to address the alarming explosion in the number of frivolous lawsuits filed by State and Federal prisoners." Title 42, United States Code, Section 1997e reads, "[n]o action shall be brought with respect to prison conditions under section 1983…or any other Federal law… until such administrative remedies as are available are exhausted." The new language of the PLRA makes exhaustion mandatory, not discretionary, as it was in CRIPA.

In 1996, the Prison Litigation Reform Act of 1995 (PLRA) was signed into law (Pub. L. No. 104-134 (1996)). That federal statute (in Title 42, U.S. Code, Section 1997e) made several significant changes to prisoner litigation in federal courts. With regard to suits relating to prison conditions, the Act provided the following:

> No action shall be brought with respect to prison conditions under … (42 U.S.C. § 1983), or any other Federal law, by a prisoner confined in any jail, prison, or other correctional facility until such administrative remedies as are available are exhausted.

The PLRA also placed other limitations on prisoner suits:

- Frivolous, malicious, and ill-founded suits could be dismissed without requiring exhaustion of administrative remedies.
- Attorney fees were limited.
- No federal civil action could be filed by an inmate for mental or emotional injury while in custody without a prior showing of physical injury or the commission of a sexual act (as defined in section 2246 of title 18).
- An inmate seeking to proceed *in forma pauperis* (without funds, and, therefore, excused from paying filing fees or other court fees), would have to submit records showing the lack of funds in his prison account in order to avoid payment of fees.
- Court orders for relief from prison conditions were strictly limited to correct only the violation of rights shown by the particular plaintiff-inmate.
- Consent decrees were limited in the scope of relief that could be ordered.
- The use and authority of special masters in prison cases were limited.

These amendments to federal statutes, and particularly to Section 1983 actions, were tested in the courts. (See Appendix 5 for one district court's "Instructions for filing a Complaint by a Prisoner Under the Civil Rights Act,

42 U.S.C. § 1983.") Meanwhile, the PLRA has achieved the main intent of the act, which is reducing the volume of prisoner rights suits brought in federal courts.

Several Supreme Court decisions have interpreted the PLRA's exhaustion requirement. In *Booth v. Churner,* 532 U.S. 731 (2001), the Court said that an inmate must complete a prison administrative process capable of addressing the inmate's complaint and providing a form of relief, even if that process does not provide for requested monetary relief. The Court said that the congressional focus was on the exhaustion of "processes," not the forms of relief. Before the passage of the PLRA, in *McCarthy v. Madigan,* 503 U.S. 140 (1992), the Supreme Court ruled that exhaustion of the Bureau of Prisons inmate grievance procedure was not required before seeking relief in a federal court, since the procedure did not give the requested monetary relief. The Court then said, "Congress, of course, is free to design or require an appropriate administrative procedure for a prisoner to exhaust his claim for money damages." The PLRA, in 42 U.S.C. § 1997e(a), does just that. In 2001, the Court in *Booth* said the PLRA's statutory history confirms that Congress meant to require exhaustion of administrative procedures regardless of the "fit" between a prisoner's requested relief and the administrative remedies possible.

The next year, in *Porter v. Nussle,* 534 U.S. 516 (2002), the Court held that the PLRA's exhaustion requirement applies to *all* prisoner suits about prison life.

> **Beyond doubt, Congress enacted § 1997e(a) to reduce the quantity and improve the quality of prisoner suits; to this purpose, Congress afforded corrections officials time and opportunity to address complaints internally before allowing the initiation of a federal case. In some instances, corrective action taken in response to an inmate's grievance might improve prison administration and satisfy the inmate, thereby obviating the need for litigation....In other instances, the internal review might "filter out some frivolous claims."...And for cases ultimately brought to court, adjudication could be facilitated by an administrative record that clarifies the contours of the controversy.**

In *Woodford v. Ngo,* 548 U.S. 81 (2006), the Supreme Court examined whether the PLRA's exhaustion requirement requires *proper* exhaustion of administrative remedies. In *Woodford,* the inmate filed his grievance outside the prison policy's required time period, resulting in prison officials rejecting the inmate's grievance. The PLRA's statutory language provides that an inmate may not sue under 42 U.S.C. § 1983 "until such administrative remedies as are available are exhausted." The inmate, taking the statutory language as written, argued that it does not matter why administrative remedies are no longer available, only that they are no longer available. The issue before the Court was whether an inmate satisfies the PLRA exhaustion requirement by filing an untimely or otherwise procedurally defective administrative grievance. The Court held it did not.

> **Proper exhaustion demands compliance with an agency's deadlines and other critical procedural rules because no adjudicative system can function effectively without imposing some orderly structure on the course of its proceedings ... The benefits of exhaustion can be realized only if the prison grievance system is given a fair opportunity to consider the grievance ... A prisoner who does not want to participate in the prison grievance system will have little incentive to comply with the system's procedural rules unless noncompliance carries a sanction ... For example, a prisoner wishing to bypass available administrative remedies could simply file a late grievance without providing any reason for failing to file on time. If the prison then rejects the grievance as untimely, the prisoner could proceed directly to federal court ... We are confident that the PLRA did not create such a toothless scheme.**

There has been criticism of the *Woodford* opinion in that the ruling holds that the PLRA prevents the filing of even meritorious claims if an inmate fails to meet the prison's procedural requirements for filing a grievance.

In *Jones v. Bock,* 549 U.S. 199 (2007), the Court considered whether inmates were required to specially plead or show exhaustion in their complaints, or whether exhaustion was an affirmative defense that the defendant must plead and show. Prior to *Jones,* there was a split in the circuits on this issue. The Court noted that the PLRA, while dealing extensively with the issue of exhaustion, did not address the issue of whether exhaustion had to be pleaded by the inmate or claimed by the defendant as an affirmative defense. In the absence of the PLRA addressing this aspect, the Court held that the usual practice was to be followed and that this meant prison officials needed to raise the issue as an affirmative defense.

> **The PLRA dealt extensively with the subject of exhaustion … but is silent on the issue whether exhaustion must be pleaded by the plaintiff or is an affirmative defense. This is strong evidence that the usual practice should be followed, and the usual practice under the Federal Rules is to regard exhaustion as an affirmative defense.**

The Court maintained that since the PLRA does not require plaintiffs to plead exhaustion, such a result must be achieved by an amendment to the Federal Rules of Civil Procedure (or by amendment of the act), and not by judicial interpretation.

Jones also held that the Sixth Circuit erred in ruling that an inmate's exhaustion was inadequate under the PLRA when a person who was later sued by the inmate is not named in the first grievance step. The Supreme Court said the PLRA did not impose such a requirement; rather, the PLRA required the inmate to comply with the agency's prison grievance process. Since the prison procedures did not mention naming particular officials, the Sixth Circuit's rule requiring this as part of the exhaustion process was not warranted. Finally, the Court held that the Sixth Circuit erred in holding that an inmate's entire claim had to be dismissed if any one claim was not properly exhausted, again pointing out that this action was not required by the PLRA. The Court observed that the effect of a total exhaustion rule might be having inmates file various claims in separate lawsuits to avoid this potential problem. Such action was seen as contrary to a main purpose of the PLRA: reducing the number of inmate suits. If a complaint contains both exhausted and unexhausted claims, the court moves forward with the exhausted and leaves the unexhausted behind.

The Supreme Court has rejected efforts to excuse noncompliance with the exhaustion requirements of the PLRA. In *Ross v. Blake*, 578 U.S. ___, 136 S. Ct. 1850 (2016), the Court addressed the issue of when administrative remedies are "available." Inmate Blake, in a state correctional system, alleged that correctional officer M had assaulted him and officer R had failed to take adequate steps to protect him. The inmate then complained to supervisory correctional staff who referred the matter to the state's Internal Investigative Unit (IIU), which was tasked with, among other duties, investigating claims of excessive force by staff. The IIU investigation made a finding condemning the conduct of officer M but made no finding as to officer R. The inmate never pursued any relief under the state's administrative remedy procedure, believing that the IIU investigation was an equivalent. The inmate then sued both officers (although officer M resigned in lieu of termination), seeking money damages under 42 U.S.C. Section 1983. A jury awarded the inmate $50,000 in damages from officer M. The district court had dismissed the claim against officer R because that officer had raised the defense that the inmate had failed to exhaust available administrative remedies. The circuit court of appeals reversed the trial court, concluding that PLRA's "exhaustion requirement is not absolute," and adopting an "extra-textual exception" originally formulated by another circuit. "[T]here are certain 'special circumstances' in which, though administrative remedies may have been available[,] the prisoner's failure to comply with administrative procedural requirements may nevertheless have been justified[,]" *Giano v. Goord*, 380 F.3d 670, 676 (2nd Cir. 2004).

The question the Supreme Court considered was: *"Did the court of appeals misapply Supreme Court precedent by ruling there is a common law "special circumstances" exception to the Prison Litigation Reform Act that relieves an inmate of his mandatory obligation to exhaust administrative remedies when the inmate erroneously believes that he satisfied exhaustion by participating in an internal investigation?"* The Supreme Court reversed the court of appeals holding the mandatory language of the PLRA **"means a court may not excuse a failure to exhaust, even to take such circumstances into account."** However, the Court went further in ruling that the PLRA itself requires only exhaustion of administrative remedies, which are available. A prisoner **"is required to exhaust those, but only those, grievance procedures that are "capable of use" to obtain "some relief for the action complained of."** The Court described at least three circumstances in which an administrative remedy is "not capable of use" and thus unavailable: (1) where **"it operates as a simple dead end—with officers unable or consistently unwilling to provide any relief to aggrieved inmates,"** (2) where an **"an administrative scheme might be so opaque that it becomes, practically speaking, incapable of use"** (such as when a procedure exists on paper but no prisoner could reasonably understand or use the system), and (3) **"when prison administrators thwart inmates from taking advantage of a grievance process through machination, misrepresentation, or intimidation."** The case was then remanded to the lower court to make an inquiry and determination as to whether administrative remedies were "available" to the inmate.

In 2016, the Supreme Court, in *Bruce v. Samuels*, 577 U.S. ___, 136 S.Ct. 627, addressed a split in the circuits as to whether the 20% payments toward an inmate's filing fee applied to each case (each case requires payment of 20% of the inmate's commissary balance) or whether the inmate was assessed 20% of their monthly commissary balance to be applied to any outstanding filing fee balance. The inmate argued that the language of the PLRA, referring to a singular "clerk of court," indicates that there is to be only one payment. In addition, a sequential position would render the filing fee for a sixth PLRA case as nothing since 100% of the inmate's commissary account would be depleted. The government countered that the PLRA intended the filing fee payments to apply to each individual case filing and that interpreting the statute to require a 20% commissary balance better promotes the purpose of the PLRA of deterring frivolous lawsuits. The question the Supreme Court considered was: *"When a prisoner files more than one case or appeal in the federal courts in forma pauperis, does § 1915(b)(2) cap the monthly exaction of filing fees at 20% of the prisoner's monthly income regardless of the number of cases or appeals for which he owes filing fees?"*

The Supreme Court ruled:

We hold that monthly installment payments, like the initial partial payment, are to be assessed on a per-case basis. Nothing in § 1915's current design supports treating a prisoner's second or third action unlike his first lawsuit.

A prisoner who utilizes the PLRA partial filing fee payments is required to pay 20% of his or her commissary balance for each PLRA action filed and such payments for each case are to be paid simultaneously.

While seeming to state the obvious, the provisions of the PLRA do not apply to persons who are not prisoners at the time of the filing of their legal action. *Lesesne v. Doe*, 712 F.3d 584 (D.C. Cir. 2013), and collected cases referenced therein. A prisoner is defined as a "person incarcerated or detained." 42 U.S. Code Section 1997e(h).

▶ Prisoners' Rights

If, despite the efforts that have been described (which, in many cases, may be helpful in avoiding a lawsuit), the corrections worker finds themselves involved in a court action, the steps outlined in a review of court appearances come into play. Again (it cannot be overemphasized), the first step and the most important way to defend a case is to obtain representation, establish good communication with counsel, and cooperate with counsel in all stages of the legal case until its conclusion.

In order to work effectively and legally, avoid lawsuits wherever possible, and have a good working relationship with counsel, the staff must be knowledgeable of the law. For torts, habeas corpus, and state or local relief, this requires knowledge of local laws and policies. For the most common legal action, as well as the most threatening (because of the risk of personal judgments and broad injunctive relief), corrections staff, in defense against Section 1983 actions in federal courts, must be aware of constitutional requirements. The balance of this book (Chapters 6 through 17) discusses the constitutional requirements that have been placed on corrections workers. On the other side of the coin, these are the prisoners' constitutional rights, as defined at this time.

This text focuses on the constitutional principles established by the Supreme Court, which are contained in a group of cases that, taken together, form the body of "corrections law," or prisoners' rights. There are many decisions—hundreds in the lower federal courts and hundreds more in state courts—that further define prisoners' rights. This text focuses on Supreme Court decisions because it establishes the constitutional standards applicable to different areas of inmate activities nationwide and these decisions are the yardstick for measuring constitutional liability under 42 U.S.C. § 1983. Lower court decisions will be covered occasionally, because they take prisoners' rights questions into new or expanded areas not yet addressed by the Supreme Court. The reader, and especially any corrections worker, is warned (again) that, besides the Supreme Court decisions, the rulings in local jurisdictions, whether from state courts (for state agencies) or from federal appellate or district courts (for state or federal workers), are also binding as to legal requirements, in practice and in court litigation in that jurisdiction.

Summary

- A prison is a special community with very specific outer boundaries. The interior components of a prison also resemble a community. To run effectively, prisons require a high degree of uniformity. The prison environment, by its very nature, may contribute to the filing of litigation.

- Prisoners' rights are principally those rights that are guaranteed under the U.S. Constitution and that apply to the situations in which inmates find themselves. Those rights are primarily pursued in the courts through a federal civil rights statute, 42 U.S.C. § 1983 (and the equivalent, Bivens suits, for federal inmates).
- In Section 1983 suits, inmates usually seek monetary damages. Courts may also give injunctive relief in such suits. Money damages are awarded against the individual officials who have been shown to be responsible for violating constitutional rights. Corrections staff, therefore, must be concerned, individually, about the impact of civil rights lawsuits that may be brought against them.
- The first, and leading, rule for corrections workers is to follow agency policy. Policy should always be written to include any current requirements guaranteed by the Constitution, as interpreted by the courts. It is the responsibility of agency administrators and lawyers to make sure that policy does reflect, at a minimum, those constitutional guarantees.
- Other rules for corrections workers are to get good training in all aspects of the job; to become familiar with the law (statutory and court rulings) that directly affects the job; to identify and follow a good mentor; and to keep good records of work performed and of any unusual incidents.
- Inmate grievance systems have been adopted by virtually all corrections agencies. These provide benefits to corrections staff and management and to inmates, in many cases. Courts have encouraged the use of administrative grievance systems. As interpreted by the Supreme Court, the exhaustion requirement of the Prison Litigation Reform Act of 1995 applies to all prisoner suits about prison life (*Porter v. Nussle*). The Court also has held that the PLRA requires the proper exhaustion of administrative remedies for inmate grievances before inmates bring Section 1983 actions into federal courts (*Woodford v. Ngo*). However, inmate needs only exhaust those administrative remedies that are available, meaning those that might give the prisoner some relief from the complained of actions (*Ross v. Blake*).
- Under the PLRA, an inmate is required to pay 20% of the balance of their prison income toward each legal action commenced using in forma pauperis status. *Bruce v. Samuels*.
- When lawsuits are filed against corrections workers, they must work closely with counsel in defense of the lawsuits.

Thinking About It

On July 1, Inmate Smith filed an institution administrative grievance alleging an officer used unnecessary force against Smith. Department of Corrections (DOC) policy provides a three tiered system of administrative grievance: the institution level, the region level (appeals) and the headquarters level (appeals). At each level an inmate is entitled to a response to their inmate grievance within twenty working days of receipt, and the inmate has twenty working days to file an appeal with the next level (region or headquarters) after receiving a response to their grievance. DOC regulations also prohibit an appeal of an administrative grievance until the inmate receives a response from the level of the DOC in which the grievance was filed. Inmate Smith did not receive a response from the institution within 20 working days and filed a grievance about the failure to respond. Inmate Smith did not receive a response from the institution on the second grievance. Sixty days after filing the initial grievance, and without receiving a response from the DOC, Smith files a lawsuit in federal court. Prison officials claim Smith has failed to exhaust administrative remedies as required by the PLRA. Smith argues the DOC's failure to respond within the time frames established by DOC policy has made the grievance system unavailable. Does a correctional system's failure to abide by its own regulations make the grievance system unavailable under the PLRA? *Robinson v. Superintendent*, 831 F.3d 148 (3rd Cir. 2016).

Key Terms

Bill of Rights
classification (corrections)
grievance (corrections)
in forma pauperis

Endnotes

1. Florida Department of Corrections Mission Statement. Available: http://www.dc.state.fl.us/about.html
2. Virginia Department of Corrections Mission Statement. Available: https://vadoc.virginia.gov/about/

3. North Dakota Department of Corrections and Rehabilitation. Available: https://www.docr.nd.gov/. Accessed February 09, 2020.

4. E.A. Carson. *Prisoners in 2018*. (Washington, DC: Bureau of Justice Statistics, U.S. Department of Justice, April 2020), Table 2. https://www.bjs.gov/content/pub/pdf/p18.pdf. Accessed November 30, 2020.

5. Marushack, L.M. & Minton, T.D. *Correctional Populations in the United States, 2017–2018*. (Washington, DC: Bureau of Justice Statistics, U.S. Department of Justice, August 2020), Table 1. https://www.bjs.gov/content/pub/pdf/cpus1718.pdf. Accessed November 30, 2020.

6. See note 5 above, Table 1.

7. West, H.C. & Sabol, W.J. *Prisoner in 2009* (Revised). (Washington, DC: Bureau of Justice Statistics, U.S. Department of Justice, October 2011), Table 1. https://www.bjs.gov/content/pub/pdf/p09.pdf. Accessed November 30, 2020.

8. See endnote 5 above, Table 1.

9. See endnote 1 above, Table 13.

10. U.S. Department of Justice, Bureau of Justice Statistics, *Prisoners in 2000* by Allen J. Beck and Paige Harrison (August 2001), page 12. https://www.bjs.gov/content/pub/pdf/p00.pdf. Accessed August 5, 2020.

11. Sykes, G. M. *The Society of Captives: A Study of a Maximum Security Prison*. (Princeton, NJ: Princeton University Press, 1974), 63–83. Occasionally, there are inmates who are not opposed to being confined. The reasons vary: there may be a desire to complete a beneficial prison vocational training program; some inmates feel they are better cared for or have more secure living conditions within the prison than they do on the outside.

12. U.S. Department of Justice, Bureau of Justice Statistics. *Challenging the Conditions of Prisons and Jails- A Report on Section 1983 Litigation* by Roger A. Hanson and Henry W.K. Daley (December 1994) Retrieved at https://www.bjs.gov/content/pub/pdf/ccpjrs83l.pdf. This report notes that the number of prisoner Section 1983 actions correlates strongly to the increase in the U.S. prison population.

13. Administrative Office for U.S. Courts. Table C-2: *U.S. District Courts—Civil Cases Filed, by Jurisdiction and Nature of Suit—During the 12-Month Period Ending March 31, 2020*. https://www.uscourts.gov/statistics-reports/caseload-statistics-data-tables

14. Florida Department of Corrections. *Inmate Grievance Procedure*. Rule Chapter 33-103. Accessed February 10, 2020. https://www.flrules.org/gateway/RuleNo.asp?title=INMATE%20GRIEVANCE%20PROCEDURE&ID=33-103.001

15. Idaho Department of Corrections. *Grievance and Informal Resolution Procedure for Offenders*. Accessed February 10, 2020. http://forms.idoc.idaho.gov/WebLink/DocView.aspx?dbid=0&id=281409&page=1&cr=1 10

16. In a survey of adult state correctional agencies and the District of Columbia, 28 agencies reported activities in their grievance systems. Those 28 agencies reported, for the year 2013, a total of 500,224 grievances filed. Kaul, P., Donley, G., Cavataro, B., Benavides, A., Kincaid, J. & Chatham, J. (2015). Prison and jail Grievance policies: Lessons from a fifty-state survey. University of Michigan School of Law. Retrieved at https://www.law.umich.edu/special/policyclearinghouse/Site%20Documents/FOIAReport10.18.15.2.pdf. Accessed March 31, 2020.

CHAPTER 6

Access to Courts

It is fundamental that access of prisoners to the courts for the purpose of presenting their complaints may not be denied or obstructed.

U.S. Supreme Court, *Johnson v. Avery*

CHAPTER OUTLINE

- Opening the Gates
- *Ex parte Hull*
- *Johnson v. Avery*
- *Shaw v. Murphy*
- *Bounds v. Smith*
- *Lewis v. Casey*
- *Murray v. Giarratano*
- *Wolff* and *Martinez*
- Access to the Courts in the Digital Age
- Frivolous Complaints and Frequent Filers
- Litigation Alleging Retaliation for the Exercise of Constitutional Rights

This chapter examines the constitutional provisions that protect the rights of prisoners by discussing how inmates get into court to get their complaints heard. Are there protections or guarantees that apply to the filing of prisoner complaints in the courts? If so, where are they found, and how far do they go? How much do prison authorities have to do, or what are they restrained from doing, according to the constitutional rights of prisoners to have access to the courts?

Look again at the list of amendments to the Constitution provided in Box 5-1 and locate the provision that you believe gives prisoners the right to get into court, even when they are confined in prison. (Please be assured that the constitutional provisions in Box 5-1 are the provisions in the Constitution that are used to ensure rights to prisoners and to measure the extent of those rights.)

There is nothing that addresses such a right, is there? Indeed, the courts (including the Supreme Court) have not always been careful to specify where such a right is found in the Constitution. In *Christopher v. Harbury*, 536 U.S. 403 (2002) the Court recognized as "unsettled the basis of the constitutional right of access to courts" and in a footnote provided the following list of constitutional sources for such a right: Article IV Privileges and Immunities Clause, (citations omitted), the First Amendment Petition Clause, (citations omitted), the Fifth Amendment Due Process Clause, *Murray v. Giarratano*, 492 U.S. 1, 11, n. 6 (1989) (plurality opinion), the Fourteenth Amendment Equal Protection, *Pennsylvania v. Finley*, 481 U.S. 551, 557 (1987), and Due Process Clauses, *Wolff v. McDonnell*, 418 U.S. 539, 576 (1974). The Court then explained that denial of access to the courts can be broadly classified into two groups- those cases where actions by public officials delay or frustrate a plaintiff's ability to prepare and file a lawsuit at the present time. Court ordered relief in these types of denial of access to the courts' claims would include providing prisoners with an adequate law library, illiterate prisoners with access to readers or services from someone trained in the law. The Court's opinion in Christopher is also important as it expressly established that having " a successful access claim requires a prisoner to show that the defendants have scuttled his pursuit of a "nonfrivolous, arguable" claim. A prisoner's right to access to the courts is not free standing, it exists only to "provide some effective vindication for a separate and distinct right to seek judicial relief for some wrong." However, as we will see in this chapter, the courts—and most importantly, the Supreme Court—have found that prisoners do have a right of access to the courts.

There is a right in Article I, Section 9, of the Constitution to seek a writ of habeas corpus. This is a specific guarantee of constitutional protection. But what of other complaints and wrongs done to prisoners? Habeas corpus provides only special relief—release from illegal confinement. And prisoners have many complaints; indeed, the great majority of their complaints are not the basis for habeas corpus relief, that is, these complaints would not entitle them to be released from custody.

▶ Opening the Gates

It is frequently said that, until the 1960s, the courts had a "hands-off" attitude toward prisons and prisoner complaints. The term "hands-off" means that, except for a few cases of habeas corpus, courts did not look behind the walls of prisons to examine the way prisoners were treated. Running the prisons was considered to be the business of wardens, the Executive Branch of government, and those charged with keeping control of persons in custody and not the business of the judiciary.

Federal courts in the 1960s opened the gates to prisoners—they started taking their hands off and looking more closely at matters behind prison walls.

▶ *Ex Parte Hull*

This is not to say that hands were kept completely off before 1960. In a landmark case that is still an important guide for corrections officials, the Supreme Court said the following in *Ex parte Hull*, 312 U.S. 546 (1941):

> **[T]he state and its officers may not abridge or impair petitioner's right to apply to a federal court for a writ of habeas corpus.**

Michigan had a regulation that required prisoners to submit all legal documents to an institution office for review before the papers could be mailed to court. If "properly drawn," the papers would be forwarded to court. If not, they would be returned to the inmate. Hull, a Michigan inmate, tried to send a petition for a writ of habeas corpus to the Supreme Court. It was refused for mailing, as was a subsequent letter to the Court. (How, you may ask, did Hull get into court? He somehow managed to get another paper to his father, who filed it with the clerk of the Court.) The Supreme Court, while not giving Hull relief on his habeas corpus petition, struck down the Michigan regulation. This is a leading ruling for the principle that prison officials may not screen, censor, or interfere with an inmate's mailings and submissions to the courts.[1]

The Supreme Court, however, while giving us a leading principle on prisoners' rights, did not identify where in the Constitution it found the protection for prisoners that it summarily (and unanimously) defined. One may surmise that the protection was inherent in the habeas corpus provision (Article I, Section 9), which we have already discussed. If that is the source of the protection, the question remains: Do the constitutional protections for accessing federal courts apply only to habeas corpus petitions and not to other types of actions, such as suits for constitutional violations under Section 1983? We will look at that question again as later opinions are given by the Supreme Court on prisoner access to courts.

▶ *Johnson v. Avery*

The leading case on prisoner access to the courts, and one that can be noted as a leading part of the abandonment of the "hands-off" doctrine in the 1960s, is *Johnson v. Avery*, 393 U.S. 483 (1969). Johnson, a Tennessee inmate, was disciplined for violating a prison regulation that stated, "No inmate will advise, assist or otherwise contract to aid another, whether with or without a fee, to prepare Writs or other legal matters"[2] The trial court (the U.S. District Court in Middle Tennessee) found that the regulation was invalid on the grounds that it was an interference with inmates' access to federal habeas corpus relief. On appeal, the Sixth Circuit Court of Appeals reversed, finding that the State of Tennessee was pursuing a legitimate purpose in preserving prison discipline and in limiting the practice of law to licensed attorneys. The Supreme Court accepted the appeal (the petition for writ of certiorari) to decide whether the state limitation on prisoner legal activities was valid. In the prison vernacular, the practice of one inmate helping another with legal work is called "jailhouse lawyering," so the Supreme Court had to decide whether it was legally permissible for Tennessee to prohibit "jailhouse lawyering."

At the outset, the Court identified its opinion as being based on concern for protecting the writ of habeas corpus. Thus, this case, like *Ex parte Hull*, is constitutionally based on the provision guaranteeing the writ of habeas corpus.

> **[I]t is fundamental that access of prisoners to the courts for the purpose of presenting their complaints may not be denied or obstructed.**

There were other earlier cases, the Court noted, that had relied on this principle. For example, according to *Smith v. Bennett*, 365 U.S. 708 (1961), a state may not make the writ available only to prisoners who can pay a filing fee. Also, a state must furnish a transcript of court proceedings to a prisoner who cannot afford to pay for that transcript when the prisoner says it is needed in order to pursue subsequent legal action. *Long v. District Court*, 385 U.S. 192 (1966).

In a statement of legal principle that was given as an aside (we call this a **dictum**), the Supreme Court said that Tennessee could not have a regulation that would forbid illiterate or poorly educated prisoners to file habeas corpus petitions. In this case, because Tennessee did not have any other source of assistance (other than the jailhouse lawyer) for such prisoners, in effect, it was doing just that by prohibiting prisoners from assisting one another with legal filings. The Court noted (we would call this taking judicial notice of facts, which are not proved in the record) that prisons have "a high percentage of persons who are totally or functionally illiterate." A crucial fact seemed to be that Tennessee did not provide any alternative kind of legal assistance for such illiterate persons to file petitions for relief. (The Court noted that some states did provide assistance to prisoners to help in drafting habeas corpus petitions. In some states, the public defender system provided attorneys who would assist with preparing petitions. Some law schools initiated programs which allows senior law students to assist prisoners. A few states have even paid attorneys to be of assistance to inmates at the prison.)

The Court further stated that there can be abuses when inmates provide legal assistance to other inmates. To help control this problem, the state could place restrictions and restraints on the "jailhouse lawyering" activities—for example, by having limitations on the time and place for such activities and prohibiting the giving of any consideration (money or other favors) for the assistance provided by another inmate. Nonetheless, the Court said:

> **[U]nless and until the State provides some reasonable alternative to assist inmates in the preparation of petitions for post-conviction relief, it may not validly enforce a regulation such as that here in issue, barring inmates from furnishing such assistance to other prisoners.**

▶ *Shaw v. Murphy*

In *Shaw v. Murphy*, 532 U.S. 223 (2001), the Supreme Court looked further at the issue of "jailhouse lawyering" and reasonable alternatives. Murphy, a Montana State Prison inmate working as an inmate law clerk, wanted to help a maximum security inmate who was charged with assaulting a correctional officer. Although prison rules did not allow this help (because of separate housing locations), the inmate law clerk wrote a letter to the charged inmate, saying, "I do want to help you with your case… Don't plead guilty because we can get at least 100 witnesses to testify that [the officer] is an overzealous guard who has a personal agenda to punish…inmates." Prison staff reviewed the correspondence and charged the inmate law clerk with violating prison rules, including interference with due process hearings. A hearing was held and Murphy was found to have committed the prohibited act.

A sanction was imposed. (This was internal disciplinary punishment.) Murphy sued, seeking injunctive and declaratory relief under 42 U.S.C. § 1983. He claimed, in part, a violation of his First Amendment rights, including the right to provide legal assistance to other inmates.

The U.S. District Court in Montana dismissed the claim. The Ninth Circuit Court of Appeals reversed, ruling that inmates have a First Amendment right to assist other inmates with their legal claims. Murphy enjoyed this right of association, the court of appeals concluded, because he was providing legal advice that potentially was relevant to the other inmate's defense. The Supreme Court reversed, holding that inmates do not have a special First Amendment right to provide legal assistance to other inmates. Such contacts between inmates are subject to the standard stated in *Turner v. Safley*, 482 U.S. 78 (1987). *Turner*, discussed in some detail in a review of the First Amendment as it applies to inmate mail, allows restrictions on an inmate's constitutional rights if those restrictions are reasonably related to legitimate penological objectives. The inmate failed to show that the prison restrictions were not related to such objectives.[3]

▶ *Bounds v. Smith*

Another leading case on prisoner access to courts is *Bounds v. Smith*, 430 U.S. 817 (1977). The Supreme Court in *Bounds* took the principles of *Johnson v. Avery* and expanded them into broader guarantees of constitutional protections.

At the outset, the *Bounds* Court stated the question it was addressing: "whether States must protect the right of prisoners to access to the courts by providing them with law libraries or alternative sources of legal knowledge." The Court, however, did not answer that question thoroughly, but it did give us more guidance about the right of accessing the courts.

In *Johnson v. Avery* and in *Ex parte Hull*, the Supreme Court had said that the state could not impede or restrict an inmate's right of access to courts. In *Bounds*, the Court held that the state must take some steps to assist inmates if they did not have alternative means of obtaining legal assistance.

This lawsuit came out of North Carolina, which had a large number of prison facilities spread over the state. (At the time of the suit, there were 13,000 inmates in 77 prison units; 65 of those units had fewer than 200 inmates each.) The district court had found that the state did not have any type of assistance to help inmates prepare their petitions to the courts. That court required the state to come up with a plan to fulfill its duty to ensure access to the courts. The district court noted that the state could choose to implement a program that provided lawyers, law students, or public defenders to provide assistance or provided law libraries for inmates to do the work themselves.

North Carolina responded with a plan to provide seven libraries in facilities around the state. Inmates who needed to work on their legal matters would be transported to one of these central libraries to work one full day (or longer, if necessary) on their legal research and writing. The state drew up a list of books that would be provided in each library, along with standard legal forms, writing paper, typewriters, and access to copying machines. Almost by default, that plan has become the constitutional standard for prison law libraries, because it was the one presented in the case considered by the Supreme Court.[4] (U.S. Code Annotated; Supreme Court Reporter; Black's Law Dictionary, 1960).

Inmates objected to this plan, saying it did not go far enough. They sought more books, a library at every institution, and legal counsel for assistance in addition to the libraries. The district court approved the state plan and held that the state did not have to provide legal assistance in addition to the libraries. On appeal, the Fourth Circuit Court of Appeals affirmed. The appeals court approved the ruling of the district court and the state's plan for law libraries, with one amendment: it required the state to ensure that female inmates would have access rights to library facilities similar to the men.

The Supreme Court affirmed the lower court's ruling and, in effect, the constitutionality of the North Carolina law library plan. In its arguments before the Supreme Court, the state contended that its only obligation (under *Johnson v. Avery*) was not to interfere with inmate "writ writers" and not to restrict communications to the courts (under *Ex parte Hull*). The Court rejected those contentions and said more was required:

> **[O]ur decisions have consistently required States to shoulder affirmative obligations to assure all prisoners meaningful access to the courts … We hold, therefore, that the fundamental constitutional right of access to the courts requires prison authorities to assist inmates in the preparation and filing of meaningful legal papers by providing prisoners with adequate law libraries or adequate assistance from persons trained in the law.**

The Supreme Court did not rule that law libraries were required—provided that the state has an alternative means of "adequate" legal assistance. What would such an alternative be? The Court noted that briefs in the case suggested these alternatives: training inmates as paralegal assistants to work under lawyers' supervision; using paralegals and law students; having a program of volunteer attorney assistance; hiring lawyers on a part-time or full-time staff basis; or using legal assistance organizations, public defenders, or legal service offices. As an aside, the Court observed that using attorneys or legal service programs would be preferable to having inmate writ writers, because the inmates who do legal work for other inmates could generate internal disciplinary problems. The Court said that it would not endorse any particular plan, however. In fact, it encouraged local experimentation, with the overriding requirement that any plan would have to provide adequate, meaningful assistance to meet constitutional standards.

Let us return to our question: Does the constitutional standard of court access apply only to habeas corpus actions (as would seem to be the limits of the holdings in *Hull* and *Johnson*)? The Court in *Bounds* expanded the principle of prisoner access to courts, but it fell short because it did not define exactly what kind of legal activities were covered. Some language in *Bounds* seems very broad indeed. The Court stated, for example, "[P]risoners have a constitutional right of access to the courts," and "States [have] obligations to assure all prisoners meaningful access to the courts." But the citations to earlier cases supporting those statements deal with habeas corpus petitions, or with attacks on convictions. Nor did this Court identify the constitutional provision that supports the principle on which it was insisting. The closest we get is this statement of the question to be decided: Do the state's programs give to inmates the opportunity "to present claimed violations of fundamental constitutional rights to the courts"? The Court's discussion seems to imply, if not conclude, that the legal assistance requirements apply to habeas corpus petitions and to civil rights (constitutional) complaints.

It is reasonable to conclude that *Bounds* guarantees access to the courts for both habeas corpus and Section 1983 actions. Whether it applies to "lesser" activities, such as common law torts and personal legal matters (such as researching domestic relations cases, for example) was not decided. This conclusion is supported by a statement in the opinion: "[T]his Court has 'constantly emphasized' [that] habeas corpus and civil rights actions are of 'fundamental importance…in our constitutional scheme' because they directly protect our most valued rights."

While a close and careful reading of *Bounds* would seem to limit the Court's **holding** to habeas corpus and Section 1983 actions, in practice, there is no distinction made in most prisons about what kinds of legal matters the inmates are working on. Because it is improper for officials to scrutinize an inmate's legal work (other than perhaps to do the most cursory examination of legal papers to be sure that they are, in fact, of a legal nature) or to interfere in any way with legal papers being sent to courts, inmates are allowed to work on any kind of legal matter. Also, because only a very few jurisdictions have an alternative legal assistance program, such as the Supreme Court encouraged be explored in *Bounds,* almost every prison in the country has a law library (see **FIGURE 6-1**).

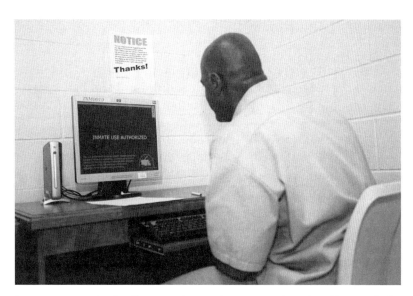

FIGURE 6-1 An inmate using a computer in the library at the maximum security prison Tecumseh State Correctional Institution in Nebraska.
© Mikael Karlsson/Alamy Stock Photo

There may be a wide variety in the size (and thoroughness) of the lawbook collections in prison libraries. Small institutions (and most jails) usually have comparatively small collections—much smaller than the one specified in *Bounds*. But the average law library in prisons is probably pretty close to the one proposed by North Carolina in *Bounds*. (Some are much larger, and, in some states, there may even be several in a single institution.) What a bonanza for the lawbook publishers! Lawbooks are expensive, statute and case reporter collections contain many books, and those books must be constantly updated. (Another problem and expense are the mutilation or loss of books—in colleges, public libraries, and prisons, books are frequently damaged or stolen. A major difference is that those in prisons must be restored or a constitutional question is raised!) The Supreme Court recognized that there is a serious economic impact for the state in providing a prison law library. Most states and localities, however, have chosen to install law libraries rather than pursue any of the alternative legal assistance programs suggested by the Court.

Recent technological changes have occurred that have altered the way prisoners access legal materials. In many prisons, paper book law libraries have been replaced with **electronic law libraries**. The Federal Bureau of Prisons has replaced its paper law libraries with an electronic version from a contract provider and most states have also begun using electronic law libraries.[5] South Dakota recently did away with its paper law library and use of contract legal services and began using an electronic law library system, which inmates access through computer tablets with which provided they are. Some states also provide inmates with legal research and document drafting training to assist other inmates in their access to the courts. For example Oklahoma selects and trains inmate research assistants who "are to assist all fellow inmates at their own facility in their legal claims for no fee or any type of renumeration other than inmate wages granted by the agency.

An **electronic law library** provides access to the same types of material as in a traditional paper library, with the difference being the format. Electronic law libraries may increase the availability of legal resources because of reduced cost and elimination or reduction in theft or destruction of resources. Electronic libraries take up less physical space, but they do involve inmate access to computer terminals and also instruction to inmates in the computer skills and research techniques needed to locate relevant material.

▶ *Lewis v. Casey*

In 1996, the Supreme Court, in *Lewis v. Casey*, 518 U.S. 343 (1996), modified its holdings and decision in *Bounds*. A lower federal court had held that the Arizona Department of Corrections was not meeting *Bounds* standards and that its law libraries and other legal assistance provided to inmates were inadequate. That court ordered Arizona to provide more training to library staff, update its legal materials, provide better photocopying services, provide better library access for lockdown prisoners, keep its libraries open during expanded times specified by the court, and prepare a videotape on legal research for inmates. Also, bilingual inmates had to be located and trained as legal assistants to help non-English speaking inmates. The Ninth Circuit Court of Appeals affirmed that judgment.

The Supreme Court, in a part (Section III) of the opinion in *Lewis* in which eight of the nine justices joined, found that the district court order was far too broad and intrusive. The lower court had failed "to accord adequate deference to the judgment of the prison authorities," and had instead used a special master (a law professor from New York) rather than the prison authorities to devise a plan that would provide better services.

The **master** had taken eight months to investigate the Arizona legal program and then drew up a 25-page injunctive order that the lower court adopted. This violated numerous warnings from the Supreme Court in other cases that courts should not become "enmeshed in the minutiae of prison operations." Instead, the Supreme Court said that the lower court should have acted as the North Carolina court had in *Bounds*, turning to the Department of Corrections to devise a program that would ensure the access to the courts that the court demanded. The plan from North Carolina, with minor changes from the court, became the approved plan for implementation and for ultimate review and approval by the Supreme Court in *Bounds*. Here, "[t]he State was entitled to far more than an opportunity for rebuttal, and on that ground alone this order would have to be set aside."

However, there was much more that the Supreme Court found objectionable in the lower court's actions. First, the Court said, there had not been a sufficient showing by inmates of actual injury to justify the district court to intervene as drastically as it did. The district court had found "a systemic *Bounds* violation," meaning that the whole Arizona prison system was failing to meet *Bounds* standards for legal assistance. Instead, the Supreme Court pointed out, there were only two inmates who, from the record, were shown to have been injured (by not getting their legal matters drafted or filed). The lower court was especially concerned with illiterate and non-English speaking inmates because of their inability to get into court with their complaints. The Supreme Court indicated that the remedy devised by the lower court should have been limited to the injuries that were shown to have been sustained by the two injured inmates. Those two instances "were a patently inadequate basis for a conclusion of systemwide violations and imposition of systemwide relief."

> *Bounds* **did not create an abstract, free-standing right to a law library or legal assistance ... [T]he inmate therefore must ... demonstrate that the alleged shortcomings in the library or legal assistance program hindered his efforts to pursue a legal claim.**

Yet another, and perhaps even more important, holding of *Lewis* was that the *Bounds* opinion had been taken too far:

> **[S]everal statements in** *Bounds* **went beyond the right of access recognized in the earlier cases on which it relied ... These statements appear to suggest that the State must enable the prisoner to discover grievances, and to litigate effectively once in court ... [W]e now disclaim [those suggestions]. To demand the conferral of such sophisticated legal capabilities upon a mostly uneducated and indeed largely illiterate prison population is effectively to demand permanent provision of counsel, which we do not believe the Constitution requires.**

The Court went on to specify what kinds of cases are covered by the prisoners' rights to have access to courts. Besides habeas corpus, earlier cases indicated that inmates could pursue direct appeals from their convictions. *Wolff* (discussed later in this chapter) extended prisoners' access rights "only slightly" to vindicate "basic constitutional rights," namely, civil rights actions under 42 U.S.C. § 1983. That is as far as the Supreme Court would go; inmates do not have to be aided to bring, and to effectively pursue, all kinds of legal actions, the Court said in *Lewis*.

> **In other words,** *Bounds* **does not guarantee inmates the wherewithal to transform themselves into litigating engines capable of filing everything from shareholder derivative actions to slip-and-fall claims. The tools it requires to be provided are those that the inmates need in order to attack their sentences, directly or collaterally, and in order to challenge the conditions of their confinement. Impairment of any other litigating capacity is simply one of the incidental (and perfectly constitutional) consequences of conviction and incarceration.**

Thus, with *Lewis v. Casey*, the guidelines of *Bounds* are severely limited, although the Court in *Lewis* did not say that it was overruling *Bounds*. Also, with a hearty slap at the freewheeling actions of the district judge in this case, the Supreme Court once more emphasized the message of deference to prison authorities that the courts should be, but often are not, showing in their handling of prison matters.

Today, states use various approaches to provide inmates with legal assistance. For example, the Washington State department of corrections' policy says "Individuals will have access to a Law Library and/or the resources of a Law Library, assistance from individuals trained in the law, and/or access to legal service contractors." [Section VIA]. With respect to inmate assistance in legal matters, the policy, in part, provides:

> [II A] An incarcerated individual may confer with another incarcerated individual in researching and preparing legal pleadings. No incarcerated individual may represent, attend, hear, or participate in another individual's legal matter before a legal tribunal unless called as a witness. [IIB]An incarcerated individual cannot, under any circumstances, receive any form of favor or payment for the time, efforts, equipment, or materials used in assisting another individual. [IIC] Incarcerated individuals may assist each other in preparing legal documents in the Law Library…unless there is a legitimate penological interest precluding the contact.

This policy provides an example of accommodating an inmate's right to legal assistance, while also addressing the concerns prison officials have to protect security and good order in the institution.[6]

▶ *Murray v. Giarratano*

In *Murray v. Giarratano*, 492 U.S. 1 (1989), inmates who were on death row in Virginia claimed that they had a constitutional right to counsel in order to pursue collateral attacks on their convictions and sentences. The Supreme Court acknowledged that, in earlier cases, such as *Gideon v. Wainwright*, 372 U.S. 335 (1963), it had ruled that, under the Sixth and Fourteenth Amendments, defendants had the right to counsel at trials on criminal felony charges. This meant that the government would have to provide counsel for defendants who were indigent. In *Douglas v. California*, 372 U.S. 353 (1963), the Court also ruled that there was a similar right to counsel, whom the government would have to appoint for indigents, for an initial appeal from conviction and sentence. However, in *Pennsylvania v. Finley*, 481 U.S. 551 (1987), the Supreme Court had held that the state did not have to provide counsel for indigent prisoners who were seeking postconviction relief (by collateral attacks on their convictions and sentences).

One question that remained—and the one that was considered in *Murray*—was whether inmates under death sentence were entitled to counsel in order to pursue collateral attacks after their initial appeals. Lower courts had ruled that they were constitutionally entitled to such legal assistance, and four justices in *Murray* agreed with that conclusion. This was primarily based on the decision of the Supreme Court in *Bounds*, which required assistance be provided to inmates to give them meaningful access to the courts. But the majority of the Court in *Murray* held that their ruling in *Pennsylvania v. Finley* had been correct and that it also applied to persons on death row, as well as those serving ordinary sentences of imprisonment.

> **In *Finley*, we ruled that neither the Due Process Clause of the Fourteenth Amendment nor the equal protection guarantee of "meaningful access" required the State to appoint counsel for indigent prisoners seeking state postconviction relief…[W]e now hold that *Finley* applies to those inmates under sentence of death as well as to other inmates, and that holding necessarily imposes limits on *Bounds*.**

▶ *Wolff* and *Martinez*

The Supreme Court has dealt with inmates' legal activities in two other cases. By coincidence, these two cases are primarily known for their rulings in other areas of constitutional law. But the Court disposed of court-access issues in both of them, with clear holdings regarding prisoners' rights. Those two cases, *Wolff* and *Martinez*, are also similar in that they both deal with issues of attorney–client (when the client is an inmate) contacts. Attorney–client communication is another aspect of prisoners' access to the courts.

A fundamental principle of our legal system is the right of a person to have confidential communications with his attorney. This principle clearly does not end just because the client is in prison. Whether the attorney is representing the inmate on an appeal of the criminal conviction that placed their client in prison, on constitutional claims about the conditions of the inmate's confinement, or on any of the whole range of civil matters in which inmates may be involved, professional legal contacts—in person, by phone, or by mail—are necessary.

Attorneys are considered to be "officers of the court," bound by codes of ethics governing their work. As officers of the court, they are entitled to a degree of special deference to their status, and they, in turn, must take their professional responsibilities seriously. Under some circumstances, attorneys have violated the trust that is given to them in their capacity as members of the bar. (For more details, see the case of *U.S. v. Novak*, 531 F.3d 99 (1st Cir. 2008), which serves as an explicit example of the violation of trust by an attorney. The focus of *Novak*, however, is the Fourth Amendment search-and-seizure provision.)

Prisons and jails have administrative and security concerns, which lead to some restrictions on prisoners having contacts with their lawyers. The prisoners and the lawyers may not be very understanding about these restrictions and the reasons for having them. What has to be arrived at is a balance between the government's needs to ensure proper oversight of all inmate activities, including legal ones, for the security and orderly running of the institution and the needs of attorneys and inmates to have adequate and specially protected opportunities for communication, in visits, phone calls, and correspondence. *Wolff* and *Martinez* address some of the specific ways in which that balance is to be achieved in a corrections setting.

Wolff v. McDonnell, 418 U.S. 539 (1974), is known as the leading case on inmate discipline. The bulk of the opinion deals with prison disciplinary requirements. In a separate section (Section VII) of the decision, the Court addressed a Nebraska regulation that governed the inspection of attorney mail addressed to inmates. The state originally provided that all incoming mail would be opened and inspected. During the course of the litigation, Nebraska modified its position to say that mail from attorneys to inmates could be opened (but not read) to inspect for contraband, as long as it was done in the presence of the inmates. The Eighth Circuit Court of Appeals had ruled that attorney mail could only be inspected by feeling it or fluoroscoping it; it could be opened only under "appropriate circumstances," presumably when officials had good grounds to suspect, from other circumstances, that there was contraband enclosed. Also, there was a question in the case about how far the prison officials had to inquire to identify mail as coming from attorneys. The holding of the Court regarding such attorney mail follows:

> **We think it entirely appropriate that the State require any such communications to be specially marked as originating from an attorney, with his name and address being given, if they are to receive special treatment.**

With respect to the issue of the "special treatment" given to attorney mail—that is, opening the mail only in the presence of the inmate—as opposed to general correspondence, which can be opened (and read) by prison staff for inspection and security purposes, the Court said:

> **As to the ability to open the mail in the presence of inmates, this could in no way constitute censorship, since the mail would not be read ... The possibility that contraband will be enclosed in letters, even those from apparent attorneys, surely warrants prison officials' opening the letters ... [W]e think [state officials], by acceding to a rule whereby the inmate is present when mail from attorneys is inspected, have done all, and perhaps even more, than the Constitution requires.**

What does the Court mean when it says that perhaps this is more than the Constitution requires? That phrase has never been fully explained by the Supreme Court or tested much in the lower courts. Today, most prison authorities take the *Wolff* decision holdings as their guidance. If anything, they may be more liberal in dealing with mail between attorneys and inmates. For example, they may not require the special attorney markings on the envelope that *Wolff* says can be required, and some may not even open mail marked as coming from an attorney (especially in lower security institutions).

Another legal issue raised by some prisoners is whether a prison policy of opening and inspecting legal mail out of the presence of the inmate violates the inmate's First Amendment free speech rights rather than access to the courts. One lower federal court has ruled that this practice and policy did violate the Constitution. In the wake of the 9-11 terrorist attacks, there were instances of public officials receiving letters contaminated with the anthrax virus. To prevent the introduction of biological toxins, prison officials determined that incoming special mail would be opened and inspected outside of the presence of the inmate, protecting the institution, staff, and inmates. The court of appeals in *Jones v. Brown*, 461 F.3d 353 (3rd Cir. 2006), held that opening and inspecting incoming legal mail out of the presence of the inmate stripped the communication of its confidentiality and burdened the prisoner's constitutional rights. The court supported its position with language in *Wolff v. McDonnell* that stated the only way to ensure a prisoner's legal mail is not read by correctional officials is to conduct the inspection in the presence of the inmate. The court of appeals then used the weighing factors identified in *Turner v. Safley* to conclude that prison officials had failed to demonstrate "a valid, rationale connection" between the new policy and a legitimate governmental interest. The court ruled that prison officials failed to demonstrate that the risks posed immediately after the 9-11 attacks still required this ongoing abridgment of the prisoner's rights. See also *Hayes v. Idaho Correctional Center*, 849 F.3d 1209 (9th Cir. 2017) (collecting circuit court cases and concluding that even isolated instances of erroneous processing of legal mail states a claim for a First Amendment violation.).

Can officials read the incoming mail from attorneys? Lower courts have split on this issue, but most cases (and most prisons) follow the Supreme Court guidance, saying that the opening of the mail is only for the purpose of ensuring that no contraband is enclosed and not for reading the content of any communications. If improper enclosures or content are discovered, the mail could be refused for delivery to the inmate. *Wright v. McMann*, 460 F.2d 126 (2nd Cir. 1972). The attorney mail, after all, is protected only for the conveyance of legal discussions. If it is used for other purposes, it has no more protection than ordinary mail. If it is used for improper purposes (enclosing any contraband, such as money or drugs, or for discussing criminal proposals, such as escape plans or future criminal activity), it should be forwarded to law enforcement officials for possible prosecution. Improper use of the mail by an attorney, or by anyone in his office, would be grounds for placing restrictions on the legal mail of that attorney and possibly of that inmate.

Can officials read <u>outgoing</u> mail from an inmate to their attorney? Does it matter if the legal mail relates to a civil case or a criminal case? A death row inmate in Arizona complained that state correctional officials inspected and read outgoing legal mail to the attorneys representing the inmate in his case. After submitting an administrative appeal, the inmate was advised that DOC policy authorized staff to read legal mail to establish the absence of contraband and ensure that the content of the mail is of legal subject matter. The inmate attempted to file a Section 1983 action, but the case was dismissed by the district court for failure to state a claim. The court of appeals in *Nordstrom v. Ryan*, 762 F.3d 903 (9th Cir. 2014) reversed, ruling that reading communications between a prisoner and his attorney would have a chilling effect on their Sixth Amendment right to counsel. While the Supreme Court has not ruled on this issue, several other courts of appeal have ruled that when prison officials read mail between a prisoner and their lawyer in a criminal case, serious issues under the Sixth Amendment (and its application, by interpretation of the Fourteenth Amendment, to state criminal defendants), which guarantees a right to counsel in criminal cases, are implicated. *Guajardo-Palmer v. Martinson*, 622 F.3d 801 (7th Cir. 2010).

In Section VIII of *Wolff v. McDonnell*, the Court also addressed the issue of legal assistance provided to Nebraska inmates. To meet *Johnson v. Avery* requirements, the warden at the Nebraska Penal Complex appointed an inmate who had some knowledge of legal matters to assist inmates. The warden limited legal assistance to the work of this one advisor. The Court did not decide whether this one advisor was sufficient but agreed with the Eighth Circuit that the case should be remanded (sent back) to the district court to ascertain whether the help given was sufficient or whether other inmates also would have to be permitted to give legal help. The Court did address the question of whether legal assistance to inmates is limited to the preparation of habeas corpus petitions (as *Hull* and *Johnson* seemed to limit them). The Court noted that "the demarcation line between civil rights actions and habeas petitions is not always clear." The Court said:

> **The right of access to the courts, upon which *Avery* was premised, is founded in the Due Process Clause and assures that no person will be denied the opportunity to present to the judiciary allegations concerning violations of fundamental constitutional rights.**

Thus, we have a ruling that these access-to-courts opinions apply to the preparation and submission of habeas corpus and civil rights (Section 1983) actions, the standard that was picked up by the Court again in *Bounds*.

In *Procunier v. Martinez*, 416 U.S. 396 (1974), the main part of the decision dealt with inmate mail restrictions. That case is known for being the lead, opening case in the Supreme Court on the issue of regulating prisoner correspondence. This case also contains a ruling on the issue of attorney visits. The question presented in the case was whether it was proper for the state (California) to restrict attorney visiting privileges to members of the bar and licensed private investigators. (California has a system of licensing legal investigators who provide investigative assistance to lawyers. They were recognized as being of such help to attorneys that they were also granted the special visiting privileges given for legal visits.) The lower court had ruled that this state regulation was "an unjustifiable restriction on the right of access to the courts." It struck down the regulation, and the Supreme Court agreed:

> **The constitutional guarantee of due process of law has as a corollary the requirement that prisoners be afforded access to the courts in order to challenge unlawful convictions and to seek redress for violations of their constitutional rights.**

Inmates and lawyers wanted the regulation stricken, because they wanted to be able to use law students or paralegals to visit the prisons and to interview inmate clients. Although the Court conceded that the prisoner-access-to-courts doctrine did not require officials to adopt every proposal that prisoners might want to facilitate their legal activities, there was no showing, in this case, that a less-restrictive regulation, allowing student and paralegal activities, would not be possible. The Court agreed that any such requested practices must be weighed against the legitimate interests of penal administration. Here, there was nothing to show that allowing the "attorney helpers" would unduly burden the prison task of screening and monitoring visitors.

As a result, prisons today must allow paralegals and law students, as well as any other professional assistants (such as the investigators in California), to have legal visits in the same manner as attorneys. As a practical matter, the attorney must identify the individual who is to have the visit, because that person is visiting in the place of the attorney, and the attorney is responsible for supervising the work (and the professional behavior) of the assistant.

There is one special caveat: prisoners who are charged with a crime have additional protection under the Sixth Amendment. (Please look at the language of that amendment; you will see that it is prefaced by the phrase, "In all criminal prosecutions.") Assistance of counsel is mentioned specifically as a guarantee for pretrial criminal defendants. Courts are very protective of these pretrial rights of detainees. Reading the mail, or even opening the mail, of pretrial defendants is very risky. The best advice is to check with local authorities, because any pretrial defendant is held under the authority of the local criminal court. In most jurisdictions, the criminal court judges will be especially protective of attorney–client communications. Attorney visits to clients awaiting trial also receive a higher degree of protection (more frequent visiting times may be required, for example). Attorney contacts, by visits, mail, or phone calls must be carefully protected, according to the expectations and rulings of the local courts, so as not to jeopardize the prosecution of criminal cases.

▶ Access to the Courts in the Digital Age

The rapid development and utilization of digital devices to foster personal communication and access to written material has impacted the operations of correctional institutions. Three of these issues are communications between attorneys and their incarcerated clients; how constitutionally mandated legal materials are provided to confined persons; and accommodating institution security and inmate's e-discovery issues.

The first issue of attorney–client privileged communication is not unique to correctional settings. The American Bar Association has recognized the importance of protecting the confidentiality of communications between clients and attorneys from inadvertent or unauthorized disclosure.[7]

Correctional organizations have adopted rules to accommodate offender access to the court by treating mail and telephonic communications between legal staff and an offender and face-to-face contact with attorneys with consideration of protecting the attorney–client privilege.

The question arises about what is the legal status of communications between an attorney and an incarcerated client using a correctional agency's electronic messaging system? Several lower courts have considered this issue and have generally held that if warnings of nonconfidentiality are given, the warnings given by the correctional agency effectively rebuts any claim to attorney–client privilege.

The use by the prosecution of communications between a pretrial detainee and her attorney using the Bureau of Prisons TRULINCS system was challenged in *Arciero, et al v. Holder, et al* (D. Ha, 2015).[8] Arciero was a pretrial detainee who used the prison electronic messaging system (EMS) system to communicate with her attorney. The plaintiffs [the inmate and her attorney] argued the BOP's system of monitoring electronic messaging between attorneys and their clients violated the Sixth Amendment. The trial court dismissed the lawsuit, concluding that the notices provided by the BOP and the contractor providing the EMS put the users on notice that their use of the system was subject to monitoring. The BOP Inmate Acknowledgment, which required an affirmative acceptance by the inmate user, warns:

Warning: This computer system is the property of the United States Department of Justice. The Department may monitor any activity on the system and search and retrieve any information stored within the system. By accessing and using this computer, I am consenting to such monitoring and information retrieval for law enforcement and other purposes. I have no expectation of privacy as to any communication on or information stored within the system.

Responsibility: I must abide by all terms prescribed in Bureau of Prisons' policy regarding my use of TRULINCS and electronic messaging systems, which I acknowledge having read and understood. I understand and consent to having my electronic messages and system activity monitored, read, and retained by authorized personnel. I understand and consent that this provision applies to electronic messages both to and from my attorney or other legal representative, and that such electronic messages will not be treated as privileged communications, and that I have alternative methods of conducting privileged legal communication. . . .

The terms and conditions of use by the contract provider additionally warned the user that use of the system constituted an agreement to the monitoring of the messages by the contractor and the correctional agency. Because of these notices to both the inmate and her attorney, any attorney–client privilege in the messages was waived. The lower courts, which have ruled that using the institution electronic messaging system waives attorney–client privilege also noted that both the detainee and the detainee's attorney retained the right to other use forms of privileged (unmonitored) communications such as postal mail, telephone, and face-to-face visitation. While email may be a preferred manner of communication for attorneys, the Constitution does not turn an attorney's preference into a legal requirement.

The second issue is how constitutionally mandated legal materials are provided to confined persons. Recent technological changes have occurred that may alter the way prisoners access legal materials. In many prisons, paper book law libraries have been replaced with **electronic law libraries**. This topic is discussed in detail earlier in this chapter after the discussion of *Bounds v. Smith*. An electronic law library provides access to the same types of material as in a traditional paper library, with the difference being the format. Electronic law libraries may increase the availability of legal resources because of reduced cost and elimination or reduction in theft or destruction of resources. Electronic libraries take up less physical space, but they do involve inmate access to computer terminals and also instruction to inmates in the computer skills and research techniques needed to locate relevant material.

The third issue involves aspects of both criminal and civil law. Many 21st century criminal prosecutions in state and federal courts involve thousands of pages of paper evidence, electronically created and stored materials, and audio/visual surveillance recordings. At the federal level, a detainee may be held in a federal correctional facility hundreds of miles away from the place of their trial (and their attorney). Relevant material in a criminal trial may include documents or materials created by several law enforcement agencies, including federal, state, county, and local, all which may have unique ways of creating, storing, and accessing the material (for example, pdf files of documents, JPEG images of photos, and recorded statements of the defendant or other persons with knowledge of the matter).

Similar issues can arise in civil matters. For example, an inmate sues state correctional officials for excessive force, and wants to review video and audio recordings of the use of force action. Federal Rules of Civil Procedure authorize the discovery of "all documents, electronically stored information, and tangible things that the disclosing party has in its possession, custody, or control and may use to support its claims or defenses". F.R.Civ. P. 26 (1)(A)(ii).

Correctional agency resources must be used to ensure material introduced into the facility are not weaponized (for example, breaking a CD rom into shards to make a stabbing weapon), time constraints in processing the material, supervision of the inmate during any review process, and obtaining and maintaining hardware necessary to review the material.[9]

Examples of how this has been addressed include the Federal Bureau of Prisons, which, in conjunction with the U.S. Marshals Service, holds a significant number of pretrial detainees in the United States. An offender's defense attorney is advised as follows:

> *(e) Inmate Access to Electronic Discovery Materials In some circumstances, an inmate may access litigation documents in various electronic formats rather than in printed form. Electronic legal materials for inmate review should be provided by an attorney on a storage device appropriate with the maintenance of the safety and security of the institution and compatible with the configuration available at the institution. Specific requests and/or questions regarding the institution's e-discovery capabilities should be directed to the Warden of the institution in which the inmate is confined. All external hard drives, thumb drives, CD/DVDs, or other removable media entering a BOP facility, or received from any source, must be scanned for viruses and malware prior to use within the facility.[10]*

▶ Frivolous Complaints and Frequent Filers

This chapter clearly shows that inmates have a right of access to the courts, but what about those inmates who abuse this process? Responding to inmate litigation can be very time-consuming and, where individual staff members are sued, can impact staff members professionally (disrupting the performance of their duties at work) and possibly even personally (such as complicating the approval of a loan). Prison litigation is also very burdensome to the courts. Although legal recourse is appropriate for substantive claims, what about those lawsuits where "no evidentiary hearing is required in a prisoner's case...when the factual allegations are incredible"?[11]

The Prison Litigation Reform Act (PLRA) of 1996 amended several sections of the United States Code. One section was Title 28 U.S. Code Section 1915, which authorized federal courts to accept filings from persons without the ability to immediately pay the full filing fee. This was known as *in forma pauperis* (IFP) (claiming lack of funds to pay certain costs). Title 28, U.S. Code, Section 1915A, requires a court to review, preferably before docketing or as soon as practicable thereafter, an inmate's complaint in a civil action in which the inmate is seeking redress from a government entity or officer or employee of a government entity. Section 1915A(b) *requires* the court to dismiss an inmate's complaint, or any portion of it, if it is frivolous, malicious, fails to state a claim on which relief can be provided or seeks monetary relief from a defendant who has immunity.

Another provision of the PLRA (in Title 28, U.S. Code, Section 1915) requires an inmate who wishes to bring a civil action or file an appeal *in forma pauperis* to pay the full amount of the filing fee. The PLRA allows for this to be paid on a time payment plan.[12] Although the statute allows for filing without payment if the inmate has no assets and no means by which to pay the initial partial filing fee in Section 1915(b) (4), payment is required when such funds exist. Institution staff is required to withdraw the funds and send them to the court to pay the inmate's filing fee obligation.

The PLRA also amended 28 U.S. Code Section 1915, addressing filing requirements for indigent persons. Section 1915g, as amended, provides as follows:

> *(g) In no event shall a prisoner bring a civil action or appeal a judgment in a civil action or proceeding under this section if the prisoner has, on 3 or more prior occasions, while incarcerated or detained in any facility, brought an action or appeal in a court of the United States that was dismissed on the grounds that it is frivolous, malicious, or fails to state a claim upon which relief may be granted, unless the prisoner is under imminent danger of serious physical injury.*

Coleman v. Tollefson, 575 U.S. 532 (2015) addressed this provision of the PLRA (28 U.S. Code Section 1915g), which denied *in forma pauperis* status (to file a suit without the pre-payment of the filing fee) to prisoners who had three previous lawsuits dismissed as frivolous, malicious or for failure to state a claim. On two earlier occasions, Michigan state prisoner Coleman had *in forma pauperis* prisoner rights suits dismissed as being frivolous, malicious, or for failure to state a claim. The dismissals of these two suits were affirmed on appeal. Coleman also had filed a third *in forma pauperis* prisoner rights lawsuit which the district court had dismissed as being frivolous, malicious or for failure to state a claim. The inmate appealed the third case dismissal, and while the appeal was pending, sought to file an additional four prisoner rights lawsuits *in forma pauperis*. The lower court denied the application *for in forma pauperis* status, citing the three-strikes rule and ruling that a case dismissed by a district court on 1915g grounds was a strike. On appeal, the judgment of the district court was affirmed, although the appellate court used different grounds. The prisoner appealed and the Supreme Court granted *certiorari* to consider this question: *Whether, under the "three strikes" provision of the Prison Litigation Reform Act, 28 U.S.C. 1915(g), a district court's dismissal of a lawsuit counts as a "strike" while it is still pending on appeal or before the time for seeking appellate review has passed.*

The Court affirmed the lower court and ruled that:

> **"[A] prisoner who has accumulated three prior qualifying dismissals under § 1915(g) may not file an additional suit in forma pauperis while his appeal of one such dismissal is pending."**

The Court relied on three rationale for its decision. The first is the language of the statute, which states a dismissal and not a dismissal and appellate review. The second rationale is that under the law, judgments of trial courts are effective when decided in the absence of a stay. The Court's third rationale considered the language of 1915g in conjunction with the purpose of the PLRA.

> **Finally, the statute's purpose favors our interpretation. The "three strikes" provision was "designed to filter out the bad claims and facilitate consideration of the good." Citing Jones v. Bock, discussed above. . . . To refuse to count a prior dismissal because of a pending appeal would produce a leaky filter. Appeals take time. During that time, a prisoner could file many lawsuits, including additional lawsuits that are frivolous, malicious, or fail to state a claim upon which relief may be granted.**

In reaching its unanimous conclusion, the Court discussed the importance of *in forma pauperis*.

> **Congress wished to ensure that no persons who were without adequate financial resources were prohibited from "commenc[ing, prosecut[ing], or defend[ing] an action, civil or criminal, in any court of the United States, solely because his poverty makes it impossible for him to pay or secure the costs." [citations omitted].**

Congress recognized that persons using *in forma pauperis* status would have no incentive to "refrain from filing frivolous, malicious, or repetitive lawsuits." After being made aware that prisoner lawsuits were a disproportionate share of all filings in federal court, Congress *"enacted a variety of reforms designed to filter out the bad claims [filed by prisoners] and facilitate consideration of the good."* [citation omitted]. One of those reforms was the "three-strikes" rule. The Court concluded that the language of the statute did not require a dismissal to include appellate review.[13]

An exception to the Section 1915(g) provision is where the inmate is under "imminent danger of serious physical injury." In *Malik v. McGinnis*, 293 F.3d 559 (2nd Cir. 2002), the Second Circuit held that the statutory intent was to make an exception for cases in which the danger existed at the time the complaint was filed; its focus was to prevent impending harm, not to revisit a harm that had already occurred and was past. This position has been adopted by other circuits.[14]

In some cases, when a lawsuit is dismissed for failure to state a claim, the dismissal is without prejudice. The Supreme Court has agreed to decide if dismissal without prejudice for failure to state a claim counts as a strike under the PLRA 28 U.S. Code 1915(g). An inmate in Colorado filed and had been dismissed for failure to state a claim for three lawsuits against correctional personnel. When he attempted to file another one, the district court required him to pay the full filing fee despite the inmate's arguments that the dismissals "without prejudice" were not strikes as used in the PLRA. The inmate appealed and the U.S. Court of Appeals affirmed, ruling that in the 10th Circuit a dismissal pursuant to 28 U.S. Code 1915(g) "without prejudice" is a strike for PLRA purposes. In *Lomax v. Ortiz-Marquez*, ___ U.S. ___ (2020) the Supreme Court affirmed the lower courts' rulings that Section 1915(g)'s three-strikes provision refers to any dismissal for failure to state a claim, whether with prejudice or without. The decision was based on the language of the statute.

> *This case begins, and pretty much ends, with the text of Section 1915(g). Under that provision, a prisoner accrues a strike for any action "dismissed on the ground that it . . . fails to state a claim upon which relief may be granted." That broad language covers all such dismissals: It applies to those issued both with and without prejudice to a plaintiff's ability to reassert his claim in a later action. (footnote omitted) A strike-call under Section 1915(g) thus hinges exclusively on the basis for the dismissal, regardless of the **decision's** prejudicial effect.*

A "dismissal without prejudice," terminates the action but allows a party to make the same claim to the same court. *Semtek International Inc. v. Lockheed Martin Corp.* 531 U.S. 497 (2001).

▶ Litigation Alleging Retaliation for the Exercise of Constitutional Rights

Correctional officials make a number of decisions every day affecting the lives of inmates in their custody such as housing, work, and other programing assignments. These decisions fall within the discretion of corrections administrators and the courts are instructed to give the administrators great deference when an administrator exercises discretion. Administrators are generally aware of the constitutional rights of prisoners-so what happens when a prisoner believes that an administrator has made a discretionary decision that negatively impacts the prisoner because the prisoner exercised a constitutional right? When a prisoner is punished for exercising a constitutional right, the courts view the conduct as retaliation which is violation of the Constitution. Courts generally agree that prison officials may not retaliate against an inmate for filing legal actions in the exercise of their constitutional right of access to the courts. For example in *Goff v. Burton*, 7 F.3d 734 (8th Cir. 1993) the inmate sued prison officials alleging he was transferred from a medium security prison to a maximum security facility because the inmate had filed lawsuits against prison officials alleging a violation of his constitutional rights. The court of appeals reversed the judgment of the district court which had concluded the transfer was retaliatory and the money judgment in favor of the inmate for over $2000 in damages. The court of appeals concluded that while the prisoner's litigation may have been a factor in the decision to transfer the inmate, the district court has applied an incorrect standard in determining what motivated the prison officials to act. The court of appeals stated the correct legal standard is whether "but for" the prisoner's protected conduct the action would not have been taken. After the case was returned to the district court, the district court applied the new standard and again awarded the inmate money damages because prison officials had retaliated against the prisoner. The second judgment was affirmed on appeal.

The Eighth Circuit has established that to state a retaliation claim a prisoner must show (1) they engaged in a protected activity, (2) the government official took adverse action against the prisoner that would chill a person of ordinary firmness from continuing in the activity, and (3) the adverse action was motivated at least in part by the exercise of the protected activity. *Spencer v. Jackson County, Missouri* 738 F.3d 907 (8th Cir. 2013). The Third Circuit has adopted a similar standard: to establish illegal retaliation for engaging in protected conduct, a prisoner must demonstrate that: (1) their conduct was constitutionally protected; (2) they suffered an adverse action at the hands of prison officials; and (3) their constitutionally protected conduct was a substantial or motivating factor in the decision to discipline him" *Watson v. Rozum*, 834 F.3d 417 (3rd Cir. 2016). The Ninth Circuit adds an additional requirement that the prisoner establish the action by correctional officials did not reasonably advance a legitimate correctional goal. *Rhodes v. Robinson*, 408 F.3d 559 (9th Cir. 2005).

The first factor is established by demonstrating the prisoner engaged in some type of constitutionally protected activity such as filing litigation or prison grievances or speaking to the media about prison conditions. The second factor-an adverse action generally requires an act or omission directed at the prisoner by prison officials that would be sufficiently onerous to deter a person of ordinary firmness from exercising their First Amendment rights. To establish the third element, the causation factor, several circuits have adopted the burden shifting frame work announced by the Supreme Court in a non- prison case - *Mount Healthy Bd. of Ed. v. Doyle*, 429 U.S. 274 (1977). In *Mounty Healthy*, the Supreme Court ruled that the plaintiff has the initial burden of proving that their constitutionally protected conduct was "a substantial or motivating factor" in the decision to take the official action. The burden then shifts to the defendant to prove by a preponderance of the evidence that it would have taken the same action even in the absence of the protected activity. Other circuits have ruled that the prisoner must demonstrate that the desire to retaliate by prison officials was the actual motivating factor for the conduct of the official. *Rouse v. Benson*, 193 F.3d 936 (8th Cir. 1999). Federal appellate courts have noted that a prisoner's claim of retaliation should be viewed skeptically by courts since "every act of discipline . . . is by definition retaliatory in the sense that it responds directly to prisoner misconduct." *Cochran v. Morris*, 73 F.3rd 1316 (4th Cir. 1986) (*en banc*).

Summary

- Inmates have a right of access to the courts; which prison officials may not obstruct. This was based, in the earlier Supreme Court decisions, on the constitutional guarantee of the writ of habeas corpus (*Ex parte Hull; Johnson v. Avery*).
- Access to the courts is also guaranteed for suits claiming civil rights violations, under 42 U.S.C. § 1983 (*Bounds v. Smith; Wolff v. McDonnell*). Prisoner access rights also have for a long time been guaranteed for direct appeals from convictions (*Lewis v. Casey*).
- A state may not forbid inmates to assist other inmates in legal matters ("jailhouse lawyering") unless there is an alternative method of assistance provided, particularly for illiterate inmates, who must also have a means to get their petitions to court (*Johnson v. Avery*).
- Inmates do not have a special First Amendment right to provide legal assistance to other inmates. Such contacts between inmates are subject to the standard stated in *Turner v. Safley* and *Shaw v. Murphy*.
- Inmates must be provided with a law library to assist them in preparing their legal papers, unless there is an alternative legal assistance program provided (*Bounds v. Smith*).
- The broad legal assistance holdings of *Bounds* were severely limited in the later decision of *Lewis v. Casey*. The Supreme Court criticized the federal trial court in *Lewis* for not deferring to the judgment of the prison authorities regarding what kind of law library and legal assistance program could be provided. Furthermore, the relief provided (a sweeping, detailed legal assistance plan) was considered to be far too broad, based on the limited legal complaints that had been proved. It was maintained that the lower court should have provided limited relief to correct the violations shown, rather than mandate a system-wide plan of corrective action. Finally, constitutional requirements for legal assistance to inmates are limited to direct appeals from convictions, habeas corpus actions, and lawsuits under Section 1983, and, as to those, the government need only ensure that there is assistance for the initial preparation and filing of papers, not for later litigating steps.
- When *Bounds v. Smith* was decided, access to an adequate law library meant access to an area with many paper volumes of statutes and case decisions. Some states have moved to providing access to these materials in an electronic format, and a very modern prison law library may consist of few books but several computer terminals that provide access to the materials that were formerly available in paper books.

- Counsel need not be provided to inmates in collateral attacks on their sentences, even in death penalty cases (*Murray v. Giarratano*).
- Attorney mail requires more protection than ordinary mail, but (as long as it is identified as attorney mail on the envelope) it may be opened and inspected (not read) in the presence of the inmate. This serves the security concerns of the prison and protects the confidentiality of the contents of the mail (*Wolff v. McDonnell*).
- Legal visits also require special protections. Not only attorneys but also paralegals, legal investigators, and law students who are under the attorneys' supervision are entitled to legal visits with the attorneys' inmate clients (*Procunier v. Martinez*).
- Recent legislative actions and court interpretations have resulted in procedures (requiring inmates to pay filing fees; mandating court dismissal of frivolous claims; and "three-strikes" provisions) to curtail inmate abuses of court filings.
- A prisoner is not entitled to file a law suit without prepayment of fees if on three or more prior occasions that prisoner has filed and had been dismissed as frivolous, malicious, or fails to state a claim upon which relief may be granted, a lawsuit unless the prisoner is under imminent danger of serious physical injury. (*Coleman v. Tollefson*).
- Prison officials may not retaliate against inmate who engage in constitutionally protected activity. Punishing an inmate for inmate exercising their right of access to the courts (including filing administrative grievances) can be the basis for a constitutional tort lawsuit against the offending prison officials even when the act or omission of the prison officials is not itself a constitutional violation.

Thinking About It

In 2015 inmate Able was housed in a 100 year old maximum security prison. Over the years. Able had sued the prison staff several times about conditions at the prison, and even was awarded money damages because of conditions at the facility. Able then filed a lawsuit against state correctional officials due to new conditions at the prison, contributed statements to the local news media about the poor medical treatment inmates at the facility, and then three days later filed an administrative grievance complaining about the nutritional value of the meals served at the facility. The warden at the facility asked to transfer Able to a different, newer, maximum security prison because Able's numerous complaints and grievances made it apparent that due to the age of the facility, the only viable solution was to transfer Able to a more modern facility. Able was transferred to the newer prison, where he was assigned a cell mate (Able was housed alone at the old facility) and the amount of time Able could spend in the law library was reduced from seven hours a week to four hours a week. Able sued alleging the transfer was retaliation for exercising First Amendment rights to right to speak to the media and access the courts without facing retaliation.

Key Terms

dictum (plural, dicta)
electronic law library
holding
master (court procedure)

Endnotes

1. In *Houston v. Lack*, 487 U.S. 266 (1988), the Supreme Court held that an inmate's appeal was considered "filed" on the date it was dropped into the prison mailbox. The inmate is unable to travel to the courthouse to file the appeal; in fact, the inmate can do little else but hand her complaint to prison officials for mailing. The inmate does not have any discretion in this process.
2. Note that prison authorities, in writing this regulation, perpetuated the common mistake made in prison circles, among inmates and staff, of calling the papers prepared by inmates "writs." As discussed earlier, only courts write, or sign, writs. Inmates prepare petitions, asking the courts to issue writs. That is the proper nomenclature for habeas corpus proceedings.
3. The Court remanded (sent back) to the lower court the issue of whether the inmate had overcome the presumption that prison officials had acted reasonably. In its ruling, the Supreme Court pointed out that prison officials had offered the charged inmate the assistance of another law clerk.
4. Regarding law books, the North Carolina plan proposed that the library would contain North Carolina statutes and reporters (the books that contain state court rulings, particularly at the appellate levels); court rules; the federal code, in certain frequently used titles (*U.S. Code Annotated*, Titles 18, 28, and 42); the *Supreme Court Reporter* (from 1960 to present) and federal court reporters (for those

same years); *Black's Law Dictionary*; and several legal reference books in the areas of habeas corpus, criminal law, and prisoners' rights. This pretty closely conforms, the Court noted, to minimum collections for law libraries in prisons, as drawn up and recommended by the American Correctional Association, the American Bar Association, and the American Association of Law Libraries.

5. BOP Program Statement 4500.12, *Trust Fund/Deposit Fund Manual*, §14.10(d) Electronic Law Library. South Dakota recently did away with its paper law library and use of contract legal services and began using an electronic law library system, which inmates access through computer tablets with which they are provided. See South Dakota DOC Policy 1.3.E.1 *Inmate Access to the Courts.* Section 6 (B). B. The DOC will provide access to legal reference materials through LexisNexis (or some other company provider), via inmate tablets and kiosks, which shall be made available to inmates at all adult DOC facilities. Available: https://doc.sd.gov/documents/Inmate%20 Access%20to%20the%20Courts8132019.pdf. Accessed February 17, 2020. See also Weiss, D.C. *South Dakota Inmates get tablets for legal research; state drops paralegal and part-time lawyer.* ABA Journal. October 3, 2017. Available: http://www.abajournal.com/news /article/south_dakota_inmates_get_tablets_for_legal_research_spurring_state_to_drop. Accessed 17 February 2020. This change is currently being litigated. Oklahoma Department of Corrections. OP 030115, effective October 29, 2019. http://doc.publishpath.com /Websites/doc/images/Documents/Policy/op030115.pdf

6. State of Washington Department of Corrections. *Legal Access for Incarcerated Individuals.* DOC Number 590.500, revised 25 September 2018. Available: https://www.doc.wa.gov/information/policies/files/590500.pdf. Accessed 12 February 2020.

7. ABA Model Rule of Professional Responsibility 1.6, *Confidentiality of Communications*: (c) A lawyer shall make reasonable efforts to prevent the inadvertent or unauthorized disclosure of, or unauthorized access to, information relating to the representation of a client. Available: https://www.americanbar.org/groups/professional_responsibility/publications/model_rules_of_professional_conduct/rule _1_6_confidentiality_of_information/.

8. Arciero v. Holder, et al. Available: https://scholar.google.com/scholar_case?case=4603312676466190119&q=Arciero+v+Holder&hl =en&as_sdt=6,24. Accessed February 17, 2020. See also *United States v. Walia*, Case No. 14-CR-213 (MKB) (EDNY, July 25, 2013) (the BOP's Trust Fund Limited Inmate Communication System (TRULINCS) does not provide for the communication of privileged information.). To address the issue of attorney–client privilege and the EMS within the Bureau of Prisons, a bill was introduced into the U.S. House of Representatives titled *Effective Assistance of Counsel in the Digital Era Act* (116th Congress—H.R. 5546, which would require the Attorney General to create a program or system to exclude from monitoring the contents of any privileged communication.

9. Turner, J. I. *Managing Digital Discovery in Criminal Cases*, 109 J. Crim. L. & Criminology 237 (2019); and Mcenanay, J & Elem, D.L. *Delivering e-discovery to Federal Pretrial Detainees.* 32 Crim. Law 49 (2017-2018).

10. *Legal Resource Guide to the Federal Bureau of Prisons 2019. (39).* Available: https://www.bop.gov/resources/pdfs/legal_guide _march_2019.pdf. Accessed February 13, 2020. See also Virginia Department of Corrections Operating Procedure 866.3. *Offender Legal Access.* As amended 01 January 2020, Section 7(V)(7). Available: https://vadoc.virginia.gov/files/operating-procedures/800 /vadoc-op-866-3.pdf. Accessed February 17, 2020. (Outlining procedure for inmate access to digital legal materials from courts and attorneys). Washington State DOC Policy 590.500 also establishes a procedure for permitting an inmate access to digital legal materials from courts, the prosecuting attorney in the inmate's criminal case on appeal, and for certain prison hearings.

11. The Seventh Circuit noted that facts alleged by inmates may be unbelievable because they are nutty or delusional! This is the language used in *Gladney, Jr. v. Pendleton Correctional Facility and Indiana Department of Corrections*, 302 F.3d 773 (7th Cir. 2002). The complaint alleges "that on numerous occasions over a span of three years unnamed guards at three different prisons unlocked the door to the plaintiff's [inmate] cell while he was asleep, allowing inmates to come in and drug and sexually assault him. He slept through all these outrages and only discovered what had happened when one day he noticed a needle mark under his lip. When he visited the prison infirmary to have the mark attended to, the medical personnel claimed not to see the mark because they were trying to make him think that he was delusional."

12. See 28 U.S.C. Section 1915(b): (b)

    (1) Notwithstanding subsection (a), if a prisoner brings a civil action or files an appeal in forma pauperis, the prisoner shall be required to pay the full amount of a filing fee. The court shall assess and, when funds exist, collect, as a partial payment of any court fees required by law, an initial partial filing fee of 20% of the greater of—

        (A) The average monthly deposits to the prisoner's account; or (B) The average monthly balance in the prisoner's account for the 6-month period immediately preceding the filing of the complaint or notice of appeal.

    (2) After payment of the initial partial filing fee, the prisoner shall be required to make monthly payments of 20% of the preceding month's income credited to the prisoner's account. The agency having custody of the prisoner shall forward payments from the prisoner's account to the clerk of the court each time the amount in the account exceeds $10 until the filing fees are paid.

        In 2016, the Supreme Court, in *Bruce v. Samuels*, 577 U.S. ___, 136 S.Ct. 627, [discussed previously in Chapter 5] addressed a split in the circuits as to whether the payments described in 28 U.S. Code 1915(b)(2) toward an inmate's filing fee applied to each case (each case requires payment of 20% of the inmates commissary balance) or whether the inmate was assessed 20% of his monthly commissary balance to be applied to any outstanding filing fee balance.

13. This restriction does not apply to an inmate who can pay the filing fee. In that instance, the court will screen the civil complaint as provided in Section 1915A.

14. See *Andrews v. Cervantes*, 493 F.3d 1047 (9th Cir. 2007); *Ciarpaglini v. Saini*, 352 F.3d 328 (7th Cir. 2003); *Abdul-Akbar v. McKelvie*, 239 F.3d 307, (3rd Cir. 2001) (en banc).

CHAPTER 7

First Amendment: Inmate Mail

When a prison regulation or practice offends a fundamental constitutional guarantee, federal courts will discharge their duty to protect constitutional rights.

U.S. Supreme Court, *Procunier v. Martinez*

We have been sensitive to the delicate balance that prison administrators must strike between the order and security of the internal prison environment and the legitimate demands of those on the "outside" who seek to enter that environment, in person or through the written word.

U.S. Supreme Court, *Thornburgh v. Abbott*

The First Amendment to the U.S. Constitution contains this phrase:

Congress shall make no law ... abridging the freedom of speech.

CHAPTER OUTLINE

- Prison Mail: The Background
- *Procunier v. Martinez*
- *Procunier v. Navarette*
- *Turner v. Safley*
- Inmate Marriages
- Correspondence in Foreign Languages
- Prisoner Use of Electronic Messaging and Social Media
- *Thornburgh v. Abbott*
- *Beard v. Banks*
- *Bell v. Wolfish*
- National Security Issues
- Inmate Postage
- Nude Photos

Freedom of speech is one of the most cherished, and frequently discussed, freedoms set out in the U.S. Constitution. However, the phrase only applies to "Congress." Is it, therefore, only applicable to the federal government? No, not really. The First Amendment does refer to the federal Congress, and, for many years, it was not clear whether there was any such protection from state action (apart from state constitutions, most of which have similar provisions to the U.S. Bill of Rights). However, in a series of opinions (e.g., *Rankin v. McPherson*, 483 U.S. 378 (1987)), the U.S. Supreme Court has ruled that the Fourteenth Amendment guarantee of due process which limits the power of the states to restrict the rights of persons incorporates various constitutional protections from the Bill of Rights, including the First Amendment freedom of speech. Therefore, decisions of the Supreme Court that interpret the First Amendment apply to the federal government and all state governments.

It is sometimes even said that freedom of speech is of the highest concern and deserving of the highest degree of protection, in the country. Some believe that the First Amendment is a "preferred" amendment, containing the most important kinds of constitutionally protected liberties. There is no set of priorities stated in the Constitution, of course, and on the face of it, all provisions are of the same degree of importance. What is meant by these statements is that the protections of the First Amendment are fundamental to our most cherished freedoms and, therefore, deserve the highest degree of concern in the courts when those freedoms are threatened. Although the First Amendment freedoms are extremely important, they are not absolute. All of them have restrictions and limitations. The Supreme Court and lower courts have addressed what, if any, First Amendment rights are retained by prisoners and the extent to which these rights may be restricted or limited by prison officials.

▸ Prison Mail: The Background

In the 1960s, the federal courts started abandoning their long-standing, hands-off attitude toward prisons. By the end of that decade, there was a torrent of prisoner litigation, challenging all kinds of prison conditions and practices. It is not surprising that many of those challenges dealt with the First Amendment.

A prime subject of inmate litigation was correspondence. Many lawsuits focused on personal, social correspondence—that is, mail sent between inmates and persons such as family and friends outside of the prisons. There was a flurry of court decisions dealing with such mail.

While inmates asserted their rights to the protections of the First Amendment, prison officials insisted that prison was a completely different world from that on the outside, requiring considerable restrictions on inmate mail. Some of the matters that prison officials were particularly concerned about included letters that discussed direct affronts to security (such as plans for escape); enclosures (such as maps or money) that could be used in illegal ventures; contents of correspondence that discussed or planned other illegal activities (such as robberies to be committed upon release, the retrieval of stolen money secreted somewhere before confinement, or threats against government officials); contents of letters that expressed viewpoints that, in the prison setting, could be inflammatory (such as an encouragement to riot, or racial or religious statements that may incite some readers to extreme actions); and pornographic content (whether in the letters themselves or, more likely, in enclosures of publications, photos, or drawings). Some authorities did not like, for obvious reasons, communications that were critical of staff (and particularly of the warden or other high officials), and they took steps to restrict them.

The practice of restricting the content of mail is sometimes called "censorship." Censorship has become an emotion-packed word, partly because of our strongly held feelings about the importance of freedom of speech, so it is commonly used by those who are opposed to any restrictions of speech. (Speech is not limited to its usual meaning of verbal, spoken communication; it also covers any kind of communication of thoughts and ideas, such as publications, written words, and even artistic representations and physical actions that communicate ideas.) In careful usage, the word *censorship* refers to the act of officials who have the authority to remove objectionable content from printed or artistic content. It has also been used to refer to the act of military authorities who review and "censor" mail, removing those portions that are thought to be threatening or damaging in any way. The Supreme Court, and other courts, are usually (but not always) careful to avoid using the word *censorship*, because it carries within it the negative connotation of interfering with a basic freedom.

What does "censorship" mean in a prison setting? Some people picture prison officials opening mail and poring over every word to make sure there is nothing objectionable. In practice, this is pretty far from the truth. So much mail is received and sent by inmates of the typical prison or jail that the thorough review of all mail is impractical. As examples, in 1990 the U.S. Court of Appeals for the Fourth Circuit noted that the federal prison system, with a population of 59,000 inmates, was processing more than 156,000 pieces of mail a week.[1] In twelve years the federal prison population had grown to over 137,000 and an investigation conducted by the Department of Justice Office of Inspector General report concluded that some federal prison mail rooms were processing "up to 3,000 pieces of mail daily, with double that amount or more on a Monday (because there is no mail delivery on weekends) and during holiday periods."[2] In litigation over its mail policies, the Maricopa County (AZ) Sheriff's Office [with an average daily population of 7,359] reported receiving and processing (sorting and searching for contraband) 2,500 to 3,000 pieces of mail daily, including postcards, legal/privileged mail, clergy/religious mail and magazines, books, and photos. That volume increased by 1,000 to 1,500 pieces per day during the holidays.[3]

Many correctional agencies address the issue of reviewing inmate mail by (1) searching the contents of incoming mail for contraband and (2) identifying those inmates (or groups of inmates) who are of most concern as security threats and look closely at their mail. Examples of such inmates of high concern are gang members, inmates who have escape histories, and inmates involved in large-scale drug or other criminal activities.

Incoming mail presents the greatest concern, because prison officials must carefully control what is introduced into the facility. What is sent out of the prison is of less concern, because once it leaves the premises it no longer poses a direct threat to internal security. In some institutions, particularly smaller ones, and especially ones of higher security; the contents of mail—both incoming and outgoing—are scanned closely. But if there is not enough staff time to inspect every piece of mail carefully, authorities can save staff time by concentrating on those inmates who must be watched most closely and hope to intercept those things that pose the greatest risks. In the final analysis, the main purpose of monitoring inmate mail is deterrence—knowing that their mail will be opened and that it may be read (assuming that it *will* be read), inmates and their outside correspondents will be deterred from sending improper content in their mail (or so it is hoped by prison officials).

This is not to say that officials have no interest in what is sent out of the prison or in the mail of the average prisoner. If only communications to and from selected, high-risk inmates are subjected to close review, those inmates can ask (or coerce) other inmates to send out or receive information that they do not want intercepted. Additionally, in the interest of running an orderly prison, it is good for staff to know if inmates are having particularly upsetting problems. In many places, officers on the night shifts, when sitting at their desks, are given mail to review to gain more knowledge about inmates under their supervision, as well as to look for more serious things such as security breaches or plans for criminal activity.

▶ *Procunier v. Martinez*

In California in the 1960s, state prison officials adopted regulations that instructed inmates not to write letters that unduly complained or magnified their grievances. The regulations declared as contraband any writings "expressing inflammatory political, racial, religious or other views or beliefs." They said inmates "may not send or receive letters that pertain to criminal activity; are lewd, obscene, or defamatory; contain foreign matter; or are otherwise inappropriate."

Procunier v. Martinez, 416 U.S. 396 (1974), was a **class action**—meaning that it was a combined lawsuit brought on behalf of all persons who were in a similar situation: in this case, all of the inmates in prisons of the California Department of Corrections. A class action is designed to save court time and to keep costs down by having a single presentation of the issues and a consolidated review of the legal status of the plaintiffs and their common complaints.

This case was unusual in that it was first considered by a three-judge federal court in the Northern District of California. In most cases in the American judicial system the first, or trial, level of cases is presided over by a single judge. Congress had enacted an exception (28 U.S. Code § 2281), providing for three judges to sit in review of a case in federal court when the lawsuit challenged the constitutionality of a statewide law (or a regulation that had the effect of a statewide law). This statute was repealed in 1976. Pub. L. 94-381. Congress enacted a new law on the use of three judge panels which was codified as 28 U.S. Code § 2284 which required 3 judge district court panels in reapportionment cases and other cases as directed by Congress. There is another unusual provision for such cases: when a three judge panel grants or denies a interlocutory, or permanent injunction (as it was in *Martinez* by the three-judge panel), a party may take a direct appeal to the Supreme Court, avoiding the ordinary route of taking an appeal to a circuit court of appeals and then petitioning the Supreme Court for a writ of certiorari. 28 U.S. Code § 1253.

In *Procunier v. Martinez*, the Supreme Court, for the first time, addressed the issue of the rights of inmates to be free of restrictions on their mail under the First Amendment. The Court noted that, historically, there was a hands-off attitude in federal courts toward prison matters. The Court here put that concept officially to rest, saying that federal courts must "take cognizance of valid constitutional claims whether arising in a federal or state institution."

> **When a prison regulation or practice offends a fundamental constitutional guarantee, federal courts will discharge their duty to protect constitutional rights.**

The Court then noted that many lower courts had been addressing freedom of speech restrictions in prison regulations. A wide range of standards had been adopted in various courts to deal with these complaints. Some courts took a hands-off approach, deferring to prison needs for censorship of mail. Another standard was that the restrictions on correspondence would have to be supported by a "rational and constitutionally acceptable concept of a prison system." (That standard certainly did not give much guidance to either side about what kind of restrictions would be allowed or tossed out.) In another court, a similar position was adopted, in which a restriction would be upheld if it was "reasonably and necessarily [related] to the advancement of some justifiable purpose." Stricter courts required that, to support a restriction of correspondence, there must be a "compelling state interest" or, at the strictest extreme, a "clear and present danger" to support First Amendment regulation by the government, even in a prison setting.

It was exactly because of these widely varying standards in the lower courts that Supreme Court review was established in the first place. But here, as in many other areas of constitutional standards, the Supreme Court did not necessarily adopt one lower court's analysis and run with it. First, the Court in *Procunier v. Martinez* noted that prisoner mail had been identified as an aspect of "prisoners' rights." However, in the case of prison mail, the Court noted that restrictions on the mail were of concern to other people besides the prisoners. So, it refrained from going so far as to decide whether a person's right to free speech survives imprisonment. Both parties to correspondence have an interest in having their mail delivered and read, the Court said. The person outside the prison has an interest in receiving or sending mail, and "it is plain that [the outside person's] interest is grounded in the First Amendment's guarantee of freedom of speech." As to restrictions on First Amendment liberties, there may be some restrictions if they are imposed "in furtherance of legitimate governmental activities."

The Court then issued its guidelines for such prison cases:

> **One of the primary functions of government is the preservation of societal order through enforcement of the criminal law, and the maintenance of penal institutions is an essential part of that task. The identifiable governmental interests at stake in this task are the preservation of internal order and discipline, the maintenance of institutional security against escape or unauthorized entry, and the rehabilitation of the prisoners …. [T]he legitimate governmental interest in the order and security of penal institutions justifies the imposition of certain restraints on inmate correspondence.**

The Court gave some examples of "order and security" concerns that would justify censorship, including letters concerning escape plans or other proposed criminal activity, and letters in code. The guidance of the Court was given in this language:

> **[C]ensorship of prisoner mail is justified if the following criteria are met. First, the regulation or practice in question must further an important or substantial governmental interest unrelated to the suppression of expression … [Prison officials] must show that a regulation authorizing mail censorship furthers one or more of the substantial governmental interests of security, order, and rehabilitation. Second, the limitation of First Amendment freedoms must be no greater than is necessary or essential to the protection of the particular governmental interest involved.**

Applying these standards, the Court affirmed the action of the district court, rejecting the California regulations. Those prison rules were found to be too broad and too vague. The regulations had been used to suppress unwanted criticism and did not establish clear restrictions based on prison concerns about security and order.

The Supreme Court also agreed with the district court in requiring state officials to provide procedural safeguards when mail was rejected. These procedures required that an inmate be notified when a letter is rejected, the author of any letter is given some opportunity to protest the rejection, and such protests are reviewed by someone other than the person who originally disapproved the correspondence. As a result, such procedures for protest and review must be built into any prison's correspondence policies and practices.

▶ *Procunier v. Navarette*

In a case decided just a few years later, the Supreme Court, in *Procunier v. Navarette*, 434 U.S. 555 (1978), showed the importance of following court rulings. Mr. Raymond K. Procunier (the Director of the California Department of Corrections) and other state officials were sued under 42 U.S.C. Section 1983. The inmate, Apolinar Navarette, sued them, claiming interference with his outgoing mail. He claimed that the officials failed to mail several correspondence items he had written in 1971 and 1972.

The officials claimed **immunity** from this lawsuit. This is what is called qualified immunity. (Qualified immunity is in contrast to absolute immunity, which protects legislators, judges, prosecutors, and jury members from being sued at all for actions taken in connection with their official duties.) It is the leading defense available to officials in the Executive branch, such as prison officials, in Section 1983 actions. By the time of this case, the qualified immunity doctrine had been settled in several cases. For example, in the case of *Scheuer v. Rhodes*, 416 U.S. 232 (1974), the Court ruled as follows:

> [A] **qualified immunity is available to officers of the executive branch [if their action is based on] the existence of reasonable grounds for the belief formed at the time and in light of all the circumstances, coupled with good-faith belief.**

This principle was explained further in *Wood v. Strickland*, 420 U.S. 308 (1975). However, in *Navarette*, the Court summarized:

> **[T]he immunity defense would be unavailing to petitioners [prison officials] if the constitutional right allegedly infringed by them was clearly established at the time of their challenged conduct, if they knew or should have known of that right and if they knew or should have known that their conduct violated the constitutional norm.**

Applying this standard, the Supreme Court agreed with the prison officers that in 1971 and 1972, when the conduct complained of in this lawsuit took place, there was no established First Amendment right of prisoners, and thus there was no basis for rejecting the qualified immunity defense. Reviewing the cases of the Supreme Court and of federal courts in California, there was no judicial ruling that announced a clearly established constitutional right protecting Navarette's correspondence. Therefore, the defendant prison officials were entitled to the qualified immunity defense as a matter of law, because they had no obligation to know at the time that their conduct was in violation of a constitutional right.

Another ground that the courts could have used to reject the qualified immunity defense would have been that the officials acted with "malicious intention," intending to deprive the prisoner of a constitutional right or intending to cause him injury. The Court concluded that there was no issue of malicious intent, because even the prisoner's claims alleged only negligent and inadvertent interference with his mail.

It should be noted that if the actions complained of had occurred in 1977 or 1978 (or today), there would be a very different outcome. Qualified immunity would not be immediately available. Courts would have to look at the officials' conduct and analyze that conduct against established constitutional standards on correspondence, which by then had been set in *Procunier v. Martinez* (in 1974) and in succeeding cases.

▶ *Turner v. Safley*

Another major Supreme Court decision on inmate mail is *Turner v. Safley*, 482 U.S. 78 (1987). There were two Missouri regulations under review in *Turner*. The first regulation governed correspondence between inmates. The authorities allowed correspondence with immediate family members in other institutions and correspondence between inmates (in different institutions) about legal matters. Other correspondence between inmates was generally disapproved.

The Court applied the principles of *Procunier v. Martinez*, observing that courts must take cognizance of the valid constitutional claims of inmates. Noting that prisoners have the right to petition for redress of their grievances and to have access to the courts (another type of correspondence that is specially protected) under *Johnson v. Avery*, 393 U.S. 483 (1969), the Court emphasized that prisoners are not barred by their prison walls from seeking the protections of the Constitution. On the other side; however, the Court acknowledged (as it did in *Martinez*) that courts are not good places to deal with problems of prison administration.

[T]he problems of prisons in America are complex and intractable, and, more to the point, they are not readily susceptible of resolution by decree. . . .

Running a prison is an inordinately difficult undertaking that requires expertise, planning, and the commitment of resources, all of which are peculiarly within the province of the legislative and executive branches of government. Prison administration is, moreover, a task that has been committed to the responsibility of those branches, and separation of powers concerns counsel a policy of judicial restraint. . . .

[W]hen a prison regulation impinges on inmates' constitutional rights, the regulation is valid if it is reasonably related to legitimate penological interests. In our view, such a standard is necessary if "prison administrators ... and not the courts, [are] to make the difficult judgments concerning institutional operations."

[The language in the first two paragraphs quoted above come from the Court's opinion in *Procunier v. Martinez*, and the third paragraph is from *Jones v. North Carolina Prisoners' Union*, 433 U.S. at 128.]

In *Turner*, the Court identified the following factors as important in determining the reasonableness of the prison regulation, which impacts constitutional rights:

[T]here must be a "valid, rational connection" between the prison regulation and the legitimate governmental interest put forth to justify it.

[A court must examine] whether there are alternative means of exercising the right that remain open to prison inmates.

[Courts must also look at] the impact accommodation of the asserted constitutional right will have on guards and other inmates, and on the allocation of prison resources generally.

[T]he absence of ready alternatives is evidence of the reasonableness of a prison regulation.

Applying these concepts to the Missouri regulation barring inmate-to-inmate correspondence, the Court ruled the justification for the regulation by prison officials was based on concern that mail between prisons could be used to communicate escape plans and to arrange assaults, retribution, and other violence. There was also a growing concern in Missouri (and in many prison departments) about prison gangs. One way to help control this problem, according to the state, was to transfer gang members into different prisons and then to restrict their correspondence. Other inmates were in protective custody, under the threat of violence from some inmates; allowing free communication between inmates in different facilities could place additional risk on the safety of these protected inmates. After applying the four determining factors noted above, the Court concluded that the Missouri regulation did not deprive inmates of all means of expression; rather, it stopped communications only with a limited group of persons—those of particular concern to prison officials. To allow the requested correspondence could result in less liberty and safety to others, both inmates and staff. Finally, the Court noted there was no obvious, easy alternative to the adopted policy. Therefore, the Court held that "the prohibition on correspondence is reasonably related to valid corrections goals." The Missouri regulation was declared to be constitutionally valid.

▶ Inmate Marriages

The second part of the *Turner* opinion dealt with another Missouri regulation, which banned inmate marriages. Prison officials claimed that marriages could lead to "love triangles" and did not carry any constitutional protection in the first place. The Supreme Court disagreed. The right to marry had been recognized as a fundamental right, under *Zablocki v. Redhail*, 434 U.S. 374 (1976). This right carries over into a prison setting, the Supreme Court ruled.

Authorities argued that restrictions on marrying in prison were necessary because of legitimate security and rehabilitation concerns. Although the right to marry could be subject to necessary restrictions inherent in incarceration, the Supreme Court ruled that there are still benefits that could accrue as the result of inmate marriages.

[W]e conclude that these [several beneficial elements of marriage] are sufficient to form a constitutionally protected marital relationship in the prison context.

The Court held that the Missouri regulation, presenting almost a complete ban on inmate marriages, was an exaggerated response to the security concerns of officials. The prison regulations were found to be not reasonably related to legitimate prison interests. Missouri could regulate the time and place and other incidents of the marriage relationship. (The Court suggested that it approved of the Federal Bureau of Prisons rule, which generally permitted marriages but allowed a warden to deny marriage if it was found to constitute a threat to security or order of the prison or to public safety. What are the differences between these two approaches? What are examples of when the federal restriction would be properly applied?) The Missouri ban on prison marriages was found to be invalid.

The Sixth Circuit Court of Appeals, in *Toms v. Taft*, 338 F.3d 519 (6th Cir. 2003), extended the *Turner* holding on inmate marriages by requiring Ohio state authorities to assist an inmate who wanted to marry someone outside of the prison. Ohio law required both parties seeking a marriage license to personally appear in the probate court to make an application. The local judge had indicated that he would be willing to appoint either an employee of the institution or an employee of the probate court to serve as a deputy clerk for the purpose of issuing the marriage license. The prison warden, however, declined the inmate's request to allow someone at the prison to act as a deputy clerk, stating, "I do not see myself or the institution being involved in this process," other than allowing for a brief marriage ceremony if a marriage license was obtained. The federal court disagreed with Ohio officials, stating the following:

[A] refusal to aid a prisoner in exercising his right to marry, where such refusal completely frustrates the right, can amount to a "prison regulation" under *Turner*. Therefore, such refusals must be reasonably related to legitimate penological interests… [T]he distinction between actively prohibiting an inmate's exercise of his right to marry and failing to assist is untenable in a case in which the inmate's right will be completely frustrated without officials' involvement … The inmate's right to marry may be curtailed only where the officials' refusal to assist the inmate is reasonably related to legitimate penological interests.

Turner instructs that a prisoner's right to marry is not absolute and must be weighed against competing governmental interests. Prison policies on marriage establish a process to assess the risk to institutional security by accommodating the inmate's (and the perspective spouse's) right to marry. The Bureau of Prisons policy on marriage provides as follows:

The Warden shall approve an inmate's request to marry except where a legal restriction to the marriage exists, or where the proposed marriage presents a threat to the security or good order of the institution, or to the protection of the public.[4]

Most states have promulgated rules on inmate marriages, and most have limited restrictions such as marrying former employees; prohibiting marriages that pose a threat to institution security or public safety; and any marriage that requires assistance from DOC staff. See, for example, Minnesota DOC Policy 302.140, Offender Marriage, 18 December 2018.[5]

A. An offender who is 18 years of age or older, or is 16 to 17 years of age with parental or guardian consent, may get married while incarcerated subject to the following limitations:
1. An offender may not marry another offender, a DOC employee, a contractor, or an employee of a contractor.
2. The marriage must not pose a threat to the safety and security of a facility, staff, the public, or other offenders.
3. DOC staff must not encourage or assist in the civil marriage in any way.

An example of when prison security issues may outweigh an offender's right to marry involve cases in which one of the couple is a current or former correctional worker. Two recent decisions by the Seventh Circuit Court of Appeals discussed the application of *Turner v. Safley* to situations in which former prison employees requested permission to marry inmates who were still confined by the Department of Corrections. In *Riker v. Lemmon, et al*, 798 F.3d 546 (7th Cir. 2015) a former contract employee requested permission to visit and marry an inmate she met while working at the correctional facility. After the plaintiff employee resigned, the ex-employee made several requests for visitation privileges but was denied by the DOC under its policy, which states *"ex-employees shall not be permitted to visit an offender if the relationship between the offender and the ex-employee started … during the ex-employee's period of employment with the Department."* The plaintiff then requested to marry the inmate but was denied permission by the DOC. The denial was premised on the possibility that the former employee would disclose sensitive security information to the incarcerated spouse. The ex-employee sued the DOC alleging her rights to marry had been violated. After the DOC was granted summary judgment by the trial court, the ex-employee appealed.

The appeals court first noted that although the plaintiff was not a prisoner, "*so far as challenges to prison regulations as infringing constitutional rights are concerned, the standard is the same whether the rights of prisoners or of nonprisoners are at stake.*" In applying the *Turner* factors, the court of appeals concluded that the state had failed to present sufficient evidence to establish how allowing the marriage "*would pose a security risk or how preventing her marriage furthers its security interests.*" . . . *The Department offers no explanation for why it could not permit [the]marriage request while simultaneously maintaining a secure facility.* The judgment of the district court granting summary judgment to the prison officials was reversed.

Two years later, a similar situation arose in Wisconsin where a former employee requested permission to marry an inmate in DOC custody. The DOC provided extensive evidence that the ex-employee had circumvented prison rules, including corresponding and having telephonic communications with the inmate under a false name. The employee had resigned, and then was re-employed by the DOC as a psychologist. After the DOC learned of her relationship with the inmate, the DOC terminated the employee for violations of the Department's fraternization policy. The DOC reported the ex-employee's relationship with the inmate to the state Psychology Examining Board (the "Board"). The Board concluded that the ex-employee had violated state regulations and suspended the ex-employee's license for one year. The court of appeals affirmed the district court's grant of summary judgment to the prison officials finding that there was a rational relationship between the denial of the request to marry and the legitimate penological interest put forward to justify the denial. The repeated efforts to conceal the true nature of the relationship was "*rationally related to the defendants' interests in maintaining a secure prison capable of effectively monitoring inmate contacts and in promoting respect for its rules.*"

In *Turner*, the plaintiff (Len Safley) was a male inmate and his intended bride was a female inmate at a facility that housed both males and females. The *Turner* Court did not conclude that the inmate status of both parties created a blanket exception to the Court's ruling. Inmates in same sex facilities were generally prohibited by state law from marrying each other. In *Obergefell v. Hodges*, 576 U.S. ___, 135 S. Ct. 2584 (2015), the Supreme Court ruled that the Fourteenth Amendment requires a state to license a marriage between two people of the same sex and to recognize a marriage between two people of the same sex when their marriage was lawfully licensed and performed out-of-state.

In a lower court case from Washington, the inmate plaintiff alleged the state's policy on inmate marriage [prohibiting marriages between confined prisoners] violated his right to marry as recognized in *Turner v. Safley* and discriminated against him because he desired to marry a same sex fellow inmate, which was contradictory to *Obergefell v. Hodges*. The district court in *Sandoval v. Obenland, et al*, W.D. WA Case No. 3:17-cv-05667-RJB-DWC concluded the state's policy did not, on its face, prohibit or discriminate against same-sex marriages but prohibited marriages between confined inmates. The state presented evidence that permitting marriages between confined offenders would impact the institution because: (i) the state would be required to assist the inmates to be present at the same location to conduct the marriage ceremony and the related security risks associated with such movement; (ii) that once married, the two inmates would be required to be housed separately to further the state's no sexual contact rule; (iii) safety and security concerns that some inmates may be coerced into marriages; and (iv) additional burdens related to housing assignments, financial arrangements, visitation, and other contact between offenders, which is usually prohibited. The court additionally concluded that while there were no alternative means for the plaintiff to exercise his right to marry, *Turner* factor 3, the cost of accommodation and 4, absence of ready alternatives favored the defendants and the constitutionality of the policy.

In a different case, the state of Nebraska's inmate marriage policy, which provided, "*Inmates will normally not be permitted to marry other inmates due to potential risks to safety, security or good order of the facility*" was declared facially invalid (Nebraska DOC Policy 205.04, 2016).[6] The court ruled that the regulation was very similar to the Missouri regulation declared unconstitutional in *Turner v. Safley*. In Nebraska, a valid marriage required the parties to "to solemnly declare in the presence of a magistrate or minister and the attending witnesses, that they take each other as husband and wife." Nebraska Statutes Section 42-109. The state argued that the statute required a physical presence, and that a valid marriage ceremony could be performed only when the parties, the officiant, and witnesses were physically present. The inmate couple conceded that since they were confined in separate facilities, transportation to one or the other institution or a courthouse to satisfy the presence requirement was not practical. However, the plaintiffs argued that presence could be achieved by way of an e-ceremony such as Skype, which would not require transportation or present security issues for the DOC. The court found that in the absence of evidence indicating an e-marriage would pose a threat to institution security, order or resources, denial of the practice did not further a legitimate governmental interest. The court granted summary judgment for the plaintiffs and permanently enjoined the state actors, their successors, and designees from denying the plaintiffs' request to participate in an electronic wedding ceremony.[7]

▶ Correspondence in Foreign Languages

Another special concern of prison administrators is the use of a language other than English in inmate correspondence. This issue (which has not been decided in the Supreme Court) was addressed in the case of *Thongvanh v. Thalacker*, 17 F.3d 256 (8th Cir. 1994). Thongvanh, a native of Laos, was an inmate at the Iowa Men's Reformatory. He was able to speak some English, but some family members (particularly his parents and grandparents) could not. Iowa officials had a rule that all correspondence, incoming and outgoing, had to be written in English. This, of course, was so that it could be monitored.

Thongvanh brought a Section 1983 action, alleging violation of his First Amendment (free speech) rights, due process, and equal protection. At trial, a jury found that there were violations of his rights and awarded him $4,000. The court of appeals affirmed that judgment.

Although the court of appeals conceded that Iowa officials had legitimate security concerns regarding the inspection of mail, that court found that officials had not shown why correspondence in Lao could not be translated and then checked. Thongvanh had been allowed to correspond with his parents and grandparents in Lao but only with them. There was a refugee service center that provided translations to the Iowa Reformatory for those letters. It was also noteworthy that Spanish-speaking inmates were excepted from the English-only mail policy. As in many prisons, there was a staff member who was able to translate Spanish correspondence. Also, the evidence showed that there was an exception made for a German speaking inmate who was allowed to correspond in German.

After considering this evidence and applying the standards of *Turner v. Safley*, the appeals court found (1) the inmate's right under the First Amendment to free expression was clearly abridged, (2) limiting correspondence in Lao to Thongvanh's parents and grandparents was arbitrary and not reasonably related to a legitimate government interest, and (3) this inmate was not treated the same as other inmates similarly situated (those who spoke Spanish and German).

The court's opinion in this case did not clearly specify what constitutional standards were applied to arrive at this verdict against Iowa prison officials. From what was stated, it is fair to assume that there were two constitutional standards violated: First Amendment freedom of speech (under *Turner* standards because there was an alternative available in Iowa to allow the speech to occur) and equal protection under the Fourteenth Amendment (because Thongvanh was, without good justification, treated so differently from other inmates who were allowed to correspond in languages other than English).

With respect to both of those conclusions, a key factor was that Iowa officials could obtain translations of the inmate's correspondence into and out of Lao. What this opinion did not address was what obligation, if any, the prison officials had to locate a translation service for mail written in Lao. What if the refugee service translators had not been available? How far would officials have to go to find translators for Lao or any other language? And if the service was not free (as the refugee service was), how much would the government be obligated to pay to achieve foreign-language translation for this, or any other, inmate?

Ortiz v. Fort Dodge Correctional Facility, 368 F.3d 1024 (8th Cir. 2004), concerned an inmate who was allowed to correspond in Spanish with a sister in Mexico City, as this was the only way they could communicate. He was not allowed to correspond in Spanish with other family members who lived in the United States, nor could he receive letters written in Spanish from these persons. This ban lasted three months, at which time the prison changed its policy to allow inmates to correspond in their preferred language. Ortiz filed suit asking for compensatory and punitive damages for the three months during which he could not write or receive letters in Spanish. The district court, applying the *Turner* factors, found in favor of the prison and Ortiz's unit manager, holding that the former policy was reasonably related to a penological interest. The appeals court affirmed. The *Ortiz* courts distinguished *Thongvanh*, saying that Ortiz did not identify a cost-free way for the prison to accommodate him. Ortiz did not present at trial what it would cost to hire an interpreter, whether the prison had Spanish-speaking employees, whether other prisons could have provided interpretation services, or whether a social service agency was willing to translate the letters on the inmate's behalf. The lack of such information failed to meet *Turner's* third and fourth factors, which require an evaluation of the alternatives to the existing regulation and their impact on the prison, inmates, and non-inmates. No ready alternative at a minimal cost was presented. The distinction between the cases? In *Thongvanh*, information was presented to show that a translation service had offered, at no cost, to translate the letters into English.

In another appellate-level case, *Kikumura v. Turner*, 28 F.3d 592 (7th Cir. 1994), the court reviewed a Federal Bureau of Prisons policy at the U.S. Penitentiary in Marion, Illinois, which acted to exclude publications in Japanese. (During the course of the litigation, the policy shifted somewhat, and officials at the penitentiary were able to find an employee in another prison who could screen the materials published in Japanese and return them.) The trial court had found that there was no clearly established constitutional right for an inmate to receive a publication in a foreign language and granted qualified immunity to Warden Turner. The appeals court upheld that ruling. (Whether Iowa officials would have been protected by qualified immunity in the *Thongvanh* case—because there was no clearly established right to receive foreign-language mail when their action was taken—was not addressed in that court opinion.) Because of procedural complexities and errors, the appeals court sent the case back for further consideration on the issue as to whether the original, total ban on the receipt of Japanese materials violated Kikumura's constitutional rights, which would have entitled him to injunctive or declaratory relief.

BOX 7-1 Controlling Contraband—Postcards and Photocopies of Incoming General Correspondence

The Supreme Court has recognized that correctional officials "ha[ve] a compelling interest in staunching the flow of contraband into and within its facilities." *Holt v. Hobbs*, 574 U.S. 362 (2015). Supreme Court cases have established "that correctional officials must be permitted to devise reasonable search policies to detect and deter the possession of contraband in their facilities." *Florence v. Board of Chosen Freeholders of Burlington County*, 566 U.S. 318 (2012). Prison officials have reported recent incidents such as identifying a letter to an inmate that had been soaked in K2 (a synthetic marijuana), finding greeting cards with strips of suboxone (a combination of two substances, which are used to treat opioid addiction) hidden behind address labels of incoming mail to a prisoner, and photographs and personal letters soaked in liquid suboxone.[8] In response, corrections officials have formulated a number of responses, such as (i) requiring that all incoming postal mail correspondence be photocopied in house or routed to a contractor who duplicates the contents and forwards a digital copy to the institution where the offender is confined;[9] (ii) prohibiting greeting cards and photographs submitted through the postal mail;[10] (iii) requiring written correspondence to inmates come on standard-sized post cards instead of letters,[11] and (iv) requiring all incoming postal mail to be sent in white envelopes.

The Virginia state policy of replacing original incoming correspondence with photocopies was found not to violate an inmate's First Amendment rights. The state presented evidence that since the policy was implemented, there were significantly fewer incidents of illegal drugs being found and that the number of drug overdoses causing death or requiring medical treatment declined. Applying the *Turner* factors, three separate district courts concluded the regulation was logically connected to the legitimate government interests of keeping offenders safe and running a secure prison system by reducing the introduction of contraband. The policy was consistent with the second *Turner* factor because inmates retained multiple alternative means of exercising their right to receive the content of the correspondence; they were able to use an electronic messaging system, to send and receive messages and receive photographs, and were able to keep photographs taken within the prison and directly from vendors. The third *Turner* factor, the impact of accommodation on the facility and staff, favored the state policy since to allow the introduction of drugs and increase inmate overdoses and overdose deaths would be "irresponsible." The fourth *Turner* factor favored the regulation because the inmate failed to point to any ready alternatives to the regulation.[12]

Postcard-only correspondence policies were upheld by several district courts and by one circuit court of appeals. In *Simpson v. County of Cape Girardeau, Mo.* 879 F.3d 273 (8th Cir. 2018), an inmate's mother challenged the county's postcard-only mail policy. The district court conducted a bench trial and concluded, considering the factors announced in *Turner v. Safley*, that the county's policy did not violate the First Amendment. The court of appeals affirmed the district court's judgment, finding that the purpose of the policy was to improve institution security and efficiency. The court of appeals cautioned its opinion was narrow, based on a fact-intensive *Turner* analysis, which requires a *"careful examination of the policies and institutions at issue in each case."*

▶ Prisoner Use of Electronic Messaging and Access to Social Media

Over the last 20 years, the increased use of email for communications has prompted correctional organizations to adopt procedures to provide inmate access to a form of electronic messaging (Electronic Messaging System, EMS). The EMS does not use the Internet but is a closed system, which requires a subscription by both the inmate and a person in the community. The EMS is provided by a contractor, and the inmate or community subscriber pays a fee for using the service. Using electronic messaging eliminates the risk of contraband items being smuggled into the facility within the mail sent to inmates. As with other inmate correspondence, the electronic message's contents are reviewed pursuant to agency policy. The use of EMS provides inmates with another means of communicating, along with regular mail, telephone, and visiting.[13]

The proliferation of social media platforms presents new issues for correctional agencies, inmates, and the family and friends of those incarcerated. In *Packingham v. North Carolina*, ___ U.S. ___, 137 S. Ct. 1730 (2017), the Court ruled that a North Carolina law, which prohibited certain convicted sex offenders from accessing commercial websites that allow children to join or have a web presence violated the First Amendment because it was not narrowly tailored to further the acknowledged compelling governmental interest of protecting children. The Court first noted that this was the first case the Court "*has taken to address the relationship between the First Amendment and the modern Internet*"; and that seven in ten Americans used at least one social media platform. Social media had become an integral part of life in America:

> ***Social media allows users to gain access to information and communicate with one another about it on any subject that might come to mind. . . . By prohibiting sex offenders from using those websites, North Carolina with one broad stroke bars access to what for many are the principal sources for knowing current events, checking ads for employment, speaking and listening in the modern public square, and otherwise exploring the vast realms of human thought and knowledge. These websites can provide perhaps the most powerful mechanisms available to a private citizen to make his or her voice heard. They allow a person with an Internet connection to "become a town crier with a voice that resonates farther than it could from any soapbox."***

The Court noted that the language of state's statute was sweeping, potentially barring a convicted, but no longer supervised, sex offender from accessing commercial websites like WebMD, Amazon, Facebook, and Twitter. States would not be prohibited from enacting "*specific, narrowly tailored laws that prohibit a sex offender from engaging in conduct that often presages a sexual crime, like contacting a minor or using a website to gather information about a minor.*" However, the state's current law violated the First Amendment.

> ***In sum, that to foreclose access to social media altogether is to prevent the user from engaging in the legitimate exercise of First Amendment rights. It is unsettling to suggest that only a limited set of websites can be used even by persons who have completed their sentences. Even convicted criminals — and in some instances especially convicted criminals — might receive legitimate benefits from these means for access to the world of ideas, in particular if they seek to reform and to pursue lawful and rewarding lives.***

The application of *Packingham* to correctional entities is developing. Several circuit courts of appeal have ruled that similar restrictions on access to computers and social media access without probation officer approval did not violate the probationer's First Amendment rights because the probationer, unlike Packingham, was still under correctional supervision. See, for example, *U.S. V. Halverson*, 897 F.3d 645 (5th Cir. 2018) ("The *Packingham* decision is inapplicable to [the defendant's] circumstances. Even while on supervised release, [the defendant] is serving his criminal sentence, and the Court has broad discretion in establishing the conditions under which [the defendant] will serve the supervised release portion of his sentence.").

The Court's statement that persons have a First Amendment right to use social media has been applied to detainees. See, for example, *Kelly v. Santiago*, Case No. 3:18-cv-01768-VAB (D.CT 2019) (detainee's allegation that detention center staff placed him in segregation (retaliated against him) for his postings on Facebook (which identified the inmate as a gang member)). Some correctional organizations have specific rules forbidding inmates from having social media accounts and from permitting family and friends from using social media on the inmate's behalf.[14] Correctional officials believe such access can pose a threat to institutional security and the public. Others feel social media is beneficial to the inmate and makes conditions in prisons and jails more transparent. This issue will likely generate a significant amount of litigation in the future.

▶ *Thornburgh v. Abbott*

Another type of inmate mail is the receipt of publications—magazines, newspapers, books, and clippings from those materials. In general, a prisoner may receive such publications in two ways: (1) by subscription or (2) as separate mailings from family or friends.

The Federal Bureau of Prisons had regulations that allowed inmates to receive publications from outside of the prison but authorized local prison authorities to reject incoming publications that were found to be "detrimental to the security, good order, or discipline of the institution or if [they] might facilitate criminal activity." Wardens were cautioned not to reject publications solely on the grounds of religious, philosophical, political, social, or sexual content, or if the content was unpopular or repugnant.

The term *publication* was defined as including books, magazines, newspapers, and other materials such as brochures, flyers, and catalogs. The regulation gave some examples of publications that could be found to pose a threat to security—for example, those depicting how to make or use weapons, ammunition, or bombs; those depicting how to make alcoholic beverages or how to manufacture drugs; those encouraging activities that could lead to group violence or disruption; those providing instruction in the commission of criminal activity; and (the most controversial example and the one most contested in the case) those containing sexually explicit material that posed a threat to the security, good order, or discipline of the institution or facilitated criminal activity. (Under the last standard, if you were a warden, what material would you exclude?) An instruction of the Bureau of Prisons gave additional guidance for this pornography standard: wardens could reject material that depicted homosexuality, sado-masochism, or bestiality but only if it was found to pose a threat to the security of the local institution (the overriding standard for any material). Sexually explicit material involving children could always be excluded, because the mailing of it is per se (in and of itself) a violation of federal laws.

In a class action suit, *Thornburgh v. Abbott*, 490 U.S. 401 (1989) addressed challenges to these regulations by inmates and by some publishers. The Supreme Court quickly identified that the inmates (and the publishers) had First Amendment interests in receiving (and sending) the contested publications. First, the Court addressed the question of what standard of review should be applied to these kinds of First Amendment rights. The Court said the standard to be applied was the one in *Turner v. Safley*, not the one in *Procunier v. Martinez*, because the latter case was limited in its analysis and application. The Court observed that outgoing mail (which may be the focus of the *Martinez* opinion) is not as great a security concern as incoming mail.

The mail regulations in the *Thornburgh* case were based on a concern for prison security, which is a purpose "central to all other corrections goals," the Court said. It was a legitimate governmental objective, and the regulation restricting inmate First Amendment rights was neutral in its application—that is, it was applied without regard to the content of the expression. Furthermore, the Court liked the fact that determinations for rejections of publications were made on individualized bases: The Bureau of Prisons required each individual magazine or book or newspaper to be examined. Inmates were not kept from subscribing to certain titles; only individual issues of a subscription could be excluded, based on a finding that those issues contained material that posed a risk to the institution's security. Using the *Turner* language, the Bureau of Prisons' regulation was found not to be exaggerated, and it was permissible, because there was no obvious alternative that could achieve the same result (of keeping such publications out of prison).

Applying the *Turner* standard, the Court concluded that the government regulations were "reasonably related to legitimate penological interests." The regulations were upheld as constitutionally valid.

While the *Thornburgh* case judicially decided the issue of receiving sexually oriented publications under First Amendment protection, the U.S. Congress has legislatively taken action to limit such publications. In Section 615 of the Commerce, Justice, State Appropriations Act of 2000 (Public Law 106-113),[15] Congress said: *"None of the funds made available in this Act to the Federal Bureau of Prisons may be used to distribute or make available any commercially published information or material to a prisoner when it is made known to the Federal official having authority to obligate or expend such funds that such information or material is sexually explicit or features nudity."* In effect, this language prevents federal prison staff from delivering these publications to inmates, even if the inmate has a subscription. The Bureau of Prisons January 2003 policy on incoming publications requires such a publication to be returned to the publisher or sender, with notification of the administrative appeal process. How did inmates and publishers react to these restrictions? In an earlier version (1996) of the restrictions, three inmates with subscriptions, along with the affected publishers, sued in a free-speech challenge. The U.S. District Court for the District of Columbia enjoined enforcement, finding it facially invalid under the First Amendment. The DC Circuit Court of Appeals, applying *Turner*, reversed in *Amatel v. Reno*, 156 F.3d 192 (DC Cir. 1998). In June of 1999, the U.S. Supreme Court, without comment, declined to review the court of appeals' decision.

▶ *Beard v. Banks*

In this case, which is an extension of the ruling in *Thornburgh v. Abbott*, the Supreme Court considered whether it was a violation of the First Amendment for Pennsylvania authorities to withhold newspapers, magazines, and personal photographs from inmates who were in a Long Term Segregation Unit. This was done, prison officials said, to motivate the inmates to adopt better behavior.

The district court found that the prison rule was acceptable and was supported by the evidence officials presented. The court of appeals reversed, holding that the prison's regulation could not be "supported as a matter of law by the record in this case."

The Supreme Court, in *Beard v. Banks*, 548 U.S. 521 (2006), reversed the appellate court and agreed with the district court's conclusion. It held that the state's justification to motivate improved behavior by inmates was a legitimate governmental purpose under *Turner v. Safley* requirements:

> **The articulated connections between newspapers and magazines, the deprivation of virtually the last privilege left to an inmate, and a significant incentive to improve behavior, are logical ones.**

The Court further said that the material presented by prison officials was sufficient to show that the policy was reasonable and inquiring into the other three factors discussed in *Turner* would not be particularly useful.

Applying language it had used in *Overton v. Bazzetta*, 539 U.S. 126 (2003), which related to visitation rights, the Court concluded:

> **[W]ithholding such privileges "is a proper and even necessary management technique to induce compliance with the rules of inmate behavior, especially for high-security prisoners who have few other privileges to lose."**

The Court added that the court of appeals had placed too high an evidentiary burden on Beard, the secretary of the department of corrections, failing to provide sufficient deference to the judgment of prison officials on these matters of prison management.

In the absence of evidence contrary to, or conflicting with, the rationale of prison authorities, the Court concluded that the policy was constitutional within the standards set by *Turner*.

▶ *Bell v. Wolfish*

In another case that is also something of an adjunct to the *Thornburgh v. Abbott* decision, the Supreme Court dealt with the constitutionality of a regulation limiting the receipt of books and magazines. *Bell v. Wolfish*, 441 U.S. 520 (1979), is primarily known and cited as a case dealing with conditions in jails, particularly with double-celling (crowding) in jails. *Bell* also dealt with a challenge to a Federal Bureau of Prisons' regulation that required inmates (most of whom were pretrial detainees but some of whom were prisoners serving sentences) to receive such publications only from the publisher (thus, the "publisher-only" rule). The Bureau of Prisons justified this restriction on security concerns; authorities claimed that books and magazines were too hard to examine thoroughly for contraband, and the greatest risk for the introduction of contraband in such materials was when they were sent by family and friends. By limiting the sender to publishers, officials believed that the threat of contraband would be minimized. During the course of the litigation, the Bureau of Prisons amended its rule to allow paperback books and magazines to be sent in by family and friends. Hardcover books were still limited to a "publisher-only" restriction.

The Supreme Court found the regulation to be a reasonable response to "an obvious security problem." The Court noted that there were other ways for inmates to obtain reading materials (mainly from a prison library). The rule had nothing to do with the content of the materials and, therefore, was content-neutral (always a First

Amendment concern of the courts). The same concern over security, in support of the regulation, applied to both pretrial detainees and to convicted inmates. The prison regulation was upheld.

▶ National Security Issues

A special interest arises from the confinement of certain types of inmates, such as spies and terrorists. In the mid-1990s, the Federal Bureau of Prisons implemented rules governing inmates associated with national security issues and acts of violence and terrorism (Title 28, Code of Federal Regulations, Sections 501.2 and 501.3). These sections authorize the implementation of special administrative measures (which govern such areas as the inmate's correspondence, interviews with representatives of the news media, use of telephone, and visiting) to prevent disclosure of classified information (for national security cases) and to protect persons against the risk of death or serious bodily injury (for acts of violence and terrorism).

For example, in the case of an inmate convicted of espionage, the inmate may have knowledge about practices and procedures used by government agencies. The "shelf life" of this information may extend many years beyond the inmate's conviction. If the information became known, the safety of United States operatives could be in danger. To address this concern, the mail, telephone conversations, and visiting activities of such an inmate may be subject to increased limitations or scrutiny under this regulation.

The section of the rule (28 CFR 501.3) on prevention of acts of violence and terrorism authorizes, under stringent procedures, "the monitoring or review of communications between [a particular inmate] and attorneys or attorneys' agents who are traditionally covered by the attorney–client privilege, for the purpose of deterring future acts that could result in death or serious bodily injury to persons, or substantial damage to property that would entail the risk of death or serious bodily injury to persons."

In *United States v. Stewart*, 590 F.3d 93 (2nd Cir. 2009), (*en banc*) re-hearing denied, 597 F.3d 514 (2nd Cir. 2010), the court of appeals upheld the validity of the section 501.3 special administrative measures as applied to communications between defendant Stewart (an attorney) and her client, Omar Abdel Rahman, a prisoner convicted of terrorist acts. The court of appeals described Rahman's status as follows:

> Rahman is serving a life sentence in a maximum-security prison for terrorism-related crimes of seditious conspiracy, solicitation of murder, solicitation of an attack on American military installations, conspiracy to murder, and a conspiracy to bomb. He is subject to "Special Administrative Measures" (SAMs) restricting his ability to communicate with persons outside of the prison in which he is incarcerated so as to prevent him from continuing to lead terrorist organizations.

Attorney Stewart signed documents saying she understood the restrictions imposed by the SAMs and agreed to abide by its terms (for example, not to use her meetings, correspondence, or phone calls with Rahman to pass messages between third parties and Rahman). After agreeing to the limitations imposed by the special administrative measures, Stewart facilitated communication of information to third parties in violation of those measures, resulting in the prosecution of herself and others. She was sentenced to 10 years in federal prison for her conduct.

▶ Inmate Postage

Does the First Amendment entitle an inmate to free writing material and postage? The Supreme Court has not addressed this question, but lower federal courts have. In *Van Poyck v. Singletary*, 106 F.3d 1558 (11th Cir. 1997), the Department of Corrections policy in Florida provided indigent inmates with free postage and writing materials to mail one first-class letter per month, for such mailing to occur on a specific day, and for an inmate to receive a maximum of 15 stamps from a person outside of the prison. Another rule limited the number of stamps an inmate could possess at any one time to 20. The inmates alleged a violation of their First Amendment, freedom of speech rights.

The Eleventh Circuit held that the First Amendment does not require prison officials to give indigent inmates unlimited free postage and materials for nonlegal mail. The Court also supported the limitation on the number of stamps received and possessed by inmates, holding that the rule was related to the legitimate security interest of eliminating the exchange of contraband among inmates.

In *Davidson v. Mann*, 129 F.3d 700 (2nd Cir. 1997), an inmate challenged a New York state prison rule that limited the number of stamps an inmate could purchase to 50 every two weeks—or to 50 per month for an inmate in special housing (ordinarily disciplinary) status. This was claimed to be a First Amendment violation of the inmate's right to send outgoing nonlegal mail. The appeals court, using the *Turner* standard, ruled in favor of the state, saying the regulation was rationally related to legitimate penological objectives. The limits on the number of stamps were seen as legitimately furthering the goal of avoiding thefts and disputes. It was also commented that inmates in New York had the choice of prioritizing their mailings or showing extenuating circumstances to warrant an exception being made.

▶ Nude Photos

Inmate Giano challenged the Clinton, New York, Correctional Facility policy that prohibited the possession of nude or seminude photos of inmates' spouses or girlfriends. He brought a Section 1983 action, claiming that the policy infringed on his First Amendment rights. *Giano v. Senkowski*, 54 F.3d 1050 (2nd Cir. 1995). Officials at Clinton allowed inmates to receive other erotic literature (such as *Playboy* magazine), but they justified the exclusion of wives' or girlfriends' photos on the grounds that possession of such photos could cause violent confrontations among inmates if they were passed around the institution or if they were possessed by the wrong inmates. Officials said that the possibility of those confrontations posed a threat to the safety, security, and good order of the institution.

Giano's girlfriend sent four photos to him; two of them were seminude. Under the prison's policy, an employee who went through the incoming mail took out the two seminude photos and sent the rest of the mail to Giano. The confiscated photos were added to Giano's personal property, which was to be stored and then given to him upon his release. The Second Circuit said that this action and this policy by Clinton officials did not violate the First Amendment. "Prison officials must be given latitude to anticipate the probable consequences of certain speech and must be allowed to take reasonable steps to forestall violence," the court said.

Other courts, it was noted, had recognized this same problem. The Ninth Circuit, in *Pepperling v. Crist*, 678 F.2d 787 (9th Cir. 1982), accepted the proposition that nude photos of wives or girlfriends are "highly emotionally charged and often lead to violent altercations among prisoners." Another court, in *Trapnell v. Riggsby*, 622 F.2d 290 (7th Cir. 1980), upheld the ban on nude photos of wives and girlfriends on the grounds that many offenders had assaultive behavior records and "the highly emotionally charged nature of the photographs" increased the likelihood of violence. The court in *Giano* concluded that the policy at Clinton was based on a valid, rational concern about maintaining prison order and security. The court, in something approaching a humorous aside, noted the proposition that "one man's pornography may be another's keepsake." But the court was also helped to reach its conclusion by the fact that the inmate had other links to his girlfriend, including ordinary correspondence and other permissible photos.

Summary

- Freedom of speech, guaranteed in the First Amendment, is a freedom that is highly protected in the courts, but it is not an absolute freedom.
- Prison officials have concerns about the content of mail—both sent and received by inmates. Contraband enclosures and illegal content in communications are the main concerns.
- Correctional agencies are implementing new policies regarding access to the Internet, e-messaging, and postcards-only correspondence.
- The Supreme Court recognized the mail sent by outside correspondents to inmates to be "speech," protected by the First Amendment. But the Court also ruled that prison officials could restrict such correspondence if it was necessary in order to further a "legitimate government interest." The government interests that could justify restrictions on correspondence are the preservation of internal order and discipline, maintenance of institutional security, and rehabilitation of prisoners (*Procunier v. Martinez*).
- In a civil rights action (under Section 1983), a prison official is protected against liability (is given qualified immunity) if the actions he took interfering with inmate correspondence were taken before the law governing such correspondence had been clearly established (*Procunier v. Navarette*).
- Conceding the very difficult problems that are inherent in running prisons, the Supreme Court held that prison officials had good security reasons to prohibit inmates from writing to inmates in other institutions in most cases (*Turner v. Safley*). In the same case, however, the Court said prison authorities had not shown

justification to ban inmate marriages. The Court provided a four-part test for examining First Amendment challenges.

- Lower federal courts have been addressing cases related to the rights of inmates marrying other inmates.
- Regarding correspondence in foreign languages, the Supreme Court has not yet ruled on the obligation of prisons to allow such correspondence. A lower court indicated that, in a case in which a translation service was available and correspondence had been allowed for other languages, prohibiting some mail in Lao was not permissible (*Thongvanh v. Thalacker*). Another lower court indicated that an official was protected by qualified immunity in a case involving receipt of Japanese publications, because the law in this area had not been clearly established (*Kikumura v. Turner*).
- The Supreme Court upheld a regulation that allowed local prison officials to reject incoming publications (magazines, newspapers, etc.) if they were found to be detrimental to the security or good order of the institution or if they might facilitate criminal activity (*Thornburgh v. Abbott*).
- A prison regulation banning newspapers, magazines, and personal photos to incorrigible, recalcitrant inmates housed in a highly restrictive housing unit was upheld as a proper, and even necessary, management approach to induce compliance with the rules of inmate behavior, especially for high-security prisoners who have few other privileges to lose (*Beard v. Banks*).
- Special administrative measures (covering such areas as inmate correspondence, news media interviews, telephone use, and visiting) have been implemented to prevent disclosure of classified information (for national security cases) and to protect persons against the risk of death or serious bodily injury (for acts of violence and terrorism). An appeals court has upheld such measures in a case involving acts of violence and terrorism (*United States v. Stewart*).
- Courts of Appeals have decided that prison officials may limit (for nonlegal mail) the number of stamps provided to an indigent inmate and may also limit the number of stamps that an inmate may purchase or have in his or her possession (*Van Poyck v. Singletary; Davidson v. Mann*).
- Federal courts upheld a New York policy that prohibited nude or seminude photos of spouses or girlfriends to be sent in to inmates (*Giano v. Senkowski*).

Thinking About It

A prison inmate writes his brother, saying there is a "beetled eye'd bit__back here who enjoys reading people's mail." The letter continues, saying the staff member was hoping to read a letter "someone wrote to their wife talking dirty sh__, so she could go in the bathroom and masturbate." (Note: the last two letters of *bit__* and *sh__* were blackened out.) The letter was reviewed by prison staff under agency policy [Divisional Rule 21, prohibited an inmate from "using abusive or obscene language ... or making a written statement, intended to annoy, offend or threaten."], and the inmate was punished under the institution's disciplinary policy. The inmate sued, claiming a violation of First Amendment rights. How do you think the court should rule? See *Loggins v. Delo*, 999 F.2d 364 (8th Cir. 1993).

Key Terms

class action
immunity

Endnotes

1. *United States of America v. Stotts*, 925 F.2d 83 (4th Cir. 1991).
2. U.S. Department of Justice, Office of Inspector General Report No. I-2003-02.
3. *Outley v. Penzone*, (D. AZ, 2020) No. CV 18-02753-PHX-GMS (JFM). Order on Defendant's Motion for Summary Judgment. The average daily population in 2016 was 7,359. Maricopa County, AZ. *Maricopa County Criminal Justice System*. https://www.maricopa .gov/Archive/ViewFile/Item/2862. Accessed February 17, 2020.
4. Federal Bureau of Prisons Program Statement 5326.05, Marriages of Inmates, September 22, 2011.
5. Minnesota DOC Policy 302.140, Offender Marriage, 18 December 2018. Available: http://www.doc.state.mn.us/DocPolicy2/html /DPW_Display_TOC.asp?Opt=302.140.htm
6. Nebraska DOC Policy 205.04. *Inmate Marriage*, June 30, 2016.
7. *Gillpatrick & Wetherell v. Frakes, et al.* D. NE Case No. 4:18CV3011, Memorandum filed June 7, 2019. Available: https://www .aclunebraska.org/sites/default/files/field_documents/gillpatrick_order.pdf. Accessed 20 February 2020. The state's policy was revised

since the court's decision and the most current at the time of publication was revised August 31, 2019: https://corrections.nebraska
.gov/system/files/rules_reg_files/205.04_2019.pdf

8. Norwood, C. *Anti-Drug Smuggling Policies are Increasingly Isolating Prisoners*. Governing. February 13, 2019. Available: https://www
.governing.com/topics/public-justice-safety/gov-prison-jails-drugs-restrictions-inmates.html. Accessed February 16, 2020.

9. See Pennsylvania DOC Policy DC-ADM-803 *Inmate Mail and Incoming Publications*, p. 1–8. October 3, 2018. Available: https://www
.cor.pa.gov/About%20Us/Documents/DOC%20Policies/803%20Inmate%20Mail%20and%20Incoming%20Publications.pdf.
Accessed February 16, 2020.

10. See for example: State of Montana Department of Corrections Policy Directive DOC 3.36, Offender Mail. June 29, 2018. (Prohibiting
greeting cards or "unusually" thick paper or stationary. Available: https://cor.mt.gov/Portals/104/Resources/Policy/Chapter3/3.3.6%20
Offender%20Mail%2006.29.2018.pdf?ver=2018-06-29-112231-043. Accessed February 16, 2020.

11. See Greene County, Missouri Sheriff's Office Offender Mail (requiring incoming correspondence to be on standard white postcard no
larger than 5 × 7. Available: https://greenecountymo.gov/sheriff/division/detention/mail.php and Walker County, Alabama, Sheriff's
Office (all incoming and outgoing mail must be on a plain white postcard (except legal mail). Available: http://walkercountysheriff
.com/visitation-policy-and-rules.html. Accessed February 16, 2020.

12. See *Couch, et al v. Clarke, et al*, Case No. 7:18:CV00049, (W.D.Va. 2019) (Order granting summary judgment to defendants), Available:
https://scholar.google.com/scholar_case?case=6500086506929084960&q=couch+v.+Clarke&hl=en&as_sdt=6,24; affirmed Case No.
19-6526, U.S. Court of Appeals, Fourth Circuit (October 29, 2019). file:///C:/Users/daryl/AppData/Local/Temp/196526.U.pdf.
Accessed February 17, 2020.

13. See New Hampshire DOC Policy and Procedure Directive 5.24, Inmate email Service: https://www.nh.gov/nhdoc/policies
/documents/5-24.pdf. Accessed February 17, 2020.

    *It is the policy of the Department of Corrections to allow inmates to send and receive e-mail correspondence through the
    contracted vendor, according to all applicable laws, policy, procedures and regulations. IIIA.*

    The Federal Bureau of Prisons provides inmate access to email using the TRULINCS system:

    *(3) Public Messaging Contacts. Inmates request to exchange emails with a person in the community by creating a contact with
    an email address. . . .*

    Program Statement 4500.12, Trust Fund/Deposit Fund Manual, March 14, 2018. Section14.10©(3). https://www.bop.gov
    /policy/progstat/4500.12.pdf. Accessed February 17, 2020.

14. Wiltz, T. *Should Social Media Be Banned in Prison?* Pew Charitable Trust Stateline. January 13, 2017. https://www.pewtrusts.org/en
/research-and-analysis/blogs/stateline/2017/01/13/should-social-media-be-banned-in-prison. Accessed February 29, 2020.

15. Section 615 of the Commerce, Justice, State Appropriations Act of 2000 (Public Law 106-113), (For more information in this area,
please go to http://www.bop.gov. Once on that website, click on "Policy/Forms" and select the 5000 series. The policy on incoming
publications is located at 5266.10.)

CHAPTER 8

First Amendment: Inmate Association Rights and Visiting

The fact of confinement and the needs of the penal institution impose limitations on constitutional rights, including those derived from the First Amendment, which are implicit in incarceration. Perhaps the most obvious of the First Amendment rights that are necessarily curtailed by confinement are those associational rights that the First Amendment protects outside of prison walls.

U.S. Supreme Court, *Jones v. North Carolina Prisoners' Labor Union*

CHAPTER OUTLINE

- Freedom of Association
- *Jones v. North Carolina Prisoners' Labor Union*
- Inmates and the News Media: *Pell v. Procunier; Saxbe v. Washington Post*
- *Houchins v. KQED, Inc.; Garrett v. Estelle; Hammer v. Ashcroft; Smith v. Coughlin*
- Inmate Visits
- *Block v. Rutherford*
- *Kentucky Department of Corrections v. Thompson*
- *Overton v. Bazzetta*
- Conjugal Visits
- Artificial Insemination

This chapter looks at another right that is protected by the First Amendment of the Constitution. Although it is not as well known as the freedoms of speech, press, and religion, which are also contained in the First Amendment, there is an association right that is found in that amendment. Most inmates want to keep in contact with family and friends. One way to do that is through correspondence. This chapter looks at the contacts that inmates maintain or establish through organizations, associations, and especially through visiting.

▶ Freedom of Association

The First Amendment does not mention the right of freedom of association, other than that of peaceable assembly. But the Supreme Court has found such a right in the First Amendment (which is applicable to the states by the Fourteenth Amendment).

In *Roberts v. United States Jaycees*, 468 U.S. 609 (1984), the Supreme Court found that there are two kinds of freedoms of association protected by the Constitution. The first protects the rights of individuals "to enter into and maintain certain intimate human relationships." This refers to family relationships and the need to protect them as well as the inherent need for seclusion from others in such relationships (that is, a right to privacy). Where does the Constitution give such protection? The Supreme Court stated in Roberts "because (editor-when enclosed by quotation marks the passage comes from a Supreme Court or other court opinion-Please do not alter the punctuation) the Bill of Rights is designed to secure individual liberty, it must afford the formation and preservation of certain kinds of highly personal relationships a substantial measure of sanctuary from unjustified interference by the State." This may be seen as the Supreme Court conducting a free-ranging interpretation of the Constitution, rather than a strict construction of the First Amendment's language.

There is not much need for this kind of associational protection in prisons, because prisoners forfeit their rights to close, intimate family relationships as a condition of their incarceration. (An exception might be those few states that allow "conjugal visitation"—the permission to receive visits from spouses or partners in a private place on the prison grounds, such as a small apartment or a trailer. See the discussion of that kind of association later in this chapter.)

For the second kind of association protected by the Constitution, the Supreme Court has recognized that citizens have a right to engage in "expressive association." This is the right to gather together (in "peaceable assembly") to take part in those activities that are specifically protected by the First Amendment: the right to speak, the right to worship, and the right to petition the government for redress of grievances.

This chapter examines to what extent prisoners retain any associational rights under the Constitution, and to what degree prison authorities may restrict or ban those associational activities?

▶ *Jones v. North Carolina Prisoners' Labor Union*

In the late 1960s and early 1970s, there was a movement to organize U.S. prisoners into prisoners' unions. This movement was based, in name and philosophy, on the U.S. labor union movement. The state of North Carolina experienced the organization of inmates in many of its institutions into a "Prisoners' Labor Union." The Supreme Court's decision in *Jones* provided the prisoner's rationale for forming a union: The union's stated purposes were "to seek through collective bargaining … to improve … working condition, … to work towards the alteration or elimination of practices and policies of the Department of Correction which it did not approve of, and to serve as a vehicle for the presentation and resolution of inmate grievances." The state originally tolerated inmates forming and joining this union, but as its size grew to 2,000 members in forty different prisons, the North Carolina Department of Corrections issued a regulation prohibiting the solicitation of members, banning union meetings in the prisons, and forbidding bulk mailings about the union from outside sources.

The union filed suit, challenging the regulation and seeking an injunction against its enforcement, pursuant to 42 U.S.C. § 1983. Because it was a challenge to the constitutionality of the statewide regulation, a three-judge district court was convened to hear the lawsuit. That court found the regulation unconstitutional in many aspect and enjoined (enjoin is a legal term meaning an order directing a party to do or not to do a specific act) its enforcement. The state took a direct appeal of that judgment to the Supreme Court, which issued its opinion in *Jones v. North Carolina Prisoners' Labor Union*, 433 U.S. 119 (1977).

The Supreme Court in *Jones* noted that the district court had based its review of the state regulation on three constitutional provisions: freedom of speech and freedom of association under the First Amendment, and equal protection of the laws under the Fourteenth Amendment. The decision of the Supreme Court is permeated with criticism of the district court's approach; the Court ruled that the lower court did not give "appropriate deference to the decision of prison administrators." Although the Court noted that constitutional rights can be claimed by prisoners, it emphasized that the needs of prisons "impose limitations on constitutional rights," even those found in the First Amendment. The Supreme Court said that courts must recognize the "wide-ranging deference to be accorded the decisions of prison administrators." The district court had given particular emphasis to the fact that North Carolina had permitted inmates to be members of the union, so it would perforce have to allow solicitation of membership. As to bulk mailings of union literature and meetings of inmate union members, the district court relied on the equal protection clause. The court held that because prison officials allowed other groups such as the Jaycees, Alcoholics Anonymous, and the Boy Scouts, to have meetings and receive literature; they could not "pick and choose" to try to limit union activities simply because they disliked the message of a group or its purposes.

The Supreme Court, however, found North Carolina's approach to be reasonable. The state had permitted membership in the union because it assumed that each prisoner was allowed to believe whatever they chose to believe. Officials had concluded that concerted group activity by the union, or the solicitation of membership, would pose problems and frictions in the operation of the state's prisons. The Supreme Court said that "[t]he ban on inmate solicitation and group meetings, therefore, was rationally related to the reasonable, indeed to the central, objectives of prison administration."

As to speech rights, the Court held that those rights were "barely implicated in this case." The only mail question was that of bulk mailings, and the advantage of those would be cost savings. Those savings did not fundamentally affect free speech values, because there were other channels of information available to the union. Nor did the ban on the solicitation of membership improperly impair free speech rights. Solicitation is more than a simple expression of ideas; in this case it could be an invitation to engage in a prohibited activity. (A North Carolina statute separately made illegal any collective bargaining for inmates with respect to pay, work hours, or other conditions of their incarceration). It was not only reasonable but necessary for the prison officials to control union activities, and that was permissible under the First Amendment free speech clause.

The Supreme Court said that association rights might have been more implicated in this case than speech rights. However, association rights are "necessarily curtailed by the realities of confinement." Further, the Court held:

> **They [association rights] may be curtailed whenever the institution's officials, in the exercise of their informed discretion, reasonably conclude that such associations, whether through group meetings or otherwise, possess the likelihood of disruption to prison order or stability, or otherwise interfere with the legitimate penological objectives of the prison environment.**

The Court recognized that preserving order in the prison is a paramount concern. The district court had rejected prison officials' concerns, because that court said those concerns were speculative rather than concrete. The Supreme Court rejected this approach taken by the district court:

> **Prison life, and relations between the inmates themselves and between the inmates and prison officials or staff, contain the ever-present potential for violent confrontation and conflagration. Responsible prison officials must be permitted to take reasonable steps to forestall such a threat, and they must be permitted to act before the time when they can compile a dossier on the eve of a riot.**

The Supreme Court also rejected the equal protection analysis of the district court. Conceding that other organizations had been allowed to operate more freely than the union, the Court found this justified. Officials had demonstrated a rational basis for distinguishing different kinds of prison organizations. Alcoholics Anonymous and Jaycees were allowed to operate in many prisons because they were seen as serving rehabilitative purposes, and they work "in harmony with the goals and desires of the prison administrators." The union, of course, differed greatly and critically from those other organizations because its stated intent was to pursue an adversarial relationship with authorities. The Supreme Court pointed out that a prison is not a public forum and does not require the protections that have been given to such fora in other cases. When it comes to different groups within prisons, the Court required discretion to be honored:

> **[T]he courts should allow the prison administrators the full latitude of discretion, unless it can be firmly stated that the two groups [those permitted and those disallowed] are so similar that discretion has been abused. That is surely not the case here. There is nothing in the Constitution which requires prison officials to treat all inmate groups alike.**

▶ Inmates and the News Media: *Pell v. Procunier;*
Saxbe v. Washington Post

In a case involving visitation (the language of which was cited in the *Jones* case), inmates in California sought to have a state regulation declared unconstitutional. The regulation prohibited face-to-face interviews between individual inmates and any representatives of the news media. The media joined the case, arguing that the freedom of the press, which is guaranteed in the First Amendment, had also been violated by the state action. A three-judge district court found that the state policy unconstitutionally infringed on the inmates' rights under the First and Fourteenth Amendments. Because the press could enter institutions to observe conditions and to interview inmates randomly, and because the inmates were given interview rights under its ruling, the district court did not award any additional protections to the media. A direct appeal was taken to the Supreme Court.

In *Pell v. Procunier*, 417 U.S. 817 (1974), and in another case that decided the same question on the same day, *Saxbe v. Washington Post*, the Supreme Court decided the issue of entitlement to media interviews by looking at the two sets of interests presented by the two types of parties involved in this litigation.

First, as to the inmates who wanted to have individual interviews, the state regulation clearly restricted one kind of communication under the First Amendment. The Court concluded that this restriction was permissible. It was noted that inmates had other means of communication available—they could send and receive mail—and this was permitted with members of the news media, as well as with family and friends. They were also allowed to have visits—not with the news media but with family, friends, attorneys, and clergy. A major concern in these cases always had been that there might be terrible treatment of an inmate or that unconstitutional conditions inside a prison would be exposed, which could be sealed off from outside knowledge by the prison restrictions. These alternative methods of communication by mail and visits, whereby inmates could communicate their complaints and grievances, ensured that the authorities did not erect an absolute barrier to knowledge about prison conditions.

> [T]he institutional objectives furthered by that regulation [banning face-to-face media interviews] and the measure of judicial deference owed to corrections officials in their attempt to serve those interests are relevant in gauging the validity of the regulation. Accordingly, in light of the alternative channels of communication that are open to prison inmates, we cannot say on the record in this case that this restriction on one manner in which prisoners can communicate with persons outside of prison is unconstitutional.

Second, the media representatives argued that the limitation on press interviews violated their rights under the First Amendment guarantee of freedom of the press which is applicable to the states by the Fourteenth Amendment. The Supreme Court understood that California authorities were not trying to conceal conditions inside prisons because the press and members of the public were allowed to visit and take tours of prison facilities. During tours, journalists could stop and speak to any inmates they encountered and could discuss with them any subject. The sole limitation was the ban on interviews with specifically requested individual inmates. This restriction was adopted in 1971 in response to a violent episode that authorities felt was at least partly attributable to face-to-face interviews. When they were permitted, it was found that the press concentrated on a few inmates, who as a result became "public figures" and gained notoriety and influence among their fellow inmates.

In the companion case, *Saxbe v. Washington Post*, 417 U.S. 843 (1974), the Federal Bureau of Prisons justified a similar ban on individual interviews on a similar theory, called the "big wheel" theory. Knowledge gained through the operation of prisons had taught administrators that a few inmates, already or potentially notorious, were spotlighted by the press attention and through "their repeated contacts with the press tend to become the source of substantial disciplinary problems that can engulf a large portion of the population at a prison." It is noteworthy that the holding stated in *Pell* and followed in *Saxbe* was a strictly legal one.

> [T]he First Amendment does not guarantee the press a constitutional right of special access to information not available to the public generally … Newsmen have no constitutional right of access to the scenes of crime or disaster when the general public is excluded. Similarly, newsmen have no constitutional right of access to prisons or their inmates beyond that afforded the general public.

Applying this constitutional standard to the Federal Bureau of Prisons regulation, the Court held that because members of the news media were given access to information available to the general public (and the public did not have a right to individual interviews with selected inmates), there was no violation of the First Amendment.

The Supreme Court holdings in *Pell* and *Saxbe* are especially significant for the support they give to prison security and good order against strong First Amendment claims. One underlying principle in the orderly running of prisons is that inmates should be treated the same, whenever possible. (In this sense, prison is or should be a great equalizer.)

According to this theory, if an inmate is given special attention in the media or has their writings published in newspapers or magazines, that special attention brings notoriety within the prison. This can lead to hostility toward someone who has gained special status or who is seen as having brought negative attention to the facility or a tightening of conditions as the result of publicity. Pressures may be placed on the inmate to tell the stories or complaints of other inmates in order to avoid negative reactions if they do not. Staff members at the prison may also treat the inmate differently; there is especially a concern that staff will be reluctant to deal with the "big wheel" inmate as strictly in accord with policy as they do with others. This fear of notoriety or exposure of staff in the media has been called a "chilling effect," when such an inmate gets special media attention.

Application of the "big wheel theory" has not been consistent since. In *Jordan v. Pugh*, 504 F.Supp. 2d 1109, (D. CO 2007), an inmate housed in the Administrative Maximum Unit, Florence, Colorado, challenged the Federal Bureau of Prisons (BOP) rule prohibiting an inmate from being published under a byline, alleging that the rule was an unconstitutional violation of the First Amendment. The prohibition was based on the "big wheel" theory. In its opinion, the district court said: "[a]t trial, the BOP presented no evidence of any instance where an inmate who published under a byline in the news media became a 'big wheel,' or more importantly, became a security risk. "The court held that the "existence of a 'big wheel' security risk arising from an inmate's bylined publication in the news media is undocumented and speculative." Using both the two-part *Martinez* test (whether the restriction furthers an important or substantial governmental interest unrelated to the suppression of expression and is no broader than necessary to protect the particular governmental interest) and the four-part *Turner v. Safley* test (rational connection between the regulation and a legitimate, neutral penological objective; whether alternative means exist; impact of the accommodation; and whether there were alternatives that could be applied at a de minimis cost), the court found the regulation violated the First Amendment rights of prisoners. (Note: The Bureau of Prisons current rule (Title 28, Code of Federal Regulations, Section 540.20) has removed language prohibiting an inmate from publishing under a byline.)

▶ *Houchins v. KQED, Inc.; Garrett v. Estelle; Hammer v. Ashcroft; Smith v. Coughlin*

In *Houchins v. KQED, Inc.*, 438 U.S. 1 (1978), the Supreme Court reviewed a legal challenge by a television station when a county sheriff refused to allow journalists to visit and photograph a portion of the county jail where a prisoner had committed suicide and conditions were allegedly very bad. The Court reaffirmed the principle of *Pell* and *Saxbe*, saying that the First Amendment does not require the sheriff to give the media access to government information, and the media did not have the right of special access to the county jail that was any greater than that given to the general public.

Another offshoot of *Pell v. Procunier*, involving a question of narrow application but of some interest, was *Garrett v. Estelle*, 556 F.2d 1274 (5th Cir. 1977). The issue was whether the media had the right to film and televise executions. Garrett, a news reporter, asked prison officials for permission to film the first execution to take place in Texas under its new **capital punishment** statute. The request was denied, pursuant to a Texas statute that prohibited press access to death row inmates and at executions. (Texas did revise its position during the litigation to allow press pool representatives at the execution, but filming was disallowed.) The Court of Appeals for the Fifth Circuit (the Supreme Court has not decided this question) ruled that the First Amendment does not require the news media to have access to matters that are not accessible to the public generally, citing *Pell*. The state contended that televising an execution would amount to reinstating public executions, which had been discontinued in Texas in 1920. (The Supreme Court, much earlier, in *Holden v. Minnesota*, 137 U.S. 483 (1890), had upheld the right of a state to restrict attendance at executions, rather than make them public.) The court upheld the right of Texas to continue a policy that barred the media access to film executions. In *Entertainment Network, Inc. v. Lappin*, 134 F. Supp. 2d 1002 (S.D. 2001), an Internet content provider sued, seeking to do a live Internet broadcast of the execution of Timothy McVeigh (the Oklahoma City bomber who had bombed the Murrah Federal Building in Oklahoma City killing 168 people. The district court reaffirmed the position that the press has no constitutional right of access to prisons or prison inmates beyond that given to the general public.

An issue arose when prison officials modified a policy to no longer allow face-to-face media interviews with death row inmates. In *Hammer v. Ashcroft*, 570 F.3d 798 (7th Cir. 2009)(en banc), cert denied 559 U.S. (2010), a prisoner on death row in a federal institution sued various prison officials, alleging this prohibition violated his rights under the First Amendment and the equal protection component of the due process clause of the Fifth Amendment.

When the federal government established the federal death row unit in the 1990s, interviews were allowed for the first nine months. Shortly after the broadcast of a television interview with a death row prisoner, the policy was reevaluated, and a decision was made to prohibit all death row offenders from this type of media communication.

The Seventh Circuit Court of Appeals, in an en banc decision, rejected the inmate's claim that allowing prison officials' discretion to permit face-to-face interviews in situations other than death row, while having a blanket prohibition for death row, violated the equal protection clause. The court, noting that the "Special Confinement Unit" was one of the most secure areas of the federal prison system, held that the Constitution is not offended by applying greater restrictions to maximum security prisoners than those requiring less security.

The court also considered arguments made by correctional administrators and accepted as legitimate by the Supreme Court in *Pell v. Procunier* and *Saxbe v. Washington Post*, that media interviews with prisoners can turn those interviewed into celebrities within the prison. Relying on the principle established in *Saxbe v. Washington Post*, that prisoners who are interviewed may "tend to become the source of substantial disciplinary problems that can engulf a large portion of the population at a prison," the court held that the regulation satisfied the "reasonably related to legitimate security interests" standard set forth in *Turner v. Safley*, 482 U.S. 78 (1987).

The prisoner's last contention, that the restriction was motivated by a desire to silence prisoners who might criticize prison officials or prison conditions, was also rejected. This appellate court found that the challenged rule was objectively reasonable and thus was permissible under *Turner* standards. The court also noted that prisoners on death row retained other means of communicating with the outside world about prison conditions, including correspondence with the media and the filing of lawsuits.

Limits placed by the state on other kinds of associational rights have also been upheld. For example, in *Smith v. Coughlin*, 748 F.2d 783 (1984), the Second Circuit Court of Appeals upheld New York's restriction on visits to death row inmates, which limited visiting to family members only and did not allow visits with friends and acquaintances.

▶ Inmate Visits

The rights of inmates to have special visits, for example, those with the news media, have been explained previously. Another example is with attorneys and/or their representatives. In addition to special visits, all prisons and jails have some provision for visitation. In more secure institutions, visiting may have restrictions regarding both the persons permitted to visit and the frequency of visits.

A facility (prison or jail) will typically advise new arrivals during the orientation process about the visitation and correspondence rules. As with mail, a prisoner will be asked to list those family members and close friends with whom they would like to receive visits from. (This same process may also apply to telephone calls in facilities where telephone contact is permitted but limited to a certain list of persons, limited in frequency, and limited in length of calls.) If an inmate has an additional person, such as a member of the clergy, with whom they would like to visit, the inmate may request that person's name be placed on the approved list. The list is reviewed to see if there are any visitors that may pose a threat to institution security or good order. The backgrounds of some visitors may be investigated, especially in high-security facilities or those with highly notorious inmates. These may include checks for criminal records or general background checks (with the police or probation officers) in the inmate's or requested visitor's community.

Visits in prisons and jails are of two kinds: contact and noncontact. In a contact visit, the inmate and their visitor are seated, perhaps at a table or in facing chairs, in a visiting area where physical contact is possible.

During such visits, the visitors are allowed to obtain food and beverages from a vending machine, use the restroom or get a drink of water. These visits are supervised by a visiting room officer, who is typically seated to observe activities anywhere in the room, and perhaps also by camera monitors. Noncontact visits are those where the inmate and the visitor are unable to have physical contact. They may be seated facing each other with a glass partition separating them. Conversation is allowed by a grill opening in the glass or a telephone used on each side. Noncontact visits are common in detention facilities (see **FIGURE 8-1**). On the other hand, contact visitation is the norm in most prisons. In some prisons and jails, visiting is further "normalized" by allowing children to play in the visiting room or an adjoining play area. Other prisons and jails do not allow small children to visit. Some facilities, especially in warmer climates, allow visiting outdoors; this is usually limited to low-security institutions.

A major concern for correctional administrators is the risk of contraband being introduced during a contact visit. Noncontact visitation tends to minimize the opportunity for a visitor to leave contraband at the institution. Correctional administrators understand that visitation can reduce the stress of incarceration and separation from family on inmates. A visit with a loved one is a way to relieve stress and to encourage a more tranquil adjustment by most inmates. While disturbances can occur in correctional facility visiting rooms, on balance most correctional administrators view visitation as a useful management tool.

Nevertheless, contraband does get passed, by any means the ingenuity of the inmate and their visitor can devise. It may be passed from mouth to mouth during a kiss when first meeting for the visit. It may be passed from hand to hand. Contraband also may be hidden somewhere in the visiting area (such as in a wastebasket, on the underside of a chair, in a vending machine, or in a restroom) to be retrieved by the inmate (or his inmate friend) at a later time.

Besides surveillance of the visiting area—by staff on the scene and perhaps by camera monitors—other security steps must be taken. The visitor is warned of the consequences of introducing contraband and may be required to check any belongings (such as a duffel bag, fanny pack, or purse) at the front entrance. The visitor will often be required to pass through a metal detector on the way to the visiting area. The inmate is searched before the visit and may be strip-searched after the visit. The inmate's clothing is also thoroughly searched before they are allowed back inside the facility. Areas where visitors have access (such as the restroom, under chairs, and in waste containers) are carefully searched after the visiting period. Small children have been used to carry contraband (such as drugs, money, and ammunition) into the prison in their diapers or candy containers.

FIGURE 8-1 A man visiting a woman in prison. This is an example of a noncontact visit.

Modern technology has generated several innovations which have altered the operations of correctional facilities. One of these innovations has been the development of equipment and procedures for video visitation. People who are familiar with Skype or the video chat programs on their smart phones are aware of the capabilities of allowing communications to be both visual and aural. Video visitation may be considered an improvement over regular telephone communication. The process allows persons to maintain visual contact with a friend or family member who is incarcerated without traveling to distant locations, allows correctional facilities to avoid labor-intensive posts in visiting room, and eliminates one source of contraband from coming into the facility. It is estimated that approximately 600 correctional facilities have implemented video visitation for inmates. However, like most technology, the innovation has its drawbacks and detractors.[1] Operational procedures vary among the facilities and states which use the process, and there are several private vendors who provide services. Some states have video visiting terminals in or near correctional facilities with inmates accessing the communication through a kiosk or other device within the correctional institution.[2] Other states have systems that allow persons who are on the inmate's approved visitor list to access video visiting from any location with a computer that has a camera.[3] Some states have implemented programs that authorize inmates to possess specially designed tablets (generally with clear plastic bodies to permit visual inspection and which are linked only to the contract system).[4] Many jails have adopted video visiting either in addition to in-person visitation or as a replacement where in-person social visits are prohibited.[5]

Rules establishing video social visitation generally provide that video visitation is a privilege, not a right, and warn both the inmate user and the visitor that communication is being recorded and is subject to monitoring. The Washington DOC has established specific rules relating to social video visits advising inmates and visitors of unacceptable behavior, such as:

Conduct

The following is prohibited during video visits:

- Any display of nudity
- Behavior or actions that are sexual in nature
- Use or display of any weapons, drugs/alcohol, or related paraphernalia
- Activity or display of graphics/paraphernalia associated with any Security Threat Group
- Unlawful activity or depiction of unlawful activity
- Incarcerated individuals who violate visit rules will be subject to disciplinary action per DOC 460.000 Disciplinary Process for Prisons.
- A visitor who engages in prohibited conduct may be suspended or terminated from video visiting privileges. Regular visiting privileges may also be suspended/terminated.

Any display of nudity; Behavior or actions that are sexual in nature; Use or display of any weapons, drugs/alcohol, or related paraphernalia; Activity or display of graphics/paraphernalia associated with any Security Threat Group; Unlawful activity or depiction of unlawful activity and sanctions for violating the visiting rules.[6]

▶ *Block v. Rutherford*

The leading case on inmate visiting, *Block v. Rutherford*, 468 U.S. 576 (1984), arose from the Los Angeles County Jail. The sheriff had a policy that allowed only noncontact visits by pretrial detainees with their spouses, relatives, and friends. A group of detainees brought a class action suit under 42 U.S.C. Section 1983, challenging that policy. The district court found that denying inmates the right to embrace their spouses or children (which they are not allowed to do in noncontact visiting) during the weeks or months they were awaiting trial was an impermissible burden. That court (and the court of appeals in affirming) found that the loss of some contacts during visitation was punitive and an exaggerated response to security concerns of jail officials. The Supreme Court reversed the lower courts' actions.

Because the case involved pretrial detainees and not prison inmates, the courts used the standard set out in *Bell v. Wolfish*, 441 U.S. 520 (1979). From *Bell*, the standard set by the Supreme Court is whether the challenged practice or condition amounts to punishment of the inmate: "A court must decide whether the disability is imposed for the purpose of punishment or whether it is but an incident of some other legitimate governmental purpose."

(In practical and legal effect, the same outcome can be expected in prison cases, because both jails and prisons use the same process to detect unconstitutionality. They must determine whether there is a legitimate government interest, usually related to security, that justifies the restriction on otherwise permissible and even constitutionally protected activity.) The Supreme Court in *Block* said:

> **The question before us, therefore, is narrow: whether the prohibition of contact visits is reasonably related to legitimate governmental objectives.**

The Court determined there was "a valid, rational connection between a ban on contact visits and internal security of a detention facility." Even the lower courts acknowledged that contact visits open an institution to the introduction of drugs, weapons, and other contraband. Visitors could conceal contraband items and transfer them during the close contact that is permitted in contact visiting. The fact that unconvicted, pretrial detainees rather than convicted prisoners were involved did not persuade the Supreme Court (although this was a factor that influenced the decisions of lower courts on this and many other pretrial issues). As in *Bell*, the Court concluded that there was no reason to conclude "that pretrial detainees pose any lesser security risk than convicted inmates." Although the Court conceded that visits from family and friends are important to inmates, it drew the following conclusion:

> **[T]he Constitution does not require that detainees be allowed contact visits when responsible, experienced administrators have determined, in their sound discretion, that such visits will jeopardize the security of the facility.**

What the Supreme Court did not decide was whether inmates have the right under the Constitution to have visits in the first place. Stated another way, could visits be banned altogether?

▶ *Kentucky Department of Corrections v. Thompson*

In *Kentucky Department of Corrections v. Thompson*, 490 U.S. 454 (1989), Kentucky officials had adopted a policy that excluded certain prison visitors. This policy covered such persons as those under the influence of alcohol or drugs, those with a record of disruptive conduct, those who were directly related to the inmate's criminal conduct, and those whose presence would constitute a clear and present danger to an institution's security. The Kentucky State Reformatory at LaGrange adopted even more restrictive grounds for excluding visitors, including former "residents" (inmates) at the facility and former employees. Inmates at the Reformatory and inmates at the State Penitentiary at Eddyville brought a class action suit under Section 1983, challenging the enforcement of these visiting regulations.

Some visitors were barred from visiting for violations of some part of the visiting rules. These suspension "orders" were entered without a hearing. The constitutional challenge centered on whether it was a violation of due process of law to terminate or suspend visiting privileges without a hearing. The lower courts in *Thompson* had ruled that there was a protected constitutional interest for prisoners to receive visits. This constitutional right required the prison officials to adopt some procedures whereby a prisoner would receive notice of, and the reasons for, any action to exclude a visitor, as well as an opportunity to respond. These procedures were called "minimum due process procedures." The Supreme Court reversed the lower courts' rulings.

In summary, the Court ruled that due process procedures are only necessary when a liberty interest is at stake. Constitutionally protected liberty interests come from two places: the due process clause itself (in the Constitution) or in the laws of the state. In this case, the suspension of visiting privileges was not guaranteed by the due process clause. It was not inherent in the Constitution itself. In several cases, the Court had rejected the idea that any changes in conditions of confinement that adversely affected inmates were sufficient to invoke due process, merely because of that adverse impact.

Whether state law had created enforceable liberty interests is a more difficult question to address, and it is made even more difficult by a 1995 Supreme Court decision in the inmate discipline case of *Sandin v. Conner*, 515 U.S. 472 (1995). According to the Court in *Thompson*, the answer depended on whether the state had adopted "substantive predicates" to guide or limit its discretion in decision making. Another analysis depended upon whether the state's regulations had "explicitly mandatory language," which required a certain outcome. If the regulation said that when certain conditions or predicates were present, a particular outcome had to follow, then the state had created a liberty interest. In the case of such mandatory conditions or predicates, the state would have created the expectation on the part of persons (including prisoners) that certain facts, conditions, or actions would lead to a certain result. The *Sandin* case has overruled the *Thompson's* Court's analysis which ruled that a constitutionally protected liberty interest could be created "outside the Constitution" by the state's statutory or regulation language. *Sandin* was an inmate discipline case, but the decision has raised serious doubt regarding the use of the *Thompson* analysis and standard in any prison cases.

The Court in *Thompson* concluded that the Kentucky regulations did not have the "requisite mandatory language." The regulations did not require a particular result to follow when certain conditions were met. The policy issuance started with the phrase, "Administrative staff reserves the right to allow or disallow visits." Visitors might be excluded if they fell into one of the listed categories, but they did not have to be excluded. Therefore, the regulations were saved from creating a liberty interest, which would have been protected by the due process clause. The Supreme Court ruled that Kentucky was not required to hold a hearing in order to terminate visiting privileges.

The Supreme Court did not expressly decide whether there is a constitutional right to visiting. Justice Anthony Kennedy, in a concurring opinion, raised a concern that the Kentucky case involved only a denial of visiting to certain visitors and not a ban on all prison visitations. He expressly cautioned that a ban on all visiting would have raised a different question, not yet decided, about whether a total ban is unconstitutional. The majority opinion ruled that if there were sound security reasons, a ban would probably be constitutional. For the stability and safe running of the institution, virtually all prison administrators concede the value of allowing inmate visitation. Therefore, the conditions for having a challenge in court on a total ban are not likely to occur. What occurs in practice is that all visits are suspended during an institutional emergency, such as the aftermath of a riot or massive disruption. That is a temporary situation and if challenged, would likely be supported by the courts as a necessary reaction to the emergency, as legitimate but temporary security concerns of the administration.

▶ *Overton v. Bazzetta*

In the early 1990s, the population of Michigan prisons increased, leading to an increase in prison visitation, which strained the resources available for prison supervision and control. Prison officials found it more difficult to maintain order during visiting and prevent smuggling or drug trafficking. Substance abuse also increased. In response to these concerns about prison security, in 1995, the Michigan Department of Corrections revised its visitation policies. Under its new regulations, visitors had to be named on an approved visitor list. The policy permitted visits by clergy and attorneys without being listed. The list contained a number of restrictions: Minors under 18 years of age could not be placed on the visiting list unless they were the children, stepchildren, grandchildren, or siblings of the inmate. If an inmate's parental rights had been terminated, the child could not visit. A child who was approved to visit had to be accompanied by an adult who was an immediate family member of either the child or the inmate or was the child's legal guardian. A former inmate could not visit unless they were a member of the inmate's immediate family and had the warden's prior approval. Inmates who committed multiple substance abuse violations were not allowed to receive any visitors, other than attorneys and members of the clergy. An inmate with the no-visitor restriction could request reinstatement of his visiting privileges after two years. The decision on the reinstatement rested with the warden.

Inmates, their friends, and their family members filed a Section 1983 action, alleging that the visiting restrictions violated the First, Eighth, and Fourteenth Amendments. The case, *Overton v. Bazzetta*, 539 U.S. 126 (2003), was certified as a class action. The focus of the litigation was on noncontact visits.

Both the district court and the appeals court ruled that the restrictions on noncontact visits were invalid. The Supreme Court disagreed. In considering whether the regulations infringed on a constitutional right of association, the Court concluded:

> **The very object of imprisonment is confinement. Many of the liberties and privileges enjoyed by other citizens must be surrendered by the prisoner. An inmate does not retain rights inconsistent with proper incarceration ... And, as our cases have established, freedom of association is among the rights least compatible with incarceration.**
>
> **We need not attempt to explore or define the asserted right of association at any length or determine the extent to which it survives incarceration because the challenged regulations bear a rational relation to legitimate penological interests.**

Holding the challenged regulations to be rationally related to a legitimate penological objective (the *Turner v. Safley* standard), the Court held it was not necessary to consider the extent to which the right of association survives incarceration. The Court noted that it accords substantial deference to the professional judgment of prison administrators, as these are the persons who define the goals of a corrections system and determine the most appropriate means to accomplish those goals.

> **The burden, moreover, is not on the State to prove the validity of prison regulations but on the prisoner to disprove it.**
>
> ***Turner* does not impose a least-restrictive-alternative test, but asks instead whether the prisoner has pointed to some obvious regulatory alternative that fully accommodates the asserted right while not imposing more than a *de minimis* cost to the valid penological goal.**

In the last part of its opinion, the Court held that the visiting restriction for inmates with two substance-abuse violations was not cruel and unusual punishment in violation of the Eighth Amendment. The withdrawal of visitation privileges for these inmates for a limited period was viewed as a regular means of affecting prison discipline. The Court further concluded that the regulation did not present any of the other concerns raised by the Eighth Amendment: it did not create inhumane prison conditions; deprive inmates of basic necessities or fail to protect their health or safety; involve the infliction of pain or injury; or amount to deliberate indifference to the basic needs of the inmates.

▶ Conjugal Visits

California[7], Connecticut, New York[8] and Washington[9] allow private family visits which could generally be described as **conjugal visits**, during which an inmate and their spouse (or, in some places, unmarried partner) are allowed some degree of privacy, during which they can engage in acts of sexual intimacy. The Supreme Court has not ruled on any request to permit such visiting as a matter of constitutional entitlement.

A case that may be somewhat suspect because of its age, but which is still one of the few reported cases ruling on the right to conjugal visitation, is *Payne v. District of Columbia*, 253 F.2d 867 (DC Cir. 1958). In *Payne*, a court in the District of Columbia rejected a claim by an inmate's wife that she was legally entitled to conjugal visits with her inmate husband.

In *Lyons v. Gilligan*, 382 F.Supp. 198 (N.D. OH, 1974), inmates of the Marion, Ohio, Correctional Institution and their wives brought a Section 1983 action to require conjugal visiting, claiming that they were denied constitutional rights of privacy (intimate familial, associational rights), and that they were thereby being cruelly and unusually punished. As to punishment, the court concluded that the absence of conjugal visitation was not excessive punishment but only a customary concomitant of incarceration. When and if additional states should adopt family visiting, there might be an "evolving standard of decency," which would require courts to address whether the denial of conjugal visits is a constitutional violation. But with the current standards of visiting, there was no constitutional right found by this court.

Perhaps a more intriguing argument is that raised by the claim in the *Lyons* case that authorities were denying inmates and their wives access to bedroom activities, which constituted an unwarranted invasion of their privacy. The federal court rejected that argument, saying that the cases that had recognized a privacy right in the First Amendment were distinguishable:

> **[T]he right of privacy on which plaintiffs rely is bottomed on the need to ensure private citizens that the police will not intrude upon their most intimate affairs. It does not follow, however, that because the state cannot pass criminal laws the enforcement of which will require such intrusion, the state is obligated by the Constitution to create private places for the conduct of marital relations… [I]mprisonment of persons convicted of crimes is not tantamount to an intrusion into the prisoner's home.**

The court concluded that there was no constitutional violation when authorities failed to provide for conjugal visits, thereby preventing acts of sexual intimacy between prisoners and their wives during their visits.

A similar outcome was attained in *Hernandez v. Coughlin*, 18 F.3d 133 (2nd Cir. 1994) when inmate Hernandez sued prison officials who had denied his request for a conjugal visit under state regulations. The inmate claimed the denial deprived him of his right to "marital privacy," a protected liberty interest, and subjected him to cruel and unusual punishment. The district court dismissed the action and the inmate appealed. The Second Circuit affirmed the dismissal holding that the Constitution creates no protection for marital privacy in prisons: *"though the right to marriage is constitutionally protected for inmates, the right to marital privacy and conjugal visits while incarcerated is not."* The right to marital privacy, like other rights of association, is necessarily abridged as a result of incarceration.

Could an inmate's religious beliefs require them to engage in sexual intercourse as part of a sincerely held religious belief? In two unreported cases decided by federal district courts, the inmate was denied a conjugal visit. *In Washington v. Cate, No. 1:11-cv-00264 GSA PC, 2014 U.S. Dist. LEXIS 12402, at *4-5 (E.D. Cal. Jan. 31, 2014)*[10] a California inmate serving a life sentence alleged Title 15 of the California Code of Regulations, section 3177(b)(2), which prohibits conjugal visits for inmates serving a life sentence, violated his rights under the First Amendment and the Religious Land Use and Institutionalized Persons Act (RLUIPA). The rule excludes from participation offenders convicted of violent offenses against a minor or family members, and for inmates with certain classifications, such as having a death sentence, being designated in "close custody," and other California state classification categories. The district court dismissed the suit for failure to state a claim, concluding that California's general denial of conjugal visits to inmates serving life sentences was not a violation of the First Amendment. The RLUIPA claim failed because denying conjugal visits to certain classes of prisoners such as those serving life sentences was the least-restrictive means of furthering a compelling governmental interest.

Recently, in the case of *Pleasant-Bey v. Tennessee*, (M.D. TN. Case No. 3-19-cv-00486 memorandum dated February 12, 2020) a federal district court in Tennessee conducted a PLRA screening review in an inmate's action in which he alleged the denial of conjugal visitation rights with his wife violated his First Amendment rights and under RLUIPA, because his sincerely held religious beliefs were substantially burdened. The district court dismissed the inmate's claim of an alleged violation of his First Amendment rights, but since the Supreme Court has not addressed the relationship, if any, between RLUIPA and conjugal visits, the suit was allowed to proceed. The court did note that California federal district courts had routinely dismissed inmate claims for conjugal visitation and declined to follow them.

A conjugal visitation program in New York State gained court approval in *Matter of Mary of Oakknoll v. Coughlin*, 475 N.Y.S.2d 644 (NY App. Div. 1984). Some inmates complained that the program was limited to those inmates (and their spouses) who could show a valid marriage certificate to verify their marital status. The court upheld the program and its restrictions. That court noted that there was no constitutional right to conjugal visitation. Prison officials had the authority, the court said, to authorize visiting programs. Conjugal visiting was, in effect, just one type of visiting. The standards for visiting of any type were for the officials to determine, based on their corrections experience and judgment. Later, another federal court confirmed that the commissioner of corrections in New York had the discretion to determine what the prison visitation program should be and which inmates would be able to participate in the conjugal visitation program. *Cromwell v. Coughlin*, 773 F.Supp. 606 (S.D. NY 1991).

An example of a current state DOC program for extended visitation is the state of Washington Extended Family Visiting Program:

I. [590.100] The Department has established an Extended Family Visit (EFV) Program in Prisons for eligible offenders to support building sustainable relationships important to offender reentry and to provide an incentive for those serving long-term sentences to engage in positive behavioral choices.
II. This program facilitates visits between an offender and his/her immediate family in a private visiting unit. Immediate family consists of the offender's birth children, stepchildren, grandchildren, great-grandchildren, birthparents or pre-incarceration adoptive parents, stepparents, grandparents, great-grandparents, siblings, and spouse/state registered domestic partner.

▶ Artificial Insemination

There is a fundamental right to procreation, as determined by the Supreme Court in *Skinner v. Oklahoma*, 316 U.S. 535 (1942). One of the six states (California) that allows conjugal visits refused an inmate's request to artificially inseminate his wife.

In *Gerber v. Hickman*, 291 F.3d 617 (9th Cir. 2002), Gerber, a 41-year-old man serving a sentence of 100 years to life plus 11 years, asked to receive a plastic collection container along with a prepaid return mailer from a laboratory; he wanted to be allowed to ejaculate into the container and to have the filled container returned to a laboratory in the prepaid mailer by overnight mail or have it picked up by his counsel. The inmate said he would pay all costs for this procedure.

The inmate sued when his request was denied. The district court in California dismissed the suit for failure to state a claim, ruling that an inmate does not have a constitutional right to procreate and that such a right is "fundamentally inconsistent with incarceration." The Court of Appeals for the Ninth Circuit affirmed:

> **[T]he Supreme Court in *Turner* recognized that an inmate's right to marry while in prison did not include the inmate's right to consummate the marriage while in prison or to enjoy the other tangible aspects of marital intimacy … [T]he Court clearly stated that the right to marry "is subject to substantial restrictions as a result of incarceration," and that inmate marriages are formed "in the *expectation* that they *ultimately* will be fully consummated." … The Court plainly envisioned that while the intangible and emotional aspects of marriage survive incarceration, the physical aspects do not.**

The Ninth Circuit's decision, however, was not unanimous. A dissenter said there was nothing in the record to show that the right to have a child is fundamentally inconsistent with incarceration; he would have remanded the case for further proceedings to determine whether legitimate penological objectives justified the restriction. A second dissenter suggested that, by allowing conjugal visiting, the state did not intend to deprive an inmate of the right to procreate. This dissenter believed that this decision suggested that the state's denial was nothing more than "the ad hoc decision of prison authorities."

An earlier Missouri case, *Goodwin v. Turner*, 908 F.2d 1395 (8th Cir. 1990), offered at least a partial response to the "ad hoc" reference in the *Gerber* dissent. In *Goodwin*, a male inmate sought habeas corpus relief after denial by the Federal Bureau of Prisons of his request that he be allowed to artificially inseminate his wife. In denying the request, the Court of Appeals for the Eighth Circuit, applying *Turner v. Safley*, said the prison regulation met the reasonable relationship standard:

> [I]f the Bureau [of Prisons] were forced to allow male prisoners to procreate, whatever the means, it would have to confer a corresponding benefit on its female prisoners. The significant expansion of medical services to the female population and the additional financial burden of added infant care would have a significant impact on the allocation of prison resources generally and would further undercut the Bureau's limited resources for necessary and important prison programs and security.

Summary

- The Supreme Court has recognized that the associational rights that persons have in the "free world" may be limited by prison officials' concerns about prison order and stability (*Jones v. North Carolina Prisoners' Labor Union*). The fact that other organizations, such as the Boy Scouts and Alcoholics Anonymous, were allowed to organize and meet in prisons did not mean that a labor union was constitutionally entitled to organize and meet under equal protection analysis. The Court held that the prison authorities had reasonable grounds for distinguishing between the groups and were not required to treat all groups alike.
- Prison regulations that banned interviews by the news media of individual inmates were upheld by the Supreme Court. Under the freedom of press guarantee of the First Amendment, members of the news media have no more right of access to prisons than the general public (*Pell v. Procunier; Saxbe v. Washington Post*). Extending the ruling about limited access by the media to prisons and jails, a federal appeals court upheld a Texas rule that excluded news media from filming executions (*Garrett v. Estelle*). Prison officials may create a blanket exclusion of face-to-face media interviews for death row inmates, while permitting such interviews with offenders in other prisons (*Hammer v. Ashcroft*).
- Visiting in prisons and jails is a valued activity. There are two kinds of visits: contact and noncontact. In noncontact visits, a physical barrier (usually glass) remains between the inmate and his visitor; in contact visits, there is no such barrier, and inmates and their visitors are seated in ordinary chairs and are permitted to have some degree of physical contact.
- The Supreme Court upheld a policy at the Los Angeles County Jail that allowed only noncontact visiting by detainees with their family and friends who visited. The Court said that there is no constitutional

requirement for contact visits and that jail administrators have adequate reasons to limit visits (*Block v. Rutherford*).

- In another visiting case, the Supreme Court ruled that prison officials were not required to provide a hearing before terminating the visiting privileges of persons who were deemed to pose a threat to institutional security or to the orderly conduct of the visiting room (*Kentucky Department of Corrections v. Thompson*). The holding of that case is probably still valid, although the reasoning the Court used is cast in doubt by a 1995 Supreme Court decision in *Sandin v. Conner*.

- The Supreme Court ruled that where a regulation bears a reasonable relation to legitimate penological interests, a visiting policy that limits visits by an inmate's children and places other restrictions on visits was constitutionally permissible (*Overton v. Bazzetta*).

- Conjugal visits are allowed in a few states. There is little in the way of constitutional law concerning conjugal visitation. The Supreme Court has not had any case ruling on this issue; however, lower federal courts have ruled that there is no constitutional right to conjugal visits (*Lyons v. Gilligan; Hernandez v. Coughlin; and Washington v. Cate*). In New York, courts ruled that visitation policies are to be determined by the prison officials and that it is permissible for New York to limit conjugal visits to spouses (*Matter of Mary of Oakknoll v. Coughlin; Cromwell v. Coughlin*).

- Several lower federal courts have determined that denying conjugal visits to inmates with religious beliefs is the least restrictive alternative for furthering a compelling state interest and does not violate RLUIPA. (Washington v. Cade). However, a federal court in another district has permitted a RLUIPA claim to proceed.

- There are few legal cases on the right of prisoners to pursue artificial insemination. Appellate courts have so far applied the *Turner* standard and have held that requests for artificial insemination may be denied by prison authorities, based on their legitimate penological concerns (*Gerber v. Hickman; Goodwin v. Turner*).

Thinking About It

In 1998, inmate John Doe was convicted of sexually assaulting a minor female and was placed on probation. Three years later, he was sentenced to 25 years in prison for armed robbery. Shortly after he was sentenced, his daughter was born and he and the mother shared joint custody. In 2004, the child, through her mother, asked to be permitted to visit her father. Wisconsin administrative rules allowed the warden to deny visits if, among other reasons, the warden has "reasonable grounds" to believe that "the inmate's offense history indicates there may be a problem with the proposed visitation" or if "the proposed visitor may be subjected to victimization." Because of Doe's past conviction for sexual assault, the Warden denied the visit until Doe completed the sex offender treatment program (SOTP). Doe declined because he felt he was not a sex offender. Five years later, after Doe was transferred to a different facility, he requested SOTP but was denied because that program was not available, and he had a low priority for the program. Doe again requested visitation privileges but without using the procedures set forth in the administrative rule. The Warden advised him to file an inmate complaint, which was denied. Doe then sued prison officials alleging a violation of his First Amendment right to association. After the district court dismissed his claim, the inmate appealed. How should the court of appeals rule? *Sterling v. Thurmer*, 880 F.3d 319 (7th Cir. 2018).

Key Terms
capital punishment
conjugal visits

Endnotes
1. Rabuy, B. & Wagner, P. *Screening Out Family Time: the for-profit video visitation industry in prisons and jails.* January 2015. Prison Policy Initiative. https://www.prisonpolicy.org/visitation/report.html. Accessed February 20, 2020.
2. Pennsylvania Department of Corrections *Video Visiting Program.* https://www.cor.pa.gov/family-and-friends/Pages/Video-Visitation.aspx. Accessed February 20, 2020.
3. Minnesota Department of Corrections *Video Visitation.* https://mn.gov/doc/family-visitor/visiting-information/video-visitation/. Accessed February 20, 2020.
4. South Dakota Department of Corrections Policy 1.5.D.4 *Inmate Access to Telephones and Tablets.* https://doc.sd.gov/documents/Inmate%20Access%20to%20Telephones%20and%20TabletsT882019.pdf. Accessed February 20, 2020.

5. Compare Washington County, Oregon Sheriff's Office Social Visiting Rule which allows both video and face-to-face visitation. https://www.co.washington.or.us/Sheriff/Jail/ContactInmate/social-visiting.cfm with Jefferson Parish, Louisiana Sheriff's Office which prohibits in-person visitation but authorizes video visitation initiated within the facility or from any location by computer. Accessed 20 February 2020. https://www.jpso.com/DocumentCenter/View/779/Inmate_visitation_rules?bidId=

6. Department of Corrections, Washington State, *Video Visits.* https://www.doc.wa.gov/corrections/incarceration/visiting/video-visits.htm Accessed February 20, 2020.

7. California, [*Adult Visiting Guidelines-Family Visits.* https://www.cdcr.ca.gov/visitors/inmate-visiting-guidelines/]. Accessed February 20, 2020.

8. New York [*Family Reunion Program.* DOC No. 4500, 01/25/2016. https://doccs.ny.gov/system/files/documents/2020/11/4500.pdf].

9. Washington [*Extended Family Visits*-DOC 590.100, 05/01/20 https://www.doc.wa.gov/information/policies/files/590100.pdf]. Accessed August 16, 2020.

10. *Washington v. Cate, No. 1:11-cv-00264 GSA PC, 2014 U.S. Dist. LEXIS 12402, at *4-5 (E.D. Cal. Jan. 31, 2014).* See also *Owens v. Kernan*, E.D. CA Case No. 2-16-cv-0167-EFBP June 6, 2016 (same outcome).

CHAPTER 9

First Amendment: Religion

Inmates clearly retain protections afforded by the First Amendment, including its directive that no law shall prohibit the free exercise of religion.

U.S. Supreme Court, *O'Lone v. Shabazz*

Another of the highly protected rights of the First Amendment, and the first one mentioned there, is religion:

Congress shall make no law respecting an establishment of religion, or prohibiting the free exercise thereof.

CHAPTER OUTLINE

- Establishment of Religion
- Faith-Based Initiatives
- *Cruz v. Beto*
- Freedom to Exercise Religion in Prisons
- *O'Lone v. Shabazz*
- Religious Freedom Restoration Act (RFRA)
- Religious Land Use and Institutionalized Persons Act of 2000 (RLUIPA)
- Other Free Exercise Issues in Prisons
  - Diet
  - Grooming
- Unusual Religious Groups

The language of this phrase applies to "Congress," and, therefore, to the federal government. The Supreme Court uses the Fourteenth Amendment to apply the religion phrases to the states. This is not one phrase but two: the establishment clause and the free exercise clause. The government cannot (1) establish religion or, (2) prohibit the exercising of one's religion. Although there are two freedoms protected, the press—and sometimes even teachers and the courts—are not careful to distinguish which of the "freedom of religion" phrases are being used. The kind of protection is different under each one.

To evaluate your understanding of "establishment" as opposed to "free exercise," consider the following, which are some of the most publicized issues decided under the First Amendment. Which of these were decided under the establishment clause and which were decided under the free exercise clause?

1. Persons handing out religious material in an airport terminal
2. Conscientious objection—not having to serve in the military because of religious reasons
3. Putting a nativity scene on the courthouse lawn
4. Polygamy—being allowed to have several wives
5. Paying for chaplains in the military with government funds
6. Persons driving around a quiet residential neighborhood with religious messages blaring from a speaker on their truck
7. Prayer, or Bible readings, in public schools[1]

▶ Establishment of Religion

The establishment of religion clause is discussed less frequently in law and practice than the free exercise clause and other First Amendment rights cases. In corrections law, there were very few cases under the establishment clause, but recently a number of cases have used the Establishment Clause to challenge perceived disparities in treatment between religious groups. "The clearest command of the Establishment Clause is that one religious denomination cannot be officially preferred over another" *Larson v. Valente*, 456 U.S. 228 (1982). A recent example is *Maye v. Klee*, 915 F.3d 1076 (6th Cir. 2019) where a member of the Nation of Islam alleged a violation of the establishment clause when prison officials declined to allow members of the Nation of Islam sect from participating in the end of Ramadan feast- Eid al-Fitr. The court of appeals concluded the establishment clause was violated because the prison practice favored one sect of Islam over another. *Zorach v. Clauson*, 343 U.S. 306 (1952).

One of the most interesting religion cases was *Theriault v. Carlson*, 339 F.Supp. 375 (N.D. GA 1973) and 495 F.2d 390 (5th Cir. 1974); also *Theriault v. Silber*, 391 F.Supp. 578 (W.D. TX 1975); and many other reported cases involving inmate–plaintiff Theriault. In *Theriault v. Carlson*, Theriault and another inmate, while confined in the Atlanta Penitentiary, challenged federal authorities to allow them to practice their religion. These inmates created a religion called Church of the New Song (CONS—its membership was restricted to those in prison!). They wrote scriptural texts and demanded group meetings and other activities. Although most of these claims in court were based on the "free exercise" clause, one claim was tied to the establishment clause: Theriault asked to be paid as a chaplain of his group, like other prison chaplains. If this didn't happen, he claimed that prison authorities should terminate religious programs funded by the government (chapels, Bibles, and Korans paid for with government money and the paid employment of chaplains on the staff).

The federal court (the main discussion on establishment is in the original district court decision in northern Georgia) held that it was permissible to have chaplaincy programs in prisons. The court compared them with those in the military, which had already been upheld by the courts. (We will look at the other claims of Theriault in the "free exercise" section later in this chapter.)

There is language in a leading Supreme Court decision that provides good guidance regarding what government should or should not do under the First Amendment. In *Abington School District v. Schempp*, 374 U.S. 203 (1963), the Supreme Court held:

> **The state must be steadfastly neutral in all matters of faith, and neither favor nor inhibit religion … [H]ostility, not neutrality, would characterize the refusal to provide chaplains and places of worship for prisoners and soldiers cut off by the state from all civilian opportunities for public communion.**

Because *Abington* was a school-prayer case and did not involve prisons, this language endorsing chaplains and chapels for the military and prisons is dictum and not the case holding. It is a strong indication, however, and a strong discouragement to litigating this issue, that the Court does not consider the use of public monies for chaplaincy programs in prison to be a violation of the establishment clause. The first sentence of the previous quotation is a generic constitutional admonition for governments to use in assessing their position in questions concerning the "establishment of religion."

The establishment clause does not specifically identify prohibited conduct, but *Abington*, and other Supreme Court decisions, such as *Everson v. Board of Education*, 330 U.S. 1 (1947), provide guidance. In *Everson*, the Court noted:

> **The 'establishment of religion' clause of the First Amendment means at least this: Neither a state nor the Federal Government can set up a church. Neither can pass laws which aid one religion, aid all religions, or prefer one religion over another. Neither can force nor influence a person to go to or to remain away from church against his will or force him to profess a belief or disbelief in any religion … Neither a state nor the Federal Government can, openly or secretly, participate in the affairs of any religious organizations or groups and vice versa.**

Bowen v. Kendrick, 487 U.S. 589 (1988), addresses another establishment question. *Bowen* concerned a challenge to the Adolescent Family Life Act, which allowed federal grants to public or nonprofit private organizations or agencies for services and research in the area of premarital adolescent sexual relations and pregnancy. Noting the complexity of the problem, the act named a number of entities, including religious organizations, whose involvement was seen as important. The district court had held that the act violated the establishment clause because it provided for the involvement of religious organizations in federally funded programs. The case was appealed directly to the Supreme Court. The Court held that the act, on its face, did not violate the establishment clause. The Court held that if both secular and religious objectives influence the government's practice, there is no violation of the establishment clause, provided that the government's expressed purposes are sincere. These holdings have a direct relevance to the current focus on faith-based initiatives, which have been government-sponsored programs that take place in corrections.

▶ Faith-Based Initiatives

Within two weeks of taking office in 2001, President George W. Bush issued Executive Orders 13198 and 13199.[2] Respectively, these orders (1) covered agency responsibilities with respect to faith-based and community initiatives and (2) established the White House Office of Faith-Based and Community Initiatives (White House OFBCI). The White House OFBCI was to "establish policies, priorities, and objectives for the Federal Government's comprehensive effort to enlist, equip, enable, empower, and expand the work of faith-based and other community organizations to the extent permitted by law." Selected federal agencies (specifically, the Attorney General and the Secretaries of Education, Labor, Health and Human Services, and Housing and Urban Development) were directed to establish a Center for Faith-Based and Community Initiatives, whose purpose would be to "coordinate department efforts to eliminate regulatory, contracting, and other programmatic obstacles to the participation of faith-based and other community organizations in the provision of social services." In December, 2002, President Bush issued Executive Order 13279, Equal Protection of the Laws for Faith-Based and Community Organizations which required the federal government to implement federal programs in accordance with Establishment Clause and the Free Exercise Clauses of the First Amendment.[3] Additional executive orders on this subject that had been issued in January of 2001 by President Bush (13199) and amendments to Executive Order 13199 by President Obama in February of 2009[4] were revoked by President Trump by an *Executive Order on Establishment of a White House Faith and Opportunity Initiative* in May of 2018.[5]

The recent introduction of faith-based initiatives in a number of states, as well as in the federal government, has generated new challenges to the establishment clause. Supporters of faith-based programs in prisons suggest that such programs can help an inmate learn self-restraint and become a better citizen upon release. These program goals appear worthwhile and are secular in nature. The issue in prison litigation may focus on exactly how this is achieved and whether the programs violate the First Amendment's establishment clause.

One example of a challenge to faith-based initiatives occurred in the Iowa state correctional system. The Iowa Department of Corrections (DOC), starting in 1999, contracted with a religious-based organization to provide programming with the purpose of providing "a positive influence in prison" and to assist prisoners, upon release, in becoming "contributing members of society." *Americans United for Separation of Church and State v. Prison Fellowship Ministries, Inc.*, 509 F.3d 406 (8th Cir. 2007). The program included both study and work based on Christian values, but a participant did not have to be Christian to participate. Participants in the program were housed in a separate unit. Participation in the program was voluntary and there were no incentives, such as early release. Until July of 2007, DOC funding made up 30-40% of the religious program's operating cost. The contracts required government funds to be used only for "the non-religious aspects" or "the non-sectarian portion" of the programs.

In analyzing whether the program violated the establishment clause of the First Amendment, the court of appeals addressed two issues: Did the state act with the purpose of inhibiting or advancing religion and did the aid have the effect of advancing or inhibiting religion? Relying on an earlier Supreme Court opinion, *Agostini v. Felton*, 521 U.S. 203 (1997), both the district court and the court of appeals concluded that the state's intention was secular—to offer inmates comprehensive programs and reduce recidivism—with no purpose of either advancing or inhibiting religion. As to the second issue, the district court found, and the court of appeals agreed, that the program, as implemented in Iowa, advanced and endorsed religion in violation of the establishment clause. The court specifically noted that the program was "dominated by Bible study, Christian classes, religious revivals, and church services." The court concluded that for an inmate to enter the program and use the government funding, the inmate had to agree to "productively participate in a program that is Christian-based." The court in *Americans United* found that the program violated the establishment clause of the First Amendment and ruled that the private religious program, Interchange Freedom Initiative (IFI), had to return to the state the funds that IFI had received after the district court decision was issued but not the funds received prior to that date. Faith-based initiatives continue to be used in some prison systems. One example of a faith-based initiative is the Georgia Department of Corrections' Faith- and Character-Based Initiative.[6] The program "consists of personal and spiritual growth and development under the supervision of a trained program coordinator. Participants are divided into four phases, which follow a 12-month curriculum (for the dorms) and a 24-month curriculum for the prison for successful completion and graduation." The DOC states the program "enhances public safety through community partnerships that will support the offender's successful transition from custody to community. Georgia's Faith and Character Based programs have been shown to have a treatment effect of 10; meaning someone is 10 times less likely to return to prison after completing a Faith and Character Based program."

▸ *Cruz v. Beto*

For many years, the only guidance from the Supreme Court on prison religion issues was in *Cruz v. Beto*, 405 U.S. 319 (1972). This was a per curiam decision of the Court, meaning that it was a summary opinion without full-blown analysis and discussion, as would be found in the regular opinions of the Court. (This per curiam decision was somewhat unusual in that two justices only concurred in the case and one justice dissented. Such divisions are uncommon in per curiam decisions.) This was a Section 1983 action by Cruz, a Texas inmate, who claimed to be a Buddhist. He was not allowed to use the prison chapel, or to correspond with a Buddhist religious advisor, and could not share his religious materials with other inmates. For his attempts to hand out literature, he was punished by being placed in solitary confinement. He also objected to other religious programs that provided Jewish and Christian Bibles and religious classes and services. The district court dismissed Cruz's complaints without a hearing, and the Fifth Circuit Court of Appeals affirmed.

The Supreme Court, although conceding that prison officials must be given wide latitude in the running of prisons (it was this deference to prison administrators' discretion that led the lower courts to dismiss the complaints), said that prison complaints based on constitutional challenges must be more closely examined. In this case, the complaints had been summarily dismissed, and the Court said that that was too hasty.

> **If Cruz was a Buddhist and if he was denied a reasonable opportunity of pursuing his faith comparable to the opportunity afforded fellow prisoners who adhere to conventional religious precepts, then there was palpable discrimination by the State against the Buddhist religion.**

This sounds like an "equal protection" analysis, reasoning that if Texas allows activities by one religious group, it must (constitutionally) be prepared to offer similar activities to other religions. Again, it is not a fully developed opinion—but it is a statement of law from the Supreme Court, and it is, therefore, binding as a constitutional standard. In addition, the Court clearly said that the First Amendment (the religion clause) was applicable to persons in prison.

▸ Freedom to Exercise Religion in Prisons

"It is a matter of some interest to correctional administrators and to lawyers that the 'correctional law revolution' can be traced to religious cases—specifically, to cases brought by Black Muslim prisoners in the early 1960s."[7] The courts had a "hands-off" attitude toward prisons for many decades. In more recent times, courts have reversed this attitude, and, indeed, there are literally thousands of prisoners' rights lawsuits filed, and many hundreds decided every year, even in the face of the discouragement intended by the Prison Reform Litigation Act. Many legal scholars assert that this opening-up of the courts to review prison programs and activities can be traced to the "Black Muslim" litigation in federal courts in the early 1960s. This religious group, led at the time by Elijah Muhammad (a former federal inmate himself), gained followers among black inmates, as well as many black citizens in the community, particularly in the large cities—Chicago, New York, Los Angeles, Washington, DC, and others. Although there were a few prisoners' rights cases before 1961, they were sporadic and led to no body of case law that protected the rights of prisoners in any significant area.

The Black Muslims made demands for prison authorities to recognize their group and allow religious activities. Some states denied that the Nation of Islam (the Black Muslims) was a religion and litigated this issue. (The early cases from New York State, for example, showed that approach to the litigation, contesting whether the Nation of Islam was, in fact, a religion.) If it was not a religion, it would not be entitled to First Amendment protection at all. Courts have been notably reluctant to tackle this issue of what is, in fact, a religion, although in *Fulwood v. Clemmer*, 206 F.Supp. 370 (D.D.C. 1962) the court did address the issue and concluded that the Black Muslim faith was indeed a religion.

Once that entry issue was decided, there was a flurry of complaints and demands from Black Muslim inmates, particularly in California, New York, and the District of Columbia. These dealt with the rights to hold services; pursue religious instruction; have visits from religious leaders; have correspondence with religious persons in the community; obtain religious writings; wear religious medals and other apparel (shawls, robes, kufis, sandals); and obtain funding for chaplains or other religious assistance and materials. As a result of this litigation, and of concessions by prison administrators because of the pressures of the litigation, Black Muslims were permitted to engage in a range of activities in prisons, at least in those jurisdictions with large urban populations where the lawsuits were brought.

▶ *O'Lone v. Shabazz*

For many years, the only Supreme Court ruling on prison religious activities was its 1972 decision in *Cruz v. Beto*. There was some guidance from lower federal courts in cases dealing with free exercise claims by various religious groups in the community, and the lower courts were embroiled in many prison cases that raised religious issues. In *O'Lone v. Shabazz*, 482 U.S. 342 (1987), the Supreme Court finally gave a clear ruling on prisoners' free exercise rights in prison.

Shabazz and other Muslim inmates at a state prison in New Jersey filed suit, claiming that prison regulations interfered with their ability to attend Jumu'ah prayers in the institution. Because of security concerns and demands on staff time, prison officials prohibited inmates who were working on outside work details from coming back inside the prison during the day, except for in emergencies. This prevented Muslims on the outside work details from attending Jumu'ah service, which the parties agreed was a religious dictate (the most important service of the week) of their sincerely held religious beliefs. The district court had held that the challenged prison rules were permissible, because they advanced the goals of security, order, and rehabilitation. The court of appeals reversed, saying that the free exercise rights of the prisoners had been violated without the state showing whether some method of accommodation could be achieved, taking into account the prison's concerns about crowding, understaffing, and the possibilities of disruption.

The Supreme Court rejected this ruling of the court of appeals, which would have required prison officials to prove there was "no reasonable method" that would have accommodated these inmates' rights to observe "a central religious practice." The Supreme Court emphasized that the courts should respect and defer to the judgment of the prison officials. Regarding the restrictions imposed in this case, the Court found that prison officials acted reasonably and with good cause. Looking at the reasons for the adoption of the prison policy, the Court found that there were no obvious, easy alternatives to the policy that New Jersey officials had adopted.

In *O'Lone*, the Supreme Court set out the standards that govern analysis of prisoners' constitutional claims:

> **To ensure that courts afford appropriate deference to prison officials, we have determined that prison regulations alleged to infringe constitutional rights are judged under a "reasonableness" test less restrictive than that ordinarily applied to alleged infringements of fundamental constitutional rights** [Citing *Jones v. North Carolina Prisoners' Labor Union*]. **We recently restated the proper standard: "[W]hen a prison regulation impinges on inmates' constitutional rights, the regulation is valid if it is reasonably related to legitimate penological interests."** [Citing *Turner v. Safley,* 482 U.S. 78 (1987)]

New Jersey had a legitimate interest in maintaining security and order at the prison, the Supreme Court said, which led officials to adopt the policy that restricted inmates' rights to exercise their religion freely by attending Jumu'ah prayers. This reasonable restriction, in furtherance of a legitimate penological objective, the Court ruled, outweighed the First Amendment claim of inmates to practice their religion.

▶ Religious Freedom Restoration Act (RFRA)

In *Employment Division v. Smith*, 494 U.S. 872 (1990), the Supreme Court declined to apply the compelling governmental interest standard to a case where two persons charged with violating a law of general application (the use of peyote) were terminated from their employment and denied unemployment benefits. The employees alleged that their conduct in using peyote as members of the Native American Church and the denial of unemployment benefits was a significant burden on their exercise of religion. In the final paragraph of the majority opinion, the Court noted that, *"Values that are protected against government interference through enshrinement in the Bill of Rights are not thereby banished from the political process."* This language has been interpreted to mean that "the political branches could shield religious exercise through legislative accommodation." *Cutter v. Wilkinson*, 544 U.S. 709 (2005) (discussed in detail below)

Responding to the *Employment Division* decision, Congress did enact legislation restoring the compelling governmental interest standard rejected by the Supreme Court. This did not overrule the Supreme Court's judgment; it provided persons with additional rights under federal law than were provided to them by the First Amendment. In 1993, Congress enacted the Religious Freedom Restoration Act (RFRA is codified at Title 42, U.S. Code, Section 2000bb). This law was proposed and enacted specifically to provide a higher standard for evaluating the government's authority to restrict an individuals' religious freedoms, as set out in *O'Lone* and other rulings of the Supreme Court on religious matters. According to its statement of purpose in enacting RFRA, Congress cited its unhappiness with the 1990 ruling in the case of *Employment Division v. Smith*. As previously stated, the Court had pulled back from its earlier rulings that government would have to show a compelling interest in order to justify restrictions on the free exercise of religion. While not citing the Supreme Court decision in *O'Lone*, Congress had been made aware of the prison ruling and asked to exempt correctional facilities from RFRA. That request, in the form of an amendment, was rejected in a vote on the floor of Congress.

RFRA provides the following:

Government may substantially burden a person's exercise of religion only if it demonstrates that application of the burden to the person—(1) is in furtherance of a compelling governmental interest; and (2) is the least restrictive means of furthering that compelling governmental interest.

"Government" as used in the law was defined (in Section 2000bb-2) as any agency or official of the United States, any state, or any subdivision of a state. Thus, by very specific language, Congress gave religious practitioners a federally protected interest in addition to the First Amendment free exercise clause. Both the First Amendment and RFRA require a person to demonstrate that some governmental action "substantially burdens" the free exercise of religion. If their free exercise is substantially burdened, the restriction is valid under RFRA only if it furthers a compelling governmental interest by the least restrictive means. So, if a government restriction is found to comply with RFRA, that restriction would almost always satisfy the First Amendment. However, not all restrictions that would satisfy the First Amendment would be in compliance with RFRA as RFRA has a more demanding standard.

City of Boerne v. Flores, 521 U.S. 507 (1997) dealt with a decision by local zoning officials in Texas to deny religious leaders a building permit to enlarge a church. The denial was based on an ordinance governing historic preservation in an area encompassing the church. The church's archbishop sued in U.S. district court, challenging the denial of the permit under RFRA. The trial court held that Congress, by enacting RFRA, had exceeded its constitutional powers. The Fifth Circuit Court of Appeals reversed, saying the act was constitutional, and the case went to the Supreme Court. That Court held that RFRA "exceeds Congress' power."

Congress does not enforce a constitutional right by changing what the right is. It has been given the power [in Section 5 of the Fourteenth Amendment] "to enforce," not the power to determine what constitutes a constitutional violation.

The power to interpret the Constitution in a case or controversy remains in the Judiciary.

It is for Congress in the first instance to "determin[e] whether and what legislation is needed to secure the guarantees of the Fourteenth Amendment," and its conclusions are entitled to much deference … Congress' discretion is not unlimited, however, and the courts retain the power … to determine if Congress has exceeded its authority under the Constitution. Broad as the power of Congress is under the Enforcement Clause of the Fourteenth Amendment, RFRA contradicts vital principles necessary to maintain separation of powers and the federal balance.

The federal government has taken the position that the Court's decision in *Boerne* was limited to state and not federal action. Accordingly, for federal agencies and activities, the test contained in RFRA (whether compelling government interests are involved and whether they are upheld by the least restrictive means) remains the standard for free exercise claims raised under the First Amendment. In 2000, Public Law 106-274 (RLUIPA) amended provisions of RFRA to remove any reference that RFRA applied to the states.

For states, the former test for prison matters was reinstated: whether the government restriction is reasonably related to legitimate penological interests (as stated in *O'Lone* and *Turner*).

In *Burwell v. Hobby Lobby Stores, Inc.* 573 U.S. 682 (2014), the Supreme Court addressed the issue of whether a for-profit corporation was a "person" as that term is used in RFRA. 42 U.S. Code Sections 2000bb-1[8]

The owners of for-profit corporations argued that complying with the provisions of the Affordable Care Act of 2010 (ACA) and the regulations implementing it (requiring provision of employee health insurance programs, which included certain types of contraceptives) violated their sincerely held religious beliefs. After concluding that the term "person" as used in RFRA included the plaintiff corporations, the Court then addressed whether the regulations substantially burdened the plaintiffs' exercise of religion.

The Court concluded that provisions of a Health and Human Services (HHS) rule promulgated pursuant to the ACA concerning the provision of health insurance for employees substantially burdened the sincerely held religious beliefs of the owners of the plaintiff corporations because failure to follow the regulations could result in fines and penalties of $1.3 million dollars a day for Hobby Lobby and $90,000 and $40,000 a day for the other two plaintiff corporations. HHS had argued that guaranteeing the cost-free access to the contraceptive methods at issue for the corporate employees was a compelling governmental interest, and the Court assumed this to be true without deciding it. Finally, the Court ruled that HHS had failed the "least restrictive alternative" because HHS already established rules to accommodate not-for-profit religious groups with religious objections to the rules.

▶ Religious Land Use and Institutionalized Persons Act of 2000 (RLUIPA)

In September of 2000, the Religious Land Use and Institutionalized Persons Act of 2000 was enacted (RLUIPA is codified in Title 42, U.S. Code, Section 2000cc), and it is applicable to state programs that use federal funding. The act focuses on two areas: (1) the protection of land use, when it is used for religious exercise and (2) the protection of religious exercise by institutionalized persons. Both contain the RFRA language the Supreme Court, in *Boerne*, had held unconstitutional as specifically applied to the states. RLUIPA prohibits states from imposing a substantial burden on the religious exercise of a person unless the government shows that imposing the burden furthers a compelling government interest and is the least restrictive means of furthering that compelling interest.

RLUIPA is a congressional effort to achieve its RFRA purposes by narrowing the focus to show a greater federal interest, one that Congress apparently believes is within its enforcement powers under Section 5 of the Fourteenth Amendment. As applied to institutionalized persons, the statute applies where the substantial burden on religious activity occurs in a program or activity that receives federal financial assistance or where the substantial burden would affect (or removal of that substantial burden would affect) commerce with foreign nations, among the states, or with Indian tribes.

As applied to institutionalized persons, would the Supreme Court find RLUIPA constitutional? In *Cutter v. Wilkinson*, 544 U.S. 709 (2005), current and former Ohio prison inmates, identifying themselves as followers of "nonmainstream" religions, claimed Ohio prison officials failed to allow their religious exercise, and that such denial was a violation of RLUIPA, section 3. This section prohibits state governments from imposing a substantial burden on an institutionalized person's religious exercise unless the government demonstrates that the burden placed on the person furthers "a compelling governmental interest" and does so by "the least restrictive means."

In response, Ohio prison officials countered the inmates' claims under RLUIPA, arguing that the act violated the establishment clause of the First Amendment.

The district court rejected Ohio's argument, saying that on the "thin record before it, the court declined to find … that enforcement of RLUIPA, inevitably, would compromise prison security. The court of appeals reversed, holding that section 3 "impermissibly advance[es] religion by giving greater protection to religious rights than to other constitutionally protected rights."

The Supreme Court reversed, saying:

RLUIPA thus protects institutionalized persons who are unable freely to attend to their religious needs and are therefore dependent on the government's permission and accommodation for exercise of their religion.

The Court first established the premise that exercise of religion not only involves beliefs but also the performance of physical acts, including assembling with others for worship and participating in religiously motivated activity. In recognizing the need of correctional administrators to balance correctional goals against religiously motivated activities, the Court said:

We do not read RLUIPA to elevate accommodation of religious observances over an institution's need to maintain order and safety.

The Court further commented that lawmakers supporting RLUIPA were mindful of this need and that the lawmakers anticipated "that courts would apply the Act's standard with 'due deference to the experience and expertise of prison and jail administrators in establishing necessary regulations and procedures to maintain good order, security and discipline, consistent with consideration of costs and limited resources.'" RLUIPA's requirements did not compel prison officials to accommodate a prisoner's religious observances at the expense of these interests. The Court, referring to the Prison Litigation Reform Act (PLRA), stated that "[s]tate prison officials make the first judgment about whether to provide a particular accommodation, for a prisoner may not sue under RLUIPA without first exhausting all available administrative remedies." Furthermore, RLUIPA section 2000cc-2(e) specifically states that RLUIPA is not to be interpreted as amending or repealing the PLRA.

In concluding that RLUIPA did not violate the establishment clause of the First Amendment, the Court noted that for more than 10 years, the Federal Bureau of Prisons had operated under the compelling governmental interest standard (established by RFRA, discussed earlier in this chapter) "without compromising prison security, public safety, or the constitutional rights of other prisoners."

A final comment on *Cutter*. In *Cutter*, Ohio officials made a **facial challenge** to the constitutionality of a RLUIPA provision. This type of challenge claims that the statute itself is unconstitutional. Ohio did not claim unconstitutionality under the facts of any specific inmate cases. The district court, noting the underdeveloped record, said a finding "that it is *factually impossible* to provide the kind of accommodations that RLUIPA will require without significantly compromising prison security or the levels of service provided to other inmates cannot be made at this juncture." The Supreme Court agreed.

The Supreme Court's next guidance on RLUIPA's application in a correctional setting came in *Holt v. Hobbs*, 574 U.S. 352 (2015). The Arkansas Department of Corrections (ADOC) implemented a rule prohibiting inmates from growing beards except for those with certain dermatological conditions for which inmates could wear a ¼ inch beard. The ADOC justified the rule because it promoted institution security in (i) minimizing the risk of inmates concealing contraband in their beards and (ii) promoting quick identification in the event an inmate would shave his beard to alter his appearance [the prison system photographed inmates so staff could easily identify them]. Inmate Holt, a Muslim, claimed that shaving his facial hair in any manner violated his religious beliefs, but he agreed to limit the beard length to ½ inch to accommodate the ADOC's security interests. The ADOC refused to accommodate the inmate's request and advised the inmate that failure to comply with the rule would result in disciplinary action. The magistrate judge who presided over a hearing for an injunction was skeptical of a person's ability to hide contraband in a ½ inch beard but still deferred to the ADOC's assessment that the policy was the least restrictive means of furthering a compelling governmental interest. The district court dismissed the suit for failure to state a claim and the court of appeals affirmed the dismissal. The Supreme Court granted *certiorari* to address this question: "Whether the Arkansas Department of Correction's grooming policy violates the Religious Land Use and Institutionalized Persons Act of

2000, 42 U.S.C. §2000cc et sec., to the extent that it prohibits petitioner from growing a one-half-inch beard in accordance with his religious beliefs."

RLUIPA allows prisoners "to seek religious accommodations pursuant to the same standard as set forth in RFRA." The ADOC had presented testimony from staff that inmates could hide contraband in a ½ long beard, although the witnesses had no personal knowledge of this ever occurring. Staff additionally testified that an inmate who escaped could shave his beard and quickly alter his appearance or shave his beard to disguise himself to permit access to restricted portions of the prison. The ADOC witnesses could not explain why these concerns could not be addressed by taking photographs of inmates with and without beards (a policy used in many correctional agencies).

The Court first set forth how cases under RLUIPA should be analyzed:

> *Under RLUIPA, petitioner bore the initial burden of proving that the Department's grooming policy implicates his religious exercise. RLUIPA protects "any exercise of religion, whether or not compelled by, or central to, a system of religious belief," § 2000cc-5(7)(A), but, of course, a prisoner's request for an accommodation must be sincerely based on a religious belief and not some other motivation, . . .* [the prisoner] *also bore the burden of proving that the Department's grooming policy substantially burdened that exercise of religion.*

The ADOC policy required the inmate to shave his beard, which violated his religious belief. Failure to comply with the policy would result in disciplinary action. The Court noted the district court and court of appeals had concluded that Holt's exercise of religion was not substantially burdened because he was authorized to use alternative means of practicing his religion such as use of a prayer rug, to contact spiritual advisors and observe a religious diet and holidays. While alternative means of practicing a religion is a consideration in First Amendment "free exercise" cases, RLUIPA assesses whether government has substantially burdened a religious exercise, not whether it has provided alternative means of exercising religious beliefs. The Court then determined that under the facts of this case, the inmate established that the ADOC policy prohibiting beards substantially burdened Holt's exercise of religion.

Once the inmate demonstrates that a policy or act substantially burdens their religious exercise, "***the burden shifted to the Department to show that its refusal to allow petitioner to grow a ½-inch beard "(1) [was] in furtherance of a compelling governmental interest; and (2) [was] the least restrictive means of furthering that compelling governmental interest."***

The ADOC argued that its policy furthered the broad compelling interest of institution safety and security. The Court concluded that more than a general referral to a broad interest is necessary to establish a compelling interest.

> *But RLUIPA, like RFRA, contemplates a "'more focused'" inquiry and "requires the Government to demonstrate that the compelling interest test is satisfied through application of the challenged law "to the person" — the particular claimant whose sincere exercise of religion is being substantially burdened."*

When determining whether the policy furthers a compelling governmental interest courts are instructed to evaluate whether application of the practice to a particular inmate furthers the governmental interest:

> *RLUIPA requires us to "'scrutiniz[e] the asserted harm of granting specific exemptions to particular religious claimants'" and "to look to the marginal interest in enforcing" the challenged government action in that particular context. [citations omitted] In this case, that means the enforcement of the Department's policy to prevent petitioner from growing a ½-inch beard.*

While recognizing the state's interest in safety and security in prisons, the Court scrutinized whether the rule furthered the state's interest. Contraband could be hidden in an inmate's hair on his head and in his clothing. If searches of those areas would divulge contraband, why couldn't searches of ½-inchbeards do the same? It was also unclear why a ¼-inch beard, permitted for medical reasons could be effectively searched, but not a ½-inch beard. These concerns demonstrated the policy was not the least restrictive means of furthering a legitimate governmental interest.

> *"The least-restrictive-means standard is exceptionally demanding," and it requires the government to "sho[w] that it lacks other means of achieving its desired goal without imposing a substantial burden*

on the exercise of religion by the objecting part[y]." [citation omitted] "*[I]f a less restrictive means is available for the Government to achieve its goals, the Government must use it.*" [citation omitted].

Two additional factors were raised by the plaintiffs, which impacted the Court's RLUIPA analysis. The first was whether the agency's own regulations permitted accommodation in other cases, a situation referred to as "under inclusiveness." The ADOC allowed inmates with medical conditions to have beards. The Court deemed that the ADOC's beard policy was underinclusive since other inmates were authorized to do what the plaintiff was not.

Although the Department's proclaimed objectives are to stop the flow of contraband and to facilitate prisoner identification, "[t]he proffered objectives are not pursued with respect to analogous nonreligious conduct," which suggests that "those interests could be achieved by narrower ordinances that burdened religion to a far lesser degree." [citation omitted].

The state also failed to address the inmate's claim that many other correctional departments do allow for religiously motivated beards. While not required to adopt procedures simply because a few other correctional organizations have adopted that procedure,

"*[t]hat so many other prisons allow inmates to grow beards while ensuring prison safety and security suggests that the Department could satisfy its security concerns through a means less restrictive than denying petitioner the exemption he seeks.*"

The Court continued to acknowledge that judges should be deferential to the expertise of correctional officials, but dismissed the notion that a court should defer to every assertion by the government that allowing a particular practice in prison would undermine institution safety and security:

RLUIPA, however, does not permit such unquestioning deference. RLUIPA, like RFRA, "makes clear that it is the obligation of the courts to consider whether exceptions are required under the test set forth by Congress." [citation omitted]. *That test requires the Department not merely to explain why it denied the exemption but to prove that denying the exemption is the least restrictive means of furthering a compelling governmental interest.*

Because the Court determined the ADOC's grooming policy violated RLUIPA insofar as it prevented Holt from growing a ½-inch beard in accordance with his religious beliefs, the judgment of the court of appeals was reversed.

Another issue that RLUIPA generated was whether a prison inmate could seek money damages for violations of the statute directly from the state. Under the concept of sovereign immunity, most sovereign governments (the federal and state governments) waived their sovereign immunity for certain types of suits (e.g., torts). In *Sossamon v. Texas*, 563 U.S. 277(2011), a state prisoner sued several defendants, including the state of Texas, alleging that a state policy, which prohibited inmates from participating in group religious activities in the prison chapel and some inmates on disciplinary restrictions from participating in group religious activities violated the prisoner's free exercise of religion rights under RLUIPA. The prisoner sought injunctive relief and money damages both from individual state officials and the state itself. The state argued that it had not waived its sovereign immunity from suits for money damages. The only question that the Supreme Court addressed is whether the state of Texas, by accepting money from the federal government, waived its sovereign immunity for money damages. The Supreme Court ruled:

We conclude that States, in accepting federal funding, do not consent to waive their sovereign immunity to private suits for money damages under RLUIPA because no statute expressly and unequivocally includes such a waiver.

The Supreme Court has not yet determined whether money damages are an appropriate remedy for RFRA claims against federal government employees. Two federal courts of appeal (*Tanvir v. Tanzin*, 894 F.3d 449 (2nd Cir. 2018) and *Mack v. Warden, Loretto FCI*, 839 F.3d 286 (3rd Cir. 2016) have interpreted RFRA to authorize money damages against federal officers in their individual capacities, while three others (*Davila v. Gladden*, 777 F.3d 1198, 1210 (11th Cir. 2015); *Oklevueha Native Am. Church of Hawaii, Inc. v. Holder*, 676 F.3d 829, 840-41 (9th Cir. 2012); and *Webman v. Fed. Bureau of Prisons*, 441 F.3d 1022, 1026 (D.C. Cir. 2006) [RFRA did not waive sovereign immunity of the United States for money damages]) have held that money damages are not authorized under the statute. In November of 2019, the U.S. Supreme Court granted *certiorari* to address the following question: *Whether the Religious Freedom Restoration Act of 1993, 42 U.S.C. 2000bb et seq., permits suits seeking money damages against individual federal employees. Tanzin v. Tanvir*, Docket No. 19-71, *certiorari granted* 22 November 2019. The Supreme Court decided this case in December, 2020 ruling that RFRA's express remedies provision permits litigants, when appropriate, to obtain money damages against federal officials in their individual capacities.

RLUIPA will continue to generate litigation about how correctional agencies must accommodate the religious rights of prisoners. These issues include questions as to when a prisoner's religious rights have been substantially burdened, whether the government's interest in restricting the rights is a compelling one, and if so, did the government choose the least restrictive means of furthering that governmental interest, which is involved under the circumstances.

▶ Other Free Exercise Issues in Prisons

Many kinds of religious activities and special provisions for religious exercise have been requested by prison inmates. When denied or restricted, lawsuits (usually under 42 U.S.C. § 1983) have been brought. It should be noted that earlier court decisions decided before RFRA (1997) and RLUIPA (2000) may receive a different analysis and holding, in light of RLUIPA. Prisoner claims may be brought for violations of both the First Amendment and either RFRA (for federal conduct) or RLUIPA (state conduct).

Diet

Both Muslim and Jewish inmates have asked that they be provided specially prepared foods, based on the religious dietary laws of their faiths. The dietary requirements of the two religions are similar in that adherents of both religions refrain from eating pork and anything that comes into contact with pork. Muslims would ask that the meat that they eat be slaughtered in special rites, with a prayer being said at the time of slaughter (Hallal). Strict Jewish diets are called kosher and follow religious laws for the preparation and serving of food (kashruth laws).

Some courts held that special meals did not have to be prepared for Muslim inmates, as long as they could nutritionally sustain themselves by eating what was served to all inmates, while refraining from eating pork or pork products. To assist them in doing this, some prisons mark (with an asterisk, for example) those items on the menu board that contain any pork. See for example, *Jones v. Williams*, 791 F.3d 1023 (9th Cir. 2015) ("When serving food items containing pork, the prison had a practice of displaying a sign to indicate the items' pork contents.") Early court decisions outlining Muslim dietary requirements are located in *Abernathy v. Cunningham*, 393 F.2d 775 (4th Cir. 1968), and *Barnett v. Rodgers*, 410 F.2d 995 (DC Cir. 1969).

Jewish dietary requirements are complex, requiring not only specially prepared foods but also the separation of pots, pans, and eating utensils (milk and meat products must be strictly separated), and the inspection of food storage, preparation, and serving areas by rabbinical authorities. Courts are divided on whether prisons must meet these dietary requirements for observant Jews, but one court held that "prison authorities must accommodate the right of prisoners to receive diets consistent with their religious scruples." *Kahane v. Carlson*, 527 F.2d 492 (2nd Cir. 1975). That court brushed aside objections that such special food preparation would be extremely burdensome and expensive for prison authorities, saying that this problem would be surmountable "in view of the small number of practicing orthodox Jews in federal prisons," which would not exceed approximately 12 persons. The problem with this estimate made by the *Kahane* court was that following the laws of Kashruth is not limited to orthodox Jews; any Jew, as an individual matter, may choose to follow these laws. When kosher foods were made available, scores of Jewish inmates requested that diet. (Whether this was as a consequence of individual religious conviction, a desire to create administrative headaches for authorities, or a perception that the kosher diet would be better than the regular inmate dining room fare was not clear.)

What is virtually impossible for prison officials to do is to base the provision of such special religious items as diet on the sincerity or the "orthodoxy" of the inmate's beliefs. The courts have shown reluctance to inquire into the sincerity of religious beliefs, and as a practical matter, testing "sincerity" is an administrative nightmare. Having said that, individual sincerity is challenged by some prison authorities and examined by some courts. If it can be shown that the inmate's dietary request is not religiously motivated, there is no First Amendment issue.

The courts have considered a few factors to determine religious sincerity: whether the inmate participates in other religious observances at the prison, whether the inmate eats food that is not consistent with their religious beliefs, and whether their purchases of commissary items are contrary to their religious views. What is not acceptable is for prison officials to make their finding based on a determination that the beliefs fall outside the main or customary tenets of the stated religion.

An example of religious diet for a different religion is *DeHart v. Horn*, 227 F.3d 47 (3rd Cir. 2000), where a state prison inmate taught himself Buddhism during his confinement. From his readings of Buddhist religious texts (Sutras), DeHart became a vegetarian, based on a precept in Buddhism that prohibits the killing of any living thing. DeHart went through the state grievance process and was denied special food. The state's position was that a vegetarian diet is not mandated by any recognized Buddhist sect. In denying preliminary injunctive relief, the circuit court said the court's task was to decide if the beliefs were sincerely held and religious in nature in the individual's "scheme of things." The case was remanded for an analysis under the *Turner* standards in order to decide whether the prison restrictions were reasonably related to a legitimate prison objective.

In *Jackson v. Mann*, 196 F.3d 316 (2nd Cir. 1999), an inmate was denied a kosher diet following a determination by the prison chaplain that the inmate failed to meet the requirement to be a Jew (either being born Jewish or completing a formal conversion process). The inmate filed suit under 42 U.S.C. § 1983. The district court granted summary judgment to the prison officials, saying the inmate had provided no proof that he was Jewish "according to the practices of the Jewish religion." The circuit court reversed and remanded, saying the focus must be on whether the inmate's belief is religious and sincerely held, not whether it follows ecclesiastical law.

Where challenged, most correctional facilities have made some accommodation to Jewish inmates' dietary requests. Like the *Kahane* court, most judges would require "the provision of a diet sufficient to sustain the prisoner in good health without violating the Jewish dietary laws." How to accomplish this is left to prison officials. Although some have attempted to set up a kosher kitchen, doing this within a prison is very difficult. Some institutions have ordered frozen or prepared foods from commercial vendors, which are certified as being kosher. Others have tried to provide a selection of food items that are regularly prepared for all inmates, such as raw fruits and vegetables, boiled eggs, and canned fish, so that the Jewish inmates can have a kosher diet by selecting those permissible items from the food line.

In *Beerheide v. Suthers*, 286 F.3d 1179 (10th Cir. 2002), the department of corrections (DOC) in Colorado appealed a district court decision, holding not only that the DOC had to provide inmates with a kosher diet but must provide the diet without requiring a contribution from the inmates. The court also found no acceptable alternative means for the inmates to exercise the right to maintain a kosher diet. The court rejected the department's suggestion that the inmates could purchase such meals in the commissary because the evidence showed that the inmate-plaintiffs were not financially able to do this. It rejected the suggestion that kosher food could be provided by members of the community, saying the Jewish community could not be expected or required to provide food to the inmates. The court also rejected the offering of the prison common fare program (which served vegetarian meals or meals prepared with no pork or pork by-products). The court held that this program did not meet such factors required by kosher rules as the storage, source, and preparation of the ingredients and the service of meals.

This federal court also rejected the DOC's proposal that inmates taking part in the kosher meal program be required to make a co-payment of no more than 25% of the additional cost of providing the meals. The district court found that under this proposal, an inmate maintaining a kosher diet would be expected to pay $90 per month, incurring a debt to his prison account if unable to pay. The court determined that an inmate living solely on earnings from prison work received a maximum of approximately $57 per month, thus incurring a debt of $30 each month. While some inmates might have more than the minimal income earned from work, the court noted, "Forcing prisoners to decide between communicating with family and legal representatives, seeking medical treatment, and following religious tenets constitutes a Hobson's choice (an apparently free choice when there is no really good alternative) rather than a true alternative."

The Colorado DOC also argued that there was an adverse impact on financial resources and staff and administrative resources. The court held that there was insufficient information provided by the department in support of its position. Finally, the district court found that providing inmates with kosher meals free of charge, coupled with a selective screening process unrelated to money, was an alternative with only a slight impact on the department's food budget. The DOC had a screening process providing guidelines for the loss of the religious diet privilege. These guidelines included being observed violating the religious dietary requirements; providing all or a portion of the specially prepared meal to other offenders; eating both the specially prepared meal and the general diet meal that is offered to the general population; and discovering that an inmate no longer practices the religion. The federal appeals court affirmed these holdings of the district court.

In another case concerning religious diet, a federal inmate at Texarkana, Texas, asked to be provided with a diet consistent with his religious beliefs, which were not of any widely known religious group but were based on his interpretations of certain Biblical texts. The inmate insisted on only organically grown produce, which was to be washed in distilled water. A lower court held that meeting the inmate's demands would put an undue burden on the prison system. In *Udey v. Kastner*, 805 F.2d 1218 (5th Cir. 1986), the appeals court held that providing such special dietary requests would lead to a probable proliferation of claims for special food. Having to process such multiple dietary claims, and trying to meet them, would pose "undue costs and administrative burdens" to the government. On this ground, the inmate's requests for the special diet were denied. Note that this case was decided before *Turner v. Safley* in 1986, and its holding is consistent with the *Turner* factor, which considers "the impact accommodation of the asserted constitutional right will have on guards and other inmates, and on the allocation of prison resources generally." *Ali v. Stephens*, 822 F.3d 776 (5th Cir. 2016) (cost reduction as a general matter is a compelling governmental interest). Courts also must consider that RLUIPA "may require a government to incur expenses in its own operations to avoid imposing a substantial burden on religious exercise." 42 U.S. Code Section 2000cc-3.

A similar concern was the basis for a federal court ruling in New York in *Benjamin v. Coughlin*, 708 F.Supp. 570 (S.D. NY 1989). There, Rastafarians asked for a special diet, based on their religious teachings. The diet involved no meat, foods raised only with organic fertilizers, and food cooked in natural materials, such as clay pots. The court in the *Benjamin* case ruled that prison authorities did not have to supply those food items, because they were too complex, and providing them would present too heavy a financial and administrative burden.

The number of different religions with special dietary needs can pose a large burden on a corrections facility that tries to accommodate all of the various demands. (This would seem to be especially true in facilities in large cities or large corrections systems.) With demands on staff for supervising the preparation and serving of special foods and the increased costs of providing special religious diets, the administrative burdens can become immense. Verifying the true dietary requirements of religious groups and making sure the special food supplies from outside the prison, as well as those separated and prepared inside the prison, meet religious requirements, add to the burden. While most administrators would like to respect religious beliefs and teachings and see inmates adhere to and strengthen their religious ties to the community, doing this equitably and respectfully in response to numerous religious requests for special diets can become an overwhelming task.

In a special dietary request that was well publicized at the time, members of the Church of the New Song (CONS, the inmate-founded religion that we discussed earlier in this chapter) requested that filet mignon and sherry be provided for a special sacramental meal. By this time, the federal court in northern Georgia had held that the inmates in CONS were entitled to First Amendment (free exercise) protection. That court, in *Theriault v. Carlson*, 339 F.Supp. 375 (N.D. GA 1973) had ordered authorities at the Atlanta Penitentiary to permit group meetings, religious instruction by the CONS leaders, and religious writings to be mailed and received. However, the request for steak and wine went too far and was not approved. Later, a different court in Texas (where Theriault was then confined) ruled that the Church of the New Song was a "masquerade," a philosophy seeking to cause disruption in prisons, and was not a religion at all. *Theriault v. Silber*, 391 F.Supp. 578 (W.D. TX 1975). We should note that federal courts in Iowa ruled that the Church of the New Song was a religion and was entitled to the protections of the First Amendment. Based on that finding, the authorities at the Iowa State Penitentiary were ordered to allow CONS to exercise their religion equally with other religions in *Remmers v. Brewer*, 494 F.2d 1277 (8th Cir. 1974).

Levitan v. Ashcroft, 281 F.3d 1313 (DC Cir. 2002) was a case involving Federal Bureau of Prisons inmates who were practicing Catholic Christians. The inmates challenged the Bureau's rule barring their drinking of small amounts of wine as part of Communion (a Catholic sacrament). Under that rule, only the supervising chaplain was allowed to consume the wine. The inmates argued that the prohibition violated the free exercise clause of the First Amendment. The district court ruled in favor of the prison officials, saying that under the First Amendment, a religious practice must be mandated by the inmate's religion. The Court of Appeals for the DC Circuit disagreed and held that the proper approach was to use the *Turner* and *O'Lone* balancing standard. Because this was not done by the district court, the decision of the lower court was reversed, and the case remanded for fact finding under a *Turner* and *O'Lone* analysis. (The decision in *Levitan* was handed down in March of 2002; in August of that year, the Bureau of Prisons revised its policy to allow inmates to receive, under the supervision of clergy, a small amount of wine as part of a religious ritual.)

Application of the requirements of RFRA or RLUIPA in the area of religious dietary practices requires additional analysis. In the first instance, a prisoner must demonstrate that his or her religious beliefs were substantially burdened. As noted above, the Supreme Court in *Holt v. Hobbs* did find that the ADOC's policy imposed a "substantial burden" on the inmate's religious belief. The lower courts have generally ruled that a "substantial burden" occurs when the government, through act or omission, puts substantial pressure on individuals to modify their behavior and violate their religious beliefs. *Thompson v. Holm*, 809 F.3d 376 (7th Cir. 2016) ("forcing an inmate to choose between daily nutrition and religious practice is a substantial burden.")

In *Lovelace v. Lee*, 472 F.3d 174 (4th Cir. 2006), the court held that a substantial burden under RLUIPA is imposed by a prison's practice of removing an inmate from what was called the Ramadan Observance pass list, as this removal precludes the inmate from not only the special pre-dawn and post-sunset Ramadan meals, but also from taking part in his religion's group prayers or services held before or after the special breakfast meal. The court said the prison's policy works "to restrict the religious exercise of any [Nation of Islam] inmate who cannot or does not fast, but who still wishes to participate in group services or prayers."

In a case involving a denial of a *halal* diet to a Muslim inmate, the court of appeals defined "substantial burden" as one that (1) requires participation in an activity prohibited by a sincerely held religious belief; (2) prevents participation in conduct motivated by sincerely held religious belief; or (3) places substantial pressure on a prisoner not to engage in, or engage in conduct contrary to, sincerely held religious beliefs. *Abdulhaseeb v. Calbone*, 600 F.3d 1301 (10th Cir. 2010). This case is significant since the inmate was housed in a private correctional facility. Both the district court and court of appeals allowed the action under RLUIPA to proceed against the private corrections employees. In *Knows His Gun v. Montana*, 866 F.Supp. 2d 1235 (D. MT, 2012) the district court expressly ruled that private corrections can be sued under RLUIPA as they are instrumentalities of the state when confining state prisoners.

Once the prisoner demonstrates that his or her religious beliefs were substantially burdened, the government must come forward with credible evidence to demonstrate that the restriction was the least restrictive means of furthering a compelling governmental interest. The Supreme Court, in *Cutter v. Wilkinson*, discussed above, concluded that prison security and order were compelling governmental interests. The Fifth Circuit Court of Appeals has concluded that budgetary and administrative considerations can be "compelling governmental interests." *Baranowski v. Hart*, 486 F.3d 112 (5th Cir. 2007). The court said that:

> [t]he uncontroverted summary judgment evidence submitted by Defendants establishes that TDCJ's [Texas Department of Criminal Justice] budget is not adequate to cover the increased expense of either providing a separate kosher kitchen or bringing in kosher food from the outside; that TDCJ's ability to provide a nutritionally appropriate meal to other offenders would be jeopardized … that such a policy would breed resentment among other inmates; and that there would be an increased demand by other religious groups for similar diets.

Once the government establishes that the restriction furthers a compelling governmental interest, it must also demonstrate that it is using the "least restrictive means" to further that compelling governmental interest.

Like the issue raised in the *Levitan* case discussed above, some correctional organizations have attempted to apply a "religiously required" test by requiring that a prisoner's desired practice must be "compelled by" or be "central to" the prisoner's faith. In *Koger v. Bryan*, 523 F.3d 789 (7th Cir. 2008), the court of appeals disagreed with prison officials who had denied a prisoner the opportunity to eat a nonmeat diet because the prisoner had been unable to establish that his faith group required the nonmeat diet.

Grooming

Inmates have claimed that their religious teachings require certain grooming, or personal appearance, standards. One of the most common is that men are not allowed to cut their facial hair, or any hair on their heads, resulting in beards and long hair.

For many years, most correctional agencies had required men to cut their hair and to be clean shaven. One of the reasons for this was a desire for a standard, military-like appearance. Also, sanitation was a concern. When challenged, the best argument of officials was that there was a security concern, because inmates had to be readily identified (by means of photo IDs, among other things). Allowing beards, mustaches, or long hair changed the appearance and made identification more difficult. With the 1960s, beards and longer hair became more common for men, and confrontation on this issue was inevitable.

Some inmates claimed that long hair was required by their religion, and a free exercise claim was generated. In *Goings v. Aaron*, 350 F.Supp. 1 (D. MN 1972), a Native American inmate claimed that he made a religious vow at his father's funeral that he would return to old traditions and would not cut his hair. He was punished in prison for refusing to have his hair cut. The federal district court, although expressing some doubt about the inmate's sincerity, ruled that he could be required to cut his hair while confined, even if not cutting it was a religious claim.

A different result was reached in *Benjamin v. Coughlin*, 905 F.2d 571 (2nd Cir. 1990), when the New York State Department of Correctional Services (DOCS) appealed a district court order that prohibited the DOCS from requiring newly admitted Rastafarian inmates to cut their hair for the taking of initial photographs. The state argued that requiring inmates to cut their hair for photographs was a legitimate governmental interest related to identifying prisoners who escape. The court of appeals agreed with the district court that the state could obtain suitable photographs by having the prisoners pull their hair back for the photographs. While giving great deference to the state's security interests, the court relied on *Turner v. Safley* to conclude that the state had failed to demonstrate that this accommodation would have more than a minimal effect on the state's legitimate penological interest.

In *Moskowitz v. Wilkinson*, 432 F.Supp. 947 (D. CT 1977), an Orthodox Jewish inmate at the Danbury Federal Correctional Institution filed suit when authorities ordered him to remove his beard, which he had grown based on his religious teachings. The government asserted its interest in requiring no beards, based on prison security, because growing a beard and shaving it would make identification of the inmate more difficult (both within the prison and outside in case identification had to be made to facilitate apprehension in the event of escape). The court found this argument weakened by experiences in other states. A survey had shown that about half the states operated without a no-beard rule. The court held that the no-beard rule was an impermissible infringement on the inmate's sincerely held religious beliefs and that punishing him for refusing to shave his beard was unconstitutional. (See also *Fromer v. Scully*, 874 F.2d 69 (2nd Cir. 1989).)

In *Pollock v. Marshall*, 845 F.2d 656 (6th Cir. 1988), inmate Pollock claimed that his religious beliefs in the teachings of the Lakota American Indians taught him that hair was sacred and that it should not be cut. Marshall, the superintendent of the Southern Ohio Correctional Facility, required Pollock to cut his hair, and Pollock sued under 42 U.S.C. § 1983. Although Marshall asserted that Pollock was not truly a believer—because he was not born a Lakota Indian and couldn't just become one by professing to be—the courts assumed, for purposes of deciding the case, that Pollock did believe in the religion of the Lakota Indians. They used the test of *Turner v. Safley*, maintaining that the regulation impinging on the inmate's constitutional rights would be valid if it was reasonably related to legitimate penological interests. The Sixth Circuit found that there were legitimate interests supporting the Ohio regulation: "Quick identification, removal of a place to hide small contraband, prevention of sanitation problems and homosexuality [prisoners with long hair were alleged by the superintendent to provide homosexual attraction to other inmates], and reduction of [physical] contact between prisoners and guards are all legitimate penological interests that are furthered by requiring inmates to keep their hair short."

The impact of correctional grooming policies under the heightened standards of RFRA and RLUIPA has been mixed. The Ohio grooming policy discussed in *Pollock* above was found not to violate a Native American prisoner's religious rights under RLUIPA. In *Hoevenaar v. Lazaroff*, 422 F.3d 366 (6th Cir. 2005), the court of appeals agreed with the district court that the prison system's ban on long hair promoted security by preventing inmates from hiding contraband in their hair and preventing prisoners from quickly changing their appearance by cutting their hair after an escape. After finding that these governmental interests were present, the court of appeals reversed the district court's order allowing the prisoner to wear a kouplock (described as a 2-inch square of hair at the base of the skull) because the district court failed to afford appropriate deference to the views and expertise of correctional officials in addressing security matters.

Some, but not all, correctional agencies have modified their grooming policies as applied to religious beliefs in response to RLUIPA and *Hobbs. v. Holt.* In *Knight v. Thompson, et al.,* 797 F.3d 934 (11th Cir. 2015) cert. *denied* ___ U.S. ___, 136 S. Ct. 1824 (2016), the court of appeals affirmed the judgment of a district court, which found that Alabama's failure to accommodate the religious beliefs of inmates concerning hair length did not violate RLUIPA. In a lawsuit that began in 1993, inmates in the Alabama Department of Corrections (ADOC) challenged the ADOC's policy requiring male inmates to wear their hair off the neck and collar. The policy did not provide for any religious exceptions. Native American inmates requested an exception because wearing long hair was a central tenet of their religion. The U.S. District Court initially granted judgment in favor of the ADOC under the First Amendment and RFRA and the inmates appealed. While the appeal was pending in the court of appeals (and RFRA was determined not to apply to the states), Congress enacted RLUIPA, and the case was returned to the district court to allow the inmates to amend their complaint to add RLUIPA claims. The district court again ruled in favor of the ADOC, and the inmates appealed again. In 2007, the court of appeals affirmed the judgment of the lower court in all aspects except the hair length claim. Because the factual findings of the district court were now over 10 years old, the court of appeals remanded the case to the district court for a full evidentiary hearing.

The sincerity of the inmates' religious beliefs, and the conclusion that the ADOC policy substantially burdened that belief was not contested. At the evidentiary hearing, the inmate plaintiffs presented testimony that 38 state DOCs and the Federal Bureau of Prisons permitted male inmates to wear long hair either generally or as a religious accommodation. Testimony was also given that the prison staff, using Photoshop, a computer program, could easily modify digital photographs to address changes in inmate appearance. Finally, the plaintiffs introduced expert testimony that "inmates have many other locations where they can more easily store contraband (e.g., socks, stitching areas in clothes, gloves, jackets, etc.), long hair does not impede inmate identification, and long hair does not pose any health risks if inmates follow basic hygiene procedures.

The state offered testimony that the state's prisons were overcrowded and understaffed, and the grooming policy was "necessary to accomplish several compelling goals, including the prevention of contraband, facilitation of inmate identification (both during the usual course of prison business and after escapes), maintenance of good hygiene and health, and facilitation of prison discipline through uniformity." A warden testified that allowing long hair presented safety concerns because long hair slows the process of looking for contraband, increased the risk that the hair would be grabbed during a fight, and would obscure scalp diseases. Another state witness stated that permitting exceptions to the grooming policy that exempts only certain inmates would allow them to identify as a special group and form gangs, eroding order and control. The state also presented testimony from the former director of the Virginia DOC who had implemented a uniform one-inch hair-length policy. This witness stated the policy was implemented after a dangerous inmate had escaped and cut his hair. The inmate was virtually unrecognizable from the pictures maintained by the DOC. This witness testified that non-exempt inmates might attack long haired exempt inmates out of jealousy; described an incident in which a black widow spider wove a nest in an inmate's dreadlocks; and how long hair can conceal scalp sores, cysts, and tumors. However, none of the state's witnesses had personal knowledge of long hair being grabbed in a fight or a longhaired inmate being attacked out of jealousy of hair length.

The court of appeals concluded that, based on the district court's findings of fact, the ADOC's short-hair policy furthered its compelling interests in security, discipline, hygiene, and safety within its prisons and in the public's safety in the event of escapes and alteration of appearances. On the issue of whether the ADOC's policy was the least restrictive means of furthering a compelling governmental interest, the court of appeals again affirmed the lower court's judgment. The ADOC had shown that Plaintiffs' proposed alternatives allowing an exemption for Native American inmates, requiring exempted inmates to search their own hair, and using a computer program to manipulate inmate photographs did not eliminate the ADOC's security, discipline, hygiene, and safety concerns. The accommodations that plaintiffs proposed on contraband and identification did not fully address the ADOC's concerns about gang-formation and hair-pulling during fights, or the concealment of infections and infestations. Finally, even though many correctional agencies granted exceptions to its hair length policies to accommodate religious beliefs, the ADOC was not compelled to implement the same accommodations. "*The RLUIPA does not force institutions to follow the practices of their less risk-averse neighbors, so long as they can prove that they have employed the least restrictive means of furthering the compelling interests that they have chosen to address."*

The United States Court of Appeals for the Fifth Circuit in *Ali v. Stephens*, 822 F.3d 776 (5th Cir. 2016) followed *Holt v. Hobbs* in affirming a district court judgment that the Texas Department of Criminal Justice (TDCJ) policy on inmate grooming violated RLUIPA. The district court ruled in favor of the inmate that the TDCJ's policy on grooming, which denied his request to grow a four-inch beard for religious reasons neither furthered a compelling governmental interest nor was the least restrictive alternative. The court of appeals ruled that contrary to the district court's conclusion, the denial of the inmate's request furthered a compelling governmental interest in controlling contraband in prisons. The TDCJ had argued the policy furthered the interest of inmate identification. However, the state failed to demonstrate how before and after photos as discussed in *Holt v. Hobbs* would not accommodate this concern. Equally important was the conclusion that inmates can quickly alter their appearance by growing, cutting or dying their hair, or wearing glasses. The court of appeals noted that the TDCJ had changed its policy to allow ½-inch long beards and concluded the TDCJ had not satisfactorily addressed how security concerns for a four-inch beard were substantially greater than for a ½-inch beard. The TDCJ had also argued that accommodating the inmate's request would require additional substantial sums of state funds. The TDCJ projected that the cost of inspecting beards might run as high as $1.1 million annually in added staff time. The district court rejected this argument as speculative and credited plaintiff's expert witness that not all Muslim men grow beards, and a reasonable estimate of additional cost for searching the beards was closer to $3,000 annually.

▶ Unusual Religious Groups

Earlier, the text discussed the Church of the New Song, certainly one of the most unusual nonmainstream organizations that has sought First Amendment protection for its activities. This was also a brilliant effort by an inmate to achieve free exercise rights for his group of inmates. The text also notes an inmate Udey, a member of a group of worshipers numbering only a few people, who held somewhat unusual beliefs. The small number of believers was not the ground for turning down his requests for a special diet; however, administrative burden to the government was the ground for that ruling.

In *Jones v. Bradley*, 590 F.2d 294 (9th Cir. 1979), an inmate at the Washington State Penitentiary asked to use the chapel and to perform marriages, claiming he was a pastor of the Universal Life Church (ULC). The district court dismissed his complaint, holding that the ULC is not a religion and, therefore, is not entitled to First Amendment protections. The court of appeals held that it was improper to inquire into the "truth" of religious beliefs or to discredit them because of their unusual nature. Rather, it decided the case on the assumption that the ULC is a religion. Given that assumption, it concluded that inmate Jones was not entitled to the activities he requested; he could not use the chapel because he did not intend to use it for the ceremonial purposes for which it was provided. (He said he wanted to have "study groups," and the court suggested that another room might be made available for that purpose.) He was not entitled to perform marriages, because that was a matter regulated by state licensing requirements, and it did not require free exercise protection.

Another group claiming First Amendment free exercise rights has been the Metropolitan Community Church (MCC). The MCC is a group of Christian churches that ministers primarily to the spiritual and religious needs of homosexuals. In Michigan, the court of appeals upheld a ban on the activities within prisons of inmates affiliated with the MCC. *Brown v. Johnson*, 743 F.2d 408 (6th Cir. 1984). Prison officials had testified that there was a strong correlation between inmate homosexuality and prison violence. Also, they asserted that attending MCC worship services (or being involved in other MCC activities) would identify the participating inmates as homosexuals, which would increase the risks for confrontation or disruptive behavior. The court accepted those concerns as a basis for concluding that there was a strong interest in maintaining internal security within the prison, which justified the ban on MCC services and activities.

In a California case, a three-judge U.S. district court was convened to review a constitutional attack on a state ban on worship services and counseling conducted by ministers of the MCC. *Lipp v. Procunier*, 395 F.Supp. 871 (N.D. CA 1975). The state first argued that the MCC was not a bona fide religion, but rather "a self-proclaimed religious and social group," without standing to assert a constitutional claim of denial of religious rights to free exercise. The court rejected this argument, finding that "the Church's ministry and work and the religion espoused by the Church … possess the cardinal characteristics associated with traditional 'recognized' religions in that it teaches and preaches a belief in a Supreme Being, a religious discipline, and tenets to guide one's daily existence." The court dismissed any consideration of the sexual orientation of the Church's adherents, noting that "the mere fact of one having homosexual proclivities does not per se deprive him of legal entitlements and constitutional immunities."

However, the court held that there could be a security concern that would justify restrictions on the activities of the MCC. "Whether the proclivities, habits or inclinations of an individual or group of prison inmates to act present a clear and present danger to prison discipline and control of prison safety to persons and property" is the question to be answered. The court deferred its final decision pending the presentation of evidence on that question. (State officials, after this court decision, withdrew the ban and allowed some activities of the MCC. Thus, there is not a ruling in this case that the MCC is entitled to engage in its activities within prisons, only a statement of what standards would have to be met, under the First Amendment, in order to justify a restriction or ban of the MCC activities.)

In *McCorkle v. Johnson*, 881 F.2d 993 (11th Cir. 1989), an inmate (McCorkle) at the Holman, Alabama, prison had filed a Section 1983 lawsuit, claiming that authorities were violating his constitutional rights by restricting his practice of his Satanic religion. The court of appeals affirmed a district court ruling that officials had not violated McCorkle's First Amendment rights. The state had first argued that Satanism was not a religion and McCorkle was not a sincere believer in that "religion." The courts refused to get embroiled in those difficult questions. (As we have already noted, proving what is, or is not, a religion and deciding the sincerity of religious beliefs are issues that courts prefer to avoid.) The courts said that, even if Satanism is a religion and McCorkle was a sincere believer, the Alabama policy was valid, because it was reasonably related to a legitimate penological interest.

Johnson (the Alabama warden) had testified that he was concerned about the Satanic teachings and actions being a threat to the security and orderly running of the prison. He noted that he had seen phrases in the Satanic "bible" that taught hatred of enemies and revenge as a top priority. McCorkle himself had testified that he wanted to practice sacrifices, draw (human) blood for initiation (he had, in fact, cut his own wrists in connection with his Satanic rituals), and eat human flesh. Desecration of Christian symbols and mockery of traditional religious morals and teachings were also taught. (The courts noted that McCorkle had been able to perform some alternative Satanic actions, such as wearing a medallion and being able to recount Satanic texts that he had memorized. It is not clear that those things had any impact at all on the courts' rulings.) Applying the standards of the Supreme Court rulings in *O'Lone v. Shabazz* and *Turner v. Safley*, these courts held that the restrictions placed on Satanic activities were a permissible response to a valid penological concern.

> It [the ban on Satanic written materials and Satanic worship] is an informed and measured response
> to the violence inherent in Satanic worship, and to the potential disorder that it might cause in prison.

Are prison officials required to treat atheism as a religion? A Wisconsin inmate argued that he was denied the opportunity to create a group within the prison to study and discuss atheism. Prison officials concluded that there was no religious basis for the group, so the application was treated as a request to form an "inmate activity group." As such, the request was denied. The inmate sued prison officials, claiming that his rights of free exercise were violated by the prison's action as well as giving favored treatment to religious groups, which was a violation of the establishment clause of the First Amendment. In *Kaufman v. McCaughtry*, 419 F. 3d 678 (7th Cir. 2005), the court of appeals affirmed the dismissal of the free exercise claim. The court ruled that the term *religion* has been interpreted broadly to include "non-theistic and atheistic beliefs, as well as theistic ones." However, the prisoner had failed to demonstrate any burden that the state had placed on his practice of atheism, and the prisoner was not prohibited from other means of practicing atheism, including individual study, informal discussion with other atheist inmates, and correspondence with atheist groups in the community.

The dismissal of the prisoner's establishment clause claim was reversed. Because atheism may be considered a religion for First Amendment purposes, the appellate court ruled that prison officials and the district court erred when concluding that the request to form an atheist study group was not a request to form a religious group. Other religious groups within the prison, including Christians, Muslims, Buddhists, and Wiccans, were authorized to conduct formal group meetings to study religious beliefs, creeds, dogma, tenets, and rituals. Accommodation of those religious groups, while denying similar privileges to an atheist group, results in promoting certain religious faiths over others, a violation of the establishment clause. In the absence of evidence demonstrating that a group meeting of atheist inmates posed a greater threat to institution security and order than those of other religious groups, dismissal of the prisoner's complaint was in error, this court of appeals ruled. After the court of appeals remanded this case back to the district court, the state revised its policy in light of the court of appeals opinion and now considers atheism a religion. The district court also ruled that the prison officials were entitled to qualified immunity for money damages as the law was not clearly established at the time of the complained about action. *Kaufman v. McCaughtry*, 422 F.Supp.2d 1016 (W.D. WI 2006).

Summary

- The First Amendment's freedom of religion provisions contain two parts: the establishment clause and the free exercise clause.
- The number of prisoner lawsuits alleging violations of the establishment clause has been increasing. The establishment clause forbids any action by the government to "establish religion." The clause also prohibits government from favoring one religion over another, or one sect of a religion over another sect of the same religion. The majority of First Amendment religion cases from prisons arise under the "free exercise" clause.
- Under the establishment clause, federal courts have upheld the use of federal money to pay prison chaplains, build chapels, and purchase religious materials (*Theriault v. Carlson*).
- Presidents Bush, Obama, and Trump have issued executive orders providing for faith-based initiatives. Program supporters believe that such initiatives will help an inmate prepare for a successful return to the community. Governmental funding for such programs may be used only for secular purposes and may not be used to advance or endorse religion (*Americans United for Separation of Church and State v. Prison Fellowship Ministries, Inc.*).
- The Supreme Court ruled that a Buddhist inmate would have to be given the opportunity to pursue his faith, comparable to the opportunity given to prisoners of other faiths (*Cruz v. Beto*).
- Litigation brought by Black Muslim inmates in the early 1960s can be credited with opening up federal courts to civil rights claims by prisoners, not only on religious freedom claims, but more broadly on claims of constitutional violations.
- The Supreme Court held that New Jersey prison officials were justified in restricting the movement of inmates in and out of the prison, which prevented Muslim inmates from coming back into the institution on Friday at noon for Jumu'ah prayers. The Court said that officials met the standard of acting reasonably, in pursuit of a valid correctional purpose, which was maintaining prison security and order (*O'Lone v. Shabazz*).
- The standard of *O'Lone* (bearing a reasonable relationship to a legitimate governmental objective) was called into question by the action of Congress in passing the Religious Freedom Restoration Act (RFRA). That act prohibits that government from substantially burdening a person's free exercise of religion unless it is necessary to further a compelling governmental interest and is the least restrictive means of achieving that interest. That law was initially applied to both state and federal prison administrators.
- In *City of Boerne v. Flores*, the Supreme Court held that RFRA was unconstitutional. The federal government interpreted the Court's ruling as applying only to the states, so RFRA is still considered to be applicable to the federal government.
- In 2000, Congress passed the Religious Land Use and Institutionalized Persons Act of 2000 (RLUIPA). This act re-established the compelling government interest and least restrictive means test of RFRA in certain cases, including for the protection of religious exercise by institutionalized persons. RLUIPA is applicable to state programs, which use federal funding. RLUIPA was applicable to states receiving federal funds. In *Cutter v. Wilkinson* (2005), the United States Supreme Court upheld the constitutionality of this statute. The court also noted that prison security and good order remain a compelling governmental interest.
- The Supreme Court's decision in *Hobbs v. Holt* held that under RLUIPA, the plaintiff has the initial burden of proving that their desired act or conduct is based on a sincerely held religious belief, and that the restriction imposed by the government substantially burdens that exercise. The burden then shifts to the government to demonstrate the restriction on that particular claimant's religious exercise is "the least restrictive means of furthering [a] compelling governmental interest." The "least restrictive means of furthering a compelling governmental interest" is "exceptionally demanding" and requires the government to "sho[w] that it lacks other means of achieving its desired goal without imposing a substantial burden on the exercise of religion by the objecting part[y]."
- Some religious groups have strict dietary requirements. In the 1960s and 1970s, some courts required prisons to provide special religious diets, such as pork-free diets for Muslims and kosher diets for Jewish

inmates. In more recent cases, some requests for religious diets by individuals or groups with only a few members have been disapproved, primarily on the basis of administrative and financial burdens.

■ Grooming cases (especially by male inmates who want to grow beards or long hair, based on religious teachings) have also gone both ways. As with religious diet cases, the Supreme Court has not ruled on these inmate complaints. Some lower federal courts have ruled in favor of inmates, saying that prison officials did not have a sufficient justification for requiring clean-shaven or short-haired inmates. Other courts have upheld prison policies that required inmates to shave or cut their hair against claims of First Amendment protections.

■ Claims for free exercise of religious beliefs have been made by many inmates who adhere to teachings that are not in the mainstream of religious groups. Courts generally are loath to become embroiled in the question of whether religious beliefs are held by adherents of a "true religion." More often, courts will concede, or assume for the purposes of deciding a case, that an individual's or a group's beliefs are religious. The courts will then decide claims for religious protections and activities based on whether the exercise of those teachings in a prison setting would pose a threat to prison order or security or would pose a significant burden on prison administration.

Thinking About It

An inmate in the custody of the department of corrections (DOC) had been receiving a special kosher diet as part of his religious beliefs. Correctional officials discovered the inmate was buying non-kosher items from the commissary and removed the inmate from the kosher diet program. The inmate sued the DOC, claiming his denial of a kosher diet violated his rights under the First Amendment and RLUIPA. The DOC responded that purchasing food inconsistent with the inmate's religious diet accommodation indicated the inmate was insincere in his beliefs. The DOC also incurred extra cost in providing the special dietary meals and had an interest in providing special diets to only those prisoners whose religious beliefs are sincere and who otherwise complied with DOC policy. The inmate acknowledged buying non-kosher items, but stated these items were provided to other inmates as part of an "inmate store."

May the DOC deny the inmate a religious diet based on the above facts. *Perrault v. Michigan Department of Corrections.* (WD Mi 2018).

Key Term

facial challenge

Endnotes

1. Please try to make your own identification of these cases, which have actually been decided under the First Amendment. Numbers 1- *International Society for Krishna Consciousness, Inc. v. Lee*, 505 U.S. 672 (1992) , 2- *United States v. Seeger*, 380 U.S. 163 (1965), 4- *Reynolds v. United States*, 98 U.S. 145 (1897), and 6-*Saia v. New York*, 334 U.S. 556 (1946) are free exercise cases. In them, persons of different religious backgrounds claimed the right to engage in certain protected, religion-dictated activity without government interference or regulation. Numbers 3- *County of Allegheny v. ACLU, Greater Pittsburgh Chapter*, 492 U.S. 573 (1989) and 5- *Karkoff v. March*, 755 F.2d 223 (2nd Cir. 1985) are establishment cases, where persons objected to government activity that seemed to give preference to or endorse a particular religious group or function (with government funding). Number 7-*Abington School District v. Schempp*, 374 U.S. 203 (1963), school prayer, perhaps the most famous constitutional religious issue in recent years, actually involves both freedoms. It is decided primarily on the basis of the establishment clause, with the assertion that the public-school system, a government function, cannot endorse a prayer or Bible reading that is presented to all children. Competing with it is a free exercise claim of students and parents, who want school children to be able to participate in some kind of religious observance in the classroom.

2. "Executive Order 13198 of January 29, 2001, Agency Responsibilities With Respect to Faith-Based and Community Initiatives," *Federal Register*, Vol. 66 (2001): 77141–77144, https://www.govinfo.gov/content/pkg/FR-2002-12-16/pdf/02-31831.pdf and "Executive Order 13199 of January 29, 2001, Establishment of White House Office of Faith-Based and Community Initiatives," *Federal Register*, Vol. 66 (2001): 8499–8500, https://www.govinfo.gov/content/pkg/FR-2001-01-31/pdf/01-2852.pdf

3. "Executive Order 13279 of December 12, 2002, Equal Protection of the Laws for Faith Based and Community Organizations," *Federal Register*, Vol 67 (2002): 77141–77144, https://www.govinfo.gov/content/pkg/CFR-2003-title3-vol1/pdf/CFR-2003-title3-vol1-eo13279.pdf

4. "Executive Order 13498 of February 5, 2009, Amendments to Executive Order 13199 and Establishment of the President's Advisory Council for Faith-Based and Neighborhood Partnerships," *Federal Register* The new Executive Order changed the Office's name from "White House Office of Faith-Based and Community Initiatives" to the new name, "White House Office of Faith-Based and Neighborhood Partnerships." https://www.govinfo.gov/content/pkg/FR-2009-02-09/pdf/E9-2893.pdf

5. "Executive Order 13831 of May 3, 2018, Establishment of a White House Faith and Opportunity Initiative," *Federal Register* Vol. 83 (2018): 20715–20717. https://www.govinfo.gov/content/pkg/FR-2018-05-08/pdf/2018-09895.pdf. President Trump's May 2018 Executive Order on Establishment of a White House Faith and Opportunity Initiative in addition to substituting "White House Faith and Opportunity Initiative" for "White House Office of Faith Based and Community Initiatives" provided for the appointment of an Advisor to head the White House Faith and Opportunity Initiative. The Initiative was instructed to "consult with and seek information from experts and various faith and community leaders from outside of the Federal Government including those from state, local, and tribal governments . . . . These experts and leaders shall be identified based on their expertise in a broad range of areas in which faith-based and community organizations operate, including poverty alleviation, religious liberty, strengthening marriage and family, education, solutions for substance abuse and addiction, crime prevention and reduction, prisoner reentry, and health and humanitarian services." The Initiative was also tasked with identifying and making proposals to reduce "burdens on the exercise of religious convictions and legislative, regulatory, and other barriers to the full and active engagement of faith-based and community organizations in government-funded or government-conducted activities and programs" in accordance with the Attorney General's October 6, 2017, Memorandum on Federal Law Protection for Religious Liberty. https://www.justice.gov/opa/press-release/file/1001891/download

6. Georgia Department of Corrections- Faith and Character Based Initiative. http://www.dcor.state.ga.us/Divisions/Facilities/Transitional/FCBI 3

7. Clair Cripe, 1976. "Religious Freedom in Institutions." Paper presented at the American Correctional Association Annual Congress, Denver, CO, 1976).

8. 42 U.S. Code Sections 2000bb-1 Provides as follows:
   (a) Government shall not substantially burden a person's exercise of religion even if the burden results from a rule of general applicability, except as provided in subsection (b).
   (b) Exception Government may substantially burden a person's exercise of religion only if it demonstrates that application of the burden to the person –
      (1) is in furtherance of a compelling governmental interest; and
      (2) is the least restrictive means of furthering that compelling governmental interest.

© EJ_Rodriquez/iStock/Getty Images Plus/Getty Images

CHAPTER 10

Fourth Amendment: Search and Seizure, and Privacy

A right of privacy in traditional Fourth Amendment terms is fundamentally incompatible with the close and continual surveillance of inmates and their cells required to ensure institutional security and internal order. We are satisfied that society would insist that the prisoner's expectation of privacy always yield to what must be considered the paramount interest in institutional security.

U.S. Supreme Court, *Hudson v. Palmer*

The Fourth Amendment to the Constitution provides:

The right of the people to be secure in their persons, houses, papers, and effects, against unreasonable searches and seizures, shall not be violated.

CHAPTER OUTLINE

- Searches in Prisons
- *Hudson v. Palmer*
- *Bell v. Wolfish*
- *Lanza v. New York*
- *United States v. Hearst*
- Attorney Visits, Communications
- Strip Searches
- Prison Rape Elimination Act PREA
- Pat Searches and Other Inmate Searches
- Prison Searches and the Eighth Amendment
- DNA Collection
- *Maryland v. King*
- Searches of Non-Inmates
  - Searches of Employees; *City of Ontario, CA. v. Quon*
  - Visitor Searches

This chapter explores whether, and to what extent, the Fourth Amendment applies within prisons and jails. The exact language of the amendment protects "persons, houses, papers, and effects." Does this include inmates in their prison cells? The amendment does not forbid all searches of persons and their homes and property but only "unreasonable" searches. The job of the courts, in looking at claims of illegal searches, is to decide two questions: Is the area of the search protected under the Constitution? If so, has a search been conducted in a reasonable or an unreasonable manner? There are special limitations on both of these concepts in a prison setting.

▶ Searches in Prisons

There are two principal kinds of searches in prisons: searches of an inmate's cell or living quarters and searches of the person. As to searches of the person, there are several kinds of inmate searches: pat or frisk searches, visual or strip searches, digital or simple instrument searches, urine testing, X-ray examinations, and blood tests. In addition to those principal kinds of searches, there are searches of all other physical areas within the facility, such as work and recreation areas and the grounds surrounding the buildings, as well as the obvious searches of inmates' living quarters (whether in cells, rooms, or dormitories). Also, there are questions of searches of visitors and employees.

On the part of inmates, some are looking for ways to escape, some are assaultive, and some are looking for ways to introduce **contraband**. Corrections officials, on the other hand, are looking for ways to stop these illegal occurrences. Searches are commonly used for this purpose. They are conducted by looking for escape implements, weapons that might be used in assaults, and all other kinds of contraband, such as drugs and money.

Cell phones are an especially dangerous form of contraband as they may be used by inmates to avoid staff monitoring of their telephone calls. Cell phones may be used to plan escapes and other crimes, threaten persons in the community, or otherwise facilitate criminal activity. In 2010 Congress enacted the Cell Phone Contraband Act of 2010 (Public Law 111-225). In part, this legislation amends 18 U.S.C. § 1791, "Providing or possessing contraband in a federal prison," by expanding the term prohibited object to include a phone or other device used by a user of commercial mobile service." The punishment for providing or attempting to provide an inmate this prohibited object, or for an inmate to make, possess or obtain, or attempt to make or obtain this prohibited object, is up to one year in prison, a fine, or both. Prisoners have used cell phones to facilitate escapes, threaten persons in the community[1] and to perpetrate fraud on persons in the community by threatening arrest for missed jury duty.[2]

The Supreme Court has provided guidance on Fourth Amendment issues related to prisoner cell searches in two leading cases.

▶ *Hudson v. Palmer*

Palmer was an inmate at the Bland Correctional Center in Virginia. Hudson, a correctional officer, and another officer conducted a **shakedown** search of Palmer's cell and locker, looking for contraband. During the search, they found a ripped pillowcase in a trash can in the cell. They filed charges against Palmer for destroying state property, and he was found guilty of that offense in a disciplinary hearing. Palmer filed a lawsuit under 42 U.S.C. § 1983, claiming that Hudson had violated his Fourth Amendment right not to be subjected to unreasonable searches and seizures.

Palmer also claimed that Hudson, during the search, destroyed some of Palmer's personal property, just to harass him. The loss of property was treated as a due process claim, which is not a Fourth Amendment issue. The Supreme Court ruled that because the state had provided a remedy to seek compensation for Palmer's lost property, there was no due process violation, even if (as alleged) the property was destroyed intentionally and without authorization. (*Parratt v. Taylor*, 451 U.S. 527 (1981), *Daniels v. Williams*, 474 U.S. 327 (1986), and *Davidson v. Cannon*, 474 U.S. 344 (1986), provide a full picture of the Supreme Court's current treatment of this kind of due process claim by inmates.)

The Fourth Amendment question in *Hudson v. Palmer,* 468 U.S. 517 (1984), was "whether [Palmer] has a right of privacy in his prison cell entitling him to the protection of the Fourth Amendment against unreasonable searches." The Fourth Circuit Court of Appeals held that an inmate had a limited privacy right in his cell. The Supreme Court reversed that ruling:

> [T]he Fourth Amendment proscription against unreasonable searches does not apply within the confines of the prison cell.

After discussing the volatile and often violent nature of prisons, the Court emphasized that prison officials "must be ever alert to attempts to introduce drugs and other contraband into the premises which, we can judicially note, is one of the most perplexing problems of prisons today." Officials must also prevent the flow of weapons into the prisons, look for escape plots or tools, and try to maintain as sanitary an environment as possible. Because of these concerns and the fact that contraband may often be hidden in cells, the Supreme Court recognized the need for cell access:

> **Unfettered access to these cells by prison officials, thus, is imperative if drugs and contraband are to be ferreted out and sanitary surroundings are to be maintained.**

As with many constitutional claims of prisoners, the Court noted that the question of privacy in prison is based on a balancing of interests: the interest of society in the security of prisons and the expectation of privacy of prisoners in their cells. The Court concluded the balance favored prison security:

> **A right of privacy in traditional Fourth Amendment terms is fundamentally incompatible with the close and continual surveillance of inmates and their cells required to ensure institutional security and internal order .... We believe that it is accepted by our society that "[l]oss of freedom of choice and privacy are inherent incidents of confinement."**

Palmer had also claimed a Fourth Amendment violation because Hudson had seized and destroyed some of his property during the search. The Court ruled, in a footnote that the Fourth Amendment's proscription of unreasonable seizures was also inapplicable in a prison cell:

> **Prison officials must be free to seize from cells any articles which, in their view, disserve legitimate institutional interests.**

The Supreme Court tersely but sweepingly held:

> **[T]he Fourth Amendment has no applicability to a prison cell.**

The significance of the *Hudson v. Palmer* decision illustrates the state of the law before the *Hudson* decision. In *United States v. Hinckley*, 672 F.2d 115 (D.C. Cir. 1982) was an expedited appeal of issue in the trial of John Hinckley in U.S. District Court in the District of Columbia for the attempt to assassinate President Ronald Reagan. At one point in the trial, an extremely important piece of prosecution evidence was excluded on the grounds of invasion of the defendant's privacy in his cell. An officer had found, in a regular search of Hinckley's cell, a diary that Hinckley was keeping. The officer noted some entries in that diary, copied them, and turned them over to authorities. A government witness, a psychiatrist, was ready to testify about Hinckley's mental state—his "sanity"—based on the writings in that diary. However, the witness was not allowed to do so on the grounds that the diary writings were protected by a privacy right and that they had been taken and copied in an "unreasonable seizure" under the Fourth Amendment. The district court ruled, and the appellate court affirmed, that the writing which the officer initially observed did not reasonably relate to correctional security, and the seizure was not warranted by correctional interests. Hinckley was found not guilty by reason of insanity and was committed to St. Elizabeth's Hospital, the psychiatric hospital of the District of Columbia until he was given a full time convalescent leave in 2016. *U.S. v. Hinckley*, 200 F.Supp. 2d 1 (D.D.C. 2016).

▶ *Bell v. Wolfish*

In *Bell v. Wolfish*, 441 U.S. 520 (1979), which dealt with several constitutional claims raised by inmates at the Metropolitan Correctional Center (MCC, a federal detention center in New York City), the Court addressed two search issues: searches of living quarters (inmates' cells) and visual strip searches. (Strip searches will be discussed later in this chapter.)

The MCC, like most jails and detention centers, held both pretrial detainees and convicted prisoners. Most inmates were unconvicted persons who were confined while awaiting trial. The convicted persons at MCC included those who were being held after their convictions, while awaiting sentencing and then transfer to a regular prison, and those who were serving short sentences. Other convicted persons were brought back to the jail from prison where they were serving sentences, for purposes of posttrial hearings on their cases, to consult with counsel on appeals, or perhaps to testify in another person's case. (The major part of the *Wolfish* opinion deals with a discussion of the issue of double-bunking pretrial detainees in a detention facility, which is discussed elsewhere in an examination of the conditions of confinement.)

Staff at the MCC conducted randomly timed, unannounced searches of inmates' living quarters. During these "shakedowns," all inmates would usually be cleared out of the particular living unit and a team of correctional officers would search each room in that unit. Inmates complained that during these searches items in the cells were left in needless disarray, and sometimes they were damaged or destroyed. They asked for permission to be present during the searches of their cells to watch the searches (and presumably to serve as a deterrent to overzealous or wrongful searching by the staff). The district court had ordered that inmates would have to be present during searches, in order to have "reasonable" searches and seizures. Prison officials said that permitting inmates to observe room inspections would lead to friction between the inmates and the security guards and would allow the inmates to attempt to frustrate the search by distracting personnel and moving contraband from one room to another ahead of the search team.

The Second Circuit Court of Appeals agreed with the district court and held the room-search policy of the MCC to be unconstitutional. (The Supreme Court complained that the court of appeals had not identified the constitutional provision on which it relied when it set aside the prison's room-search rule. The district court had said that the pretrial detainees retained a right of privacy, which was found in the Fourth Amendment.) The Supreme Court disagreed and reversed the lower courts' rulings.

For both unsentenced (pretrial) detainees and persons serving sentences, the Supreme Court said that an inmate has no privacy right with respect to his room or cell. The MCC's room-search rule was found *not* to violate the Fourth Amendment.

> **[R]oom searches represent an appropriate security measure … [E]ven the most zealous advocate of prisoners' rights would not suggest that a warrant is required to conduct such a search … The room search rule simply facilitates the safe and effective performance of the search which all concede may be conducted. The rule itself, then, does not render the searches "unreasonable" within the meaning of the Fourth Amendment.**

The question of whether an inmate has a right to be present during a search of his cell was raised again in the case of *Block v. Rutherford*, 468 U.S. 576 (1984), even though it had been recently decided in *Wolfish*. (*Block* also concerned pretrial detainees at the Los Angeles County Jail and dealt mainly with the issue of contact visiting.) The Supreme Court in *Block* reiterated its stand on the cell-search rule and held (again) that prisoners have no constitutional right to be present to observe a search of their cells.

▶ *Lanza v. New York*

Although *Hudson* and *Wolfish* constitute the definitive word from the Supreme Court on room searches in prison, some other cases gave forewarning of the *Hudson* approach and cast some light on other types of prison searches.

In *Lanza v. New York*, 370 U.S. 139 (1962), Lanza had a visit from his brother in a local jail. The two conversed in the visiting room. Unknown to them, there was an electronic device hidden in the room that picked up their conversation and a transcript was made of what was said. A state legislative committee, which was investigating possible corruption in the state parole system, called Lanza to testify, based on the content of the transcript of the jail conversation. Lanza refused to testify and was convicted for that refusal. He claimed that it was improper for the jail officials to electronically intercept and record his visiting room conversation. He further claimed that it was a violation of his constitutional rights when he was punished for refusing to talk about the contents of that intercepted conversation.

The Supreme Court disagreed with Lanza and upheld his conviction. The Court first pointed out that Lanza's claim that the officials' action was a violation of the Fourth Amendment was based necessarily on the assumption that the visiting room of the jail was a constitutionally protected area and that the surreptitious eavesdropping in that room was an unreasonable search and seizure.

> **But to say that a public jail is the equivalent of a man's "house" or that it is a place where he can claim constitutional immunity from search or seizure of his person, his papers, or his effects, is at best a**

novel argument ... [I]t is obvious that a jail shares none of the attributes of privacy of a home, an automobile, an office, or a hotel room. In prison, official surveillance has traditionally been the order of the day.

However, the Supreme Court observed that the legislative committee had other grounds to question Lanza. Therefore, his prosecution for refusing to testify (even when given immunity from prosecution) was permissible, even if there had been a constitutional problem with the intercepted conversation. Thus, there is not a clear holding that there was no Fourth Amendment protection in the visiting situation at the jail. However, the language quoted previously shows the predilection of the Supreme Court to find no privacy in a prison or jail, even in a conversation with a person from the outside community. (In an aside, the Court did note that relationships that have special legal protection, such as attorney–client relationships, would have at least as much protection in a jail as in the outside world. In effect, the Court found no fault with the jail intercepting a conversation with a social, family member visitor but warned that "special relationships" must be carefully protected in jail.)

▶ *United States v. Hearst*

Of similar import is the case involving the prosecution of Patty Hearst. In *United States v. Hearst*, 563 F.2d 1331 (9th Cir. 1977), cert. denied, 435 U.S. 1000 (1978), the court of appeals upheld Hearst's conviction over an objection that it was obtained using evidence of an intercepted conversation Hearst had in jail. While she was held in the San Mateo County (California) Jail shortly after her arrest, Hearst had a visit from a friend. They communicated over a phone, while viewing each other through a glass window (typical noncontact visiting). The conversation was monitored and recorded by jail staff, which was often done in that jail. The tape of this conversation was delivered to the Federal Bureau of Investigation (FBI) and the tape was later used against Hearst at trial; some portions were read to the jury and other parts of the tape were used by the prosecution in Hearst's cross-examination.

The question raised on appeal of Hearst's conviction was whether making that tape and using it at her trial was a violation of the Fourth Amendment. The court of appeals noted the *Lanza* decision and the fact that *Lanza* was still a valid statement of the law. In the *Hearst* case, jail officials had a justifiable security purpose in monitoring and recording conversations of inmates with their visitors, the court said. Once the government established a justifiable purpose for its intrusion on individuals' rights, the question of the constitutionality of the jail's actions was to be resolved in its favor. This was because courts should show a deference to the needs of prison (and jail) administration and because there were obviously "traditional notions regarding surveillance of prisoners." The court further noted the Supreme Court decision in *Procunier v. Martinez*, 416 U.S. 396 (1974), which allowed the reading of prisoner correspondence when justified on the grounds of institutional security and order. "It would be anomalous indeed to permit prison officials to intercept written correspondence ... while prohibiting the interception of oral communications between prisoners and visitors conducted for essentially the same purposes: prison security and order." The court further noted that it was permissible for the jail to turn the tapes over to law enforcement personnel (the FBI). Once the tapes were legitimately under government control, they could be used as evidence by the government.

In *United States v. Paul*, 614 F.2d 115 (6th Cir. 1980), cert. denied, 446 U.S. 941 (1980), correctional officers at a federal prison monitored a telephone call in which inmate Pierce was telling an unidentified woman to "bring the material" and that he would "have the money." The following day, Pierce, prior to going to a visit, was searched and found to have an unauthorized $5.00 bill on his person. Susan Paul, who came to visit Pierce, was taken to the warden's office and strip-searched, but nothing was found. Through subsequent monitoring of a telephone conversation between another inmate and a woman identified as Susan, the staff heard the woman say she had "ditched the stuff" under the chair. With that lead, hashish was located, and Pierce and Paul were prosecuted for introducing drugs into a federal prison.

During the trial process, the defendants argued that the testimony regarding the monitored telephone conversations should have been suppressed and that the taping was in violation of the federal wiretapping statute, under Title 18, U.S. Code, Sections 2510 et seq. The district court refused to suppress testimony regarding the monitored telephone conversations and held that the facts of this case fell under Section 2510(5)(a) of the law, which permits interception of wire communications when done by a law enforcement officer in the ordinary course of his duties. The circuit court agreed, referring to *Lanza* and *Hearst*.

Section 2511(2)(c) is another provision of this act (the "wiretap" law) that is used to uphold the monitoring of prison telephone conversations. This section allows monitoring where "one of the parties to the communication has given prior consent to such interception." As part of the rules in many prisons and jails, and supported by a notice posted in the telephone area, every inmate is advised of the potential for monitoring and that the inmate's use of the telephone constitutes her consent for this monitoring. In *United States v. Amen*, 831 F.2d 373 (2nd Cir. 1987), cert. denied, 485 U.S. 1021 (1988) the court approved this policy:

> **If security concerns can justify strip and body-cavity searches … and wholly random cell searches … then surely it is reasonable to monitor prisoners' telephone conversations, particularly where they are told that the conversations are being monitored.**

▶ Attorney Visits, Communications

To protect the privacy of attorney–client communications, most prisons and jails have special areas where attorneys can meet with their clients without prison officials being in a position to hear the conversations. Prison officials must take appropriate steps to ensure the privacy of these conversations. In *Lonegan v. Hasty*, 436 F. Supp. 2d 419 (E.D. NY 2006), the court refused to grant qualified immunity protection to prison officials who secretly audio-taped communications between detainees and their attorneys. The court noted that while prisons are not usually places where a person expects privacy, the Fourth Amendment protects communications between attorneys and clients in prison, especially those communications taking place in an area designated for attorney–client meetings.

In *United States v. Hatcher*, 323 F.3d 666 (8th Cir. 2003), the prisoners and attorneys were aware that their conversations were being recorded by prison officials. However, the district court ruled that the tapes were protected by the attorney–client privilege and refused to order their disclosure. The court of appeals disagreed, ruling that carrying on a conversation knowing it was being monitored by a third party was a waiver of any attorney–client privilege.

A variation of this is *United States v. Novak*, 531 F.3d 99 (1st Cir. 2008). Inmate Holyoke contacted attorney Novak through telephone calls made from the Barnstable County Jail in Massachusetts. The jail randomly recorded and monitored inmate phone calls. Pursuant to state and federal regulations, attorney-inmate calls may not be monitored; however, the procedures in place to prevent such monitoring failed in this instance, and the law enforcement officer hearing the inmate-attorney call learned of planned criminal activity. Government officials asked Holyoke for his cooperation in an investigation of attorney Novak. Holyoke agreed, and in later conversations Novak agreed to launder what he believed were the proceeds of drug trafficking. Novak was subsequently arrested for endeavoring to obstruct justice and money laundering. He filed a motion to suppress the recordings, claiming that the first instance of monitoring violated the Fourth Amendment. While the district court agreed and suppressed the evidence, the First Circuit reversed, saying Novak had limited his suppression arguments to a Fourth Amendment claim. (The Sixth Amendment would protect the defendant's right to the assistance of counsel.) The court said that the monitoring posed a "significant Sixth Amendment issue," but since this was not raised by Novak, it would not be considered by the court. As for the Fourth Amendment, the court observed that a "telephone call can be monitored and recorded without violating the Fourth Amendment so long as one participant in the call consents to the monitoring."

▶ Strip Searches

The appellate court, in *Forts v. Ward*, 621 F.2d 1210 (2nd Cir. 1980), said, "the modern sensitivity to the significance of gender in American life and law has made it inevitable that cases will arise where gender-based legal contentions conflict." This case arose out of the Bedford Hills Correctional Facility in New York, a women's prison. In 1977, there was a change of policy whereby, for the first time, male corrections officers were assigned to duty in the facility's sleeping quarters. Female inmates filed suit under 42 U.S.C. § 1983, claiming that their constitutional rights to privacy were violated when male officers were able to routinely view them while partially or completely unclothed. The union representing the corrections officers joined administrators in opposing the lawsuit. The officers' argument was based primarily on their equal employment opportunity rights. They claimed that excluding them from certain positions violated Title VII of the Civil Rights law and (in this situation) disadvantaged male officers.

One part of the solution, developed earlier in the case by the administration, was to remove men from night-shift duties, when they would encounter female inmates disrobed more frequently, as the inmates prepared for bed or were in bed. The cells at Bedford Hills had solid doors, with a clear glass window (6"x9"). The inmates were allowed to close their doors and to cover their door windows for 15-minute intervals (for privacy, presumably when changing their clothes or preparing for bed). Taking the men off night-shift duty not only reduced the job-assignment opportunities for men but also for women, because the women would have to cover all night-shift posts and would, therefore, have reduced opportunities to work the day shift, which most staff preferred.

The district court in *Forts* had found that female inmates were entitled to be protected from being viewed by male officers when they were partially or completely unclothed. This included while they were sleeping (inmates also complained that male officers would view them unnecessarily while they were sleeping), while they were receiving medical treatment in the hospital, while showering, and while using toilet facilities. That court (the trial court) upheld the nighttime ban on male officers in the housing quarters but allowed men to work the daytime shifts, because female inmates could cover their cell windows when they needed privacy.

The court of appeals was concerned about the district court's order because the officers' Title VII equal employment rights still seemed to be infringed. Without describing just where in the Constitution the inmates' privacy rights were found, the appeals court noted that there was a direct conflict here between the privacy rights of inmates in their cells and the employment rights of the officers. The court of appeals tried to accommodate both concerns by endorsing a plan that changed the supervision and living arrangements. The state had agreed to allow inmates to cover their windows when they were changing their clothes or using the toilet. The court approved this change, which would cover nighttime hours as well as daytime. Prison officials proposed to solve the problem of inmates complaining that they could be viewed while sleeping by issuing to anyone who wanted them one-piece pajamas. The district court had rejected this offer because the pajamas were unattractive and uncomfortably warm, but the court of appeals said those concerns were not sufficient to outweigh equal employment rights. The court directed the parties to explore what kind of sleepwear could be agreed on to achieve the privacy protection desired by inmates. That privacy protection covered only the involuntary viewing of private parts of the body by male officers and did not extend (as inmates argued) to a protection against being viewed at all while asleep. These two concessions by the state satisfied the appellate court by achieving some accommodation of the competing rights of the parties. While these accommodations were practical for Bedford Hills facility, there are security issues that arise when inmates, who are authorized to prevent their viewing by staff for even limited periods of time, could facilitate inmate misconduct or be used to commit crimes or engage in self-destructive activity.

The Supreme Court decision in *Bell v. Wolfish*, 441 U.S. 520 (1979) dealt with the issues of cell searches (discussed above) and body cavity searches during strip searches. At all Federal Bureau of Prison facilities, inmates were required to undergo a strip search (by an officer of the same sex) after every contact visit with a person from outside of the institution. As part of these searches, the inmates were required to expose their body cavities for visual inspection. Prison officials testified that these were necessary to find, and to deter, the introduction of contraband into the institution. The district court had allowed the strip searches but had banned the body cavity searches, unless there was probable cause that the inmate was concealing contraband. The court of appeals affirmed, finding that this "gross violation of personal privacy" was not justified by the government's security interest in conducting the search.

The Supreme Court commenced its discussion on the legality of body cavity searches by noting that "this practice instinctively gives us the most pause." On this one issue, an additional justice dissented, making this a five-to-four decision on the body cavity searches, while all other issues in *Bell* were decided in favor of the government by a six-to-three vote. The Court's decision was specifically stated to apply both to the convicted prisoners and to the pretrial detainees, both of whom were housed at the New York MCC and were subject to these searches after visiting.

The Supreme Court assumed, for the purpose of making its constitutional analysis, that the inmates retained some Fourth Amendment rights while in the jail facility. It pointedly did not decide that they did have any such rights; it only assumed so for purposes of deciding the case and pointing out what searches could be conducted. Searches under the Fourth Amendment, the Court said, would be impermissible only if they were unreasonable. "The Fourth Amendment prohibits only unreasonable searches, and under the circumstances, we do not believe that these searches are unreasonable." The Court further explained this point:

The test of reasonableness under the Fourth Amendment is not capable of precise definition or mechanical application. In each case it requires a balancing of the need for the particular search against the invasion of personal rights that the search entails … A detention facility is a unique place

fraught with serious security dangers … [I]nmate attempts to secrete [contraband] items … by concealing them in body cavities are documented in this record, and in other cases.

Stating further that they did not underestimate "the degree to which these searches may invade the personal privacy of inmates," the Court held that such searches, conducted in a reasonable manner (and not abusively), could be conducted at the conclusion of visits, without a necessary finding of probable cause or **reasonable suspicion** (which some others, including dissenting justices, would require) before a body cavity search could be conducted. The probable cause standard for searches (and arrests) is found in the Fourth Amendment. The standard is objective and measured by the facts and circumstances (the totality of the circumstances) within the officer's knowledge, or based upon reliable information, would lead to what an officer would believe to be evidence of crime to be found at the location searched. The Supreme Court has defined the concept as "fluid," *Illinois v. Gates* 462 U.S. 213 (1983) and "incapable of precise definition or quantifications into percentages." *Maryland v. Pringle*, 540 U.S. 366 (2003). In *Texas v. Brown*, 460 U.S. 730 (1983) the Court ruled the probable cause standard does not require showing an officer's "belief [is] correct or more likely true than false." The concept of reasonable suspicion was first announced by the Supreme Court in *Terry v. Ohio* 392 U.S. 1 (1968). The reasonable suspicion standard is less demanding than the probable cause standard and "requires a showing considerably less than preponderance of the evidence." *Illinois v. Wardlow*, 528 U.S. 119 (2000).

Following *Bell v. Wolfish*, a number of lower courts concluded that the constitutional rights of detainees were violated by blanket strip search policies for all persons processed into a jail's general population. Strip searches would not violate the privacy rights of detainees when correctional officials had reasonable suspicion that the detainee was concealing contraband. See, for example, *Roberts v. Rhode Island*, 239 F.3d 107 (1st Cir. 2001), *Masters v. Crouch*, 872 F.2d 1248 (6th Cir. 1989), and *Shain v. Ellison*, 273 F.3d 56 (2nd Cir. 2001). Some circuits had extended the "reasonable suspicion" policy to include some felonies. *Kennedy v. Los Angeles Police Department*, 901 F.2d 702 (9th Cir. 1989) (strip search of a person arrested for a felony property offense was unreasonable.). Beginning in the 2000s, some circuits reassessed its earlier case law and determined that blanket strip searches without individualized reasonable suspicion did not violate the Fourth Amendment.

In 2008, the *en banc* Eleventh Circuit Court of Appeals reversed its precedent and ruled that a jail's blanket policy of strip searching all arrestees upon entering the facility was reasonable even in the absence of individualized suspicion. *Powell v. Barrett*, 541 F.3d 1298 (11th Cir. 2008) (en banc). In 2010, the *en banc* Ninth Circuit Court of Appeals also reversed its precedent and upheld a blanket policy of strip searching all arrestees before they entered San Francisco's general jail population. *Bull v. City and County of San Francisco*, 595 F.3d 964 (9th Cir. 2010) (en banc). San Francisco operated six different jails, and the county justified its procedures as an effort to control the introduction of drugs, weapons, and other contraband. Records maintained by the sheriff established that in the almost four years that the policy was in effect, 1,574 items of contraband (for example, drugs, homemade knives, and jail-made handcuff keys) were uncovered during the searches. The searches were required to be performed in a professional manner by an officer of the same sex in an area affording privacy to the arrestee.

The district court held the policy violated the Fourth Amendment rights of those persons who were searched. The court of appeals focus was on the inmate's challenge to the jail's blanket policy and practice of searching pre-arraignment arrestees; it did not consider individual cases.

The court of appeals first determined that the searches conducted by the Sheriff's Department did not differ in scope, manner, or justification from the searches approved by the Supreme Court in *Bell v. Wolfish*. In addition, the record of contraband intercepted in the San Francisco searches far exceeded what had been used to justify the searches in *Bell v. Wolfish*.

The court of appeals in *Bull* also considered the strip search policy under the standards established in *Turner v. Safley*, 482 U.S. 78 (1987), and concluded that the policy was reasonably related to legitimate penological interests. The court of appeals found that the strip search policy furthered a legitimate governmental purpose of restricting the introduction of contraband. Without the policy, the jail would experience increased contraband introduction, leading to utilization of greater resources in order to detect and confiscate the contraband, this court said. The court also noted that the plaintiffs had not shown that the policy was an exaggerated response to the prison's concerns over contraband introduction. The court held that the policy requiring strip searches of all arrestees placed into the jail's general custodial population was reasonable under the Fourth Amendment. The court in *Bull* stated that it was overruling its own panel opinion in *Thompson* (previously discussed in this section), which held "that a blanket policy of stripping arrestees was per se unconstitutional." The court also made it clear that it was not disturbing its prior opinions dealing with "searches of arrestees who were not classified for housing in the general jail or prison population." An example of this is an intoxicated person who is released upon becoming sober. Surprisingly, the issue of strip searches recently arose within the context of a middle school. *Safford Unified School District v. Redding*, 557 U.S. 364 (2009).

In 2010, the Third Circuit decided *Florence v. Chosen Board of Freeholders* 621 F.3d 296 (3rd Cir. 2010). For the first-time, the court of appeals was addressing in that circuit jail policies that authorized jail officials to strip search all persons placed in general jail populations. The court noted the split in circuit authority and determined that the position announced by the 11th (*Powell v. Barrett*) and 9th Circuits (*Bull v. San Francisco*) was correct. In *Florence v. Chosen Board of Freeholders*, 566 U.S. 318 (2012), the Supreme Court resolved a split among the circuit courts of appeal concerning the constitutionality of jails performing visual searches of all persons admitted to the jails' general population, regardless of individualized suspicion of risk to the facility. The precise question the Court addressed was: *Whether the Fourth Amendment permits a jail to conduct a suspicionless strip search of every individual arrested for any minor offense no matter what the circumstances.*

Mr. Florence had failed to make timely installment payments on a fine imposed for two crimes, and a warrant was issued for his arrest. The fine was later paid, but the warrant was never withdrawn. He was arrested pursuant to that warrant during a traffic stop and transported to jail. The intake processing at the first jail where Florence was held *"required every arrestee to shower with a delousing agent. Officers would check arrestees for scars, marks, gang tattoos, and contraband as they disrobed. . . . Petitioner claims he was also instructed to open his mouth, lift his tongue, hold out his arms, turn around, and lift his genitals."* When Florence was transferred to a second jail, he underwent a similar intake screening, although the Court noted that apparently there was no physical contact between staff and the Mr. Florence during the process. Florence was released without charges being filed. He then filed a Section 1983 action alleging that the searches violated his rights to be free from unreasonable searches and seizures. The court of appeals ruled that the jails' policies on visual searches were constitutionally valid, and Mr. Florence sought review in the Supreme Court.

The Court's analysis began with a recitation of the issues facing jail administrators and staff and then addressed the importance of maintaining security and order within correctional facilities: ***"Maintaining safety and order at these institutions [jails] requires the expertise of correctional officials, who must have substantial discretion to devise reasonable solutions to the problems they face."*** In noting its earlier decision in *Bell v. Wolfish* that had upheld the Bureau of Prisons' visual search policy despite only one incident of contraband being recovered, the Court stated:

> The Court nonetheless upheld the search policy. It deferred to the judgment of correctional officials that the inspections served not only to discover but also to deter the smuggling of weapons, drugs, and other prohibited items inside. *[citation omitted]*. The Court explained that there is no mechanical way to determine whether intrusions on an inmate's privacy are reasonable. *[citation omitted]* The need for a particular search must be balanced against the resulting invasion of personal rights.

The importance of the visual searches at issue served a number of important governmental interests in detecting contraband (weapons, drugs, alcohol, currency, lighters, and matches concealed by new detainees); the presence of wounds, communicable diseases, or lice; and tattoos or other identifying marking of gangs or other disruptive groups that would pose a threat to the safety of inmates and staff.

The Court then explained the many justifications for having a policy of general application rather than trying to carve out exceptions for certain detainees, which is exacerbated by the large number of detainees processed and the short duration of many detentions. These include: the difficulty of identifying which detainees might pose a risk of violence, escape, or drug smuggling and that the deterrent value of searches for contraband depends on the unpredictability of the searches. The record developed in this case demonstrated that even persons arrested and booked into jail for minor offenses had been found with contraband hidden by their genitals or in their rectal cavities. Persons may be coerced by others to attempt to smuggle contraband into a correctional facility by being arrested for a minor offense.

While acknowledging the burden placed on detainees by the general policy of visual searches for persons entering the general population of a jail, the Court concluded that the balancing between the rights of detainees and the security needs of the facility favored the policy:

> ***These cases establish that correctional officials must be permitted to devise reasonable search policies to detect and deter the possession of contraband in their facilities. [citation omitted] ("[M]aintaining institutional security and preserving internal order and discipline are essential goals that may require***

limitation or retraction of retained constitutional rights of both convicted prisoners and pretrial detain-ees"). The task of determining whether a policy is reasonably related to legitimate security interests is "peculiarly within the province and professional expertise of corrections officials." [Citation omitted]. This Court has repeated the admonition that, "'in the absence of substantial evidence in the record to indicate that the officials have exaggerated their response to these considerations courts should ordi-narily defer to their expert judgment in such matters.'"

The Fourth Amendment requires that authorized searches must be performed in a reasonable and professional manner. Reasonable and professional searches are those done in as private a place as possible, not within view of other inmates or even of other staff who do not need to see them (and certainly never within view of outsiders, such as visitors). They must also be performed as calmly and as matter-of-factly as possible.

In *Goff v. Nix*, 803 F.2d 358 (8th Cir. 1986), inmates at the Iowa State Penitentiary complained about the strip searches that were conducted before and after their contact visits (including visits with lawyers and clergy) and before and after going to medical facilities, to court, and to exercise areas. The district court banned the strip searches in relation to lawyer and medical care visits, finding that some inmates were discouraged from engaging in these constitutionally protected visits because of their dislike for the strip searches. The court of appeals reversed and upheld the necessity for the searches in all of these cases, noting that inmates could smuggle contraband in body cavities if the searches were not conducted. The court of appeals strictly prohibited one aspect of the searches: those that involved situations in which officers, during strip searches, made "rude and offensive" comments or otherwise verbally harassed the inmates. Such verbal misconduct was found to be demeaning, bearing no relationship to the prison's need to conduct the searches. Other circuits have ruled that convicted prisoners maintain some reasonable expectations of privacy while in prison and "[T]he Fourth Amendment protects prisoners from searches and sei-zures that go beyond legitimate penological interests. Searches of prisoners must be conducted in a manner that is reasonable under the facts and circumstances in which they are performed." *Stoudemire v. Michigan DOC*, 705 F.3d 560 (6th Cir. 2013).

The Second Circuit in *Harris v. Miller, et al*, 818 F.3d 49 (2nd Cir. 2016) reaffirmed its position that inmates retain a limited right to bodily privacy under the Fourth Amendment. A female inmate alleged prison staff threw her to the ground and lifted her clothing to allow a male correctional officer to view her genital area to ascertain if any cotton was there. The inmate had blocked the window to her cell with her mattress, had removed some of the cotton and pasted it to the cell window. The inmate sued the staff alleging her rights under the Fourth and Eighth Amendment were violated. The district court dismissed the claims and the inmate appealed. The court of appeals reaffirmed its ruling in *Covino v. Patrissi*, 967 F.2d 73 (2nd Cir. 1992) that inmates retain a limited right to bodily privacy under the Fourth Amendment. In returning the case to the district court, the court of appeals instructed that the district court should analyze the inmate's claim to determine (1) did the inmate have a subjective expec-tation of bodily privacy; and (2) if so, determine if prison officials had a sufficient justification for their conduct. Because the search was an isolated incident and not part of a formal policy, the lower court should use the four fac-tors set forth in *Bell v. Wolfish*: ([1] the scope of the particular intrusion, [2] the manner in which it is conducted, [3] the justification for initiating it, and [4] the place in which it is conducted) in determining the correctional justification for the search. The court also reinstated the inmate's claim alleging excessive use of force in the search.

In *King v. McCarty*, 781 F.3d 889 (7th Cir. 2015) an Illinois state inmate sued correctional officials under the Fourth and Eighth Amendments arising out of a transfer from one institution to another. The inmate alleged prison staff required him to wear a see-through jump suit which exposed his genitals and buttocks. Prison staff dis-puted the allegations but admitted the jump suit was "less than opaque." The district court dismissed King's claim under the Eighth Amendment but allowed the Fourth Amendment claim to proceed. The action was dismissed later after it was established that King failed to exhaust administrative remedies under the PLRA. The court of appeals reversed. It first concluded that the inmate's transfer made access to the administrative remedy procedures unavailable. The court also stated that based on Seventh Circuit precedent, and the Supreme Court's decision in *Florence v. Chosen Board of Freeholders*, (2012), the Fourth Amendment's objective reasonableness standard for visual strip searches had not been extended to convicted prisoners. The inmate's Fourth Amendment action was dismissed for failure to state a claim. The court also concluded an inmate states a colorable claim under the Eighth Amendment "when he plausibly alleges that the strip search in question was motivated by a desire to harass or humiliate rather than by a legitimate justification, such as the need for order and security in prisons." In the Sev-enth Circuit, a convicted prisoner's claim that a search violated the Eighth Amendment "will require [proof] that the defendants acted without a legitimate correctional purpose and for the purpose of humiliating him and/or subjecting him to gratuitous psychological injury. . . . The Fourth Amendment imposes, by contrast, an objective standard of reasonableness, so [the inmate] can prevail under the Fourth Amendment without necessarily having to prove the defendants acted with bad intent."

In *Henry v. Hulett*, 930 F.3d 836 (7th Cir. 2019), a divided panel of the Seventh Circuit re-affirmed its ruling in *King v. McCarty* that the Fourth Amendment did not apply to noncontact visual cross-gender strip searches. A number of female prisoners were searched by DOC cadets in a training exercise, and the inmates sued, alleging violations of the Fourth and Eighth Amendments. The inmates were never physically touched by staff, and there were male staff present when the searches were conducted. The district court granted summary judgment on the Fourth Amendment claim to the DOC defendants based on *King v. McCarty* and a trial was held on the Eighth Amendment claim. A jury returned a verdict in favor of the DOC staff and the inmates appealed, asking the court of appeals to reinstate their Fourth Amendment claim. The court noted that the circuits have reached different conclusions as to whether convicted prisoners retain a Fourth Amendment privacy interest in their bodies, such as the *Harris v Miller* decision discussed above. The court also noted: "For more than 20 years it has been established in [the Seventh] [C]ircuit that the Fourth Amendment does not apply to visual inspections of prisoners. It is best to leave the law of the circuit alone, unless and until the [Supreme Court] suggest that it needs change."

▶ Prison Rape Elimination Act PREA

In 2003, Congress enacted the Prison Rape Elimination Act (PREA) to address the significant issue of sexual violence and abuse in America's jails and prisons. The purposes of PREA were to:

(1) establish a zero-tolerance standard for the incidence of rape in prisons;

(2) make the prevention of prison rape a top priority in each prison system;

(3) develop and implement national standards for the detection, prevention, reduction, and punishment of prison rape;

(4) increase the available data and information on the incidence of prison rape, consequently improving the management and administration of correctional facilities;

(5) standardize the definitions used for collecting data on the incidence of prison rape;

(6) increase the accountability of prison officials who fail to detect, prevent, reduce, and punish prison rape;

(7) protect the Eighth Amendment rights of federal, state, (no these words are capitalized in the statute and I do not have authority to change the language Congress uses!) and local prisoners;

(8) increase the efficiency and effectiveness of federal, (no this word is capitalized in the statute and I do not have authority to change the language Congress uses!) expenditures through grant programs such as those dealing with health care; mental health care; disease prevention; crime prevention, investigation, and prosecution; prison construction, maintenance, and operation; race relations; poverty; unemployment; and homelessness; and

(9) reduce the costs that prison rape imposes on interstate commerce.

34 U.S. Code, Section 30302.

The act also created the National Prison Rape Elimination Commission (NPREC) [34 U.S. Code Section 30306] and charged it with developing draft standards for the elimination of prison rape. The NPREC prepared draft standards and submitted them to the U.S. Attorney General. The Department of Justice then prepared and published proposed rules implementing the standards in the Federal Register for comment in 2009. In 2012, the Department of Justice published comprehensive rules pursuant to the directive of PREA stating: "The goal of this rulemaking is to prevent, detect, and respond to sexual abuse in confinement facilities, pursuant to the Prison Rape Elimination Act of 2003." The PREA rules are found at 28 CFR 115. June 20, 2012. The rules addressed many facets of correctional operations including development of policies and procedures, which announced the facility's zero tolerance for sexual abuse or harassment; limited cross gender viewing and searches; established requirements for the training of staff; established guidelines for screening inmates for risk of sexual victimization and abuse; established guidelines for reporting and investigating allegations of sexual abuse; requirements for the disciplining of staff and inmates who violate rules; and of the collection of data and the reporting of that data. While these rules are mandatorily applied to the Federal Bureau of Prisons, a failure by states to incorporate the standards into their correctional accreditation program would result in the withholding of 5% of certain federal grant funds. States seeking to be in full compliance are subject to audits every 3 years.

The PREA Standards directed that strip searches be subject to the following rules:

§ 115.15 Limits to cross-gender viewing and searches.

(a) The facility shall not conduct cross-gender strip searches or cross-gender visual body cavity searches (meaning a search of the anal or genital opening) except in exigent circumstances or when performed by medical practitioners.

(b) As of August 20, 2015, or August 21, 2017 for a facility whose rated capacity does not exceed 50 inmates, the facility shall not permit cross-gender pat-down searches of female inmates, absent exigent circumstances. Facilities shall not restrict female inmates' access to regularly available programming or other out-of-cell opportunities in order to comply with this provision.

(c) The facility shall document all cross-gender strip searches and cross-gender visual body cavity searches, and shall document all cross-gender pat-down searches of female inmates.

(d) The facility shall implement policies and procedures that enable inmates to shower, perform bodily functions, and change clothing without nonmedical staff of the opposite gender viewing their breasts, buttocks, or genitalia, except in exigent circumstances or when such viewing is incidental to routine cell checks. Such policies and procedures shall require staff of the opposite gender to announce their presence when entering an inmate housing unit.

(e) The facility shall not search or physically examine a transgender or intersex inmate for the sole purpose of determining the inmate's genital status. If the inmate's genital status is unknown, it may be determined during conversations with the inmate, by reviewing medical records, or, if necessary, by learning that information as part of a broader medical examination conducted in private by a medical practitioner.

(f) The agency shall train security staff in how to conduct cross-gender pat-down searches, and searches of transgender and intersex inmates, in a professional and respectful manner, and in the least intrusive manner possible, consistent with security needs.

The PREA contains no express provision allowing for private enforcement through litigation by an aggrieved person. Several lower federal courts, in reported decisions, have ruled that the PREA standards do not create a private cause of action for inmates to sue correctional staff for a violation of the standards. *McCloud v. Peck*, et al, 55 F.Supp. 2d 478 (WDNY 2014) and *Green v. Martin*, 224 F.Supp. 2d 154 (D. Conn. 2016).

▶ Pat Searches and Other Inmate Searches

Another type of search is the pat search. Pat searches (or frisks) are commonly done as inmates move from one place to another in an institution, as they work or engage in other activities in a variety of places within the prison or jail, or as they enter or exit the institution. All staff members are trained to conduct pat searches. (These involve running the hands over all parts of the inmate's body on top of the clothes. In addition, contents of pockets and anything being carried are examined separately, and hats, gloves, and jackets are removed for visual and tactile examination.). While most correctional agencies had authorized uniform cross gender pat searches, promulgation of PREA rules has prompted correctional agencies to modify their policy to prohibit cross-gender pat searches of female inmates except in exigent circumstances, Two examples of current Department of Corrections pat search policy using PREA guidance are New York Department of Corrections Directive 4910 III (B) (3) (NY DOC Directive 4910, 2019).[3] and Kansas Department of Corrections Internal Management Policy and Procedure 12-103D Paragraph II A.[4]

While the PREA standards are not constitutional requirements, courts decisions addressing the constitutionality of cross-gender searches are still applicable. For example, some courts have placed constitutional restrictions on cross-gender searches, such as saying a cross-gender search is permissible as long as it does not involve touching genital areas or breasts. (For example, see *Grummett v. Rushen,* 779 F.2d 491 (9th Cir. 1985) and *Smith v. Fairman*, 678 F.2d 52 (7th Cir. 1982)).

In *Watson v. Jones*, 980 F.2d 1165 (8th Cir. 1992), two male inmates complained that a female officer fondled their genitals and anuses when she conducted pat searches. This officer, they said, conducted almost daily pat searches of them, and, during her searches, she engaged in "prolonged rubbing and fondling of the genitals and anus area." They claimed, in a Section 1983 action, that this was a violation of the Fourth Amendment. The trial court had dismissed the claim, granting summary judgment to the officer, mainly because she stated that she never did such crotch searches, except when she knew "something was there." The appeals court agreed that it was constitutionally permissible for a female officer to conduct pat searches of male inmates. *Timm v. Gunter*, 917 F.2d 1093 (8th Cir. 1990), had approved that practice. The appeals court in *Watson* distinguished *Timm*, on the grounds that the *Timm* case involved a claim by male inmates that it was in all situations a violation of their rights to be pat searched by female officers. The court in *Timm* held that it was not a per se violation for female officers to pat-search male inmates.

However, the allegations by the inmates in *Watson* went beyond the basic issue of cross-gender pat searches. The court said that summary judgment in the lower court had been improper, because that court had not looked into the allegations that the officer had subjected the inmates to "sexually harassing and physically intrusive pat-down searches." The case was returned for further inquiry into whether the searches were unreasonable, and, therefore, unconstitutional, because they were excessively intrusive or sexually harassing. (That is, it was remanded in order to determine whether the searches had occurred in the crotch area more than was necessary for a routine tactile search for contraband.)

In *Jordan v. Gardner*, 986 F.2d 1521 (9th Cir. 1993) the court ruled that cross-gender pat searches of female inmates could not be conducted in prison. This holding was arrived at, not based on an analysis of the Fourth Amendment, but using the Eighth Amendment. Because so many female inmates had been physically and sexually abused before they came into prison, cross gender pat searches by male officers would cause the female inmates to be traumatized.

▶ Prison Searches and the Eighth Amendment

While the Supreme Court has not addressed whether the Eighth Amendment places restrictions on prison searches, the circuits have created a body law, which analyzes when a prison search can violate the Eighth Amendment. As noted above, *Jones v. Gunter* established that the particular characteristics of the person being searched may result in Eighth Amendment liability. Other circuits have generally held that searches that are done to degrade the inmate or which have no penological purpose can violate the Eighth Amendment.

In *Crawford v. Cuomo, et al*, 796 F.3d 252 (2nd Cir. 2015), the court addressed the dismissal of two male inmates' claim that a male correctional officer fondled their genitals for personal gratification and without penological justification in violation of the Eighth Amendment. The inmates did not allege a Fourth Amendment violation, but an Eighth Amendment violation. The district court had dismissed the inmates' complaint after applying circuit precedent that sexual abuse only states a cognizable Eighth Amendment claim if it occurs on more than one occasion, is "excessive in duration," involves direct contact with an inmate's genitalia (rather than contact through an inmate's clothing, as was alleged by the inmates in the *Crawford* complaint), or causes "physical injury, penetration, or pain." The court of appeals reversed, holding that "[a] corrections officer's intentional contact with an inmate's genitalia or other intimate area, which serves no penological purpose and is undertaken with the intent to gratify the officer's sexual desire or to humiliate the inmate, violates the Eighth Amendment." The court's analysis also found that evolving standards of decency as an Eighth Amendment measure were reflected in the criminalization of sexual contact between prisoners and staff; and enactment of PREA, which was designed to protect inmates from sexual abuse.

The Third Circuit followed the Second Circuit in ruling that an inmate who alleges that sexual abuse occurred during the course of a search may state a violation of the Eighth Amendment. In *Ricks v. Shover, et al*, 891 F.3d 468 (3rd Cir. 2018) the inmate alleged a male correctional officer sexually abused him during a pat search by rubbing his clothed genitalia over the inmate's clothed buttocks. The court of appeals established that such a sexual abuse claim should be analyzed as an Eighth Amendment claim using the subjective and objective component framework from *Hudson v. McMillian* (which is discussed in greater detail in the chapter on use of force). In evaluating the subjective prong, a court can consider whether "the official had a legitimate penological purpose or if he or she acted "maliciously and sadistically for the very purpose of causing harm." Factors that might establish the subjective prong include an actor's harassing comments or the overly invasive nature of the search. The objective prong may be assessed using the evolving standards of decency as announced in *Crawford v. Cuomo* above. The court of appeals returned this case to the district court for further consideration.

In addition to the searches already mentioned, inmates may also be subject to searches by simple instruments or X-rays. These would occur when staff have a reasonable belief that an inmate is concealing contraband inside or upon his person and when a visual search is either not possible or would not be sufficient to reveal the hidden contraband. In those instances, medically trained staff may be allowed by policy (and provided that the local courts have not disapproved of the practice) to use a medical instrument or an X-ray to look for the contraband. X-rays, of course, must be handled by medical staff in order to ensure that excessive exposure to radiation is avoided and proper procedures are followed. In some cases, blood or urine tests may be used to detect drug use, and breathalyzer or other on-the-spot tests may be used to detect alcohol use.

What must be emphasized is that the staff in any location must check with and receive legal advice from counsel to make sure what the position of local courts may be on any of these kinds of searches of the person. Courts in many places are very sensitive about simple instrument or x-ray search situations and have awarded money damages against staff members who performed unreasonable searches, particularly searches of the opposite gender and searches that were physically intrusive.

▶ DNA Collection

On almost any day of the week, a person can watch a crime program on television where law enforcement solves the case through analysis of DNA (deoxyribonucleic acid). While the current science of DNA testing and identification is more complex than depicted in the media, the use of DNA to identify perpetrators and as evidence of criminal involvement cannot be underestimated. Because each person's DNA is unique (with the exception of identical twins), collecting this evidence from a crime scene can implicate or eliminate a suspect. DNA evidence can also be used in analyzing unidentified remains and can help solve cases that may be many years old (DNA Initiative, 2011).[5]

In 1994, Congress first instructed the Federal Bureau of Investigation (FBI) to initiate a data bank for collecting, storing, and analyzing DNA samples to assist in crime solving. Many states passed similar legislation directing state officials to gather DNA specimens for analysis. In 2000, Congress passed the DNA Analysis Backlog Elimination Act (42 U.S.C. § 14135, et seq), which directed that all persons convicted of specified federal felonies be compelled to provide a specimen for DNA analysis. Four years later, Congress passed the Justice for All Act (42 U.S.C. § 14135a(d)), which required that all persons convicted of *any* federal felony provide a DNA specimen. The effect of this legislation resulted in prison, parole, and probation officials requiring persons under their supervision to provide specimens of bodily fluids, usually a blood sample, for delivery to the FBI for inclusion in its Combined DNA Index System (CODIS). For a more complete description of the collection process and CODIS, see the Supreme Court opinion in *Maryland v. King*, 569 U.S. 435 (2013) which is discussed below. As of September 2020, the FBI's National DNA Index (NDIS) contained over 14,328,685 offender (convicted, detainee, and legal profiles) profiles, 4,117,039 arrestee profiles, and 1,055,000 forensic profiles. As of January 2020, CODIS has produced over 533,268 hits assisting in more than 521,562 investigations (FBI, 2020).[6]

Prison officials were then tasked with developing procedures to collect specimens from inmates and to forward the specimens of bodily fluid for DNA analysis. Early testing required the collection of a blood sample (the current collection method is a swab of the mouth), a process that required a trained medical professional to extract the blood using a needle. One legal question posed by a number of prisoner lawsuits was whether the collection of blood for DNA analysis without warrant, probable cause, or reasonable suspicion violated the Fourth Amendment rights of the prisoners.

The U.S. Supreme Court has never decided the issue of whether the government could extract blood for DNA testing from a convicted felon. Shortly after the enactment of the DNA Analysis Backlog Elimination Act, two convicted federal prisoners filed a *Bivens* lawsuit against prison officials claiming that collection of bodily fluid pursuant to the statute violated their right to be free from unreasonable search and seizure under the Fourth Amendment. In *Groceman v. U.S. Department of Justice*, 354 F.3d 411 (5th Cir. 2004), the Fifth Circuit held that the Fourth Amendment is implicated by the extraction of blood from a prisoner to collect a DNA sample. In upholding the statute against Fourth Amendment challenge, the court concluded that collection of DNA specimens from a prisoner is reasonable in light of (1) a prisoner's diminished expectation of privacy, (2) the minimal intrusion involved in collecting the specimen, and (3) the legitimate governmental interest furthered by having DNA to investigate and prosecute crimes.

A similar analysis was used by federal courts of appeal in *Shaffer v. Saffle*, 148 F.3d 1180 (10th Cir. 1998), analyzing a state DNA collection statute, and in *United States v. Sczubelek* 402 F.3d 175 (3rd Cir. 2005), holding that "[t]he government's interest in building a DNA database for identification purposes, similar to its interest in maintaining fingerprint records, outweighs the minimal intrusion into a criminal offender's diminished expectation of privacy."

Other courts have upheld the collection of DNA exemplars from prisoners under a "special needs" analysis, referring to a need beyond the ordinary law enforcement need. The Supreme Court has ruled that the Fourth Amendment prohibits only unreasonable searches and seizures and that usually a search without "reasonable suspicion" is per se unreasonable. When the search is done for the purpose of collecting evidence of criminal wrongdoing, a warrant is usually required. In several non-law enforcement cases, the Supreme Court ruled that searches on less than "reasonable suspicion" may not violate the Fourth Amendment if the search serves "special needs beyond the normal need for law enforcement." *Griffin v. Wisconsin*, 483 U.S. 868 (1987) (search of probationer) and *Indianapolis v. Edmond*, 531 U.S. 32 (2000) (stop of vehicle at DUI checkpoint).

In *Nicholas v. Goord*, 430 F.3d 652 (2nd Cir. 2005), cert. denied 549 U.S. 963 (2006), several inmates in New York state custody challenged New York's DNA collection statute, seeking money damages and injunctive relief in a suit under 42 U.S.C. § 1983. The Second Circuit concluded that the extraction of DNA from a prisoner implicated the Fourth Amendment and served a special need. The court said, "Because the state's purpose in conducting DNA indexing is distinct from the ordinary 'crime detection' activities associated with normal law enforcement concerns, it meets the special needs threshold." The special needs analysis is discussed below in more detail.

▶ *Maryland v. King*

By 2013, all states had enacted laws requiring DNA specimens to be collected from convicted felons. Some states extended the testing requirement to all persons <u>arrested</u> for certain violent state offenses. Maryland was one of those states and after King was arrested for threatening people with a weapon, one of the designated violent offenses, staff at the jail collected a DNA specimen, pursuant to the Maryland law, using a buccal swab (applying a cotton swab or filter paper to the inside of a person's cheeks). The specimen was tested and matched a sample taken from the victim of an unsolved rape. King was questioned by Maryland state law enforcement, and an additional specimen was collected and used at King's trial for the rape. He was convicted and sentenced to life in prison. King appealed his conviction to the Maryland Court of Appeals (Maryland's highest state court), which concluded that the state law authorizing the collection of DNA specimens from arrestees was an unlawful seizure because obtaining and using the cheek swab was an unreasonable search of the person. The Supreme Court granted certiorari to address this question: *Does the Fourth Amendment allow the States to collect and analyze DNA from people arrested and charged with serious crimes?*

At the Supreme Court, the state argued that collection of an arrestee's DNA furthered an important governmental interest of ensuring the accurate identification of the person arrested. This interest was then balanced against the individual's expectation of privacy. Both the State and King agreed that the collection of biological material using a buccal swab was a search. Because the process was a search, the Fourth Amendment was implicated. After concluding that the manner in which the biological material was collected using a buccal swab was a minimal intrusion, the Court noted that the *"fact that an intrusion is negligible is of central relevance to determining reasonableness"* of a search.

The next step in the Court's analysis was to balance the interest of the government against the privacy interest of the person searched:

> *[W]e balance the privacy-related and law enforcement-related concerns to determine if the intrusion was reasonable." [citation omitted]. This application of "traditional standards of reasonableness" requires a court to weigh "the promotion of legitimate governmental interests" against "the degree to which [the search] intrudes upon an individual's privacy."*

The Court identified that one of the state's interest was **"the need for law enforcement officers in a safe and accurate way to process and identify the persons and possessions they must take into custody."** The collection of DNA for identification purposes was important because a person arrested for a serious charge could lie or attempt to mislead the police as to their true identity. While using fingerprints had become the primary method of ensuring the accurate identification of an arrestee, the Court concluded that DNA testing was even more accurate and not much more intrusive. Another important state interest was ensuring the accurate identification of detainees by the agency detaining the person. Positive identification would allow the detaining authority to know the risk the detainee poses to staff, other inmates, and for the new detainee. Whether the detainee is wanted on other charges, has a record, including a history of violence or suffers from a mental illness, can be ascertained through identification procedures and other official records. Accurate identification also furthers the interest of the government in ensuring the detainee is available for future judicial proceedings (if granted pre-trial release):

> *"A person who is arrested for one offense but knows that he has yet to answer for some past crime may be more inclined to flee the instant charges, lest continued contact with the criminal justice system expose one or more other serious offenses."*

This same information can be used to accurately consider if, and on what conditions, an offender should be granted pretrial release. Finally, the collection of DNA and

> *"the identification of an arrestee as the perpetrator of some heinous crime may have the salutary effect of freeing a person wrongfully imprisoned for the same offense."*

The Fourth Amendment requires the governmental interest be balanced against the privacy interest of the person searched. The context of the search is an important consideration in determining whether a search is reasonable. In determining reasonableness, one factor is the reasonable expectation of privacy that the person searched has. In the custodial context, a person arrested and held in detention has a diminished expectation of privacy:

> *"Once an individual has been arrested on probable cause for a dangerous offense that may require detention before trial, however, his or her expectations of privacy and freedom from police scrutiny are reduced."*

When balanced against the interests of the government in accurate identification of persons arrested and detained for a serious offense, the diminished expectation of privacy and the minimal intrusion of having a buccal swab to collect biological material was not unreasonable.

> *In light of the context of a valid arrest supported by probable cause respondent's expectations of privacy were not offended by the minor intrusion of a brief swab of his cheeks. By contrast, that same context of arrest gives rise to significant state interests in identifying respondent not only so that the proper name can be attached to his charges but also so that the criminal justice system can make informed decisions concerning pretrial custody. Upon these considerations the Court concludes that DNA identification of arrestees is a reasonable search that can be considered part of a routine booking procedure. When officers make an arrest supported by probable cause to hold for a serious offense and they bring the suspect to the station to be detained in custody, taking and analyzing a cheek swab of the arrestee's DNA is, like fingerprinting and photographing, a legitimate police booking procedure that is reasonable under the Fourth Amendment.*

As discussed earlier, some courts of appeal had upheld blood draws from convicted felons under a "special needs" analysis. In *King*, the Court considered whether "special needs" applied in this case.

> *The special needs cases, though in full accord with the result reached here, do not have a direct bearing on the issues presented in this case, because unlike the search of a citizen who has not been suspected of a wrong, a detainee has a reduced expectation of privacy.*

This would be especially applicable to a person convicted of an offense, who would have a more diminished expectation of privacy than a detainee.

▸ Searches of Non-Inmates

In Neumeyer v. Beard, 421 F.3d 210 (3rd Cir. 2005) the court of appeals noted was posted at the prison entranceways and in front of the visitor parking lot at the Pennsylvania Department of Corrections' State Correctional Institute at Huntingdon.

> [WARNING.] THIS IS A STATE CORRECTIONAL INSTITUTION. ALL PERSONS, VEHICLES AND PERSONAL PROPERTY ENTERING OR BROUGHT ON THESE GROUNDS ARE SUBJECT TO SEARCH. DRUG DETECTION DOGS AND ELECTRONIC DEVICES MAY BE USED FOR THIS PURPOSE.

Similar signs are common at correctional facilities and provide notice that a person entering prison grounds is subject to a search of their person, vehicle, and personal property to prevent the introduction of contraband and to help ensure prison security and good order.

Persons in custody share the correctional environment with prison staff and visitors (e.g., inmate visitors, attorneys, government and community representatives, volunteers, and vendors). Courts have long taken notice that correctional institutions are unique places "fraught with serious security dangers" (*Bell v. Wolfish*). Prison security and good order are central objectives of correctional staff and administration. In order to promote prison security and good order, correctional administrators have the responsibility to prevent the introduction of contraband into the prison. In some cases, sources of contraband introduction are prison staff and visitors to the institution. Several important questions are raised in this context: What expectations of privacy do prison employees and visitors have? And, how do prison administrators accommodate these privacy interests, if any, with the interest in maintaining security by prohibiting the introduction of contraband? A sign, similar to the one at the beginning of this section often is found at the entranceways to prisons and serves to put on notice those persons entering prison property that they, their vehicles, and their personal property are subject to search.

Searches of Employees; *City of Ontario, CA. v. Quon*

Staff searches are very sensitive and generally are conducted only on a finding of reasonable suspicion. See for example, *Braun v. Maynard*, 652 F.3d 557 (4th Cir. 2011) (visual strip search of correctional employees based on "reasonable suspicion" after positive Ionscan test). Some searches of correctional workers have been justified under the "special needs" doctrine. *Washington v. Unified Government of Wyandotte County, et al*, 817 F3d 1192 (10th Cir. 2017) (random urinalysis of correctional employee having contacts with juvenile detainees furthered governmental interest of safety and well-being of the juvenile; and employees with law enforcement duties who have access to, and direct contact with, inmates, or may be called upon to secure a correctional facility, illegal drug use presents a significant potential threat to the inmates and the security of the facility). For visitors and staff, the suspicion is often founded on confidential information, sometimes provided by an inmate. This requires assessing the reliability of the informant and determining whether there is any corroborating information or circumstance.

Staff members should be advised, throughout their training, that their persons and anything they bring into an institution are subject to search. (Signs, as noted above, are also posted to warn visitors that they are not to bring in contraband and that they may be subject to search to ensure that contraband is not brought in.) Prison staff are not immune from violating the law themselves. Consider the following three examples of staff criminal conduct involving introduction of contraband into a correctional facility. In 2019, six employees of the South Carolina Department of Corrections plead guilty to charges of accepting bribes to smuggle contraband into a state prison.[7] In 2019, a former Ohio state corrections officer was sentenced to 30 months in federal prison for smuggling illegal drugs and tobacco into a state prison.[8] In 2019, a former chaplain at a federal prison in New Hampshire was sentenced to forty months for smuggling drugs, cellular phones, tobacco and other contraband into a federal prison.[9]

Security is the prime concern of correctional facilities. Some correctional systems limit the amount of personal property that staff members may bring into the institution; others may subject staff to a routine metal detector and pat search. If the propriety of a search is in doubt, turning the employee away (just as the visitor can be turned away) while the matter is investigated may sometimes be the best solution. But to collect evidence and to be certain that allegations or suspicions are well-founded, searches of employees' lockers, cars, clothes, purses and wallets, and searches of their persons may be necessary.

In 2001, a police department in California acquired alphanumeric pagers to be used to contact SWAT members in the event of an emergency. The contract for service was with the city, and the city paid the monthly fees. When the pagers were issued, the officers were advised that use of the pagers could be monitored by the city, and that the officers should have no expectation of privacy or confidentiality during such usage. The city's contract with the service provider permitted a limited number of characters for each pager each month, and any overage was billed at an additional cost. The city noted that some officers were exceeding their monthly character limits and initially offered the officers the opportunity to reimburse the city for the overage rather than have an audit done of the messages. When the overages continued, the city conducted an audit of the usage of those officers to determine if the contracted limits were sufficient for city business. After transcripts of the messages were collected and reviewed, it was determined that at least one officer was using the pager for personal messages and was conducting personal business while on duty. After the city initiated disciplinary action against the officer, litigation began. One of the issues was the privacy interest that a public employee maintains when using city-owned electronic communication devices.

In *City of Ontario, CA v. Quon*, 560 U.S. 746 (2010), the Supreme Court addressed the issue of whether a public employee had an expectation of privacy protected by the Fourth Amendment in personal communications made using a government-owned communications device, and if so, did the city's action of reviewing such communications amount to a "reasonable" search? The Court first noted that the Fourth Amendment applies to conduct by officers of the government in situations other than investigations of criminal activity. The Fourth Amendment also applies to the government in its capacity as an employer. Public employees do not lose the protections of the Fourth Amendment merely because they work for the government rather than a private employer. The Court also noted that the function and operation of the government create "special needs" beyond normal law enforcement needs that make the usual requirements of a warrant or probable cause impractical in the government workplace.

To answer the first question, whether the police officer had an expectation of privacy protected by the Fourth Amendment, the Court first considered the non-law enforcement case of *O'Connor v. Ortega*, 480 U.S. 709 (1987). *O'Connor* dealt with the warrantless search of an office and files of a state hospital employee. The Court noted that *O'Connor* held that workplace conditions in the public sector can vary significantly and that there may be certain circumstances in public sector employment where an employee will have no reasonable expectation of privacy. However, these instances must be determined on a case-by-case basis. To decide the *Quon* case, the Supreme Court presumed that the officer had a reasonable expectation of privacy in the communications—that obtaining and reviewing a transcript of the communications constituted a search under the Fourth Amendment and that principles of law applicable to searches of physical office space apply with at least the same force as electronic communications.

The last issue for the Court to decide was whether the search was reasonable. While the Fourth Amendment usually requires a judicial warrant for a search to be reasonable, there are exceptions, including "special needs of the workplace." A warrantless search by a government employer, which is conducted for a:

> **noninvestigatory, work-related purpos[e] or for the investigatio[n] of work-related misconduct ... is reasonable if it is justified at its inception and if the measures adopted are reasonably related to the objectives of the search and not excessively intrusive in light of the circumstances giving rise to the search [internal quotations omitted].**

In this case, the search was "valid at its inception" because its purpose was to determine if the city's contract provided a sufficient amount of coverage to carry out public business and to ensure that the city was not using public funds to pay for an employee's extensive personal communications. The scope of the search was also reasonable because only two of several months of communications were reviewed, and only communications made while the officer was on duty were reviewed. The Court also concluded that the extent of the expectation of privacy is important. In this case, the officer was advised that the communications were subject to audit.

> **As a law enforcement officer, he would or should have known that his actions were likely to come under legal scrutiny, and that might entail an analysis of his on-the-job communications.**

The precise impact and application of *Quon* in the correctional setting are unclear. The "special needs of the workplace," as applied to the public sector work environment, certainly may impact the status of the law in the areas of prison employee and visitor searches. One example is whether the "special needs of the workplace" standard justifies warrantless and suspicionless searches of prison employees' vehicles parked on prison grounds. In *True v. Nebraska*, 612 F.3d 676 (8th Cir. 2010), the state had a policy that authorized prison personnel, without warrant, probable cause, or reasonable suspicion, to search employee vehicles parked on prison grounds. The vehicles that were searched were chosen randomly by location. Before a search was made, the employee was asked to consent to the search, and if consent was refused, no search would be done, but the employee could be disciplined. In *True*, the employee refused to consent, no search was made, and the employee was disciplined. The court of appeals first noted that while correctional workers retain certain expectations of privacy, the fact that the employee works in a prison diminishes any subjective expectation of privacy. The next questions were whether the search was justified by "special needs of the workplace" and if the search was reasonable. In upholding the policy, the court ruled that search of a vehicle is less intrusive than a search of a person. The court also ruled that conducting random searches of vehicles parked on prison grounds where inmates might have access to the vehicle was a reasonable practice to prevent the introduction of contraband. The court's decision held that prison security and order are factors to consider in determining whether "special needs of the workplace" exist. In deciding this case, factual determinations such as whether vehicles are in an area accessible to inmates, and whether the selection of vehicles to be searched was based on a uniform or systematic random selection, were important.

Appellant True also alleged that by conducting random searches of employees' cars, but not the cars of visitors, there was an equal protection violation. The appeals court disagreed, affirming the lower court's grant of summary judgment for the defendants. The appeals court held that the differential treatment was "rationally related to a legitimate state interest." Those interests were institutional security, contraband interdiction, and administrative efficiency. The court noted that employee cars are at the prison daily, conceivably making it easier to smuggle contraband. The court held that there was no violation of the equal protection clause.

Earlier in this chapter, it was stated that the issue of when prison officials may conduct strip searches of inmates caused the Supreme Court in *Bell v. Wolfish* "the greatest pause." The Court concluded that a reasonable response to the security needs of the prison was to conduct strip searches of inmates who had access to persons or places where contraband could be obtained. One issue that was not addressed by *Bell v. Wolfish* is under what conditions, if any, can prison employees be subjected to strip searches? This is a question the Supreme Court has not yet answered, but several lower courts have provided guidance to prison officials. Jurisdictions that have addressed the issue have generally held that correctional workers may be strip searched without a warrant only when there is reasonable suspicion that the employee is transporting contraband. *McDonell v. Hunter*, 809 F.2d 1302 (8th Cir. 1987). Reasonable suspicion requires that the search be based on "specific objective facts and rational inferences they [officials] are entitled to draw from those facts in light of their experience. It requires individualized suspicion, specifically directed to the person who is targeted for the strip search." *Hunter v. Auger*, 672 F.2d 668 (8th Cir. 1982). The courts have applied a balancing test: weighing the privacy interests of employees (which are diminished because of their workplace) with the legitimate governmental interest of promoting institution security and good order by preventing the introduction of contraband. Again, law enforcement officials and counsel should be consulted and local court rulings on searches must be carefully followed. Generally, reasonable suspicion that an employee is carrying contraband is the minimum standard for conducting a search, but a search warrant is always the safest way to go.

Visitor Searches

Visitors to prisons or jails no doubt retain some degree of Fourth Amendment protection, and they have a greater expectation of privacy than inmates have. Nonetheless, once they enter the jail or prison, security concerns are pervasive, and prison and jail staff can take necessary steps to protect the security and good order of the facility. This means that, in all facilities, visitors may be constantly monitored, which may include camera surveillance; they may be asked to check their possessions, such as bags and purses, in lockers at the entrance; and they may be asked to walk through a metal-detecting device. Some places require, and courts have approved, routine pat downs (conducted by a staff member of the same sex) and searches of bags and briefcases before entering a corrections facility. If a person refuses, the visitor may be permitted to turn around and leave. (This practice of allowing a visitor to leave, which, of course, is not an option for an inmate, prevails simply because the prime interest of prison or jail officials is to prevent the introduction of contraband into the institution. When the visitor leaves, the introduction of contraband has probably been prevented, at least for that visit.) Not all correctional systems offer the departure option, and one court has refused to suppress evidence found in a search of a vehicle on prison grounds after the visitor refused to give express consent for the search. *United States v. Prevo*, 435 F.3d 1343 (11th Cir. 2006). In that case, the court relied on the fact that this visitor had driven her car onto prison grounds several times and was aware that her vehicle could be subject to search. The court of appeals concluded that implicit consent could not be withdrawn once law enforcement officers determined to search the vehicle. The search of the vehicle produced a loaded firearm, drugs and drug paraphernalia, and over $20,000 in cash.

In another instance, a court used a balancing test to conclude that the "special needs" of a prison in preventing the introduction of contraband outweighed the minor inconvenience of a search of a prison visitor's vehicle without warrant or probable cause. *Neumeyer v. Beard*, 421 F.3d 210 (3rd Cir. 2005). Like the facts in *United States v. Prevo*, a notice that vehicles were subject to search was prominently posted, and the visitors had parked in the visitor parking lot several times before the search. The court did question the absence of any written standards by the state directing how vehicles were to be randomly selected and how the searches were to be conducted, but in the absence of any evidence of abuse of discretion, this was not sufficient to warrant finding the search unreasonable.

While the Supreme Court has not addressed the issue of what level of suspicion will warrant a strip search of a prison visitor, several federal appellate courts have ruled that the appropriate standard is "reasonable suspicion" based upon particular and individualized suspicion that contraband will be found on the visitor's person. See for example, *Wood v. Clemmons*, 89 F.3d 922 (1st Cir. 1996); *Spear v. Sowders*, 71 F.3d 626 (6th Cir. 1995), *Romo v. Champion*, 46 F.3d 1013 (10th Cir. 1995) and *Calloway v. Lokey*, 948 F.3d 194 (4th Cir. 2020). Because of the sensitivity of strip searches of non-inmates, and because any illegal material such as drugs or other contraband may result in criminal prosecutions, it is a good practice, when time permits, to involve local law enforcement officials in decisions related to conducting a strip search of a visitor. To best limit the potential liability of correctional staff and to ensure the admissibility of evidence collected during the search in a criminal trial, a good option, when time allows (which often is not the case), is to involve appropriate law enforcement personnel in the jurisdiction to obtain a judicial **search warrant** for a strip search of a visitor or even for a pat search or search of a visitor's possessions (including a car). Nevada Department of Corrections Administrative Regulation 422.05 requires correctional staff to advise all visitors when a search is to be performed and to obtain the written consent of the visitor before the search is performed. Visitors may refuse, but will be denied access to the facility that day. The refusal can be the basis for future denials of visitor access. Strip searches are done without written consent only pursuant to a judicial search warrant and in the presence of a state peace officer.[10]

Summary

- The Fourth Amendment prohibits unreasonable searches and seizures. In determining the constitutionality of any search, courts are instructed to balance the privacy interest of the person searched against the needs of the government for that search.
- Conducting searches of persons and of property and places in prisons and jails is essential to maintaining security.
- The Supreme Court held that the Fourth Amendment does not apply to a prison cell. An inmate has no protected right of privacy in prison. Officers may conduct searches of cells to the extent that they believe it is necessary in order to maintain security and order. They may also seize articles that are found during searches and that are deemed to be contraband (*Hudson v. Palmer*). An inmate has no right to be present during the search of his cell (*Bell v. Wolfish*).
- There is also no right to privacy in other areas of a jail. It was held to be permissible for authorities to eavesdrop, and record, a conversation in the visiting room between an inmate and his brother (*Lanza v. New York*). A recording made in such a visiting situation may be turned over to law enforcement officials and used in prosecution of the inmate (*United States v. Hearst*).
- Under the federal statute on wiretapping (interception of communications, 18 U.S.C. § 2510 et seq.), prison officials, within the ordinary course of business, may monitor inmate telephone conversations without obtaining judicial approval. Monitoring may also occur with the consent of one party to the conversation (*United States v. Paul; United States v. Amen*).

- There is no Fourth Amendment protection when a party consents to their conversation with an attorney being recorded and monitored by others (*United States v. Novak*). When attorneys and their clients carry on communications knowing their communications are being recorded and monitored by third parties, there can be no claim to attorney–client privilege in the communication (*United States v. Hatcher*).

- Strip searches of inmates cause special concerns to the courts. The Supreme Court upheld a policy of conducting body cavity searches after all contact visits in a jail (*Bell v. Wolfish*). Cross-gender pat searches of female inmates were once a widely accepted correctional practice, but promulgation of PREA regulations now make such searches only under exigent circumstances. Strip searches should be performed by officers of the same sex as the inmates or by medical professionals.

- A federal court in New York required prison authorities to accommodate the privacy of female inmates ensuring that male officers working in female inmate living units would not be able to observe female inmates unclothed (*Forts v. Ward*).

- In *Florence v. Chosen Board of Freeholders* (2012), the U.S. Supreme Court resolved a split in the circuits and ruled that blanket strip search policies for all persons booked into the general population of a detention facility did not violate the Fourth Amendment. These searches furthered compelling governmental interests in security and safety.

- Appellate courts have held that the collection of DNA specimens from a prisoner is reasonable (and not a violation of the Fourth Amendment) in light of a prisoner's diminished expectation of privacy; the minimal intrusion involved in collecting the specimen; and the legitimate governmental interest furthered by having DNA to investigate.

- In *King v. Maryland*, (2015), the Supreme Court ruled that state laws authorizing the collection of biological material from all persons arrested for serious crimes did not violate the Fourth Amendment. The State's interest in accurate identification of persons arrested and detained for serious charges, coupled with the minimal intrusion to the person who had a diminished expectation of privacy, was reasonable

- Pat searches of inmates are commonly done as inmates move about the institution. Enactment of PREA regulations have severely limited the use of cross-gender pat searches, and restrictions may be placed on such searches. Another type of search is by simple instruments or X-rays, with these performed by medical personnel.

- In most jurisdictions, visitors and employees may be subject to searches when prison or jail staff have reasonable suspicion that they may be carrying contraband. Most facilities post warnings, advising visitors that they are not to bring any contraband into the facilities and that they may be subject to searches of their persons or property.

- The application of the "special needs" test may permit the government to conduct warrantless searches, without reasonable suspicion, of the vehicles of visitors and employees. In this area of searches, because the Supreme Court has not ruled and there is clearly a constitutional right involved, prison or jail administrators must make certain what the local state of the law is. If there is doubt about the propriety of a search and if no search warrant has been obtained, it is usually better to turn the visitor (or employee) away and refuse entry into the facility, rather than risk an unlawful search.

- The Supreme Court has held that a warrantless search of a government employee by his employer conducted for a noninvestigatory, work-related purpose or to investigate work-related misconduct is reasonable. The search must be justified at its inception and the adopted measures must be reasonably related to the search objectives and not excessively intrusive in light of the circumstances that gave rise to the search (*City of Ontario, CA v. Quon*).

Thinking About It

Angela traveled to a state correctional facility to visit Travis who was confined there. Travis had recently been transferred there after he was found to have attempted to introduce contraband into the facility where he was previously confined. Staff at the new facility were both aware of Travis' previous conduct and had received confidential information from an inmate that an inmate named Travis was looking to introduce contraband into the prison. Supervisory correctional staff cautioned visiting room staff to be alert for attempts to introduce contraband by visitors for Travis. When Angela arrived at the facility staff observed she appeared "frazzled and kind of nervous." The visiting room was monitored by officers in the room and by video cameras observed "live time" by other staff in a monitoring room. During the visit staff monitoring the video cameras (who had experience detecting attempts to introduce contraband through the prison visiting room) observed that Angela appeared nervous, was fidgeting with the waist band of her slacks and that Travis was watching correctional officers supervising the visiting room. About an hour into the visit the monitoring room officer observed Angela adjusting her slacks in a manner consistent with reaching into the inside of her pants. Other staff were notified and the visit was terminated. Staff asked Angela to consent to a strip search. It was disputed whether Angela understood the request for consent and she stated she feared prison staff would not let her leave unless she consented. The search was conducted by same sex staff in a professional manner, and no contraband was found. Angela sued several correctional staff alleging a violation of Fourth Amendment right to be free from unreasonable search and seizure. How should the court rule? *Calloway v. Lokey*, 948 F.3d 194 (6th Cir. 2020).

Key Terms

contraband (corrections)
reasonable suspicion
search warrant
shakedown (corrections)

Endnotes

1. Burke, T. and Owen, S. 2010. *Cell Phones as Prison Contraband. FBI Law Enforcement Bulletin,* 10–15.
2. Shadel, D. *Criminals Operate Jury Duty Scam From Inside State Prison.* AARP Magazine, February 7, 2020. Available https://www.aarp.org/money/scams-fraud/info-2020/prison-jury-duty-scam.html. Available https://www.aarp.org/money/scams-fraud/info-2020/prison-jury-duty-scam.html
3. Cross Gender Pat Frisks
   a. Male Inmates: Pat frisks will be performed by Officers regardless of gender. However, a female Officer shall not perform a non-emergency pat frisk of any male Muslim inmate over the objection of the inmate if a male Officer is present at the location where the pat frisk is to be conducted and is available to perform the pat frisk. This in no way restricts the ability of a female Officer to perform a pat frisk on a male Muslim inmate when there is an articulable basis to suspect that the inmate may possess contraband, or in emergency situations.
   b. Female Inmates
      (1) Facilities shall not permit cross gender pat frisks of female inmates, absent exigent circumstances. Facilities shall not restrict female inmates' access to regularly available programming or other out-of-cell opportunities in order to comply with this provision. Exigent circumstances mean any set of temporary and unforeseen circumstances that require immediate action in order to combat a threat to the security or institutional order of a facility. When exigent circumstances require the cross gender pat frisk of female inmates, the provisions of Section III-B-3-b-2 will be followed.
      (2) A male officer may perform emergency pat frisks of female inmates when exigent circumstances exist and a female officer is not present at the location where the frisk is to be conducted or, if present, is not available to perform the pat frisk. When a male officer performs emergency pat frisks of female inmates when exigent circumstances exist and no female officers are available, then the pat frisk shall be conducted in a location where there is regular access and traffic by staff, inmates, or both rather than in a more remote or less traveled area. In facilities with CCTV capabilities, pat frisks should also be conducted in the area where a camera is present. NOTE: When a male Officer is to conduct a pat frisk of a female inmate, the male Officer shall record the date, time, place, and the reason for the pat frisk on Form #1140CGPF, "Report of Cross Gender Pat Frisk –Female Inmate."
      (3) When a male Officer pat frisks a female inmate, the Officer shall not use the palm of the hand when frisking the clothed breast area of the female inmate. Instead, the Officer shall use the back and side of the hand only and shall use care not to pat the clothed nipples of the inmate. When frisking the clothed upper thigh of a female inmate, a male Officer shall use care not to pat the clothed genital area of the inmate. The Officer shall conduct himself professionally, alert to the perceived sensitive nature of the cross gender pat frisk.
      NY DOC Directive 4910, *Control of & Search for Contraband.* June 28, 2019. Available: https://doccs.ny.gov/system/files/documents/2019/08/4910%20Control%20of%20%26%20Search%20for%20Contraband.pdf. Accessed March 20, 2020.
      See also Kansas DOC Internal Management Policy and Procedure 12-103D. December 12, 2017. Available at https://www.doc.ks.gov/kdoc-policies/AdultIMPP/chapter-12/12-103d/view. Accessed March 20, 2020.

4. Kansas DOC Internal Management Policy and Procedure 12-103D II (A). December 12, 2017.

    II. Pat-Down, Full-Frisk, and Canine (K-9) Searches

        A. A pat-down or full-frisk search of offenders may be conducted at any time or place.

            1. Pat-down searches of male offenders may be conducted by trained staff of the same or opposite gender as the offenders being searched.

            2. Pat-down searches of female offenders and all juvenile offenders shall be conducted by a trained staff member of the same gender only, except in exigent circumstances. (28 C.F.R. § 115.15)

            3. Staff shall be cognizant of transgender and intersex offenders and shall conduct searches in a respectful, and least intrusive, manner as possible.

            4. The facility shall document all cross-gender pat searches of female offenders as well as any cross-gender strip searches or cross-gender visual body cavity searches if such searches cannot be avoided.

        Available at https://www.doc.ks.gov/kdoc-policies/AdultIMPP/chapter-12/12-103d/view. Accessed March 20, 2020.

5. DNA Initiative. "Advancing Criminal Justice Through DNA Technology." Accessed January 14, 2011.

6. Federal Bureau of Investigation. "CODIS-NDIS Statistics." Accessed November 17, 2020. https://www.fbi.gov/services/laboratory/biometric-analysis/codis/ndis-statistics

7. *Eight Former SCDC Employees Plead Guilty to Federal Crimes Associated with Accepting Bribes to Smuggle Contraband into SCDC Facilities.* U.S. Attorney, District of South Carolina press release. September 23, 2019. https://www.justice.gov/usao-sc/pr/eight-former-scdc-employees-plead-guilty-federal-crimes-associated-accepting-bribes. Accessed March 2, 2020.

8. U.S. Attorney, Southern District of Ohio press release. November 22, 2019. *https://www.justice.gov/usao-sdoh/pr/former-corrections-officer-sentenced-prison-smuggling-drugs-state-prison.* Accessed March 2, 2020.

9. A former chaplain at a federal prison in New Hampshire was sentenced to forty months for smuggling drugs, cellular phones, tobacco and other contraband into a federal prison. U.S. Attorney, District of New Hampshire press release. August 1, 2019. *https://www.justice.gov/usao-sdoh/pr/former-corrections-officer-sentenced-prison-smuggling-drugs-state-prison.* Accessed March 2, 2020.

10. Nevada Department of Corrections Administrative Regulation 422- Search and Seizure Standards. Effective November 16, 2016. Accessed August 21, 2020. http://doc.nv.gov/uploadedFiles/docnvgov/content/About/Administrative_Regulations/AR%20422%20Search%20and%20Seizure%20Standards%20Final%2011-15-16.pdf

CHAPTER 11

Fifth and Fourteenth Amendments: Due Process—Inmate Discipline

There is no iron curtain drawn between the Constitution and the prisons of this country. Prisoners may also claim the protections of the Due Process Clause. They may not be deprived of life, liberty, or property without due process of law.

U.S. Supreme Court, *Wolff v. McDonnell*

Due process is found at two places in the U.S. Constitution: the Fifth Amendment and the Fourteenth Amendment.

The Fourteenth Amendment, Section 1, says:

No State shall … deprive any person of life, liberty, or property without due process of law; nor deny to any person within its jurisdiction the equal protection of the laws.

This amendment was adopted after the Civil War and guarantees protections against state actions (which also include local government actions) that would take away the life, liberty, or property of its citizens.

There is also a due process clause in the Fifth Amendment, which protects citizens against federal government actions that would take away life, liberty, or property:

No person shall be … deprived of life, liberty, or property, without due process of law.

CHAPTER OUTLINE

- The Fifth and Fourteenth Amendments
- The Importance of Inmate Discipline
- How Prison Discipline Works

- *Wolff v. McDonnell*
- *Sandin v. Conner*
- *Baxter v. Palmigiano*
- Double Jeopardy
- *Superintendent v. Hill*
- *Hewitt v. Helms*
- Confidential Informants

This chapter analyzes how the due process provisions of the Constitution protect inmates against unfair actions of the government (state and local inmates are protected by the Fourteenth Amendment, federal inmates by the Fifth Amendment) in the context of inmate discipline. A separate chapter discusses due process with respect to classification, transfers, personal injuries, and property loss.

▶ The Fifth and Fourteenth Amendments

The language of the due process clauses requires that two inquiries to be made in any claim of constitutional protection against state action. The first question is, has there been any deprivation of life, liberty, or property? Not every type of government action that offends a person raises a due process question. A person claiming violation of the due process clause must show that life, liberty, or property has been taken or is adversely affected. If there has been deprivation of a constitutionally protected liberty interest by the government the second question is, what process is due to the person who has been deprived? This is a matter that the courts have called "fundamental fairness." The purpose of due process is to ensure that the government has taken action that it is justified to take or that it has taken the action with procedural steps that ensure fairness. What makes an action fair? Generally speaking, the courts have said that fairness means providing steps ensuring that the facts are as the government claims they are and that the action taken is authorized by law (that is, the government agency or official taking the action has been given the legal authority to act). Beyond those general statements, the exact procedure that must be followed—the "process that is due" to the individual affected—varies greatly from one situation to another.

Courts generally agree that the more serious the loss is to the individual, the more procedural protections (due process) must be provided by the government. For example, what is the most serious kind of deprivation that the government can take? Most would agree that taking a convicted offender's life as punishment for a capital offense is the highest kind of deprivation. In response to that analysis, beyond the stringent procedural requirements for criminal trials in general, even more detailed procedural protections are established before capital punishment can be imposed. At the other extreme would be a minor loss of property, in which a person is entitled to an administrative (informal) claim procedure to evaluate the claim and to reimburse the person for their loss. Some actions in prison carry a high degree of procedural protection, and others carry low degrees of due process entitlement—or none at all (even though the offended person claims there has been a "deprivation" by the government).

▶ The Importance of Inmate Discipline

This chapter deals with the most frequently contested and litigated type of action involving inmates: inmate **discipline.** Why is disciplinary action against inmates so often contested? The action taken can be very serious to the individual inmate, affecting their sentence (as when good time is taken away, or their parole date is moved back) and thus their liberty in getting to the streets. Or disciplinary action may take away their property, confiscating some item they have in their cell, or ordering them to pay for damage they have done to someone else's property. The disciplinary action may adversely affect the conditions of confinement; for instance, placement in highly restricted **disciplinary confinement** (which is variously called detention, segregation, isolation, or "the hole" and can be thought of as a jail within the prison). Their privileges may also be taken away, such as recreation, visiting, or commissary purchases.

Typically, a number of inmates who are disciplined are those who have trouble adjusting to the regimen and rules of prison life and who are contesting, or trying to circumvent, those rules almost every day of their incarceration. As an example, in its 2020 Annual Report, the Ohio Department of Rehabilitation and Correction reported the

Rules Infraction Board processed 69,151 conduct violations in fiscal year 2019, with violations of Rule 19 (fighting), Rule 39 (drugs/intoxicating substance) and Rule 23 (refusal to accept an assignment) making up almost 30% of all infractions. Its inmate population in fiscal year 2020 was 45,813.[1] Inmates commonly use prison administrative grievance procedures to appeal disciplinary actions. In grievance procedures (in those jurisdictions that allow administrative appeals of the disciplinary actions), complaints regarding disciplinary actions are the most common type of complaints filed by inmates. The ultimate appeal (through legitimate channels) is to file an action in court, challenging the disciplinary sanction that was taken. Lawsuits in which inmates have raised due process questions about the fairness of the actions taken by prison staff, disciplinary actions are frequently cited complaints.

A disciplinary process that sanctions inmates for infractions of the rules is vitally necessary. A legitimate question may be raised as to why corrections institutions wonder why additional punishment is necessary need to impose disciplinary sanctions on inmates who are already locked up and who are thereby already being punished severely for their criminal activity. The answer is complex and is open to discussion, but the main reasons are these: most prisons today are surprisingly (to an outsider) free-flowing and tolerant of a wide variety of activities, and inmates, in large numbers, move from living quarters to dining hall, to work, to recreation, to visiting, to school.

The large varieties of activities and programs that are offered today, even in a highly regimented prison or jail environment (there are, of course, fewer programs and much less inmate movement in jails than in prisons), provide many benefits. These include a greater normalization of the living environment, which reduces tensions for inmates and, thereby, also for staff; a greater variety of programs, which assist the inmates in rehabilitation efforts and in preparing them for return to the community; and greater opportunities for interaction with others, both inmates and staff, which assist inmates in having more positive interpersonal relationships. Although there are many benefits to such activities, there are also increased risks, the most important being an increased risk to security. Flowing numbers of inmates moving from place to place in the institution increase the opportunities for misconduct, such as planning escapes, assaults (on other inmates and on staff), and trafficking in contraband. In high-security institutions and in antiquated facilities in which the supervision of inmate movement and programs is difficult, there will be a lesser flow of inmate traffic within the institution and a decreased variety of programs.

Because the majority of inmates want to adjust as well as they can to the requirements of prison life (doing their time quietly and with as few confrontations as possible), it is the goal of the staff to help those inmates by providing a safe and secure environment. To accomplish this, those who create trouble must be held accountable, either by coercing them into conforming their behavior to expected prison norms or by removing them from the population where they disrupt and intimidate others. As a side benefit, staff are hoping to instill better self-control skills and the ability to adjust to societal norms of behavior, producing inmates who respect authority and the rules that protect the safety and the rights of all.

▶ **How Prison Discipline Works**

There is a need for a firm and fair internal disciplinary system in every correctional facility. Upon admission to the facility, every inmate in the orientation procedure should be given notification (preferably both written and oral) of the prison's rules and the procedures for enforcing those rules. Central to this orientation procedure, and underlying inmate discipline, is a purpose of instilling in inmates a sense of responsibilities, which go along with freedoms and liberties that they may have while confined. (These freedoms and rights are significantly reduced compared with those of persons on the outside, but it is important to emphasize the ones that inmates do retain.) **BOX 11-1** provides a model set of rights and responsibilities addressed to inmates.

Staff must also be trained in disciplinary procedures (since an offense may be committed in the presence of any staff member, everyone must be taught the requirements of the system and how misconduct by inmates is handled). The most basic training starts with the list of prohibited conduct inside the institution and also the list of sanctions that may be imposed. There is a large list of acts and omissions which are prohibited by prison rules (some things, such as murder, assault, and theft, are just like offenses on the outside, while others, such as escape, riot, and offenses involving contraband, are peculiar to prisons). At the end of this text is Appendix 6, which presents a model misconduct code for a prison. It sets out a list of typically prohibited prison acts, indicating their degree of seriousness and providing the types of sanctions that may be imposed when an inmate commits a particular prohibited act. (It must be emphasized—this is a model code and not one that is legally required or judicially approved.) This appendix identifies major and minor disciplinary offenses and sanctions (see the "Low moderate" category). Examples of minor offenses include single incidents of using obscene language, or malingering (feigning illness). Sanctions for such one-time offenses do not involve a substantive loss

BOX 11-1 Inmate Rights and Responsibilities

Bureau of Prisons, Justice
§ 541.12 Inmate rights and responsibilities.

Rights	Responsibilities
Reprinted from the Federal Bureau of Prisons, Program Statement 5270.09, Inmate Discipline, Appendix C effective August 1, 2011.	

1. You have the right to expect that as a human being you will be treated respectfully, impartially, and fairly by all personnel.

1. You have the responsibility to treat others, both employees and inmates, in the same manner.

2. You have the right to be informed of the rules, procedures, and schedules concerning the operation of the institution.

2. You have the responsibility to know and abide by them.

3. You have the right to freedom of religious affiliation and voluntary religious worship.

3. You have the responsibility to recognize and respect the rights of others in this regard.

4. You have the right to health care, which includes nutritious meals, proper bedding and clothing, and a laundry schedule for cleanliness of the same, an opportunity to shower regularly, proper ventilation for warmth and fresh air, a regular exercise period, toilet articles, and medical and dental treatment.

4. It is your responsibility not to waste food, to follow the laundry and shower schedule, to maintain neat and clean living quarters, to keep your area free of contraband, and to seek medical and dental care as you may need it.

5. You have the opportunity to visit and correspond with family members, and friends, and correspond with members of the news media in keeping with Bureau rules and institution guidelines.

5. It is your responsibility to conduct yourself properly during visits. You will not engage in inappropriate conduct during visits to include sexual acts and introduction of contraband, and not to violate the law or Bureau guidelines through your correspondence.

6. You have the right to unrestricted and confidential access to the courts by correspondence (on matters such as the legality of your conviction, civil matters, pending criminal cases, and conditions of your imprisonment).

6. You have the responsibility to present honestly and fairly your petitions, questions, and problems to the court.

7. You have the right to legal counsel from an attorney of your choice by interviews and correspondence.

7. It is your responsibility to use the services of an attorney honestly and fairly.

8. You have the right to participate in the use of law library reference materials to assist you in resolving legal problems. You also have the right to receive help when it is available through a legal assistance program.

8. It is your responsibility to use these resources in keeping with the procedures and schedule prescribed and to respect the rights of other inmates to the use of the materials and assistance.

9. You have the right to a wide range of reading materials for educational purposes and for your own enjoyment. These materials may include magazines and newspapers sent from the community, with certain restrictions.

9. It is your responsibility to seek out and utilize such materials for your personal benefit, without depriving others of their equal rights to the use of this material.

Rights	Responsibilities
10. You have the right to participate in education, vocational training, counseling, and employment as resources permit, and in keeping with your interests, needs, and abilities.	10. You have the responsibility to take advantage of activities, which may help you live a successful and law-abiding life within the institution and in the community. You will be expected to abide by the regulations governing such activities.
11. You have the right to use your funds for commissary and other purchases, consistent with institution security and good order, for opening bank and/or savings accounts, and for assisting your family.	11. You have the responsibility to meet your financial and legal obligations, including, but not limited to, DHO and court-imposed assessments, fines, and restitution. You also have the responsibility to make use of your funds in a manner consistent with your release plans, your family needs, and for other obligations that you may have.

The Federal Bureau of Prisons, published in Title 28 CFR, § 541.12 (Revised as of July 1, 2010).

of "liberty" (such as a recommendation for parole date rescission or retardation, or the imposition of disciplinary segregation). Instead, lesser sanctions may consist of a change in housing, a reprimand and warning, or extra duty. Offenses warranting more serious sanctions are handled by an institution's disciplinary authority (typically a committee or a hearing officer).

Often, as is shown in the Bureau of Prisons Inmate Discipline Program [see Appendix 6 on the Navigate eBook site on jblearning.com], offenses are of different categories of severity, and sanctions may be imposed in a range, according to the severity of the offense that has been committed. Sanctions are of many kinds. In those jurisdictions with parole, serious misconduct is usually reported to the parole board, and serious problems regarding misconduct in the prison may adversely affect parole decisions. Most jurisdictions have some sort of good time provision. This is time taken off the full length of the sentence, so that an inmate can be released early (if they are not paroled first) using an accumulation of good time credits. (Good time in some places is also applied to the parole eligibility or parole grant date, so that earning good conduct time can advance a parole release date, as well.) Most often, good time is given for good conduct for each month the sentence is served (or for working in a factory or in the fields, or for an unusually meritorious event, such as assisting staff in a riotous situation). In some states, it is given at the beginning of the sentence, according to the number of years in the sentence, and the inmate retains that "lump sum" of good time unless there is reason to take it away. Taking good time from an inmate is, thus, a significant sanction, especially under some circumstances in which many months can be taken from the inmate (good time **forfeiture**).

A common type of disciplinary sanction is to place the inmate for a certain length of time in disciplinary confinement inside the prison (disciplinary segregation or detention) for a proscribed length of time. Property may also be taken away or privileges revoked. Assignments to a preferred job or preferred housing may be changed. The inmate may be ordered transferred to a higher-level institution. For some offenses, only one or two types of sanctions are available; for others, there may be a whole range and combination of sanctions which may be applied for the individual offender and his offenses (just as in sentencing in criminal court).

There is also a specific procedure established for deciding whether the inmate committed the prohibited act before deciding the sanctions that are appropriate. (In some systems [and court opinions], inmates and staff [and judges] use the terms guilt and innocence when referring to disposition of administrative disciplinary matters. However, these terms are better applied to criminal prosecutions, and are not used in this text.) An inmate accused of violating prison rules is given the opportunity to appear before a disciplinary authority, which may be a single individual or a committee. The committee is usually composed of staff members who are experienced in prison matters and have been trained to conduct such hearings. To ensure impartiality, the staff on the disciplinary authority may not have been directly involved in the alleged incident. In *Pigge v. Cotton*, 342 F.3d 660 (7th Cir. 2002) the court of appeals ruled that prison disciplinary authorities, as adjudicators, are "entitled to a presumption of honesty and integrity" absent clear evidence to the contrary and that staff hearing officers are not deemed biased simply because they are employees of the correctional department. (A few states have tried using a hearing officer, who has a greater degree of independence and is from outside of the prison.)

The inmate receives a written copy of the charges before the hearing (the constitutional requirements for the different elements of the proceedings are discussed later in this chapter). At the hearing, the inmate may have someone assist them (ordinarily not an attorney or someone from the outside) or may appear without assistance. Some states, such as Minnesota, permit an attorney to appear as a representative on behalf of inmate.[2] The inmate may present their version of what happened. The disciplinary authority considers the evidence and decides whether or not the inmate committed the prohibited act, as charged. If the disciplinary authority concludes that they did, the same authority decides what sanction to impose (again, as with the terms *guilty* and *innocent,* inmates and staff may use the term *sentence* taken from criminal court terminology). Often, the decisions regarding whether the inmate committed the prohibited act, and which sanction is to be imposed, may be reassessed by a reviewing authority, at the institution or at a higher level of the agency. Some jurisdictions allow the inmate to appeal an adverse decision through the inmate grievance procedure, and some provide for automatic review of all disciplinary actions, at least when they are of a higher degree of severity.

▶ *Wolff v. McDonnell*

Wolff v. McDonnell, 418 U.S. 539 (1974), is the genesis of inmate discipline decisions. As in many other prison cases dealing with all sorts of prison operations, lower courts had diverged widely on the disciplinary issues regarding whether inmates were entitled to any due process protections at all, and if so, what the constitutional due process requirements were. With *Wolff,* the Supreme Court provided the constitutional standards. Later cases decided subsidiary issues or refined the holdings in *Wolff,* but this case remains the leading, landmark decision on due process in prison hearings.

McDonnell was a Nebraska inmate who filed a Section 1983 action, claiming that disciplinary proceedings did not comply with the due process clause. (The *Wolff* decision also addressed the issue of attorney mail, and there was a question about the adequacy of the legal assistance program provided to inmates. But *Wolff* is known principally as the "inmate discipline case.") McDonnell was found guilty of serious misconduct. Under Nebraska rules, infractions that were less than serious could be punished only by loss of privileges. For "flagrant or serious misconduct," the inmate could have their good time credits taken away, and they also could be placed in a disciplinary cell. Loss of good time not only potentially lengthened the time to be held in prison, but it also had to be reported to, and considered by, parole authorities. Nebraska argued that the procedure for disciplining inmates was a matter of internal policy which raised no constitutional issues. McDonnell argued that his liberty was seriously affected by the state's actions in taking his good time credits, which required due process protections.

First, the Supreme Court rejected the contention that prisoners had no due process rights:

Prisoners may … claim the protections of the Due Process Clause. They may not be deprived of life, liberty, or property without due process of law.

The Court also held that 42 U.S.C. Section 1983 was a proper way for the prisoner to raise this question in federal courts. The Court recognized that there are special problems in prison administration that must be balanced with any rights claimed by the prisoner.

[T]here must be mutual accommodation between institutional needs and objectives and the provisions of the Constitution that are of general application … But here the State itself has not only provided a statutory right to good-time but also specifies that it is to be forfeited only for serious misbehavior … Since prisoners in Nebraska can only lose good-time credits if they are guilty of serious misconduct, the determination of whether such behavior has occurred becomes critical, and the minimum requirements of procedural due process appropriate for the circumstances must be observed.

Determining when action taken against a prisoner is so serious that it triggers due process is, as pointed out previously, the entry question in any due process analysis. The kinds of actions that trigger due process requirements had been discussed and developed in many Supreme Court decisions that dealt with nonprison matters. That discussion is now mainly of interest only to lawyers in their historical analysis of due process rights in prisons. It has been put to rest, at least for now, in the decision of *Sandin v. Conner,* which follows in this chapter. *Sandin* gave us the answer about how to evaluate entitlement to due process rights in prisons.

What *Wolff* provided were the procedural requirements that must be followed by prison officials in those cases where due process is required. The Court said that what is required in some other kinds of actions affecting inmates, such as revocation of probation or parole, is not required in a prison disciplinary hearing. The Court reviewed the background of prison proceedings, which "take place in a closed, tightly controlled environment peopled by those who have chosen to violate the criminal law and who have been lawfully incarcerated for doing so." The Court noted the argument that disciplinary proceedings further "the institutional goal of modifying the behavior and value systems of prison inmates sufficiently to permit them to live within the law when they are released." Because of the nature of prisons, "there would be great unwisdom in encasing the disciplinary procedures in an inflexible constitutional straitjacket that would necessarily call for adversary proceedings typical of the criminal trial."

The Court then specified the minimal due process standards for a prison disciplinary hearing, which are far short of criminal trial proceedings.

[There must be, in a prison hearing] advance written notice of the claimed violation and a written statement of the fact findings as to the evidence relied upon and the reasons for the disciplinary action taken … At least a brief period of time after the notice, no less than 24 hours, should be allowed to the inmate to prepare for the appearance before the [Disciplinary] Committee … [T]he inmate facing disciplinary proceedings should be allowed to call witnesses and present documentary evidence in his defense when permitting him to do so will not be unduly hazardous to institutional safety or correctional goals … Where an illiterate inmate is involved … or where the complexity of the issue makes it unlikely that the inmate will be able to collect and present the evidence necessary for an adequate comprehension of the case, he should be free to seek the aid of a fellow inmate, or if that is forbidden, to have adequate substitute aid in the form of help from the staff or from a sufficiently competent inmate designated by the staff.

The Court also suggested that impartiality of the disciplinary committee was necessary when it ruled that the Nebraska Adjustment Committee was sufficiently impartial to satisfy the due process clause.

These are the minimum procedural requirements for a prison hearing. In a footnote, the Court noted that these requirements are set for a serious sanction, such as the loss of good time, and are not required for "lesser penalties such as the loss of privileges." Also very important in the decision is what the Court did *not* require. There is no requirement that the inmate must be given the right to appeal to a higher authority. Although the inmate is given the right to call witnesses, the court noted the potential for disruption that this could cause and said that "[p]rison officials must have the necessary discretion to keep the hearing within reasonable limits and to refuse to call witnesses who may create a risk of reprisal or undermine authority." Also, if the committee did not call the witnesses the inmate requested, the Court said it would be good to give its reasons for not calling those witnesses. Confrontation and cross-examination were also recognized to present special hazards in a prison setting. The Court declined to require them, saying, "the Constitution should not be read to impose the procedure at the present time and … adequate bases for decision in prison disciplinary cases can be arrived at without cross-examination."

A major due process concern was the right to counsel at prison hearings. Although a few states had allowed attorneys or outside representatives at hearings, most did not. The Court noted that allowing counsel would "inevitably give the proceedings a more adversary cast and tend to reduce their utility as a means to further correctional goals." The Court said that "we are not prepared to hold that inmates have a right to either retained or appointed counsel in disciplinary proceedings." Note that the Supreme Court ruled that assistance in an inmate disciplinary hearing was not required unless the issues were complex or the inmate was illiterate. Because these are difficult standards to apply in most prison cases, many, if not all, state correctional agencies give every inmate charged with violating prison rules an opportunity to have a staff, or inmate counsel, substitute. An example is Maine which requires an inmate accused of violating prison rules to be advised of their right to have a staff or inmate counsel substitute assist them, to identify the person they wish to assist them, and that the disciplinary authority may appoint a staff counsel substitute when necessary.[3]

The Court also noted that the procedures specified were "not graven in stone. As the nature of the prison disciplinary process changes in future years, circumstances may then exist which will require further consideration and reflection of this Court." Although this statement fairly invites challenges to its decision "at some future time," the ruling about the procedural requirements still stands. (**BOX 11-2** provides an example of some aspects of one state's inmate discipline policy, including its coverage of the *Wolff* requirements.)

BOX 11-2 Inmate Discipline

POLICY:

A. The New Mexico Corrections Department (NMCD) shall provide a safe and secure environment for both staff and inmates through the implementation and maintenance of reasonable standards of control and discipline. Staff and inmates will be provided access to copies of this policy and procedure additions/revisions as they are implemented. This policy and procedure shall be reviewed at least annually and updated as necessary.

B. There are written rules of inmate conduct that specify the acts prohibited within the institutions and the penalties that can be imposed for various degrees of violation. [4- 4226]

C. A rulebook containing chargeable offenses, ranges of penalties, and disciplinary procedures shall be given to each inmate and staff member and shall be translated into those languages spoken by significant numbers of inmates. Signed acknowledgement of receipt of the rulebook shall be maintained in the inmate's file. When a literacy or language problem prevents an inmate from reading the rulebook, a staff member or translator shall assist the inmate in reading the rules. [2-CO-3C-01] [4-4228]

D. All personnel who work with inmates shall receive sufficient training so that they are thoroughly familiar with the rules of inmate conduct, the rationale for the rules, and the sanctions available. [4-4229]

E. This policy includes written guidelines for resolving minor inmate infractions, which includes a written statement of the rule violated, and hearing and decision within seven days, excluding weekends and holidays, by a person not involved in the rule violation; inmates may waive their appearance at the hearing. [4-4230] [2-CI-5A-6]

F. When an inmate allegedly commits an act covered by criminal law, the case shall be referred to the appropriate court or law enforcement officials for consideration for prosecution. [4-4231] The NMCD shall provide a safe and secure environment for both staff and inmates. In order to implement this policy, it is essential that reasonable standards of control and discipline are established and maintained. Staff and inmates will be provided access to copies of this policy and procedure and additions/revisions as they are implemented. This policy and procedure shall be reviewed at least annually and updated as necessary.

G. The disciplinary process of the industry program shall be in accordance with this policy. [2-CI-5A-5]

H. When a rule violation requires a formal resolution, staff members shall prepare a disciplinary report and forward it to the designated supervisor (Shift Sgt/Lt/Cpt.). [4- 4232]

I. Disciplinary reports by staff members should include at a minimum: [4-4233]
    ▪ Specific rule(s) violated;
    ▪ A formal statement of the charge;
    ▪ Any unusual inmate behavior;
    ▪ Any staff witnesses;
    ▪ Any physical evidence and its disposition;
    ▪ Any immediate action taken, including the use of force; and,
    ▪ Reporting staff members signature and date and time of report.

J. When an alleged rule violation is reported, an appropriate investigation shall begin within twenty-four (24) hours of the time the violation is reported and shall be completed without reasonable delay, unless there are exceptional circumstances for delaying the investigation. [4-4234]

K. An inmate charged with rule violations that is place (sic) on pre-hearing detention status shall be reviewed by the Warden or designee within seventy-two (72) hours, including weekends and holidays. [4-4235]

L. An inmate charged with a rule violation shall receive a copy of the disciplinary report, which includes the written statement of the charge(s), a description of the incident and specific rules violated. The inmate shall be given a copy of the report no less than twenty- four (24) hours prior to the scheduled hearing with the Hearing Officer. The hearing may be held within the twenty-four (24) hours with the inmate's written consent. [4-4236]

M. An inmate may waive his or her right to a hearing provided that the waiver is documented and reviewed by a Deputy Warden. [4-4237]

N. An inmate charged with rule violations shall be scheduled for a hearing as soon as practicable, but no later than seven days, excluding weekends and holidays, after being charged with a violation. Inmates shall be notified of the time and place of the hearing at least twenty-four (24) hours in advance of the hearing. [4-4238]

O. Continuances of the disciplinary hearing shall be for a reasonable period of time and for good cause. [4-4239]

P. Disciplinary hearings on rule violations shall be conducted by an impartial person. A written record of the proceedings shall be made and maintained in accordance with state archive rules; a taped record of all major level proceedings shall be made and maintained for at least one year. [4-4240]

Q. An inmate charged with rule violations shall be present at the hearing unless they waive that right in writing or through their behavior. Inmates may be excluded during the testimony of any inmate whose testimony must be given in confidence; the reason for the inmate's absence or exclusion shall be documented. [4-4241]

R.   An inmate shall have an opportunity to make a statement and present documentary evidence at the hearing and can request witnesses on their behalf; the reasons for denying such a request shall be stated in writing. [4-4242]

S.   A staff member or an agency representative will assist an inmate at disciplinary hearings if assigned. The institutional Facility warden will develop a representative list with the minimum of three appointed staff members to choose from to assist inmates if the need for a representative is required. A representative shall be appointed when it is apparent an inmate is not capable of collecting and presenting evidence effectively on his or her own behalf. [4-4244]

T.   The hearing officer's decision shall be based solely upon information obtained in the hearing process, including staff report, the statements of the inmate charged, and evidence derived from witnesses and documents. [4-4244]

U.   A written record shall be made of the decision and the supporting reasons and a copy shall be kept in the inmate's file and in the disciplinary archive file. [4-4246]

V.   If an inmate is found not guilty of an alleged rule violation, the disciplinary report shall be removed from the inmate's file. [4-4246]

W.   The Warden's appeal form in this policy is the mandatory form to be used by the designated Appeals Disciplinary officer and shall not be modified. This mandatory statewide facility form is to ensure continuity between all facilities (Public and Private).

X.   A Deputy Warden or applicable Facility designee shall review all disciplinary hearings and dispositions to assure conformity with policy and procedures. [4-4247]

Y.   All major misconduct reports, administrative, and inmate disciplinary infraction data shall be entered into the Criminal Management Information System (CMIS) by the local facility disciplinary officer within five (5) working days of delivering to inmate.

AA. Data on disciplinary infractions shall be used to determine assault rates on NMCD staff and inmates.

BB. Inmates have the right to appeal any decision of the hearing officer to the Warden. Inmates shall have up to fifteen (15) calendar days of receipt of the decision to submit an appeal. The appeal shall be decided within thirty (30) calendar days of its receipt by the Warden's office and the inmate shall be promptly notified in writing of the results. [4- 4248]

CC. The Warden or shift supervisor can order immediate segregation when it is necessary to protect the inmate or others. The action shall be reviewed within seventy-two (72) hours by the appropriate authority. [4-4250]

DD. There is a sanctioning schedule Category "A" Sanction Chart Attachment (CD- 090101.C) and Category "B" Sanction Chart Attachment (CD-090101.D). [4-4255]

EE. Inmates in Disciplinary Restrictive Housing shall be personally observed by a correctional officer at least every thirty (30) minutes on an irregular schedule. Inmates who are violent or mentally disordered or who demonstrate unusual or bizarre behavior shall receive more frequent observation. [4-4257]

FF. An inmate can be placed in disciplinary detention for a rule violation only after a hearing by the Hearing Officer. [4-4252]

New Mexico Department of Corrections. Inmate Discipline (CD-090100). 05/28/19, reviewed/revised 05/28/19. Pages 5-8. Accessed 20 March 2020. *Available:* https://cd.nm.gov/wp-content /uploads/2019/06/CD-090100.pdf

Note: The numerical references at the end of some paragraphs refer to the Commission on Accreditation for Corrections Standards.

▶ *Sandin v. Conner*

The Supreme Court *did* reconsider its ruling on the first part of prison disciplinary due process analysis in *Sandin v. Conner,* 515 U.S. 472 (1995). Recall that the first question to be answered in any due process case is: Has there been a deprivation of life, liberty, or property that triggers activation of the clause, requiring some due process protection? The *Sandin* case revisits the issue of "the circumstances under which state prison regulations afford inmates a liberty interest protected by the Due Process Clause."

Conner, a Hawaii inmate, was charged with serious misconduct, found guilty of the charges before an adjustment committee, and sanctioned with 30 days in disciplinary segregation. He was not allowed to call witnesses to testify at his hearing before the committee. The Ninth Circuit Court of Appeals held that Conner had a liberty interest in remaining free from disciplinary segregation and that he had not received the due process required by *Wolff* when he was not allowed to present any witnesses. The Supreme Court reversed that judgment.

There is an excellent discussion of the history of prison due process decisions in *Sandin,* if you are interested in reading it. The Court noted that its analysis of due process entitlement in prison had culminated in the decisions of *Greenholtz v. Inmates,* 442 U.S. 1 (1979), and *Hewitt v. Helms,* 459 U.S. 460 (1983). Essentially, those decisions held that due process turned on whether state action was mandatory or discretionary. That is, if officials were required (mandated) to reach a certain result if certain facts existed, then some due process was required. A clue to whether an action is mandatory is use of the word "shall" in regulations or policy. From the opposite perspective, if the official action was totally discretionary (for example, when policy used the word "may"), no due process was required. The Court in *Sandin* abandoned that standard, finding it too mechanical and cumbersome. It found two major problems with that standard: it encouraged states to avoid due process by always writing discretionary language ("officials may" do this or that) into their rules, and it led to over-involvement of the courts in the day-to-day management of the prisons. Furthermore, it encouraged inmates to comb through regulations, looking for mandatory language on which they could bring a due process challenge.

Finally, the Court said that the legalistic search for mandatory language in prison rules "strayed from the real concerns undergirding the liberty protected by the Due Process Clause." The purpose of prison discipline is to effectuate prison management and prisoner rehabilitative goals, according to the Supreme Court. Prison discipline does not ordinarily impose any sanction or retribution beyond that contained in the sentence being served. As long as it does not add on to that sentence or go beyond the conditions contemplated in the sentence, the disciplinary action does not create a liberty interest.

> **We hold that Conner's discipline in segregated confinement did not present the type of atypical, significant deprivation in which a state might conceivably create a liberty interest ... Conner's confinement did not exceed similar, but totally discretionary confinement in either duration or degree of restriction ... The regime to which he was subjected as a result of the misconduct hearing was within the range of confinement to be normally expected for one serving an indeterminate sentence of 30 years to life.**

Thus, the question is not whether the inmate is sanctioned, or even sanctioned (in their view) severely. The question is whether the sanction is within the range of conditions, restrictions, and sanctions that are contemplated while serving a sentence of confinement. If the sanction extends the duration of the sentence, some due process would be required. In Hawaii, although the parole board must consider prison misconduct, it is not required to deny parole for the misconduct record of an inmate. The parole board itself has procedural protections at its hearings that allow the inmate to explain their misconduct record. That process protects the parole decision making as far as due process is concerned, and no additional protection is needed at the prison's disciplinary hearing.

> **We hold, therefore, that neither the Hawaii prison regulation in question nor the Due Process Clause itself afforded Conner a protected liberty interest that would entitle him to the procedural protections set forth in *Wolff*.**

Sandin, of course, has led to a flurry of court decisions interpreting disciplinary procedures in light of the new standard (and it has also triggered reexaminations by corrections agencies of their rules). This process will continue, as adjustment is made to the starker (and somewhat simpler) standard, in deciding whether due process applies to prison hearings.

▸ *Baxter v. Palmigiano*

In *Baxter v. Palmigiano*, 425 U.S. 308 (1976), the Supreme Court considered several disciplinary issues. One was whether inmates were entitled to counsel at disciplinary hearings. Two courts of appeals had held that counsel must be provided if the misconduct charges involved crimes punishable under state criminal statutes. (Both of those cases were considered together in this opinion under the name of *Baxter v. Palmigiano. Baxter v. Palmigiano* was a Rhode Island case on writ of certiorari from the Court of Appeals for the First Circuit. *Enomoto v. Clutchette*, on certiorari from the Ninth Circuit, involved California prison hearings and was decided as a companion case with *Baxter*) The Supreme Court disagreed with the two courts of appeals and reaffirmed its holding in *Wolff*:

> **[W]e are not prepared to hold that inmates have a right to either retained or appointed counsel in disciplinary proceedings.**

Another issue that was already considered in *Wolff* was raised again in *Baxter*. The Ninth Circuit Court of Appeals had required providing in writing to an inmate if he was denied the right to cross-examine or confront witnesses against him at the hearing. The Supreme Court also reversed this requirement. It pointed out that, in

Wolff, it recommended, but did not require, written reasons for denying inmates the right to call witnesses on their own behalf, but it made no such requirement for confrontation and cross-examination. In the prison setting, those hearing steps carry inherent dangers, the Court said, and there is no due process requirement for prison officials to allow confrontation and cross-examination.

A new issue raised in *Baxter* was the right of the inmate to remain silent at his disciplinary hearing. Inmate Palmigiano was told that he was not required to testify at his hearing, that he could remain silent, but that his silence could be used against him. The First Circuit Court of Appeals held that this violated the self-incrimination privilege of the Fifth Amendment, made applicable to the States by reason of the Fourteenth Amendment, and that adverse inferences could *not* be drawn from an inmate's failure to testify. The Supreme Court disagreed:

> **[A]n inmate's silence in and of itself is insufficient to support an adverse decision by the Disciplinary Board … [P]ermitting an adverse inference to be drawn from an inmate's silence at his disciplinary proceedings is not, on its face, an invalid practice.**

Furthermore, the Court noted that if an inmate was compelled to furnish evidence that might incriminate him in a later criminal proceeding (that is, he was ordered to testify), he would have to be given immunity regarding the use of that testimony in the criminal proceedings. *Baxter* instructs that an inmate in a disciplinary proceeding can be advised that their silence can be used against them, but that the silence is not enough by itself to convict the inmate (there must be other evidence); if the inmate is ordered to testify, they must be given immunity from use of that testimony in a criminal proceeding.

Finally, the Ninth Circuit (in the companion case of *Enomoto v. Clutchette*) had ruled that minimum due process was necessary even when inmates were deprived of privileges. The Supreme Court rejected that ruling. As the Supreme Court in *Sandin made clear,* that loss of privileges is certainly not the type of disciplinary sanction that would require due process.

▸ Double Jeopardy

The discussion of the rights of inmates in *Baxter* raises a question about **double jeopardy**, when inmates are subject to both disciplinary sanctions for misconduct in prison and also criminal prosecution in criminal court for the same misconduct. The Double Jeopardy Clause is found in the Fifth Amendment:

> **[N]or shall any person be subject for the same offence to be twice put in jeopardy of life or limb.**

The Supreme Court has not ruled specifically on this issue. But lower courts have consistently held that it is not a constitutional violation to proceed against a prisoner in both forums—in a prison disciplinary action and in a criminal prosecution. These courts have ruled that it is permissible to have both institutional sanctions and a criminal sentence imposed for the same misconduct.

For example, see the case of *Porter v. Coughlin,* 421 F.3d 141 (2nd Cir. 2005). Porter had participated in a riot at his New York prison. He was ordered to be confined for three years in a Special Housing Unit, following a disciplinary hearing. He was additionally convicted for that same offense in state court and sentenced to an additional three to six years of incarceration. This court noted that the Supreme Court has said (but it was not in a prison discipline case) that the Double Jeopardy Clause "protects only against the imposition of multiple *criminal* punishments for the same offense." *Hudson v. United States,* 522 U.S. 93 (1997). Criminal prosecution and prison disciplinary proceedings based on the same offense do not implicate double jeopardy concerns.

In *United States v. Simpson,* 546 F.3d 394 (6th Cir. 2008), inmate Simpson had escaped from a Tennessee jail where he was held as a federal prisoner following conviction on several federal crimes. He was charged for the escape in a disciplinary hearing and was given 60 days in disciplinary segregation, 40 days of good time disallowed, and a 6-month loss of visitation privileges. Simpson was then indicted in federal court for escape. He received an additional 18-month consecutive sentence for the escape. He challenged that federal prosecution for the same escape. This court said that this action did not constitute double jeopardy, noting that he was twice put in jeopardy only if he was at risk for *criminal* punishments for the same offense. "Every circuit court of appeals to consider this question has given the same answer. The Double Jeopardy Clause was not intended to inhibit prison discipline, and disciplinary changes in prison conditions do not preclude subsequent criminal punishment for the same misconduct."

▶ *Superintendent v. Hill*

The question in *Superintendent (of the Massachusetts Correctional Institution at Walpole) v. Hill*, 472 U.S. 445 (1985), concerned the degree of evidence that must be present to support a finding of guilt in a prison disciplinary hearing. Inmate Hill was found guilty of assault based on testimony from a prison guard (officer) that he heard some commotion, went to investigate, and found an assaulted inmate. He saw Hill (and two other inmates) running away and no other inmates in the area. He charged the three inmates with the assault. The disciplinary board also considered the guard's written report. They found the charged inmates guilty of the assault. Hill lost 100 days of good time and was placed in isolation for 15 days. He filed suit in state court, which found insufficient evidence to support the finding of guilt. The Massachusetts Supreme Judicial Court affirmed that ruling. The U.S. Supreme Court reversed the Massachusetts courts.

> [R]evocation of good time does not comport with "the minimum requirements of procedural due process," unless the findings of the prison disciplinary board are supported by some evidence in the record … [D]ue process in this context requires only that there be some evidence to support the findings made in the disciplinary hearing.

The Court found that the minimal evidence in this case—testimony from the prison guard and copies of his written report—was "some evidence" and thus was sufficient to meet due process requirements.

What this case does point out is that courts in many situations are unaccustomed to dealing with the obviously lessened levels of procedure that are constitutionally required in prison hearings. The evidence in *Superintendent v. Hill* was minimal, but sufficient, the Supreme Court said, to satisfy the low levels of protection required in prison hearings. This same understandable predilection of courts (as in the Massachusetts courts here) to apply court-hearing standards to prison administrative hearings can be found in many situations, especially in the lower courts.

▶ *Hewitt v. Helms*

Hewitt v. Helms, 459 U.S. 460 (1983), involved the placement of inmate Helms in administrative segregation status at the Huntingdon, Pennsylvania, State Correctional Institution. There was a major disruption at the institution involving several assaults on prison officers and the destruction of property. Helms was removed from his cell after order was restored and placed in restrictive confinement for questioning during the investigation of the riot. He was given a minimal hearing some five days later. The question was whether moving Helms from his regular cell in the general population to administrative segregation required due process, and, if so, what amount of process was required.

> [T]he transfer of an inmate to less amenable and more restrictive quarters for nonpunitive reasons is well within the terms of punishment ordinarily contemplated by a prison sentence.

The Court then concluded that placement in more restrictive, segregated confinement did not create any liberty interest. So Helms did not have any due process entitlement found in the Constitution itself.

However, this is the case that spelled out that there was another source of liberty interest in the Fourteenth Amendment—namely, state rules that mandated certain actions if certain facts were found. The Court found that Pennsylvania had used explicit mandatory language in its rules for placement in prison segregation, and, thereby, a right to due process was created. This is the analysis that *Sandin* later specifically rejected (overruled), so, in the *Sandin* analysis, Helms was not entitled under the Constitution to any due process whatsoever for his placement in administrative segregation.

In *Hewitt*, the Supreme Court went on to hold that the small amount of procedural protection used by Pennsylvania was sufficient. All that was required was "some notice of the charges against him and an opportunity to present his views to the prison official charged with deciding whether to transfer him to administrative segregation." That decision maker would then review the charges and the evidence (including the inmate's statement). This very minimal procedure was all that would be required to satisfy due process requirements.

A case of similar concerns is *United States v. Gouveia*, 467 U.S. 180 (1984). Gouveia, a federal inmate, was placed in administrative detention while authorities investigated the murder of an inmate. Correctional systems uniformly have a location or status to isolate offenders charged with violating prison rules and who pose a threat to institutional security. In *Hewitt v. Helms* this status was called administrative segregation, and in *Gouveia* it was called administrative detention. In both cases it was the same type of status- it is a more restrictive type of housing than the general population of the facility used to isolate inmates from the general population for safety and security reasons. Administrative segregation is not being used as a sanction for misconduct, and while on this administrative status, the inmate may receive the same general privileges given to an inmate in the general prison population, such as access to education programs, counseling, commissary, visiting, and use of a radio. Although the inmate cannot move about the prison in the same way as a regular inmate, the conditions and privileges of administrative detention are generally more liberal than in disciplinary segregation.

He remained in administrative detention for 19 months, until he was indicted and arraigned in federal court. During the time that he was in detention, he had no counsel. He claimed this was a violation of his Sixth Amendment right to counsel, but the trial court denied that claim. He was convicted of murder.

The Ninth Circuit Court of Appeals reversed his conviction on the ground that Gouveia had to be given counsel after 90 days in prison detention or else be released back into the general prison population. The Supreme Court reversed, holding that inmates were not constitutionally entitled to the appointment of counsel while they were in administrative segregation and before any judicial proceedings had been initiated against them. Neither is an inmate, during this investigation period, entitled to someone who will investigate the case on his behalf.

The right to counsel attaches only at or after the initiation of adverse judicial proceedings against the defendant.

▶ Confidential Informants

Another issue that is of continuing concern in prison discipline cases is the use of confidential informant evidence. The Supreme Court has not addressed this issue. The legal guidance used by correctional systems comes from federal courts of appeals and state courts.

In the prison setting, staff receive information from a variety of sources, which assists them in maintaining security and control of the facility. As inmates have become more sophisticated, as gangs in prisons present a threat to the safety of inmates and staff, and as drugs and other contraband are continuing, if not increasing, problems, prison staff must use any information they can acquire to make institutions as safe and secure as possible. One of the oldest and most common sources of information is the inmate **informant** (in prison jargon, a "snitch" or a "rat").

Often, information from these informants leads to prison disciplinary action, bringing charges against the inmate based on the informant evidence. The question is, how is this information to be used in disciplinary hearings? The Supreme Court at least tacitly recognized the difficulty of this problem when, in *Wolff* and in *Baxter*, it held that, in a prison, there was no right to confrontation and cross-examination of adverse witnesses. This allows prison staff to protect the identity of the informants. The confidentiality of the informants protects both their own safety and the opportunity to continue to use their information in the future.

But how does one ensure the fairness of the prison proceeding based on informant evidence? How can one protect against an inmate fabricating information or pointing a finger at a person with whom they just want to get even? Corrections officials and courts have struggled with this issue, and, in general, they have come up with the conclusion that there must be some way that officials can utilize to ascertain the reliability of the informant's story. Often, the hearing officer or committee is required to make a statement in the record that informant information has been used as evidence in the case and that the officer or committee is satisfied that that information is reliable. Such a conclusion about reliability may be based on a review of the background and the circumstances that support reliability by the hearing officer themself, or it may be based on a report from an investigative officer who presents to the committee their reasons for believing the inmate. All of this consideration about the inmate informant is discussed out of the presence of the inmate who is charged, of course. This protects the inmate "snitch" against reprisals. The informant's reliability may be established by reliability in other situations (the informant has provided reliable information in the past), by detailed accounts that could only be known by someone who was there, or by corroborative evidence developed in the case.

For an examples of cases in which the courts of appeal have required such an inquiry into the reliability of the informant to be placed into a confidential record of the proceedings, see *McCollum v. Williford*, 793 F.2d 903 (7th Cir. 1986) and *Zimmerlee v. Kinney*, 831 F.2d 183 (9th Cir. 1987). This is one of several areas in which different courts have arrived at different requirements for prison officials to follow. Until the Supreme Court addresses these questions, prison staff will have to ascertain what courts in their jurisdiction have said and follow those rulings regarding legal requirements in inmate disciplinary hearings.

Summary

- Due process is a concept that is guaranteed in two places in the Constitution: the Fifth Amendment (for federal actions) and the Fourteenth Amendment (for state actions).
- There are two inquiries in due process cases: (1) whether a person has been deprived of life, liberty, or property and (2) if there was such deprivation, whether procedural protections (due process) were provided.
- The disciplining of inmates is an important part of prison and jail administration. It is essential for the safety and orderly running of a corrections facility. It must be done fairly and evenhandedly, in accordance with written rules.
- The Supreme Court held, in the leading case on inmate discipline, that inmates are entitled to the protection of the due process clause. In cases of serious sanctions, inmates must be given these procedural rights: advance written notice of the charges; some time to prepare for the hearing; the right to call witnesses and present documentary evidence (unless to do so would be hazardous); a right to assistance, for illiterate inmates or in complex cases; and a written statement of the findings, including the evidence relied on and the reasons for the action taken. There is no need to provide an appeal process or to provide legal counsel (*Wolff v. McDonnell*).
- More recently, the Supreme Court has said that prison disciplinary action does not deprive an inmate of liberty and does not require due process, unless the sanction adds on to the sentence or goes beyond the conditions contemplated in the sentence. In that case, the Supreme Court held that the inmate's placement in disciplinary segregation (a common sanction in prison cases) did not create a liberty deprivation that required a due process hearing. It was a punishment "within the range of confinement to be normally expected" (*Sandin v. Conner*).
- The Supreme Court (disagreeing with some appellate courts) held that counsel did not have to be provided at prison disciplinary hearings, even when the misconduct amounted to criminal misconduct. Also, the Court ruled that an inmate could be advised at a disciplinary hearing that he had the right to remain silent, but that if he did, his silence could be used against him. The silence by itself could not support an adverse decision. If the inmate was ordered to give evidence that could incriminate him in a later criminal proceeding, he would have to be given immunity as to the use of that testimony in a criminal trial (*Baxter v. Palmigiano*).
- An inmate may receive disciplinary sanctions for misconduct committed inside the prison (or jail) where they are confined. In addition, they may be prosecuted and sentenced in criminal court for the same misconduct. This is not a constitutional violation under the Double Jeopardy Clause. Several courts of appeal (but not the Supreme Court) have adopted this ruling.
- At a prison disciplinary hearing, the amount of evidence required to support a finding that an inmate committed misconduct is "some evidence" (*Superintendent v. Hill*).
- The holding of *Hewitt v. Helms*, that in some cases staff would have to provide a minimal due process hearing before placing an inmate into restrictive confinement within the prison, has been overruled by the due process analysis of *Sandin v. Conner*.
- Confidential informants are often used in prison security investigations and disciplinary matters. The Supreme Court has not ruled on the standards for using evidence from confidential informants. Lower courts have held that hearing officials must, at a minimum, satisfy themselves of the reliability of the information that has been provided by any inmate informants.

Thinking About It

During a search of inmate Berry's cell, officers found three pieces of tobacco under the pillow on Berry's bed. DOC rules prohibit an inmate from possessing tobacco products. Berry was given an incident report for a prison rule violation. At a disciplinary hearing, Berry denied possessing the tobacco. She did not dispute that tobacco was found under her pillow, but since three other inmates were present in the pod when it was searched, she claimed the tobacco was planted. The prison disciplinary committee found that Berry had committed the prohibited act and sanctioned her with 10 days loss of good conduct time. Inmate Berry sued correctional staff alleging she was denied good conduct time without due process. What should the court rule? Was there some evidence to support the committee's sanction?

Key Terms

disciplinary confinement
discipline (corrections)
double jeopardy
forfeiture
informant

Endnotes

1. Ohio Department of Rehabilitation and Correction. 2020 Annual Report, 28, 13. Accessed November 16, 2020. https://www.drc.ohio .gov/Portals/0/ODRC%20FY2020%20Annual%20Report%202%202%281%29.pdf
2. Minnesota Department of Corrections, Policy No. 303.010 *Offender Discipline*, effective July 1, 2019. Accessed August 23, 2020. http:// www.doc.state.mn.us/DocPolicy2/html/DPW_Display_TOC.asp?Opt=303.010.htm
3. Maine Department of Corrections, Policy No. 20.1 *Inmate Discipline*. Effective July 2, 2002, last revised November 6, 2019. Accessed August 23, 2020. https://www.maine.gov/sos/cec/rules/03/chaps03.htm

© EJ_Rodriquez/iStock/Getty Images Plus/Getty Images

CHAPTER 12

Fifth and Fourteenth Amendments: Due Process— Classification, Transfers, Personal Injuries, and Property Loss

Confinement in any of the State's institutions is within the normal limits or range of custody which the conviction has authorized the State to impose. That life in one prison is much more disagreeable than in another does not in itself signify that a Fourteenth Amendment liberty interest is implicated when a prisoner is transferred to the institution with the more severe rules.

U.S. Supreme Court, *Meachum v. Fano*

CHAPTER OUTLINE

- The Nature of Classification
- *Meachum v. Fano; Montanye v. Haymes*
- *McKune v. Lile*
- *Howe v. Smith*
- *Olim v. Wakinekona*
- *Vitek v. Jones*
- *Wilkinson v. Austin*
- *Young v. Harper*
- *Kansas v. Hendricks; Kansas v. Crane*

- *Farmer v. Brennan*
- International Transfers
- Consular Notification and Access
- Loss of Property and Personal Injuries
  - *Parratt v. Taylor*
  - *Hudson v. Palmer*
  - *Daniels v. Williams*
  - *Davidson v. Cannon*
- Use of Excessive Force

This chapter examines the wide range of other actions, primarily in prisons, where due process claims have been made. Under the due process clauses of the Fifth and the Fourteenth Amendments, no person may be "deprived of life, liberty, or property, without due process of law." Action is not taken in prisons to deprive persons of their lives, except in death penalty cases, although property and liberty deprivation claims are common. This chapter addresses cases in which inmates raise due process claims because of the loss of their property, and some cases (other than discipline), in which claims have been made that the liberty of inmates has been taken away by the actions of prison officials.

▶ The Nature of Classification

One of the most important functions in running prisons is the classification of prisoners. Classification involves several decisions about the individual inmate, including where (to what institution) they should be sent to serve their sentence and where they should be assigned (within an institution) for housing, special programs, and work. There are, in every corrections agency, staff members who are specially trained to make those decisions about the classification of inmates. Written policies in the agency set the rules for classification.

Procedures for classifying inmates take into account numerous factors, including: (1) the age and sex of the offender; (2) the criminal sophistication of the offender; (3) geographic concerns (such as where the offender's home has been, where his family is located, from what location he is likely to get visitors, and to what area he is likely to be released); (4) special needs, focusing first on any medical or psychiatric problems and then on other special needs, such as education and vocational training; (5) special security problems, such as other offenders from whom this inmate should be separated (whether codefendants, gang members, persons with whom he has been confined before, informants, law enforcement or public officials, etc.) and whether the inmate is known to be an escape risk; (6) special factors, such as recommendations from the sentencing court; and (7) the availability of space in appropriate facilities.

The last factor (7) involves another classification process—the classification of facilities. Institutions in the corrections department are classified according to security level, the types of inmates they receive, and the programs they offer. Obviously, each institution has a geographic location, which often enters into classification decision making. Classification officials must know well the different types of institutions and what kinds of inmates go to each one.

Institutions are typically classified as *minimum, medium,* and *maximum* security. Other titles may also be used. The level of security is decided by physical factors, such as the type of perimeter security (such as a wall, fencing, or no fencing at all) and type of housing inside (single cells are most desirable for high-security inmates; and open housing, as in dormitories, is best for low-security inmates), and levels of staffing. The old-style penitentiary or state prison, with high walls and towers spaced around the walls where armed guards keep watch, is thought of as high security. More recent prison architecture does not include walls (mainly because of expense), although high-security features can be built on the perimeter of the institution, which, it is claimed, give just as high a degree of security. Those features typically include a double fence, with barbed (now usually razor) wire on the top and coils of razor wire laid between the fences and on the ground next to the fences. Inside a prison, security features are many: gates to the institution, typically a double set at each entry point, which are operated from a remote, protected location; grilled doors located on corridors into the main part of the institution and at strategic points in the facility where there is inmate movement; security cameras, which allow surveillance of most areas of the institution and enable correctional staff to watch remote locations; heavily secured gates and doors, which may be operated electronically or by keys; and alarm systems, which are triggered by improper movement or other breaches of security. The most important security feature is trained staff, who are alert to possible problems and who move through an assigned area to make sure all is well. Communication between staff, whether by phone, radio, or electronic means, is also a vital security feature. From these many factors, a security assessment is made of the facility, so that classification and assignment to the right institution may be made for the individual inmate.

Institutions are also classified according to the kinds of programs they offer. Some have highly specialized medical or psychiatric units. Some have vocational or educational programs of a specialized nature. Some have more internal security units, so they can take more people who may need separation for protection, detention, or disciplinary housing. Of course, some facilities are for women and others for men. (Nationwide, there are a few institutions that take both male and female inmates into the same facility.) Some institutions specialize in programs for younger offenders. By sheer numbers, a very large prison system will have a larger variety of institutions and a greater number of classification choices for the individual. A very small system will have very few choices—perhaps only one male institution and a much smaller one for women.

As a basic rule of classification (or at least a desirable rule of institution assignment), an inmate will be sent to an institution as close to their home as possible. All of the other classification factors will enter into the decision: the offender must be sent to a facility that is appropriate for their security level and that has special features or programs that they need (including medical and psychiatric care, educational programs, and separation from certain other people). In order to make these decisions, the staff needs as much reliable information about the offender as possible. At initial classification, this information will usually come from the defendant's presentence report and from law enforcement or court authorities (who will provide the offender's criminal history, rap sheet, and special information, such as escape or suicide attempts). If the inmate has been confined in the system before, their records from the previous incarceration will be used. The classification officer (or team), on the basis of review of the records (sometimes, with a face-to-face interview, especially in those states that have an initial diagnostic and reception center, one of the main purposes of which is to make a better-informed classification decision for each inmate), then makes a decision to send the inmate to a certain facility. Later, there may be a decision to reclassify the inmate, based on factors that come to light after the offender is serving their sentence. These factors for reclassifying the inmate may include information in any of the areas mentioned previously, such as moving the inmate to a place of higher security (because of discipline or escape problems), relieving crowding in the inmate's present facility, moving the inmate closer to home as they approach release, or moving the offender to a facility where special programs they may need are available (see **FIGURE 12-1**). Here is what two states say about classification:

> The NMCD [New Mexico Corrections Department] shall establish procedures to implement and monitor an inmate's status relating to [the inmate's] risk assessment, program assignment, good time and release preparation. This will include consideration of any special needs of the inmate. The NMCD shall ensure that all inmates are classified into the most appropriate custody level based on security and custody considerations with the intent of balancing the inmate's program and treatment needs .... The NMCD utilizes an objective rating process to assign inmates to the most appropriate custody level consistent with the safety of the general public, staff, and other inmates (New Mexico Corrections Department, 2016).

In Alaska, the following policy has been established:

> Purpose: To establish a uniform system to assess the custody and rehabilitative needs of prisoners in the custody of the Alaska Department of Corrections and to designate prisoners to the appropriate correctional facility. . . . Policy: A. Prisoners shall be classified to the least restrictive custody level based on the assessment of behavioral risk factors, supervision needs, rehabilitative needs, and institutional behavior. B. The classification process shall identify prisoners' rehabilitative and reentry requirements that promote public safety and provides for the responsible reformation and reintegration of offenders. C. Prisoners shall be housed based on their custody level. D. Regular reviews of each prisoner's custody and rehabilitative status shall be completed (Alaska Department of Corrections, 2014).

The main constitutional issue in classification decision making is due process: Is the inmate entitled to any process or any kind of hearing before he is classified to a particular institution or before he is moved to a particular place?

FIGURE 12-1 A Hearing at the Community Corrections Center in Lincoln, Nebraska.
© Mikael Karlsson/Alamy Stock Photo

▶ *Meachum v. Fano; Montanye v. Haymes*

Meachum v. Fano and *Montanye v. Haymes,* both Supreme Court cases and both decided on June 25, 1976, address the due process question for inmate classification and transfers. They involve just slightly different aspects of transfers of prisoners.

Meachum v. Fano, 427 U.S. 215 (1976), involved the transfer of inmate Fano and five others from the Massachusetts Correctional Institution at Norfolk, a medium security facility, to a maximum security prison. The transfer was based on information that authorities received, indicating that the inmates were involved in criminal conduct—namely, the possession of weapons or ammunition during a time when the institution was caught up in several disturbances. None of the inmates were punished by the loss of good time or by disciplinary confinement; they were transferred to a place where living conditions were "substantially less favorable than those at Norfolk." The question to be decided, as stated by the Supreme Court, was "whether the Due Process Clause of the Fourteenth Amendment entitles a state prisoner to a hearing when he is transferred to a prison the conditions of which are substantially less favorable to the prisoner."

The Supreme Court held that there was no due process entitlement in such a transfer.

> **We reject at the outset the notion that *any* grievous loss visited upon a person by the State is sufficient to invoke the procedural protections of the Due Process Clause …. Similarly, we cannot agree that *any* change in the conditions of confinement having a substantial adverse impact on the prisoner involved is sufficient to invoke the protections of the Due Process Clause …. [G]iven a valid conviction, the criminal defendant has been constitutionally deprived of his liberty to the extent that the State may confine him and subject him to the rules of its prison system so long as the conditions of confinement do not otherwise violate the Constitution. The Constitution does not require that the State have more than one prison for convicted felons; nor does it guarantee that the convicted prisoner will be placed in any particular prison if, as is likely, the State has more than one correctional institution. The initial decision to assign the convict to a particular institution is not subject to audit under the Due Process Clause, although the degree of confinement in one prison may be quite different from that in another. The conviction has sufficiently extinguished the defendant's liberty interest to empower the State to confine him in *any* of its prisons.**

This Supreme Court decision is full of language of the same sort, emphasizing that a liberty interest was not created by placing an inmate in a particular kind of confinement that is more disagreeable than another might be. Many federal courts previously had held that if an inmate suffered a "grievous loss" or if there was a "substantial deprivation" imposed by prison officials, there would have to be a due process hearing before that transfer action was taken in order to protect the constitutional rights of the inmate. The Supreme Court rejected those standards and said specifically that they did not trigger due process entitlements.

> **Transfers between institutions, for example, are made for a variety of reasons and often involve no more than informed predictions as to what would best serve institutional security or the safety and welfare of the inmate …. That an inmate's conduct, in general or in specific instances, may often be a major factor in the decision of prison officials to transfer him is to be expected unless it be assumed that transfers are mindless events. A prisoner's past and anticipated future behavior will very likely be taken into account in selecting a prison in which he will be initially incarcerated or to which he will be transferred to best serve the State's penological goals …. Massachusetts prison officials have the discretion to transfer prisoners for any number of reasons …. Holding that arrangements like this are within reach of the procedural protections of the Due Process Clause would place the Clause astride the day-to-day functioning of state prisons and involve the judiciary in issues and discretionary decisions that are not the business of federal judges …. Our holding is that the Due Process Clause does not impose a nation-wide rule mandating transfer hearings.**

The language of the *Meachum* opinion is mostly in terms of the "transfer" of prisoners, but you can see that the language also covers what called classification decisions. From *Meachum,* the Court's guidance is that an agency's classification and transfer actions, as a general principle, are not subject to due process requirements.

The companion case of *Montanye v. Haymes,* 427 U.S. 236 (1976), followed the same track as *Meachum,* with just slightly altered facts. Inmate Haymes was transferred from the Attica Correctional Facility in New York to Clinton Correctional Facility, both of them maximum-security prisons. Haymes claimed that Superintendent Montanye transferred him for disciplinary reasons, because Haymes was circulating a petition among inmates complaining of Haymes being removed from his work assignment as an inmate clerk in the law library. As a clerk, Haymes had been providing legal assistance to other inmates. Those inmates also claimed that they were deprived of that assistance as a result of Haymes's work reassignment. When Haymes filed suit, complaining of the prison actions against him, the district court ruled that there had been no violation of his constitutional rights. The court of appeals reversed and sent the case back for further consideration on the grounds that Haymes's transfer was a disciplinary action, not an administrative one. That court reasoned that the transfer, like other serious disciplinary actions, could not be taken without certain procedural protections; that is, the consequences of the transfer were so burdensome that they probably triggered due process clause protections, necessitating a hearing.

The Supreme Court disagreed with the reasoning of the court of appeals and reversed.

> **We held in *Meachum v. Fano,* that no Due Process Clause liberty interest of a duly convicted prison inmate is infringed when he is transferred from one prison to another within the State, whether with or without a hearing …. As long as the conditions or degree of confinement to which the prisoner is subjected are within the sentence imposed upon him and are not otherwise violative of the Constitution, the Due Process Clause does not in itself subject an inmate's treatment by prison authorities to judicial oversight. The Clause does not require hearings in connection with transfers whether or not they are the result of the inmate's misbehavior or may be labeled as disciplinary or punitive.**

That language used in *Montanye,* "as long as the conditions … are within the sentence imposed upon him," is especially noteworthy, because it anticipates the standards for due process entitlement adopted in *Sandin v. Conner,* 515 U.S. 472 (1995). In *Sandin,* the Court rejected and overruled a due process analysis that had been adopted in another type of special transfer, namely, the transfer of a prisoner from the general population of a prison into administrative segregation. In *Hewitt v. Helms,* 459 U.S. 460 (1983), the Court had said that placement in segregated confinement did not, in and of itself, create a liberty interest, which would necessitate a due process hearing. However, the Court noted that the state had used mandatory language in its rules, and that kind of language triggered due process entitlement for that kind of transfer. The *Sandin* decision rejected that analysis, saying that due process is not required when action is taken against the inmate "within the range of confinement to be normally expected for one serving" a sentence of confinement. Therefore, we can add the transfers of inmates from the regular population to administrative detention or segregation to those transfers that will not require due process hearings.

▸ *McKune v. Lile*

In *McKune v. Lile,* 536 U.S. 24 (2002), Kansas inmate Lile refused to participate in the prison's mandatory Sexual Abuse Treatment Program (SATP). Part of SATP required the inmate to sign an "Admission of Responsibility" form, accepting responsibility for the crimes for which he had been sentenced and detailing all prior sexual activities, even those not charged. No legal immunity was provided. Failure to comply would result in the reduction of prison privileges and transfer to a potentially more dangerous unit. The inmate refused to cooperate with the SATP requirements and sued for injunctive relief, claiming a violation of his Fifth Amendment right against self-incrimination. The district and appeals courts held in favor of the inmate. The Supreme Court reversed. Citing *Meachum,* the Court held that no transfer hearing was required. Although *McKune* deals with the privilege against compelled self-incrimination, not due process, the Court saw *Meachum* as controlling authority for its position that, by the fact of their convictions, inmates must expect significant restrictions on rights and privileges that free citizens take for granted. No liberty interests (such as eligibility for good time credits or parole, which would affect an inmate's release date) were implicated.

> **No one contends … that the transfer is intended to punish prisoners for exercising their Fifth Amendment rights. Rather, the limitation on these rights is incidental to Kansas' legitimate penological reason for the transfer: Due to limited space, inmates who do not participate in their respective programs will be moved out of the facility where the programs are held to make room for other inmates …. It is well settled that the decision where to house inmates is at the core of prison administrators' expertise …. For this reason the Court has not required administrators to conduct a hearing before transferring a prisoner to a bed in a different prison, even if "life in one prison is much more disagreeable than in another." … This logic has equal force in analyzing respondent's self-incrimination claim.**

The *McKune* decision was not unanimous. The opinion of the Court, including one concurring opinion, was divided in a five-to-four split. The dissenting justices noted that, although Kansas's goal of reducing **recidivism** among sex offenders was admirable, an inmate should not be compelled to forfeit the privilege against self-incrimination simply because the ends are legitimate or because the conviction is for a sex offense. The dissenting justices asked the question, "[W]hat if this is one of those rare cases in which the jury made a mistake and he is actually innocent?"

▸ *Howe v. Smith*

This case flowed from the decision of officials in Vermont to "get out of the prison business." In December of 1974, the Vermont commissioner of corrections announced that he would close the state prison at Windsor, the only high-security facility in the state. This would leave only community correctional centers (for minimum security inmates) and the diagnostic treatment facility at St. Albans as state corrections facilities for adult inmates, inside the state. Howe was serving a life sentence for first-degree murder. The Department of Corrections Classification Committee decided that he should be kept in a maximum security facility. When the decision was made to close Windsor, it was proposed that Howe should be transferred to a federal prison. The Federal Bureau of Prisons had agreed to take up to 40 Vermont prisoners. This was done pursuant to Title 18, U.S. Code, Section 5003(a), which allowed the director of the Bureau of Prisons to take state prisoners upon certification that there were federal facilities that could accommodate them (such a certificate was made). Howe was given a hearing in Vermont, with advance notice of the proposal and the reasons for it. The hearing officer recommended that Howe be transferred to a federal institution, because Howe was dangerous and could not be placed in a community-based program. The hearing officer also found that Howe was an escape risk (he had previously escaped from the maximum security wing at St. Albans) and that he needed long-term, maximum-security supervision.

In *Howe v. Smith,* 452 U.S. 473 (1981), the Supreme Court upheld the validity of the transfer. The legal analysis turned principally on the federal statute that authorized the Bureau of Prisons to take state prisoners, 18 U.S.C. § 5003, and not on constitutional protections. "The plain language, the legislative history, and the longstanding administrative interpretation of [Sec.] 5003(a) clearly demonstrate that the provision is a broad charter authorizing the transfer of state prisoners to federal custody. There is no basis in [Sec.] 5003(a) for the petitioner's challenge to his transfer to federal custody."

▶ *Olim v. Wakinekona*

Olim v. Wakinekona, 461 U.S. 238 (1983), involved another type of prisoner transfer. Wakinekona was serving a life sentence in the Hawaii State Prison. Because he was a serious troublemaker, a "Program Committee" recommended his transfer to a prison on the mainland. He was later transferred to Folsom State Prison in California. Wakinekona filed a Section 1983 action against state officials, claiming that he had been denied procedural due process, because he had not been given a hearing before he was transferred. The Supreme Court reviewed the case because it presented the new question of whether the due process clause protects inmates in cases of interstate transfers.

The Court noted that Hawaii, like many other states, had statutes that allowed it to transfer inmates to other states or to federal prisons. It also noted that "[o]vercrowding and the need to separate particular prisoners may necessitate interstate transfers." Another frequent reason for interstate transfer would be the one in Wakinekona's case: for the orderly running of an institution, it may be very desirable to transfer a troublemaker out of the system to another state. Thus, an inmate "has no justifiable expectation that he will be incarcerated in any particular State," just as he has no justifiable expectation that he will be placed into a particular prison within a state.

> **The reasoning of *Meachum* and *Montanye* compels the conclusion that an interstate prison transfer, including one from Hawaii to California, does not deprive an inmate of any liberty interest protected by the Due Process Clause in and of itself.**

▶ *Vitek v. Jones*

The prior cases on inmate transfers identify situations in which no due process rights are implicated. The Court, however, has set some limits on transfer actions. *Vitek v. Jones,* 445 U.S. 480 (1980), is a case that can best be interpreted, in contrast to the other transfer cases we have just discussed, as a transfer made outside the range of conditions normally to be expected by one serving a sentence of confinement. Jones was serving a sentence of three to nine years in the Nebraska state prison. Jones was placed in the penitentiary hospital, apparently for displaying psychiatric and behavioral problems. Two days later, he was placed in solitary confinement, where he set his mattress on fire, burning himself. He was treated for the burns in a nearby private hospital. Then, based on reports that he was suffering from a mental illness or defect and a finding that he could not receive proper treatment for that condition in the penal complex, he was transferred to the Lincoln Regional Center, a state mental hospital. Jones and other inmates challenged the Nebraska procedures, claiming that they were not given due process protections when they were transferred from the prison complex to the mental hospital. A three-judge U.S. district court, convened to consider the constitutionality of the state law and procedure, agreed with the inmates that their transfer, without adequate advance notice and opportunity for a hearing, deprived them of liberty without due process of law in violation of the Fourteenth Amendment.

The Supreme Court agreed to review the case, to decide whether the involuntary transfer of a state prisoner to a mental hospital affected a liberty interest that is protected by the due process clause. The Court first reviewed the recent prison cases that involved due process (*Meachum, Montanye, Greenholtz v. Inmates,* 442 U.S. 1 (1979), [a parole case], and *Wolff v. McDonnell,* 418 U.S. 539 (1974) [an inmate discipline case]). After this review, the Court concluded that Jones was entitled to due process because Nebraska had set up a procedure that created the expectation that action would not be taken against him unless he demonstrated specified behavior. These would be the factual substantive predicates, under the "mandatory language" analysis, which the Supreme Court later rejected in *Sandin v. Conner.*

However, apart from that reliance on mandatory language in the state statute, the Supreme Court also found that, by the very nature of the transfer, "the transfer of a prisoner from a prison to a mental hospital must be accompanied by appropriate procedural protections." The transfer of a prisoner from a regular prison facility to a mental hospital, the Court found, implicated a liberty interest that is protected under the due process clause. The Court noted that an ordinary citizen would be entitled to due process before they could be involuntarily sent to a mental health facility.

> **We conclude that a convicted felon also is entitled to the benefit of procedures appropriate in the circumstances before he is found to have a mental disease and transferred to a mental hospital .... A criminal conviction and sentence of imprisonment extinguish an individual's right to freedom from**

confinement for the term of his sentence, but they do not authorize the State to classify him as mentally ill and to subject him to involuntary psychiatric treatment without affording him additional due process protections.

The Court concluded that there were stigmatizing consequences of a transfer to a mental hospital for involuntary psychiatric treatment (which could involve subjecting the patient to mandatory behavior modification treatments). Those consequences constituted the kinds of deprivation of liberty that due process was established to protect. Although the state had an interest in placing the inmate in a specialized psychiatric facility for treatment, the inmate still had a strong interest in not being arbitrarily or wrongly classified as mentally ill, and then being subjected to unwanted treatment.

The Supreme Court identified the amount of due process—that is, the hearing requirements—which would have to be observed before transferring a prisoner to a mental hospital. The process would have to include: (1) advance written notice to the prisoner that a transfer was being considered; (2) a hearing, with disclosure of the evidence that officials were relying on and an opportunity for the prisoner to be heard in person and present documentary evidence; (3) an opportunity at the hearing to present witnesses and confront and cross-examine state witnesses, unless there was a finding of good reason not to permit witnesses or confrontation and cross-examination; (4) an independent decision maker; (5) a written statement by the factfinder as to the evidence relied on and the reasons for the action that was recommended; (6) availability of counsel, furnished by the state, if the inmate was not able to provide his own; and (7) effective and timely notice of all these hearing rights. It must be noted that item 6 in the procedures, providing counsel to the prisoner, was not agreed to by a majority of the Court. A five-to-four decision settled all other aspects of the case. Justice Powell departed from the majority on the right-to-counsel issue. He voted to require only some "competent help" at the hearing and disagreed that the state would have to provide legal counsel. Therefore, item 6 cannot be considered to be part of the majority decision of the Court, and the right to legal counsel cannot be considered to be a constitutional due process requirement in these hearings.

▶ *Wilkinson v. Austin*

Since the 1980s, partly in response to increased violence in prisons, many states and the federal government have established increased high security or "supermax" prisons. The state of Ohio did this at the Ohio State Penitentiary (OSP). This facility was designed to house 504 inmates in single cells. The conditions were more restrictive than anywhere else in the state system, with prisoners confined to their 7×14-foot cells for 23 hours a day (with one hour a day allowed for exercise at an indoor recreation cell), a light (dimmed at night) burning in each cell at all times, meals provided and eaten in the cells, and "inmates being deprived of almost any environmental or sensory stimuli and of almost all human contact." Further, placement at the OSP was indefinite, and prisoners at the OSP were ineligible for parole. The purpose was to "separate the most predatory and dangerous prisoners from the rest of the … general [prison] population."

In *Wilkinson v. Austin*, 545 U.S. 209 (2005), the Supreme Court determined "what process the Fourteenth Amendment to the United States Constitution requires Ohio to afford to inmates before assigning them to Supermax." Noting the severe conditions at the OSP, the Court concluded:

> **While any of these conditions standing alone might not be sufficient to create a liberty interest, taken together they impose an atypical and significant hardship within the correctional context. It follows that respondents [the prisoners] have a liberty interest in avoiding assignment to OSP.**

Having determined that placement at the OSP deprived inmates of a protected liberty interest, it follows that they were entitled to due process protection before that action was taken. What procedure were they entitled to? Looking at standards established in other due process cases, the Court said that the Ohio policy met constitutional standards for procedural protections. That policy provided for a prison official to conduct a classification review, a three-tiered further review process if there was a recommendation that the inmate be placed in OSP, notice to the inmate of the factual basis leading to the OSP placement recommendation, and an opportunity for the inmate to submit objections prior to final determination, including a fair opportunity for rebuttal at a hearing (but without the opportunity to call witnesses). These procedures met the factors that had to be considered in satisfying due process: the inmate's interest in avoiding erroneous placement in OSP, minimizing the risk of making an erroneous placement in OSP, and satisfying the concerns of prison management to ensure the safety of prison personnel, the public, and the prisoners themselves. The Court specifically refrained from saying just what procedural steps would be required to meet the due process concerns in any such placement decision, but said Ohio's policy was satisfactory, providing sufficient procedural protection to the inmate.

▸ *Young v. Harper*

In *Young v. Harper,* 520 U.S. 143 (1997), the Court considered whether *Meachum* applied in a situation in which an inmate was removed from a preparole program. In *Young*, Oklahoma's Preparole Program became effective whenever state prisons became overcrowded (when the prison population exceeded 95% of capacity). The program authorized the release by administrative action of inmates before their sentences expired. This was called conditional release. Harper had served 15 years of a life sentence for two murders. Following a review by state officials, he was released, spending five months in the community. Subsequently, the governor, pursuant to his authority under this program, denied Harper parole and Harper was returned to prison. He then filed a petition for a writ of habeas corpus, claiming deprivation of his liberty without due process. The state argued that *Meachum* was controlling, claiming that reincarceration of a preparolee was nothing more than a "transfer to a higher degree of confinement." The Supreme Court disagreed, supporting the appeals court holding that preparole "more closely resembles parole or probation than even the more permissive forms of institutional confinement .... [D]ue process therefore mandates that program participants receive at least the procedural protections described in *Morrissey*." The Supreme Court said the "conditional release" was just like parole and that due process requirements for parole actions applied.

▸ *Kansas v. Hendricks; Kansas v. Crane*

These two Supreme Court decisions dealt with Kansas's Sexually Violent Predator Act. In 1994, Kansas passed this act, which set procedures for civilly committing persons who, due to a "mental abnormality" or "personality disorder," are likely to become involved in "predatory acts of sexual violence." The statute was used for Hendricks, an inmate with a long history of sexually molesting children. In 1984, he was convicted for taking "indecent liberties" with two 13-year-old boys. After serving nearly 10 years for those offenses, he was due for release from prison shortly after the law became effective. The state filed a petition, seeking his confinement under the new law. Hendricks challenged the law on various points, alleging a lack of due process and also that he was subjected to double jeopardy and **ex post facto** statutory punishment.

At a hearing on his commitment, Hendricks admitted he had repeatedly abused children when not confined; that this occurs whenever he "get[s] stressed out"; that he "can't control the urge"; and that the "only sure way he could keep from sexually abusing children in the future was 'to die.'" He did not object to the diagnosis that he suffered from pedophilia.

The Kansas Supreme Court invalidated the act, holding that the precommitment condition of a "mental abnormality" did not meet what the court saw as the due process requirement that involuntary civil commitment must be based on a finding of "mental illness." Kansas petitioned the U.S. Supreme Court for a writ of certiorari and Hendricks filed a cross petition, reasserting his claims of double jeopardy and ex post facto violations.

The Supreme Court, in *Kansas v. Hendricks,* 521 U.S. 346 (1997), upheld the Kansas act, likening it to state civil commitment procedures for mental patients that it had previously approved.

> **The challenged Act unambiguously requires a finding of dangerousness either to one's self or to others as a prerequisite to involuntary confinement. Commitment proceedings can be initiated only when a person "has been convicted of or charged with a sexually violent offense," and "suffers from a mental abnormality or personality disorder which makes the person likely to engage in the predatory acts of sexual violence." ... The [Kansas] statute thus requires proof of more than a mere predisposition to violence .... The precommitment requirement of a "mental abnormality" or "personality disorder" is consistent with the requirements of ... other statutes that we have upheld in that it narrows the class of persons eligible for confinement to those who are unable to control their dangerousness.**

Indeed, we have never required State legislatures to adopt any particular nomenclature in drafting civil commitment statutes. Rather, we have traditionally left to legislators the task of defining terms of a medical nature that have legal significance.

The Supreme Court also looked at Hendricks's claims of double jeopardy and ex post facto, rejecting each of them:

Where the State has "disavowed any punitive intent"; limited confinement to a small segment of particularly dangerous individuals; provided strict procedural safeguards; directed that confined persons be segregated from the general prison population and afforded the same status as others who have been civilly committed; recommended treatment if such is possible; and permitted immediate release upon a showing that the individual is no longer dangerous or mentally impaired, we cannot say that it acted with punitive intent. We therefore hold that the Act does not establish criminal proceedings and that involuntary confinement pursuant to the Act is not punitive. Our conclusion that the Act is nonpunitive thus removes an essential prerequisite for both Hendricks' double jeopardy and ex post facto claims.

The Supreme Court in *Hendricks* found no indication on the face of the statute to suggest that the intent of the legislature was anything other than an action, using civil commitment proceedings, intended to protect the public from harm.

Several years later, in *Kansas v. Crane*, 534 U.S. 407 (2002), the Supreme Court looked again at the Kansas procedure for committing sexual predators. The Court examined the question of whether *Hendricks* required a finding that the person is "*completely* unable to control his [dangerous] behavior." Crane was a previously convicted sexual offender who was diagnosed as suffering from exhibitionism and antisocial personality disorder. After a hearing before a jury, the district court ordered his civil commitment. The Kansas Supreme Court reversed, holding that the district court did not meet the *Hendricks* requirement of finding that Crane could not control his dangerous behavior.

The Supreme Court held that *Hendricks* established no requirement of *total* or *complete* lack of control but disagreed with the state's position that *Hendricks* allows commitment without *any* determination at all of lack of control.

[W]e recognize that in cases where lack of control is at issue, "inability to control behavior" will not be demonstrable with mathematical precision. It is enough to say that there must be proof of serious difficulty in controlling behavior. And this, when viewed in light of such features of the case as the nature of the psychiatric diagnosis, and the severity of the mental abnormality itself, must be sufficient to distinguish the dangerous sexual offender whose serious mental illness, abnormality, or disorder subjects him to civil commitment from the dangerous but typical recidivist convicted in an ordinary criminal case.[3]

▶ *Farmer v. Brennan*

Farmer v. Brennan, 511 U.S. 825 (1994), raised serious questions about the proper classification of an inmate. The inmate, Farmer, was a transsexual. He was medically identified as a male, because he possessed male sex organs. (He would have much preferred being treated and classified as a female; he thought of himself as a female and had taken steps before his incarceration to physically change to a female.) The case was decided as an Eighth Amendment case in order to consider Farmer's claim that he had been subjected to cruel and unusual punishment when he was placed in a male penitentiary, where he was sexually assaulted and injured.

Farmer is discussed here to emphasize the difficult problems that can be encountered in properly classifying an inmate. Farmer was an inmate who presented complex questions about how best he could be placed and treated inside the prison system. Providing for inmate safety, according to the Supreme Court and many lower courts, is a requirement demanded by the Eighth Amendment. Prison officials, however, are not guarantors of the safety of inmates, courts have said. But the officials must take steps to protect inmates, particularly when the officials are on notice that a risk is presented by a particular inmate's behavior.

There are two possible types of liabilities under such circumstances: common law tort liability and liability for violating the inmate's constitutional rights. If officials are negligent in taking protective steps (when they have received some notice of danger to the inmate and the inmate is then assaulted because of officials' inaction), their liability would fall under traditional, common law tort standards. An official could also be held constitutionally liable, as the Supreme Court said in *Farmer,* if he knows that an inmate faces a substantial risk of serious harm and the official disregards that risk and fails to take reasonable steps to avoid it.

To be sure, some responsibility is also placed on the inmate: if he knows he is in danger, he has some obligation to let prison officials know that. If officials are proposing to place him in the regular prison population, and he fears for his safety if that happens, he should let prison staff know of his fears and the basis for them. But the decision in *Farmer* emphasizes that, even though the standards for constitutional liability under the Eighth Amendment are rigorous, the mistaken classification of an inmate may expose staff to constitutional (Section 1983) liability in cases of "unnecessary and wanton infliction of pain." If that high standard is not proved, there may still be regular, common law tort liability for classifying an inmate mistakenly, particularly when decisions were not made according to commonly accepted correctional guidelines.

Would inmate Farmer have a constitutional claim against prison officials for "wrongly" classifying him? Does a prisoner have a liberty interest, protected by the due process clause, in prison classification? The Supreme Court in *Moody v. Daggett,* 429 U.S. 78 (1976) ruled that prisoners (at least federal prisoners) have no liberty interest, protected by the due process clause, in prison classification:

> **We have rejected the notion that every state action carrying adverse consequences for prison inmates automatically activates a due process right. In *Meachum v. Fano* … for example, no due process protections were required upon the discretionary transfer of state prisoners to a substantially less agreeable prison, even where that transfer visited a "grievous loss" upon the inmate. The same is true of prisoner classification and eligibility for rehabilitative programs in the federal system. Congress has given federal officials full discretion to control these conditions of confinement**.

In those jurisdictions where prisoner classification is vested in the discretion of prison officials, a prisoner would not have a constitutionally protected liberty interest in any particular classification.

▶ International Transfers

Another type of transfer, of more recent vintage, is the transfer of an inmate from one country to another. For the United States, these transfers were initiated by discussions with Canada in 1975. There is heavy and fairly free movement of persons between Canada and the United States. This large volume of traffic results in the prosecution and conviction of many persons who commit crimes in the neighboring country. The main concern underlying the initial discussion regarding the international transfer of inmates was a humanitarian and practical one: to get the offenders closer to home and under the supervision of the laws and customs of their home country. At first, the discussion focused on setting up legal arrangements to transfer the supervision of parolees from one country to the other. But this soon expanded to the consideration of all types of sentences—probation, imprisonment, parole, and even juvenile dispositions.

Issues of sovereignty are involved in such transfers. These transfers are called *international* or *foreign transfers* of prisoners and not prisoner exchanges. In these transfer cases, there is no requirement that one prisoner be exchanged for another or that there must be any kind of equality or balancing of numbers when prisoners are transferred. The supervision over the criminal sentence is being "exchanged" between the two sovereign countries but *transfer* is the preferred term for this program. Considerations of the principles of international law are necessarily present. The enforcement of criminal laws is an essential part of a nation's sovereignty. When a person is transferred out of a country, that sovereign nation is giving up a degree of control in a central aspect of its sovereignty. There are also extremely practical, and sometimes troublesome, questions of differences between the criminal laws of the two nations. No two nations have identical laws. (The criminal approaches of Canada and the United States are quite similar, which was helpful in working out transfers between those two countries. But some things are different. For example, all sentences—for any crimes—of greater than two years in Canada are served in federal institutions and not provincial ones. Of course, in the United States, every state plus the federal government administers its own criminal sanctions, of all lengths and of every type, and every state as well as the federal government has institutions for different lengths of sentences.) Attributes of sentences are often different. Such things as parole eligibility, good-conduct allowances, and inmate discipline vary (after all, as previously mentioned, these things even vary greatly from jurisdiction to jurisdiction within the United States). Also, there may be some serious differences regarding how each nation views the seriousness of particular offenses. The question then is, when a prisoner is transferred, does the exact length of the sentence they have to serve become the sentence in the receiving country (their home country), and do all the other aspects of their sentence (such as parole, probation, good time, disciplinary sanctions) apply after their transfer?

Shortly after the discussions were held with Canada, the same kind of talks took place between the United States and Mexico. There was somewhat more urgency with Mexico, because the numbers of prisoners were greater on both sides of the border. Concerns of families of U.S. citizens who were arrested in Mexico (and then of the members of Congress with whom those families talked) and of the State Department over conditions in Mexican jails and prisons and about Mexican criminal procedures encouraged the talks. There were more differences between the Mexican and American systems, so the talks with Mexico presented more practical problems than those with Canada. With the election of President Carter in 1976, there was a decisive push to finalize the discussions on prisoner transfers, because he was meeting with the president of Mexico soon after his election, and an issue was sought that could be held out as an example of goodwill and cooperation between the two countries. Ultimately, an announcement was made at that meeting that the two nations were signing a treaty to allow for sentenced offenders to be sent from one country to the other.

From the talks with Canada, and as an accommodation for the concerns of sovereignty and the differences between the criminal justice systems in the two countries, the following principles were agreed on: (1) Transfers would occur only for those who were convicted of offenses that were recognized as criminal violations in both countries. For example, if there is an offense in Country A of impersonating the president, which is not a crime in Country B, the offender in Country A convicted of that offense would not be a candidate for transfer to Country B. Otherwise, the offender would be imprisoned in Country B for activity that is not considered criminal in Country B. (2) The transfer would always be based on a tripartite agreement. This meant that the holding country (where the offender was tried and sentenced), the receiving country (their home country), and the offender would have to agree to the transfer. Because the main purpose of the program was humanitarian, if the offender did not want to return to their home country to serve their sentence, they should not have to go. (3) The fact of the conviction and the sentence would be given full recognition in the receiving country. The length of sentence would be transferred intact from one nation to the other. The other attributes of the sentence, such as the eligibility for parole on the length of a sentence, the requirements for parole supervision, remission (good time) credits, disciplinary procedures, and all kinds of programs that might be offered, would be governed by the law and procedures of the receiving country. (4) All appeals of the conviction or sentence would have to be completed before the transfer. A prisoner would not be considered "legally ready" for transfer consideration if appeals were still pending. (5) For sheer administrative convenience, a prisoner should have a certain length of time still remaining on his sentence in order to be eligible for a request for transfer. At the beginning, this was one year; later, it was reduced to six months. It takes some length of time just to process the transfer papers through diplomatic and corrections channels. If an inmate is very close—less than six months, for example—to release, there are often ways to reduce the remaining time to be served in confinement or under supervision and effect the release without having to go through the international transfer process. (6) The transfer of probation and parole, including both supervision and revocation authority, was authorized.

These principles became the foundation for the treaties entered into with Mexico on November 25, 1976, and with Canada on March 2, 1977. The Constitution mandates that only the federal government in the United States can enter treaties or any kind of agreements or transactions with foreign nations. (Article II, Section 2 of the Constitution gives the power to make treaties to the president. Two-thirds of the Senate must vote to ratify a treaty.) To achieve the international transfer of prisoners, treaties had to be negotiated and signed with each country and then sent to the Senate for ratification. Besides the treaties, it was recognized that, in the United States, implementing legislation would be needed. In 1977, a federal statute was passed (it is codified in Title 18, U.S. Code, Sections 4100 and following). It sets up the mechanics for transfers from and to the United States, primarily through the Department of Justice. The Department of State must also be involved in every case. States (in the United States) are authorized to send offenders who are foreign nationals to their home countries through this mechanism, and they can also receive back (to their home states in the United States) offenders from foreign countries.

Through the intervening years, treaties have been negotiated and signed with many countries. Presently, the United States has treaties with more than 85 countries and territories. In 2018, pursuant to these treaties, there were 311 inmates transferred, with 27 American citizens coming to the United States and 284 foreign nationals from the Federal Bureaus of Prison facilities leaving the United States (DOJ International Prisoner Transfer Program, 2018).[4]

Prisoners who were returned under the transfer treaty often brought lawsuits challenging their custody after they were back in the United States. The leading case considering challenges to the treaty process and the authority to hold prisoners under sentences imposed in foreign countries is *Rosado v. Civiletti*, 621 F.2d 1179 (2nd Cir. 1980). In that case, Rosado and three other U.S. citizens had been arrested in Mexico and charged with narcotics offenses. After their arrests, they claimed that they were stripped, bound, beaten, and tortured with electric prods. They had no access to attorneys or family members, they said. They refused to sign confessions that were prepared by authorities. They were transferred into a regular prison, where they alleged that they were told that the charge for a cell (and other amenities) would be $2,000. After a month, they were taken to court and were asked to confirm the statements that prosecutors had prepared for them. They denied them and were returned to prison. Sometime later, they were advised that the judge in their cases had convicted each of them for the drug offenses and had sentenced each one to nine years of imprisonment. At no time did they see the judge, an attorney, or any of the witnesses against them. These were the allegations of the plaintiffs in *Rosado*.

The appeals court in *Rosado* noted that, at the Senate hearings on the transfer treaties, complaints had been heard from many U.S. citizens who had been held in Mexican jails and prisons. Those stories provided compelling arguments to approve a transfer process. The prisoners in *Rosado* had been advised, while confined in Mexico, that the treaty had been approved in 1977, and they were informed of the necessary procedures to initiate a transfer. One of the conditions of the transfer, which had to be agreed to by the prisoners, was that there would be no legal remedy available to challenge their convictions or sentences once in the United States. This was part of the established principle that any appeals or challenges to the underlying conviction and sentence had to be brought and completed in the sending country. Also, as part of the process and the protection given to inmates, on the part of the United States, all prisoners (in this case, all of those who were in Mexican custody) were interviewed and advised by a U.S. public defender, who explained to them in detail the workings of the transfer treaty. Also, as a part of the transfer process, a U.S. magistrate went to the foreign country (or met the inmates at the border) and made certain that the inmates understood the consequences of the transfer. The inmates were also advised that nothing in the treaty prevented them from challenging their custody status, the legality of the treaty, or the manner in which their sentences were being executed once they returned to the United States. Any such challenge would have to be by means of petition for habeas corpus.

The *Rosado* plaintiffs challenged the constitutionality of their detention by habeas corpus action. A U.S. district court ordered their release, finding that their consents to be transferred were not voluntarily given (in view of the coercive nature of the conditions under which they were held in Mexico). The court of appeals disagreed and upheld the constitutionality of the transfer procedure.

First, the court noted that the law was clear that the U.S. Constitution only applied to actions taken in the United States or to actions taken by U.S. agents working in a foreign country. The Bill of Rights does not protect U.S. citizens against any actions that might be taken by a foreign nation's officials. A major concern in the litigation was the voluntariness of the prisoners' consent to be returned to the United States. The court applied the same standards used to test voluntariness of pleas of guilty in U.S. criminal cases: whether it was a deliberate, intelligent choice. The court concluded that the inmates' decisions were voluntarily and intelligently made.

> **[B]ecause the statutory procedures governing transfers of these prisoners to United States custody are carefully structured to ensure that each of them voluntarily and intelligently agreed to forego his right to challenge the validity of his Mexican conviction, and because we must not ignore the interests of those citizens still imprisoned abroad, we hold that the present petitioners are estopped from receiving the relief they now seek.**

In other words, this appeals court approved the concept and the legality of the international transfer process. The court recognized the desirability of having the transfer procedure available and did not want to jeopardize the chances of other prisoners to transfer out of Mexico. (After all, if a court had found that Mexican procedures and conditions were so bad that these prisoners in *Rosado* had to be released, it would probably eliminate the chances for others to transfer back to the United States. The U.S. government, in effect, would have been blocked from trying to assist its citizens to transfer, because an essential element of the treaty was that a transferred prisoner would be held in custody under the sentence that had been imposed in the sending country.) There was also concern about the impact, if such a ruling were made, on the relations between the two countries: Mexico would no doubt be offended and might itself abandon the treaty or any efforts to assist U.S. citizens if American courts intensively reviewed conditions in Mexico, based on the prisoners' assertions about what happened, and found the conditions and procedures so bad that they were serious violations of U.S. constitutional requirements.

In any event, the international transfer program has withstood constitutional attack in the courts. Inmates in the United States, however, are allowed to challenge any conditions or actions of U.S. officials after they are returned to U.S. custody. These challenges are brought, as for any American prisoner, using habeas corpus or Section 1983 actions to challenge the legality of their custody or the conditions under which they are held.

Another aspect of the treaty transfer program was challenged in *Marquez-Ramos v. Reno,* 69 F.3d 477 (10th Cir. 1995). Marquez-Ramos was a Mexican national serving a sentence in a federal prison. He sought a writ of **mandamus** (under Title 28, U.S. Code, Section 1361), asking the court to require the U.S. Attorney General to transfer him to Mexico. The court noted that, under the Treaty on the Exercise of Penal Sentences between the United States and Mexico, a request for transfer by an inmate is to be transmitted by the Transferring State (in this case, the United States) to the Receiving State (Mexico) only if the authority of the Transferring State "finds the transfer of an offender appropriate." The treaty, and its implementing statute in the United States, gave the authority to review such requests to the U.S. Attorney General. The treaty also set out the factors to be considered in reviewing a request for transfer. Those factors include whether the transfer will contribute to the social rehabilitation of the offender, the nature and severity of his offense and previous criminal record, and the strength of his family relationships and of his other connections of residence (whether in the United States or in his native country). In this case, the attorney general denied Marquez-Ramos's transfer request, mainly because of his serious offense and his ties to the United States. The district court and the court of appeals ruled that Marquez-Ramos had no entitlement to mandamus relief, because the attorney general had total discretion to make the transfer decision within the framework of the treaty. Mandamus was not available to challenge the discretionary authority of the attorney general, the courts said.

▶ Consular Notification and Access

The Vienna Convention on Consular Relations, of which the United States is a signatory provides that when a foreign national of a signatory country is arrested or detained, the detaining authority (1) must notify the detainee's consular authorities of the arrest or detention when the foreign national's home country has a mandatory notification requirement under the treaty even if the detainee does not request notification; (2) if mandatory consular notification is not required, the detaining authority must advise the detainee that they may request that consular officials be notified of the arrest or detention without delay; (3) consular officials should be permitted to have communication and access to the foreign national in detention and to provide consular assistance to the detainee; (4) law enforcement or an other government official notifying a foreign national's consular office when the foreign national dies, suffers a serious injury or suffers a serious illness.[5]

The Federal Bureau of Prisons and most, if not all, local jails and state departments of corrections have policies implementing these notification procedures. The State Department recommends that detaining authorities fully document the steps that are taken to comply with the Consular notifications, and steps are usually taken to ensure consular visits, if desired by the detainee, are afforded privacy.

But what happens if the government either fails, or is unable, to document that consular notifications were made? In *Sanchez-Llamas v. Oregon,* 548 U.S. 331 (2006), a foreign national was arrested for attempted murder. The detainee was advised of their *Miranda v. Arizona* rights, but the notices required by the Vienna Convention were not given. Statements made by the detainee while in police custody were introduced at trial over the objections of the detainee that the failure to provide the consular notifications warranted suppression. After the state courts denied the detainee relief, an appeal was made to the Supreme Court. The Court did not address the broader issue of "*whether the Vienna Convention grants individuals enforceable rights*" but affirmed the lower court's denial of relief because there was no expressed authority for private enforcement actions in the treaty and the failure to notify consular officials was at best only remotely connected to the gathering of evidence in this case. In a companion case decided at the same time, a foreign national was arrested in Virginia for state law violations and no consular notification was made. The detainee did not raise the issue at trial or on direct appeal but did challenge the failure to notify in a postconviction habeas action in state court. The state court denied relief because the detainee should have raised the claim at trial and on direct appeal. The Supreme Court affirmed the lower courts that the detainee had procedurally defaulted on his claim and was not entitled to relief.

Two years later, the Supreme Court in *Medellin v. Texas,* 553 U.S. 1346 (2008), decided a similar issue but with different facts. In 2004, the International Court of Justice (ICJ) had ruled in *Case Concerning Avena and Other Mexican Nationals* (Mex v. U.S. 2004 I.C.J. 12 (*Avena*) that the United States had violated the terms of Article 36(1)(b)[the consular notification provisions] of the Vienna Convention on Consular Relations and that the 51 identified individuals were entitled to a review and reconsideration of their state court convictions and sentences. Petitioner Medellin was one of the individuals identified by the ICJ in the *Avena* decision. After the Supreme Court's decision in *Sanchez-Llamas* discussed above, President Bush issued a Memorandum "stating that the United States would "discharge its international obligations" under *Avena* "by having State courts give effect to the decision." Medellin was on Texas' death row awaiting execution and he challenged his conviction and death sentence on the grounds that he had not been informed of his Vienna Convention consular rights. State courts in Texas denied him relief because he had failed to raise the claim on direct appeal in state court. The Supreme Court considered two issues:

> ***First, is the ICJ's judgment in Avena directly enforceable as domestic law in a state court in the United States? Second, does the President's Memorandum independently require the States to provide review and reconsideration of the claims of the 51 Mexican nationals named in Avena without regard to state procedural default rules? We conclude that neither Avena nor the President's Memorandum constitutes directly enforceable federal law that pre-empts state limitations on the filing of successive habeas petitions. We therefore affirm the decision below.***

Medellin had been convicted of murdering two women in Texas in 1993 and sentenced to death. After the Supreme Court's decision, Texas executed Medellin in April of 2008.

While the Supreme Court has not ruled on the issue, some lower federal courts have refused to allow suits for money damages against state officials who do not provide the required consular notifications. See, for example, *Mora v. New York*, 524 F.3d 183 (2nd Cir. 2008). Not all of the circuits are in agreement—see, for example, *Jogi v. Voges*, 480 F.3d 822 (7th Cir. 2007), in which the Seventh Circuit has held that "Article 36 of the Vienna Convention by its terms grants private rights to an identifiable class of persons — aliens from countries that are parties to the Convention who are in the United States" and that a person may bring a Section 1983 for damages when that right is violated.

▶ Loss of Property and Personal Injuries

The due process clause also protects against the unlawful deprivation of property. The Supreme Court decided two cases (*Parratt* and *Hudson*) that dealt with property deprivation. The remaining cases in this section deal with the loss of liberty that may be caused by personal injury.

Parratt v. Taylor

Historically, it is important to consider *Parratt v. Taylor*, 451 U.S. 527 (1981), although it was later overruled. Taylor was an inmate at the Nebraska Penal and Correctional Complex. He ordered some hobby materials, for which he paid $23.50. Somehow, the materials were lost after they had arrived at the prison and before they got to Taylor. Taylor brought suit under Section 1983, claiming that his property had been taken (*deprived,* to use the constitutional language) without due proce ss of law. The Supreme Court noted that his claim was that the property was negligently lost and that the court analysis would have to focus on whether the essential elements of a Section 1983 claim were present: (1) whether the loss was caused by a person who was acting under color of state law, and (2) whether that state official's conduct deprived Taylor of a right given him under the Constitution.

The Court found that Taylor had been deprived of his property under color of state law. Thus, the first question was answered in the affirmative. To answer the second question, the Court had to look to the constitutional provision invoked, which was the due process clause. Taylor's claim did involve an alleged loss of his property. That part of the due process clause (a deprivation of life, liberty, or property) was met. However, the second part of the clause, that he was deprived of his property without due process of law, was not met. This was because Nebraska provided a remedy to persons who suffered a loss of property at the hands of the state because of state negligence. This state tort claims procedure was available to inmates. "The remedies provided could have fully compensated [Taylor] for the property loss he suffered, and we hold that they are sufficient to satisfy the requirements of due process."

Thus, the Supreme Court held that a loss of property could be the basis of a claim for the deprivation of constitutional rights under Section 1983, if the state did not have an adequate remedy (due process) to compensate the inmate for that deprivation. In this case, though, Nebraska had a process for compensation to the inmate, and the existence of that tort claim procedure allowed the state to have the Section 1983 action dismissed for failure to state a claim under the statute (Section 1983) and under the Constitution.

Hudson v. Palmer

Hudson v. Palmer, 468 U.S. 517 (1984), is a case that involves both a Fourth Amendment cell search (and whether there is any privacy right in prisons) and a claimed deprivation of property without due process. Palmer claimed that the officers destroyed some of his personal property in the cell just to harass him. The Supreme Court extended its holding in *Parratt,* saying that even though there was a claim of intentional destruction of Palmer's property, the requirements of due process had been met in this case, because the state (Virginia) gave Palmer a remedy. He could file a claim for compensation for his lost or damaged property, and that remedy precluded bringing a claim for constitutional deprivation under Section 1983. Thus, even intentional damage to property is not the basis for a constitutional claim, as long as the state has a remedy for the inmate to use to be compensated for his loss.

Daniels v. Williams

Daniels sued under 42 U.S.C. § 1983, seeking damages for back and ankle injuries he sustained when he fell on a stairway at the city jail in Richmond, Virginia. He claimed that a jail officer had negligently left a pillow on the stairs, which caused his fall. This, he claimed, deprived him of his liberty interest to be free from bodily injury. The Supreme Court, in *Daniels v. Williams,* 474 U.S. 327 (1986), said that the due process clause was intended to secure individuals from abuse of power by government officials. The Constitution does not say one way or the other whether ordinary negligence is enough to state a constitutional claim. Therefore, the Court had to address that issue.

The word *deprive* in the Constitution connotes more than a negligent act, according to the Supreme Court.

> **[We] overrule *Parratt* to the extent that it states that mere lack of due care by a state official may "deprive" an individual of life, liberty, or property under the Fourteenth Amendment …. Far from an abuse of power, lack of due care suggests no more than a failure to measure up to the conduct of a reasonable person. To hold that injury caused by such conduct is a deprivation within the meaning of the Fourteenth Amendment would trivialize the centuries-old principle of due process of law.**

The Court held that a state official's negligent act that caused unintended loss of life, liberty, or property did not implicate the due process clause. There was no constitutional claim made by Daniels when he alleged he was injured by the negligent act of the jail officer.

Davidson v. Cannon

Davidson v. Cannon, 474 U.S. 344 (1986), was a companion case to *Daniels* and was decided by the Supreme Court on the same day. Davidson was an inmate in the New Jersey State Prison. He sent a note, saying that he had been threatened by another inmate, to the assistant superintendent of the prison, who, in turn, sent it on to a corrections sergeant. The sergeant failed to read the note right away and left the prison. Later, Davidson was assaulted and injured by the inmate he had identified in his note. Davidson brought suit under Section 1983, alleging that his constitutional rights had been violated under the Eighth and Fourteenth Amendments. The U.S. district court ruled that prison officials had failed to take reasonable steps to protect Davidson and that, for this reason, he was injured. Using *Parratt* standards, that court found that Davidson was deprived of his liberty interest in his own personal security and that New Jersey did not have a law or procedure that would compensate him for his injury.

Therefore, the trial court said, he had been deprived of his liberty without due process of law, and he was awarded damages of $2,000 against the prison officials.

The court of appeals reversed the lower court's judgment. The Supreme Court agreed to review the matter. Applying its reasoning in *Daniels,* the Supreme Court agreed with the court of appeals:

> **[W]here a government official is merely negligent in causing the injury, no procedure for compensation is constitutionally required …. [The officials'] lack of due care in this case led to serious injury, but that lack of care simply does not approach the sort of abusive government conduct that the Due Process Clause was designed to prevent.**

Here, rather than abuse of power, the officials mistakenly believed that the situation was not too serious, and the sergeant simply forgot about the note from Davidson. The government—in this case, prison officials—is not required by the Constitution to use due care in all situations, the Court ruled; the Constitution does not guarantee against officials making mistakes or being unintentionally negligent.

Davidson had indicated that he just wanted some kind of remedy. New Jersey did not have one for him for this kind of injury, and he wanted some compensation, such as Nebraska had for inmate Taylor (for his lost hobby materials) or Virginia had for Daniels (for his injuries sustained in the fall on the jail stairs). But the Supreme Court held that the Constitution does not require that the state provide a remedy in situations in which there has been no deprivation of a protected interest (life, liberty, or property). The Court said that it might indeed be good for the state to have a means of compensating for such injuries, but the Constitution does not require it, and federal courts cannot require it as a constitutional matter.

▶ Use of Excessive Force

Use of force by government actors may be the basis of a denial of substantive due process rights. Use of force is covered in more detail in the chapter on conditions of confinement. The cases of *Whitley v. Albers,* 475 U.S. 312 (1986), and *Hudson v. McMillian,* 503 U.S. 1 (1992), particularly involve questions of convicted and sentenced inmates being injured as a result of force and whether those actions were excessive, creating constitutional liability. Those cases were brought and analyzed by the courts as Eighth Amendment cases, because the convicted inmates claimed that they had been punished cruelly and unusually by staff actions.

In *Whitley v. Albers,* discussed extensively in the chapter on cruel and unusual punishment, the Court expressly rejected the inmate's claim that the same use of force would state a claim under the Eighth Amendment "cruel and unusual punishment" and for a violation of substantive due process of the Fourteenth Amendment. In *Whitley,* the parties seemed to agree that the Fourteenth Amendment was an overlapping source of protection for state action involving the use of force. Because the inmate was convicted, the primary source of protection was the Eighth Amendment, and considering the standard for substantive due process claims compared with Eighth Amendment excessive force claims, *"in these circumstances the Due Process Clause affords respondent no greater protection than does the Cruel and Unusual Punishments Clause."*

In 2015, the Supreme Court decided *Kingsley Hendrickson,* ___ U.S. ___, 135 S.Ct. 2466 (2015), which ruled that a pretrial detainees' claim of excessive force claims should be evaluated by determining if the force used by the officer was "objectively reasonable." This case is discussed in greater detail in the chapter on jails.

Summary

- Classification—assigning each inmate to the proper institution within the prison system and to the proper housing and programs within that institution—is a central part of good prison management.
- The Supreme Court has ruled that a corrections agency may assign an inmate to any institution within the agency, without implicating any due process concerns under the Constitution (*Meachum v. Fano; Montanye v. Haymes; McKune v. Lile*).
- A state inmate may be transferred to any institution in the federal system (*Howe v. Smith*) or out of the state without a hearing (*Olim v. Wakinekona*).
- The transfer of an inmate from a prison to a mental hospital, however, involves a protected liberty interest and requires a hearing. The requirements include advance written notice to the prisoner; a hearing, with disclosure of evidence relied on to support the transfer; the opportunity to present witnesses and to confront

and cross-examine official witnesses; an independent decision maker; a written statement of the evidence relied on and the reasons for the action taken; and assistance by someone at the hearing (*Vitek v. Jones*).

■ A prisoner has a liberty interest in avoiding transfer to a prison (such as a Supermax) where the conditions of confinement at the new facility pose "an atypical and significant hardship on the inmate in relation to the ordinary incidents of prison life" (*Wilkinson v. Austin*). The procedures provided by the state, including advance written notice, an opportunity to object, and a right to receive a written statement as to why placement was made, satisfied due process for such a transfer to a Supermax facility.

■ The Court has held that due process considerations are required with respect to the reconfinement of an inmate participating in a preparole program (*Young v. Harper*).

■ Committing dangerous sex offenders, beyond their confinement for sex crimes, was found in Kansas to be permissible, comparable to civilly committing dangerous mental patients (*Kansas v. Hendricks; Kansas v. Crane*).

■ While prison officials are not guarantors of inmate safety, the mistaken classification of an inmate may expose staff to liability when that mistake results in "unnecessary and wanton infliction of pain" to the inmate (*Farmer v. Brennan*).

■ There is now, by treaty, a procedure for transfers of prisoners between the United States and many other countries. This procedure requires the application and approval of the transfer by both countries and the inmate. The procedure has been upheld in federal courts against claims that criminal proceedings in the foreign country violated due process standards (*Rosado v. Civiletti*) and claims by a U.S. prisoner that he should be returned to his native country even though the U.S. government did not approve of the transfer (*Marquez-Ramos v. Reno*).

■ Based on the Vienna Convention on Consular Relations, foreign nationals who are arrested or detained in the United States require either notice to the foreign national's consul or be advised that notice may be requested. Most correctional agencies have protocols to ensure that such notices are given.

■ Property claims—inmate claims that property has been lost, damaged, or destroyed by government officials—at first found support as stating constitutional violations (because of deprivation of property) in *Parratt v. Taylor. Parratt* was overruled by later Supreme Court decisions, which held that mere claims of government negligence would not support a constitutional claim under 42 U.S.C. § 1983. To state a constitutional claim, there must be abusive conduct by government officials (*Daniels v. Williams; Davidson v. Cannon*). For such claims of property loss or personal injury as a result of negligence on the part of government employees, the remedy in most states is a tort claims procedure.

■ In *Kingsley v. Hendrickson*, the Supreme Court ruled that claims of excessive force under the due process clause consider whether an officer's use of force was reasonable. The case is discussed in greater detail in the chapter on jails.

Thinking About It

Inmate Bee was housed in a medium security prison (MSP). Prison officials transferred inmate M, who had a history of violent conduct in prison including twice stabbing another inmate within the last five years, from a maximum-security prison (MAX) to the MSP. When M arrived at MSP, he tested positive for methamphetamine. After threatening his first cellmate, M was moved into a cell with Bee. Less than 45 days after M and Bee became cellmates, M beat Bee so badly that Bee went into an irreversible coma. Bee's family sued prison officials, alleging that their classification of M violated Bee's Eighth Amendment right to be protected from harm by another inmate. What do you think the outcome will be? *Shauf v. Rios*, 313 F.Supp. 2d 1262 (W.D. OK 2018).

Key Terms

ex post facto
mandamus
recidivist (recidivism)

Endnotes

1. New Mexico Corrections Department. Policy No. CD-080100. *Institutional Classification, Inmate Risk Assessment and Central Office Classification.* Revised August 24, 2016. Page 7. Santa Fe: State of New Mexico, 2016. Available from https://cd.nm.gov/wp-content/uploads/2019/06/CD-080100.pdf. Accessed March 5, 2020.

2. Alaska Department of Corrections. Policy # 700.01. *Prisoner Classification.* Effective November 25, 2014. Juneau: State of Alaska. 2014. Available from https://doc.alaska.gov/pnp/pdf/700.01.pdf. Accessed March 5, 2020.

3. Congress enacted a sexual predator commitment statute (18 U.S.C. § 4248) similar to the Kansas statutes discussed in the text. The statute was challenged by persons whom the United States sought to commit, and one basis of the challenges was that Congress lacked constitutional authority to enact such a statute. After several lower courts had declared the statute unconstitutional, concluding that Congress lacked authority under the "necessary and proper" clause to enact such a statute, the issue was addressed by the Supreme Court. In *United States v. Comstock,* 560 U.S. 126 (2010) the Supreme Court ruled that enactment of 18 U.S.C. § 4248 did not exceed Congress's authority under the necessary and proper clause of the Constitution.

4. See U.S. D.O.J International Prisoner Transfer Program, updated August 31, 2018. Available at: https://www.justice.gov/criminal-oia/iptu. Accessed March 5, 2020. Also see Federal Bureau of Prisons Program Statement 5140.39, Transfer of Offenders to or from Foreign Countries.

5. *Consular Notification and Access*, 5th Edition. U.S. Department of State. Available at: https://travel.state.gov/content/dam/travel/CNAtrainingresources/CNA%20Manual%205th%20Edition_September%202018.pdf. Accessed March 6, 2020. Article 36 of the Vienna Convention on Consular Relations (Vienna Convention or Convention), Apr. 24, 1963, [1970] 21 U. S. T. 77, 100-101, T. I. A. S. No. 6820, addresses communication between an individual and his consular officers when the individual is detained by authorities in a foreign country.

CHAPTER 13

Fourteenth Amendment: Equal Protection—Female Offenders and Others

To withstand constitutional challenge, classifications by gender must serve important governmental objectives and must be substantially related to achievement of those objectives.

U.S. Supreme Court, *Craig v. Boren*

The Fourteenth Amendment, which we have just examined in many correctional practices that have been raised in the courts under the due process clause, also contains the equal protection clause:

No State shall … deny to any person within its jurisdiction the equal protection of the laws.

CHAPTER OUTLINE

- Female Offenders
- *Pargo v. Elliott*
- Noncitizens (Foreign Offenders)
- Other Equal Protection Cases
- Racial Discrimination
- *Johnson v. California*
- Sexual Identity

A BRIEF PRIMER ON EQUAL PROTECTION

The Fifth Amendment (applicable to the federal government) provides, in part, as follows:

No person shall . . . be deprived of life, liberty, or property, without due process of law; . . . .

The Fifth Amendment does not contain an express guarantee of equal protection, but since the 1950s, the Supreme Court has ruled that the Due Process Clause of the Fifth Amendment contains an equal protection component similar to the express component of the Fourteenth Amendment.

The Fourteenth Amendment applicable to the states provides, in part, as follows:

No state . . . [shall] deny to any person within its jurisdiction the equal protection of the laws.

In order to establish a case of illegal government discrimination in violation of equal protection, a plaintiff must present facts establishing that they have been "treated differently by a [government] actor than others who are similarly situated simply because [they] belong to a particular protected class." Generally, the government must treat similarly situated persons alike. If groups are not similarly situated, the government need not treat them alike. *City of Cleburne v. Cleburne Living Center*, 473 U.S. 432 (1985). Once a plaintiff has established that they are similarly situated to another group and that the government is treating the two groups differently in a harmful way, courts will use one of three tests to determine if the classification is legal: strict scrutiny, intermediate scrutiny, and rational relationship.

Strict scrutiny is applied in cases that impact a fundamental right or involve a suspect classification such as differential treatment based on race, religion, national origin, or alienage. A suspect classification will be ruled constitutional only when the government can demonstrate that the classification serves a compelling governmental interest AND that the classification is necessary to serve that compelling government interest.

Intermediate or heightened scrutiny is applied in cases in which the classification impacts a protected class of persons, such as classification by gender or illegitimacy. A classification impacting a protected class will be ruled constitutional only when government shows that the classification serves an important governmental interest and the classification is substantially related to that important governmental interest.

The rational basis test is applied to all other forms of government classification. The classification will be upheld as constitutional if it is rationally related to a legitimate governmental interest.

While much of the case law developing equal protection analysis deals with classes of people, the Supreme Court has recognized that there can be a "class of one." A "class of one" equal protection claim may be stated when the person alleges that they have "been intentionally treated differently from others similarly situated and that there is no rational basis for the difference in treatment." *Village of Willowbrook v. Olech*, 528 U.S. 562 (2000) *per curiam*. Class of one claims in the correctional setting may be limited as so many actions taken by correctional workers "involve discretionary decision making based on a vast array of subjective, individualized assessments." *Enqquist v. Oregon Department of Agriculture*, 553 U.S. 591 (2008). Allowing class of one claims under these circumstances *"would undermine the discretion public officials are entrusted to exercise."*

The Supreme Court may use an equal protection analysis to protect the rights of inmates, even in cases in which there may be another constitutional provision, which one would think might be applicable. For instance, in the case of *Cruz v. Beto*, 405 U.S. 319 (1972), the Supreme Court said that if the Buddhist inmate who brought that lawsuit was being denied the opportunity to pursue his faith comparable to the opportunity given to other prisoners of other faiths, there was impermissible discrimination by the state of Texas against him. One may have thought there would have been more analysis under the First Amendment (freedom of religion), but "equal protection" seemed to be the basis of the Court's reasoning. It can also be called, as in that ruling about religious activities in prisons, the "non-discrimination" requirement of the Constitution.

▶ **Female Offenders**

The most striking (albeit recent) application of the equal protection clause is in the realm of female offenders. Females made up 7.4% of the total sentenced correctional population in 2018 compared with 5.4% in 1980 (Bronson & Carson, 2020).[1] Because of the smaller number of female offenders (even though the number of female offenders is markedly higher than 20 or 30 years ago (See **FIGURE 13-1** which depicts the growth of females in federal and state prisons from 1986 to 2018), most states have only one corrections facility for women (see **FIGURE 13-2**). Even in the larger states, where there are larger numbers of both male and female offenders, there are many more male institutions than female. For example, the Texas Department of Criminal Justice (TDCJ) Correctional Institution Division with 165,000 inmates operates 92 correctional facilities, 12 of which are designated as female facilities and one (a medical treatment center) is designated co-gender.[2] The state of Vermont confines approximately 1,400 inmates and operates seven facilities with one designated as a female facility, the Chittenden Regional Correctional Facility, which is a 172-bed correctional facility primarily for women. The facility houses pretrial and sentenced women for all custody levels.[3] These basic differences in numbers (along with ideas about the way women offenders should be treated) lead to many of the complaints about disparity in treatment, which will be examined using several court decisions.

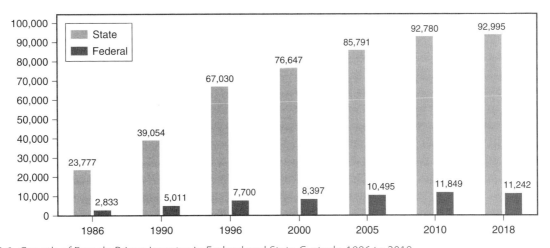

FIGURE 13-1 Growth of Female Prison Inmates in Federal and State Custody, 1986 to 2018.

Data from Bureau of Justice Statistics-Prisoners in _____. Available at: https://www.bjs.gov/index.cfm?ty=pbse&tid=0&dcid=0&sid=40&iid=0&sortby=&page=paging&curpg=3. Accessed 17 March 2020.

One early reference to the constitutional requirement of comparable treatment for women was in the case of *Bounds v. Smith,* 430 U.S. 817 (1977). In *Bounds,* a district court had required North Carolina to come up with a plan for law libraries in its prison system to enable inmates to do legal research and prepare legal papers in order for them to have access to the courts. The state drew up a plan, which provided for a sizable collection of law books to be placed in several facilities throughout the state. Inmates who were not located in one of those facilities would be transported to a facility with a law library, upon request, to do their legal research. This plan was approved by the district court and the Fourth Circuit Court of Appeals, except that the court of appeals required the state to modify its plan to ensure that female inmates had access to similar legal research facilities. The Supreme Court approved the North Carolina plan (without a specific discussion of the availability of law-books to female inmates).

In the case of *Bukhari v. Hutto,* 487 F.Supp. 1162 (E.D. VA 1980), the court considered complaints from female inmates in Virginia that they were treated differently—and more poorly—than males. The court noted in its opinion that, for many centuries (in Anglo-American practice), there had not been separate facilities for male and

FIGURE 13-2 A Corrections Officer Addresses a Group of Inmates in the Female Unit of the Santa Ana, California, City Jail.

© Marmaduke St. John/Alamy Stock Photo

female inmates: all were confined together. It was considered a great improvement when reformers insisted upon separate institutions for males and females. The court observed that in Virginia (and the same is true in many states) the female institution was more campus like, smaller, and more relaxed than male institutions. There was just one state facility, the Virginia Correctional Center for Women, which took most of the female offenders. Although there was a higher staff-to-inmate ratio there, there also were fewer programs than were available for males. The court set down the principles for further consideration of female's claims: the state would have to justify its reasons for treating female inmates separately and differently from males. The equal protection clause requires parity of treatment for females, the court said, but not identical treatment. Further hearings were ordered to look into the justifications for the disparate treatment.

In *Batton v. State Government of North Carolina,* 501 F.Supp. 1173 (E.D. NC 1980), female inmates claimed that they were sent from all over the state to one institution, the North Carolina Correctional Center for Women in Raleigh. This resulted in many of them being farther from their homes than male inmates were. Also, it meant that there was no classification of female offenders according to their ages, the seriousness of their offenses, and their custody requirements. The female inmates also claimed that they had fewer opportunities for programs and activities than males had; they had fewer work-release placements, less vocational training, lower wages for their prison work, less access to medical and psychiatric care, and a less adequate law library. The court noted that only 4% of the 15,000 North Carolina inmates at that time were female. Under the Constitution, to evaluate the females' claims of unconstitutional, disparate treatment, the court took the standard from the Supreme Court decision in *Craig v. Boren,* 429 U.S. 190 (1976):

> **To withstand constitutional challenge … classifications by gender must serve important governmental objectives and must be substantially related to achievement of those objectives**.

Although not a prison case, the *Craig* language has been widely quoted as the constitutional statement of equal protection to be used in assessing equal protection claims by female offenders. (*Craig* was a Supreme Court case reviewing an Oklahoma statute, which prohibited sales of 3.2% beer to males under 21 and to females under 18. The Court said that the gender-based differential in Oklahoma law constituted a denial of equal protection to males who were between 18 and 20 years of age. In the *Craig* case, the Court said Oklahoma had not shown that the different treatment was necessary to further the legitimate objective of the statute, which was traffic safety.)

The federal court in *Batton* said that it would defer to state officials' judgment whenever possible in assessing the treatment of female offenders. Applying the *Craig v. Boren* standard, quoted above, the court found that, with respect to medical and psychiatric care, disparate wage rates, and the law library, the state had shown its justification for different treatment of females. Summary judgment was granted to state officials for those issues. On other issues (parole, work-release and vocational training opportunities, education, recreation, classification, and the housing of offenders), the court said that further evidence would have to be developed to see whether there was a substantial relationship between the reasons for those female programs being disparate and the achievement of legitimate government objectives.

In *Glover v. Johnson,* 478 F.Supp. 1075 (E.D. MI 1979), a federal district court ruled that educational and vocational programs offered by Michigan to female inmates were markedly poorer than those offered to male inmates. The court ruled that this lack of parity denied equal protection to the females. The court ordered that there be an evaluation and report made of the educational and vocational interests and capabilities of female inmates. Then, with those facts in hand, the state would be required to establish a program substantially equivalent to the one offered throughout the state to male inmates.

Another issue addressed by the courts has been the difference in the treatment of females in their transfers, especially outside the state of their residence and conviction. A federal court, in *Park v. Thompson,* 356 F.Supp. 783 (D. HI 1973), held that it was unconstitutional for Hawaii not to have any long-term facilities for females in the state. Inmate Park challenged, by habeas corpus, her transfer to a federal prison in California to serve her sentence. (The court first ruled that habeas corpus could be used to test the validity of the place of confinement, as well as the underlying validity of the confinement—the traditional purpose of the habeas corpus writ.) The court ruled that it was an equal protection violation to transfer females outside of the state, when males could remain in the state under similar circumstances. (This case may have been decided differently after the Supreme Court's ruling in *Olim v. Wakinekona,* 461 U.S. 238 (1983), where the Court found no constitutional violation in the transfer of inmates to facilities in other states, specifically from Hawaii to California. That decision was based on a due process analysis. The decision in *Park* was based on disparate treatment for females under the equal protection clause. The *Olim* decision would take care of the due process arguments, but the equal protection concerns, as they existed in 1973, still would remain on the facts of *Park v. Thompson.*)

A very different result on out-of-state transfers of female inmates was reached in *Pitts v. Thornburgh,* 866 F.2d 1450 (DC Cir. 1989). Female inmates complained that they were transferred some 260 miles to a federal facility for females in rural West Virginia, whereas male inmates, in most cases, stayed in facilities close to home (the District of Columbia). The trial court had ruled that these transfers caused no violation of constitutional rights, because there was no evidence to show that facilities or programs at the female facility were inferior to those for males in the District of Columbia (D.C). The court of appeals affirmed that ruling, finding no "invidious discrimination" against females and no violation of equal protection rights, because the government had an important objective to achieve: the relief of severe overcrowding in the D.C. facilities.

A similar ruling occurred in *Jackson v. Thornburgh,* 907 F.2d 194 (DC Cir. 1990). In *Jackson,* the District of Columbia Good Time Credits Act of 1986 granted early release to inmates serving sentences in D.C. prison facilities. The purpose was to reduce overcrowding. Female D.C. inmates housed in a federal prison, and thus not covered by the law, challenged its constitutionality on the basis of equal protection, claiming, in part, unlawful gender discrimination. The court denied the claim, holding that the act's distinction was not based on gender, either overtly or covertly.

With respect to inmate visiting rights, there have been opinions both supporting and rejecting (for constitutional violations) jail programs that are different for male and female inmates. In *Molar v. Gates,* 159 Cal. Rptr. 239 (1979), a county jail's practice of providing minimum security status and facilities for male inmates when they were not provided for female inmates was found to be unconstitutional, violating the equal protection clauses of both the federal and state constitutions. Because of the much larger numbers of male inmates, a greater variety of living units and programs, with differing levels of security, was provided for the male inmates. Female inmates were all treated alike. Consequently, there were no minimum-security privileges for females. Importantly for this case, minimum security for male inmates meant they could have contact visits. No females were allowed to have contact visits. The court found this disparate treatment to be unsupportable.

However, in *Morrow v. Harwell,* 768 F.2d 619 (5th Cir. 1985), the federal appeals court upheld a visiting program in a county jail that allowed more visitation time for males than for females. In the jail, more than 90% of the inmates were male. Female inmates complained because on visiting days more time was set aside for male visits than for female visits. This amounted to one more hour of visiting time overall for all males. A magistrate at the trial level had ruled that this visiting disparity violated the equal protection standards of the Fourteenth Amendment. However, no inmate, because of the large number of inmates, was allowed more than 15 minutes for a visit. The appellate court held that allowing more overall time for males was justified, because a greater percentage of the population was male. No violation of equal protection was found on the appeals level.

▶ *Pargo v. Elliott*

A major lawsuit with an involved litigation history is *Pargo v. Elliott,* 49 F.3d 1355 (Pargo 1) and 69 F.3d 280 (8th Cir. 1995) (Pargo 2) (8th Cir. 1995). Inmates at the Iowa Correctional Institution for Women (ICIW) filed a Section 1983 action, claiming that their equal protection rights were violated because prison programs and services at the ICIW differed substantially from those provided to male inmates in Iowa institutions. The U.S. district court had initially used the case of *Klinger v. Department of Corrections,* 31 F.3d 727 (8th Cir. 1994), as its guide. In the *Klinger* case, the court of appeals had reversed the district court's judgment that Nebraska state correctional officials had violated the Equal Protection rights of female inmates in the provision of prison programs and services. The *Klinger opinion* concluded that male and female inmates in Nebraska were not similarly situated. In *Klinger,* the court of appeals concluded that male inmates in the Nebraska state penitentiary were not similarly situated to female inmates in Nebraska because of the size of the institution used for comparison, the length of sentences being served, and the custody classification levels of the two groups of inmates.

Believing that the ruling in *Klinger* was controlling, the district court in *Pargo* after conducting a trial over two months and accumulating a trial transcript of over 1,000 pages of witness testimony entered judgment for the correctional officials because male and female inmates were not similarly situated in Iowa. (First *Pargo* district court decision- *894 F.Supp. 1239 (S.D. IA 1994).* The plaintiffs appealed and the court of appeals and in

Pargo v. Elliot, 49 F.3d 1355 (8th Cir. 1995) *(Pargo 1)* the court of appeals vacated the district court's judgment and instructed the lower court to make detailed findings of facts and conclusions of law which were necessary to determine if male and female inmates were similarly situated. The Eighth Circuit, in *Pargo 1,* stated that the ruling in *Klinger* does not stand for the proposition that male and female inmates can never be similarly situated. In the district court in *Pargo*, female inmates argued that males and females with the same custody levels and sentence length had very different programs and services available to them. The plaintiffs argued that these facts distinguished the *Pargo* case from the facts in *Klinger*. The court of appeals also cautioned that the Supreme Court's guidance in *Turner v. Safley* related to deference to prison administrators' judgment should not foreclose using heightened scrutiny in evaluating prisoner equal protection claims.

The case was sent back (remanded) to the district court, with instructions to make detailed findings and conclusions, on the issue of the similar or dissimilar situation of the Iowa inmates.

The district court, on the remand of the case, prepared 115 pages of findings and conclusions in *Pargo v. Elliot,* 894 F.Supp. 1243 (S.D. IA 1995) (district court decision 2). The district court's principal conclusion was that male and female inmates in the Iowa prison system were not similarly situated. The findings spelled out the custody levels Iowa used for classifying male and female inmates and the programs that were available, in each custody level, to females compared with males. The district court concluded that there was no evidence of "invidious discrimination" (a term given by the Supreme Court in *Personnel Administrator of Massachusetts v. Feeney,* 442 U.S. 256 (1979), to test discrimination allegations). The programs and services for males and females, the district court concluded, taken as a whole or compared by custody level, were substantially similar. Any differences in programs and services had been justified by state prison officials. The court of appeals, in its second opinion (reported at *Pargo* II- 69 F.3d 280), affirmed the district court's judgment. The major focus left in the case was whether female inmates who were classified as "minimum live-out" (MLO) were disparately and unconstitutionally treated compared with their male counterparts.

Female inmates in MLO status claimed that they lived in more confined housing, with fewer furloughs, fewer off-grounds work opportunities, less library and yard time, different substance abuse programs, and more restrictive settings for their visits. The courts found that the differences in these programs were not because of "invidious discrimination." Female plaintiffs who were in other security levels also complained that, compared with men in the same security classification, they had fewer legal assistance programs, less work-release time, fewer therapy programs, and fewer yard and library privileges. The district court found, and the appeals court approved, that any differences in these programs were "rationally related to legitimate penological interests, such as security and rehabilitation." The Iowa prison officials prevailed in this large-scale challenge to practices in their institutions.

In *Archer v. Reno,* 877 F.Supp. 372 (E.D. KY 1995), 13 female inmates at the Federal Medical Center at Lexington, Kentucky, had been enrolled in a dental education course or had worked in the dental lab there. They brought a Bivens action (the federal equivalent of Section 1983), seeking an injunction against their transfers out of Lexington. They complained that their transfers would deny them the opportunity to complete their dental training program and to become certified dental technicians. (There were five dental labs in the federal prison system, all of which were located in male institutions once the Lexington institution became an all-male institution.) The Bureau of Prisons had decided to convert Lexington to a male institution because of population pressures and consideration of the types of facilities that were available for men and women. (A new medical facility was then being opened in Fort Worth, Texas, and that facility would, in effect, replace Lexington for female inmates with medical needs, including medical training needs.)

The federal district court ruled that the female inmates had no right to specific educational or vocational programs; there was no constitutional right to be rehabilitated (citing *Rhodes v. Chapman,* 452 U.S. 337 (1981) and *Garza v. Miller,* 688 F.2d 480 (7th Cir. 1982)). The court further noted that inmates had no constitutional right to be assigned to a particular job (citing *Flittie v. Solem,* 827 F.2d 276 (8th Cir. 1987) and *Twyman v. Crisp,* 584 F.2d 352 (10th Cir. 1978)). In addition, the inmates had no constitutional right to remain in a particular institution (citing the Supreme Court transfer cases *Meachum v. Fano,* 427 U.S. 215 (1976), *Montanye v. Haymes,* 427 U.S. 236 (1976), and *Olim v. Wakinekona,* 461 U.S. 238 (1983)). The court found that the Bureau of Prisons had presented justification for its decisions about the classification of institutions and of inmates, which were related to its legitimate security and penological interests. It is noteworthy that the court did not undertake any discussion of equal protection rights of the female inmates or of the Supreme Court standard in *Craig v. Boren,* which other courts have used in disparate treatment cases. One must assume that it was not raised by the plaintiff-inmates and did not occur to the court.

▶ Noncitizens (Foreign Offenders)

The number of noncitizens in the United States is increasing, both in general and in the country's jails and prisons. On December 31, 2018, state and federal prisons housed 104,273 non-U.S. citizens. The Federal Bureau of Prisons held 33,420 of these noncitizen inmates.[4] (See Appendix 13-1, Female and National Origin Offender Data Bullets, on the Navigate eBook site on jblearning.com). In fiscal year 2019, non-U.S. citizens made up 44.6% of persons sentenced in U.S. district courts under the U.S. sentencing commission guidelines, with 79% being charged with immigration offenses.[5]

Does the equal protection clause protect only citizens of the United States? The language of the Fourteenth Amendment, states that it protects "persons" and not just citizens. And yet, there are court rulings that state that persons who have entered the United States illegally are not protected by some constitutional provisions. This is based on the theory that, if persons are taken into custody at the border or at any place (such as an airport terminal or a dock) where they are trying to enter the country without authorization, they are "excludable aliens." In that status, they are legally considered not to have entered the country. (No matter where they are subsequently confined, they are considered to have been caught "at the border.") Consequently, they are not entitled to all of the rights of persons who are legally within the jurisdiction of the United States and under the protection of the Constitution.

Despite these legal distinctions of immigration law, courts have given protections to noncitizen, foreign-born inmates. In the case of *Thongvanh v. Thalacker,* 17 F.3d 256 (8th Cir. 1994), for example, dealing with inmate mail that was written in a foreign language (Lao), the court applied an equal protection analysis to conclude that, because translations were already being made for Spanish-speaking inmates, an effort had to be made to provide translators who could review mail written in Lao. Noncitizen inmates may also be more likely to request religious activities or materials that are related to religions that are outside of the "mainstream" of religious observances in the United States. The Supreme Court decision in *Cruz v. Beto,* in particular, relied on equal protection analysis to conclude that if prison authorities provided religious privileges to other religious groups, they would have to show why they could not do the same for Buddhist inmates. (Technically, that is a First Amendment, freedom of religion case, but the reasoning of the court was couched very much in equal protection terms.)

▶ Other Equal Protection Cases

Equal protection can also be raised on the other side (in a claim of reverse discrimination) by men claiming disparate treatment, with more favorable treatment being given to women. In *Hill v. Estelle,* 537 F.2d 214 (5th Cir. 1976), six Texas male inmates brought a Section 1983 action, claiming violation of their constitutional (equal protection) rights because female inmates were not held to the same grooming standards (they were allowed to have long hair of different styles); females, unlike men, could make telephone calls to their families; and females, unlike men, were allowed to decorate their cells. The court of appeals conceded that there was some disparate treatment between the men and the women, but it held that the state's policies on these matters did not amount to constitutional violations. The court found that no fundamental right was infringed, and that the disparity was not of an unreasonable or egregious level.

▶ Racial Discrimination

Racial discrimination can also be raised by inmates as an equal protection violation. The Supreme Court, in *Lee v. Washington,* 390 U.S. 333 (1968), held that prisoners are protected against discrimination based on race. Inmates in Alabama had challenged the segregation of prisoners in the Alabama system. Officials claimed that segregation was necessary to protect institutional security. The federal district court had conceded that, in isolated instances, it might be necessary to separate races for a limited period of time, but held that complete and permanent segregation of the races in all Alabama penal facilities was unconstitutional. The Supreme Court, in a per curiam opinion, supported that decision.

In *Woods v. Edwards,* 51 F.3d 577 (5th Cir. 1995), an inmate in the Louisiana State Penitentiary at Angola filed a Section 1983 action, claiming that his extended lockdown (for nearly four years) was because of his race and was, therefore, a violation of his equal protection rights. (The court stated that his race was presumed to be Black; apparently that was not specified in the pleadings or the record!) The inmate claimed that similarly situated White inmates had been released from lockdown status much earlier than he had been released. The court of appeals noted that, to prove his case, the inmate would have to show that prison officials acted with a discriminatory purpose. According to the court in *United States v. Galloway,* 951 F.2d 64 (5th Cir. 1992), "Discriminatory purpose in an Equal Protection context implies that the decision maker selected a particular course of action at least in part because of, and not simply in spite of, the adverse impact it would have on an identifiable group." The defendants had shown that the inmate's lockdown had been extended because of the repeated seriousness of his behavior, including writing threatening letters and forging another inmate's name on letters. The court said the inmate had provided no proof of discriminatory intent on the part of officials. Lacking any evidence of discriminatory intent, and, to the contrary, finding officials had a nondiscriminatory reason for their actions, the action of the district court, granting summary judgment to the prison-official defendants, was affirmed.

▸ *Johnson v. California*

Because of concerns over violence that might occur between prison racial gangs, California had an unwritten policy of segregating by race all inmates housed in two-person cells at the state's reception centers. For up to 60 days, these centers housed all newly admitted male inmates and those male inmates transferred from other state facilities. Other areas within the institution, such as recreation and dining, were not subject to the segregation rule. The separation practice was challenged by an African American inmate who had been placed in segregated housing several times during his incarceration in the state. The inmate argued that such segregation violated his right under the equal protection clause of the Fourteenth Amendment. The district court granted the prison officials qualified immunity, and the court of appeals affirmed. The court of appeals had reviewed the racial discrimination issue using the deferential standard of *Turner v. Safley,* 482 U.S. 78 (1987) and ruled that there was a "'common sense connection' between the policy and prison violence."

In *Johnson v. California,* 543 U.S. 499 (2005), the Supreme Court applied its earlier decision in *Lee v. Washington* to reaffirm that all governmental classifications that use race are viewed with "strict scrutiny." The use of race as a factor in classification presents serious concerns.

> **Racial classifications raise special fears that they are motivated by an invidious purpose. Thus, we have admonished time and again that, "[a]bsent searching judicial inquiry into the justification for such race-based measures, there is simply no way of determining … what classifications are in fact motivated by illegitimate notions of racial inferiority or simple racial politics."**

Strict scrutiny generally applies to "suspect" classifications (such as race) and requires that the government establish that its classification furthers a *compelling* governmental objective and is narrowly tailored to further that objective. This is a different, and higher, standard than that applied in *Craig v. Boren,* discussed above, which required that gender-based classification serve an *important* governmental objective, and the classification must be substantially related to the achievement of the objective. The least stringent level of review is called a "rational basis" and requires the government to demonstrate only that classification bears a rational relationship to a legitimate purpose.

The Court also noted that racial classification has led to stigmatization and increased racial hostility, and that virtually all states and the Federal Bureau of Prisons are able to safely manage prison populations without using racial segregation. The state had argued that the more relaxed standard of review was appropriate because the state's policy was based on its need to maintain the safety and security of prisons, an area in which prison officials are provided significant discretion. In rejecting the use of the *Turner v. Safley* deference standard given to prison administrators, the Court ruled:

> **The right not to be discriminated against based on one's race is not susceptible to the logic of *Turner*. It is not a right that need necessarily be compromised for the sake of proper prison administration. On the contrary, compliance with the Fourteenth Amendment's ban on racial discrimination is not only consistent with proper prison administration, but also bolsters the legitimacy of the entire criminal justice system. Race discrimination is "especially pernicious in the administration of justice." …. Granting the CDC an exemption from the rule that strict**

scrutiny applies to all racial classifications would undermine our "unceasing efforts to eradicate racial prejudice from our criminal justice system."

The Court's decision did not prohibit all race-based classifications in a correctional setting but only directed that race-based classifications further a compelling governmental interest and be narrowly drafted to further that purpose. The case was remanded back to the lower courts to determine, under the strict scrutiny standard, if the state could demonstrate that these conditions were met.

▶ Sexual Identity

One lower federal court has noted that "There is no question that prison officials have a challenging path to navigate in determining how best to handle "transgender" prisoners, in part because the term "transgender" is not clearly defined and covers a large spectrum of both male and female prisoners. *Jones v. Union County Sheriff's Office*, Civil Action No. 3:18-CV-00509-KDB-DCK. Recognizing the complexity of the issues in addressing the needs of the inmate population and legitimate security needs, the National Institute of Corrections has made available a *Policy Review and Development Guide* to assist agencies in formulating policy that best meets the needs of inmates and the agency.[6] Many correctional agencies have policies to address the medical and other concerns such as housing, searches, property, and programming.[7] Some issues have been litigated since the 1980s, such as housing inmates in facilities consistent with their identified gender rather than their gender identity at birth. Many of the issues in current litigation arise out of alleged Eighth Amendment violations concerning denial of necessary medical care and are addressed in another chapter.

The PREA Standards adopted by the Department of Justice include a section on screening to assess the vulnerability of an inmate for the risk of sexual abuse and abusiveness. 28 CFR section 115.41 recommends that the screening consider, at a minimum, the following factors: (1) Whether the inmate has a mental, physical, or developmental disability; (2) The age of the inmate; (3) The physical build of the inmate; (4) Whether the inmate has previously been incarcerated; (5) Whether the inmate's criminal history is exclusively nonviolent; (6) Whether the inmate has prior convictions for sex offenses against an adult or child; (7) Whether the inmate is, or is perceived to be gay, lesbian, bisexual, transgender, intersex, or gender nonconforming; (8) Whether the inmate has previously experienced sexual victimization; (9) The inmate's own perception of vulnerability; and (10) Whether the inmate is detained solely for civil immigration purposes. An initial assessment should be made within 30 days of the inmate's arrival at an institution and the standards suggest conducing a reassessment when deemed appropriate, such as inmate request, a referral, or an incident of sexual abuse.

PREA Standard 115.42(c) states:

> In deciding whether to assign a transgender or intersex inmate to a facility for male or female inmates, and in making other housing and programming assignments, the agency shall consider on a case-by-case basis whether a placement would ensure the inmate's health and safety, and whether the placement would present management or security problems.

PREA Standard 115.42(e) states:

A transgender or intersex inmate's own view with respect to his or her own safety shall be given serious consideration.

PREA suggests that correctional policies related to transgender persons may include classification factors such as: an inmate's security threat level; criminal and disciplinary history; current gender expression; medical and mental health information; vulnerability to sexual victimization; and likelihood of perpetrating abuse. The policy will likely consider facility-specific factors as well, including inmate populations, staffing patterns, and physical layouts.

While the Supreme Court has not addressed all of these issues, but in *Farmer v. Brennan*, 511 U.S. 825 (1994), the Court addressed a classification claim by an inmate plaintiff who alleged he was a transsexual. The case concerned whether the inmate was appropriately transferred from one prison to another. The case is discussed in detail elsewhere in the text.

Some lower federal courts have considered and ruled on several issues. In *Doe v. Massachusetts Department of Corrections, et al*, D. MA Civil No. 17-12255-RGS (2018), a transgender female was housed in a male facility. Litigation was initiated under the Americans with Disabilities Act and the Due Process and Equal Protection Clause of the Fourteenth Amendment to compel the DOC to transfer the plaintiff to a female facility. The court granted a preliminary injunction to the plaintiff directing the DOC to "where feasible, (1) arrange for appropriate (done by female correctional workers) strip searches, (2) continue to house her in an individual cell, and (3) ensure private showering." The state of Massachusetts recently enacted legislation Mass. Gen. Laws ch. 127, § 32A:

> Section 32A: *Treatment of prisoner having gender identity differing from prisoner's sex assigned at birth*
> Section 32A. A prisoner of a correctional institution, jail or house of correction that has a gender identity, as defined in section 7 of chapter 4, that differs from the prisoner's sex assigned at birth, with or without a diagnosis of gender dysphoria or any other physical or mental health diagnosis, shall be: (i) addressed in a manner consistent with the prisoner's gender identity; (ii) provided with access to commissary items, clothing, programming, educational materials and personal property that is consistent with the prisoner's gender identity; (iii) searched by an officer of the same gender identity if the search requires an inmate to remove all clothing or includes a visual inspection of the anal cavity or genitals; provided, however, that the officer's gender identity shall be consistent with the prisoner's request; and provided further, that such search shall not be conducted for the sole purpose of determining genital status; and (iv) housed in a correctional facility with inmates with the same gender identity; provided further, that the placement shall be consistent with the prisoner's request, unless the commissioner, the sheriff or a designee of the commissioner or sheriff certifies in writing that the particular placement would not ensure the prisoner's health or safety or that the placement would present management or security problems.

There has also been litigation by female-born inmates who feel threatened by the presence of transgender female inmates, including those who are still anatomically male.[8] This is a rapidly evolving area and is likely to generate significant litigation in the coming years.

Summary

- The controlling principle for the treatment of female offenders is that there must be parity of treatment for male and female inmates. This means that there must be substantially equivalent facilities and treatment programs for both men and women. Because of the difference in numbers and needs, there cannot be total equivalency. Identical treatment is not required for men and women (*Pargo v. Elliott*).
- The equal protection clause requires that any disparity in treatment between male and female inmates must be justified by important government objectives and must be substantially related to advancing those objectives (*Craig v. Boren*).
- Equal protection also serves to protect other classes of inmates from discrimination. When considering programs and services, in order to justify different treatment for racial and ethnic minorities, the elderly and youths, noncitizen inmates, and other groups (persons with disabilities are now covered by their own protective statute, the Americans with Disabilities Act), there must be a substantial government (correctional) reason for the difference. Absent that, corrections officials can expect courts to examine closely, and perhaps reject, any significant differences in treatment.
- The Supreme Court has not yet addressed equal protection rights for inmates, except in the case of racial discrimination, which it has forbidden (*Lee v. Washington*).
- While prison officials may consider race in making classifications, such classifications must further a compelling governmental interest and be narrowly tailored to further that purpose (*Johnson v. California*).

Regulations promulgated pursuant to the Prison Rape Elimination Act direct correctional officials to assess the risk of housing and programming for non-gender conforming inmates.

Thinking About It

A state DOC policy on legal assistance to prisoners provides that the state will contract with a private law firm or entity to provide legal assistance to inmates in civil matters but not representation except that the state contracts for a full time attorney to represent the inmates at the state's female correctional facility in family matters including, but not limited to, divorces, child custody, and Department of Children and Families proceedings. Inmate Y, a male, requested state paid representation assistance to reverse a parental rights termination order. The state refused to provide such assistance. Inmate Y then sues correctional officials, alleging that the provision of family law legal assistance and representation to female prisoners but not to male prisoners violates the equal protection clause of the Fourteenth Amendment. How should the court rule? *Harnage v. Dzurenda*, et al., 176 F.Supp.3d 40 (D.Conn. 2016).

Endnotes

1. Jennifer Bronson, and E. Ann Carson. *"Prisoners in 2017."* Washington, D.C., Bureau of Justice Statistics, U.S. Department of Justice. April 2019.
2. *TDCJ Unit Directory*. Available: https://www.tdcj.texas.gov/unit_directory/index.html. Accessed March 22, 2020.
3. Vermont's incarcerated population on October 31, 2020 was 1371 inmates including 1273 males, 84 females and 14 transgender inmates. Vermont Department of Corrections, *Population Report* October 31, 2020. https://doc.vermont.gov/sites/correct/files/documents/PopulationReport_10-31-20.pdf
4. See note 1 above, Table 11.
5. Glenn R. Schmitt, and Amanda Russell. *Overview of Federal Criminal Cases Fiscal Year 2019*. April 2020. United States Sentencing Commission. Available: https://www.ussc.gov/sites/default/files/pdf/research-and-publications/research-publications/2020/FY19_Overview_Federal_Criminal_Cases.pdf. Accessed November 17, 2020.
6. U.S. Department of Justice. National Institute of Corrections. *Policy Review and Development Guide,* Lesbian, Gay, Bisexual, Transgender, and Intersex Persons in Custodial Settings (2015). Available at https://info.nicic.gov/sites/info.nicic.gov.lgbti/files/lgbti-policy-review-guide-2_0.pdf. Accessed March 17, 2020.
7. See for example, Federal Bureau of Prisons Program Statement 5200.04, *Transgender Offender Manual*, January 18, 2017 (change notice 5200.04 CN-1 May 11, 2018), and Minnesota DOC Directive 202.045- *Management of Transgender/Gender Non-Conforming/Intersex Offenders*, June 19, 2018. Available: http://www.doc.state.mn.us/DocPolicy2/html/DPW_Display_TOC.asp?Opt=202.045.htm. Accessed March 17, 2020.
8. See for example *Guy v. Espinoza, et al,* E.D. CA. Case No. 1:19-cv-00498-AWI-EPG (PC). Report and Recommendation of Magistrate Judge to dismiss claims with prejudice January 17, 2020. Available: https://scholar.google.com/scholar_case?case=17292084137669022002&q=transgender+AND+female+AND+prisoners&hl=en&as_sdt=6,24&as_ylo=2019

CHAPTER 14

Eighth Amendment: The Death Penalty and Other Sentencing Issues

The basic concept underlying the Eighth Amendment is nothing less than the dignity of man. While the State has the power to punish, the Amendment stands to assure that this power be exercised within the limits of civilized standards.

U.S. Supreme Court, *Trop v. Dulles*

CHAPTER OUTLINE

- Sentencing
- Death Penalty Sentences
- Death Row Conditions
- Legal Challenges to the Method of Execution
- Cruel and Unusual Punishment in Noncapital Sentencing Cases

▶ Sentencing

The whole of the Eighth Amendment reads as follows:

> **Excessive bail shall not be required, nor excessive fines imposed, nor cruel and unusual punishments inflicted.**

All the components of the Eighth Amendment refer to criminal processes and sanctions. The first two clauses have less significance in a study of corrections because the excessive bail clause deals primarily with the pretrial release of arrestees, and the excessive fines clause deals with a particular type of criminal sentencing (imposing fines).

If the wording of the amendment is realigned, the language that is of direct and frequent importance to corrections is, "cruel and unusual punishments shall not be inflicted." The Supreme Court has used the **cruel and unusual punishment** clause to weigh sentencing. That is one of the main uses of the clause. Criminal sentences have been challenged as being too harsh and, thus, in violation of the Constitution. In *Trop v. Dulles*, 356 U.S. 86 (1958), the Court found that the sanction of loss of nationality following conviction by military court martial of desertion during wartime was too severe and, therefore, was cruel and unusual punishment. Perhaps more importantly, the *Trop* case provided some of the standards for judging what "cruel and unusual" means. The Court said that the Eighth Amendment is tied to a concern for "the dignity of man."

> **The Amendment must draw its meaning from the evolving standards of decency that mark the progress of a maturing society.**

This is a frequently quoted phrase, used to help interpret the amendment's language. But does it really help? Where does a court find the currently evolved "standards of decency"? The statement clearly says that "cruel and unusual punishment" is an evolving standard. A court's responsibility in applying the Eighth Amendment may require it to assess the subjective consciousness of society to determine the "evolving standards of decency". Some may criticize this function for its lack of objectivity, but the term "cruel and unusual punishment" is inherently subjective.

Another sentencing case that gives us some guidelines about what *cruel and unusual* means is *Weems v. United States*, 217 U.S. 349 (1909). There, the sentence given was 12 to 20 years at hard labor, with ankle and wrist chains to be worn during the entire service of sentence and perpetual loss of civil rights. The crime for which that sentence was imposed was being an accessory to falsification of a government document. The Supreme Court overturned the sentence as being too harsh. Again, more important than the specific holding regarding that a particular "excessive" sentence is the language the Supreme Court used to analyze when punishment is cruel and unusual. The Court noted that a punishment is cruel and unusual if (1) it is greatly disproportionate to the offense for which it has been imposed or, (2) it goes far beyond what is necessary to achieve a sentencing aim, even if that aim is justified. The second guideline may be taken to say that a punishment is cruel and unusual if it is unnecessarily severe for whatever sentencing purpose a court is using.

Over 50 years after *Trop* and 100 years after *Weems*, the Supreme Court continues to look at the issues of "evolving standards of decency" and "proportionality" with regard to punishments. In *Atkins v. Virginia*, 536 U.S. 304 (2002), the Court said:

> **A claim that punishment is excessive [and therefore disproportionate to the offense] is judged not by the standards that prevailed in 1685 when Lord Jeffreys presided over the "Bloody Assizes" or when the Bill of Rights was adopted, but rather by those that currently prevail.**

> **Our independent evaluation of the issue reveals no reason to disagree with the judgment of "the legislatures that have recently addressed the matter" and concluded that death is not a suitable punishment for a mentally retarded criminal. We are not persuaded that the execution of mentally retarded criminals will measurably advance the deterrent or the retributive purpose of the death penalty. Construing and applying the Eighth Amendment in the light of our "evolving standards of decency," we therefore conclude that such punishment is excessive.**

Atkins will be reviewed in greater detail in the next section on death penalty sentences.

▶ Death Penalty Sentences

The constitutionality of the death penalty has been analyzed under the cruel and unusual proscription of the Eighth Amendment. This analysis has been overlaid with concerns under the due process clause. Starting with *Furman v. Georgia*, 408 U.S. 238 (1972), the Supreme Court closely examined the use of the death penalty itself, and it considered under which circumstances, or with which procedural protections, it *could* be used. In earlier days, the Court had assumed that the death penalty was a permissible sanction. Cases only looked at whether the particular means of executing the defendant were cruel and unusual or constitutional. For example, in *Wilkerson v. Utah*, 99 U.S. 130 (1878), the Supreme Court upheld the constitutionality of execution by firing squad against an Eighth Amendment challenge. In an example of an applied challenge to a method of execution, a 410 pound Washington state inmate (Rupe) argued his execution by hanging would violate the Eighth Amendment. After hearing expert testimony as to the physical impact of the hanging, a federal judge concluded that hanging Rupe would risk decapitating him. The court ruled that placing Rupe on the gallows would offend "basic human dignity" and "public perceptions of standards of decency."[1]

In the *Furman* case, the Supreme Court called a halt to the prior (some would say widespread, although a number of states had already repealed capital punishment) use of the death penalty. The Court found that it was imposed, like other sentences, at the complete discretion of the judge or jury, and it held that this practice was a violation of the Eighth Amendment. The practice led to such arbitrary and varied results that the Court found "no meaningful basis for distinguishing the few cases in which it is imposed from the many cases in which it is not."

The states (at least those that wanted to use the death penalty) scrambled to find procedures that would satisfy the Supreme Court's concerns. These procedures were found in *Gregg v. Georgia*, 428 U.S. 153 (1976), where the Court again looked at the constitutionality of the death penalty.

> **It is apparent from the text of the Constitution itself that the existence of capital punishment was accepted by the Framers. At the time the Eighth Amendment was ratified, capital punishment was a common sanction in every State. Indeed, the First Congress of the United States enacted legislation providing death as the penalty for specified crimes .... The Fifth Amendment, adopted at the same time as the Eighth, contemplated the continued existence of the capital sanction by imposing certain limits on the prosecution of capital cases: "No person shall be held to answer for a capital, or otherwise infamous crime, unless on a presentment or indictment of a Grand Jury ... nor shall any person be subject for the same offense to be twice put in jeopardy of life or limb ... nor be deprived of life, liberty, or property, without due process of law ..."**

> **And the Fourteenth Amendment, adopted over three-quarters of a century later, similarly contemplates the existence of the capital sanction in providing that no State shall deprive any person of "life, liberty, or property" without due process of law.**

As mentioned, in *Gregg*, a formula for sentencing that would meet Eighth (and Fourteenth) Amendment standards was found. (The Court noted that, after the *Furman* ruling, 35 states and the federal government had enacted new statutes for death penalty sentencing.) Under the Georgia scheme, at least one aggravating factor had to be found by the jury to exist beyond a reasonable doubt before a death sentence could be imposed. This was intended to meet the Supreme Court's concern in *Furman* that death sentences were imposed in an arbitrary or capricious manner. Besides the minimum of one aggravating factor, the jury in death penalty cases could consider other relevant aggravating and mitigating factors. Also, Georgia provided that there would be an automatic appeal of all death sentences to the Georgia Supreme Court. Besides reviewing all the procedural proprieties for such cases, the state Supreme Court was charged with comparing the death sentence with those sentences imposed on all similarly situated defendants in the state. These procedures satisfied the U.S. Supreme Court.

> **No longer can a jury wantonly and freakishly impose the death sentence; it is always circumscribed by the legislative guidelines ... [T]he statutory system under which Gregg was sentenced to death does not violate the Constitution.**

In the course of its opinion, the Supreme Court also looked at the history of the Eighth Amendment and reviewed those standards that reflect "standards of decency" and make punishments constitutionally acceptable. At its simplest, the "cruel and unusual punishment" clause means that punishments must not be excessive, but what does *excessive* mean?

> **First, the punishment must not involve the unnecessary and wanton infliction of pain. Second, the punishment must not be grossly out of proportion to the severity of the crime.**

Is the death penalty, in all cases, excessive and, therefore, cruel and unusual? Two justices gave their opinions that it is. They would vote to ban all capital punishment as cruel and unusual. But the majority of the Supreme Court held that it is not an unconstitutional punishment per se.

> **[T]he decision that capital punishment may be the appropriate sanction in extreme cases is an expression of the community's belief that certain crimes are themselves so grievous an affront to humanity that the only adequate response may be the penalty of death .... [In this case,] we are concerned ...**

only with the imposition of capital punishment for the crime of murder, and when a life has been taken deliberately by the offender, we cannot say that the punishment is invariably disproportionate to the crime. It is an extreme sanction, suitable to the most extreme of crimes. We hold that the death penalty is not a form of punishment that may never be imposed.

This is a somewhat indirect statement by the Supreme Court, in which it found that the death penalty is not per se unconstitutional.

Along with, and following *Gregg*, numerous other death penalty sentencing formulas have been reviewed in the Supreme Court. Most have been approved. The Supreme Court in *Maynard v. Cartwright*, 486 U.S. 356 (1988), however, rejected a death penalty imposed in a case in which Oklahoma required the jury to find an aggravating circumstance to support a death sentence. One egregious circumstance, which Oklahoma law specified could be used to support a death sentence, was that a murder was "especially heinous, atrocious, or cruel." The Supreme Court said that language was too vague and could result in arbitrary results; a person might believe, for example, that "every unjustified, intentional taking of human life is 'especially heinous.'"

The standards that Georgia adopted, which the Court approved in *Gregg*, was not the only constitutional capital sentencing scheme. For example, in *Pulley v. Harris*, 465 U.S. 37 (1984), the Court upheld the California capital sentencing scheme, which did not include a review of the death penalty compared with other similar cases in the state. This comparison, part of Georgia's capital sentencing scheme, had been approved by state supreme court on mandatory appeal, and was approved by the U.S. Supreme Court in *Gregg*. (In other words, the Supreme Court ruled that the comparative proportionality review of sentences, as Georgia had established, is not required in every state's review of death sentences.) What is required is a system of procedural checks and precautions that prevents arbitrariness, according to the Court in *Pulley*.

Is it permissible to have a death penalty system that mandates the death penalty for all offenses of a certain kind? Does this avoid arbitrariness? North Carolina passed a law that mandated the death sentence for all convictions of first-degree murder. In *Woodson v. North Carolina*, 428 U.S. 280 (1976), the Supreme Court rejected that statute as unconstitutional. Besides the two justices who would find all death sentences unconstitutional, three other justices voted against this statute on the grounds that it did not meet "civilized standards" and that it was contrary to "contemporary values," being "unduly harsh and unworkably rigid." The Court was also concerned that this mandatory kind of sentencing eliminated consideration of the individual defendant, which the Court stated was an important (and apparently necessary) sentencing requirement, at least for death penalty cases. The North Carolina scheme (and others that tried to cure *Furman* problems with mandatory sentencing) was rejected.

A sentencing statute in Nevada, which mandated the death penalty in all cases of murder by an inmate who was serving a life sentence without parole, was also rejected in *Sumner v. Shuman*, 483 U.S. 66 (1987). But in *Blystone v. Pennsylvania*, 494 U.S. 299 (1990), the Supreme Court upheld a death penalty statute that required the jury to impose the death sentence in a murder case if the jury found that aggravating circumstances outweighed any mitigating circumstances. The Pennsylvania death penalty statute required a jury to impose a death sentence when at least one aggravating circumstance and no mitigating circumstances were found. Blystone's death sentence was upheld.

In *Kansas v. Marsh*, 548 U.S. 163 (2006), the Supreme Court held that a state statute which required a jury to impose a death sentence when it found an equal number of aggravating and mitigating circumstances was constitutional. The Court ruled that the state did not create an unconstitutional presumption in favor of the death penalty. In explaining the differences between state statutes and what the Constitution requires in this regard, the Court noted that a state capital sentencing system is constitutional when it (1) "rationally narrows the class of death-eligible defendants" and (2) "permits a jury to consider any mitigating evidence relevant to its sentencing determination."

The Court has clearly indicated that its concern for individualizing the sentence requires the jury to consider mitigating circumstances in all death penalty cases. This is supported in *Hitchcock v. Dugger*, 481 U.S. 393 (1987); *Eddings v. Oklahoma*, 455 U.S. 104 (1982); and *Lockett v. Ohio*, 438 U.S 586 (1978). From *Eddings*, the Court provided the guidance that a death penalty system must be "at once consistent and principled but also humane and sensible to the uniqueness of the individual." The Court in *Eddings* applied the following rule from its earlier decision in *Lockett*:

[W]e conclude that the Eighth and Fourteenth Amendments require that the sentencer … not be precluded from considering, as a mitigating factor, any aspect of a defendant's character or record

and any of the circumstances of the offense that the defendant proffers as a basis for a sentence less than death.

In *Coker v. Georgia*, 433 U.S. 584 (1977), the Supreme Court held that the death penalty for the crime of rape of an adult woman is unconstitutional on the grounds that it is disproportionate to the offense. In *Kennedy v. Louisiana*, 554 U.S. 407 (2008), the Supreme Court ruled that imposition of the death penalty for the rape of a child under 12 was disproportionate to the offense and violated the Eighth Amendment. When death did not occur or was not intended, the Court said its determination of the constitutionality of the death penalty has been guided by "objective indicia of society's standards, as expressed in legislative enactments and state practice with respect to executions."

After reviewing the authorities informed by contemporary norms, including the history of the death penalty for this and other non-homicide crimes, current state statutes and new enactments, and the number of executions since 1964 [none for child rape], we conclude there is a national consensus against capital punishment for the crime of child rape.

While noting both the devastating impact of rape on its victims and the general public abhorrence of the crime of rape of a child, the Court ruled:

Consistent with evolving standards of decency and the teachings of our precedents we conclude that, in determining whether the death penalty is excessive, there is a distinction between intentional first-degree murder on the one hand and nonhomicide crimes against individual persons, even including child rape, on the other. The latter crimes may be devastating in their harm, as here, but "in terms of moral depravity and of the injury to the person and to the public," … they cannot be compared to murder in their "severity and irrevocability."

However, the death sentence is not reserved solely for offenders who actually commit a murder. In *Tison v. Arizona*, 481 U.S. 137 (1987), for example, the Court ruled that it was not cruel and unusual to impose the death penalty on a defendant who did not commit the murder himself, but who was a significant accomplice. In that case, the defendant, Tison, by assisting his father and another inmate to escape from prison and then to commandeer a car in which all four passengers were killed, showed "reckless indifference to human life." The Court further noted that Tison "knowingly engaged in activities known to carry a grave risk of death."

In *Thompson v. Oklahoma*, 487 U.S. 815 (1988), a statute that allowed the death penalty for persons aged 15 or younger was held to be unconstitutional. But the Court held, in *Stanford v. Kentucky*, 492 U.S. 361 (1989), that death sentences imposed on persons aged 16 and 17 were constitutional. In 2005, the Supreme Court in *Roper v. Simmons*, 543 U.S. 551 (2005), declared that the execution of a person for a crime committed as a juvenile violates the Eighth and Fourteenth Amendments.

All states forbid the execution of persons who are (or have become) insane. The Supreme Court approved, in *Ford v. Wainwright*, 477 U.S. 399 (1986), the rule that the Eighth Amendment prohibits the execution of a person who is presently insane.

The Court, in *Penry v. Lynaugh*, 492 U.S. 302 (1989), upheld the death penalty of a person who was, as described by the court, "mentally retarded." *Penry* was abrogated by the Court's decision in *Atkins v. Virginia*, 536 U.S. 304 (2002). Atkins was convicted of abduction, armed robbery, and capital murder. In assessing punishment, a forensic psychologist testified that Atkins was "mildly mentally retarded." The U.S. Supreme Court reviewed the death sentence, saying it was doing so, in part, "in light of the dramatic shift in the state legislative landscape that has occurred in the past 13 years." Holding the executions of mentally retarded criminals as cruel and unusual punishment in violation of the Eighth Amendment, the Court said in *Atkins*:

[T]he public reaction to the execution of a mentally retarded murderer in Georgia apparently led to the enactment of the first state statute prohibiting such executions. In 1988, when Congress enacted legislation reinstating the federal death penalty, it expressly provided that a "sentence of death shall not be carried out upon a person who is mentally retarded." In 1989, Maryland enacted a similar prohibition. It was in that year that we decided Penry, and concluded that those two state enactments, "even when added to the 14 States that have rejected capital punishment completely, do not provide sufficient evidence at present of a national consensus."

The Court in *Atkins* noted that much had changed over the intervening years. State legislatures, responding to the national attention received by the execution of Jerome Bowden and the *Penry* decision, began to address the issue. Jerome Bowden, a person identified as suffering from mental retardation, was scheduled for execution in Georgia in June 1986. The Georgia Board of Pardons and Paroles granted a stay, following public protests over his execution. A psychologist, selected by the state, evaluated Bowden and determined he had an I.Q. of 65, which is consistent with mental retardation. Nevertheless, the board lifted the stay and Bowden was executed the next day. The board concluded that Bowden understood the nature of his crime and his punishment, and, therefore, the execution, despite his mental deficiencies, was permissible.[2] The Court identified 16 additional states since 1990 that prohibited the execution of the mentally retarded.

> **It is not so much the number of these States that is significant, but the consistency of the direction of change. Given the well-known fact that anticrime legislation is far more popular than legislation providing protections for persons guilty of violent crime, the large number of States prohibiting the execution of mentally retarded persons (and the complete absence of States passing legislation reinstating the power to conduct such executions) provides powerful evidence that today our society views mentally retarded offenders as categorically less culpable than the average criminal …. And it appears that even among those States that regularly execute offenders and that have no prohibition with regard to the mentally retarded, only five have executed offenders possessing a known IQ less than 70 since we decided *Penry*. The practice, therefore, has become truly unusual, and it is fair to say that a national consensus has developed against it.**

The Court's ruling in *Atkins* left open the question of how to determine if a person has an intellectual disability and whether that disability forecloses a person's execution. Florida attempted to resolve the issue by enacting a statute, which defined "intellectual disability" as having an IQ test score of 70 or lower. In *Hall v. Florida*, 572 U.S. 701 (2014), a death sentenced offender claimed he was intellectually disabled and could not legally be executed. Because the inmate had taken several IQ tests with scores above 70, the state courts refused to permit other testimony concerning the existence of an intellectual disability. The Court noted that: *"Previous opinions of this Court have employed the term "mental retardation." This opinion uses the term "intellectual disability" to describe the identical phenomenon."* In summarizing its previous rulings, the Court again stated that the Eighth Amendment prohibits the execution of intellectually disabled persons.

> *No legitimate penological purpose is served by executing a person with intellectual disability. [citation omitted]. To do so contravenes the Eighth Amendment, for to impose [T]he harshest of punishments on an intellectually disabled person violates his or her inherent dignity as a human being. "[P]unishment is justified under one or more of three principal rationales: rehabilitation, deterrence, and retribution." [citations omitted]. Rehabilitation, it is evident, is not an applicable rationale for the death penalty. [citation omitted]. As for deterrence, those with intellectual disability are, by reason of their condition, likely unable to make the calculated judgments that are the premise for the deterrence rationale. They have a "diminished ability" to "process information, to learn from experience, to engage in logical reasoning, or to control impulses … [which] make[s] it less likely that they can process the information of the possibility of execution as a penalty and, as a result, control their conduct based upon that information." [citation omitted]. Retributive values are also ill-served by executing those with intellectual disability. The diminished capacity of the intellectually disabled lessens moral culpability and hence the retributive value of the punishment. [citation omitted]. "If the culpability of the average murderer is insufficient to justify the most extreme sanction available to the State, the lesser culpability of the mentally retarded offender surely does not merit that form of retribution".*

Florida's categorical approach to determining intellectual disability was found to violate the Eighth Amendment. The Court ruled that Florida's mandatory reliance on the IQ score to determine intellectual disability was inconsistent with accepted medical practice because medical science utilizes other forms of evidence to assess disability and the IQ test itself is imprecise. One year later in *Brumfield v. Cain*, 576 U.S. ____, 135 S.Ct. 2269 (2015), the Court further cautioned that consideration of an IQ test when determining if a legally sufficient intellectual disability exists in a capital case must take into account the test's margin of error (Standard Error of Measurement-SEM).

In *Madison v. Alabama*, 586 U.S. ___, 139 S.Ct 718 (2019), a death sentenced inmate experienced strokes and was diagnosed with dementia. As a result of these occurrences, the inmate could no longer recall committing the acts he was sentenced to death for. He claimed his lack of memory rendered him mentally incompetent to be executed. Madison's petition in the state court was denied, and the inmate appealed. The Court ruled:

> *First, a person lacking memory of his crime may yet rationally understand why the State seeks to execute him; if so, the Eighth Amendment poses no bar to his execution. Second, a person suffering from dementia may be unable to rationally understand the reasons for his sentence; if so, the Eighth Amendment does not allow his execution.*

Because the Court was unsure if the lower courts had committed any legal errors in finding that Madison was competent to be executed, the case was returned to the state courts for reconsideration.

What is the current status of the death penalty in the United States? At year-end 2018, 34 states and the federal government had statutes authorizing the death penalty. There were 2,628 persons confined by these jurisdictions under a sentence of death. In 2017, there were 23 executions in the United States. All 23 executions were carried out by lethal injection. Fifteen of the persons executed were White, and eight were Black.[3] In 2018, 25 executions were carried out, fourteen of the persons executed were White, six were Black and five were Hispanic. In 2017 and 2018 all the persons executed were males. From 2017 to November 2020, 85 persons have been executed in the United States, 80 by lethal injection and 5 by electrocution (all five in Tennessee).[4] In 2019, the National Conference of State Legislatures reported 29 states, the federal government and U.S. Military still retained the death penalty.[5] In 2020, Colorado abolished capital punishment, and the Death Penalty Information Center now identifies 28 states with capital punishment and 22 without.[6] In 2018, the average elapsed time from sentence to the date of execution was almost 20 years[7] because there are lengthy appeals and other legal proceedings in connection with the death sentence.

▶ Death Row Conditions

Another aspect of the death penalty is a consideration of the conditions under which persons who have been sentenced to that penalty are held. In those states (and the federal government) where the death penalty is authorized, it has long been the practice to have a separate prison area called "death row." All those with a death sentence are assigned to it (there are separate facilities for women who may receive a death sentence), and they are held there, in a segregated unit from other inmates, for as long as they are in custody with the death penalty in place. Security conditions are high, and program opportunities are few, although there are often recreation facilities inside the unit or attached to it. Prisoners are allowed out of their cells to shower and to receive visitors. Food is brought to the unit to be eaten there, and medical staff visit the unit to check on medical complaints and to take care of as many problems as possible inside the unit. If the inmate is taken out of the unit, for example to a community medical facility, a court, or even a clinic or visiting area inside the prison, he is usually handcuffed and shackled. These conditions, of course, typically go on for many years. (In 2017, the average elapsed time from sentence to the date of execution was 20 years, 3 months[7] because there are lengthy appeals and other legal proceedings in connection with the death sentence.) This separate, often harsh confinement, like so many other aspects of corrections, can be traced historically to English law, which required solitary confinement as "a further terror and peculiar mark of infamy" attached to the death penalty. This language is quoted in *In re Medley*, 134 U.S. 160 (1890).

The *Medley* case was the first taken to the Supreme Court to complain of death row conditions. Medley, under death sentence in Colorado for killing his wife, challenged his solitary confinement conditions while awaiting execution. He brought a habeas corpus action directly into the Supreme Court, which held that Medley's solitary confinement was "additional punishment" and, under the circumstances of his case, was unconstitutional. (This was because Colorado's law that required the solitary confinement was enacted after the offense and was, therefore, an ex post facto law—increasing the penalty for the offense after the offense had been committed. There was no ruling that the conditions were themselves unconstitutional.)

The Supreme Court has not subsequently set any constitutional requirements for death row conditions of confinement. It has given some indication that the question of whether many years spent on death row, in and of themselves, raises a question of cruel and unusual punishment. On March 27, 1995, the Supreme Court denied certiorari in the case of *Lackey v. Texas*, 514 U.S. 1045 (1995). Lackey sought review of the question of whether the

17 years he had spent on death row violated the Eighth Amendment. Although the Court refused to issue a ruling on that question, Justice Stevens noted that it was, for several reasons, a significant question, which would have to be addressed eventually. He suggested that the issue would best be considered in the Supreme Court after it had been addressed by some additional lower courts.

Since *Lackey*, three federal courts of appeal have held that long confinement on death row awaiting execution does not violate the Constitution. *Thompson v. Secretary for the Department of Corrections*, 517 F.3d 1279 (11th Cir. 2008); *Allen v. Ornoski*, 435 F.3d 946 (9th Cir. 2006) cert. denied 546 U.S. 1136 (2006); and *Chambers v. Bowersox*, 157 F.3d 560 (8th Cir. 1998). In *Knight v. Florida* and *Moore v. Nebraska*, 528 U.S. 990 (1999) (two cases considered at the same time), the Supreme Court was asked to consider whether the Eighth Amendment prohibits as "cruel and unusual punishment," the execution of persons who have spent nearly 20 years or more on death row. The Supreme Court declined to review those cases. In a dissenting opinion, Justice Breyer argued for consideration of the Eighth Amendment claim, stating that both cases involved "astonishingly long delays flowing in significant part from constitutionally defective death penalty procedures." Justice Breyer also noted, "A growing number of courts outside the United States—*courts that accept or assume the lawfulness of the death penalty*—have held that lengthy delay in administering a *lawful* death penalty renders ultimate execution inhuman, degrading, or unusually cruel." It is anticipated that the Supreme Court, at some point, will review this Eighth Amendment issue in detail. Until then, the Justices of the Supreme Court continue to discuss this issue in concurring or dissenting opinions related to denial of petitions for certiorari. A recent example is *Thompson v. McNeil*, 556 U.S. 114 (2009). In addressing the denial of the petition for writ of certiorari, Justice Stevens noted that "[t]hirty-two years have passed since petitioner was first sentenced to death." Further, he said, "our experience during the past three decades has demonstrated that delays in state-sponsored killings are inescapable and that executing defendants after such delays is unacceptably cruel. This inevitable cruelty, coupled with the diminished justification for carrying out an execution after the lapse of so much time, reinforces my opinion that contemporary decisions to 'retain the death penalty as a part of our law are the product of habit and inattention rather than an acceptable deliberative process.'"

The Supreme Court has given much attention and many opinions in the last 40 years on constitutional requirements for imposing the death penalty. Conditions on death row have been challenged in lower courts, and there is some guidance from those courts. In short, the case law instructs that death row inmates cannot be held in "barbarous and torturous" conditions. But they can be held in segregated confinement—that is, in units segregated from inmates serving regular terms of imprisonment—for the many years that death sentence appeals take.

Recent scientific research on the psychological and physical impact of long-term isolation present in death row conditions has sparked a new round of litigation concerning the conditions of death rows. In *Porter v. Clarke*, 923 F.3d 348 (4th Cir. 2019), the court of appeals affirmed the conclusions of the district court that the conditions of confinement that had existed in Virginia's death row before 2015 violated the Eighth Amendment. The district court made detailed findings of fact concerning the size of cells [71 square feet], cell features such as windows and doors, out of cell activities [exercise and shower], types of contacts that death row inmates had with other inmates, staff and persons in the community [contact and noncontact visiting and telephone calls]. The district court considered testimony from experts in psychology and determined "that the conditions of confinement on Virginia's death row"—particularly inmates' prolonged periods of isolation—"created, at the least, a significant risk of substantial psychological or emotional harm."

The court of appeals ruled that the objective component of Eighth Amendment conditions of confinement analysis announced in *Farmer v. Brennan* was met because "[t]he challenged conditions of confinement on Virginia's death row—under which Plaintiffs spent, for years, between 23 and 24 hours a day "alone, in a small ... cell" with "no access to congregate religious, educational, or social programming"—"pose a "substantial risk" of serious psychological and emotional harm." The subjective component [deliberate indifference] was also established because Virginia state officials were aware of the substantial risk of "the psychological or emotional harm posed by solitary confinement." Virginia's own state policies limited placement of non-death row inmates in similar isolation to 30 days. The court also noted that the "extensive scholarly literature describing and quantifying the adverse mental health effects of prolonged solitary confinement that has emerged in recent years provides circumstantial evidence that the risk of such harm 'was so obvious that it had to have been known.'" The court of appeals affirmed the district court's grant of injunctive relief prohibiting the previous death row conditions. However, the dissent to the panel opinion noted that even the plaintiffs conceded that modifications that the state made to death row conditions in 2015 [substantially increasing the contact that inmates were allowed to have with their family members and each other, increased recreational opportunities, and a $2 million construction project, which created a new dayroom and a new outdoor recreation yard], "rendered the current conditions on Virginia's death row constitutional."

In a very early case challenging conditions of death row, inmate Sinclair complained of many conditions on Louisiana's death row in *Sinclair v. Henderson*, 331 F.Supp. 1123 (E.D. LA 1971). Among other conditions, Sinclair complained of unsanitary food; inadequate plumbing, ventilation, bedding, and medical attention; the use of inmate guards; and a lack of physical exercise. All of the complaints were rejected, except for the last one. The court supported the need for regular exercise:

> **Confinement for long periods of time without the opportunity for regular outdoor exercise does, as a matter of law, constitute cruel and unusual punishment …. [I]t is feasible both economically and from a security standpoint for the defendant to make arrangements for all prisoners on Death Row to have regular outdoor exercise opportunity.**

Although confinement without exercise for short periods might be tolerable (for Eighth Amendment assessment), because of the long periods of time that death row inmates are held, regular out-of-cell exercise is viewed as a necessity. This is true of other conditions on death row as well. What might be constitutionally permissible over a short time may become unconstitutional when it continues over a long period of time.

In *Gates v. Cook*, 376 F.3d 323 (5th Cir. 2004), Mississippi death row inmates complained about their conditions of confinement. The court of appeals affirmed the district court's order directing the Department of Corrections to ensure that death row cells were adequately cleaned before assigning an inmate to that cell; provide adequate cleaning materials; develop a plan to control insects, including use of screens; improve plumbing, lighting, and ventilation on the death row unit; and improve the process for dealing with mental health issues. The concerns identified in *Gates* occurred in a death row unit, and this case could easily be considered a discussion on the conditions of confinement. For example, the trial court in *Gates* found that some cells were "extremely filthy" with crusted fecal matter, urine, dried ejaculate, peeling and chipping paint, and old food particles on the walls. The court of appeals agreed with the trial court that such conditions would present a substantial risk of serious harm to the inmates, and, therefore, violated the Eighth Amendment. The court also required plumbing problems to be addressed, including fixing a problem resulting in inmates being exposed "to each other's feces for over a decade."

A prison policy in Oklahoma that prohibited contact visits by death row inmates (or other "high-maximum" security inmates) with their attorneys was struck down by a federal appeals court in *Mann v. Reynolds*, 46 F.3d 1055 (10th Cir. 1995). The principal problem for the state was that prison officials allowed these same inmates to have contact during visiting with other persons, but they singled out attorneys for the special ban. The state did not provide "an explanation why they have singled out attorneys for the restricted contact." Apparently, there had not been any particular problems with attorney visits, except for "isolated occasions when cigarettes, chewing gum, pens, and paper clips have been unwittingly passed by uninitiated lawyers to inmates." Absent such a showing that the ban on contact visiting with attorneys was necessitated by prison security concerns, the court said it was not rational to enforce such a ban.

In the case of *Smith v. Coughlin*, 748 F.2d 783 (1984), the Second Circuit Court of Appeals ruled that it was permissible for prison authorities in New York to restrict the visits made to death row inmates. There, visits were limited to members of the inmate's immediate family, and the court said that policy, based on security and administrative concerns, was justified and not unconstitutional.

In 2015, the court of appeals for the Fifth Circuit found that conditions on Louisiana's death row violated the Eighth Amendment because the conditions did not adequately address the issues of heat. Death row inmates were in their cells 23 hours a day. The cell area was not air conditioned, but rather cooled by fans in windows, which provided moving air through an 8 × 6 inch grille into the cell. The cells provided limited access to water, and ice was available, but needed to be delivered to each cell by staff or other inmates when the inmate was not in a common area. Medical testimony reflected that high temperatures could have serious consequences for a person with some health conditions. The trial court concluded that the inmates established an Eighth Amendment claim, and the relief ordered was to air condition the housing units. The court of appeals affirmed the judgment that the inmates' Eighth Amendment rights had been violated but vacated the injunction for air conditioning because the relief was not sufficiently tailored as required by the PLRA. *Ball v. LeBlanc*, 792 F.3rd 584 (5th Cir. 2015).

▶ Legal Challenges to the Method of Execution

In *Wilkerson v. Utah*, mentioned earlier in this chapter, the Court ruled that the method of carrying out the sentence of death by firing squad was governed by the Constitution and could not be cruel or unusual. Twelve years later in *In re Kemmler*, 136 U.S. 436 (1890), the Court ruled that execution by the newly developed electric chair did not violate the Constitution, since the method was enacted by the state legislature and designed to reduce the suffering that might occur when a death penalty is carried out. In its opinion, the *In Re Kemmler* Court noted that Section 505 of New York's Code of Criminal Procedure was amended in 1888 to read as follows: "§ 505. The punishment of death must, in every case, be inflicted by causing to pass through the body of the convict a current of electricity of sufficient intensity to cause death, and the application of such current must be continued until such convict is dead."

By the 1980s, most states that authorized the use of capital punishment had adopted lethal injection as the method of execution. Lethal injection uses one or more commonly available drugs to cause death. In the last several years, the Supreme Court decided several cases related to both procedural and substantive aspects of carrying out capital punishment. The distinction between prisoner litigation as habeas corpus or Section 1983 is not always clear. In *Nelson v. Campbell*, 541 U.S. 637 (2004), without deciding the difficult legal question of what the appropriate legal procedure is—habeas or Section 1983—for challenging a method of execution, the Court ruled that because the prisoner was claiming that a procedure in the execution process to be used by prison officials would cause unnecessary pain and suffering, the prisoner could use Section 1983 to obtain injunctive relief. Two years later, in *Hill v. McDonough*, 547 U.S. 573 (2006), the Court did rule that a prisoner under sentence of death may use Section 1983 to challenge particular execution procedures.

In *Baze v. Rees*, 553 U.S. 35 (2008), death-sentenced inmates in Kentucky claimed the state's protocol (procedure) for carrying out executions by lethal injection violated the Eighth Amendment ban against cruel and unusual punishment. The Supreme Court affirmed the Kentucky Supreme Court's ruling that the procedures used by the state, including its use of a three-chemical combination to cause death, did not violate the Constitution. The three drugs commonly used by the states (and by Kentucky at the time of the *Baze* decision) were sodium thiopental, which induces unconsciousness; pancuronium bromide, which is a paralytic that causes breathing to cease; and potassium chloride, which interrupts electrical activity of the heart. *In Re Bureau of Prisons' Execution Protocol*, 955 F.3d 106 (D.C. Cir. 2020) *cert denied sub nom Bourgeois v. Barr*, Supreme Court Docket No. (19A1050) (June 29, 2020).

In *Baze v. Rees*, Chief Justice Roberts wrote the controlling opinion and was joined by two other justices in the outcome and the rationale. Two other justices concurred in the result but on a different basis then stated by Chief Justice Roberts. There was no majority opinion in this case. In *Baze*, the inmates conceded that if the state's execution protocol was carried out properly, there would be no violation of the Eighth Amendment. The inmate's constitutional objection to the protocol was premised on a perceived significant risk the protocol would not be carried out properly. The most significant risk the inmates identified was that the first drug, sodium thiopental, would not be administered properly and the condemned individual would suffer unnecessary pain during the administration of the second and third drugs. The inmates argued that if the state adopted certain alternative procedures such as using only a single drug and requiring the state to utilize trained personnel to ensure the sodium thiopental was administered properly would eliminate these risks. Chief Justice Roberts agreed that the risk of future pain and suffering can violate the Constitution, but only when the risk is "sure or very likely to cause serious illness or needless suffering." The Chief Justice concluded the potential risks that the protocol would not be carried out properly failed to establish "a substantial risk of harm, an objectively intolerable risk of harm."

> **Much of petitioners' case rests on the contention that they have identified a significant risk of harm that can be eliminated by adopting alternative procedures, such as a one-drug protocol that dispenses with the use of pancuronium and potassium chloride, and additional monitoring by trained personnel to ensure that the first dose of sodium thiopental has been adequately delivered. Given what our cases have said about the nature of the risk of harm that is actionable under the Eighth Amendment, a condemned prisoner cannot successfully challenge a State's method of execution merely by showing a slightly or marginally safer alternative. . . . Instead, the proffered alternatives must effectively address a "substantial risk of serious harm." [citation omitted] To qualify, the alternative procedure must be feasible, readily implemented, and in fact significantly reduce a substantial risk of severe pain. If a**

State refuses to adopt such an alternative in the face of these documented advantages, without a legitimate penological justification for adhering to its current method of execution, then a State's refusal to change its method can be viewed as "cruel and unusual" under the Eighth Amendment. The Supreme Court affirmed the Kentucky Supreme Court's ruling that the procedures used by the state for lethal injection. Including the use of the three chemical combination to cause death, did not violate the Constitution.

In *Glossip v. Gross*, 576 U.S. ___ (2015), the Supreme Court addressed the constitutionality of Oklahoma's three-drug lethal injection protocol. Several death row inmates had challenged the protocol on the basis that the state had substituted midazolam for sodium thiopental as the first drug in the protocol. The purpose of the first drug is to render the inmate "insensate" to the potentially noxious effects of the second and third drugs. The manufacturer of sodium thiopental had refused to sell the drug to the states for the purpose of lethal injection, so alternative drugs were considered. The district court conducted a three-day hearing and concluded that the inmates had failed *"to identify a known and available method of execution that presented a substantially less severe risk of pain than the method that the State proposed to use and .... [and] that Oklahoma's protocol did not "present a risk that is 'sure or very likely to cause serious illness and needless suffering,' amounting to 'an objectively intolerable risk of harm.'"* The state protocol called for administration of 500 milligrams of midazolam and the district court found, based on testimony from medical experts that the dose *"would make it a virtual certainty that any individual will be at a sufficient level of unconsciousness to resist the noxious stimuli which could occur from the application of the second and third drugs."* The court of appeals affirmed concluding that the inmates (i) failed to identify a readily available alternative for the state to use; (ii) failed to prove the use of midazolam would create "a demonstrated risk of severe pain"; and (iii) that the district court's conclusions concerning the use of midazolam were not clearly erroneous.

The Supreme Court affirmed the circuit court judgment concluding that the prisoners had:

> **failed to identify a known and available alternative method of execution that entails a lesser risk of pain, a requirement of all Eighth Amendment method-of execution claims. {citation omitted} [and that] . . . the District Court did not commit clear error when it found that the prisoners failed to establish that Oklahoma's use of a massive dose of midazolam in its execution protocol entails a substantial risk of severe pain.**

In previous decisions, the Court had upheld as constitutional a state's use of a firing squad, the electric chair, and the three-drug lethal injection protocol described in *Baze, and "[the Supreme Court]* **has never invalidated a State's chosen procedure for carrying out a sentence of death as the infliction of cruel and unusual punishment."** Because the Court has held that the death penalty is constitutional,

> **[i]t necessarily follows that there must be a [constitutional] means of carrying it out. [citation omitted] And because some risk of pain is inherent in any method of execution, we have held that the Constitution does not require the avoidance of all risk of pain.**

The district court did not commit a clear error in finding the use of midazolam in the state's execution protocol did not create a substantial risk of severe pain. The Court considered four factors in making that determination: (i) the general deference appellate courts have for the findings of facts made by trial courts; (ii) the plaintiffs failed in their burden to demonstrate *"that the use of midazolam is sure or very likely to result in needless suffering"*; (iii) the deference paid to the numerous lower state and federal courts that had concluded the use of midazolam *"is likely to render an inmate insensate to pain that might result from administration of the paralytic agent and potassium chloride"*: and (iv) while acknowledging the responsibility of courts to identify and invalidate unconstitutional methods of execution, challenges to execution protocols *"test the boundaries of the authority and competency of federal courts"* who should not involve themselves in ongoing scientific controversies beyond their expertise.

The Court's rulings in *Baze* and *Glossip* were facial challenges to a state's execution procedures. In *Bucklew v. Precythe*, ___ U.S. ___, 139 S.Ct 1112 (2019), the Court considered an applied challenge to Missouri's execution protocol due to the prisoner's specific medical condition. The inmate proposed that the state execute him by "nitrogen hypoxia." Nitrogen hypoxia occurs when oxygen in the air, which is breathed, is replaced with another gas such as nitrogen. The lack of oxygen effectively suffocates the individual. In 2018, three states, Alabama,

Mississippi, and Oklahoma, had provisions for using nitrogen hypoxia but only Alabama allowed inmates to choose that method.[8]

The inmate in *Bucklew* had been convicted of capital murder and other crimes and sentenced to death. For almost 20 years, Missouri had litigated its execution procedures, and like Oklahoma, had revised its protocol based on the availability of chemicals. The Court expressly noted that the opinion in *Baze v. Rees* authored by Chief Justice Roberts was the controlling opinion for determining the constitutionality of execution protocols, and that the analysis for determining the constitutionally of a state's execution protocol is the same for both facial and as-applied challenges. In order to succeed on a claim that an alternate method of execution should be used the inmate must first demonstrate that their proposed alternative method is "***sufficiently detailed to permit a finding that the State could carry it out "relatively easily and reasonably quickly.***" [Citations omitted]. In this case, the inmate had failed to present any evidence about how the procedure would be carried out such as whether the gas would be administered through a mask or in a tent, the concentration of nitrogen in the gas, how quickly the gas should be administered, and any safety concerns for staff conducting the execution. In determining whether the proposed alternate method is available, states may consider its legitimate concern of using an untested method of execution that had never been used before. The *Baze/Glossip* standard requires the person challenging the state's chosen method of execution to demonstrate that the proposed "***readily available alternative, . . . would significantly reduce a substantial risk of severe pain.***" An inmate may propose a method of execution used by other jurisdiction but not currently used by that state—such as firing squad, electrocution, lethal gas, or another state's lethal injection protocol. The Court affirmed the lower courts' judgment upholding the constitutionality of the state's execution procedures.

The federal Constitution is not the only resource to challenge methods of execution. In 2008, the Nebraska Supreme Court ruled that the state statute authorizing execution by electrocution violated the state constitution's ban against cruel and unusual punishment. *State v. Mata*, 745 N.W. 229 (Nebraska 2008). The court said it's holding that a method of execution (electrocution) was cruel and unusual punishment was not directed to the validity of the sentence but only to the legality of the execution of the sentence.

State law may also require that execution procedures be promulgated using the state's administrative procedure act, which may require public notice, comment, and even public hearings before adopting the procedures to be used in executions.[9]

▶ Cruel and Unusual Punishment in Noncapital Sentencing Cases

The Supreme Court has also considered the cruel and unusual punishment clause in cases in which the sentence was less than the death penalty. (Recall the discussion of the historic cases of *Weems v. United States* (1909) and *Trop v. Dulles* (1958), in which the Supreme Court found the sentences (having to wear ankle and wrist chains throughout the service of a 20-year sentence in *Weems* and the loss of nationality for military desertion in *Trop* unconstitutional, because they were too severe.)

In sentencing cases since *Weems* and *Trop*, the Supreme Court considered the heavy sanctions imposed for repeat offenders. (The recent "three-strikes-and-you're-out" laws are not new legislative ideas!) In *Rummel v. Estelle*, 445 U.S. 263 (1980), Texas had enacted a law that required life imprisonment for a person who was convicted the third time for a felony. Rummel was charged with felony theft for obtaining $120.75 under false pretenses. The jury convicted him of that offense and also found that he had two prior felonies (fraudulent use of a credit card, by which he obtained $80 in goods and passing a forged check, which was $28.68 in value). A life sentence was imposed, as required by the state statute. (The Supreme Court noted that, at that time, Washington and West Virginia also had mandatory life sentences for the commission of a third felony. Several other states had mandatory life sentences upon conviction of a fourth felony. Others required at least one of the felonies to be of a violent nature to support a life sentence.) The Court observed that the purpose of the recidivist statute was to deter repeat offenders and to segregate the recidivist from society for a lengthy period of time. The mandatory life sentence was upheld, and it was not found to be cruel and unusual or unconstitutional.

Three years later, in *Solem v. Helm*, 463 U.S. 277 (1983), the Supreme Court found a South Dakota recidivist sentence to be unconstitutional. The sentencing statute required that a person convicted of a felony who had at least three prior felony convictions was to be sentenced as a Class 1 felon, which meant life imprisonment without parole. Helm had been convicted of six prior nonviolent felonies. He then was convicted of writing a "no account" check for $100. The ordinary penalty for that offense alone would have been a maximum of five years imprisonment. Noting that the Eighth Amendment cases had established that a sentence must be proportionate to the crime the defendant has committed, the Court examined the gravity of Helm's current offense and the harshness of his sentence and held that his sentence was "significantly disproportionate to his crime" and, therefore, was in violation of the Eighth Amendment.

The *Solem* decision is very hard to reconcile with the Court's ruling in *Rummel*. But the Court specifically did not overrule the *Rummel* decision. It said that the South Dakota (*Solem*) sentence was "far more severe" than the life sentence in *Rummel*. Why? Apparently, the key factor for the Court was that Rummel was eligible, under Texas law, for parole on his sentence, whereas Helm was not eligible for parole. The only way for Helm to be released was by commutation of his sentence by the Governor; that relief had been granted very rarely on life sentences. Also, the Court noted that only one other state had such a severe recidivist statute with a nonparolable life sentence as punishment.

In *Ewing v. California*, 538 U.S. 11 (2003), the Supreme Court examined the constitutionality of California's three-strikes law. Under the law, a defendant who is convicted of a felony and has previously been convicted of at least two serious or violent felonies must receive an indeterminate life-imprisonment term. Ewing, on parole from a nine-year term for first-degree robbery and residential burglary, tried to walk out of a golf club's pro shop with three golf clubs, valued at $399 each, concealed in his pants leg. He was convicted of felony grand theft. Ewing was sentenced under the three-strikes law to a term of 25 years to life. The Supreme Court affirmed the California sentence, with four justices dissenting. The Court's opinion in *Ewing* held that the punishment was not grossly disproportionate to the severity of the crimes committed and did not violate the Eighth Amendment ban on cruel and unusual punishment. In reaching its decision, the *Ewing* Court stated that it was being guided by Justice Kennedy's concurrence in *Harmelin v. Michigan*, 501 U.S. 957 (1991). Harmelin was convicted under Michigan law of having in his possession over 650 grams of cocaine. He received a mandatory life sentence with no possibility of parole. The Supreme Court rejected Harmelin's claim that his sentence was cruel and unusual because it was "significantly disproportionate" to his crime. Justice Kennedy's concurrence identified four considerations of a proportionality review: substantial deference to legislative determinations; the variety of legitimate penological schemes; the nature of our federal system, which recognizes that differing attitudes and perceptions of local conditions could result in different, yet rational conclusions on the length of prison terms; and proportionality guided by objective factors to the fullest extent possible. Justice Kennedy also stated that the Eighth Amendment does not require strict proportionality between crime and sentence, but rather forbids only extreme sentences that are grossly disproportionate to the crime.

Throughout the States, legislatures enacting three strikes laws made a deliberate policy choice that individuals who have repeatedly engaged in serious or violent criminal behavior, and whose conduct has not been deterred by more conventional approaches to punishment, must be isolated from society in order to protect the public safety .... Our traditional deference to legislative policy choices finds a corollary in the principle that the Constitution "does not mandate adoption of any one penological theory." ... A sentence can have a variety of justifications, such as incapacitation, deterrence, retribution, or rehabilitation .... Some or all of these justifications may play a role in a State's sentencing scheme. Selecting the sentencing rationales is generally a policy choice to be made by state legislatures, not federal courts.

Ewing's sentence is justified by the State's public-safety interest in incapacitating and deterring recidivist felons, and amply supported by his own long, serious criminal record .... To be sure, Ewing's sentence is a long one. But it reflects a rational legislative judgment, entitled to deference, that offenders who have committed serious or violent felonies and who continue to commit felonies must be incapacitated.

The dissenting justices concluded that Ewing's sentence was grossly disproportionate to the "triggering offense conduct"—stealing three golf clubs—that led to the sentence.

In *Lockyer v. Andrade*, 538 U.S. 63 (2003), a companion case (also from California) to *Ewing*, the Court declined to accept the argument that two consecutive terms of 25 years to life for stealing about $150 in video tapes were grossly disproportionate to the offense committed and in violation of the Eighth Amendment. Andrade, like Ewing, had a long criminal history and was, therefore, subject to the three-strikes penalty. The Supreme Court again held that the three-strikes sentences were not grossly disproportionate and not a violation of the Eighth Amendment.

The Supreme Court, in *United States v. DiFrancesco*, 449 U.S. 117 (1980), upheld an imposition of a greater sentence by an appellate court (as that court was authorized by statute to do). Such an increase was not considered unconstitutional but rather a variety of a "two-stage" sentencing procedure.

The problem of recidivism among persons released from prisons continues to create significant issues for society. In a study of recidivism which covered 30 states and over a period of nine years, the study found that 83% of persons released from prison were re-arrested within nine years of release.[10] The highest percentage (44%) of re-arrest took place in the first year after release.

What of the sentencing that requires a convicted sex offender to be castrated or allows the defendant to choose castration to avoid many years of imprisonment? The Supreme Court has not ruled on the constitutionality of such statutes, and the lower court opinions have split. For cases that seem to go in both directions, see *State v. Brown*, 326 S.E.2d 410 (SC 1985) (holding that castration, a form of mutilation, violates the South Carolina state Constitution, which prohibits cruel and unusual punishment; thus, castration as a condition to suspension of sentence and placement on probation was void); and *People v. Foster*, 124 Cal.Rptr.2d 22 (CA App. 4 Dist. 2002) (upholding a plea agreement where Foster, "having bargained for a 30-year sentence that included the possible imposition of hormone suppression treatment in exchange for the dismissal of myriad serious felony charges … cannot then maintain on appeal that such treatment cannot be imposed because it would violate prohibitions against cruel and unusual punishment. To do so would be to have his cake and eat it too.")

What can be seen in these cases, and in those involving conditions of confinement, is that the Supreme Court and the lower courts, in dealing with the Eighth Amendment, come up with paraphrases, or interpretive yardsticks, to define what "cruel and unusual" means. How easy it would be to say that "this sentence" or "this condition in prison" is cruel and unusual and is, therefore, unconstitutional. That would entail an entire decision of only one or two paragraphs, of no more than 10 sentences. But there is no such simple court opinion. Is *cruel and unusual* too difficult a phrase to understand? The Court has never said so. It has never ducked away from giving us an interpretation of what the phrase means in a sentencing or prison situation merely because the concept of *cruel and unusual* is too complex to understand. The words are not uncommon, and they are certainly not legalistic, but they apparently require some degree of judicial translation to turn them into an understandable concept. At least the courts seem to believe that we readers of the opinions need such help in understanding and applying what *cruel and unusual* means as a constitutional concept.

Summary

- The Eighth Amendment's proscription of cruel and unusual punishments has been interpreted and applied by using many other phrases and definitions, supposedly to make it easier to understand what "cruel and unusual punishments" means.

- In sentencing, a sanction is cruel and unusual if it is disproportionate to the offense for which it is imposed or if it goes far beyond what is necessary to achieve a justified sentencing goal (*Weems v. United States*). The Supreme Court has recognized that "cruel and unusual" is an evolving standard, tied to "the progress of a maturing society" (*Trop v. Dulles*).

- With respect to the death penalty, the Supreme Court, in 1972 (*Furman v. Georgia*), struck down sentencing that was "arbitrary" and "unprincipled."

- The death penalty, the Supreme Court has ruled, is not per se cruel and unusual punishment (*Gregg v. Georgia*). The Court has reviewed cases from many states and has approved death sentences when there are procedural protections that ensure consideration of the individual's background and situation and when there are adequate review procedures. The death penalty was disapproved in cases in which the result was "unduly harsh and rigid," such as requiring the death penalty in all cases of murder and in cases in which the penalty was found to be disproportionate or excessive. The death penalty was also disapproved when used for the crime of rape of an adult woman (*Coker v. Georgia*), the rape of a child under age 12 (*Kennedy v. Louisiana*), and when imposed upon persons who were not yet 18 when they committed their capital offense (*Roper v. Simmons*). The Supreme Court has also ruled that executing a person who is currently insane (*Ford v. Wainwright*), or who is developmentally disabled (*Atkins v. Virginia*), violates the Eighth Amendment.

- *Hall v. Florida* and *Brumfield v. Cain* provide guidance on what constitutional limitations are placed in determining developmental disability for purposes of the death penalty.

- The conditions of confinement on death row have not been considered by the Supreme Court regarding the constitutional standards that apply there. Lower courts have acknowledged that death row inmates may need to be confined in housing that is segregated from other prisoners. Confining inmates for long periods of time without the opportunity to have outdoor exercise was held to be cruel and unusual by one court. One court has required that death row conditions not violate the Eighth Amendment in such areas as the ventilation that is provided, pest control, and adequate plumbing and lighting. Visiting for death row inmates may need to be limited, but restrictions must be justified by significant administrative or security considerations.

- The method that is used to carry out an execution is governed by the Constitution and may not be cruel and unusual (*Wilkerson v. Utah*). It is legislatures that provide for the method of execution in each jurisdiction (*In re Kemmler*).

- An inmate who is sentenced to death may use Section 1983 to challenge the specific procedures (claiming they will cause unnecessary pain and suffering) that will be used to carry out the execution (*Nelson v. Campbell* and *Hill v. McDonough*).

- The Supreme Court approved Kentucky's three-drug execution protocol, holding that a method of execution violates the Eighth Amendment only if the method creates an objectively intolerable risk of unnecessary pain and suffering (*Baze v. Rees*).

- In *Glossip v. Gross*, the Supreme Court approved Oklahoma's three-drug execution protocol using midazolam and established that for a condemned prisoner to prevail on an Eighth Amendment challenge to a state's method of execution the inmate must identify a known and readily available alternative method of execution that would substantially reduce a significant risk of pain.

- In *Bucklew v. Precythe*, the Supreme Court ruled that a condemned prisoner's as-applied Eighth Amendment challenge to a state's method of execution is evaluated using the same standards as the facial challenges outlined in *Baze/Glossip*.

- The Supreme Court upheld a severe recidivist sentencing statute in one case (*Rummel v. Estelle*), in which a mandatory life sentence was required for a third-time felony conviction. However, it disapproved of a similar law (*Solem v. Helm*), apparently because the life sentence, imposed for a fourth-time felony conviction, did not carry any opportunity for parole release and was, therefore, too harsh and excessive. More recently, the Court upheld California's three-strikes law (*Ewing v. California*; *Lockyer v. Andrade*), holding that the punishment was not grossly disproportionate to the severity of the crimes committed.

Thinking About It

Washington State enacted a Persistent Offender Accountability Act (POAA) which required courts to impose a life sentence without parole on offenders who are convicted of a third "most serious offense". Defendant Moretti was convicted at age 20 of breaking into a vacant home and setting it on fire, receiving a sentence of 20 months imprisonment. At age 26 Moretti was convicted of vehicular assault causing serious bodily injury while under the influence and received a prison sentence of 13 months. At age 32 Moretti and another man were convicted of first degree assault and second degree robbery of two men. During this crime, Moretti beat one of the victims with a baseball bat. Because of Moretti's previous two convictions, he was labeled a "persistent offender" under Washington's POAA statute and sentenced to life in prison without parole. Moretti challenged the life sentence on state constitutional and Eighth Amendment grounds because the sentencing judge should have considered his young age at the time of the first two offenses. Can states categorically utilize serious crimes committed by young adults in enhancing a sentence to include a life without possibility of parole? *State v. Moretti*, 446 P.2d 609 (WA. 2019).

Key Term

cruel and unusual punishment

Endnotes

1. *Rupe v. Wood*, 863 F.Supp. 1307 (W.D. Wa. 1994).
2. See footnote 8 in the opinion in *Atkins v. Virginia*, 536 U.S. 304 (2002).
3. Snell, T. *Capital Punishment, 2018: Selected Findings—Statistical Tables*. Page 1 and Table 2. (Washington, DC: Bureau of Justice Statistics, U.S. Department of Justice. September 2020). Available- https://www.bjs.gov/content/pub/pdf/cp18st.pdf Accessed

November 30, 2020. In this reference, the author notes that at year end 2018, 34 states the federal government and U.S. Military authorized the death penalty, though Wyoming had no death sentenced inmates.

4. The Death Penalty Information Center reported that in 2018 there were 25 executions carried out and in 2019 there were 22 executions carried out. All the persons executed were males, and 43 of the 47 executions were carried out by lethal injection. Tennessee executed four persons by electrocution. https://deathpenaltyinfo.org/executions/execution-database

5. *States and Capital Punishment.* June 12, 2019. Available at https://www.ncsl.org/research/civil-and-criminal-justice/death-penalty .aspx. Accessed March 3, 2020.

6. *DPIC Fact Sheet,* March 23, 2020. Available- https://files.deathpenaltyinfo.org/documents/pdf/FactSheet.f1585003454.pdf

7. See endnote 2, table 11.

8. *Alabama Replaces Lethal Injection in Favor of Nitrogen Gas,* Death Penalty Information Center, July 12, 2018. https://deathpenaltyinfo .org/news/alabama-prisoners-end-execution-lawsuit-state-will-drop-lethal-injection-in-favor-of-nitrogen-gas. Accessed November 30, 2020.

9. Compare *Bowling v. Kentucky Department of Corrections,* 301 S.W. 3d 478 (KY 2009) (corrected 2010) and *Morales v. California Department of Corrections and Rehabilitation,* 168 CA App. 4th 729 (2008) (requiring adoption pursuant to state Administrative Procedures Act, APA) with *Porter v. Commonwealth,* 661 SE 2d 415 (VA 2008) (state APA not applicable to state execution procedures) and *Middleton v. Missouri DOC,* 278 S.W. 3d 193 (MO 2009). (Missouri execution protocol is not a rule and is not subject to promulgation under state APA).

10. Mariel Alper, Matthew Durose, and Joshua Markham, Bureau of Justice Statistics Special Report. *2018 Update on Prisoner Recidivism: A 9-Year Follow-up Period (2005-2014).* Bureau of Justice Statistics. Washington D.C. 2018. https://www.bjs.gov/content/pub /pdf/18upr9yfup0514.pdf

CHAPTER 15

Eighth Amendment: Conditions of Confinement—Cruel and Unusual Punishment

No static "test" can exist by which courts determine whether conditions of confinement are cruel and unusual, for the Eighth Amendment must draw its meaning from the evolving standards of decency that mark the progress of a maturing society. But the Constitution does not mandate comfortable prisons.

U.S. Supreme Court, *Rhodes v. Chapman*

As a reminder, the Eighth Amendment reads as follows:

Excessive bail shall not be required, nor excessive fines imposed, nor cruel and unusual punishments inflicted.

CHAPTER OUTLINE

- Conditions in prisons
- Opening the gates
- Crowding in prisons and jails
- Effect of the prison Litigation Reform Act
- *Bell v. Wolfish*
- *Rhodes v. Chapman*
- *Brown v. Plata*
- *Whitley v. Albers*
- *Wilson v. Seiter*
- *Hudson v. McMillian; Wilkins v. Gaddy*
- *Farmer v. Brennan*
- *Helling v. McKinney*
- Qualified immunity

This chapter continues the examination of the phrase "cruel and unusual punishments." It is this language that is used, constitutionally, to weigh the variety of conditions under which prisoners are held. Courts, particularly by the Supreme Court, have addressed conditions of confinement using the Eighth Amendment as the yardstick. At what point do punishments become "cruel and unusual" and, therefore, unconstitutional? How does a correctional worker (or a judge, lawyer, or inmate) tell whether certain actions or conditions amount to cruel and unusual punishment?

▶ Conditions in Prisons

Prior to the 1960s, the courts took a "hands-off" attitude toward prisons and did not give any constitutional guidelines for the management of correctional facilities. This "hands-off" attitude applied to the conditions under which individual prisoners were held. Courts, including the Supreme Court, generally did not consider lawsuits addressing the circumstances under which prisoners were held. The prison wall was a barrier behind which the courts were loath to look. While there were some conditions that deserved scrutiny from the outside, the courts in those days took the position that the Constitution did not give them the keys to unlock the doors and evaluate the conditions behind the prison and jail walls. From the 1960s to the 1980s, that changed!

▶ Opening the Gates

One of the cases (and there were many) that started the opening of the prison gates for court examination under the Eighth Amendment was *Wright v. McMann,* 387 F.2d 519 (2d Cir. 1967). A prisoner at Clinton State Prison in New York alleged that the conditions under which he was held in the solitary confinement unit of that prison (where he had been placed for violating prison rules) were deplorable. To name just a few of those conditions, the cell was dirty, without means of cleaning it; the toilet and sink were encrusted with slime and human excrement residue; the prisoner was left nude for several days, after which he was given only a pair of underwear to wear; he had no hygiene items—no soap, towel, toilet paper, toothbrush, or comb; he was not permitted to sleep during daytime hours, between 7:30 A.M. and 10:00 P.M.; the windows in his cell were left open, causing exposure to the cold winter air during subfreezing temperatures; the cell had no furniture except the toilet and sink, so he had to sleep on the cold concrete floor without bedding; and his food was served in bowls that were placed on the floor of his cell. Wright claimed he was kept in this cell for 33 days beginning in February of 1965 and for another 21 days the following year.

These were the allegations made by Wright without the assistance of any counsel. The district court dismissed the complaint on the grounds that it did not make a showing of a denial of constitutional rights. If Wright did have a remedy, the court said, it was in the New York state courts. Because the district court had dismissed Wright's suit without any hearing, the appeals court accepted the facts alleged in the plaintiff's complaint as true.

The case was brought under Section 1983 of the Civil Rights Act. The court of appeals noted that, for many years, federal courts failed to review prisoner complaints about disciplinary proceedings in state prisons. One reason for this had been that the courts thought the Eighth Amendment did not apply to state prisoners. Also, courts were reluctant to interfere in the internal operations of state prisons and preferred to see the state courts look at such complaints. Those views, by the time of the *Wright* case, had been set aside. First, there was no question that the Eighth Amendment applied to the states, which had been demonstrated in *Robinson v. State of California,* 370 U.S. 660 (1962). Further, a state prisoner could bring an action under the Civil Rights Act, as held in *Cooper v. Pate,* 378 U.S. 546 (1964). Also, the Supreme Court made it clear in *Monroe v. Pape,* 365 U.S. 167 (1961), that the Civil Rights Act could be used for relief (in that case, against city police officers) without having to exhaust state remedies first. Finally, noting a number of recent cases (many of them involving Black Muslim claims), this court drew the following conclusion:

> **[W]hile federal courts are sensitive to the problems created by judicial interference in the internal discipline of state prisons, in appropriate cases they will not hesitate to intervene.**

The court of appeals in *Wright* then gave a brief overview of the history of the Eighth Amendment. What was its purpose? The writers of the amendment had in mind the abuses of certain English monarchs, the court said, and primarily intended to prevent "torture and barbarous punishments, such as pillorying, disemboweling, decapitation, and drawing and quartering." By the 1800s, the cruel and unusual punishment clause was thought to be dead, because those historic punishments had disappeared. The Supreme Court, however, revitalized the amendment in *Weems v. United States*, 217 U.S. 349 (1910), saying that a constitutional principle "must be capable of wider application than the mischief which gave it birth." The Court in *Weems* noted that the Constitution:

> **... is not fastened to the obsolete, but may acquire meaning as public opinion becomes enlightened by a humane justice**.

Thus was born the concept that what "cruel and unusual punishment" means is found in an evolving, ever-changing state of public opinion—that is, in the views of American society. In *Wright*, the court of appeals applied these broad standards of justice and decency to arrive at these conclusions:

> [T]he debasing conditions to which Wright claims to have been subjected would, if established, constitute cruel and unusual punishment in violation of the Eighth Amendment .... We are of the view that civilized standards of humane decency simply do not permit a man for a substantial period of time to be denuded and exposed to the bitter cold of winter in northern New York State and to be deprived of the basic elements of hygiene such as soap and toilet paper .... The Eighth Amendment forbids treatment so foul, so inhuman, and so violative of basic concepts of decency.

The case was returned to the trial court. That court was required to conduct a hearing on Wright's charges to see if they were true. If they were proved, Wright had been subjected to cruel and unusual punishment and would be entitled to relief under Section 1983. A concurring judge, while agreeing that the case had to be returned for a hearing, warned that there was a flood of complaints waiting to be released by opening the gates with an approval of closer examination by federal judges of Section 1983 complaints. That judge noted that "the great majority of prisoners are prone to make whatever charge they have reason to believe will get them a hearing, with little or no regard for the truth of their allegations." Whether that cynical viewpoint is accurate might be debated; what is clearly accurate is that judge's prediction of letting loose a flood of prisoner petitions and the greatly increased burden that flood would produce in the workload of the federal courts. The number of prisoner petitions filed in federal courts grew from approximately 23,000 in 1980 to a peak of over 68,000 in 1996. In the twelve month period ending September 30, 2019, 29,445 prisoner civil rights or conditions of confinement cases were filed in U.S. Courts.[1]

▶ Crowding in Prisons and Jails

There have been many things written on the topic of crowding, and it is universally agreed that the prisons and jails in the United States are crowded, in many jurisdictions, beyond their most desirable **capacity**.[2] The Department of Justice has developed a system of evaluating prison capacity based on several factors, including <u>design capacity</u> (The number of inmates a facility can hold set by the architect or planner); <u>rated capacity</u> (The number of inmates or beds a facility can hold set by a rating official) and <u>operational capacity</u> (The number of inmates a facility can hold based on staffing and services). These three figures are not always the same. Maximum capacity uses the highest figure of the three. On December 31, 2019, based on these definitions, the federal system and seven states were operating above their prisons' maximum rated, operational, and design capacity.[3]

It is also generally agreed that this crowding leads to other problems in corrections facilities by straining budgets, diluting programs, and creating tensions in everyday living conditions. (Most people refer to this problem as "overcrowding," but the author finds the frequent and loose use of that word inaccurate. Use of the term *overcrowded* can imply that the level of the prison population is bad. Typically, whenever a prison's population exceeds its designed or planned capacity, the prison is said to be overcrowded and carries the judgment with it that it is, therefore, bad. In fact, prisons and jails can be decently run at something over design or ideal capacity. Adequate funding and staffing, along with many other factors, contribute to a well-run, though crowded, facility. The term *overcrowding* should be reserved for those conditions in which the population has reached a truly risky or unmanageable level. Otherwise, the term *crowding* should be used when a facility's population rises above "normal" or planned levels.)

Crowding in prisons and jails, with its companion problems, has led to huge numbers of lawsuits, most of them under Section 1983, with many of them leading to court orders or consent decrees requiring corrective action.[4] At least 40 states, plus the District of Columbia, Puerto Rico, and the Virgin Islands, have been under such orders or decrees. About 500 jails have been under such orders. In many cases, the corrections administrators entered into the consent decrees (that is, they agreed to the decrees and signed them). **Consent decrees** are agreements by the parties, and approved by the court handling the case, that certain steps will be taken to improve conditions. Later in this chapter, legislative enactments, such as the Prison Litigation Reform Act (PLRA), which directly impact existing and new consent decrees, are discussed.

Many administrators of corrections systems (superintendents of jails if not the elected sheriff) are political appointees, whose tenures can be short. (As of October 2001, the average tenure of adult correctional agency directors was 3.3 years.[5]) Besides other problems that are created by this too-frequent turnover of top administrators, the presence of a consent decree is presents constraints that pass from one administrator to the next. Administrators may come into a new job expecting to be able to manage things with changes or methods of their choosing, only to find that the playing field is already severely restricted by the requirements of a consent decree.

There are myriad other problems created by these court orders, or consent decrees, in conditions cases. One pervasive problem is that changes usually require outlays of money—in some cases, very large outlays, which a court has no authority to appropriate. The moneys must come from legislative appropriations. Although some initial funding may be obtained (at the request of and with the support of the current governor, county executive, mayor, or sheriff), the funding ordinarily must be continued over a period of time. Subsequent executives or legislatures may have differing views about appropriating money or using limited resources for prison or jail problems. It makes no difference: the order or decree remains an ongoing obligation on the correctional system and the administrator, who can be found in contempt and be punished for failing to carry out its terms, even though it may be a decree with which they disagree and that they might never have signed themselves. The enactment of the PLRA provides corrections administrators with a means to address these concerns.

Some Section 1983 cases have involved individual inmate–plaintiffs who seek relief in the form of money damages. In addition, you will recall that Section 1983 actions can provide for injunctive relief, and this is sought in many cases. When cases are expanded to be class actions on behalf of all inmates in a particular facility, or even in an entire corrections system, injunctive relief is the principal remedy sought. In many of these cases that govern conditions of prisons or jails, the courts may appoint a master to assist in the administration of the relief that is granted. In the past, these masters, although theoretically limited to be assistants to the judges who appoint them, had in fact been given such wide authority, by judges in some cases, that they became involved in the day-to-day running of the prisons or were authorized to look over the shoulders of administrators in many different aspects of their jobs.

It should be noted that many defendant–administrators willingly signed consent decrees because they agreed with their provisions and wanted to see the changes made that were demanded by inmates (or by the attorneys for inmates' rights groups). The administrators knew that an agreement for better prisons or jails would result in additional or new facilities, more staff, expanded programs, better health care, and better food service. This leads to a very complex public administration problem: by what authority does an administrator bind a state or local government to spend large sums of money on future corrections expenditures? The short and somewhat too-easy answer is that the administrator has no such right or authority, because the power to raise money for the government, and to decide where it is spent, is first and foremost with the political arm of government, which is directly answerable to the people—namely, the legislature.

▶ Effect of the Prison Litigation Reform Act

Although a consent decree is not the same as a court order entered after trial, it is binding and enforceable by the court. Until 1996, it could go on indefinitely. However, changes occurred with passage of the Prison Litigation Reform Act (PLRA). The PLRA was enacted by Congress in 1996 in response to concerns over inmate-related litigation. While the PLRA does not change an inmate's substantive rights, it does establish guidelines (such as requiring exhaustion of grievances). It also focuses on the use of consent decrees by federal judges.[6]

The PLRA defines *consent decree* as "any relief entered by the court that is based in whole or in part upon the consent or acquiescence of the parties but does not include private settlements." *Relief* is defined as all relief that may be granted or approved by the court and includes consent decrees. Under the PLRA, the court may not grant or approve prospective relief in any civil action with respect to prison conditions unless it finds (1) the relief is narrowly drawn, (2) extends no further than necessary to correct the violation of a federal right, and (3) is the least intrusive means necessary to correct that violation. The court is also required to give substantial weight to any adverse impact that the proposed relief has on public safety or the operation of a criminal justice system. As noted in the prior section, historically, many consent decrees had not met these guidelines. The PLRA places strong constraints on consent decrees in prisoner suits.

The PLRA also addresses existing consent decrees. It provides for termination of a decree, upon the motion of any party or intervener, no later than two years after the date the court granted or approved the prospective relief; one year after the court has entered an order denying termination of prospective relief; or, for orders issued on or before the date of enactment of the PLRA, two years from the date of the law's enactment. A party can move for immediate termination of the prospective relief if the conditions mandated by the statute are not met. A different section of the PLRA concerns special masters and includes limitations on their powers and duties, including a prohibition against their making findings or communications *ex parte* (on one side only). These provisions reflect Congress's intent to limit judicial management of prisons.

The case of *Miller v. French,* 530 U.S. 327 (2000), dates back to 1975, when inmates at the Pendleton (Indiana) Correctional Facility brought a class action lawsuit under 42 U.S.C. Section 1983. The district court found constitutional violations of the Eighth Amendment, and the appeals court affirmed in part. Injunctive relief was ordered, remaining in effect through the current litigation, with the last modification occurring in 1988. In 1997, the state, citing the PLRA, filed a motion to end the relief and the continuing oversight of the federal courts. Inmates sued, asking the district court to stop implementation of the PLRA's automatic stay provision[7] (here, involving temporary suspension of the court-ordered injunctive relief), saying that it violated the separation of powers doctrine. The lower courts held that the statutory stay provision impermissibly limited the courts' powers. The Supreme Court disagreed and reversed, with the language:

> **The entry of the stay does not reopen or 'suspend' the previous judgment …. [T]he stay merely reflects the changed legal circumstances—that prospective relief under the existing decree is no longer enforceable, and remains unenforceable unless and until the court makes the findings required by [18 U.S.C.] § 3626(b)(3).**

Gilmore v. People of the State of California, 220 F.3d 987 (9th Cir. 2000), examined the constitutionality of the provisions of the PLRA that require termination of prospective relief in prison condition cases. Pursuant to the PLRA, state officials filed for the termination of court orders (dating back to 1972) and consent decrees (dating back to 1980). The federal appeals court noted the following: "No circuit court has found the PLRA to violate due process or the Equal Protection Clause …. We decline to stray from these precedents."

The court in *Inmates of Suffolk County Jail v. Rouse,* 129 F.3d 649 (1st Cir. 1997), also rejected the inmates' attack on the PLRA's termination provisions. The case dated back to 1971 and involved conditions of confinement, primarily the double-bunking of pretrial detainees. A 1979 consent decree ratified an architectural plan for a new facility with single-occupancy cells and a phasing out of the old jail. For various reasons, the new facility was not completed until mid-1990, and there was difficulty from the start in providing single occupancy in its cells. Modifications of the consent decree occurred in 1985, 1990, and 1994. Passage of the PLRA was followed by the state government asking the court to terminate the consent decree. The district court upheld the PLRA's constitutionality and said it would not order enforcement of the consent decree's provisions. The court, however, refused to vacate the decree or terminate its obligations because these were undertaken by agreement of the parties and with court approval. An appeal was filed by both parties.

The appeals court ordered termination of the consent decree. This appeals court found the PLRA legislation to be rational and upheld its provisions against the constitutional objections that inmates had brought. The court drew the following conclusion:

> Under the PLRA, the courthouse doors remain open and the withdrawal of prospective relief—above and beyond what is necessary to correct the violation of federally protected rights—does not diminish the right of access …. [W]hile there is a constitutional right to court access, there is no complementary constitutional right to receive or be eligible for a particular form of relief.
>
> A statute that neither abridges a fundamental right nor operates against a suspect class receives rational basis review when it is challenged under the Equal Protection Clause …. The PLRA is such a statute: … it does not impair a fundamental right.

In *Imprisoned Citizens v. Ridge,* 169 F.3d 178 (3rd Cir. 1999), an appellate court reached a similar conclusion:

> The termination provision [of the PLRA] does not deny prisoners "a reasonably adequate opportunity to present claimed violations of fundamental constitutional rights to the courts." ***Lewis v. Casey,*** 518 U.S. 343, 351 (1996) …. The provision therefore does not infringe any identified fundamental right, and is subject to only rational basis review.
>
> While [18 U.S.C.] § 3626(b)(2) [providing for immediate termination of prospective relief] admittedly singles out certain prisoner rights cases for special treatment, it does so only to advance unquestionably legitimate purposes—to minimize prison micro-management by federal courts and to conserve judicial resources …. "[I]t is not the role of courts, but that of the political branches, to shape the institutions of government in such fashion as to comply with the laws and the Constitution."

At this point, you may think that the PLRA's termination provisions provide almost a sure way for prison administrators to end obligations previously agreed to (either by themselves or their predecessors). Keeping in mind that pre-PLRA consent decrees were likely to be broader in scope, this may be a fair assumption. However, as shown in *Benjamin v. Fraser,* 264 F.3d 175 (2nd Cir. 2001), this is not always the case.

The plaintiffs in *Benjamin* and several related cases were pretrial detainees. Suit was first brought in 1975, alleging that conditions in New York City jails violated the inmates' constitutional rights. The original consent decrees dated to 1978 and 1979. The New York City Department of Corrections attempted to terminate operation of the decrees, pursuant to PLRA provisions. The district court granted relief, terminating consent decrees that called for judicial supervision over restrictive housing, inmate correspondence, and law libraries. But the court denied termination of the decrees that involved attorney visitation and the proper use of restraints on inmates.

The district court's action was appealed. Looking just at the issue of attorney visitation, the appeals court supported the lower court's retention of this part of the earlier decrees. The court observed that the corrections department offered no justification for allowing family visits, but not attorney visits, during counts; no reasons why the process of bringing detainees to the counsel rooms could not begin upon the attorney's arrival at the prison, rather than his arrival at the visiting area[8]; and no reasons why a space reservation policy could not be used in those institutions with limited visiting areas. The appeals court found the measures ordered to be reasonable to safeguard the detainees' constitutional rights at minimal cost to the department and without impairing institutional concerns. The appeals court affirmed the "continuing need for prospective relief to correct an ongoing denial of a federal right, and that the relief ordered was sufficiently narrow to satisfy the requirements of the PLRA." When there are good, historic reasons, the provisions of a consent decree (even though it is many years old) may be continued, even though the PLRA facilitates the termination of many decrees.

The PLRA does not inhibit a federal court from ensuring that prisons are operated in a constitutional manner when challenged under Section 1983. When it comes to the constitutional requirements of running government, the courts must have some means of ensuring that constitutional standards are met. The government (theoretically) does not have to run prisons. (In the 1970s, Vermont, because of increasing prison problems, tried to get out of the prison business altogether by closing its prisons and sending all people who were sentenced in Vermont courts to places outside the state, which were willing to contract to take them. See *Howe v. Smith,* 452 U.S. 473 (1981). But, if a state is going to run a prison, it must meet the minimum constitutional standards set for prisons. (Vermont had to see that its prisoners were properly cared for—court action by inmates transferred out of the state ensured that.) The courts have the challenge of enforcing the orders to bring prison or jail conditions up to those minimum constitutional standards. Prior to the PLRA, one widespread problem was that court orders and consent decrees of the 1970s and 1980s dealt with literally hundreds of items that inmates (as well as judges, and even administrators) wanted to see changed but that had no relationship to a constitutional requirement. The PLRA has addressed this concern about court orders and consent decrees that cover multiple issues for unlimited amounts of time. More on judicial intervention in prison conditions will be discussed later; in particular, see the Supreme Court's discussion in *Wilson v. Seiter* that appears later in this chapter.

▶ *Bell v. Wolfish*

The first Supreme Court case dealing with conditions of confinement and interpreting the Eighth Amendment was *Bell v. Wolfish,* 441 U.S. 520 (1979). You will recall that this case was discussed earlier on several collateral issues: the publisher-only rule for incoming publications and the inspection of personal packages, as well as the requirement for inmates to be present during searches of their rooms and the issue of searches of body cavities during strip searches. *Wolfish* arose as a class action by the inmates of the Metropolitan Correctional Center (MCC) in New York City, operated by the Federal Bureau of Prisons. The MCC housed pretrial detainees who were awaiting trial in federal court, along with a number of inmates who were already convicted and serving sentences. It was opened in 1975. That same year, inmates filed the suit, challenging the conditions in the MCC on almost every front.

The planned capacity for the MCC was 449 inmates, who were to be housed primarily in rooms designed for single occupancy. About 60 inmates were to be housed in dormitories, large open rooms with bunks and minimal physical separations for privacy. Because of rapid increases in the numbers of commitments from the local courts, the number of persons confined at the MCC rose quickly. The MCC's planned capacity was exceeded shortly after it opened. To provide sleeping space, the single bunks in the dormitories and in the single rooms were replaced with double bunks. Often, new arrivals had to sleep on cots in the common areas (used for watching television or other recreation purposes) until space became available in the regular rooms. While the complaints of the inmates, and the orders of the lower court in this case, dealt with many issues, we will address the principal issue and holding of the case, the so-called double-bunking issue. The constitutional question was, is it permissible to place two (or more) inmates in a space planned or designed for one person? Is it a constitutional violation to "overcrowd"— that is, to place many more people into a jail than it was designed to hold?

In *Wolfish,* the Supreme Court addressed overcrowding, or double bunking, with respect to pretrial detainees. The lower courts had started (as most federal courts had done in other jail cases) with the premise that these people were to be treated as innocent until they were proved guilty. This was not the same as requiring compliance with "contemporary standards of decency," which would be required by the cruel and unusual punishment clause of the Eighth Amendment. Rather, pretrial detainees, according to those lower courts, could be subjected only to those "restrictions and privations" that were inherent in the confinement itself (restriction of their freedom to come and go as they pleased), which were justified by compelling necessities of jail administration. The insistence on showing "compelling necessity" was central to the rulings for the inmates in the lower courts, which had found double-bunking unconstitutional. It was a prevalent approach among federal courts before *Wolfish.*

The Supreme Court rejected the "compelling necessity" test, finding no source for it in the Constitution. The Court also dismissed the "presumption of innocence" analysis, pointing out that that presumption is only a doctrine that governs the burden of proof in criminal trials and that it has no application to a determination of the rights of an accused person who is being confined before trial.

It is the due process clauses of the Constitution, not the Eighth Amendment, which protects a pretrial detainee from certain conditions and restrictions. (The Eighth Amendment deals with punishments, which cannot be cruel and unusual. A pretrial detainee, having not been convicted, cannot be punished at all. Therefore, the "cruel and unusual" proscriptions of that amendment do not apply.)

[W]hat is at issue when an aspect of pretrial detention that is not alleged to violate any express guarantee of the Constitution [such as a free speech, religion, or search question] is challenged, is the detainee's right to be free from punishment …. In evaluating the constitutionality of conditions or restrictions of pretrial detention … we think that the proper inquiry is whether those conditions amount to punishment of the detainee.

Under the due process clauses, the detainee is entitled to be protected against deprivation of their liberty without due process of law. That is the standard for evaluating the conditions of their confinement in general, and in particular, whether double bunking is permissible:

For under the Due Process Clause, a detainee may not be punished prior to an adjudication of guilt in accordance with due process of law.

Therefore, to ascertain whether there has been a due process—a constitutional—violation, the question is whether the detainee has been punished. How does one ascertain that?

Not every disability imposed during pretrial detention amounts to "punishment" in the constitutional sense …. [The government, everyone agrees, can detain a person awaiting trial, and it must be able to use the devices necessary to achieve detention.] Loss of freedom of choice and privacy are inherent incidents of confinement in such a facility. And the fact that such detention interferes with

the detainee's understandable desire to live as comfortably as possible and with as little restraint as possible during confinement does not convert the conditions or restrictions of detention into "punishment."

But how does a court ascertain whether the conditions amount to "punishment"?

A court must decide whether the disability is imposed for the purpose of punishment or whether it is but an incident of some other legitimate governmental purpose. Absent a showing of an expressed intent to punish on the part of detention facility officials, that determination generally will turn on "whether an alternative purpose to which [the restriction] may rationally be connected is assignable for it, and whether it appears excessive in relation to the alternative purpose assigned [to it]."

The Court summarized as follows:

[I]f a particular condition or restriction of pretrial detention is reasonably related to a legitimate governmental objective, it does not, without more, amount to "punishment."

On the other hand,

[I]f a restriction or condition is not reasonably related to a legitimate goal—if it is arbitrary or purposeless—a court permissibly may infer that the purpose of the governmental action is punishment that may not constitutionally be inflicted upon detainees.

With these holdings, correctional officials have the yardstick to measure whether conditions in a jail are unconstitutional. The Court then applied these criteria to the specific jail conditions claims made by the detainees in *Wolfish*:

[T]he Government must be able to take steps to maintain security and order at the institution .... Restraints that are reasonably related to the institution's interest in maintaining jail security do not, without more, constitute unconstitutional punishment .... On this record, we are convinced as a matter of law that "double-bunking" as practiced at the MCC did not amount to punishment and did not, therefore, violate [inmates'] rights under the Due Process Clause .... While confining a given number of people in a given amount of space in such a manner as to cause them to endure genuine privations and hardship over an extended period of time might raise serious questions under the Due Process Clause as to whether those conditions amounted to punishment, nothing even approaching such hardship is shown by this record.

Wolfish is important on two critical points: it provides the standard for measuring the constitutionality of conditions for pretrial detainees, and it ruled that double-bunking is not per se unconstitutional. (Many courts had ruled that double-bunking was per se unconstitutional and that putting more inmates into a living space than the number it was designed for was always impermissible. The Court in *Wolfish* said that crowding, at least under the conditions at the MCC, was permissible and not a constitutional violation.[9]) Once a court creates a baseline of constitutionally acceptable conditions, challenges to other jail conditions are made by alleging the conditions are far worse than those spelled out at the New York MCC. (This is called "distinguishing the case." Attorneys for jail inmates who claim crowded or other unconstitutional conditions will you point out to the court how different the conditions are in their client's jail, distinguishing those conditions from the MCC and the "double-bunking is okay" ruling of *Wolfish*.) The *Wolfish* decision has allowed jails to be double-bunked and otherwise crowded, so long as conditions do not become "genuine privations and hardship over an extended period of time." The prevention of such privations and hardships is a challenge for jail administrators, one that can often be met by sound correctional management and the effective use of those resources that are available, even though they may be less than ideal.

The *Wolfish* opinion also establishes the necessity for identifying the precise constitutional source of the right sought to be protected. Pretrial detainees are not protected by the prohibition against "cruel and unusual punishment" in the Eighth Amendment. Instead, protection is found in the due process clauses of the Fifth (for persons in federal custody) and Fourteenth (for persons in state custody) Amendments. When analyzing a claim that would fall under the Eighth Amendment if made by a convicted and sentenced prisoner, it is imperative to identify the precise status of the prisoner making that claim so that the proper constitutional analysis can be considered and applied.

▶ *Rhodes v. Chapman*

In *Estelle v. Gamble* (1976) (discussed in detail in Chapter 16 on Healthcare) the Supreme Court announced that the Eighth Amendment is violated when prison officials are deliberately indifferent to the serious medical needs of an inmate. This requires an analysis of two separate components: the objective component-is the alleged injury sufficiently serious, and a subjective component-what was the state of mind of the government actor, which in *Gamble* was deemed to be deliberate indifference. Subsequent Supreme Court cases have continued this dual component standard when addressing the Eighth Amendment claims in prisons by providing guidance on either the subjective or objective component of the standard. In reviewing the following cases, please consider whether the issue before the Court relates to the objective or subjective component, or in some cases, both.

Because of the way the *Wolfish* case developed, the double-bunking issue was decided in *Wolfish* only for pretrial detainees. (The other issues, concerning searches and mail, were decided for both the pretrial detainees and the sentenced inmates.) This left double-bunking in prisons for sentenced inmates as an issue to be decided in another case, which the Supreme Court did very soon thereafter in *Rhodes v. Chapman,* 452 U.S. 337 (1981). The single issue in that case was "whether the housing of two inmates in a single cell at the Southern Ohio Correctional Facility is cruel and unusual punishment prohibited by the Eighth and Fourteenth Amendments."

Ohio inmates brought this Section 1983 action, claiming that double celling in the maximum-security state prison at Lucasville resulted in inmates having to live too closely together and further claiming that this crowding strained the prison's facilities and staff. Like the MCC, in *Wolfish,* the Lucasville prison was new. It opened in the early 1970s and contained 1,620 cells, with each cell measuring 63 square feet. (The number of square feet in a cell, or per inmate, was very important in prison standards and guidelines, which were published by professional organizations and others and had been relied on in a number of court decisions in deciding whether conditions were unconstitutional.) Each cell at Lucasville had a bed, a nightstand, a sink, and a toilet. When commitments to Ohio prisons rose, double-tiered bunks were placed in the cells. Like most prisons, there were also "day rooms," which were adjacent to the cell block areas, which were furnished with television sets, card tables, and chairs. At the time of the lawsuit, Lucasville held 2,300 inmates, most of whom were serving either life or long-term sentences. Most inmates had to spend about 25% of their time in their cells; they were allowed to spend the rest of the time at work, at meals, in the showers, in the day rooms, at school, in the library, or other recreation areas. Some inmates were restricted to their cells for longer hours for security and control purposes.

The district court (trial court) had concluded that double celling at Lucasville was cruel and unusual punishment. This decision was based on five factors: (1) inmates were serving long terms of imprisonment there; (2) the institution was 38% over its "design capacity," and this led to limitation of movement as well as "physical and mental injury from long exposure"; (3) the court relied on studies that recommended that each person in a prison should have 50 to 55 square feet of living-quarters space; (4) a prisoner who was double celled had to spend most of his time in his cell with a cellmate; and (5) double celling had become the long-term practice at Lucasville—it was not temporary.

The Supreme Court rejected the district court's reliance on those five factors as showing constitutional violation of the cruel and unusual punishment clause: "These general considerations fall far short in themselves of proving cruel and unusual punishment …. At most, these considerations amount to a theory that double celling inflicts pain."

The Court presented a brief review of the standards that have been used to interpret those three words—cruel and unusual. The Court noted that it is not a static test but one that has been interpreted "in a flexible and dynamic manner." Clearly, the Eighth Amendment goes beyond the original concern over barbarous physical punishments:

Conditions must not involve the wanton and unnecessary infliction of pain, nor may they be grossly disproportionate to the severity of the crime warranting imprisonment.

That is the current "standard of decency" that must be used to measure whether conditions amount to cruel and unusual punishment.

In an interesting observation in a footnote, the Court brushed aside reliance on experts, or the standards adopted by various organizations as pointing the way to "contemporary standards of decency." Regarding an organization's standards, "they simply do not establish the constitutional minima; rather, they establish goals recommended by the organization in question." As to the opinions of experts, the Court said that they cannot weigh as heavily in determining contemporary standards of decency as "the public attitude toward a given sanction" (citing

Gregg v. Georgia, 428 U.S. 153 (1976), a death penalty case). The Court observed, "We could agree that double celling is not desirable, especially in view of the size of these cells. But there is no evidence in this case that double celling is viewed generally as violating decency." Very few correctional administrators would prefer to manage a double-bunked institution rather than one that is single celled.

Applying these "contemporary standards of decency," the Supreme Court found no cruel and unusual punishment in double-bunking per se, or in the conditions that prevailed at the Lucasville prison.

> **[T]here is no evidence that double celling under these circumstances either inflicts unnecessary or wanton pain or is grossly disproportionate to the severity of crimes warranting imprisonment.**

Along the way, the Court also made some interesting observations:

> **[T]he Constitution does not mandate comfortable prisons.**

Prisons of necessity produce some discomfort, the Court said. It is up to prison administrators and legislators, rather than courts, to weigh the conditions and decide how best to resolve problems of prison population pressures. Inquiries in lawsuits into prison conditions "spring from constitutional requirements … rather than a court's idea of how best to operate a … facility."

> **Courts certainly have a responsibility to scrutinize claims of cruel and unusual confinement, and conditions in a number of prisons, especially older ones, have justly been described as "deplorable" and "sordid" [citing *Wolfish*]. When conditions of confinement amount to cruel and unusual punishment, "federal courts will discharge their duty to protect constitutional rights" [citing *Procunier v. Martinez*, 416 U.S. 396 (1974)].**

▶ *Brown v. Plata*

A major decision on overcrowding—a decision with huge impact on statewide prison operations—was *Brown v. Plata*, 563 U.S. 493 (2011). California prisons had been under class action litigation in two cases (one case involving inmates with serious mental disorders and the second involving inmates with serious medical conditions) for many years. Each district court determined that to correct the constitutional violation, a reduction in the California Department of Corrections' prison population was needed. Pursuant to 18 U.S.C. § 3626(a) of the Prison Litigation Reform Act (PLRA), the district court judges in each case independently requested a three-judge court be convened. The Chief Judge of the Court of Appeals for the Ninth Circuit agreed, and the two cases were consolidated. The three-judge court found deplorable conditions which amounted to impermissible, unconstitutional treatment of inmates. After other attempts to correct the problems failed, the lower (three-judge) court concluded that the only way to achieve that result was to require reduction of the overall prison population in the state. An order to that effect was entered and was appealed by the state to the Supreme Court. (A direct appeal to the Supreme Court was authorized from a finding of unconstitutional action by a three-judge court.)

The Supreme Court first had to determine whether the case was properly handled in the courts by the stringent requirements of the PLRA. The Court found that, pursuant to the PLRA, the three-judge court was a proper way to review the sweeping allegations of unconstitutional state actions. Only a three-judge district court could order release of prisoners to cure systemic violations of constitutional rights; a single-judge court could not. Further, the lower courts had given the state several years to remedy the conditions, including actions beyond simply reducing the prison population. The unconstitutional, Eighth Amendment violations continued.

The Court found that the procedural requirements of the PLRA were met and that the case was ripe for Supreme Court review. But what was the violation of the Constitution? From the earlier cases on prison crowding courts have ruled that having prison populations over (even considerably over) planned capacity does not in itself create a constitutional violation. There must be a separate violation (or several violations) found, to warrant court intervention. Remedies taken must be designed to remedy those specific violations.

Here, the constitutional violations centered on two factors: the failure to provide minimal, basic care to inmates with serious mental illnesses and deficiencies in adequate medical care (the state had even conceded that medical care was so deficient as to be in violation of inmates' Eighth Amendment rights). Attempts to provide adequate medical and mental health care had failed. The basic cause of this system-wide deficiency was found to be the overcrowded state of the prisons.

FIGURE 15-1 Inmates at the California Institute for Men in Chino, CA, sit in crowded conditions.
© Anonymous/AP/Shutterstock

California's prisons were designed to hold about 80,000 inmates. At the time of trial, the population was about 156,000. For many years, the prisons had operated with almost double the numbers they were designed for, which resulted in exceptionally severely crowded conditions. See **FIGURE 15-1**. (In an unusual step in a Court opinion, photographs of some living conditions were included in the opinion. They show, for example, where "as many as 200 prisoners may live in a gymnasium, monitored by as few as two or three correctional officers.") How does this become a constitutional violation? Because, as the lower court concluded, and the Supreme Court agreed, there is an overwhelming demand placed on the medical and mental health staff and facilities that are available. (The situation was exacerbated by the fact that there were high vacancy rates for medical and mental health staff.) It was noted, for example, that there could be backlogs of up to 700 prisoners who were waiting to see a doctor, a suicide rate "approaching an average of one per week," and urgent specialty referrals "pending for six months to a year." The crowding was found to create unsanitary living conditions and increased violence, which are problems by themselves, but which could also aggravate mental health problems in prisoners with latent illnesses.

The Court concluded that overcrowding was the "primary cause" (the required finding under 18 U.S.C. § 3626(a)(3)(E)) of the violations of prisoners' constitutional rights. The Eighth Amendment violation, the cruel and unusual punishment of the prisoners, was found in their "severe and unlawful mistreatment … through grossly inadequate provision of medical and mental health care."

The Court concluded:

> **For years the medical and mental health care provided by California's prisons has fallen short of minimum constitutional requirements and has failed to meet prisoners' basic health needs. Needless suffering and death have been the well-documented result. Over the whole course of years during which this litigation has been pending, no other remedies have been found to be sufficient. Efforts to remedy the violation have been frustrated by severe overcrowding in California's prison system.**

The lower court's order for relief, requiring reduction of the prison population by about 46,000 inmates, was affirmed. (It had been found that, to achieve proper conditions, the population would have to be capped at 137.5% of design capacity.) The Court recognized that the required release of large numbers of prisoners was an exceptional step and a matter of "grave concern."[10] It was emphasized that the release was to be carefully monitored and that the "three-judge court must remain open to a showing or demonstration by either party that the injunction should be altered to ensure that the rights and interests of the parties are given all due and necessary protection." While new construction and out-of-state transfers might accomplish some population reduction, releasing some prisoners before their sentences were fully served would undoubtedly be required.

The state could propose other measures (diverting lower-risk offenders might be one way) to mitigate the severe impact of the order.

The population reduction potentially required is nevertheless of unprecedented sweep and extent.

The reduction of population ordered by the district court was to occur within two years. The Supreme Court noted though that the state should be given latitude to adjust its efforts to correct the constitutional violations, consistent with concerns for public safety, which might allow for extending the time for remedial action up to five years. However:

Without a reduction in overcrowding, there will be no efficacious remedy for the unconstitutional care of the sick and mentally ill in California's prisons.

▶ *Whitley v. Albers*

The two Supreme Court decisions in *Wolfish* and *Rhodes* take care of the broad question of general conditions in a prison facility and the specific questions of double-bunking and crowding. Those cases provide the constitutional standards (the paraphrasing of the Eighth Amendment and Due Process clause language) for evaluating conditions cases. The next cases discussed will consider cruel and unusual punishment claims by an individual inmate, based on the way they were treated.

In *Whitley v. Albers,* 475 U.S. 312 (1986), the Supreme Court considered the claim of an inmate who was shot and seriously injured inside the Oregon State Penitentiary. The shooting occurred during a riot at that prison. Inmates took control of a two-tiered cell block where inmate Albers lived. An officer was taken hostage on the upper tier. Officers formed an assault squad to regain control of the cell block. The security manager, Captain Whitley, led the assault and proceeded to the second tier himself to try to free the hostage. Three officers who were armed with shotguns followed Whitley into the cell block and were given instructions to shoot low at any prisoners who tried to climb the stairs, because they would be a threat to Whitley or the hostage. When Albers started up the stairs, after Whitley had run up, an officer fired a shot that struck Albers in the left knee. (A warning shot had been fired into the wall when the officers first entered the barricaded cell block. Another inmate was shot on the stairs, and several others on the lower tier were also wounded by gunshots.) The hostage was rescued, and the cell block was retaken. Albers filed a Section 1983 claim, alleging Eighth Amendment deprivations because of the physical damage to his knee and mental and emotional distress.

The Supreme Court noted that it is "the unnecessary and wanton infliction of pain" that constitutes cruel and unusual punishment. (This language is cited from *Estelle v. Gamble,* 429 U.S. 97 (1976). The four dissenting justices would limit the standard to those words, "unnecessary and wanton infliction of pain." They objected to the extension of that standard, which the majority adopted.) The Court elaborated further:

It is obduracy and wantonness, not inadvertence or error in good faith, that characterize the conduct prohibited by the Cruel and Unusual Punishments Clause.

Thus, an inmate would have to prove that the injury suffered was caused by an unnecessary and wanton infliction of pain to support a cruel and unusual claim. To some extent, the *Whitley* decision turns on the unusual circumstances that prison authorities faced. Those circumstances posed substantial risks to the safety of prison staff and inmates. In any event, to ascertain whether there was a constitutional violation, the Court identified the following standard:

[W]hether the measure taken inflicted unnecessary and wanton pain and suffering ultimately turns on "whether force was applied in a good faith effort to maintain or restore discipline or maliciously and sadistically for the very purpose of causing harm" [citing *Johnson v. Glick,* 481 F.2d 1028 (2nd Cir. 1973)].

The Court then reviewed and analyzed the factual situation at the Oregon State Penitentiary that led to the shooting and injury of inmate Albers. The Court said that the situation was "dangerous and volatile ... Under these circumstances, the actual shooting was a good-faith effort to restore prison security. As such, it did not violate [Albers'] Eighth Amendment right to be free from cruel and unusual punishments."

Albers also claimed that his rights were violated by taking away his liberty under the Fourteenth Amendment without due process of law. The Court quickly disposed of this claim:

> **We think the Eighth Amendment, which is specifically concerned with the unnecessary and wanton infliction of pain in penal institutions, serves as the primary source of substantive protection to convicted prisoners in cases such as this one, where the deliberate use of force is challenged as excessive and unjustified.**

Thus, a due process claim under the Fourteenth Amendment was summarily dismissed.

When discussing the use of deadly force, it is useful to consider the Supreme Court decision in *Tennessee v. Garner,* 471 U.S. 1 (1985). Although that case involved the shooting of a fleeing suspect by a police officer, its language substantially changed the assumption about when **deadly force** can be used. The Supreme Court established three standards to be met for the use of deadly force: (1) the force must be necessary to prevent the escape of the suspect; (2) there must be probable cause for the officer to believe that the suspect poses "a significant threat of death or serious physical injury to the officer or others"; and (3) if possible, there must be some kind of warning given to the fleeing person before deadly force is used. Especially notable is the fact that there is no reliance on the previous "fleeing felon" rule, which had been used by many U.S. police departments.

In the correctional setting, staff may be called upon to use force against three distinct classes of persons-convicted persons who are protected by the Eighth Amendment; un-convicted detainees protected by the due process clauses of the Fifth (for persons in federal custody) or Fourteenth (for persons in state custody) and free world persons (arrests (seizures) are governed by the Fourth Amendment). The Supreme Court has not decided, and the lower courts are divided, on when an arrestee who has Fourth Amendment protection, becomes a pretrial detainee who has due process clause protection. *Aldini v. Johnson* 609 F.3d 658 (6th Cir. 2010) (arrestee status and Fourth Amendment protection extends at least through booking) and *Miranda-Rivera v. Toledo-Davila,* 813 F.3d 64 (1st Cir. 2016) (the Supreme Court decision in *Kingsley v. Hendrickson* holds that a use of force against a detainee is governed by objective reasonableness on the part of a government actor).

In *Graham v. Conner,* 490 U.S. 386 (1989) the Supreme Court ruled that when an "excessive force claim arises in the context of an arrest or investigatory stop of a free citizen, it is most properly characterized as one invoking the protections of the Fourth Amendment, which guarantees citizens the right "to be secure in their persons . . . against unreasonable. . . seizures" of the person." In *Graham*, the Court also noted:

> **that** *" that the Due Process Clause protects a pretrial detainee from the use of excessive force that amounts to punishment. See* <u>*Bell v. Wolfish,*</u> *(1979). After conviction, the Eighth Amendment "serves as the primary source of substantive protection . . . in cases . . . where the deliberate use of force is challenged as excessive and unjustified."* <u>*Whitley v. Albers,*</u> *(1986). . . . all claims that law enforcement officers have used excessive force — deadly or not — in the course of an arrest, investigatory stop, or other "seizure" of a free citizen should be analyzed under the Fourth Amendment and its "reasonableness" standard, rather than under a "substantive due process" approach."*

Consider the case of an escape from a county jail which houses both sentenced and un-convicted persons. Staff observe two inmates scaling a fence and running towards a vehicle which appears to be operated by two persons in non-prison issue clothing. What level of force can be used, and against which of the individuals? How do staff know if either or both of the two inmates are un-convicted or convicted? What force, if any, can staff use against the free world persons who might be accomplices, or hostages? The differences in the legal standards regarding the use of force towards different classes of persons by correctional staff must be kept in mind in correctional situations. The scope of the issue is magnified if the interaction of prison staff with escaped inmates (and accomplices) occurs away from the institution. While most states authorize the use of force to re-capture escaped offenders, it is not completely clear if the standard used to assess the constitutionality of force is the Eighth, Fourth, Fifth or Fourteenth Amendment?

Every corrections facility should establish a policy on the use of force and should especially define those limited circumstances when deadly force may be used. All staff should be fully trained on those policy guidelines. Failure to follow the facility's use of force procedures could result in the staff member facing criminal prosecution.[11]

▶ *Wilson v. Seiter*

The meaning of the cruel and unusual punishment clause as applied to an individual inmate is rounded out in the decision of the Supreme Court in *Wilson v. Seiter,* 501 U.S. 294 (1991). Wilson, an inmate at the Hocking Correctional Facility in Ohio, claimed under Section 1983 that his Eighth Amendment rights were infringed by his treatment, which involved "overcrowding, excessive noise, insufficient locker storage space, inadequate heating and cooling, improper ventilation, unclean and inadequate restrooms, unsanitary dining facilities and food preparation, and housing with mentally and physically ill inmates."

After reviewing the line of cases that had been used in the development of the guidance for interpreting the Eighth Amendment, the Supreme Court particularly qualified the *Whitley* decision, which was just discussed as applying to circumstances in which officials were reacting to an emergency situation. Wanton misconduct would have to be shown by actions taken "maliciously and sadistically for the very purpose of causing harm." All agreed that the very high state of mind required by *Whitley* does not apply to general prison conditions cases, such as in *Wilson.* But, the Court said, whether the conduct is wanton depends on the state of mind of the prison official. Using the standard of *Estelle v. Gamble,* which relates to health care, the Court said that "deliberate indifference" to the needs of the inmate was the state of mind of the prison official that must be found in order to constitute cruel and unusual punishment.

> **Whether one characterizes the treatment received … as inhumane conditions of confinement, failure to attend to his medical needs, or a combination of both, it is appropriate to apply the "deliberate indifference" standard articulated in *Estelle.***
>
> **The source of the intent requirement is … the Eighth Amendment itself, which bans only cruel and unusual punishment. If the pain inflicted is not formally meted out as punishment by the statute or the sentencing judge, some mental element must be attributed to the inflicting officer before it can qualify.**

This statement increases the burden on inmates to show deliberate indifference by prison officials to support a claim of cruel and unusual punishment. In many instances, the conditions complained about may be a result of such factors as older facilities or a lack of funds. When these are the cause, there is no "mental element," no adverse intent, and thus no "deliberate indifference" to the needs of the inmate.

Another important component of the *Wilson* decision is the Court's consideration of the inmate's claim that a court must look at the overall conditions to decide whether there was cruel and unusual punishment. This approach had been followed by many federal courts in deciding that a prison's conditions were unconstitutional. The Supreme Court rejected that approach.

> **Nothing so amorphous as "overall conditions" can rise to the level of cruel and unusual punishment when no specific deprivation of a single human need exists.**

It is true that some conditions may be viewed in combination with others, the Court said, when they have a "mutually enforcing effect," such as when cells are at a low temperature at night and there are no blankets issued to keep warm. Other cases cited with approval involved the provision of outdoor exercise, which was required in *Spain v. Procunier,* 600 F.2d 189 (9th Cir. 1979), when prisoners were confined in small cells for almost 24 hours a day, but which was not required in *Clay v. Miller,* 626 F.2d 345 (4th Cir. 1980), when prisoners had access to a day room for 18 hours per day.

The Supreme Court, in this part of its decision, is endorsing the approach of *Wright v. Rushen,* 642 F.2d 1129 (9th Cir. 1981), which said that, in examining the constitutionality of conditions of confinement,

> a court should examine each challenged condition of confinement, such as the adequacy of the quarters, food, medical care, etc., and determine whether that condition is compatible with "the evolving standards of decency that mark the progress of a maturing society." Any condition of confinement which passes this test is immune from federal intervention. If no challenged condition fails to meet the test, the entire facility and its administration are immune from Eighth Amendment attack.

Flowing from this approach, if a court finds a violation with respect to a specific condition, the court should order relief with respect to that condition. It does not entitle the court to adopt remedies to bring all aspects of the prison into accord with the court's ideas of what is right and proper for a prison.

In the *Wilson* decision, the case was remanded to the lower courts to determine whether any individual condition violated the "deliberate indifference" standard.

▶ *Hudson v. McMillian; Wilkins v. Gaddy*

The *Hudson* case considered the question of what degree of injury is required before an inmate can claim an Eighth Amendment—cruel and unusual punishment—violation. Hudson, a Louisiana inmate, claimed that he was beaten by guards while he was handcuffed and shackled. He said he sustained minor bruises, some facial swelling, loosened teeth, and a cracked dental plate. The court of appeals set aside an award of damages to Hudson, ruling that to constitute an injury recoverable under the Eighth Amendment there must have been "significant injury," whereas Hudson only showed minor injuries that required no medical attention. The Supreme Court reversed in *Hudson v. McMillian*, 503 U.S. 1 (1992), giving the following reasons:

> **[W]henever prison officials stand accused of using excessive physical force in violation of the Cruel and Unusual Punishments Clause, the core judicial inquiry is that set out in *Whitley*: whether force was applied in a good-faith effort to maintain or restore discipline, or maliciously and sadistically to cause harm …. [T]he extent of injury suffered by an inmate is one factor that may suggest "whether the use of force could plausibly have been thought necessary" in a particular situation …. Thus, courts considering a prisoner's claim must ask both if "the officials act[ed] with a sufficiently culpable state of mind" and if the alleged wrongdoing was objectively "harmful enough" to establish a constitutional violation.**

Regarding the specific question raised by this case, the Court held that a serious injury was not necessary for an inmate to pursue a cruel and unusual punishment claim. A court must look at the particular circumstances of the case. The Court stated that the unjustified striking of an inmate would raise a serious question about the "concepts of dignity, civilized standards, humanity, and decency" that lie behind the Eighth Amendment. This is true, without regard to how severe the inmate's injuries are. Hudson had a claim about cruel and unusual punishment, the Supreme Court said, which had to be looked into by the courts.

In *Wilkins v. Gaddy*, 559 U.S. 34 (2010) (per curiam), Wilkins, the prisoner, stated that the officer had entered his cell and without provocation assaulted him by slamming him to the concrete floor and punching, kicking, kneeing, and choking him. The prisoner stated that because of the beating, he suffered a bruised heel, lower back pain, increased blood pressure, migraine headaches, and dizziness, as well as psychological trauma and mental anguish. The district court dismissed the suit, ruling that Wilkins' injuries were minimal (de minimis) and did not state a claim under the Eighth Amendment. The dismissal was affirmed on appeal. The Supreme Court rejected the lower courts' interpretation that prisoners alleging the use of excessive force must demonstrate a "significant injury" to state an Eighth Amendment claim.

> **Injury and force, however, are only imperfectly correlated, and it is the latter that ultimately counts. An inmate who is gratuitously beaten by guards does not lose his ability to pursue an excessive force claim merely because he has the good fortune to escape without serious injury.**

The court further explained that the ruling in *Hudson v. McMillian* intended to

> **… shift the "core judicial inquiry" from the extent of the injury to the nature of the force—specifically, whether it was nontrivial and "was applied … maliciously and sadistically to cause harm** [citing *Hudson v. McMillian*].

A case further developing the standard of *Hudson* is *Smith v. Mensinger*, 293 F.3d 641 (3rd Cir. 2002). Smith, an inmate in the Pennsylvania prison system, received prison misconduct reports, including one for punching an officer in the eye. Smith alleged he was later handcuffed behind his back. Shortly thereafter, he claimed several officers rammed his head into walls and cabinets and knocked him to the floor, where one officer kicked and punched him. While this was occurring, Smith claimed that another officer saw the beating but made no effort to intervene or restore order. Smith filed suit, alleging constitutional violations of his rights under 42 U.S.C § 1983. The lawsuit named several officers as defendants, including the officer who only saw the beating. The federal court of appeals held that the officer who observed, but did not intervene, could be held liable, provided he had a reasonable opportunity to intervene and simply refused to do so.

> The approving silence emanating from the officer who stands by and watches as others unleash an unjustified assault contributes to the actual use of excessive force, and we cannot ignore the tacit support such silence lends to those who are actually striking the blows. Such silence is an endorsement of the constitutional violation resulting from the illegal use of force.

The court cited *Hudson,* where the supervisor allegedly stood by and told officers who were beating the inmate "not to have too much fun." The court in *Smith* did acknowledge that there could be an even greater degree of "dereliction of duty" for a supervisor than for an officer of lower rank.

As discussed above, the guidance of *Whitley v. Albers, Hudson v. McMillian* and *Wilkins v. Gaddy* provide the constitutional standard for use of force against convicted persons. Until 2015, the Supreme Court had not provided a standard for evaluating use of force claims against un-convicted detainees, and some courts of appeal had used a standard similar to the *Whitley, Hudson, Wilkins* line of cases which evaluated the objective seriousness of the injury and the subjective state of mind of the actor.

An example was *Lewis v. Downey,* 581 F.3d 467 (7th Cir. 2009), a case where the court of appeals was faced with a plaintiff (inmate) who had been found guilty but was awaiting sentencing and the entry of final judgment. The inmate stated that while he was in his cell, correctional staff had ordered him to stand up, but due to illness (he had been on a hunger strike), he was unable to promptly comply. Correctional staff then tasered the inmate. The district court had granted summary judgment to the correctional personnel, in part because the district court concluded that use of the taser was a minimal use of force. The court of appeals reversed the district court's grant of summary judgment for the officer who fired the taser. In its decision, the court noted that the Supreme Court has not decided what precise constitutional provision protects a detainee from excessive force. The court of appeals ruled that conduct which would violate the Eighth Amendment "cruel and unusual punishment" clause would also violate the due process rights of the detainee under the Fourteenth Amendment. The court of appeals also ruled that a legal analysis of excessive force claims must assess the pain suffered, not necessarily the injury caused. The court concluded that the use of a taser against a prisoner is more than a minimal use of force. The court noted this conclusion shifted the focus "*away from the act and to the actor, away from the objective to the subjective …. What matters—and what will generally be the decisive factor in cases such as this—is the mindset of the individual applying the force.*"

In *Kingsley v. Hendrickson,* 576 U.S. 389 (2015), the Court provided guidance on how claims of excessive use of force arising under the Due Process clause should be analyzed. Michael Kingsley was a detainee in a county jail and alleged jail officials had used excessive force against him. The Court noted that circuit courts were split as to whether such claims required an assessment of the state actor's subjective state of mind or whether the conduct should be analyzed under the "objectively reasonable" standard which required no analysis of the actor's state of mind. The Court reversed the court of appeals and ruled that a detainee alleging an excessive use of force must only prove the force was objectively unreasonable.

In reaching this conclusion the Court relied on its previous cases addressing the rights of detainees. In *Bell v. Wolfish* the Court had ruled that in the absence of an expressed intent to punish, "*a pretrial detainee can prevail by providing only objective evidence that the challenged governmental action is not rationally related to a legitimate governmental objective or that it is excessive in relation to that purpose.*"

In determining reasonableness, courts may consider the following factors:

> *. . . the relationship between the need for the use of force and the amount of force used; the extent of the plaintiff's injury; any effort made by the officer to temper or to limit the amount of force; the severity of the security problem at issue; the threat reasonably perceived by the officer; and whether the plaintiff was actively resisting. . . . We do not consider this list to be exclusive.*

This case is discussed in greater detail in Chapter 20 Jails.

▶ *Farmer v. Brennan*

Farmer was a biological male who was medically diagnosed as a transsexual. Before being committed to prison, he had undergone estrogen therapy, received silicone breast implants, and undergone unsuccessful testicular surgery. He was placed in the Federal Penitentiary at Terre Haute, Indiana. He wore clothes in a feminine manner and took hormonal drugs (he said) that were smuggled to him in prison. He was usually segregated from the general prison population because of his own misconduct and also for his safety. (He was in a male institution, because doctors said he was still biologically a male.) He was released into regular population at the Terre Haute prison, without any objection by him. Within two weeks, he said he was beaten and raped by another inmate.

Farmer filed a Bivens suit (the equivalent of a Section 1983 action) against federal officials, claiming that he had been cruelly and unusually punished when he was transferred to the prison where officials knew there were assaultive inmates and where Farmer would be particularly vulnerable to sexual attack. He claimed that this was deliberate indifference to his personal safety, and he sought damages and an injunction that he not be placed in a penitentiary (a high-security institution) in the future. The lower courts granted summary judgment to the prison officials on the grounds that they could be held liable only if they had actual knowledge of a potential danger to Farmer, which had not been shown. In *Farmer v. Brennan*, 511 U.S. 825, (1994), the Supreme Court vacated the judgment of the lower courts and remanded the case for further consideration based on the guidelines that it laid down.

The Court made these observations and holdings:

The [Eighth] Amendment imposes duties on [prison] officials, who must provide humane conditions of confinement; prison officials must ensure that inmates receive adequate food, clothing, shelter and medical care, and must "take reasonable measures to guarantee the safety of the inmates" [citing *Hudson v. Palmer*, 468 U.S. 517 (1984)] …. [P]rison officials have a duty … to protect prisoners from violence at the hands of other prisoners.

This does not mean, however, that every injury suffered by an inmate at the hands of another inmate leads to constitutional liability for the prison officials.

[A] prison official violates the Eighth Amendment only when two requirements are met. First, the deprivation alleged must be, objectively, "sufficiently serious" [citing *Wilson v. Seiter*] … The second requirement follows from the principle that "only the unnecessary and wanton infliction of pain implicates the Eighth Amendment." To violate the Cruel and Unusual Punishments Clause, a prison official must have a "sufficiently culpable state of mind." In prison-conditions cases that state of mind is one of "deliberate indifference" to inmate health or safety.

Taking those principles from *Wilson,* the Court held:

[A] prison official may be held liable under the Eighth Amendment for denying humane conditions of confinement only if he knows that inmates face a substantial risk of serious harm and disregards that risk by failing to take reasonable measures to abate it.

In *Farmer,* the case was remanded to see whether the conditions met these standards laid down by the Court. The district court had given great weight to the fact that Farmer had not given officials notice of the risk of harm that he feared. That fact, the Court said, was not enough to dispose of the case. The lower court would have to examine the evidence, the Supreme Court said, to see if officials had other reason to know that the inmate faced "substantial risk of serious harm" and failed to take reasonable steps to avoid that risk.

▶ *Helling v. McKinney*

Helling v. McKinney is a case that could be classified as one relating to healthcare. However, the case also addresses the standard for determining what is cruel and unusual punishment in conditions of confinement.

McKinney, a Nevada inmate, filed suit under 42 U.S.C. § 1983. He claimed that his involuntary exposure to environmental tobacco smoke (ETS) posed an unreasonable risk to his health in violation of the Eighth Amendment. In *Helling v. McKinney,* 509 U.S. 25 (1993), the Supreme Court agreed that he had a good constitutional claim.

McKinney complained that he was assigned to a cell with an inmate who smoked several packs of cigarettes a day. He also said that cigarettes were sold in the prison without warning of the health hazards they posed to nonsmoking inmates and that some cigarettes were burning continuously, releasing chemicals into the prison air. Finally, he claimed to suffer from health problems that were caused by exposure to ETS.

The first court that considered McKinney's claims granted a directed verdict to the defendant prison officials, ruling that the inmate had no constitutional right to be free from tobacco smoke. The Ninth Circuit Court of Appeals reversed that ruling, saying that the inmate had stated a valid claim under the Eighth Amendment by alleging that he had been exposed to levels of ETS that posed an unreasonable risk of harm to his future health. The Supreme Court sent that ruling back to the court of appeals, to reconsider its decision in light of the intervening decision in *Wilson v. Seiter* (in other words, to apply the standard of that case). The court of appeals reinstated its previous ruling, using the *Wilson* standard.

In its *Helling* decision, the Supreme Court restated the basic rule that, under the Eighth Amendment, prison authorities may not be deliberately indifferent to an inmate's health problems. But does this standard apply only to current health problems, or does it also apply to the risk of future problems?

The Amendment ... requires that inmates be furnished with the basic human needs, one of which is "reasonable safety." It is "cruel and unusual punishment to hold convicted criminals in unsafe conditions." It would be odd to deny an injunction to inmates who plainly proved an unsafe, life-threatening condition in their prison on the ground that nothing yet had happened to them.

In an amicus brief (a brief filed by an interested person who is not a party in the case before the court), the United States (the federal government) agreed that there might be situations in which exposure to toxic or dangerous substances would pose a risk of sufficient likelihood and magnitude that the protection of the Eighth Amendment should be given, even though the effects might not be shown for some time. But the government argued that exposure to ETS was not a sufficiently grave and certain risk to pose a "serious medical need" (the preliminary and objective standard for examining health claims), keeping in mind that the amendment is to be used to protect "current standards of decency." The Supreme Court did not agree with this argument but approved the approach of the court of appeals, which said that McKinney's claim alleged ETS exposure, which posed an unreasonable danger to his future health.

McKinney also argued that current standards of decency do not support such involuntary exposure as he was required to encounter in the prison and that prison officials were deliberately indifferent to his concerns. The case was returned for the lower court to inquire into his allegations (by trial or by discovery), to see whether he could prove an Eighth Amendment violation based on ETS exposure.

McKinney states a cause of action under the Eighth Amendment by alleging that [prison officials] have, with deliberate indifference, exposed him to levels of ETS that pose an unreasonable risk of serious damage to his future health.

The Court ended by pointing out things that McKinney would have to prove: (1) that he was being exposed to unreasonably high levels of ETS; (2) that the intervening adoption of a smoking policy in the prisons, including the establishment of a number of nonsmoking areas, did not sufficiently reduce risks to McKinney; (3) that the risks he complained of violated "contemporary standards of decency," as opposed to risks that today's society chooses to tolerate; and (4) that the prison officials had shown "deliberate indifference" to substantial risks to McKinney's future health by their attitudes and conduct. The first two elements are difficult enough for the inmate to prove, but the last two—proving society's current attitudes and proving officials' indifference to ETS risks—would likely be extremely difficult. Indeed, the Supreme Court concluded its opinion by noting that the adoption by Nevada officials, while the case was being litigated, of a smoking policy that offered protections to nonsmokers (and how it was in fact enforced) might indeed make it very difficult to show that officials were ignoring the dangers of ETS.

The third and fourth elements outlined by the Court were later addressed in another case, *Atkinson v. Taylor*, 316 F.3d 257 (3rd Cir. 2003). Atkinson was a blind, diabetic prisoner in Delaware and was a former pack-a-day smoker. He shared a cell with constant smokers. One of his complaints was that he was exposed, with deliberate indifference, to constant smoking (ETS) in his cell for more than seven months, leading to nausea, the inability to eat, headaches, chest pains, difficulty breathing, and other symptoms. Atkinson's requests to prison officials to change these conditions essentially went unanswered. He filed suit under 42 U.S.C. § 1983, claiming prison officials violated his Eighth Amendment rights by exposing him to ETS that created a serious medical need and posed unreasonable risk of harm.

As to "contemporary standards of decency," the court of appeals noted that, since 1993, "almost every Court of Appeals that has addressed this issue has recognized that a prisoner's right to be free from levels of ETS that pose an unreasonable risk of future harm was clearly established by *Helling*." Also, the court noted that Atkinson had presented evidence that "society has become unwilling to tolerate the imposition on anyone of continuous unwanted risks of second-hand smoke."

As to whether officials were deliberately indifferent, the court observed that a prisoner cannot simply walk out of his cell whenever he wishes. "When a susceptible prisoner is confined to a cell, a small and confined space, with a 'constant' smoker for an extended period of time, such symptoms may transform what would otherwise be a passing annoyance into a serious ongoing medical need." Atkinson produced evidence that, after telling prison officials about his sensitivity to ETS, no change was made in his housing conditions. This evidence, the court concluded, demonstrated deliberate indifference on the part of prison officials.

In *Reilly v. Grayson,* 310 F.3d 519 (6th Cir. 2002), an asthmatic inmate, Reilly, charged state prison officials in Michigan with violation of his Eighth Amendment right to be free from cruel and unusual punishment. Reilly said he complained repeatedly to prison officials that his medical problems were made worse by failure to house him in an area free of second-hand smoke (ETS). He claimed that this exposed him to an unreasonable risk of harm to his health and constituted deliberate indifference to his serious medical needs. In the district (trial) court, he was awarded $36,500 in compensatory damages and $18,250 in punitive damages against the officials, plus attorney fees in the amount of $51,786.

The federal appeals court for the Sixth Circuit followed the Supreme Court's decision in *Helling* and one of its own circuit cases, both of which emphasized the right to be free from exposure to second-hand smoke. This court emphasized the defendants' failure to respond to the repeated medical staff recommendations that Reilly be moved to a smoke-free environment. The court found sufficient evidence in the record to show that the inmate suffered both an increase in the severity of his asthma and the risk of future damage to his health as a result of his exposure to ETS. Punitive damages were seen as appropriate based on the defendants' "reckless ... disregard of Reilly's rights." Indicative of the potential impact of an adverse ruling in a Section 1983 action, the *Reilly* holding required that all compensatory and punitive damages and attorney fees be paid by the warden and two deputy wardens who were found liable in their personal capacities for the harm caused and for the constitutional violations of Reilly's rights.[12]

▶ Qualified Immunity

Many of the cases in this text revolve around the grant or denial of qualified immunity to defendants. *Immunity* is a legal concept usually encountered in the criminal setting—persons are given immunity when they are in a protected status and cannot be sued (prosecuted). This may be because they have cooperated with law enforcement personnel or have given testimony to assist prosecutors. This kind of immunity from criminal prosecution is similar to this discussion of immunity from liability in civil cases. Specifically, immunity in Section 1983 actions, in which officials may be personally sued because of alleged violations of the constitutional rights of others.

In the civil area, the broadest kind of immunity is absolute immunity. Under the status of absolute immunity, persons cannot be sued because their actions are protected in the interest of public policy, so long as the actions are taken as part of their official duties. This immunity is available to legislators, judges, prosecutors, and jury members. Absolute immunity is not granted to government officials in the executive branch (except the president). Prison staff members are considered to be executive branch officials.

Lawyers for prison staff members did try to claim absolute immunity for their clients in the case of *Cleavinger v. Saxner,* 474 U.S. 193 (1985). They argued that the purpose of giving immunity is to protect the independence of decision makers and that persons who acted like judges in their government roles should be protected, as judges are. This kind of protection (absolute immunity) had been given to people in government who acted like judges, such as hearing examiners and administrative judges who heard evidence and ruled on controversies (for example, the Federal Trade Commission). The *Cleavinger* case involved a suit against prison disciplinary committee members who had "tried" a case involving an inmate's misconduct, found the inmate "guilty" of that conduct, and imposed punishment for that offense.

The Supreme Court rejected the argument and held that prison officials, even in disciplinary hearings, were not the same as judges and did not have absolute immunity. The Court found that the disciplinary committee members were not independent enough, were not professional hearing officers, and were not bound to procedural requirements that are imposed on judicial officers. The Court compared the prison committee membership to a school board disciplinary process, for which it was decided in *Wood v. Strickland,* 420 U.S. 308 (1975), that members were protected by only qualified immunity and not absolute immunity.

Therefore, qualified immunity, rather than absolute immunity, from personal liability in civil cases is available to prison officials. Claiming qualified immunity is a common defense used by prison staff in Section 1983 lawsuits.

How does this immunity work? In a Section 1983 action, the plaintiffs (inmates) must show that the conduct complained about was in violation of a constitutional right. (Where in the Constitution is protection given against this kind of action?) If this can be shown, it must further be shown that that right was clearly established at the time of the action that is complained about. (What evidence exists to show that the action taken by prison staff members was already prohibited by court decisions prior to the occurrence of that action?) If officials can show that either of these requirements is not met, then they are entitled to qualified immunity—protection against being sued for constitutional violations, under Section 1983. Typically, this argument is made by filing motions on behalf of the defendants (prison officials). If the judge is convinced by the arguments, they will dismiss the lawsuit.[13]

An example of the qualified immunity defense is demonstrated in the case of *Hope v. Pelzer,* 536 U.S. 730 (2002). Hope, who was an inmate in Alabama, had been handcuffed to a hitching post at the prison because of his disruptive conduct. He was cuffed with his hands above the height of his shoulders, and he alleged that this was painful. The first time he was cuffed to the post, he was offered drinking water and was given a bathroom break every fifteen minutes. On a second occasion, he was involved in an altercation with an officer at his chain gang's worksite. Hope was sent back inside the prison, ordered to take off his shirt, and forced to spend the next seven hours attached to the post. This time, he was given one or two water breaks but no bathroom breaks. He filed a Section 1983 action against prison officials, alleging violation of his Eighth Amendment rights. Lower courts granted the officials qualified immunity, with the court of appeals concluding that, although the hitching-post punishment was cruel and unusual, it was not an action that was clearly established as being unconstitutional at the time the officers acted in that way.

The Supreme Court in *Hope* disagreed with the lower courts. At the first stage of analysis, the Court concluded that there had been an Eighth Amendment violation. This was found in the officers' actions of tying Hope to the hitching post when there was no emergency situation that mandated that action, resulting in serious discomfort, including the deprivation of bathroom breaks. Citing *Trop v. Dulles,* 356 U.S. 86 (1958), the Court found that this conduct was a violation of the "basic concept underlying the Eighth Amendment, [which] is nothing less than the dignity of man."

On the second element of qualified immunity analysis, the Court said that the constitutional law was clearly established at the time of the officials' actions. The Court cited the cases of *Gates v. Collier,* 501 F.2d 1291 (5th Cir. 1974), which held that it was unconstitutional to handcuff inmates to the fence or to cells for a long period of time, and *Ort v. White,* 813 F.2d 318 (11th Cir. 1987). In Ort, an inmate had been denied water after he refused to do his assigned work on a farm. That court noted that "physical abuse directed at the prisoner *after* he terminated his resistance to authority would constitute an actionable eighth amendment violation." As a further consideration, the Department of Justice had studied the use of the hitching post in Alabama and had advised the state to discontinue its use of the post in order to meet constitutional standards. In the *Hope* case, the Supreme Court drew the following conclusion:

> **[The prison officials] violated clearly established law …. Hope was treated in a way antithetical to human dignity—he was hitched to a post for an extended period of time in a position that was painful, and under circumstances that were both degrading and dangerous. This wanton treatment was not done of necessity, but as punishment for prior conduct. Even if there might once have been a question regarding the constitutionality of this practice, the [court rulings, buttressed by the Department of Justice report] put a reasonable officer on notice that the use of the hitching post under the circumstances alleged by Hope was unlawful.**

Because the law can change, it is essential that prison policy be kept up to date regarding court decisions or statutory changes establishing the standards for constitutional conduct. Then, it is essential that prison staff carefully follow the policy of the agency. Staff members should be able to rely on written policy as being a correct reflection of current constitutional requirements. If these two steps are taken, prison officials should be able to assert the defense of qualified immunity in any Section 1983 action.

Summary

- With respect to prison conditions, an early case (*Wright v. McMann*) showed that the courts, starting in the 1960s, were willing to use the Eighth Amendment to prohibit "debasing conditions" in prisons that violated "civilized standards of humane decency."

- The Prison Litigation Reform Act (PLRA) was enacted by Congress to address concerns over the burgeoning numbers of inmate litigation cases in federal courts. One part of the PLRA was directed toward the widespread use of consent decrees in prison and jail cases.

- The PLRA provided for the termination of long-standing decrees and has been used by numerous federal courts to end court supervision of prison and jail conditions.

- As prisons and jails became more and more crowded, a major issue was whether cells could be double-bunked—that is, whether two inmates could be placed into a cell that was designed for one person. In two leading cases, the Supreme Court held that it was not per se unconstitutional to practice double-bunking. As to pretrial detainees, the Court in *Bell v. Wolfish* held that, under the Constitution, inmates could not be punished before they were convicted. (This was decided by application of the due process clause, not the cruel and unusual punishment clause of the Eighth Amendment.) The crowded jail conditions were found not to amount to punishment, because they were incidental to a legitimate government purpose and were not done with an intent to punish. In the other case, *Rhodes v. Chapman*, the Court ruled that the standard for applying the Eighth Amendment on conditions of confinement for convicted prisoners was whether the conditions caused the wanton and unnecessary infliction of pain. The Court found that the double celling in that case did not inflict wanton or unnecessary pain and was, therefore, constitutional.

- Analysis of Eighth Amendment claims requires evaluation of two separate components: the objective component-is the alleged injury sufficiently serious and a subjective component-what was the state of mind of the government actor. The state of mind component varies with the alleged violation.

- With respect to sentenced inmates, the Supreme Court in *Rhodes v. Chapman* addressed the objective component (was the alleged injury sufficiently serious) and when applying the "contemporary standards of decency," the Court found that the conditions at the prison, including double bunking, were not sufficiently serious to constitute cruel and unusual punishment.

- The Supreme Court, in a sweeping order requiring California to eliminate constitutional violations in its prison population, said that large-scale reduction of the prison population in the state would be required. The violations were a serious and longstanding deprivation of basic health care for the sick and mentally ill inmates in the system. That was the constitutional, Eighth Amendment violation. To correct it (along with other steps that might be taken), the state would have to comply with a lower court order to reduce its prison population to 137.5% of its designed capacity within two years (*Brown v. Plata*).

- The subjective component of the Eighth Amendment standard (the actor's state of mind) was addressed in *Whitley v. Albers. In Whitley* an inmate was shot during a prison disturbance. The Supreme Court held that "obduracy and wantonness, not inadvertence or error in good faith" would show cruel and unusual punishment. Because force (the shooting) was used in a good-faith effort to restore order, and not "maliciously and sadistically for the very purpose of causing harm," there was no Eighth Amendment violation (*Whitley v. Albers*).

- In *Wilson v. Seiter,* the Supreme Court noted that the very high mental standard noted in *Whitley* ("maliciously and sadistically for the very purpose of causing harm") applied only to officials who were handling emergency situations. In the more general poor-conditions cases, such as *Wilson,* the state of mind (subjective component) of prison officials was determinative, but what would have to be shown to sustain a finding of cruel and unusual punishment was deliberate indifference on the part of officials to the basic needs of inmates. Each need of inmates, or each claimed violation of constitutional standards, would have to be examined individually to determine whether officials had been deliberately indifferent to that need. It was found to be improper to look at "overall conditions" to decide whether there was cruel and unusual punishment.

- The Supreme Court ruled that when there were allegations of the use of excessive physical force against a convicted inmate, the deciding factor would be whether force was used in a good-faith effort to maintain discipline or, to the contrary, maliciously and sadistically to cause harm. Injury to the inmate does not have to be severe or even "significant." If malicious or sadistic wrongdoing was involved, any amount of harm inflicted on the inmate could sustain a finding of constitutional violation (*Hudson v. McMillian; Wilkins v. Gaddy*).

- In *Kingsley v. Hendrickson*, (2015), the Court provided guidance on how claims of excessive use of force arising under the Due Process clause should be analyzed. The Court ruled that in order to state a Due Process clause claim for excessive use of force the detainee must only prove that the force was objectively unreasonable.

- Claims by an inmate that he was placed in a prison population in which he was known to be at high risk for being assaulted and where he later alleged he was beaten and raped, raised sufficient factual issues to preclude summary judgment for prison officials on allegations of cruel and unusual punishment. The Supreme Court said that prison officials must take reasonable steps to protect the safety of inmates. In the case of this inmate (who was a transsexual), an official would be liable if he knew that the inmate faced a substantial risk of serious harm and then disregarded that risk by failing to take precautions to protect the inmate (*Farmer v. Brennan*).

- An inmate's claim of being treated cruelly and unusually by being exposed to environmental tobacco smoke was held by the Supreme Court to raise a possible Eighth Amendment violation. Much like other situations we have discussed, this could be proved if the inmate could show that the officials were deliberately indifferent to significant risks to the inmate's future health. The inmate, in order to show deliberate indifference, would have to prove that the officials exposed him to unreasonably high levels of smoke and failed to take sufficient steps to reduce the levels of smoke, that the exposure to the smoke violated "contemporary standards of decency," and that officials showed deliberate indifference to the inmate's health by their attitudes and conduct (*Helling v. McKinney*).

- Prison officials have a defense of qualified immunity against Section 1983 (constitutional violations) lawsuits. To obtain this immunity, officials must show that their actions were taken in accord with clearly established constitutional law, as of the time of their actions (*Cleavinger v. Saxner; Hope v. Pelzer*).

Thinking About It

Inmate Staples was housed in a cell in the special housing unit of a correctional facility. Staff decided to move Staples to a new cell and advised him to be handcuffed so he could be moved. Staples refused. After consulting with supervisory staff, staff once again ordered Staples to be handcuffed to be moved. Staples again refused. Supervisory staff were notified, and the use of pepper spray to obtain compliance with staff orders was discussed. State DOC policy expressly authorized the use of pepper spray to obtain compliance with an officer's order to leave an inmate's cell. Supervisory staff approached Staple's cell, again ordered him to be handcuffed so he could be moved and warned him that non-compliance would result in the use of pepper spray. Staples again refused. Staff dispersed pepper spray for about nine seconds into Staples' cell using a cone which creates a mist rather than spraying a stream directly on the inmate. Staples had faced away from the spray and had covered his face with a blanket. Ten minutes later staff asked Staples if he needed medical attention and Staples refused. Staff brought a nurse to Staples' cell and after examination the nurse deemed the inmate "medically cleared." About ninety minutes later Staples was offered a cell change to another cell which he accepted, was handcuffed and moved. Staff also provided Staples with an opportunity to shower which he accepted.

Staples sued prison staff alleging the use of the pepper spray while he was locked in his cell was an excessive use of force in violation of the Eighth Amendment. The district court granted the officers' motion for summary judgment. The inmate appealed. Was the officers' use of pepper spray on an inmate in a locked cell an excessive use of force? *Staples v. Gerry*, 923 F.3d 7 (1st Cir. 2019).

Key Terms

capacity (corrections)
consent decree
deadly force

Endnotes

1. Administrative Office of the U.S. Courts. *2019 Annual Report of the Director: Judicial Business of the United States Courts.* Table C-2 U.S. District Courts-Civil Cases Commenced by Basis of Jurisdiction and Nature of the suit. Washington, DC. https://www.uscourts .gov/sites/default/files/data_tables/jb_c2_0930.2019.pdf. With respect to civil rights (including prison conditions) petitions, in 1995, there were 41,679 civil rights petitions filed in U.S. district courts by state and federal prison inmates. Congress, in 1996, passed the Prison Litigation Reform Act (PLRA) in an effort to reduce the number of prisoner civil rights lawsuits. The PLRA requires an inmate to exhaust administrative remedies prior to filing suit. This act appears to have resulted in a decrease in such filings; 25,504 civil rights petitions were filed in 2000. The filing rate—the number of civil rights petitions filed per one thousand inmates—fell from 37 to 19. Scalia, J. *Prisoner Petitions Filed in U.S. District Courts, 2000, with Trends 1980-2000.* Page 1. (Washington, DC: Bureau of Justice Statistics, U.S. Department of Justice, 2002).

2. Every five years, the Bureau of Justice Statistics (BJS) compiles a census of state and federal correctional facilities. In 2005, adult correctional facilities were operating at 11% above rated capacity, an increase from 2% in 2000. Federal facilities were operating at a rate of 37% above capacity, state facilities at a rate of 8% above rated capacity, and private facilities were operating at 5% under rated capacity. Stephan, J. *Census of State and Federal Correctional Facilities, 2005*. Pages 1–3. (Washington, DC: Bureau of Justice Statistics, U.S. Department of Justice, 2008).One problem in approaching these figures is that there is not a universally accepted way of defining or measuring rated capacity. This is true among corrections agencies, and it is certainly a problem in court definitions of what amounts to acceptable "capacity" for prisons or jails.

3. Carson, E.Ann. Prisoners in 2019. October 2020. Terms and Definitions, p.2 and Table 17. U.S. Department of Justice, Bureau of Justice Statistics.

4. As of December 30, 2005, 44 correctional facilities under state or federal authority were under court order to limit the size of their inmate population, with 27 of these facilities restricted to housing fewer than 250 inmates. Two hundred eighteen correctional facilities were under court orders or consent decrees for specific conditions of confinement. Crowding, along with the lawsuits and court rulings that have accompanied it, has led to large expansions in prison and jail facilities. Between 2000 and 2005, the number of state and federal correctional facilities increased by 9%, while the number of offenders confined increased by 10%. Maximum security facilities increased by 12% (332 to 372), medium security facilities decreased by 8% (522 to 480), and minimum-security facilities increased by 19% (814 to 969). Stephan, J.—see endnote 2.

5. Camp, C. G., ed. *The 2002 Corrections Yearbook—Adult Corrections*. Page 150. (Middletown, CT: Criminal Justice Institute, 2003). See also National Governors Association, The Book of States 2017, Selected State Administrative Officials, Method of Selection. Table 4.10. http://knowledgecenter.csg.org/kc/system/files/4.10.2017.pdf. Accessed 04 March 2020.

6. The PLRA does not apply to relief entered by a state court that is based only upon claims arising under state law.

7. The PLRA provides for an automatic stay to begin 30 days after a motion is made to modify or terminate prospective relief under the PLRA; courts can postpone the entry of the automatic stay for up to 60 days for "good cause," which cannot include general congestion of the court's docket. Title 18, U.S. Code Section 3626[e](2) and (3).

8. The district court found that attorneys were forced to wait 45 minutes to 2 hours, or longer, after arriving. The reasons given by the department involved a scarcity of meeting rooms, a need for escort officers to accompany some of the detainees, and the fact that inmates were not brought to meetings during prison counts, although they could be taken for regular visiting.

9. During an oral argument in the Supreme Court, one justice asked the inmates' counsel, "Are bunk beds punishment? Because if they are, I am going to apologize to my sons." (This is confirmed in the transcript of the hearing.)

10. The text, as a rule, does not comment on dissents (or the number of votes in a case decision) in discussing a ruling. In this case, however, we note that there were four dissenting justices, and two dissenting opinions written. They expressed unusually strong opinions in opposition to the majority opinion. Justice Scalia said: "Today the Court affirms what is perhaps the most radical injunction issued by a court in our Nation's history: an order requiring California to release the staggering number of 46,000 convicted criminals." "There comes before us, now and then, a case whose proper outcome is so clearly indicated by tradition and common sense, that its decision ought to shape the law, rather than vice versa. One would think that, before allowing the decree of a federal district court to release 46,000 convicted felons, this Court would bend every effort to read the law in such a way as to avoid that outrageous result. Today, quite to the contrary, the Court disregards stringently drawn provisions of the governing statute [the PLRA], and traditional constitutional limitations upon the power of a federal judge, in order to uphold the absurd." "The proceedings that led to this result were a judicial travesty. I dissent because the institutional reform the District Court has undertaken violates the terms of the governing statute, ignores bedrock limitations on the power of Article III judges, and takes federal courts wildly beyond their institutional capacity." "In his dissenting opinion, Justice Alito wrote:" "The decree in this case is a perfect example of what the Prison Litigation Reform Act … was enacted to prevent. The Constitution does not give federal judges the authority to run state penal systems. Decisions regarding state prisons have profound public safety and financial implications, and the States are generally free to make these decisions as they choose." [Citing *Turner v. Safley,* 482 U.S. 78 (1987)]" "In this case, a three-judge court exceeded its authority under the Constitution and the PLRA. The court ordered a radical reduction in the California prison population without finding that the current population level violates the Constitution."

11. In some instances, actions by correctional personnel which violate the rights of persons in their custody have resulted in criminal prosecution of the staff. Title 18, U.S.C. § 242 permits prosecution of persons, including law enforcement officers and correctional officers, for willfully violating the civil rights of an individual. One such example came out of the arrest of Rodney King in California and the allegations of excessive force, which were documented on video. After the officers were acquitted on state criminal charges, the United States prosecuted some of the officers, alleging their conduct violated King's constitutional rights. *Koon v. United States,* 518 U.S. 81 (1996). Examples of similar civil rights prosecutions of correctional staff include *United States v. LaVallee,* 439 F.3d 670 (10th Cir. 2006), involving charges of conspiracy to violate and violating the rights of inmates at a federal penitentiary by 10 federal correctional officers. One of the officers received a federal prison term of 30 months, and two others each received terms of 41 months. In another case, a former correctional worker received a life sentence after being convicted of conspiracy to violate the rights of a detainee, which led to the detainee's death from the injuries suffered in an assault and subsequent denial of medical care (*United States v. Conatser,* 514 F.3d 508 (6th Cir. 2008)).

12. In *Grass v. Sargent,* 903 F.2d 1206 (8th Cir. 1990), the court of appeals held there was no constitutional right to smoke in prison. Perhaps as a result of the *Helling* opinion and related litigation, many prisons have gone smoke-free, both for inmates and staff.

13. See *Saucier v. Katz,* 533 U.S. 194 (2001). In *Saucier,* the Court noted that, where a defendant seeks qualified immunity, a ruling on the request should be made early in the proceedings. A favorable judicial determination of qualified immunity is an entitlement for the person not to stand trial or to face the other burdens of litigation. This rationale was again emphasized in *Pearson v. Callahan,* 555 U.S. 223 (2009).

CHAPTER 16

Eighth Amendment: Health Care

The government [has an] obligation to provide medical care for those whom it is punishing by incarceration. An inmate must rely on prison authorities to treat his medical needs.

It is but just that the public be required to care for the prisoner, who cannot, by reason of the deprivation of his liberty, care for himself.

U.S. Supreme Court, *Estelle v. Gamble*

CHAPTER OUTLINE

- *Estelle v. Gamble*
- *West v. Atkins*
- *Washington v. Harper; Sell v. United States*
- Other Involuntary Treatment Cases
- Inmate Suicides
- *Logue v. United States*
- Special Health Care Needs of Female Prisoners
- HIV and AIDS
- Tuberculosis in Prisons
- COVID-19 and Correctional Institutions
- An Aging Prison Population
- LGBTI Health Issues in Correctional Institutions

It is evident that correctional facilities must provide inmates with health care. Health care is one of the basic needs of prisoners that the courts have recognized, *Estelle v. Gamble*, 429 U.S. 97 (1976). After the seminal case in *Estelle*, courts continue to identify healthcare as a basic need which the government must provide to incarcerated persons. See for example *Lewis v. Casey* 518 U.S. 343 (1996) and *Estate of Clark v. Walker*, 865 F.3d 544 (7th Cir. 2017).

As a consequence of being incarcerated by the government, inmates are obviously cut off from ordinary sources of health care that they might have in the community. The Supreme Court, in the quotation from

Estelle v. Gamble set out at the beginning of this chapter, recognized that basic requirement: for prisons to provide health care to inmates. In some states, statutes or even the state constitution may specify that health care is to be provided to inmates. The statutes may be detailed, or they may just require generally that at least the emergency health needs of detainees and the necessary health care of prisoners should be provided by the government.

A few facilities in this country allow inmates to obtain their own health care in the community. This may be more prevalent in jails, and it is especially more common for inmates who have already commenced treatment for a condition and wish to continue treatment with the same provider. And, of course, it is a more likely circumstance for an inmate who has resources (health insurance or cash) to pay for their own medical care. Most prisons, as a matter of principle, do not allow inmates to obtain their own health care from a provider of their choice in the community after they are incarcerated. It is generally accepted that, as another equalizing factor whereby all inmates are treated the same, health care will be provided at a minimum for the treatment of injuries, for the diagnosis and treatment of medical conditions that require ongoing care, and for a serious medical problem that must be looked after before the inmate's release.

In *City of Revere v. Massachusetts General Hospital*, 463 U.S. 239 (1983), a suspect was shot and wounded by the Revere city police. The wounded individual was taken by ambulance to Massachusetts General Hospital (MGH) and treated. After the suspect's discharge, he was arrested, held in jail, and provided additional medical services by MGH. MGH sent a bill for almost $13,000 to the city for medical services, which the city refused to pay. The city was then sued in state court, and a state trial court dismissed the hospital's claim. The hospital appealed and the Supreme Judicial Court of Massachusetts reversed the trial court in part, ruling that in order to ensure that persons in police custody received necessary medical care, "the Eighth Amendment to the United States Constitution [as applied to the States through the Fourteenth Amendment], requires that Revere be liable to the hospital for the medical services rendered to [the suspect]. . . . "The Supreme Court reversed, ruling that it was the Due Process Clause of the Fourteenth Amendment, which protects unconvicted persons in police custody, and the Fourteenth Amendment protects the right to receive needed medical care, not who pays for it. The Court noted in a footnote that "[nothing] we say here affects any right a hospital or governmental entity may have to recover from a detainee the cost of the medical services provided to him."

A development over the last 25 years has been the introduction of charges to inmates for routine health care (co-pays). In 1995, only nine corrections agencies imposed such charges. By 2017, 42 states and the Federal Bureau of Prisons were authorized to collect co-pays for medical services, although, since then several states, including California and Illinois, have repealed laws authorizing such payments.[1] Most states charged five dollars or less, and no state charged more than $10.00.[2] In 2000, the Federal Prisoner Health Care Copayment Act of 2000 was enacted.[3] This legislation authorized charging inmates confined in an institution under the Bureau of Prisons' jurisdiction, and those charged with, or convicted of, an offense against the United States, a fee for health care services. The legislation specifies that an inmate may not be refused treatment for financial reasons and also identifies a number of areas where fees may not be charged, such as for preventative healthcare services and mental health care. **BOX 16-1** shows the Bureau of Prisons rule (published in Title 28, Code of Federal Regulations—CFR) relating to Fees for Health Care Services.

This move toward charging inmates for services rendered was initiated for a variety of reasons. The soaring cost of providing health care was one factor—charging for the care would make a small dent in those costs, but it was hoped that it would make a greater impact by reducing unnecessary inmate visits to medical services. Charging for visits and services would also bring the prison experience closer to the community one. There are some detractors to the policy of charging co-payments, and their reasons include: The system creates two tiers of patients—those who can pay and those who cannot pay; charging for minor ailments may prevent an inmate from seeking care for a condition that becomes serious or that might infect the inmate population; and that the costs of administering the co-payment system is greater than the revenue received.[4]

Setting the policy is one thing; carrying it out may be a very different and difficult thing. For example, how are the funds collected? (Inmates don't walk around with lots of cash or credit cards in their pockets—at least, not in most corrections facilities.) Most prisons and jails have a "canteen" or "commissary" where an inmate may purchase some desirable items that are not provided by the government, such as snacks, toiletries, and stationery items. Purchases there are paid for by the use of a revolving account; the inmate or their family makes deposits to their account, and purchases are debited against that account. Charges for health services may be debited against that same account. What if an inmate is covered by health insurance? Collecting from insurers for small items may be more costly than it is worth, but using that insurance (including even Medicare) may be attempted for more costly procedures.[5]

BOX 16-1 Subpart F-Fees for Health Care Services

§ 549.70 Purpose and scope

(a) The Bureau of Prisons (Bureau) may, under certain circumstances, charge you, an inmate under our care and custody, a fee for providing you with health care services.

(b) Generally, if you are an inmate as described in § 549.71, you must pay a fee for health care services of $2.00 per health care visit if you:

  (1) Receive health care services in connection with a health care visit that you requested, (except for services described in § 549.72); or

  (2) Are found responsible through the Disciplinary Hearing Process to have injured an inmate who, as a result of the injury, requires a health care visit.

§ 549.71 Inmates affected

This subpart applies to:

(a) Any individual incarcerated in an institution under the Bureau's jurisdiction; or

(b) Any other individual, as designated by the Director, who has been charged with or convicted of an offense against the United States.

§ 549.72 Services provided without fees

We will not charge a fee for:

(a) Health care services based on staff referrals;

(b) Staff-approved follow-up treatment for a chronic condition;

(c) Preventive health care services;

(d) Emergency services;

(e) Prenatal care;

(f) Diagnosis or treatment of chronic infectious diseases;

(g) Mental health care; or

(h) Substance abuse treatment.

§ 549.73 Appealing the fee

You may seek review of issues related to health service fees through the Bureau's Administrative Remedy Program (see 28 CFR part 542).

§ 549.74 Inmates without funds

You will not be charged a health care service fee if you are considered indigent and unable to pay the health care service fee. The Warden may establish procedures to prevent abuse of this provision.

The Federal Bureau of Prisons, published in Title 28 CFR, Subpart F - Fees for Health Care Services (Revised as of July 1, 2010).

Court cases have upheld the concept of charging an inmate a fee. In *Gardner v. Wilson*, 959 F. Supp. 1224 (C.D. CA 1997), the court said there was no Eighth Amendment violation for requiring an inmate to pay a $5.00 copayment for medical care. The court noted that assuring that inmates do not abuse their access to limited medical resources is a legitimate government purpose. In *Reynolds v. Wagner*, 128 F.3d 166 (3rd Cir. 1997), an appellate court similarly ruled that charging inmates modest fees for medical services is not per se unconstitutional. That court said that this practice teaches prisoners financial responsibility and deters the abuse of sick call—goals that are within the scope of legitimate penological objectives. In the same context, a federal court, in *Hutchinson v. Belt*, 957 F.Supp. 97 (W.D. LA 1996), said there was no constitutional right to *free* medical care Examples of states that have had its co-pay policies upheld against inmate legal challenges include: Texas[6], Illinois[7], Nevada[8] and Pennsylvania.[9]

What does the Constitution require of a correctional entity in providing health care to those in custody? Is a prisoner entitled to medical treatment and care for any health problems they may have? How much health care does the state have to provide? Under what circumstances will a prison official be liable, under the U.S. Constitution, for failing to provide health care? These questions, as far as defining constitutional violations and the requirements under 42 U.S.C. § 1983, are decided under the Eighth Amendment. (For pretrial detainees, as pointed out in *Bell v. Wolfish*, 441 U.S. 520 (1979), they are decided under the Fourteenth Amendment on the basis of the due process clause. While the Supreme Court has never decided the correct legal standard to apply to health care claims by pretrial detainees, most of the circuits used the "deliberate indifference" standard announced in *Estelle v Gamble*. After the *Kingsley v. Hendrickson* decision in 2015, which addressed analysis of Due Process claims in the area of excessive use of force, some circuits reconsidered their previous precedent. At the time of this text's printing, three circuits have adopted the objective reasonableness standard for allegations related to the provision of medical care. This will be discussed later in more detail. There may, of course, be different standards established locally by state or local legislation or by court rulings about what is required for detainees.)

▸ *Estelle v. Gamble*

The governing constitutional case on providing health care in prisons is *Estelle v. Gamble*, 429 U.S. 97 (1976), which announced the principle that the government must provide medical care to those whom it has imprisoned.

Gamble was an inmate in the Texas Department of Corrections. He was injured at work when a bale of cotton fell on him. When he complained, he was sent to the hospital. From there, he was sent to his cell to rest. When he returned to the hospital with increased pain, he was given pain pills. The next day, he saw a doctor, who prescribed a pain reliever and a muscle relaxant. He was placed on medical orders on "cell-pass," meaning he stayed in his cell except for showers. After a week, the doctor prescribed another pain reliever. Despite continuing pain, the doctor said Gamble could return to light work. When Gamble refused to work, he was taken before a prison disciplinary committee, which ordered him to be seen by another doctor. This second doctor ran tests and prescribed additional medication. Gamble was ordered several times to go to work, but he continued to refuse, saying he was in too much pain. He eventually was placed in solitary confinement as a disciplinary sanction for refusing to work. He then claimed chest pains and "blank outs." He was seen one time in the hospital for these complaints. When he reported continuing pains to guards in administrative segregation, he was twice refused permission to see a doctor. He filed his complaint in court, under Section 1983, claiming cruel and unusual punishment in his medical care.

The core of the Supreme Court's opinion is based on a concern over denial of medical care to prisoners, which leads to unnecessary pain and suffering. Such unnecessary suffering would be inconsistent with "contemporary standards of decency," which of course is the concern of the "evolving" Eighth Amendment proscription against cruel and unusual punishments.

> **We therefore conclude that deliberate indifference to serious medical needs of prisoners constitutes the "unnecessary and wanton infliction of pain" proscribed by the Eighth Amendment. This is true whether the indifference is manifested by prison doctors in their response to the prisoner's needs or by prison guards in intentionally denying or delaying access to medical care or intentionally interfering with the treatment once prescribed. Regardless of how evidenced, deliberate indifference to a prisoner's serious illness or injury states a cause of action under Section 1983.**

The Court then went on to note that "an inadvertent failure to provide adequate medical care" would not be a "wanton infliction of unnecessary pain" so as to constitute a constitutional violation. More to the point,

> **[A] complaint that a physician has been negligent in diagnosing or treating a medical condition does not state a valid claim of medical mistreatment under the Eighth Amendment. Medical malpractice does not become a constitutional violation merely because the victim is a prisoner. In order to state a cognizable claim, a prisoner must allege acts or omissions sufficiently harmful to evidence deliberate indifference to serious medical needs. It is only such indifference that can offend "evolving standards of decency" in violation of the Eighth Amendment.**

Applying these standards to the claims written and filed by inmate Gamble, the Court concluded that he had not shown that there was deliberate indifference to his medical complaints. He was seen by medical personnel on 17 occasions during a three-month period. He was treated for three conditions that they identified after examining and testing him. Although Gamble claimed more testing should have been done, especially regarding his lower-back complaints (and the court of appeals had agreed with him on that), the patient complaining of that particular problem points to "a classic example of a matter for medical judgment," the Court said. Failure to order certain tests or medications does not constitute cruel and unusual punishment. At most, it would suggest negligence, or medical malpractice, and that is not a constitutional level of concern. (It would be properly considered, the Court indicated, under the Texas Tort Claims Act.)

▶ *West v. Atkins*

Having decided the constitutional standard to assess health care in prisons, other litigation explores the reach of the "deliberate indifference" standard of *Estelle v. Gamble* or looks at how it may apply under different kinds of circumstances. One question is whether the Eighth Amendment (and its application by Section 1983) applies to private physicians and other health care providers who offer services to prison or jail inmates. Corrections is turning more and more frequently to the private sector to provide services in different areas of prison and jail operations. Some jurisdictions have contracted with private companies to build and run complete institutions for the state or local government. Others have contracted to provide one area of services for an institution or for an entire state. The two most commonly contracted services are food services and health care. (There are companies specializing in providing food or health services just for corrections agencies.)

In *West v. Atkins*, 487 U.S. 42 (1988), the Supreme Court addressed the question of "whether a physician who is under contract with the State to provide medical services to inmates at a state-prison hospital on a part-time basis acts 'under color of state law' within the meaning of 42 U.S.C. § 1983, when he treats an inmate." West, an inmate at a North Carolina prison, tore his Achilles tendon while playing volleyball. He was sent to the Central Prison Hospital in Raleigh, the principal medical facility for state inmates. There, Dr. Atkins, a private physician who worked under contract with the state, provided orthopedic services and treated West. West was not allowed, as a prisoner, to see a physician of his own choosing. Atkins placed West's leg in a series of casts. West alleged in his lawsuit that Atkins said surgery would be necessary but that the doctor refused to schedule it. West sued under Section 1983, claiming violation of his constitutional right to be free from cruel and unusual punishments. He alleged that Dr. Atkins was deliberately indifferent to his serious medical needs when he failed to provide adequate treatment (the surgery the doctor himself had recommended).

Lower courts took different positions on the claim (as to whether Section 1983 would apply to the contract physician), but the Fourth Circuit ended up affirming and applying the position it had taken in *Calvert v. Sharp*, 748 F.2d 861 (4th Cir. 1984), where it held that a contract physician who provided services to Maryland inmates did not act "under color of state law," which was required to pursue a Section 1983 action. The Supreme Court reversed.

Acting under color of state law is an essential element of pursuing a Section 1983 action, and it is an implicit element of pursuing a claim of violation of the Fourteenth Amendment (which applies to "State" actions). The Eighth Amendment also requires state action, or inaction, because cruel and unusual punishments can only be inflicted by the states—not by private parties (who have no authority to punish at all). The Court in *West* relied on the guidance of other Section 1983 decisions that:

> [A]cting under color of state law requires that the defendant in a [Section] 1983 action have exercised power "possessed by virtue of state law and made possible only because the wrongdoer is clothed with the authority of state law." ... It is firmly established that a defendant in a [Section] 1983 suit acts under color of state law when he abuses the position given to him by the State.

This requirement is comparatively easy to apply when the action is taken by a government official, because a state employee acts under color of state law whenever they act in their official capacity, exercising their responsibilities under the law. (One type of government employee is exempted from Section 1983 by a Supreme Court decision: a public defender. The defender has been shielded from Section 1983 liability on the grounds that they retain the attributes of a private attorney, especially keeping their independence from state interference, indeed, operating often in opposition to the state. The Court in *West* distinguished the role of a prison doctor from that of the public defender.)

The Supreme Court said that it is the physician's function for the prison system, not the nature of his employment, which determines whether their actions are attributable to the state.

> Contracting out prison medical care does not relieve the State of its constitutional duty to provide adequate medical treatment to those in its custody, and it does not deprive the State's prisoners of the means to vindicate their Eighth Amendment rights ... It is the physician's function while working for the State, not the amount of time he spends in performance of those duties or the fact that he may be employed by others to perform similar duties, that determines whether he is acting under color of state law. In the State's employ, [Dr. Atkins] worked as a physician at the prison hospital fully vested with state authority to fulfill essential aspects of the duty, placed on the State by the Eighth Amendment

and state law, to provide essential medical care to those the State had incarcerated. Doctor Atkins must be considered to be a state actor.

The case was remanded to pursue the Section 1983 action in trial court—that is, to determine whether Dr. Atkins acted with deliberate indifference to West's serious medical needs and, thus, violated his constitutional right to be free from cruel and unusual punishment.

▶ *Washington v. Harper; Sell v. United States*

Another important aspect of medical treatment, and one that is as pressing an issue in prison health care as it is in private community medical treatment, is the question of involuntary treatment of the patient. This becomes especially important in the care of mentally ill patients, where staff must know when they are permitted to intervene without the patient's consent to provide treatment. The Supreme Court, in *Washington v. Harper*, 494 U.S. 210 (1990), addressed this question.

Sometimes, medical staff must make the decision to provide treatment when the patient cannot decide for themself—for example, when they are unconscious or mentally incompetent. For the unconscious prison patient, the decision would be made on the same grounds as it would be in the outside community: if care must be given to avoid or ameliorate a life-threatening situation, or if circumstances, which if left untreated, could result in serious, long-term adverse consequences, the medical staff are justified in taking those emergency steps to assist the patient.[10] For the incompetent patient, there may be a guardian who has been given authority to make decisions regarding medical care on behalf of the patient. In some jurisdictions, courts have said that wardens or jail superintendents stand in the place of guardians, and if medical care is needed for the benefit of the inmate patient, in a serious, health-threatening situation, the warden or superintendent may make that decision on behalf of the inmate. If there is no guardian who is known, or who is available to give the necessary consent, application may need to be made to a court to appoint a guardian. Advice of counsel should always be sought to determine what the local judicial view is on the authority of the warden or superintendent to act and whether the appointment of a guardian should be sought.

The second situation for providing involuntary medical care arises when the patient does not wish to be treated. The question then becomes, when do inmates have the constitutional right to refuse medical treatment? In many states the unconsented provision of medical care or treatment would constitute a battery. Unfortunately, the decision in *Harper* does not provide definitive guidance about the constitutional standards to be used in assessing circumstances which may require treatment over the patient's objections. Harper was an inmate in the state of Washington who was given antipsychotic medication despite his refusal to take it. Although the case would seem to have some Eighth Amendment concerns embedded in it, it was decided as a due process case under the Fourteenth Amendment. The Court held that the decision to involuntarily medicate the inmate did involve his liberty interest— his desire to make his own decisions to remain unmedicated. Therefore, due process protections would apply to the decision-making process. In other words, the patient did have a constitutional right to refuse medication.

That right of the inmate to refuse treatment (medication) could be overcome by the state, the Court said, based on the context of his status of confinement.

> **The State has undertaken the obligation to provide prisoners with medical treatment consistent not only with their own medical interests, but also with the needs of the institution. Prison administrators have not only an interest in ensuring the safety of prison staffs and administrative personnel … but the duty to take reasonable measures for the prisoner's own safety …. Where an inmate's mental disability is the root cause of the threat he poses to the prison population, the State's interest in decreasing the danger to others necessarily encompasses an interest in providing him with medical treatment for his illness.**

The Due Process Clause requires analysis of substantive and procedural components. *"[T]he substantive issue involves a definition of th[e] protected constitutional interest, as well as identification of the conditions under which competing state interests might outweigh it. The procedural issue concerns the minimum procedures required by the Constitution for determining that the individual's liberty interest actually is outweighed in a particular instance."* In this case, the substantive issue is what factual circumstances must exist before the State may administer antipsychotic drugs to the prisoner against his will; the procedural issue is whether the State's nonjudicial mechanisms used to determine the facts in a particular case are sufficient.

The Court determined that a convicted prisoner in state custody had a liberty interest in avoiding arbitrary and unwanted treatment that was created by both state law and by the federal constitution. Washington authorities had well-established, nonjudicial administrative procedures that had to be followed prior to involuntarily medicating a prisoner, and the Supreme Court approved the state's approach. The state's policy required that the inmate had to first be diagnosed with a mental disorder and that as a result of that disorder, was gravely disabled or posed a likelihood of serious harm to self, others, or property. Treatment had to be ordered by a psychiatrist. A hearing committee was formed consisting of a psychiatrist, a psychologist, and the Assistant Superintendent of the facility, all of whom could not be presently involved in the inmate's treatment, who would consider evidence and make a decision concerning involuntary treatment. The inmate was entitled to receive advanced notice of the hearing, including treatment staff's tentative diagnosis and the basis for the treatment recommendations. At the hearing before the committee, the inmate was entitled to attend, call witnesses, cross examine witnesses, present evidence, and have the assistance of a lay advisor who was not involved with the inmate's treatment and who understood the psychiatric issues. The inmate had 24 hours to appeal an adverse ruling to the facility superintendent, who had 24 hours to decide the appeal. The inmate retained the right to seek judicial review. Finally, the regulation required subsequent reviews by the committee and justification by the treating psychiatrist.

The Court applied the four-factor test announced in *Turner v. Safley* and concluded that the state's policy furthered the significant government interest of addressing an inmate's danger to themself or others and its obligation to provide necessary medical treatment consistent with the patient's interest and the needs of the institution.

Where an inmate's mental disability is the root cause of the threat he poses to the inmate population, the State's interest in decreasing the danger to others necessarily encompasses an interest in providing him with medical treatment for his illness.

The inmate claimed due process required a judicial fact finder and a right to be represented by counsel. The Court concluded *"that an inmate's interests are adequately protected, and perhaps better served, by allowing the decision to medicate to be made by medical professionals rather than a judge. The Due Process Clause "has never been thought to require that the neutral and detached trier of fact be law trained or a judicial or administrative officer."* Consistent with the conclusions in *Vitek v. Jones* that law-trained advisors are not required by the Due Process clause in issues related to medical treatment, legal counsel was not required. Because the Court decided that Washington's procedures were constitutionally adequate, it is not clear just how much less than Washington's procedures might also be acceptable. The Court did specify that treatment could not be given just to control or improve the inmate's disruptive or difficult behavior.

The state policy was approved, because:

[I]ts exclusive application is to inmates who are mentally ill and who, as a result of their illness, are gravely disabled or represent a significant danger to themselves or others. The drugs may be administered for no purpose other than treatment, and only under the direction of a licensed psychiatrist.

The Court rejected the inmate's argument that, rather than forced administration of the drugs, alternative means of treatment, such as physical restraints or seclusion, should have been used. The Court said that it had not been shown that those alternatives would be as effective as medication.

We hold that, given the requirements of the prison environment, the Due Process Clause permits the State to treat a prison inmate who has a serious mental illness with antipsychotic drugs against his will, if the inmate is dangerous to himself or others and the treatment is in the inmate's medical interest.

The concept of *Harper* was carried further in the Supreme Court decision in *Sell v. United States*, 539 U.S. 166 (2003). The case involved the issue of whether the government could administer antipsychotic medication against the defendant-inmate's will, solely to render him competent to stand trial for serious, but nonviolent offenses. Sell, a dentist, was charged with making false representations in connection with healthcare payments. An initial mental health assessment determined that he was competent to stand trial, but there existed potential for a psychotic episode. While on bail, he was accused of attempting to intimidate a witness and was brought before a magistrate judge. His behavior in the judge's words was "totally out of control" at this hearing and included his spitting in the judge's face. Sell's bail was subsequently revoked, and he was detained. A new indictment was later brought against him, charging him with an attempt to kill a witness and an FBI agent.

Sell was sent to the Medical Center for Federal Prisoners in Springfield, Missouri. He was determined by two clinicians to need antipsychotic medication to restore him to competency, so that he could stand trial. Sell said he did not want to take the medication. Lower federal court rulings held that Sell could be forcibly medicated in order to make him competent to stand trial. The case was taken to the Supreme Court, which followed the guidelines it had set forth in *Harper*.

> **In *Harper*, this Court recognized that an individual has a "significant" constitutionally protected "liberty interest" in "avoiding the unwanted administration of antipsychotic drugs."**

> **[T]he Constitution permits the Government involuntarily to administer antipsychotic drugs to a mentally ill defendant facing serious criminal charges in order to render that defendant competent to stand trial, but only if the treatment is medically appropriate, is substantially unlikely to have side effects that may undermine the fairness of the trial, and, taking account of less intrusive alternatives, is necessary significantly to further important governmental trial-related interests.**

The Court in *Sell* further noted that in *Riggins v. Nevada*, 504 U.S. 127 (1992), it had again stated that a person has a "constitutionally protected liberty 'interest in avoiding involuntary administration of antipsychotic drugs'— an interest that only an 'essential' or 'overriding' state interest might overcome."

The Court in *Sell* continued by providing detailed directions. The Court stated that a court must find that there are important governmental interests at stake; that administration of the drugs is substantially likely to make the defendant competent to stand trial; that involuntary medication is necessary to further those interests; that there are no alternative, less intrusive treatments; and that administration of the drugs is in the patient's best medical interests. With these detailed directions for a trial court to use, the case was remanded (returned) for consideration as to whether the guidelines were met in Sell's case and would support a continuing order for forced medication.

It must be emphasized that *Sell* applies to persons awaiting trial. It is of interest, therefore, primarily to trial courts and to the lawyers (prosecutors and defense counsel) who handle criminal cases in which the mental competency of the defendant is at issue. These concerns are often of interest to prison and jail staff, because those pretrial inmates are usually held in prison or jail hospitals (as Sell was).

▸ Other Involuntary Treatment Cases

In the seminal case of *Cruzan v. Director, Missouri Department of Health*, 497 U.S. 261 (1990), the Supreme Court concluded that the Due Process Clause gives a mentally competent person the right to refuse unwanted medical care. Cruzan was severely injured in a car accident, and physicians believed her brain had been deprived of oxygen for 12–14 minutes. The lack of oxygen resulted in physicians describing her condition as "a persistent vegetative state: generally, a condition in which a person exhibits motor reflexes but evinces no indications of significant cognitive function." The physicians also believed there was almost no chance Ms. Cruzan would regain her mental faculties. Her mother and father, who were her guardians, requested that the feeding tube which was providing nutrition and hydration to their daughter be removed. Because this removal would almost certainly cause Ms. Cruzan's death, the state hospital required the guardians to obtain a court order authorizing the removal. The state circuit court conducted a hearing and after taking testimony from family and friends about Ms. Cruzan's beliefs about life, granted the petition. The state appealed and a divided Missouri Supreme Court reversed the circuit court holding that Missouri had a strong policy favoring preservation of life, and in the absence of a living will, or other clear, convincing and reliable evidence "no person can assume that choice for an incompetent." The U.S. Supreme Court, in part relying on its decision in *Washington v. Harper*, ruled that persons did have a Due Process right under the Fourteenth Amendment to refuse unwanted medical care, and assumed in this case, that Due Process "would grant a competent person a constitutionally protected right to refuse lifesaving hydration and nutrition." The Court recognized that in some cases, the individual's right must be exercised through a surrogate. Missouri's requirement of clear, convincing, reliable evidence to establish an incapacitated person's wishes was not prohibited by the Fourteenth Amendment, and the Missouri Supreme Court's judgment was affirmed.[11] In the 30 years since the Cruzan decision, many state DOCs have promulgated policies on living wills, advanced directives, and do not resuscitate orders.[12]

Medical treatment comes in many forms, including testing and treatment for communicable diseases; providing nutrition and hydration necessary to maintain life; or receiving other medical interventions, such as insulin for diabetes, or kidney dialysis treatment. While the interests of the state are also diverse, lower federal courts and the highest appellate courts of some states have identified several important governmental interests that might outweigh the individual's right to refuse medical treatment: (1) preservation of life; (2) protection of innocent third parties; (3) the prevention of suicide; and (4) the maintenance of the ethical integrity of the medical profession. For the incarcerated individual, a fifth interest—maintaining prison security and orderly administration—can be added. *McNabb v. Department of Corrections*, 180 P.3d 1257 (Wash. 2008). This case was decided after *Harper* and *Cruzan*, and the inmate argued, and the state court resolved, the case under state constitutional law.

In *Commissioner of Corrections v. Myers*, 399 N.E.2d 452 (MA 1979), the prisoner refused to continue with kidney dialysis treatment as a form of protest over his placement in a medium, rather than a minimum security prison. The court specifically noted that the inmate's refusal had "little to do with his disease," was unrelated to any religious objections, nor did he wish to die. The *Myers* court weighed the factors of preservation of life, protection of third parties, prevention of suicide, the ethical integrity of the medical profession, and the integrity of the correctional system, and ruled the state's interest in prison operation justified intervention:

> [T]he State's interest in upholding orderly prison administration tips the balance in favor of authorizing treatment without consent. Our evaluation of this interest takes account of the threat posed to prison order, security and discipline by a failure to prevent the death of an inmate who attempts to manipulate his placement within the prison by refusing life-saving treatment.[13]

A similar situation existed in *Singletary v. Costello*, 665 So.2d 1099 (Fla. Ct. App. 1996). Costello fasted to protest his punitive transfer to another institution and also to protest what he said was a false disciplinary report. Medical staff determined that failure to intervene in his case would result in his death (in effect, his suicide). The issue was whether the inmate had the legal right to refuse medical treatment and intervention. As in *Myers*, this inmate did not actually want to die; rather, his fast was done as a form of protest, with the object of resolving his complaints.

The Florida court held that the inmate (so long as he was competent) had the fundamental right to refuse medical treatment. This right was based on both state and federal law, and the court expressly referenced the *Cruzan* decision. The task was balancing this right against the state's interest. This court held that the state's interest in the preservation of life was not sufficient to overcome the inmate's fundamental right to refuse life-sustaining medical treatment. Refusing medical treatment would not endanger public health, the court said. Furthermore, the interest in the protection of innocent third parties did not apply in this case, as there was no evidence of minor children depending upon the inmate. Thus, this inmate could refuse medical treatment and pursue his self-induced hunger strike.

Two similar fact patterns resulted in two apparently different holdings. The word "apparently" is used because the court in *Singletary* noted that the state had not produced any evidence that Costello's hunger strike had posed any security risk to the correctional facility.

In *Thor v. Superior Court*, 855 P.2d 375 (CA 1996), an inmate who was serving a life sentence fractured a cervical vertebra while in prison and became paraplegic as a result. The inmate refused to be fed and refused medication and other treatment. Psychiatrists said he was depressed, but he was mentally competent to understand his medical condition and the consequences of his actions, which were leading to his severe deterioration and ultimate death. Health staff members went to court to get permission to forcibly medicate and feed the inmate. The Supreme Court of California ruled that, under California law, the competent inmate had a right to refuse unwanted medical treatment, even though it would certainly result in his death. Unlike the prisoner in *Myers* discussed above, the prisoner's refusal to eat and receive treatment was not an attempt to manipulate prison officials or to undermine prison integrity or public safety. In denying the petition, and allowing the prisoner to refuse treatment, the court said:

> [A] competent, informed adult has a fundamental right of self-determination to refuse or demand the withdrawal of medical treatment of any form irrespective of the personal consequences … [I]n the absence of evidence demonstrating a threat to institutional security or public safety, prison officials, including medical personnel, have no affirmative duty to administer such treatment and may not deny a person incarcerated in state prison this freedom of choice.

There are many peripheral questions that spin off this basic question of involuntary medical treatment. One is the administration of drugs for the purpose of the rehabilitation of the inmate. In *Knecht v. Gillman*, 488 F.2d 1136

(8th Cir. 1973), inmates complained that they had been injected with the drug apomorphine without their consent. Prison staff members testified that the drug was used for its negative, adverse effects; it was used for inmates who had disruptive behavioral problems. A physician said that the drug was used when inmates did not get out of bed or when they swore or lied to the staff. The drug-induced vomiting for 15 minutes to an hour. Although the drug was prescribed and administered in a medical facility of the prison system where patients were sent for treatment of mental incompetency and mental illnesses, its use, as shown in this case, was for the behavior modification of disorderly inmates. The Eighth Circuit Court of Appeals disapproved this practice:

> [T]he act of forcing someone to vomit for a fifteen minute period for committing some minor breach of the rules can only be regarded as cruel and unusual unless the treatment is being administered to a patient who knowingly and intelligently has consented to it …. The use of this unproven drug for this purpose on an involuntary basis, is, in our opinion, cruel and unusual punishment prohibited by the Eighth Amendment.

A case of the same sort, which does not deal with health care at all but is an interesting case of involuntary treatment for the good of the inmate, is *Rutherford v. Hutto*, 377 F.Supp. 268 (E.D. AR 1974). Rutherford, an inmate at the Cummins Unit in Arkansas, complained that he was being forced to attend school against his will. He said that this constituted cruel and unusual punishment in violation of the Eighth and Fourteenth Amendments.

Rutherford was 43 years old and illiterate. He had very little formal education, because, he said, his parents took him out of school in the first or second grade when he had typhoid fever, and he never returned to school. He testified that sitting in a classroom made him extremely nervous. He claimed that he had a constitutional right to remain ignorant and illiterate. Prison officials said that he had to attend classes eight hours a day, one day each week. The prison (like most prisons) offered the equivalent of a 12-grade school, with academic and vocational courses. Inmates were required to attend classes until they reached the fourth-grade level in their education. (That has been a commonly used standard to measure literacy.) Participation in school programs was voluntary beyond the fourth grade. Rutherford had even made some progress in school, despite his objections, because he was reading at the second-grade level when the lawsuit was filed, and he had shown some improvement in arithmetic skills. The federal district court supported the program.

> [A] State clearly has a right to undertake to rehabilitate its convicts …. Granting the right of a State to try to rehabilitate the inmates of its penal institutions, the Court does not think that it should necessarily be left up to an individual convict to determine whether or not he is to participate in a rehabilitative program such as the one involved here …. [T]he Court does not consider that a convict has any more right to refuse to be given a chance to benefit from a rehabilitative program than he has to refuse to work or to obey other lawful orders that may be given to him by prison personnel.

Finally, and emphatically, this district court stated:

> The "constitutional right to be ignorant" or the "constitutional right to remain uneducated," which petitioner postulates, simply does not exist …. [T]he Court holds that a State has a sufficient interest in eliminating illiteracy among its convicts to justify it in requiring illiterate convicts, including adults, to attend classes designed to bring them up to at least the fourth grade educational level.

If the inmate refused to attend classes, he could be disciplined by prison officials, the court said.

Although the term "involuntary treatment" is ordinarily used to refer to medical or mental health care, *Rutherford* is a case that shows that courts will also support prison officials in pursuing other programs "for the good of the inmate." Sensitivity to requiring attendance at school is probably not as strong as forcing unwanted medication or other medical treatment, but the principle is very similar.

With respect to federal offenders, the rehabilitative aspect of prison was recently addressed in *Tapia v. U.S.*, 564 U.S. (2011). The Court reversed the lower courts' decisions to increase a convicted drug offender's prison sentence to allow them to participate in the Bureau of Prisons Residential Drug Abuse Treatment Program. The Court ruled that Title 18, U.S. Code, Section 3582 (a) which reads in part "imprisonment is not an appropriate means of promoting correction and rehabilitation"; it does not permit a court to lengthen or impose a sentence of imprisonment to foster rehabilitation.[14]

▸ Inmate Suicides

It is an unfortunate fact that suicides are a significant problem that corrections administrators deal with. In 2016, 6% of the 4,117 deaths of state and federal prison inmates and 31.1% of the 1,071 deaths of persons in local jails were caused by suicide.[15] Many persons confined in jails and prisons have mental health problems and/or substance abuse issues. The Bureau of Justice Statistics reported that during the years 2007–2009, 63% of sentenced jail inmates met the DSM-IV criteria for drug abuse or dependence and that over half of those inmates had used drugs in the month before their crime of conviction.[16] The stress of confinement adds to the concerns of those people. Depression, no doubt, is as prevalent among inmates as it is among the general citizenry. An estimated 26% of jail inmates and 14% of state prisoners met the threshold for serious psychological distress in the previous 30 days, and 31% of jail inmates and 24% of state prisoners reported they had been diagnosed with a major depressive disorder.[17] Staff members must always be on the lookout for suicidal tendencies among inmates and should be trained to look for the symptoms of a suicidal inmate. Suicide prevention programs have been instituted in many facilities and are recommended for all types of institutions. A review of available records about an inmate should always include looking for signs of suicidal inclinations. The screening of an inmate at admission should also involve an attempt to spot the suicide problem case. Courts have emphasized this concern that correctional officials must address.

> **A psychological or psychiatric condition can be as serious as any physical pathology or injury, especially when it results in suicidal tendencies. And just as a failure to act to save a detainee from suffering from gangrene might violate the duty to provide reasonable medical care absent an intervening legitimate government objective, failure to take any steps to save a suicidal detainee from injuring himself may also constitute a due process violation under *Bell v. Wolfish*.**

The above quotation is from *Partridge v. Two Unknown Police Officers*, 791 F.2d 1182 (5th Cir. 1986). Although corrections staff must always be on the alert for the suicidal inmate in their facility, the fact that an inmate has committed suicide does not necessarily mean that officials are constitutionally liable for the death. Deliberate indifference to the suicidal tendencies of the inmate must be shown in the circumstances of each case. It has been observed in *Freedman v. City of Allentown*, 853 F.2d 1111 (3rd Cir. 1988), that jail officials cannot guarantee the safety of inmates and that inmates who are truly intent on killing themselves will probably be able to do so eventually. Deliberate indifference requires a "strong likelihood" rather than a "mere possibility" that self-inflicted harm will occur. *Gish v. Thomas*, 516 F.3d 952 (11th Cir. 2008).

In the case of *Heflin v. Stewart County*, 958 F.2d 709 (6th Cir. 1992), the court upheld a jury award to the family of a jail inmate who hanged himself. Inmate Heflin was found hanging in his cell, but the deputy sheriff ordered that his body should remain hanging until a doctor or emergency medical staff arrived. When medical staff did arrive (after some 20 minutes), Heflin was cut down, but he died soon thereafter. The appeals court in *Heflin* noted a basic principle:

> **[P]retrial detainees have a constitutional right to the same protection afforded convicted prisoners who have serious medical needs.**

While the Supreme Court has not yet affirmed this same principle, it appears to be a sound holding, based on the language and concerns of *Bell v. Wolfish*. Applying that principle to the facts of this case, the court of appeals in *Heflin* agreed with the result in the lower (trial) court, finding that the deputy sheriff should have immediately cut down the inmate and administered CPR, because he was trained in that procedure. Under these circumstances, "the unlawfulness of doing nothing to attempt to save Heflin's life would have been apparent to a reasonable official in [the deputy's] position." Thus, there was a finding of negligence on the part of the deputy. There was also apparently deliberate indifference (the constitutional standard) toward the condition of the inmate. These facts and findings would support both a common law tort claim, and a claim of constitutional violation of the inmate's rights.

Reed v. Woodruff County, 7 F.3d 808 (8th Cir. 1993), another case of a jail suicide, had similar facts but a very different result. A trustee prisoner was found hanging in a shower stall, where it was determined that he had died (apparently unintentionally) while engaging in "autoerotic asphyxiation"—using hanging to bring about sexual gratification. Staff had been aware that the inmate was not in his cell. They had not found him until he had hanged himself, and he was dead when he was found. His family claimed that his death was the result of negligence and that there was also a violation of his constitutional rights. Under Arkansas law, the county was immune from a negligence suit. The family said that the jailer who found the inmate (the jailer was a trained emergency medical technician) should have attempted to resuscitate him and that his failure to do so showed deliberate indifference, a constitutional violation. The federal court of appeals disagreed (and reversed a lower court), holding that there was no obligation to try to revive the prisoner when the trained jailer determined that he was dead. There was no evidence that an attempt to resuscitate could have succeeded, and, therefore, there was no constitutional violation.

Myers v. County of Lake, 30 F.3d 847 (7th Cir. 1994), involved an attempted suicide by a juvenile detainee. The 16 year old tried to hang himself in a county facility but was unsuccessful. However, he suffered permanent brain damage and was awarded $600,000 in a suit alleging state law negligence against the county officials. (A claim for a constitutional violation had been dismissed by a magistrate, who found there was no evidence of deliberate indifference to support a constitutional-level claim.) Applying Indiana state law, a jury had found that the detention facility was negligent in not taking adequate precautions against suicide attempts. The federal appeals court upheld this judgment, concluding that state law required institutions to use reasonable care to prevent suicides by their wards. The court acknowledged that not all suicides could be prevented but said that taking reasonable measures to prevent them was required. The county argued that it was severely "starved" for funds and that the facility in question was shorthanded, so appropriate steps could not be taken to identify and protect those who were suicide risks. The court rejected this as a defense. Although the lack of funds and adequate staffing might have meant that no individuals were negligent, the county could not use lack of funds to defend against a claim that it had failed to perform its legally required functions.

There are a number of cases in which courts held that the circumstances were not sufficient to show deliberate indifference because there was not enough evidence to make officials aware of the suicidal risk. In *Freedman v. City of Allentown*, 853 F.2d 1111 (3rd Cir. 1988), officers were not liable because they did not realize that scars on the inmate's wrists and neck were from previous suicide attempts. In *State Bank v. Camic*, 712 F.2d 1140 (7th Cir. 1983), signs that an arrestee was intoxicated, unruly, and violent were not enough to conclude that there was a high risk of suicide. In *Boyd v. Harper*, 702 F.Supp. 578 (E.D. VA 1988), an arrestee who was crying continuously in his cell just before he committed suicide did not show a strong likelihood of being suicidal.

As mentioned earlier, the Supreme Court opinion in *Kingsley v. Hendrickson* has changed how some federal courts of appeal analyze failure to protect cases initiated by detainees rather than convicted prisoners. When the Supreme Court announces a major decision that impacts legal standards in one area in deciding a case, the district courts and courts of appeal are generally left to initially decide how expansive or restrictive an application the new standard has. In this case, did the *Kingsley* opinion apply only to use of force actions brought under the Due Process Clause of the Fourteenth Amendment, or should its rationale apply to all Due Process claims? The courts of appeal had typically assessed a pretrial detainee's medical care, use of force, and conditions of confinement claims using the Eighth Amendment standards applicable to convicted persons, reasoning that pretrial detainees are entitled to at least that much protection.

The Ninth Circuit refined its application of *Kingsley* in two recent opinions. *Castro v. County of Los Angeles*, 833 F.3d 1060 (9th Cir. 2016) was a failure to protect case. After Mr. Castro was arrested for public intoxication, he was seriously assaulted by another inmate in a county sobering cell. Mr. Castro suffered significant injuries, and he sued the county and individual deputies alleging a Fourteenth Amendment failure to protect claim. At trial, the jury found all the defendants liable and awarded Mr. Castro $3 million in damages. The county appealed and a panel affirmed the judgment against the individual defendants but reversed the judgment against the county using the Eighth Amendment standard announced in *Farmer v. Brennan*. One of the panel judges concluded that the new standard announced in *Kingsley v. Hendrickson* was the appropriate standard. The appeal was reheard *en banc* and the court of appeals overruled its previous precedent. The *en banc* opinion repeated that the civil rights statute, Title 42 U.S. Code Section 1983, contains no state of mind requirement. The state of mind requirement must be determined by the underlying federal right which is alleged to be violated. Under previous Ninth Circuit precedent, the courts applied the same standard for failure to protect claims under both the Eighth and Fourteenth Amendments. The Supreme Court in its *Kingsley* opinion noted that:

The language of the two Clauses [8th and 14th Amendments] differs, and the nature of the claims often differs. And, most importantly, pretrial detainees (unlike convicted prisoners) cannot be punished at all, much less `maliciously and sadistically. . . . [A] pretrial detainee can prevail by providing only objective evidence that the challenged governmental action is not rationally related to a legitimate governmental objective or that it is excessive in relation to that purpose.

The Ninth Circuit concluded that this language did not limit the announced standard to cases of excessive use of force, but applied to any governmental action, including failure to protect.

Applying *Kingsley* to the *Castro* case, the court of appeals first concluded that the deputies' physical act of placing the other inmate in a cell with Castro was intentional. The second question in the *Kingsley* standard is:

was there a substantial risk of serious harm to the plaintiff that could have been eliminated through reasonable and available measures that the officer did not take, thus causing the injury that the plaintiff suffered?" That inquiry differs from the inquiry with respect to an Eighth Amendment failure-to-protect claim: There, "the deprivation alleged must objectively be sufficiently serious; and the prison official must subjectively have a sufficiently culpable state of mind.

The Ninth Circuit next applied this standard to an inmate suicide scenario in *Horton by Horton v. City of Santa Maria*, 915 F.3d 592 (2019). In *Horton*, the 18-year-old detainee attempted to hang himself when he was placed in a police holding cell after being arrested for vandalism. Police received various information from Horton himself, his mother, and girlfriend about his mental health, and while Horton was unsupervised for about 30 minutes, he "removed his belt, fed it through the cell door bars, and hanged himself, causing permanent and severe brain damage." The mother of the detainee sued the city, the city police department, and individual officers, including officer B, for violating Horton's Fourteenth Amendment right to be safeguarded from injury.

The court of appeals reversed the district court denial of qualified immunity for officer B based on analysis under the "old deliberate indifference standard" [requiring a subjective component and objective component] which was the law at the time of Horton's injury. The court ruled "there was no case law at the time of the incident clearly establishing that a reasonable officer should have perceived the substantial risk."

The court then addressed the "current deliberate indifference standard" by restating that in the Ninth Circuit, "Fourteenth Amendment failure-to-protect claims must be analyzed under a *purely* objective standard. [citation omitted]. [W]e ask whether there was "a substantial risk of serious harm to the plaintiff that could have been eliminated through reasonable and available measures that the officer did not take, thus causing the injury that the plaintiff suffered." [citation omitted]. There is no separate inquiry into an officer's subjective state of mind.

The Seventh Circuit has also adopted the *Kingsley* standard for Fourteenth Amendment medical claims. In *Miranda v. County of Lake*, 900 F.3d 335 (7th Cir. 2018), Lyvita Gomes was arrested and held in the Lake County Jail. Her condition deteriorated. Correctional medical staff noted she was experiencing medical and mental health issues and moved her to the jail's medical unit. Staff also noted she was not eating and drinking. Fifteen days after being admitted to the jail, a contract physician for the facility ordered Lyvita transferred by ambulance to a local hospital. She died five days later and the medical examiner stated that the manner of death was suicide caused by complications from starvation and dehydration.

The family sued and a jury trial was held on the family's claims related to Lyvita's death. The jury did not find liability on the contract medical staff, but did find a social worker liable and awarded damages of $119,000. The estate appealed the judge's jury instructions in the area of intent. The court of appeals first ruled that it believed *Kingsley* should be applied to other Fourteenth Amendment claims brought by detainees including failure to protect from self-harm. The Seventh Circuit then provided additional instructions on how this new standard should be applied in Fourteenth Amendment Due Process claims within the circuit. The first issue was that the *Kingsley* standard did not constitutionalize medical malpractice. The new objective standard differs from the old Eighth Amendment standard, which required courts to assess a government actor's subjective state of mind, For example, did the defendant subjectively believe there was a significant risk of harm to the detainee? The new objective requires that a plaintiff only establish that a defendant's conduct was *objectively* unreasonable.

The court also noted that several other circuits, the Eighth, Eleventh, and Fifth, have not adopted this expansive application of *Kingsley*.

Finally, in *Taylor v. Backes*, ____ U.S. ___, 135 S.Ct. 2042 (2015) the Supreme Court reversed a lower court judgment denying qualified immunity to prison officials after an inmate committed suicide while in custody. The deceased inmate had a history of mental illness, substance abuse, and had attempted suicide in the past. He was arrested and taken to a state correctional facility in Delaware. The facility had a suicide prevention protocol, and the survivors of the deceased inmate alleged that the state officials failed to monitor the contract medical staff at the institution. The intake protocol required staff to ask a number of questions of the detainee to ascertain the risk of self-harm. The inmate did advise the intake personnel of two prior suicide attempts but not three other ones. The inmate also advised medical personnel that he was not currently contemplating committing suicide.

Although the inmate's wife stated that her husband had told her he was planning to kill himself on the day before the suicide, this information was not communicated to the correctional facility. On the day of the suicide, the inmate was checked by staff at 10:45 a.m., 10:50 a.m., and 11:00 a.m. but he was found dead at 11:35 a.m. The court of appeals had concluded that the correctional staff were not entitled to qualified immunity because in November of 2004, a prisoner had a right under the Eighth Amendment "to the proper implementation of adequate suicide prevention protocols." In its *per curiam* opinion, the Court noted that no "decision of this Court establishes a right to the proper implementation of adequate suicide prevention protocols. No decision of this Court even discusses suicide screening or prevention protocols." A review of then circuit law also demonstrated "that the weight of that authority at the time of [the inmate's] death suggested that such a right did *not* exist." The Court noted that a right is clearly established, for qualified immunity purposes, when "existing precedent has placed the statutory or constitutional question beyond debate." The judgment of the court of appeals denying qualified immunity was reversed.

▶ *Logue v. United States*

In *Logue v. United States*, 412 U.S. 521 (1973), the Supreme Court dealt with the death of a jail inmate. Logue was arrested by U.S. marshals on charges of smuggling marijuana into the United States. He was placed in the Nueces County Jail in Texas to await trial. (Most federal detainees awaiting trial were, and are, placed in state and local jails, which contract with the federal government to hold a certain number of inmates. This is because, in most localities, there are so few federal defendants being held that it is not economically feasible to build a separate federal jail. The federal government has built jails in some large cities, such as the Metropolitan Correctional Center in New York City, which was discussed in *Bell v. Wolfish*.) Logue committed suicide in the jail by hanging himself. His parents sued the United States for his wrongful death under the Federal Tort Claims Act.

The Supreme Court held that, even though Logue was placed in the jail as a federal prisoner by a deputy U.S. marshal, he was under the control of the local sheriff and his staff and not that of the marshal. To be liable under the Tort Claims Act, any negligent act or omission had to be the conduct of a "federal agency." The jail was a contractor with the federal government, not a federal agency. The Tort Claims Act specifically excluded a contractor with the United States from the definition of a federal agency. This insulated the United States from liability for the negligent acts or omissions of the jail's employees. However, there was a question whether the deputy U.S. marshal, knowing that Logue had some suicidal tendencies, should have alerted the jail officials to that problem and should have made sure there were arrangements to place Logue under constant surveillance. The Supreme Court said that knowing that there was a serious suicidal risk and failing to take steps to avoid the suicide could have amounted to negligence, the standard for liability under the Tort Claims Act. The case was sent back for the lower courts to ascertain whether the federal employee was negligent regarding that one aspect of the inmate's death.

▶ Special Health Care Needs of Female Prisoners

At times, it may become necessary for prisoners to be hospitalized for necessary medical care. During these hospitalizations, correctional personnel supervise and, when necessary, apply appropriate restraints, including shackling the offender to minimize the risk of escape. In *Nelson v. Correctional Medical Services*, 583 F.3d 522 (8th Cir. 2009), the court of appeals addressed the issue of whether the application of restraints (shackling both legs to the opposite side rails of a hospital bed) to a female prisoner who was in active labor constituted deliberate indifference to a serious medical need. The prisoner argued that the shackling had caused "extreme mental anguish and pain, permanent hip injury, torn stomach muscles, and an umbilical hernia [that required] surgical repair." Prison policy authorized the use of shackles "only when circumstances require the protection of inmates, staff, or other individuals from potential harm or to deter the possibility of escape."

The court of appeals upheld the denial of qualified immunity to the escorting officer who was responsible for applying the restraints. The court ruled that based on medical evidence presented to the trial court, shackling a prisoner in active labor posed a danger both to the prisoner and the fetus. The court also ruled that a fact finder could conclude the officer was subjectively aware of the prisoner's pain and that the officer was aware that it would be unnecessary to shackle a very sick inmate or pregnant inmate in active labor. Other federal courts have concluded that shackling pregnant females without individual assessment of health and security needs violates the Constitution. See for example, *Mendiola-Martinez v. Arpaio*, 836 F.3d 1239 (9th Cir. 2016) and *Villegas v. Metropolitan Government of Nashville*, 709 F.3d 563 (6th Cir. 2013) (finding the constitutional right to be free from shackling during labor, but right must be balanced against legitimate penological interests). The shackling of female inmates who were in labor prompted legislation at both the state and federal level. The First Step Act of 2018 (P.L. 115-391) was passed by Congress and signed by President Trump in December of 2018. Among the statute's many provisions, the law prohibited the use of restraints on pregnant inmates in the custody of BOP and the U.S. Marshals Service. The prohibition on the use of restraints does not apply if the inmate is determined to be an immediate and credible flight risk or poses an immediate and serious threat of harm to herself or others that cannot be reasonably prevented by other means, or a healthcare professional determines that the use of restraints is appropriate for the medical safety of the inmate. In 2015, the American Medical Association had determined that at least 21 states had laws prohibiting the practice of shackling pregnant prisoners during labor (Arizona, California, Colorado, Delaware, Florida, Hawaii, Idaho, Illinois, Louisiana, Maryland, Massachusetts, Minnesota, Nevada, New Mexico, New York, Pennsylvania, Rhode Island, Texas, Vermont, Washington, and West Virginia).[18]

The medical needs of female prisoners must also be considered when she elects to terminate a pregnancy. In *Victoria W. v. Larpenter*, 369 F.3d 474 (5th Cir. 2004), a female prisoner serving a short sentence learned she was pregnant. She advised officials she wished to have an elective abortion. The facility had a policy requiring all prisoners seeking any elective medical treatment to obtain a court order. Officials met with the inmate and explained the policy to both her and her attorney. The prisoner's attorney filed a motion with the local court to have the prisoner released from her sentence but did not seek a court order authorizing her release and transport to receive an abortion. By the time of her release, the month following her hearing, it was too late to have an abortion. She sued various correctional officials and the political subdivision (a Louisiana parish), claiming her rights to obtain an elective abortion and to be free from cruel and unusual punishment were violated. The district court granted summary judgment in favor of the defendant, and the court of appeals affirmed. The court of appeals used the factors set forth in *Turner v. Safley*, 482 U.S. 78 (1987), to rule that the policy was constitutional. Because prison officials in *Victoria W.* presented evidence that the policy was based on legitimate penological grounds, including security, the policy was found to be reasonable: "The policy's aim is to maximize inmate security and avoid liability. Nothing suggests that its purpose or effect was to deter abortions .... To the contrary, because the policy is reasonably related to legitimate penological interests, we find that it was constitutionally permissible."[19]

Another case dealing with a female prisoner's right to choose to have an elective abortion is *Roe v. Crawford*, 514 F.3d 789 (8th Cir. 2008). In 2005, the Missouri Department of Corrections (MDC) changed its policy from one of providing transportation for inmates wanting to terminate their pregnancies to one of allowing such transportation only where the abortion is indicated "due to threat to the mother's life or health, and if approved by the Medical Director in consultation with the Regional Medical Director." In *Roe*, a female prisoner requested transportation to obtain an elective abortion and was denied. She sued, challenging the policy as a violation of her rights under the Fourteenth and Eighth Amendments. After the case was certified as a class action (on behalf of all female prisoners in the custody of the department of corrections), the district court struck down the new policy as violating the inmates' rights under both the Fourteenth and Eighth Amendments. The appeals court affirmed the lower court's judgment but did find that the district court erred in its Eighth Amendment analysis and on one part of its *Turner* analysis.

In holding the new policy unconstitutional, the district court applied the four-factor analysis used in *Turner v. Safley*. The appeals court determined that the state did provide a valid, rational security concern (the first *Turner* factor) by its reference to "the existence of protesters and the configuration of the clinic result[ing] in higher risks to the guards and inmates, as well as a greater potential for inmates to escape." The appeals court, citing the deference owed prison officials, held that the district court erred in finding the MDC policy irrational because there had been no prior problems.

Examining the other three *Turner* factors, the courts found these were not met in *Roe*. The second factor, alternative means of obtaining an elective abortion, did not exist. Once incarcerated in the MDC, an elective abortion, which the Supreme Court determined is a liberty interest protected under the Fourteenth Amendment, is *entirely* unavailable. (Emphasis in original.) By completely eliminating any alternative means of obtaining an elective abortion, the MDC policy represents precisely the "exaggerated response to ... security objectives" that *Turner* forbids.

In similar manner, the third and fourth factors of *Turner* were found not to be in favor of the MDC. On the third *Turner* factor, impact on other inmates and prison resources, the court found "the policy does not logically reduce the overall number of [trips]" and that cost savings would be minimal. Finally, the court ruled that the correctional department's previous policy of permitting elective abortions "represents a ready alternative." Following its analysis, the court of appeals held that the new policy violated the Fourteenth Amendment rights of female prisoners.

The court of appeals, however, reversed the district court's finding that the policy violated the Eighth Amendment rights of prisoners. The state had argued that an elective abortion was, by definition, not necessary and, therefore, could not be a serious medical need. The court of appeals ruled:

> We hold an elective, non-therapeutic abortion does not constitute a serious medical need, and a prison institution's refusal to provide an inmate with access to an elective, non-therapeutic abortion does not rise to the level of deliberate indifference to constitute an Eighth Amendment violation.[19]

Readers are reminded that the *Roe v. Crawford* opinion is binding only within the Eighth Circuit and that the policy was found not to violate a prisoner's Eighth Amendment rights. This part of the ruling must be read in conjunction with its earlier portion that found that the state's policy, which prohibited all elective abortions, violated the prisoner's rights under the Fourteenth Amendment.

▶ HIV and AIDS

The following section addresses the response to HIV and AIDS by correctional entities. Although historical, the discussion and judicial decisions on similar healthcare scenarios remain applicable. The 1980s and 1990s required correctional agencies to address extremely challenging issues in which medical knowledge only slowly evolved. To better understand the context of correctional agency actions and court decisions, the reader is encouraged to read the Centers for Disease Control and Prevention's (CDC) *HIV and AIDS in the United States 1981-2000*.[20] From the early 1980s to 2000, the incidence of HIV and AIDS increased rapidly in the United States, as did their incidence in U.S. correctional facilities. By December 31, 2000, 58% of persons diagnosed with AIDS had died. In U.S. prisons and jails, HIV and AIDS was a major issue. In 1991, 2.3% of all state and federal prison inmates were HIV positive. AIDS was the attributed cause of death in 28% of state prison inmate deaths and 24% of jail inmate deaths.[21]

The most recent figures show that at the end of 2015, there were 17,150 inmates in state and federal prisons in the United States who were HIV-positive. At year-end 2015, 1.3% of all male and female inmates held in state or federal prisons were HIV-positive.[22] This is the lowest rate of infection calculated by the Bureau of Justice Statistics since beginning to track these data in 1991. There were 45 AIDS-related deaths of state and federal prisoners in 2015. From a historical perspective, the number of AIDS-related deaths in state prisons is declining, dropping from 1,010 in 1995 to 45 in 2015.

The AIDS cases were concentrated in the prisons of certain states and were virtually unknown in others. At the end of 2015, three states—Florida (2,571), Texas (2,129), and New York (1,820)—accounted for over ⅓ of all confirmed HIV-positive cases. Four states reported 10 or fewer confirmed AIDS cases at the end of 2015. By comparison, in 2008, prison AIDS cases were also concentrated in certain states and virtually unknown in others. The four states with the highest number of patients—Florida (3,626), New York (3,500), Texas (2,450), and California (1,402)—accounted for almost half of all confirmed AIDS or HIV-positive cases. Four states reported fewer than 10 confirmed AIDS cases at the end of 2008.[23]

The Supreme Court has issued two opinions that have some impact on dealing with HIV/AIDS within the prison setting. In *Pennsylvania Department of Corrections v. Yeskey*, 524 U.S. 206 (1998), inmate Yeskey was denied placement in a motivational boot camp due to his hypertension. He sued, alleging a violation of the Americans with Disabilities Act (ADA). The Supreme Court agreed, holding that the ADA applied to inmates in state institutions.

During the same term, the Court decided *Bragdon v. Abbott*, 524 U.S. 624 (1998). Although this case deals with a private citizen, not an inmate, its holding, which interprets the ADA, gives guidance to prison and jail officials. In 1994, Abbott, who was infected with HIV, went to a dental appointment. In completing the registration form, she mentioned her HIV infection. Upon discovering a cavity, Dr. Bragdon told Abbott that he would fill the cavity at a hospital at no added cost for his services, as his policy was not to fill cavities of HIV-infected persons in his office.

Abbott was told; however, that she would have to pay costs for using the hospital facilities. Abbott sued, in part, under Section 302 of the ADA, which provides the following:

> **No individual shall be discriminated against on the basis of disability in the full and equal enjoyment of the goods, services, facilities, privileges, advantages, or accommodations of any place of public accommodation by any person who …. operates a place of public accommodation.**

Within the context of this discussion, disability is defined in the statute as "a physical or mental impairment that substantially limits one or more of the major life activities of such individual." The district and appeals courts held that Abbott's HIV infection satisfied the definition of "disability." The Supreme Court agreed. Thus, the protections of the ADA apply to persons with HIV infections.

One of the most sweeping decisions on AIDS in prisons was made in *Harris v. Thigpen*, 941 F.2d 1495 (11th Cir. 1991); 727 F.Supp. 1564 (M.D. AL 1990). Alabama had a program for the mandatory testing of all inmates and for the segregation of those found to be HIV-positive. There was a broad attack on the state's approach, supported by outside organizations. The district court held that the mandatory testing program, conducted for all inmates at admission, was a reasonable means of trying to address the threat of AIDS to the inmate population. It was upheld against challenges of unreasonable search and seizure, cruel and unusual punishment, and due process violations. Both the district and appellate courts held that the placement of HIV-positive inmates in segregated confinement was not cruel and unusual and that no due process hearing was required before their placement. Inmates challenged the state's lack of medical care, particularly when AZT (a drug commonly used in the attempted prevention of HIV infection from developing into full-blown AIDS) was not used for the treatment of HIV-positive inmates to the extent that it was recommended in the outside community (or in some other state prison systems). These courts found that there were no constitutional violations (no deliberate indifference to health needs) by Alabama and that the failure to provide the AZT treatment was permissible (justifying its conclusion in large part on the high cost of the drug treatments).

In a somewhat unusual twist, a number of non-HIV-infected inmates joined the *Harris* case in support of the state officials and asked the court to approve the testing and segregation program, so that they would be protected from the spread of HIV infection. The district court acknowledged their concerns but refused to say that they were entitled to the testing and segregation program as a matter of constitutional right and protection. In other words, the court refused to order the state to provide its program of segregating HIV-positive inmates as a constitutional entitlement for the inmates. (But the court did uphold the decision of the state to adopt the program as a justifiable policy for the good of the corrections system and its inmates.)

Inmates who were HIV-positive also objected to the fact that they were not eligible for placement in programs, such as vocational training and work release, which would help them upon release. The courts held that they were not entitled to such programs as a matter of law and that the decision to limit their access to such programs was one for the prison officials to make on the basis of their informed correctional judgment. The appeals court did send the case back for further fact-finding by the district court on the issue of whether the segregated HIV-positive inmates were excluded from programs that were available to other inmates and whether this was a violation of the Rehabilitation Act of 1973 (Title 29, U.S. Code, Section 794). The court indicated particular concern over the complaints of inmates that they did not have access to the law library materials and that this denied them equal access rights to the courts. Thus, on virtually all fronts, the concerns of the inmates were turned aside by these courts, in a big showing of deference to the policies and approaches of the corrections managers.

Eight years later, the Eleventh Circuit Court of Appeals issued its opinion on whether Alabama's policies were in violation of Section 504 of the Rehabilitation Act. In *Onishea v. Hopper*, 171 F.3d 1289 (11th Cir. 1999), cert. denied, 528 U.S. 1114 (2000), HIV-positive inmates sued the Alabama Department of Corrections under that act to force integration (mixing HIV-positive and HIV-negative inmates) in prison recreational, religious, and educational programs.

The district court denied relief, finding that sexual conduct, intravenous drug use, and bloodshed were always a possibility in prison when staff were not watching; that prison life is unpredictable; and that because HIV is transmitted by the previously listed actions, HIV transmission in prison is more than a "theoretical possibility." Since such conduct can occur within a prison and due to the catastrophic severity that would result if it did, the court held that integrating the programs would present a significant risk of HIV virus transmission and that HIV-positive inmates were not "otherwise qualified" for the benefits provided in the federal statute. On appeal, the circuit court, in an en banc decision, agreed with the district court. In framing the issue of the case, the court cited *School Board of Nassau County v. Arline*, 480 U.S. 273 (1987):

> A person who poses a significant risk of communicating an infectious disease to others in the workplace will not be otherwise qualified for his or her job if reasonable accommodation will not eliminate that risk.

As to the element of risk in AIDS management, this appeals court joined three other circuits in holding:

> [S]aying a risk of an event is small does not mean that it will not happen. And each time the event occurs, it is real people … that suffer the consequences. Saying that only one in 42,000 persons will die if exposed to a risk does not make that one's death insignificant.

The facts that prisons have violence, intravenous drug use, and sexual conduct and that these acts may cause blood-to-blood contact, providing the opportunity for transmission of the virus, was sufficient to conclude that there was significant risk. This risk removed the inmates from the protective benefits of the Rehabilitation Act.

The court also held that there was a legitimate penal concern here. Security concerns and costs were identified as such legitimate government concerns. The appeals court affirmed the decision of the district court, denying relief to the inmates. A writ of certiorari was filed with the U.S. Supreme Court in this case and was denied in *Davis v. Hopper*, 528 U.S. 1114 (2000).

In 2012, the Alabama policy on segregating HIV positive inmates was found to violate the Americans with Disabilities Act, Title II and Section 504 of the Rehabilitation Act. *Henderson v. Thomas*, 913 F. Supp. 2d 1267 (MD Ala. 2012). The parties later entered into an agreement to settle the lawsuit. The only other state that had segregated HIV positive inmates in 2012 was South Carolina, and that state discontinued the practice in 2013.[24]

As to the right of an HIV-positive inmate to be involved in programs alongside other inmates, in *Gates v. Rowland*, 39 F.3d 1439 (9th Cir. 1994), the court of appeals held that California officials did not have to place the HIV-infected inmates in work assignments in food service. A lower court had enjoined the prison officials from denying those regular work assignments to any HIV-positive inmates. Although recognizing that there was little risk of spreading the virus through the food service work, the appeals court upheld the rationale of the prison officials for their decision. The government's argument had been that other inmates would perceive a threat, even if medically there was little or none there, and that maintaining positive attitudes among the inmates about the safety and sanitation of their food was particularly important in the prison setting. The court ruled that these were legitimate penological concerns and that the state would not be required to assign HIV-positive inmates to food service jobs.

There is some basis for asserting that the HIV (positive) test results and AIDS diagnosis are matters of particular sensitivity to individuals. It may be argued that inmates may have privacy rights, so that those facts should not be revealed to persons outside of the immediate healthcare staff who have an obvious need to know about them. The court in *Harris v. Thigpen* did not find much in the way of privacy protections for HIV/AIDS inmates. But the federal court in *Doe v. Coughlin*, 697 F.Supp. 1234 (N.D. NY 1988), did find that there was a privacy interest retained by the inmate patient, who should have control over who has access to information about his medical status.

In *Doe v. Delie*, 357 F.3d 309 (3rd Cir. 2001), the court of appeals ruled that prisoners do have a right to medical privacy, subject to legitimate penological interests, protected by the Fourteenth Amendment. Doe alleged that prison officials did not maintain the privacy of his HIV status in the following ways: (1) advised escorting officers of his status; (2) during physician visits, maintained an open-door policy, allowing others to hear his communications with the physician; and (3) when administering medication, the staff loudly announced the name of the medication, permitting others (inmates) to know his status. The court of appeals ruled that a person's HIV status is entitled to privacy protection because disclosure may result in stigma, harassment, and other risks of harm.

The court also held that while a prisoner lacks an expectation of privacy in his cell (*Hudson v. Palmer*, 468 U.S. 517 (1984)), "the right to nondisclosure of one's medical information emanates from a different source and protects different interests than the right to be free from unreasonable searches and seizures." The court said that a right to privacy in medical information for a prisoner is necessarily limited by correctional necessity, and the right against disclosure of confidential medical information does not mean that Doe may expect to "conceal this diagnosed medical condition from everyone in the corrections system."

The interest of staff in knowing who is HIV-positive relates to inmates' privacy concerns. There are at least two potential areas of staff interest. The first is one of wanting to know who in a prison's general population is HIV-infected so that staff may take appropriate safety precautions. Another, more problematic issue concerns the assault upon a staff member by an inmate in which there may be exposure to blood. Should the staff member be notified if the inmate is HIV-positive? To provide this information could raise the privacy concerns mentioned before, although the employee's interest in knowing is certainly understandable.[25] One approach in such an instance is to offer the employee periodic testing, with pretest and posttest counseling. Costs in this situation would be absorbed by the agency, and if the employee chooses to go to a private physician, a claim for reimbursement might be made through workman's compensation.

Each correctional facility should check the state and local requirements for reporting HIV/AIDS cases to the local health authorities. Most jurisdictions have requirements for reporting these cases. Especially on an inmate's release, requirements of state, county, and city departments of health must be followed regarding the notification that must be made. The United States Centers for Disease Control and Prevention (CDC) periodically updates guidelines for the care and treatment of HIV in correctional institutions.[26]

▶ Tuberculosis in Prisons

It is important to comment on the prevalence of tuberculosis infection and disease (TB) in prisons and jails. It is now well known that there was a resurgence of tuberculosis in the United States in the 1980s. The spread of TB is a special concern in corrections institutions because of the close living environment, which can facilitate the spread of the disease, and the interaction that has been identified between TB and HIV infection, which is also prevalent in many corrections institutions.

The close, and often-crowded, conditions in jails and prisons create an environment of increased risk for the spread of TB. Compounding this problem is the discovery of drug-resistant strains of TB, which further increase the risk of spreading the disease. It has been found that the presence of immune suppressions in an individual (the presence of HIV, for example) may cause the individual not to be reactive to a TB skin test. This means, of course, that that person can elude detection for a long time and continue to spread the disease, while receiving no treatment for himself due to his negative test results.

The prevalence of TB remains much higher among prison inmates than the U.S. general population. In 2018, correctional facilities accounted for almost 4% of TB cases nationwide.[27] Three factors have been cited as contributing to this high rate. First, a significant number of persons in prison pose a high risk for TB (for example, drug users; persons with HIV; and persons who, prior to confinement, often did not receive standard public health interventions or nonemergency medical care). Second, as noted above, there is the institution's physical structure (close living quarters, crowded conditions, and poor ventilation). The third factor is the movement of inmates in and out of "overcrowded and inadequately ventilated facilities," joined with the existing inmate risk factors for TB.[28]

Most state and federal prison systems follow the recommendations of the Centers for Disease Control and Prevention on the screening of inmates. In a 2005 survey, 94% of the 47 responding state and federal prison systems required mandatory skin testing for TB within two weeks of prison admission. More than 90% of the state/federal systems conduct annual TB screening of all inmates.[29] Those who are diagnosed as infectious should be isolated from other inmates. The preferred method of isolation is placement in a negative-pressure isolation room (a room with ventilation that does not flow into the general ventilation system). Treatment for active cases is a combination of drugs. Inmates who show positive test results but are asymptomatic should be given preventive drug therapy and should be directly and periodically observed by health staff to detect any TB symptoms. When infected inmates are scheduled for release, it is important that they are referred to local health departments, and, if possible, arrangements for continued treatments and follow-up checks should be made.

With respect to legal issues, the main concerns have been lawsuits brought alleging failures to take adequate steps to prevent the spread of the disease, thereby placing other inmates (and staff) at increased risk. One court of appeals, in *DeGidio v. Pung*, 920 F.2d 525 (8th Cir. 1990), held that an agency's failure to take adequate steps to detect and fight the disease could show a pattern that would amount to deliberate indifference to the serious medical needs of inmates (the constitutional standard for liability under *Estelle v. Gamble*). In *Blumhagen v. Sabes*, 834 F.Supp. 1347 (D. WY 1993), an inmate in Wyoming alleged that officials had screened all inmates for TB but had failed, after testing, to isolate the infectious TB cases. In this case, the federal district court held that the allegations showed only differences of opinion about how TB cases should be treated, and the court concluded that the actions of Wyoming officials did not amount to indifference to the prisoners' medical needs. The court did note, however, that the inmate might have a claim for malpractice under Wyoming tort law and suggested that the inmate look into that as a possible remedy.

Those two cases point out the standards that would be recommended for corrections officials: (1) Due to the prevalence of the disease and its highly dangerous nature in prisons, corrections officials should regularly consult with health officials about the adoption of detection and treatment programs according to current guidelines (from the CDC and others) about TB care in corrections facilities. To fail to do so could expose officials to a claim of indifference to the medical needs of inmates and thus expose those officials to personal liability under 42 U.S.C. § 1983, pursuant to constitutional standards. (2) Even if programs are implemented, officials are well-advised to update them and to ensure that staff members follow through with all recommended testing and treatments to avoid tort claims of medical malpractice.

A second legal issue involves inmates' objections to being tested when there is a mandatory, universal testing program in an institution or agency. The Massachusetts Appeals Court, in *Langton v. Commissioner of Corrections*, 614 N.E.2d 1002 (1993), upheld the state's policy (required by a state law) that inmates were required to be tested for TB. This court noted that the commissioner had a responsibility to protect the health of all inmates and staff. Because of legitimate concerns for inmate security and safety, the court said that the policy for mandatory testing was lawful and justified and that the inmate could be disciplined for refusing to take the TB test.

Another case dealing with this issue appears to come down on the other side. In *Jolly v. Coughlin*, 894 F.Supp. 734 (S.D. NY 1995), aff'd., 76 F.3d 468 (2nd Cir. 1996), Jolly, a New York inmate was a Rastafarian who refused to take the TB screening test based on his religious beliefs. Pursuant to the corrections department's TB control program, inmates refusing the test were put in "medical keeplock," meaning they had to stay in their cells at all times, except for showering. (They were not placed in respiratory [negative pressure] isolation, as active cases were.) Inmate Jolly was in keeplock status for more than three and a half years. He never displayed any symptoms of TB, and his three X-ray tests were negative.

Applying the standards of the Religious Freedom Restoration Act, the court found that officials were substantially burdening Jolly's exercise of his religious beliefs and that there was not a compelling governmental interest in doing so. Although conceding that there was a compelling interest in preventing the spread of TB (and that interest would support universal testing programs, one might note, even against religious objections), the defendant prison officials did not convince the court that their means of dealing with this inmate (placing him in indefinite keeplock) was the least restrictive means of furthering their interest in fighting the spread of TB. Officials, in fact, conceded that Jolly was not contagious. The court ordered Jolly released from keeplock status and enjoined prison officials from placing him there.

These TB testing cases demonstrate that, under most circumstances, mandatory and universal testing is a wise medical and correctional decision, and it can be defended in court. Cases of religious objections to the testing program must be evaluated on an individual basis and reviewed with legal counsel. The merits of individual cases should be explored, along with any alternatives may be available to handle the conscientious religious objector.

▶ COVID-19 and Correctional Institutions

Beginning in 2020 correctional organizations were faced with a new and challenging issue - how to address the health and safety of inmates and staff from COVID-19 infection. The COVID-19 virus is highly infectious and can be transmitted from person to person. COVID-19 fatality rates increase with age and underlying health conditions such as cardiovascular disease, respiratory disease, diabetes, and immune compromise. If contracted, COVID-19 can cause severe complications or death. Because there is no current vaccine, the Centers for Disease Control and Prevention ("CDC") recommends preventative measures to decrease transmission such as physical distancing, mask wearing, and increasing focus on personal hygiene such as additional hand washing.

Congress and a number of federal courts have addressed some issues related to the disease. In March 2020 Congress enacted the "Corona Virus Aid, Relief and Economic Security Act" (CARES Act). Pub. L. 116-136 which addressed a number of issues related to public health and the national economy, Among the many provisions of the CARES Act provided a supplemental appropriation of $100,000,000 for additional salaries for Bureau of Prisons (BOP) staff to address the COVID-19 emergency; authorized the Department of Health and

Human Services to provide personal protective equipment and testing kits to the BOP (Section 12003 (b)(1); authorized the Director of the BOP to extend the maximum period of time an offender could be placed on home confinement pursuant to Title 18 U.S. Code Section 3624(c)) (Section 12003 (b)(2)), and authorized the BOP to waive fees related to video visiting during the national Covid-19 emergency Section 12003 (c)). The BOP also developed and implemented a number of procedures to address the emergency, including suspending face to face social visiting, suspending transfers of inmates between correctional facilities, testing new admissions to the BOP, developing self-report criteria for staff. *BOP Implementing Modified Operations*, https://www.bop.gov /coronavirus/covid19_status.jsp.

States responded by enacting policies and procedures, in many cases based upon recommendations and guidance from the Centers for Disease Control and Prevention (CDC). See for example, *Interim Guidance on Management of Coronavirus Disease 2019 (COVID-19) in Correctional and Detention Facilities*, U.S. Centers for Disease Control and Prevention, July 14, 2020, updated July 20, 2020. https://www.cdc.gov/coronavirus/2019 -ncov/community/correction-detention/guidance-correctional-detention.html. Litigation related to the states' response to COVID-19 was initiated, generally seeking temporary and permanent injunctions compelling states to implement various practices designed to prevent the spread of COVID-19 in correctional facilities.

One such lawsuit was filed in March 2020 and involved inmates at the Park Unit of the Texas Department of Criminal Justice (TDCJ). The Park Unit is a facility for the aged and infirm, and inmates there alleged policies and procedures implemented by the TDCJ violated the Eighth Amendment "cruel and unusual punishment" clause and the Americans with Disabilities Act because the policies did not provide enough protection to the inmates. Following several days of hearings, the federal district court issued a temporary injunction compelling the TDCJ to undertake 14 different modifications to its COVID-19 procedures ranging from providing inmates with unrestricted access to hand soap and disposable hand towels, providing 60% alcohol hand sanitizer in housing areas, dining area, clinic, commissary, and laundry exchange area; requiring common areas in housing areas, lavatory facilities and the dining hall to be cleaned every 30 minutes with bleach based cleaning agents; posting signage and information about the spread of Covid-19 and instructions on how to properly wash hands; development within three days on a plan to test all Pack Unit inmates for COVID-19 and for quarantining those who test positive and a plan for testing staff and minimizing positive staff contact with inmates. In making its ruling, the district court noted that the terms of the injunction exceeded the recommendations of the CDC; that many of the measures imposed by the injunction overlapped with current TDCJ COVID-19 policy, but were necessary to promote TDCJ's compliance with its own policy; and that compliance with the CDC guidelines could create unconstitutional conditions of confinement. The state appealed and the court of appeals stayed the district court's temporary injunction in April 2020. *Valentine v. Collier*, 956 F.3d 797 (5th Cir. 2020). In staying the district court's preliminary injunction, the court of appeals noted:

> As with every other part of the country, our Nation's correctional facilities have not escaped the reach of COVID-19. To mitigate the spread of the virus, the Texas Department of Criminal Justice ("TDCJ") has adopted and implemented several rounds of measures guided by ever-changing CDC recommendations. Plaintiffs are two inmates at the TDCJ Wallace Pack Unit ("Pack Unit"), a prison for the elderly and the infirm. They say TDCJ's measures don't go far enough

When considering to grant a stay of an injunction a court considers four factors: (1) has the applicant for the stay made a strong showing that the party is likely to prevail on the merits of the case; (2) will the party seeking the stay be irreparably harmed without a stay; (3) would issuing a stay substantially injure the other parties in the proceeding; and (4) where the public interest in the outcome lies. *Nken v. Holder*, 556 U.S. 418 (2009).

The court of appeals concluded the TDCJ was likely to prevail on an appeal. While first noting that an Eighth Amendment finding of deliberate indifference is "an extremely high standard to meet" the court of appeals concluded that Plaintiffs had failed to show a substantial risk of serious harm that amounts to "cruel and unusual punishment" and that the district court had committed a legal error in its application of *Farmer v. Brennan*. While the TDCJ had acknowledged that COVID-19 can pose a serious and fatal risk of harm to prison inmates, the inmate plaintiffs had failed to demonstrate that taking into account the protective measures (such as providing access to soap, tissue, gloves, masks, regular cleaning of common areas, signs educating the inmate population of the risks of COVID-19 and the quarantine of new inmates transferring into the unit) implemented by the TDOJ that there was a substantial risk of serious harm to the plaintiffs. The district court had concluded that additional measures beyond what was recommended by the CDC and implemented by the TDCJ. The court of appeals found no legal precedent which ruled that compliance with CDC guidelines would violate the Eighth Amendment.

The court of appeals also ruled the district court erred in entering an injunction to compel the state to comply with its own regulations. The Supreme Court's ruling in *Pennhurst State Hospital v. Halderman*, 465 U.S. 89 (1989) concluded the Eleventh Amendment prohibits a federal court from enjoining state facilities to follow state law.

The court of appeals concluded, assuming the plaintiffs had established an objective risk of substantial harm, they had not demonstrated the defendants were subjectively deliberately indifferent. The district court determined the correct Eighth Amendment standard was whether the defendants "reasonably abate[d] the risk" of infection. The court of appeals concluded that this analysis resembled the standard for civil negligence, not constitutional "deliberate indifference: The evidence established the TDCJ was taking measures to abate the risks of COVID-19 infections relying on information and guidance from the CDC and medical professionals. The plaintiffs (and the district court's) disagreement with the TDCJ did not establish deliberate indifference.

Concluding the TDCJ would prevail on the first element necessary to obtain a say of an injunction, the court of appeals then concluded that the state would be irreparably harmed because any time a state is enjoined from effecting its statutes enacted by representatives of the people, there is a form of irreparable injury. Texas law provided the TDCJ with the authority to implement policy in the state's prisons, so the injunction prevented the state from implementing the will of its state legislature. The court of appeals also concluded the injunction would "interfere with the rapidly changing and flexible system-wide approach" the TDCJ had implemented to address the COVID-19 outbreak. In reaching this conclusion the court of appeals noted that the TDCJ had implemented an initial policy based on the guidance of the CDC and the TDCJ's own medical experts. When the CDC modified its guidelines in both March and April the TDCJ updated and modified its policy. The court of appeals concluded the injunction would significantly hamper the TDCJ's ability to adjust its policy, and "locks in place a set of policies for a crisis that defies fixed approaches." The remaining two factors also favored the state. The plaintiffs sought to lift the stay in the Supreme Court, but the Supreme Court declined to lift the stay. *Valentine v. Collier*, __ U.S. ___, 140 S.Ct. 1598 (2020). The court of appeals later vacated the injunction concluding the state had substantially complied with its terms. *Valentine v. Collier*, 960 F.3d 707 (5th Cir. 2020). In October 2020, the 5th Circuit granted the state's motion to stay enforcement of the district court's permanent injunction rendered in this case, concluding that "TDCJ's response, albeit imperfect, did not amount to deliberate indifference under the Eighth Amendment."

Similar issues were raised in a pretrial setting in *Mays v. Dart* related to the conditions of the Cook County Jail and its response to COVID-19. A federal district court had granted plaintiff inmates' motion for a temporary restraining order on a number of issues, including requiring the Sheriff to provide hand soap and sanitizer to all detainees and to provide face masks to detainees in quarantine. The district court also placed limits on the Sheriff's ability to double cell inmates and to provide group (dormitory style housing with many inmates sleeping in a single room on closely spaced bunk beds). The court of appeals, while commending the district court for the handling of the case, found three distinct legal errors and reversed that part of the preliminary injunction related to socially distanced housing. The three legal errors found by the court of appeals were the district court's: (1) failure to consider the Sheriff's conduct in response to COVID-19 in its entirety; (2) failure to afford the Sheriff proper deference in adopting policies related to safety and security; and (3) applying an incorrect legal standard in evaluating the Plaintiffs' likelihood of success on the merits. The opinion of the court of appeals is unique in that it applies the recent Supreme Court ruling in *Kingsley v. Hendrickson*, 576 U.S. 389 (7th Cir. 2015) [this case is discussed in greater detail in this chapter and the chapter on jails] which directed that conditions of confinement claims for pretrial detainees should be evaluated under the objective reasonableness standard rather than the more challenging deliberate indifference standard. The court of appeals first set forth the requirements for a party to obtain a preliminary injunction: a plaintiff must show: (1) that without the relief request, the party would suffer irreparable harm; (2) that traditional legal remedies would be inadequate, and (3) the party demonstrates some likelihood of prevailing on the merits of their lawsuit.

The court of appeals found error with the district court's focus on Sheriff's response to the social distancing of housing and its failure to consider the totality of everything the Sheriff had done to address the systemic challenges of COVID-19. On the second issue of deference to the professional judgment of correctional administrators, the court of appeals relied upon the Supreme Court's decision in *Bell v. Wolfish* that directed courts to "afford prison administrators wide-ranging deference in the adoption of policies and practices that in their judgment are needed to preserve internal order and discipline and to maintain institutional security." In affirming other aspects of the preliminary injunction, the court of appeals found that the district court's ruling followed closely the *Guidance on*

Management of Coronavirus Disease 2019 (COVID-19) in Correctional and Detention Facilities. While noting that these guidelines do not establish constitutional minima, the guidelines were relevant to determining the objective reasonableness of an agency's actions:

> The CDC Guidelines—like other administrative guidance—do not themselves set a constitutional standard. [Citing Bell v. Woflish]. . . . But even if not dispositive, implementation (and proper execution) of guidelines that express an expert agency's views on best practices are certainly relevant to an objective reasonableness determination. . . . This is particularly true here, where the CDC Guidelines provide the authoritative source of guidance on prevention and safety mechanisms for a novel coronavirus in a historic global pandemic where the public health standards are emerging and changing.

Litigation concerning correctional response to the COVID-19 pandemic will continue to be filed in courts. As of September 28, 2020, a review of the Google Scholar legal research platform indicated that there were 6,820 results produced by using the search term "COVID 19 AND prisons."

▶ An Aging Prison Population

Data establishes that an increase in the elderly prison population has occurred, and continues to occur, across America. As of December 31, 2018, it was estimated that 21% of the nation's 1.41 million sentenced prisoners under state or federal jurisdiction were age 50 or older.[30] (this is the age commonly used to report on, or count the elderly). In 2009, prisoners over the age of 50 made up only 10% of the sentenced prison population. This elderly inmate population will likely continue to increase because of two principal factors: the increased number of elderly in the general population produces an increased pool of older offenders (although crime slows down with aging, it does not disappear); and longer sentences (including three-strikes statutes), many without parole, in many jurisdictions ensure that the existing inmate population will age while in prison and become part of that elderly group of inmates. Of the almost 64,000 persons charged in federal courts with criminal conduct in FY 2016 (October 1, 2015-September 30, 2016), 14% were age 50 years or older and the percentage of defendants sentenced to federal prison aged 50 years and older increased from 14% in FY 2006 to 20.5% in FY 2016.[31]

The increased number of elderly inmates presents several management problems that are more or less unique to this age group. While different correctional systems define elderly in different terms, either by chronological age or assessment of needs, the group as a whole possesses special needs in such areas as programming, housing, and treatment. For example, physical ailments and the general deterioration of energy levels and muscles produce problems in the classification of elderly inmates regarding housing units, job assignments, and other programs. Nutritional needs are different for aging inmates and may require the consideration of different dietary planning. Some activities, such as practicing religion, watching television, and participating in prison organizations, may be more attractive to the elderly than to younger inmates. The elderly can become easier targets for other inmates to prey on.

Because many persons in prison come from poor backgrounds, many failed to receive suitable healthcare treatment in the community. This lack of adequate health care, when coupled with use of tobacco, alcohol, and illegal drugs, and high-risk sexual activities, increases the risk that the elderly prisoner will suffer from a chronic or serious disease, violence, or some other condition that will impact bodily function or mobility. The healthcare needs of the elderly are usually greater than those of younger inmates, as the elderly inmate may suffer more frequently from physical ailments such as hypertension, diabetes, and heart disease. The older inmate more often has chronic ailments, such as hearing or vision loss, incontinence, confusion, and digestive system ailments. As a result of these conditions, it is more common to see the use of canes, wheel chairs, hearing aids, and special clothing by elderly inmates.[32]

How prison administrators react to these special problems varies. There is no set approach or agreed-upon response. Prison administrators do agree that the special situation of the aging is present and that some coordinated response must be adopted in each agency. In some agencies, the elderly (especially those needing special attention or care) are placed in certain institutions where staff members are trained to look after their needs. At some facilities, the elderly are housed together. Those with significant physical disabilities (such as those in wheelchairs or those who can walk only with a cane) are likely to be assigned to first-floor living quarters. A federal statute that has impact on corrections is the Americans with Disabilities Act (ADA), enacted in 1990. The Act was amended in 2010. Among its provisions are standards for accessible design. These standards have the objective of making prison facilities readily accessible to, and usable by persons with disabilities. In addition, the ADA also has new provisions on "discrimination prohibited." See Title 28, Code of Federal Regulations, Section 35.152, paragraph (b).

Some institutions have jobs that are largely sedentary and easy to get to, which are set aside for assignment to the elderly (and disabled) inmates. There is no agreement, among staff or among inmates, about whether elderly inmates should be totally segregated or should be mixed with younger inmates as long and as far as possible. Many of the elderly prefer separate, quieter quarters and generally find living with their own age group less stressful.

The legal problems of dealing with the elderly are essentially the same as dealing with the general prison population, but the terms "aging" or "elderly" are placed in front of the issues and the legal answers. For example, prisons obviously have a basic requirement to look after the health needs of all inmates, including the elderly. Constitutionally, the standard is the same as for all: prison officials must not show deliberate indifference to the serious medical needs of the inmates, and in this case, the increased medical needs of elderly inmates. In a similar way, common law tort (malpractice) standards are the same as those for the general population, with modification needed to reflect the recognized degree of care that must be provided to the special needs of the elderly population. As part of those broad concerns for the well-being of the elderly inmates, decisions on food service, special accommodations for visiting and other contacts with family and friends, and assignments to special housing or special programs must all reflect some sensitivity to their specialized needs. (Ignoring these problems completely could result in claims of indifference to the needs of the elderly inmates and, thus, possible exposure to individual constitutional liability under Section 1983.)

The growth in this segment of the inmate population has been gradual, but it is demonstrable. Standards of the American Correctional Association call for prison and jail administrators to take this group's special needs into account in their planning, and in the facilities and activities that are provided. Although there is no universal or easy answer to the issues presented, it is clear that corrections administrators are aware of the problem and have taken some steps to address it.

Several jurisdictions have attempted to address this issue by enacting legislation to permit release of prisoners who reach a certain age. Persons in federal custody can be recommended for early release when they have reached the age of 70 and have served more than 30 years of their sentence. This so-called "safety valve" legislation is found in Title 18, U.S.C. § 3582. The statute requires that a reduction may be considered by the sentencing court only upon recommendation of the Director of the Bureau of Prisons. There are several lower court opinions that have denied consideration of an inmate's petition to be released earlier because there was no such recommendation. *Morales v. U.S.*, 353 F.Supp. 2d 204 (D. MA 2005). In another case, while noting that the court lacked jurisdiction because there was no recommendation, the court ruled that the decision not to recommend early release had been reviewed by several levels of prison officials and was not arbitrary or capricious because the prisoner suffered only from chronic ailments. *Leja v. Sabol*, 487 F.Supp. 2d 201 (D. MA 2007).[33]

The 2018 First Step Act (P.L. 115-391) reauthorized and modified the requirements of the Second Chance Act related to elderly and terminally ill federal prisoners. The Bureau of Prisons (BOP) was instructed to commence a pilot program of placing eligible[34] elderly (over 60) and terminally ill offenders on home detention status until the expiration of their prison terms. 34 U. S. Code Section 60541(g). The transfer can be made on the BOP's own action or upon request from an eligible offender. This legislation has led to a large number of inmate lawsuits seeking home confinement under the program. The Tenth Circuit, in an unpublished opinion, *Marshal v. Hudson*, Case No. 19-3236 (March 9, 2020) ruled that federal courts have no authority to order the BOP to place an inmate in a particular pilot program. These are issues of where to house an inmate that are within the prerogative of the executive branch.

Two additional special medical concerns, not discussed in this chapter on health care, are covered in the discussion of the Fifth and Fourteenth Amendments: Due Process. The cases are *Vitek v. Jones*, 445 U.S. 480 (1980), which considers the due process rights of a prisoner when he is transferred from a regular prison to a psychiatric hospital; and *Farmer v. Brennan*, 511 U.S. 825 (1994), which discusses the problems presented in properly classifying a transsexual inmate in a prison. Although those cases have definite healthcare aspects and could have been discussed in this chapter, they are included in the discussion of due process, which addresses the classification of inmates and the transfers of inmates from one institution to another.

▶ LGBTI Health Issues in Correctional Institutions

In *Wellman v. Faulkner*, 715 F.2d 269 (7th Cir. 1983) *cert. denied* 484 U.S. 935 (1987), the Seventh Circuit Court of Appeals concluded that gender dysphoria was a serious medical need and failure of prison officials to address the specific needs of transgender prisoners would state a claim for a violation of the Eighth Amendment. In that case, the state DOC had failed to provide any treatment for the inmate's condition. A number of federal circuit court opinions addressing the same issue followed: *Farmer v. Haas*, 999 F.2d 319 (7th Cir. 1993); cer*t. denied* 510 U.S. 963 (1993); and *White v. Farrier*, 849 F.2d 322 (8th Cir 1988) (gender dysphoria is a medically recognized psychological disorder). Presently, the Federal Bureau of Prisons and most, if not all, state and local correctional facilities have policies addressing the needs of transgender and gender nonconforming detainees.[35]

While the management of LGBTI [Lesbian, Gay, Bi-Sexual, Transgender and Intersex] persons in correctional facilities present a number of issues, this section will address the highly litigated area of gender reassignment surgery. The Supreme Court has not made any rulings on this issue, so analysis comes from the several courts of appeal that have addressed the issue. In 1992, an inmate in Massachusetts seeking care for Gender Identity Disorder (GID) sued prison officials. In a case that was litigated over 20 years, a federal district court concluded in 2012 that inmate Kosilek's GID was a serious medical need, and that based on the Standards of Care formulated by the World Professional Association for Transgender Health [WPATH], which established a "triadic treatment sequence" comprised of (1) hormone therapy; (2) a real-life experience of living as a member of the opposite sex; and (3) sex reassignment surgery (SRS), SRS was the only adequate treatment for Kosilek's serious medical need. The state DOC had argued it had provided treatment in the form of hormones, electrolysis, feminine clothing and accessories, and mental health services aimed at alleviating Kosilek's distress. The DOC argued that these alternatives were medically appropriate, and SRS was not the only treatment option for treating Kosilek's GID. The DOC had also stated the decision to not authorize SRS was based on security needs: the risks of placing a postoperative female inmate in a male correctional institution, or housing a postoperative female with a history of violence toward women (Kosilek was serving life in prison for murdering his wife) in a female correctional facility where many of the inmates were victims of domestic abuse. The head of the DOC also testified that it was not good correctional policy to grant concessions to an inmate who threatened suicide or self-mutilation, and an out-of-state transfer was considered and rejected because such transfers were voluntary with the receiving agency and could be revoked at any time. After the judgment was initially affirmed by the court of appeals, the court reheard the case en banc and reversed the district court judgment.

In *Kosilek v. Spencer*, 774 F.3d 63 (1st Cir. 2014) *en banc*, the court first recognized that Kosilek's GID was a serious medical need. The legal issue, as framed by the court of appeals, *"is whether the decision[by the DOC] not to provide SRS-in light of the continued provision of all ameliorative measures currently afforded Kosilek and in addition to antidepressants and psychotherapy—is sufficiently harmful to Kosilek so as to violate the Eighth Amendment. It is not."* The DOC's decision was *"one of two alternatives-both of which are reasonably commensurate with the medical standards of prudent professionals, and both of which provide Kosilek with a significant measure of relief—is a decision that does not violate the Eighth Amendment."*

In 2005, the Wisconsin legislature enacted *The Inmate Sex Change Prevention Act*, which prohibited the Wisconsin DOC from utilizing state funding, resources, or federal funding passing through the state, to *"provide or to facilitate the provision of hormonal therapy or sexual reassignment surgery."*[36] In *Fields v. Smith*, 653 F.3 550 (7th Cir. 2011), the court of appeals affirmed a district court judgment that the law was facially unconstitutional and as applied violated the Eighth Amendment rights of Wisconsin inmates.

Eight years after *Fields v. Smith* was decided, the Seventh Circuit addressed the issue of sexual reassignment surgery in *Campbell v. Kallas*, 936 F.3d 536 (7th Cir. 2019). An inmate in the DOC was diagnosed with GID and was provided treatment by the DOC, which included hormone therapy as medically approved, counseling, and other treatments deemed necessary. The inmate sought sexual reassignment surgery (SRS), and the DOC obtained two outside consultations on the suitability of additional treatment. The consultant noted that the current WPATH standards recommendation for a presurgery 12 month "real-life experience as the opposite sex . . . could not be fully implemented in the prison setting." After a second consultation, the expert suggested that the DOC reassess its ability to provide a real-life experience of living as the opposite sex in a correctional environment. The DOC denied the inmate's request for SRS and litigation was commenced. The state defendants moved for summary judgment on the basis of qualified immunity, which was denied by the district court because it was clearly established that denying effective treatment for gender dysphoria violates the Eighth Amendment. The court of appeals reversed, holding that the district court had framed the legal question too broadly. The proper inquiry for qualified immunity purposes is whether then-existing caselaw clearly established a constitutional right to gender-dysphoria treatment beyond hormone therapy. While providing no treatment at all would violate the Eighth Amendment, the defendants provided the inmate with *"extensive treatment in the form of hormone therapy, counseling, and various lifestyle accommodations."* The judgment of the district court denying the defendant's qualified immunity was reversed, and the case was dismissed.

Four days after the Seventh Circuit decided the *Campbell v Kallas* case, the Ninth Circuit decided *Edmo v. Corizon, Inc, et al*, 935 F.3d 757 (9th Cir. 2019), affirming a district court's conclusions that the denial of gender confirmation surgery (GCS) [formerly identified as sex reassignment surgery] to a prisoner suffering from severe gender dysphoria violated the Eighth Amendment. Medical staff for the Idaho DOC had diagnosed the inmate with GID and had provided hormonal therapy and supportive counseling to treat the condition. After extensive pretrial discovery, the district court conducted a three-day evidentiary hearing. At the hearing, both the state and inmate presented expert testimony on the appropriate treatment for GID. The inmate's experts included two physicians who had treated multiple persons with GID, including pre- and postoperative GCS. The district court ruled: the inmate suffered from GID, which is a serious medical need; that GCS was a medically necessary treatment for the inmate; and that the state was deliberately indifferent to the inmate's gender dysphoria because it *"fail[ed] to provide her with available treatment that is generally accepted in the field as safe and effective, despite her actual harm and ongoing risk of future harm including self-castration attempts, cutting, and suicidal ideation."* The district court ordered the state to provide the inmate with GCS.

On appeal, the state argued that the decision not to provide GCS to the inmate was a difference of prudent medical opinion and, therefore, not deliberately indifferent. Because the district court had granted injunctive relief, the state argued that the inmate would not be irreparably harmed without an injunction and finally that the injunction was overly broad. Previous opinions of the Ninth Circuit had established that deliberate indifference to a serious medical need may be proven by showing that the course of treatment offered by the state was medically unacceptable under the circumstances and that the state chose this course in conscious disregard of an excessive risk to the patient's health. The appellate court restated the rule that differences of opinions between an inmate and a treating physician or between different physicians concerning appropriate medical care is not deliberate indifference. However, *"accepted standards of care and practice within the medical community are highly relevant in determining what care is medically acceptable and unacceptable."* In determining whether the Eighth Amendment has been violated, courts must weigh the views of "prudent professionals in the field" against the treatment decisions of prison authorities to decide whether the treatment provided was "medically acceptable." After reviewing the record and district court's evidentiary findings, the court of appeals determined that the inmate had proven that the "course of treatment" provided to the inmate to treat GID by the DOC "was medically unacceptable under the circumstances." The court of appeals affirmed the lower court's judgment.

In affirming the district court's judgment, the court of appeals distinguished the First Circuit's decision in *Kosilek* because the Idaho DOC never argued that safety and security were at issue if GCS was performed. Another circuit court's opinion, *Gibson v. Collier*, 920 F.3d 212 (5th Cir 2019) *cert. denied* _____ U.S. _____ (2019) had categorically determined that "[a] state does not inflict cruel and unusual punishment by declining to provide [GCS] to a transgender inmate" was distinguished because, contrary to the opinion of the Fifth Circuit, there was no medical consensus that GCS was necessary or effective for treating GID. The panel of the Ninth Circuit concluded that the record developed in the district court in the *Edmo* case established, and the state did not seriously refute, that there was *"medical consensus that GCS was effective and medically necessary in appropriate cases."* Finally, the Ninth Circuit affirmed the district court's conclusion that the inmate's "severe, ongoing psychological distress and the high risk of self-castration and suicide" without GCS was clearly an irreparable harm.

The varied outcomes from the three different courts of appeal indicate that the issues of the treatment of GID will continue to present challenges to correctional agencies. The court decisions concerning the medical suitability of GCS are very fact driven. However, two general legal principles can be drawn from the cases: (1) GID can be a serious medical need for which the Eighth Amendment requires prison officials to not be deliberately indifferent; and (2) the Eighth Amendment does not require GCS for all cases of GID, but when a case is severe, providing no treatment at all will potentially create constitutional liability.

A discussion of the placement of transgender women in a correctional setting matching their birth gender identity is discussed in the chapters on inmate classification. A number of states have enacted legislation directing placement of transgender inmates in facilities with their identified rather than birth sex. See for example, California Penal Code Section 2606 (a) (3) [a part of the state's "The Transgender Respect, Agency, and Dignity Act." California Senate Bill 132: (a) An individual incarcerated by the Department of Corrections and Rehabilitation who is transgender, nonbinary, or intersex, regardless of anatomy, shall:

(3) Be housed at a correctional facility designated for men or women based on the individual's preference, ...

Summary

- Prisons and jails must provide health care to inmates, because the inmates are not in a position to obtain health care for themselves. Under certain circumstances, an inmate may be charged a fee (medical co-pay) for healthcare services.

- The governing case for prison health care is *Estelle v. Gamble.* In that case, the Supreme Court held that the prison staff (whether doctors or officers or any others) violated the Eighth Amendment if they were deliberately indifferent to the serious medical needs of prisoners. Such deliberate indifference shows the unnecessary and wanton infliction of pain that the cruel and unusual punishment clause prohibits.

- Instances of medical malpractice, mistaken judgments in providing medical care, and differing opinions about what care should be provided, do not amount to "deliberate indifference." They are not constitutional violations but may state claims under tort claims procedures, where negligence is the standard.

- In *West v. Atkins*, a private physician, who was under contract to provide health care to inmates, was found to be acting "under color of state law" and was, therefore, potentially liable for constitutional violation on an inmate's claim that he was deliberately indifferent to the inmate's serious medical needs.

- The Supreme Court ruled that an inmate could be given involuntary treatment (against his wishes) when he had a serious mental illness and treatment was necessary to alleviate a significant danger that the inmate posed to himself or to others. The treatment also had to be in the best medical interest of the inmate (*Washington v. Harper*). In another case, it was held that the government may medicate a mentally ill inmate against his will to render him competent to stand trial when the criminal charges are serious and with other precautions for his treatment (*Sell v. United States*).

- Lower federal courts and the highest appellate courts of some states have identified several important governmental interests that might outweigh the incarcerated individual's right to refuse medical treatment: preservation of life; protection of innocent third parties; the prevention of suicide; the maintenance of the ethical integrity of the medical profession; and maintaining prison security and orderly administration (*McNabb v. Department of Corrections*).

- In other involuntary treatment cases, lower federal courts held that aversive treatment to control disruptive behavior was cruel and unusual and, therefore, impermissible (*Knecht v. Gillman*) and that an inmate could be required to attend classes, against his will, in order to achieve a justifiable rehabilitative goal of the state to attain literacy among inmates (*Rutherford v. Hutto*).

- Inmate suicides present challenges to prison and jail officials. Staff members must be on the lookout for signals of suicidal tendencies and must take steps to try to prevent suicides in order to provide for the safety and medical well-being of inmates and to avoid showing deliberate indifference to inmates' serious needs.

- Prison officials need to ensure that appropriate procedures are in place to meet the particularized needs of female prisoners. The needs of pregnant female offenders require careful consideration of restraint policies (*Nelson v. Correctional Medical Services*). Correctional policies that prevent a female prisoner from obtaining an elective abortion may violate the prisoner's rights under the Fourteenth Amendment (*Victoria W. v. Larpenter* and *Roe v. Crawford*).

- HIV/AIDS presents additional serious medical and management problems to corrections administrators. The protections of the Americans with Disabilities Act (ADA) apply to persons with HIV infections (*Bragdon v. Abbott*). A leading case on the treatment of HIV/AIDS inmates is *Harris v. Thigpen*. Alabama had instituted universal, mandatory HIV testing for all inmates at admission and placed all HIV-positive inmates in separate housing. The components of this program, to which the segregated inmates objected, were approved in most aspects against the inmates' constitutional and statutory claims. Other claims about HIV/AIDS programs are being litigated in federal and state courts. In *Doe v. Delie*, the court ruled that prisoners have a right to privacy in their HIV status, and prison officials should take appropriate steps to prevent the unnecessary disclosure of the prisoner's condition.

- Corrections officials must be aware of the risks presented by the presence of TB in prisons and jails. For the protection of inmates (and to avoid a showing of deliberate indifference), jail and prison staff should take steps to test for and treat the disease, in accordance with currently recommended standards of control and care.

- The COVID-19 pandemic has presented new and unique challenges to correctional administrators and courts are being asked to make legal judgments about a rapidly evolving situation.

- Care for the elderly is another area that administrators must be aware of and appropriately respond to. The special needs of these offenders, who have been identified as a constantly increasing component of expanding corrections populations, must be met.
- Correctional agencies need to be aware of the medical and legal issues associated with addressing the special needs of LGBTI offenders. Some courts of appeal have required that DOCs provide sexual reassignment (also called gender confirming) surgery.

Thinking About It

Joel Caulk was a 36-year-old inmate in the New Hampshire State Prison system. He was serving a 10- to 20-year sentence for aggravated felonious sexual assault, and he had a separate 5- to 10-year sentence for burglary, which would begin when Caulk completed the 10- to 20-year sentence. In addition, Caulk had other charges pending in New Hampshire, as well as in California, and he claimed that he had a 20- to 30-year sentence in Massachusetts. Not wishing to spend the rest of his life in prison, Caulk stopped eating solid food, and he drank certain liquids as his only nourishment. He said that he chose this method of dying so that he could remain competent. He stated that he was not committing suicide, but rather allowing himself to die. He had no life-threatening or terminal illness, and he did not make any demands or ask for anything in return. The prison administration filed in court, seeking court authorization to "feed and nourish Joel Caulk over his objection[s]." How do you think the court ruled? This case is reported in *In re Caulk*, 480 A.2d 93 (NH 1984).

Endnotes

1. Sawyer, W. *The Steep Cost of Medical Co-Pays in Prison Puts Health at Risk*. Prison Policy Initiative. April 19, 2017. Available at https://www.prisonpolicy.org/blog/2017/04/19/copays/ Accessed March 7, 2020. The states without co-pays in 2017 were Missouri, Montana, Nebraska, New York, Oregon, Vermont, and Wyoming. The average co-pay among the states and federal government was $3.47 with the exception of Texas, which charged inmates $100 a year.
2. Ollove, M. No Escaping Medical Copayments, Even in Prison. Pew Charitable Trust-Stateline. July 22, 2015 available at: https://www.pewtrusts.org/en/research-and-analysis/blogs/stateline/2015/07/22/no-escaping-medical-copayments-even-in-prison. Accessed March 7, 2020.
3. Federal Prisoner Health Care Copayment Act of 2000 (Pub. L. 106-294, October 12, 2000, 114 Stat. 1038). The language is codified in 18 U.S.C. § 4048.
4. *Charging Inmates a Fee for Health Care Services*, National Commission on Correctional Health Care. Available at https://www.ncchc.org/charging-inmates-a-fee-for-health-care-services. Accessed March 7, 2020.
5. The Affordable Care Act (ACA) extended Medicaid eligibility to an expanded number of persons and can include persons in custody. While Medicaid will not usually reimburse a governmental entity for medical services provided to an incarcerated person, it may provide reimbursement for incarcerated persons receiving health care outside of an institution. Since the enactment of the ACA, several states have received large reimbursements for inmate health care provided in the community: Arkansas ($2.8 million), Colorado ($10 million), Kentucky ($16.4 million), and Michigan ($19 million). *How and When Medicaid Covers People Under Correctional Supervision*. Pew Charitable Trust, August 2, 2016. Available at: https://www.pewtrusts.org/en/research-and-analysis/issue-briefs/2016/08/how-and-when-medicaid-covers-people-under-correctional-supervision. Accessed March 7, 2020.
6. *Morris v. Livingston*, 739 F.3d 740 (5th Cir. 2015) ["[T]he deliberate indifference standard of does not guarantee prisoners the right to be entirely free from the cost considerations that figure in the medical-care decisions made by most non-prisoners in our society."] (Texas) *cert. denied* 573 U.S. 909 (2014).
7. *Poole v. Isaacs*, 703 F.3d 1024 (7th Cir. 1024 (7th Cir. 2012) [the "Eighth Amendment does not compel prison administrators to provide cost-free medical services to inmates who are able to contribute to the cost of their care"]; (Illinois).
8. *Shapley v. Nevada Board of State Prison Commissioners*, 766 F.2d 404 (9th Cir. 1983).
9. *Reynolds v. Wagner*, 128 F.3d 166 (3rd Cir. 1997) [there is "no general constitutional right to free health care."] (Pennsylvania).
10. The "emergency privilege" is an exception to the rule that healthcare providers must have consent of the patient before providing treatment. The seminal case in American jurisprudence on this issue is *Canterbury v. Spence*, 464 F.2d 272 (D.C. Cir. 1972). The emergency privilege "comes into play when the patient is unconscious or otherwise incapable of consenting, and harm from a failure to treat is imminent and outweighs any harm threatened by the proposed treatment. When a genuine emergency of that sort arises, it is settled that the impracticality of conferring with the patient dispenses with need for it. Even in situations of that character the physician should, as current law requires, attempt to secure a relative's consent if possible. But if time is too short to accommodate discussion, obviously the physician should proceed with the treatment."
11. This case was returned to the Missouri courts and after the circuit court conducted an additional hearing, it determined that the family had established by clear and convincing evidence Ms. Cruzan's wishes and again issued an order allowing her guardians to withdraw hydration and nutrition. Nancy Cruzan died on December 26, 1990. After the Supreme Court's decision in *Cruzan*, Congress passed the Patient Self-Determination Act [Public Law No: 101-508], which amended the Social Security Act "to require hospitals, skilled nursing facilities, home health agencies, hospice programs, and health maintenance organizations to: (1) inform patients of their rights under State law to make decisions concerning their medical care; (2) periodically inquire as to whether a patient executed an advanced

directive and document the patient's wishes regarding their medical care; (3) not discriminate against persons who have executed an advance directive; (4) ensure that legally valid advance directives and documented medical care wishes are implemented to the extent permitted by State law; and (5) provide educational programs for staff, patients, and the community on ethical issues concerning patient self-determination and advance directives. That requires hospitals, nursing facilities, hospices, home health care programs, and health maintenance organizations to inform patients about their right to make forward-looking care and treatment decisions through the use of advance directives." Most states have enacted living will and advanced directive statutes.

12. See, for example, Idaho DOC Standard Operating Procedure 401.06.03.086, *End-of-Life Decision Making*, Adopted March 1, 2001, reviewed June 11, 2012. Available at http://forms.idoc.idaho.gov/WebLink/0/edoc/283167/End-of-Life%20Decision%20Making.pdf or Kentucky DOC Policies and Procedures -13.5- *Advance Healthcare Directives*. August 5, 2016. Available: https://corrections.ky.gov/About/cpp/Documents/13/CPP%2013.5.pdf

13. The *Myers* decision includes, as an appendix, portions from an affidavit done by the commissioner of corrections at that time. Describing the situation, the commissioner stated: "In dealing with a prisoner such as Myers, he [commissioner] had only two options if the law gave him no right to compel submission to treatment: 'One would be to simply grant the demands. There would be great pressure for me to do this since the only other option is to let the man die. Nevertheless, submitting to the demands would be intolerable, because it would violate my legal responsibilities (particularly, in this case, my duty to protect the public) and greatly undermine my ability to effectively and fairly manage the Department of Correction …. [T]o allow Myers, or other inmates in similar situations, to destroy themselves while in prison would create very serious practical problems in prison administration. One very serious practical problem is that it would be very difficult to make the prisoners, their families and the correction department staff understand that I had done everything legally possible to prevent a death of a prisoner in my charge. Faith in the correctional system's ability to protect inmates would be seriously undermined. More immediately, one could expect an explosive reaction by other inmates to the death and to the failure of the commissioner to prevent it by simply releasing Myers to minimum security. In my opinion, such a reaction is much more likely in a situation where Myers is permitted to die, than where he is subjected to involuntary treatment to keep him alive."

14. Tapia was convicted of alien smuggling. She was sentenced to 51 months, with the district court judge saying, "[t]he sentence has to be sufficient to provide needed correctional treatment, and here I think the needed correctional treatment is the 500 hour drug program." Tapia argued that the lengthening of her prison term was contrary to the provisions of 18 U.S.C. § 3582(a), which specifically states that the federal court in imposing or determining the length of a prison term shall recognize that imprisonment is not an appropriate means of promoting correction and rehabilitation. The appeals court upheld the district court decision. In reversing, the Supreme Court pointed to the clear statutory language—" what Congress said was that when sentencing an offender to prison, the court shall consider all the purposes of punishment except rehabilitation—because imprisonment is not an appropriate means of pursuing that goal." The Supreme Court noted that a sentencing court is without decision-making authority as to where the federal offender serves her sentence or in what program she becomes involved. The court can recommend, but not order, a particular facility placement or program involvement, with this authority resting with the Federal Bureau of Prisons.

15. Carson, E. A. & Cowhig, M. P. *Mortality in State and Federal Prisons, 2001-2016-Statistical Tables*. Table 2. (Washington, DC: Bureau of Justice Statistics, U.S. Department of Justice, February 2020). Also, Carson, E.A. & Cowhig, M. P. *Mortality in Local Jail, 2001-2016-Statistical Tables*. Table 2. (Washington, DC: Bureau of Justice Statistics, U.S. Department of Justice, February 2020).

16. Bronson, J., Stroop, J., Zimmer, S., & Berzofsky, M. *Drug Use, Dependence and Abuse Among State Prisoners and Jail Inmates, 2007-2009*. Bureau of Justice Statistics, Washington, D.C. June 2017. 1. Available: https://www.bjs.gov/content/pub/pdf/dudaspji0709.pdf. Accessed March 23, 2020.

17. Bronson, J. & Berzofsky, M. Indicators of Mental Health Problems Reported by Prisoners and Jail Inmates, 2011-2012. 1. Bureau of Justice Statistics. Washington, D.C. June 2017. Available: https://www.bjs.gov/content/pub/pdf/imhprpji1112.pdf

18. Advocacy Resource Center. American Medical Association. 2015. Available: file:///C:/Users/daryl/AppData/Local/Temp/shackling-pregnant-prisoners-issue-brief-3.pdf. Accessed March 23, 2020.

19. In *Victoria W.*, the court, noting her attorney's delay both in filing for the court order and in requesting an early release, rather than release or transport to receive an abortion, said, "… regardless of the policy's requirements, it functioned properly in this case. Her attorney's action, not the policy, denied Victoria an abortion."

20. *HIV and AIDS—United States, 1981–2000. U.S.* Centers for Disease Control, June 01, 2001. Available: https://www.cdc.gov/mmwr/preview/mmwrhtml/mm5021a2.htm

21. The information in the preceding two paragraphs of the text was taken from Harlow, C. W. *HIV in U.S. Prisons and Jails*. 1 (Washington, DC: Bureau of Justice Statistics, U.S. Department of Justice, September 1993). Available: https://www.bjs.gov/content/pub/pdf/hivuspj.pdf

22. The information in the preceding two paragraphs of the text was taken from Maruschak, L. M. *HIV in Prisons*, 1–3, Appendix Table 1. (Washington, DC: Bureau of Justice Statistics, U.S. Department of Justice, August 2017).

23. See endnote 22. Maruschak, L. M. *HIV in Prisons, 2015*. Appendix Table 3.

24. On March 28, 2011, a class action complaint for Declaratory and Injunctive Relief was filed in the United States District Court for the Middle District of Alabama (Northern Division). An amended complaint was filed on May 11, 2011. The case filing is *Henderson, et al. v. Bentley, et al.* (Civil Case No. 2:11cv224-MHT). The complaint alleged that a majority of state correctional systems in the 1980s, reflective of "a tidal wave of public fear over the HIV/AIDS epidemic" adopted policies "requiring the segregation of prisoners with HIV." The complaint further alleged that as new medications developed, the methods of HIV transmission were more clearly identified and the myths "debunked. In 2011 only two states continued to segregate inmates with HIV "in separate, specially designated housing units." The litigation, in part, was requesting a declaration that the state be enjoined (stopped) "from engaging in discriminatory policies and practices" on the basis of the inmates' HIV status and a declaration that the Alabama Department of Corrections HIV segregation policy violates Title II of the Americans with Disabilities Act and Section 504 of the Rehabilitation Act. In response to the filing, the state commissioner of corrections, in late March 2011, issued a statement saying that the Department

of Corrections would "zealously" defend against the "false and misinformed allegations that regrettably ignore this Department's important obligations to provide health care, prevent the transmission of sexually transmitted diseases, and manage the prison population in such a way to ensure the safety of that population, Departmental staff, and the public at large."

25. For an approach addressing an employee's concern, see 18 U.S.C. § 4014, Testing for human immunodeficiency virus. Paragraph (b) states, "If the Attorney General has a well-founded reason to believe that a person sentenced to a term of imprisonment for a Federal offense, or ordered detained before trial … may have intentionally or unintentionally transmitted the [HIV] virus to any officer or employee of the United States, or to any person lawfully present in a correctional facility who is not incarcerated there, the Attorney General shall … [have] the person who may have transmitted the virus to be tested … and communicate the test results to the person tested [and also "… inform any person … who may have been exposed to such virus of the potential risk involved and, if warranted by the circumstances, that prophylactic or other treatment should be considered."]."

26. Centers for Disease Control and Prevention. *Correctional Health-* HIV/AIDS- https://www.cdc.gov/correctionalhealth/rec-guide.html

27. Centers for Disease Control and Prevention. TB cases among residents of correctional facilities 1993—2018. Available: https://www.cdc.gov/tb/statistics/surv/surv2018/images/Slide30.PNG

28. Centers for Disease Control and Prevention. Prevention and control of tuberculosis in correctional and detention facilities: Recommendations from CDC. Pages 1–3. MMWR 2006; 55 (No. RR-9).

29. Hammett, T., Kennedy, S., and Kuck, S. *10th NIJ/CDC National Survey of Infectious Diseases in Correctional Facilities: Tuberculosis Screening, Treatment and Education. Final Report.* Pages 1, 9–10. November 9, 2006.

30. Carson, E. A. *Prisoners in 2018*, Table 9. (Washington, DC: Bureau of Justice Statistics, U.S. Department of Justice, April 2020).

31. Motivans, M. *Federal Justice Statistics 2015-2016.* Tables 5 and 8. (Washington, DC: Bureau of Justice Statistics, U.S. Department of Justice, January 2019).

32. Anno, B., Graham, C., Lawrence, J., and Shansky, R. *Correctional Health Care: Addressing the Needs of Elderly, Chronically Ill, and Terminally Ill Inmates.* Washington, DC: National Institute of Corrections, U.S. Department of Justice, 2004.

33. A more direct approach was H.R. 223—Federal Prison Bureau Nonviolent Offender Relief Act of 2011—introduced in the U.S. House of Representatives on January 7, 2011. This proposed legislation would require the Federal Bureau of Prisons, pursuant to a good time policy, to release from confinement an inmate who has served at least one-half of her prison term if that inmate is at least 45 years of age, has never been convicted of a crime of violence, and has not had a violation of prison disciplinary regulations involving violent conduct. In 2017, the bill was reintroduced as H.R. 64. It was referred to the House Committee on the Judiciary, Subcommittee on Crime, Terrorism, and Homeland Security committee and died there.

34. BOP OPS-Memo 001-2019. *Home Confinement Under the First Step Act.* April 4, 2019. An eligible elderly offender is one who meets the following criteria: Eligible elderly offender means an offender in the custody of the Bureau- (1)who is not less than 60 years of age; (2) who is serving a term of imprisonment that is not life imprisonment based on conviction for an offense or offenses that do not include any crime of violence (as defined in Section 16 of Title 18), sex offense (as defined in Section 20911(5) of this title), offense described in Section 2332b(g)(5)(B) of Title 18, or offense under chapter 37 of Title 18, and has served 2/3 of the term of imprisonment to which the offender was sentenced; (3) who has not been convicted in the past of any Federal or State crime of violence, sex offense, or other offense described in paragraph (2), above. (4) who has not been determined by the Bureau, on the basis of information the Bureau uses to make custody classifications, and in the sole discretion of the Bureau, to have a history of violence, or of engaging in conduct constituting a sex offense or other offense described in paragraph 2 above; (5) who has not escaped, or attempted to escape, from a Bureau of Prisons institution (to include all security levels of Bureau facilities); (6) with respect to whom the Bureau of Prisons has determined that release to home detention under this Section will result in a substantial net reduction of costs to the Federal Government; and (7) who has been determined by the Bureau to be at no substantial risk of engaging in criminal conduct or of endangering any person or the public if released to home detention.

35. See for example: BOP Policy No. 5200.94, *Transgender Offender Manual*, May 11, 2018; Arizona DOC Department Order 810, *Management of LGBTI Inmates.* November 26, 2015. Available: https://corrections.az.gov/sites/default/files/policies/800/0810_032519.pdf

36. Wisconsin Statutes 302.386 (5m). A transgender DOC inmate challenged the law and the district court concluded that the law violated the Eighth Amendment and declared it unconstitutional. The court of appeals in *Fields v. Smith*, 653 F.3 550 (7th Cir. 2011) affirmed the district court's judgment.

© EJ_Rodriquez/iStock/Getty Images Plus/Getty Images

CHAPTER 17

Probation and Parole, Community Corrections, and Fines

Due process is not so rigid as to require that the significant interests in informality, flexibility, and economy must always be sacrificed.

U.S. Supreme Court, *Gagnon v. Scarpelli*

CHAPTER OUTLINE

This chapter examines the constitutional decisions that affect the work of probation and parole officers. This is the part of corrections that is nonincarcerative. It is sometimes called "alternative sentencing" or **community corrections**. Besides probation and parole, this includes the use of fines and other types of community sanctions. Fines are included here because, although they are not a large part of corrections administration, they are widely used as sentencing options for many offenses (particularly less serious ones). In addition, technically, a fine may be considered a community corrections alternative, because the offender remains in the community, whether the fine is used as the only sanction or in combination with probation (a common sentencing combination).

It is important to clearly distinguish between probation and parole. Although they have many similarities, they are very different in their functions from a sentencing standpoint.

▶ How Probation and Parole Work

Probation and parole are both parts of the sentencing phase of criminal justice. They are similar in that persons who are placed on probation or parole live in the community, rather than in corrections facilities. The essence of their status is that they (probationers and parolees) are under the supervision of trained officers, and they are legally placed under conditions or restrictions on their release status. A key distinction is that probation is a judicial function (under court auspices), while parole is administrative (under executive authority).

Probation is a form of sentencing, so it is imposed by a court. In one type of probation, a court will impose a sentence of jail time, imprisonment, or even a fine or restitution and then **suspend** that sentence while the defendant is placed on probation. This kind of probation is called a suspended execution of sentence. In another type of probation, the court suspends the imposition of the sentence and places the defendant on a term of probation. In this kind of probation (called a suspended or deferred imposition), no set term of imprisonment hangs over the probationer's head; but if they violate probation, the court may impose any sentence that might originally have been imposed. In both types of probation, a specified length of time is set for the probation to last, and, during that time, the probationer is typically assigned to a supervising officer, to whom they must report at regular intervals. Reporting may be in person—the probationer goes to see the probation officer at their office, or, less frequently, the officer meets the probationer at home or at work—or reporting may be done by telephone, mail, or newer electronic technology like GPS monitoring and the use of kiosks. The degree of supervision may range greatly, from minimal contact with the probation officer to intensive probation, where the probationer is frequently seen and talked to by the officer to make sure they are doing well. Probation is by far the most common correctional supervision, with an estimated 3.54 million people on probation at year's-end 2018.[1]

Parole, on the other hand, is release to the community after serving time in prison. There is a paroling authority, often called a parole board or a parole commission, which can be staffed by full-time board members who are appointed, for a certain length term, by the governor of the state. (Some states utilize part-time appointees.) Usually, a hearing is conducted with each eligible inmate at the prison where they are confined. In some states, the board members themselves conduct the hearings; in others, hearing examiners or parole officers conduct the hearings, and they make their reports to the members, who vote to parole or not to parole. Eligibility for parole is determined by law. The parole statute for the state will indicate when parole may be considered.

In some states, sentencing statutes provide that the court at sentencing may set the parole eligibility date for the defendant, within ranges specified by the legislature. Some states use indeterminate sentencing where the court may impose, for example, a sentence of one year to five years. The one-year date is the parole eligibility date—the earliest the defendant can be released on parole. Or the sentence may be eighteen months to five years, which means parole eligibility occurs at eighteen months. Other states use determinate sentencing where courts only impose the full-term length of the sentence (for example, five years, or in some states, 60 months). Parole eligibility is then set at a date that is figured by a formula (such as one-third of the sentence—such as after serving 40 months of a 60 month sentence), which is set by the parole law. Also, there may be so-called indeterminate parole sentences, whereby the court imposes a single term (for example, five years), and the defendant is immediately eligible for parole and may be paroled at any time during the sentence at the total discretion of the parole board. For a life sentence, the parole eligibility date may be set by state statute or specified as part of the sentence imposed by the court. (For example, in a sentence of 15 years to life, the "15 years" may be a statutory date or may be chosen by the sentencing judge, depending on the law.) The legislature may make some offenses nonparolable or may even eliminate parole altogether.

TABLE 17-1 Parole as of 2018	
Jurisdictions with Parole	**Jurisdictions without Parole**
Alaska, Alabama, Arkansas, Colorado, Connecticut, Georgia, Hawaii, Iowa, Idaho, Kentucky, Louisiana, Maryland, Massachusetts, Michigan, Missouri, Montana, North Dakota, Nebraska, New Hampshire, New Jersey, Nevada, New York, Oklahoma, Pennsylvania, Rhode Island, South Carolina, South Dakota, Tennessee, Texas, Utah, Vermont, West Virginia, and Wyoming.	Arizona, California, District of Columbia, Delaware, Florida, Illinois, Indiana, Kansas, Maine, Minnesota, New Mexico, North Carolina, Ohio, Oregon, USA, Virginia, Washington, and Wisconsin

Modified from In Depth: Sentencing Guidelines and Discretionary Parole Release. February 23, 2018. University of Minnesota Sentencing Guidelines Resource Center. Available- https://sentencing .umn.edu/content/depth-sentencing-guidelines-and-discretionary-parole-release. Accessed 01 April 2020.

By the end of 2000, 16 states had abolished discretionary parole for all inmates; four additional states had abolished it for certain violent offenses or other crimes against a person. The federal government also has abolished parole. In 2018, 16 states, the District of Columbia, and the federal government were without parole. See **TABLE 17-1** for a list of those agencies. Please keep in mind that the abolition of parole does not mean that parole boards and paroling authorities no longer exist. These entities continue to function for those offenders who were sentenced prior to the abolition of parole. What it does mean is that, over time, there should be fewer people released by way of discretionary parole (released based on parole board decision). In 2001, there were approximately 161,000 discretionary releases, representing about 36% of adults entering parole. In 2018, discretionary parole represented 44% of persons released to parole supervision.[2]

Besides the possibility of being paroled, inmates also usually earn good conduct allowances, which are subtracted from the full-term date of the sentence and, in some cases, from the parole eligibility date as well. In other words, good conduct may (if established by state law) reduce the time the prisoner has to wait for their first parole hearing. In other states, good time is only subtracted from the full-term date of the sentence; if the inmate is not paroled, they will be released, by operation of the law, when that good time date is reached. In 2018, almost 90,000 prisoners were released under mandatory provisions—releases from prison were not decided by a parole board (20% of releases).[3]

Besides the persons who are released on parole by favorable action of the parole board, in most jurisdictions, prisoners who are released with good conduct allowances are also treated as if they were released on parole, and the releasee is under some degree of community supervision. The parolee is supervised, much like a probationer, in the community, with the conditions and restrictions of the release set by the parole board, rather than by a court. In some jurisdictions, a separate office handles the supervision of parolees; in other states, parolees are supervised by probation officers.

The essence of the probation or parole release is supervision. To enforce supervision, revocation of the probation or parole is a necessary component. Revocation occurs when the supervising officer makes a negative report, which may recommend revocation. For a probationer, this report goes to the court, which reviews it and decides whether the actions of the probationer are serious enough to terminate probation by a revocation action. When probation is revoked, the court may impose the original sentence (or any part of it) that was imposed and suspended. When the court suspended the imposition of any prison term at the original sentencing and placed the offender on probation, upon revocation, any length of sentence to imprisonment that could have originally been imposed may be imposed. If probation is revoked, the probationer is sent to jail or prison to serve the term specified by the court. This can be the original prison term that was imposed and suspended or a lesser amount. In some places, but not in all jurisdictions, the court may also add more supervision time or additional conditions of probation onto the sentence as another option at the revocation hearing.

To enforce parole, a similar revocation process for a parolee may occur, except that a negative report from the supervising officer goes to the parole board, which is given the power to revoke parole. The case is then reviewed (this aspect will be discussed in detail later in this chapter). If a decision is made to revoke parole, the person is returned to prison to serve out the balance of the sentence, computed in accordance with the laws of the state. (These rules of computation of sentences are fairly complex and vary from state to state.) In most places, the person returned from parole can earn good time again on the balance of the sentence to be served and may be paroled again. It is possible that on a longer sentences, an inmate may be paroled and returned to prison two, three, or more times on a single sentence.

On January 1, 2018, 3.6 million people were reported to were on probation in the United States, and 50%, about 1.9 million people, successfully completed their terms of probation. However, the other 50% did not successfully exit probation, either being reincarcerated for new criminal conduct or for the offense that resulted in their probation as well as a number of other technical reasons. Females made up 25% of persons on probation. Of the persons on probation, almost 60% had been convicted of a felony, and 22% had been convicted of a violent offense. Drug and property offenses made up almost 51% of the probation caseload. As for parole, almost 54% (240,500 persons) successfully completed their term of parole in 2018, and more than 205,000 parolees did not successfully complete their term of parole and were reincarcerated with a new sentence, a parole revocation, to receive treatment, or for other, unknown reasons.[4]

▶ *Jones v. Cunningham*

In this case, a Virginia parolee raised the question of whether he could go into federal court and challenge his state sentence under the federal habeas corpus statute, 28 U.S.C. § 2241. Jones originally filed his challenge to his sentence, while he was in the state penitentiary, against Cunningham, the penitentiary superintendent. (Habeas corpus actions are always brought against the prisoner's custodian.) Before his case was decided in the court of appeals, Jones was paroled. Jones tried to add or substitute the parole board members as respondents in the habeas corpus action, but the court refused, saying that he was no longer in custody but rather was "at large." In *Jones v. Cunningham*, 371 U.S. 236 (1963), the Supreme Court agreed to decide the question of whether a parolee is "in custody" within the meaning of the federal habeas corpus statute and the Constitution.

The Court reviewed the history of the Writ of Habeas Corpus in the Constitution and in English law, from where it was historically and legally derived. The Court concluded that the writ could be used for more than just physical incarceration.

> **History, usage, and precedent can leave no doubt that, besides physical imprisonment, there are other restraints on a man's liberty, restraints not shared by the public generally, which have been thought sufficient in the English-speaking world to support the issuance of habeas corpus.**

Habeas, for example, has been used by an alien seeking entry into the United States after being detained at the border. It has been used to question the legality of induction into the military service. It has even been used to test child custody when there is a dispute between the parents. Here, when Jones was paroled, his habeas corpus case against the penitentiary superintendent was ended (it "became moot"), because the superintendent's custody of Jones had ended. But can the parole board be considered to have Jones in its custody so that he can use habeas corpus to challenge the parole restraints on his liberty?

The Court noted that the Virginia parole restraints were significant: Jones was limited to a particular community, house, and job, unless it was changed by his parole officer. He had to report to the parole officer and allow the parole officer to visit his home and job to check on him. He had to "keep good company and good hours, work regularly, keep away from undesirable places, and live a clean, honest, and temperate life." He could be rearrested, at any time, at the order of the board or his parole officer, and he could be required to serve the balance of his sentence (the sentence that he claimed was illegal). (These conditions, although using language that may sound a little dated, are fairly typical of the restraints placed on parolees. Therefore, the *Jones* case is not unique or distinguishable on the grounds that the conditions were more strenuous or very unusual.) Based on these factors, the Court recognized Jones's right to pursue a habeas corpus action.

> **[The parole conditions and restrictions] significantly restrain petitioner's liberty to do those things which in this country free men are entitled to do. Such restraints are enough to invoke the help of the Great Writ .... While petitioner's parole releases him from immediate physical imprisonment, it imposes conditions which significantly confine and restrain his freedom; this is enough to keep him in the "custody" of the members of the Virginia Parole Board within the meaning of the habeas corpus statute.**

After the Court's ruling, state parolees were able to use the habeas corpus statute to challenge the conditions of their custody, just as prisoners do. Probationers and parolees may use 42 U.S.C. § 1983 to challenge conditions they claim are a constitutional violation, because all citizens are allowed to do that.)

▶ *Morrissey v. Brewer*

Morrissey had been paroled from serving his sentence at the Iowa State Penitentiary. Seven months later, he was arrested and charged with being a parole violator. After review of his parole officer's report, the board of parole revoked Morrissey's parole and ordered that he be returned to prison. He challenged the revocation action, using habeas corpus, on the grounds that he was given no hearing. The Supreme Court, in *Morrissey v. Brewer*, 408 U.S. 471 (1972), addressed the question of whether a parolee is entitled to due process—that is, to some kind of hearing—before being returned to prison by revocation of his parole status.

The Court first examined the nature of parole, noting that it was "an established variation on imprisonment of convicted criminals. Its purpose is to help individuals reintegrate into society as constructive individuals as soon as they are able, without being confined for the full term of the sentence imposed." The Court further noted that "the parolee is entitled to retain his liberty as long as he substantially abides by the conditions of his parole." The Court also noted that "the revocation of parole is not part of a criminal prosecution and thus the full panoply of rights due a defendant in such a [prosecution] proceeding does not apply to parole revocations." Whether the person is entitled to due process rights under the Constitution turns on whether the person's interest in remaining on parole is a liberty interest, within the meaning of the Fourteenth Amendment. The Court concluded that remaining on parole was such an interest.

> [T]he liberty of a parolee, although indeterminate, includes many of the core values of unqualified liberty and its termination inflicts a "grievous loss" on the parolee and often on others.

Therefore, some process is due to the parolee, and the Court described what was needed: "an informal hearing structured to assure that the finding of a parole violation will be based on verified facts and that the exercise of discretion will be informed by an accurate knowledge of the parolee's behavior."

With that guidance in mind, the Court defined the precise minimal requirements needed for parole revocation. These are the requirements of an informal, due process hearing:

> [D]ue process [requires] that some minimal inquiry be conducted at or reasonably near the place of the alleged parole violation or arrest and as promptly as convenient after arrest …. Such an inquiry should be seen as in the nature of a "preliminary hearing" to determine whether there is probable cause or reasonable ground to believe that the arrested parolee has committed acts that would constitute a violation of parole conditions.

This "preliminary hearing" requires determination by an impartial party—someone not directly involved in the case (that is, never the supervising parole officer). The parolee must be given notice that the hearing will take place and must be informed of the parole violations that have been alleged. The parolee must be allowed to "appear and speak in his own behalf; he may bring letters, documents, or individuals who can give relevant information to the hearing officer." A person who has given adverse information on which the revocation may be based must be available, at the parolee's request, for questioning in the parolee's presence. The hearing officer must make a summary or digest of the hearing and should determine whether there is probable cause to hold the parolee for a final decision. The officer should also state the reasons for his determination and the evidence on which he relied.

After this preliminary hearing and within a reasonable time (the Court indicated that two months was a reasonable amount of time, even though the parolee may have been delivered to prison within that time), there must be a "final hearing." Rather than determining whether there is probable cause to hold the parolee on revocation charges (which is the purpose of the preliminary hearing), the final hearing determines whether the facts warrant revocation. "The parolee must have an opportunity to be heard and to show, if he can, that he did not violate the conditions, or, if he did, that circumstances in mitigation suggest that the violation does not warrant revocation." The Court emphasized that each state must write its own procedures to cover parole revocation hearings, but these are the minimum requirements to satisfy due process:

> [The state must provide:] (a) written notice of the claimed violations of parole; (b) disclosure to the parolee of evidence against him; (c) opportunity to be heard in person and to present witnesses and documentary evidence; (d) the right to confront and cross-examine adverse witnesses (unless the hearing officer specifically finds good cause for not allowing confrontation); (e) a "neutral and detached" hearing body such as a traditional parole board, members of which need not be judicial officers or lawyers; and (f) a written statement by the factfinders as to the evidence relied on and reasons for revoking parole.

The Court specifically noted that it did not "reach or decide the question whether the parolee is entitled to the assistance of retained counsel or to appointed counsel if he is indigent." That question was reached in the following case, *Gagnon v. Scarpelli*.

▸ *Gagnon v. Scarpelli; Mempa v. Rhay*

Scarpelli pleaded guilty to armed robbery in Wisconsin. He was sentenced to 15 years imprisonment, but the judge suspended that sentence and placed him on probation for 7 years. He was allowed to reside in Illinois, where he was under supervision under the interstate compact for probation.[5] He was later arrested during the course of a house burglary by Illinois police. His probation was revoked by Wisconsin without any hearing. He was later sent to the State Reformatory at Green Bay to serve the 15 years that had originally been imposed. He challenged the revocation of his probation by petitioning for a writ of habeas corpus. Before that was decided, he was placed on parole, but the court held that his petition was not moot because he was still under the restraints of his parole.

The Supreme Court, in *Gagnon v. Scarpelli*, 411 U.S. 778 (1973), addressed the question of due process at probation revocation proceedings. The Court first noted its decision in *Mempa v. Rhay*, 389 U.S. 128 (1967), which involved an unusual sentencing procedure in the state of Washington. Mempa, with appointed counsel assisting him, had been convicted on a guilty plea. He was placed on probation for two years on condition that he spend 30 days in the county jail (just a "taste" of jail!), and the imposition of a further sentence was deferred. Four months later, he was brought into court on charges of a burglary. He was not represented by counsel, nor was he asked whether he wanted counsel. The court revoked his probation and imposed the maximum sentence of 10 years (but with a recommendation to the parole board that he serve only one year and then be paroled). Six years later, Mempa filed for a writ of habeas corpus, claiming a due process violation in the denial of counsel at his sentencing and probation revocation proceeding. The "deferred sentencing" procedure in Washington was held by the Supreme Court to have been such an important proceeding that due process required the presence of counsel. In effect, it was a combination of probation revocation and sentencing.

In *Gideon v. Wainwright*, 372 U.S. 335 (1963), the right to counsel had been established as a basic right in felony cases. This was done by application of the Sixth and the Fourteenth Amendments. The right was extended by the Court to a defendant in a deferred sentencing and probation revocation proceeding in *Mempa*. As the Court said in *Mempa*, there is a constitutional right to counsel in felony cases "at every stage of a criminal proceeding where substantial rights of a criminal accused may be affected." At his sentencing, albeit "deferred," Mempa was entitled to the appointment of counsel, the Supreme Court said, because his rights (his liberty interest) were so substantially affected.

The second decision, heavily relied on by the Court in *Gagnon* was *Morrissey v. Brewer*, the parole revocation case that was discussed earlier in this chapter.

> **Even though the revocation of parole is not a part of the criminal prosecution, we held [in *Morrissey*] that the loss of liberty entailed is a serious deprivation requiring that the parolee be accorded due process.**

The Court held that the revocation of probation and the revocation of parole are so similar that the right to due process is the same for each one. Therefore, for revocation of probation, the Supreme Court held that:

> **[A] probationer, like a parolee, is entitled to a preliminary and a final revocation hearing, under the conditions specified in *Morrissey v. Brewer*.**

At the preliminary hearing for probation revocation (just as for parole revocation), there must be advance notice of the alleged violations, an opportunity to appear and to present evidence, a conditional right to confront adverse witnesses, an independent decision maker, and a written report of the hearing. (The condition on the right to confront adverse witnesses is that the hearing judge or officer may decline confrontation of a witness in cases in which it is determined to pose a risk to the safety of the witness.) The minimum requirements at a final hearing are very similar; the one additional requirement for final hearings is that the parolee (or probationer) should be advised of what evidence there is against him.

The Court then went on in *Gagnon* to decide the issue left undecided in *Morrissey*: whether there is also a right to counsel (either retained or, for indigents, appointed) at revocation hearings. The Court accepted neither the argument that counsel should be provided in all hearings nor the argument that there is no due process requirement to provide counsel at all. In many cases, the Supreme Court said, the probationer or parolee has been convicted of committing another crime or has admitted those charges against him. In those cases, there is no need to provide counsel in order to relitigate those criminal charges as a basis for revocation. The probationer or parolee may want to present mitigating reasons why (even if there has been criminal or other violative conduct) revocation is not appropriate. Those reasons, however, are not usually so complicated that they necessitate counsel, according to the Court.

The Court also expressed concern that the introduction of counsel into revocation proceedings would change the nature of those proceedings and make them more adversarial and confrontational.

> **It is neither possible nor prudent to attempt to formulate a precise and detailed set of guidelines to be followed in determining when the providing of counsel is necessary .... [C]onsiderable discretion must be allowed the responsible agency in making the decision. Presumptively, it may be said that counsel should be provided in cases where, after being informed of his right to request counsel, the probationer or parolee makes such a request, based on a timely and colorable claim (i) that he has not committed the alleged violation of the conditions upon which he is at liberty; or (ii) that, even if the violation is a matter of public record or is uncontested, there are substantial reasons which justified or mitigated the violation and make revocation inappropriate, and that the reasons are complex or otherwise difficult to develop or present.**

Thus, for probation or parole revocation proceedings, there is a right to counsel but only under limited circumstances: when the charges are contested or when there are substantial mitigating reasons for the violative conduct and those reasons are complex or difficult to present. While the Supreme Court's ruling provided considerable flexibility with regard to providing counsel in revocation hearings, the guidance is complex. Accordingly, most jurisdictions take the reasonable precaution of allowing counsel to appear at probation and parole revocation proceedings. Courts, of course, have the authority to appoint counsel (or obtain representation from a local defender's office). Parole boards typically do not have such authority, so they must set up some procedure to obtain counsel for indigents when the need exists, based on the Supreme Court standard, or perhaps in all revocation hearings.

▶ Supervised Release and Revocation Under Federal Law

In 1984, Congress passed the Sentencing Reform Act, which, among other things, abolished parole for federal offenses committed on, or after, November 1, 1987. To continue a system of supervision after release from incarceration, federal judges were authorized to impose a term of supervised release under terms and conditions set by the court and monitored by federal probation officers. Title 18 U.S. Code Section 3583(a). The maximum term of the supervised release period was established by statute, was dependent upon the class of the offense committed (federal felonies were classed with the more serious offenses permitting longer periods of supervised release) and ranged from 1–5 years. Courts could impose longer periods of supervised release in cases involving child victims, terrorism, and drug, or sex offenses. Title 18 U.S. Code Section 3583(j)-(k). Some of the conditions of supervised release were mandatory, and others were discretionary.

If a person on supervised release is believed to have violated the terms and conditions of their supervision, a petition is filed in the sentencing federal district court for revocation or other action by the court. At a revocation hearing before a federal judge, the releasee has a number of rights, including: (1) written notice of the alleged violation; (2) disclosure of the evidence against him/her, (3) an opportunity to appear, present evidence, and question adverse witnesses; (4) counsel; and (5) the opportunity to make a statement and present any mitigating information. F.R.Crim. P. 32.1. Violations of the terms and conditions of supervised release need only be established by a preponderance of the evidence. Title 18 U.S. Code Section 3583(e). *U.S. v. Petersen*, 848 F.3d 1153 (8th Cir. 2017). If the court finds a violation of the conditions of supervised release, the court may modify the conditions, terminate the supervised release before its original end date, extend the term of supervised release, or revoke and impose an additional term of imprisonment. Title 18 U.S. Code Section 3583(e). If imprisonment is imposed, there are statutory limitations on the additional imprisonment term. Title 18 U.S. Code Section 3583(e)(3). Supervised release is similar to parole in that it is a term of supervision following incarceration. It differs in that it does not replace incarceration; supervised release is imposed in addition to a term of incarceration. *U.S. v. Reyes*, 283 F.3rd 486 (2nd Cir. 2002).

▸ A Brief Refresher on Fourth Amendment Search Law

In a different chapter, the application of the Fourth Amendment in correctional institutions was discussed. The Fourth Amendment prohibits unreasonable searches and seizures and generally requires searches to be based on probable cause. What is reasonable as used in the Fourth Amendment is determined by balancing the privacy interest of the individual against the needs of the state. In *Hudson v. Palmer*, the Supreme Court ruled that because of the significant state interest in prison safety and security, a convicted prisoner had no legitimate expectation of privacy in their cells and things in their cells. The law is less clear as to a prisoner's expectation of bodily privacy. Earlier, the Court had ruled in *Bell v. Wolfish* that pretrial detainees had no legitimate expectation of privacy in their cells based on institution safety and security. Because not everyone who enters a prison is a prisoner, such as employees and visitors, the Fourth Amendment recognizes their greater expectation of privacy, but one which is still balanced against governmental needs to search.

At this point, it is useful to introduce the "possible punishments continuum," as it directly impacts how the guidance in Supreme Court opinions dealing with persons in the criminal justice system is framed and applied. In *Griffin v. Wisconsin* (discussed later), the Court stated: "Probation is simply one point (or, more accurately, one set of points) on a continuum of possible punishments ranging from solitary confinement in a maximum-security facility to a few hours of mandatory community service." The different points on the continuum also represent differences in the expectation of privacy that the Fourth Amendment will protect. The continuum begins upon a valid conviction. At one end, are convicted prisoners who have the least expectation of privacy in their surroundings and likely in their bodily privacy. On the opposite end of the continuum, are people who have minimal supervision such as unsupervised probation. These persons are subject to criminal punishment (probation) and while their expectation of privacy is diminished, it is greater than that of a prisoner. While there are many points on the continuum, for the purpose of this text, consider unsupervised probation, supervised probation, parole, supervised release, and incarceration as distinct points. At each point moving toward incarceration, the legitimate expectation of privacy is diminished, and the interests of the state increase.

As you read the case summaries and portions of judicial opinions, think about what class of persons are on the continuum that the court is addressing.

▸ *Griffin v. Wisconsin; United States v. Knights; Samson v. California; Pennsylvania Board of Probation and Parole v. Scott*

When they are under supervision, it is clear that the rights of probationers and parolees are significantly limited, mainly by the conditions and restrictions that are placed on them in the terms of their probation or parole. Their constitutional rights may also be limited compared with ordinary citizens, as was shown in *Griffin v. Wisconsin*, 483 U.S. 868 (1987). Probation officers went to Griffin's apartment and searched it without a warrant after the police advised them that he might have guns there. Police officers went along during the search, and a gun was found. Griffin was convicted of possession of a firearm by a convicted felon.

The Court noted that a probationer's home, like those of free world persons, is provided protection by the Fourth Amendment and the requirement that searches be reasonable. When the government has "special needs" beyond the "normal needs of law enforcement, application of the warrant and probable cause standard requirement arc impractical." Probationers do not have the same level of liberty of free persons because of the state's needs to ensure the probationary period as one of rehabilitation and the protection of the public. The probation system then has special needs beyond those of "normal law enforcement that may justify departures from the usual warrant and probable-cause requirements."

> **Supervision [on probation], then, is a "special need" of the State permitting a degree of impingement upon privacy that would not be constitutional if applied to the public at large. That permissible degree is not unlimited, ...**

The Supreme Court also noted the very practical problems that obtaining a search warrant would present, as opposed to the need for efficiently supervising a probationer. There could be delays in obtaining a warrant, and the court deciding upon issuing a search warrant would have the authority to decide whether this degree of supervision was necessary. The burden of having to show probable cause, as a basis for issuance of the search warrant, would probably not have been met in this case. Although searching without probable cause and without a warrant clearly can operate to the detriment of the probationer, their situation as a person under close supervision by their probation officer overrides their personal protections, the Court said, which are otherwise guaranteed by the Constitution.

> **[T]he probation agency must be able to act based upon a lesser degree of certainty than the Fourth Amendment would otherwise require in order to intervene [by conducting a search] before a probationer does damage to himself or society.**

The Wisconsin state regulation under which the probationer was supervised in the community provided that a probation officer could search a probationer's home without a warrant as long as the officer's supervisor approves and there were "reasonable grounds" to believe that contraband (items that the probationer cannot possess under the probation conditions) was present. The Court held that the warrantless search of the probationer's home did not violate the constitutional rights of the probationer.

In *Griffin*, the right to search was granted to probation officers by a state regulation that gave them permission to search a probationer's residence when there were "reasonable grounds" to believe that there was something illegal or impermissible in his home. Other states may also have statutes that provide such authority to search. Alternatively, state authorities may have probationers sign a consent that permits searches of their homes or possessions (such as a car) when they are placed on probation. This agreement, in effect, becomes part of the order that places the probationer on probation. Similarly, the search authority may be incorporated into the standard conditions of probation that are given to (and should be explained to) the probationer when he is ordered into probation status.

In *United States v. Knights*, 534 U.S. 112 (2001), the Supreme Court discussed the breadth of this concept. As a condition of placing Knights on probation, a California court's order provided that Knights' person, property, vehicle, residence, and personal effects would be subject "to search at any time, with or without a search warrant, warrant of arrest or reasonable cause by any probation officer or law enforcement officer." Knights signed the order, acknowledging this condition.

Shortly after being placed on probation, Knights was suspected of being involved in criminal activity. Police surveillance was set up. Based on reasonable suspicion, but without a warrant and pursuant to Knight's probation condition, police [not probation agents] searched his apartment, where they found, among other items, a detonation cord, ammunition, and liquid chemicals. Knights was arrested and subsequently indicted. Knights moved to suppress the evidence found during the search of his apartment. The district court, with the court of appeals affirming, held that the search was impermissible. The appeals court held that the search condition in Knights' probation order had to be seen as limited to probation searches and did not extend to those for investigation purposes. The Supreme Court reversed, holding that the Fourth Amendment did not limit searches pursuant to this probation condition to those with a probationary purpose.

> **When an officer has reasonable suspicion [rather than probable cause, which is a higher standard ordinarily required by the Fourth Amendment] that a probationer subject to a search condition is engaged in criminal activity, there is enough likelihood that criminal conduct is occurring that an intrusion on the probationer's significantly diminished privacy interests is reasonable.**

The Court decision in *Knights* did not rely upon the "special needs" assessment set forth in *Griffin v. Wisconsin*, but on the general totality of the circumstances balancing rationale. The consent form executed by Knights agreeing to searches by probation and other law enforcement officers was a factor in assessing the probationer's expectation of privacy. "*The probation order clearly expressed the search condition and Knights was unambiguously informed of it. The probation condition thus significantly diminished Knights' reasonable expectation of privacy.*" The Court did not decide the question of whether the probation condition constituted a valid waiver of Knights' Fourth Amendment rights, but only that the search was reasonable in light of the probationer's diminished expectation of privacy balanced against the state's governmental interests: rehabilitation of the offender and protection of the public. The probationer's diminished expectation of privacy coupled with the police officer's reasonable suspicion of criminal activity justified the warrantless search of Knights' home.

Griffin and *Knights* concerned probationers, but similar search conditions are placed on persons released on parole and generally to the authority of supervising parole officers. Because parolees are also clearly under sanction of a sentence, their expectations of privacy are similarly diminished. The governmental interests of rehabilitation and public safety are the same. The rationale for restrictions on a parolee's rights (even constitutional ones), as spelled out in *Griffin* and *Knights*, would equally apply.

A question left unresolved by *Griffin* and *Knights* was "whether a condition of release can so diminish or eliminate a released prisoner's reasonable expectation of privacy that a suspicion less search by a law enforcement officer would not offend the Fourth Amendment." It was this question that the Supreme Court answered in *Samson v. California*, 547 U.S. 843 (2006).

California enacted a law requiring that persons released on state parole had to agree with, in writing, to searches of their person by a parole officer or other law enforcement officer at any time without warrant or cause. Samson was released on parole after expressly agreeing to the search condition, as well as other conditions of parole. His status as a parolee was known by local police, and acting under the belief there was a parole warrant for Samson, local police stopped him. After learning there was no warrant, local police, pursuant to the state statute authorizing the search of a person on parole, conducted a search of Samson's person. During the search, illegal drugs were found on Samson. After the state courts concluded that the search was constitutional, Samson appealed to the Supreme Court.

Relying heavily on its previous *Griffin* and *Knights* opinions, the Court first noted that on the continuum of criminal punishment, a parolee has "fewer expectations of privacy than probationers, because parole is more akin to imprisonment than probation is to imprisonment." A person placed on parole remained under the custody of the state Department of Corrections and was subject to a number of mandatory restrictions, such as drug testing, limitations on travel and association, and requirements for reporting to a parole officer. The nature and extent of these restrictions "demonstrate that parolees ... have severely diminished expectations of privacy by virtue of their status alone." As a condition of being allowed to serve the parole term in the community, Samson had to agree to suspicionless searches by a parole officer or other law enforcement officer; his agreement "significantly diminished" his reasonable expectation of privacy.

The Court next ruled that the state has "an 'overwhelming interest' in supervising parolees because 'parolees ... are more likely to commit future criminal offenses.'" The state has an interest in reducing recidivism and promoting both reintegration into the community and the positive citizenship of offenders. These substantial governmental interests justify "privacy intrusions that would not otherwise be tolerated under the Fourth Amendment." The Court agreed with the state that the "ability to conduct suspicionless searches of parolees serves [the state's] interest in reducing recidivism, in a manner that aids, rather than hinders, the reintegration of parolees into productive society."

The Court concluded that the search by law enforcement officers of a parolee like Samson was reasonable under the totality of circumstances. The Court considered, but rejected, the argument that most other states and the federal government are able to safely monitor the behavior of offenders on community supervision and both reduce recidivism and promote reintegration while mandating that searches of parolees be based on some degree of individualized suspicion.

> **That some States and the federal government require a level of individualized suspicion is of little relevance to our determination whether California's supervisory system is drawn to meet its needs and is reasonable, taking into account a parolee's substantially diminished expectation of privacy.**

In *Pennsylvania Board of Probation and Parole v. Scott*, 524 U.S. 357 (1998), Scott, as a condition of his release, agreed not to own or possess any firearms or other weapons. His parole agreement, which he signed, allowed state probation and parole authorities to search his person, property, and residence, without warrant, and to seize and use as evidence in revocation proceedings any violative items found.

Five months into his parole, an arrest warrant was issued. Three parole officers arrested Scott. Prior to being transferred to a correctional facility, Scott gave the officers the keys to his residence. The officers went to his house and conducted a search without warrant. There they discovered five firearms, a compound bow, and three arrows. This discovery was a contributory factor, along with alcohol consumption charges, to the decision to revoke Scott's parole and recommit him to prison.

Scott filed suit in the Commonwealth Court of Pennsylvania—both that court and, later, the Pennsylvania Supreme Court found a violation of Scott's Fourth Amendment right against unreasonable searches, regardless of Scott's signing of the parole agreement. The United States Supreme Court disagreed and held that the search was permissible, and the revocation action taken was proper.

> **The costs of allowing a parolee to avoid the consequences of his violation are compounded by the fact that parolees ... are more likely to commit future criminal offenses than are average citizens ... Indeed, this is the very premise behind the system of close parole supervision. Because parole**

revocation deprives the parolee not "of the absolute liberty to which every citizen is entitled, but only of the conditional liberty properly dependent on observance of special parole restrictions," … States have wide latitude under the Constitution to structure parole revocation proceedings.[6]

The Supreme Court, in these holdings, is clearly distinguishing the rights (and the conditional liberty) of probationers and parolees from the liberty afforded to regular, law-abiding citizens.

While the Supreme Court has not addressed the issue, lower federal courts have considered the privacy interests of persons on federal supervised release. The lower courts have generally agreed that a supervised releasee's status produces a diminished expectation of privacy. The court of appeals in *U.S. v. Lifshitz*, 369 F.3d 173 (2nd Cir. 2004) stated: *"Supervised release, parole, and probation lie on a continuum. The most severe is 'supervised release,' which is … followed, in descending order, by parole, then probation[.]"(citation omitted)*. Thus, as the district court noted, *"the current case involves the most circumscribed expectation of privacy."*

It is important to remember that the cases discussed above were heavily dependent upon state law and regulation, which may vary and produce different results. In a fact situation very similar to *Samson v. California*, the court of appeals for the 10th Circuit held that the state regulation governing the supervision of parolees in Kansas did not permit city police officers to conduct suspicionless searches of parolees. *U.S. v. Freeman*, 479 F.3d 743 (10th Cir. 2007). State courts may also interpret state laws and the state constitution to afford persons on parole or probation a greater expectation of privacy than what is provided by the Fourth Amendment. In *State v. Ochoa*, 792 N.W. 2d 260 (Iowa 2010), the state supreme court concluded that the state constitution afforded greater protection to the homes of parolees than the Supreme Court found in *Samson v. California*.

▶ *Martinez v. California*

An interesting sidelight of parole status is presented in *Martinez v. California*, 444 U.S. 277 (1980). Thomas was convicted of attempted rape and sentenced to 20 years, with a recommendation that he not be paroled. Nevertheless, after five years in prison he was paroled. Five months later, Thomas tortured and killed a 15-year-old girl. Her family brought suit in state court against California and its parole authorities, alleging that her life had been taken without due process of law and claiming that the parole authorities were, therefore, liable for the wrong decision made in releasing Thomas.

According to the record (allegations by the plaintiffs), it was more than a poor decision. The parole was made despite Thomas's record and the warning in his record that he was likely to commit another violent crime. Also, it was alleged that Thomas was not properly supervised while on parole. The actions of officials were described, in the plaintiffs' pleadings, as "reckless, willful, wanton, and malicious." The key to the outcome of the case, however, was a California statute that provided that government officials were not liable for any injury resulting from a decision to release a prisoner on parole, from determining the conditions of his parole, or whether to revoke his parole. This was held to be a complete defense for the defendants in the case, giving them absolute immunity from a suit for damages.

Noting that the availability of the statutory defense might have encouraged the parole board to take greater risks in their decision making than they would otherwise have done, the Supreme Court upheld the legality of the immunity statute and the dismissal of the case that was brought by the victim's family.

This [immunity] statute merely provides a defense to potential state tort law liability …. Whether one agrees or disagrees with California's decision to provide absolute immunity for parole officials in a case of this kind, one cannot deny that it rationally furthers a policy that reasonable lawmakers may favor …. We therefore find no merit in the contention that the State's immunity statute is unconstitutional.

Martinez (the deceased's family) had also filed action under 42 U.S.C. § 1983, claiming a constitutional violation of the victim's rights in depriving her of her life without due process of law. The statute granting immunity did not apply to this claim, because the California immunity statute only protected defendant officials in state tort law actions. The Section 1983 action, although a federal law, was accepted for adjudication in the state courts under precedent, in *Testa v. Katt*, 330 U.S. 386 (1947), that allowed states to entertain claims under federal statutes for enforcement in state courts.

The Supreme Court reasoned as follows: Section 1983 protects persons from injuries suffered because of violations of rights that are secured by the U.S. Constitution. The plaintiffs here claimed a constitutional violation when the victim's life was taken from her without due process of law. "But the Fourteenth Amendment protected her only from deprivation by the 'State of life without due process of law.'" The Court explained further:

> **Although the decision to release Thomas from prison was action by the State, the action of Thomas five months later cannot be fairly characterized as state action .... Her life was taken by the parolee five months after his release. He was in no sense an agent of the parole board .... [The victim's] death is too remote a consequence of the parole officers' action to hold them responsible under the federal civil rights law.**

The action by a court placing a defendant on probation is even more clearly immunized from suits for damages, such as those claiming a poor or even reckless decision, because judges have long been held to be immune from lawsuits arising from their judicial decisions, and the same applies broadly to judicial officers. See *Stump v. Sparkman*, 435 U.S. 349 (1978). Judges enjoy a sweeping kind of immunity, which bars any money-damages suit whenever the judge is performing a judicial act.

But that does not mean that a judge is immune to all lawsuits and can never be held liable. In *Forrester v. White*, 484 U.S. 219 (1988), Judge White had hired Forrester as an adult and juvenile probation officer. The Supreme Court in the *Forrester* case observed that judicial immunity is an accepted principle in this country:

> **[T]his Court [has] found that judicial immunity was "the settled doctrine of the English courts for many centuries, and has never been denied, that we are aware of, in the courts of this country."**

Nonetheless, such immunity only applies to the court's adjudicative functions and not employment or other administrative functions. When Judge White fired the probation officer, he was acting in an administrative capacity, the Court held, and the judge in that situation was not entitled to absolute immunity. (The Court did note that qualified immunity, similar to that enjoyed by officials in the executive branch of government, would be available to judges in their employment decisions, such as this one.)

▸ *Payne v. Tennessee; Greenholtz v. Inmates; Swarthout v. Cooke; Board of Pardons v. Allen*

An essential area of probation and parole is the initial decision to place the defendant on probation or the inmate on parole. As to probation, the law is clear that, because placing the defendant on probation is an imposition of a sentence, the due process protections of a criminal trial apply; this entitles the defendant to the opportunity to be present, and to present evidence, for mitigation of the sentence and to be heard himself (the right of **allocution**). Procedures at sentencing are somewhat more relaxed, and due process requirements are not as strict as they are in the main part of the trial, when the court or jury is considering the defendant's guilt or innocence. This is because the main inquiry at sentencing is to find the most appropriate sanction for the particular defendant in light of their past behavior and (at least in some courts) their rehabilitative needs. Individualization of the sentence has been recognized by the Supreme Court as an important sentencing objective, as emphasized in *Williams v. New York*, 337 U.S. 241 (1949).

As noted in *Mempa v. Rhay*, even in the case of deferred sentencing, there is a right to counsel at every significant stage of the proceedings, which includes any sentencing hearing or procedure. There are many rules that are developed locally regarding sentencing requirements. For example, recently, there has been a strong movement affording more rights to victims and their families at sentencing, and, in some jurisdictions, a "victim impact statement" (VIS) must be presented to the court. The Supreme Court has noted this procedure and approved it in *Payne v. Tennessee*, 501 U.S. 808 (1991).

> **We thus hold that if the State chooses to permit the admission of victim impact evidence and prosecutorial argument on that subject, the Eighth Amendment erects no per se bar. A State may legitimately conclude that evidence about the victim and about the impact of the murder on the victim's family is relevant to the jury's decision as to whether or not the death penalty should be imposed. There is no reason to treat such evidence differently than other relevant evidence is treated.**

This is consistent with *Williams v. New York*, cited previously, which encourages sentencing courts to gather all kinds of information about the defendant in order to individualize the sentence. The *Williams* case has never been overruled, but it has been cited in later years in numerous cases as a guiding Supreme Court ruling with regard to sentencing standards. In any event, some basic due process rights apply at sentencing when the defendant is placed on probation. These are the same rights that any defendant has at the sentencing stage of his criminal prosecution.

The more contentious question is whether due process is required at the time the decision is made to place an inmate on parole—that is, at the hearing on his parole release. In *Greenholtz v. Inmates*, 442 U.S. 1 (1979), the Supreme Court noted that "parole *release* and parole *revocation* are quite different. There is a crucial distinction between being deprived of a liberty one has, as in parole [revocation], and being denied a conditional liberty that one desires." (The Court notes a wonderful quote from Judge Henry Friendly: "There is a human difference between losing what one has and not getting what one wants.") The Court in *Greenholtz* applied this concept:

> **That the state holds out the possibility of parole provides no more than a mere hope that the benefit will be obtained. [That is] a hope which is not protected by due process.**

Thus, the Court in *Greenholtz* held that the paroling process—the review and decision making on whether an inmate should be paroled—involves subjective and discretionary assessments. There is no liberty interest inherent in the parole-release procedures and, therefore, no constitutional right to due process inherent in those procedures.

However, the Court found that there was another possible source of a liberty interest, which was in the language of the parole statute. The Nebraska statute provided that the parole board "shall order" the release of an inmate unless it found that one of four conditions prevailed. The Court concluded that this language created an expectation of release that entitled an inmate to some due process during the consideration of his parole. How much due process?

> **Merely because a statutory expectation exists cannot mean that in addition to the full panoply of due process required to convict and confine there must also be repeated, adversary hearings in order to continue the confinement …. The Nebraska procedure affords an opportunity to be heard, and when parole is denied it informs the inmate in what respects he falls short of qualifying for parole; this affords the process that is due under these circumstances.**

Those seem to be the minimal due process steps that the Court would require when the state statutes or rules have mandatory, nondiscretionary language that governs parole board actions. Nebraska, in fact, had some additional procedural protections, but those were not required in the Court's holding just quoted. The more formal hearing, which included more procedures, that the court of appeals had ordered was found to be too heavy and was not endorsed by the Supreme Court. The appellate court had ordered advance written notice, the right to appear and present documentary evidence (but not witnesses), a written record of the proceedings, and a written explanation of the facts relied on and the reasons for the board's actions. As a result of the Court's rejection of these requirements, due process entitlement at parole release hearings is limited to the few requirements referred to in the previous quotation.

The Court reaffirmed this position in *Swarthout v. Cooke*, 562 U.S. 216, (2011). In *Swarthout* (and the companion case *Cate v. Clay*), the Ninth Circuit Court of Appeals had held that California's parole statute created a liberty interest protected by the due process clause and that the state's statutory language of "some evidence" to support a parole board decision was a component of the federally protected liberty interest. The Supreme Court disagreed. The Supreme Court said the proper analysis under the due process clause has two steps: "We first ask whether there exists a liberty or property interest of which a person has been deprived, and if so we ask whether the procedures followed by the State were constitutionally permissible." On the first point, the Court held that whatever liberty interest did exist, it was created by state law, adding that, "no opinion of ours supports converting California's 'some evidence' rule into a substantive federal requirement." The Court continued, saying when such an interest is created, "the minimum procedures adequate for due process protection of that interest are those set forth in *Greenholtz*."

In *Board of Pardons v. Allen*, 482 U.S. 369 (1987), the Court underscored the holding of *Greenholtz*. This was a case brought by Montana inmates who claimed, under 42 U.S.C. Section 1983, that they had been denied due process rights in parole release procedures. The Montana statute stated that "the Board shall release on parole [an inmate] … when in its opinion there is reasonable probability that the prisoner can be released without detriment to the prisoner or to the community." The Court held that this language created a liberty interest in parole release under the due process clause, because it used mandatory ("shall") language that created a presumption that parole release would occur when the designated findings were made.[7]

▶ *Connecticut Board of Pardons v. Dumschat; Ohio Adult Parole Authority v. Woodard*

In *Connecticut Board of Pardons v. Dumschat*, 452 U.S. 458 (1981), the Supreme Court dealt with a challenge to the actions of the Connecticut Board of Pardons. Dumschat was serving a life sentence and applied for a **commutation** of sentence.[8] When his application for commutation of sentence was summarily denied, Dumschat claimed that he should have been given a hearing by the pardons board. The Connecticut law gave total discretion to the board to grant or deny pardons or commutations. Dumschat, however, contended that he had some expectation of receiving a commutation, because 85–90% of life sentences in the state were commuted. The Supreme Court denied his contention.

> **[A] Connecticut felon's expectation that a lawfully imposed sentence will be commuted or that he will be pardoned is no more substantial than an inmate's expectation, for example, that he will not be transferred to another prison; it is simply a unilateral hope …. No matter how frequently a particular form of clemency has been granted, the statistical probabilities standing alone generate no constitutional protections; a contrary conclusion would trivialize the Constitution. The ground for a constitutional claim, if any, must be found in statutes or other rules defining the obligations of the authority charged with exercising clemency.**

The Court relied on both *Greenholtz* and *Dumschat* in *Ohio Adult Parole Authority v. Woodard*, 523 U.S. 272 (1998). The Ohio constitution gives the governor the power to grant clemency as they believe proper. The legislature may regulate the application and investigation process (which it has delegated largely to the Ohio Adult Parole Authority), but it may not curtail the governor's discretionary authority.

Woodard was sentenced to death for aggravated murder, which he committed in the course of a carjacking. His conviction was affirmed, and the Supreme Court declined to review the conviction. As his date for execution approached, the Ohio Adult Parole Authority, as required, notified Woodard that he could have a clemency interview on September 9, 1994, if he wished, and that his clemency hearing would be on September 16, 1994. Woodard objected to the short notice for the interview and requested counsel be allowed to participate. Ohio did not allow counsel at this interview. The Supreme Court held that there was no due process violation in these procedures.

> **Despite the Authority's mandatory procedures, the ultimate decisionmaker, the Governor, retains broad discretion. Under any analysis, the Governor's executive discretion need not be fettered by the types of procedural protections sought by respondent [Woodard] …. There is thus no substantive expectation of clemency. Moreover …. the availability of clemency, or the manner in which the State conducts clemency proceedings, does not impose "atypical and significant hardship on the inmate in relation to the ordinary incidents of prison life." … A denial of clemency merely means that the inmate must serve the sentence originally imposed.**

Nor did the Court see a violation of Woodard's right under the Fifth Amendment to be free from self-incrimination.

> **It is difficult to see how a voluntary interview could "compel" respondent to speak. He merely faces a choice quite similar to the sorts of choices that a criminal defendant must make in the course of criminal proceedings, none of which has ever been held to violate the Fifth Amendment.**

▶ *United States v. Addonizio; California Department of Corrections v. Morales; Garner v. Jones; Lynce v. Mathis*

These cases look at the question of whether the parole rules may be changed after the defendant has been sentenced. In *United States v. Addonizio*, 442 U.S. 178 (1979), Addonizio complained that the U.S. Parole Commission had changed its rules while he was confined and that the change of rules resulted in his being imprisoned longer than the sentencing judge intended. The action brought was a collateral attack on Addonizio's sentence under a federal statute (Title 28, U.S. Code, Section 2255) that permits a challenge when a prisoner contends that their sentence is constitutionally or legally invalid. (All jurisdictions have procedures for such a post-sentencing attack on the validity of the sentence. In common law, the procedure was called petitioning for a writ of **coram nobis**. Most U.S. jurisdictions have abandoned that old nomenclature but provide for the same type of judicial review by some statutory or procedural authorization.) Addonizio had been sentenced to 10 years imprisonment, but the judge had indicated that he expected, with good institutional behavior, Addonizio would be released when he became eligible for parole after serving one-third of his sentence. The U.S. Parole Commission adopted new policies three years after Addonizio was sentenced, giving much heavier weight to the seriousness of the offense in determining parole release and resulting in the postponement of Addonizio's consideration for parole. When he applied to his sentencing court, that court found that its sentencing expectations had been frustrated by the commission's actions and ordered Addonizio released, reducing his sentence to "time served."

The Supreme Court held that the action by the sentencing court was invalid. In effect, it said that frustrating the desires of the sentencing judge was not a basis for setting aside the sentence.

> **[T]he sentence was and is a lawful one …. Congress has decided that the [Parole] Commission is in the best position to determine when release is appropriate, and in doing so, to moderate the disparities in the sentencing practices of individual judges …. The import of this statutory scheme is clear: the judge has no enforceable expectations with respect to the actual release of a sentenced defendant short of his statutory term …. [T]he actual [parole] decision is not his to make, either at the time of sentencing or later if his expectations are not met.**

In *California Department of Corrections v. Morales*, 514 U.S. 499 (1995), Morales was serving a sentence of 15 years to life and became eligible for parole in 1990. He was given his first parole hearing in 1989, and parole was denied. Under rules in effect at the time when he committed his offense, Morales would have been entitled to subsequent hearings every year on his suitability to be paroled. The law was then amended to allow the Board of Prison Terms to defer suitability hearings for up to three years if the inmate had been convicted of more than one offense involving the taking of life (Morales had been convicted twice of murder). Pursuant to this change in the law, the board rescheduled Morales for a hearing in three years; that is, he would be heard in 1992 rather than in 1990. Morales filed a habeas corpus petition, claiming the amendment constituted an ex post facto law in violation of the Constitution.

The Constitution forbids (in Article I, Section 10) passing any "ex post facto Law." This phrase has been interpreted to mean that laws may not be enacted that alter the definition of a crime after it has been committed, or that increase the punishment for criminal acts after their commission. The California statute clearly did not change the definition of Morales' crime, so the question is whether the amendment of the parole law increased the punishment for his crime. The Supreme Court held that it did not. It did allow the board to change the times when it would hold parole hearings, but this was only a procedural change. Here, the change only applied to a class of inmates for whom the likelihood of release on parole was fairly remote (inmates who had taken more than one life). The Court held that the California amendment did not violate the ex post facto clause, because it created "only the most speculative and attenuated risk of increasing the measure of punishment attached to the covered crimes."

The *Morales* decision led to *Garner v. Jones*, 529 U.S. 244 (2000). Jones was serving a life sentence in Georgia for murder. After five years, he escaped, during which time he committed a second murder, receiving a second life term. Under Georgia law, the Georgia Parole Board was required to consider parole for inmates serving life sentences after seven years. At the time Jones was convicted of his second murder, the board's rules required reconsideration every three years. In 1985, after Jones began serving his second life sentence, the board amended its rules to provide reconsideration hearings for inmates serving life sentences at least every eight years.

At his 1989 hearing, Jones was told he would next be considered for parole in 1997. In 1991, the Court of Appeals for the Eleventh Circuit, in a separate case, held that the retroactive application of the eight-year rule violated the ex post facto clause. The Georgia Parole Board, therefore, returned to its three-year rule. Accordingly, Jones appeared before the board in 1992 and 1995, being denied on both occasions.

Following the Supreme Court's 1995 *Morales* ruling, the board again began to schedule eight-year reconsiderations. The board had the option to make the period shorter but chose not to do so for Jones because of his multiple offenses and the circumstances and nature of the second offense. Jones sued, alleging violation of the ex post facto clause. The Supreme Court saw the Georgia law as reasonable, allowing it to put its resources to better use, stating that "By concentrating its efforts on those cases identified as having a good possibility of early release, the Board's Rules might result in the release of some prisoners earlier than would have been the case otherwise."

Based on the record in this case, the Court could not conclude that the change lengthened Jones's period of actual confinement, noting that the Georgia rule allowed for earlier consideration when warranted.

> **In *Morales*, we relied upon the State's representation that its parole board had a practice of granting inmates' requests for early review .... The policy statement here, by contrast, is a formal, published statement as to how the Board intends to enforce its Rule .... Absent any demonstration to the contrary from respondent [Jones], we respect the Board's representation that inmates, upon making a showing of a "change in their circumstance(s)" or upon the Board's receipt of "new information," may request expedited consideration.**

The Court thus gave deference to the Georgia Parole Board and, by extension, to other correctional professionals, allowing them to retain the flexibility needed to manage the parole process for the benefit of all.

Lynce v. Mathis, 519 U.S. 433 (1997), is a prison case in which the Supreme Court held that there was an ex post facto violation. In 1986, Lynce received a 22-year (8,030 days) sentence for attempted murder. In 1992, he was released from prison after the Florida Department of Corrections determined he had earned five different types of early-release credits, totaling 5,668 days. In addition, 1,860 of those days (called provisional credits) were awarded as a result of the state's plan to reduce overcrowding in its prisons. Shortly after being released, the Florida attorney general issued an opinion interpreting a 1992 statute as having retroactively canceled all provisional credits awarded to inmates who had been convicted of murder or attempted murder. Lynce was one of the 164 offenders Florida released who suddenly had an arrest warrant issued because of this change in the law providing provisional release credits. He was returned to custody with a new release date in 1998.

In his petition for a writ of habeas corpus, Lynce claimed the retroactive cancellation of provisional credits violated the ex post facto clause. The Supreme Court agreed. To be ex post facto, the Court said the law had to be retrospective—it would have to apply to events occurring before its enactment—and it must disadvantage the affected offender. The Court held that the operation of the 1992 statute, which canceled the overcrowding credits and required Lynce's reconfinement, was clearly retroactive. On the issue of whether Lynce had been "disadvantaged," the Court stated the following:

> **The 1992 statute has unquestionably disadvantaged the petitioner because it resulted in his rearrest and prolonged his imprisonment. Unlike the California amendment at issue in *Morales*, the 1992 Florida statute did more than simply remove a mechanism that created an opportunity for early release for a class of prisoners whose release was unlikely; rather it made ineligible for early release a class of prisoners who were previously eligible—including some, like petitioner, who had actually been released.**

A key distinction between *Morales* and *Lynce* is that *Morales* did not affect the length of punishment being served; *Lynce* did, by canceling provisional credits the inmates had previously earned and, as in Lynce's case, resulting in pulling some people back into prison.

▶ *Jago v. Van Curen*

What if officials give an inmate a break, but then change their minds? Van Curen was sentenced to a term of 6 to 100 years in prison. He would have been eligible for parole in 1976. Ohio passed a "shock parole" statute, which allowed earlier parole of first offenders who had served at least six months in prison for nonviolent crimes. Under this statute, Van Curen was evaluated by the Ohio Adult Parole Authority (OAPA), which approved his early release in 1974. He attended prerelease classes and was measured for civilian clothes. But then, soon after his parole interview, the Parole Authority learned that Van Curen had not been truthful in the interview or in the parole plan he had submitted for his release. He said he had embezzled $1 million when, in fact, he had embezzled $6 million; he said that he was planning to live with his half-brother if paroled, when, in fact, he intended to live with his homosexual lover. Because of these revelations, OAPA rescinded its earlier action and continued his case to a later date. Van Curen received no hearing with regard to the parole rescission action.

The court of appeals ruled that, once the decision to release Van Curen on shock parole was made, he was entitled to a hearing to explain the false statements that became the basis for the rescission decision. In *Jago v. Van Curen*, 454 U.S. 14 (1981), the Supreme Court disagreed and reversed.

> **We do not doubt that respondent suffered "grievous loss" upon OAPA's rescission of his parole. But we have previously "reject[ed] … the notion that any grievous loss visited upon a person by the State is sufficient to invoke the procedural protections of the Due Process Clause." *Meachum v. Fano* …. We hold that the Court of Appeals erred in finding a constitutionally protected liberty interest … We think that the reasoning of *Greenholtz … Dumschat …* and the Court of Appeals' own concession that Ohio law creates no protected "liberty" interest, require reversal of the holding of the Court of Appeals that respondent was entitled to a hearing prior to denial of his parole.**

▶ *Moody v. Daggett*

Moody was on parole from a federal rape conviction and was sentenced to new 10-year sentences for manslaughter and second-degree murder. He was serving those sentences when the U.S. Board of Parole issued a warrant that charged him with violating the terms of his parole release. This warrant was lodged (as is frequently done) with prison authorities as a detainer. Moody asked that the warrant be executed at once, so any prison time he had to serve for violation of the terms of his parole could run concurrently with his homicide sentences. The parole board denied his request and ordered the warrant to be held until his release on the homicide sentences, at which time the board intended to execute its warrant and take Moody into custody for his parole violation. (This meant that any term for parole violation would be served consecutively to his new prison terms—not concurrently, as Moody would have liked.) Moody filed a habeas corpus petition, claiming primarily that he had been denied a prompt parole revocation hearing.

In *Moody v. Daggett*, 429 U.S. 78 (1976), the Supreme Court held that there had not been an illegal loss of liberty caused by the lodging of the warrant against Moody and that he was not entitled to an immediate parole revocation hearing. The Court noted that the loss of liberty that Moody was suffering came from his sentences on his two homicide convictions. Even though Moody claimed that the existence of the warrant was a heavy cloud over his head and might adversely affect his eligibility for some privileges while confined, the Court said that there were good reasons for the board to defer its decision and consider Moody for release or revocation of his parole when he finished his current sentences.

> **With only a prospect of future incarceration which is far from certain, we cannot say that the parole violator warrant has any present or inevitable effect upon the liberty interests which *Morrissey* [that is, the decision in *Morrissey v. Brewer*, discussed earlier in this chapter] sought to protect. [*Morrissey*] established execution of the warrant and custody under that warrant as the operative event triggering any loss of liberty attendant upon parole revocation …. [T]he loss of liberty as a parole violator does not occur until the parolee is taken into custody under the warrant …. [W]e hold that he has been deprived of no constitutionally protected rights simply by issuance of a parole violator warrant.**

The practice of lodging warrants for violations of parole or probation against inmates who are in custody on new charges continues. A **detainer** is often held on file until the inmate is released from the sentence(s) they are serving on their new (more recently committed) offenses. The *Moody* decision tells us that there is no constitutional violation in that practice. Indeed, the Supreme Court pointed out that there may be very good reasons for the parole or probation authorities to wait until the new sentence is served, allowing them to make a more informed judgment about whether the probation or parole status of the inmate should be revoked. (Not infrequently, the revocation authority may decide that the new sentence is punishment enough and that the inmate may be released to the street after that sentence is served, usually returning to supervision under the earlier probation or parole status.)

▶ *Smith v. Doe; Connecticut Department of Public Safety v. Doe*

Are there crimes that are thought to be so reprehensible as to require continuing governmental oversight even after the criminal has paid his debt to society? *Kansas v. Hendricks*, 521 U.S. 346 (1997), discussed the Court's upholding civil commitment for persons who complete their criminal sentences and who, due to "mental abnormality" or "personality disorder," are likely to become involved in "predatory acts of sexual violence." But are there other steps that may be taken, short of confinement? The answer is yes. In *Smith v. Doe*, 538 U.S. 84 (2003), and its companion case, *Connecticut Department of Public Safety v. Doe*, 538 U.S. 1 (2003), the Supreme Court upheld the constitutionality of sex offender registration. In *Smith*, the challenge was made based on ex post facto arguments. In *Connecticut*, the challenge was based on allegations of due process violation.

Smith concerned the Alaska Sex Offender Registration Act. That Act required every sex offender or child kidnapper in the state to register with the department of corrections within 30 days prior to release from custody. If the offender was not confined, registration with local law enforcement agencies had to occur within a working day of the conviction or of the offender's entrance into the state. Periodic verification of the submitted information (which included name, address, and other specified information) was required, with the frequency (quarterly or annually) determined by the individual's type of criminal behavior. Similarly, the criminal behavior determined whether the verification was to continue for 15 years or for life. Nonconfidential information about the offender (such as name, address, photograph, place of employment, and nature of conviction) would also be made available to the public. The Act allowed the state to choose the means for making the public aware of the nonconfidential information, and the state chose to do this through the Internet. The Act's registration and notification requirements were to be retroactive.

The Doe respondents (two anonymous offenders) in *Smith* were convicted sex offenders. They had been released from prison and had completed sex offender treatment programs. Their convictions occurred before the act's passage, but pursuant to the Act they were required to register as sex offenders.

Doe I and Doe II and the wife of Doe I brought suit under 42 U.S.C. § 1983, asking that the Act be declared inapplicable to them under the ex post facto clause (of Article I of the Constitution) and the due process clause (of the Fourteenth Amendment). The district court ruled for the State; however, the appeals court held that the registration requirements were violations of the ex post facto clause because of the act's punitive and retroactive effects.

The Supreme Court, as it did in *Hendricks*, saw the threshold question as being whether the legislature meant to establish civil proceedings. If the Act was civil in nature, the question would be whether the statutory scheme was so punitive in purpose or effect as to negate the state's intent (that is, to turn the procedure into criminal proceedings, despite what the legislature said).

In considering the first question, the Court examined what the state legislature identified as the law's objective—protection of the public. To assist in this process, the legislature believed it was beneficial to release certain information about sex offenders to public agencies and the general public. The Act mandated no specific procedures, leaving this to the Department of Public Safety, an agency responsible for enforcing both criminal and civil regulatory laws. The Court found this to be persuasive in determining the legislative intent of the law to be civil and not criminal.

In considering the second question, the Court did not see the Act's statutory scheme as being punitive.

Our system does not treat dissemination of truthful information in furtherance of a legitimate governmental objective as punishment.

Although the public availability of the information may have a lasting and painful impact on the convicted sex offender, these consequences flow not from the Act's registration and dissemination provisions, but from the fact of conviction, already a matter of public record. The State makes the facts underlying the offenses and the resulting convictions accessible so members of the public can take the precautions they deem necessary before dealing with the registrant.

[T]he Act has a legitimate nonpunitive purpose of "public safety, which is advanced by alerting the public to the risk of sex offenders in their community."

The Court rejected the appeals court's view that the registration requirement was parallel to probation or supervised release (parole), as to the degree of restraint imposed. The Court pointed out that probation and supervised release have a number of mandatory conditions. The Court observed that, unlike probation or supervised release, offenders subject to the registration system were free to move where they wished and to live and work as other citizens, with no supervision. For example, the registration system could not impose on the registrant any curfew restrictions or ban against alcohol consumption, as probation or parole could.

A person's failure to abide by these conditions can result in the person's return to prison. By contrast, sex offenders who are subject to the Act's registration requirements do not have such constraints.

The Court also said that features of the Act, such as its application to all convicted sex offenders without regard to their future dangerousness, the duration of the reporting requirements, and the wide dissemination of the information, did not make the law punitive.

The excessiveness inquiry of our ex post facto jurisprudence is not an exercise in determining whether the legislature has made the best choice possible to address the problem it seeks to remedy. The question is whether the regulatory means chosen are reasonable in light of the nonpunitive objective. The Act meets this standard.

The Supreme Court looked at another challenge to sex offender registration, based on a due process complaint, in *Connecticut Department of Public Safety v. Doe*. This Doe filed on behalf of himself and other similarly situated sex offenders, claiming he was not a dangerous sex offender and that his being listed without a hearing deprived him of a liberty interest—his reputation combined with the alteration of his status under state law—and was violative of his due process rights. The district court enjoined the law's public disclosure provisions, and the appeals court affirmed.

In reversing the lower courts' decisions, the Supreme Court relied on Connecticut's legislative intent in passing the act. The Court said the state's intent was to facilitate access to publicly available information about persons convicted of sexual offenses. There was no assessment of the specific risk of reoffending or of current dangerousness. Persons included on the registry were listed because of their conviction record and state law, and the main purpose of providing this information on the Internet was to make it more easily available, not to warn about any specific person. The Court held that the state's legislative scheme would govern.

[E]ven if respondent [Doe] could prove that he is not likely to be currently dangerous, Connecticut has decided that the registry information of all sex offenders—currently dangerous or not—must be publicly disclosed. Unless respondent can show that that substantive rule of law is defective (by conflicting with a provision of the Constitution), any hearing on current dangerousness is a bootless exercise.

▶ Community Corrections

Correctional approaches, as a group, are somewhat difficult to define. Community corrections include a diverse group of programs that are based in the community and offer sentencing alternatives to incarceration. Probation and parole fall under this broad category. Also included are facilities with such titles as prerelease centers, group homes, halfway houses, residential reentry centers, and community treatment centers (see **FIGURE 17-1**). The degree of security and staff supervision in these facilities may vary greatly, but as discussed in this text, all belong to the field of community corrections, because their security features are less restrictive than the traditional jail or prison. (This distinction tends to blur at the upper end of community facilities and the lower end of confinement facilities. Some community facilities enforce strict restrictions on residents' movements, allowing them to leave the "house" or "center" only for work, job interviews, or school, while some low security corrections facilities enforce

FIGURE 17-1 Front Entrance of the Community Corrections Center in Omaha, Nebraska.
© Mikael Karlsson/Alamy Stock Photo

very few restrictions.) The distinguishing feature is that in community corrections, the offender has some degree of freedom to move around in the surrounding community and also some gradual freedom to visit home and family.

Another kind of community corrections is the sentencing alternative, which avoids placing the defendant in a prison or jail. Probation is obviously one such type of sentencing alternative. Restitution and fines, strictly speaking, are sentencing alternatives because they are often used in place of a jail term, but they are not considered community corrections because they do not involve any supervisory action, other than the passive one of collecting the fine or the restitution payment from the offender.

▶ Use of Fines

Fines are one of the oldest kinds of sentences. They are also the most common sanction used for minor offenses. For some serious offenses—particularly those involving financial gain, such as embezzlement, tax evasion, and drug offenses—they may be imposed in combination with other sanctions, including imprisonment. The Supreme Court has considered constitutional questions in connection with fines in a few instances.

▶ *Williams v. Illinois; Tate v. Short*

In *Williams v. Illinois*, 399 U.S. 235 (1970), Williams had been sentenced to one year in jail and a $500 fine for petty theft. He did not have the money to pay the fine. Under an Illinois law, Williams was to be kept in jail until he "worked off" his fine at the rate of $5 a day. This meant that he would be kept in jail 100 days longer than he would have been had he been able to pay the fine. This extended sentence also was 100 days longer than the maximum jail sentence authorized for the crime he committed. The Supreme Court held that it was a violation of the equal protection clause to require an indigent defendant to serve longer than the most that could be served by a nonindigent defendant.

In the case of *Tate v. Short*, 401 U.S. 395 (1971), the Court extended its protection of indigents in fine cases. In this case, the defendant was convicted of several traffic offenses, none of which authorized sentences of incarceration. He was given a fine, which he was unable to pay. The court ordered him to the prison farm, where he was to "work off" his fine at the rate of $5 a day. The Supreme Court held that this too was impermissible discrimination against an indigent defendant in violation of the Fourteenth Amendment. Here, confinement was ordered "solely because of his indigency." This was an equal protection violation, which could not stand. Through these rulings, the old practices of "working off" fines have been abolished; the sentence of "$100 or 10 days," as well as its many variations, is no longer allowed.

▶ *Bearden v. Georgia*

In *Bearden v. Georgia*, 461 U.S. 660 (1983), Bearden had been placed on probation, with a condition that he pay a fine of $500 and $250 in restitution. He paid $200 toward his fine, but he lost his job and was unable to pay more. When the balance of his fine and restitution came due (the court had given him four months to make the payments), Bearden told the probation office that he was going to be late with his payments because he could not find a job. He was taken before the trial court for a revocation hearing. Based on his failure to pay the fine and restitution, the court revoked probation and sentenced him to serve the balance of his probationary term (nearly three years) in prison. The Georgia Court of Appeals and the Georgia Supreme Court rejected Bearden's claim that imprisoning him for inability to pay his fine violated the equal protection clause. Courts in other states had held that revoking the probation of indigents for failure to pay their fines did violate the equal protection clause. The U.S. Supreme Court agreed to review this question to resolve the differences in the rulings of lower courts.

Which side did the Supreme Court come down on, the Georgia position (that it was permissible to revoke probation for an indigent's failure to pay a fine) or the opposing position (that it was unconstitutional to revoke probation because of an indigent's inability to pay)? Well, the Court chose neither side. As in a number of other cases, the Supreme Court refused to answer with a simple yes or no, forging a new (somewhat complex) rule, which accommodated competing interests. The Court recognized that an indigent should not be excused from punishment if they willfully refused to pay the fine (or restitution). But if the indigent probationer had made good efforts to pay the fine and could not do so, the Court held that "it is fundamentally unfair to revoke probation automatically without considering whether adequate alternative methods of punishing the defendant are available." All of these considerations were influenced by the Court's earlier decisions in *Williams v. Illinois* and *Tate v. Short*. There, the Supreme Court noted, it had ruled that a state cannot "impose a fine as a sentence and then automatically convert it into a jail term solely because the defendant is indigent and cannot forthwith pay the fine in full." In *Bearden*, the Court held:

> **[I]n revocation proceedings for failure to pay a fine or restitution, a sentencing court must inquire into the reasons for the failure to pay. If the probationer willfully refused to pay or failed to make sufficient bona fide efforts legally to acquire the resources to pay, the court may revoke probation and sentence the defendant to imprisonment within the authorized range of its sentencing authority. If the probationer could not pay despite sufficient bona fide efforts to acquire the resources to do so, the court must consider alternative measures of punishment other than imprisonment. Only if alternative measures are not adequate to meet the State's interests in punishment and deterrence may the court imprison a probationer who has made sufficient bona fide efforts to pay.**

The case was sent back to the lower courts to apply the new rule for revoking probation, taking into account the indigency of the probationer.

Other sentences that avoid confinement are orders for community service and other creative orders, which require certain activities or contributions by the defendant in lieu of sentencing to confinement.

Electronic monitoring is a recent technological innovation, which allows offenders to remain in the community when, in some cases, they would otherwise be sent to prison. Such monitoring, which keeps track of the offender's location, verifying that they are at home, work, or other approved place or, to the contrary, indicating that they have gone outside their permitted areas. Electronic monitoring is often used in conjunction with probation (or parole) supervision. It can also be structured to work outside of regular probation supervision, such as when it is administered by a private company, under court specifications, to monitor the whereabouts and activities of offenders. In 2015, the Pew Charitable Trust conducted a survey of the companies that comprise 96% of the market for manufacture, sale, or use of electronic tracking devices. From that survey, it was estimated that 125,000 convicted or pretrial offenders were subjected to electronic monitoring.[9] One issue that arises is the costs of these programs and their impact on indigent offenders. Many jurisdictions have contracted the operation of electronic monitoring to private companies that charge a fee for services. While many offenders are willing and able to pay the fee and continue to live at home and work, for others, the fee can be challenging to pay and leads to increased contact with the criminal justice system when outstanding fees are not paid.

Drug testing is a similar tool. It is usually used as a condition of probation, but it may be used as an independent kind of sentencing, operated by a private company, a drug treatment clinic, or other facility, to monitor the drug-free status of the defendant, when that is specifically ordered by the sentencing court.

Also included within community corrections are those programs that release the offender from a confinement facility into the community under special conditions, while the constraints of the term of imprisonment still hang over their head. Under this definition, parole is the most common type of such release into the community. Other community programs, which are used in many jurisdictions, are furloughs and work (or study) releases. These are available to prison and jail officials in jurisdictions where they have been specifically authorized by statute. **Furloughs** are releases of inmates for short periods of time, usually for participation in or attendance at important functions, such as a hospital visit to a very sick relative, attendance at a child's wedding, or attending a school graduation. Inmates must meet eligibility requirements for furloughs, which usually include establishing trustworthiness, having good conduct, and having no criminal record of violence, sex offenses, or escape. Sometimes, furloughs are authorized for offenders of higher security risk to attend a very important event, such as the funeral of a parent, to which the inmate is escorted by officers. (The cost of these escorts may have to be paid for by the inmate or his family.)

Work release is a program that allows low-risk inmates to leave the prison or jail during the day to go to a job and to return to the institution at night and on weekends. Study release is a similar program, which allows inmates to go out during limited hours to attend school and then to return to sleep and eat at the corrections facility. The term includes such categories as halfway houses, residential treatment centers, restitution centers, and prerelease centers. In 2018, the Florida DOC had 4% of its prison population in a re-entry center, state run community release centers, or private community release centers.[10] Work release, like furloughs, do not involve a liberty interest protected by the Due Process Clause of the U.S. Constitution. *Asquith v. Dept. of Corrections*, 186 F.3d 407

(3rd Cir. 1999). However, the closer a furlough or work release program comes to parole (*Moody v. Daggett*) or pre-parole (*Harper v. Young*—discussed in the chapter on due process), courts may conclude that the due process clause requires some type of procedural due process protection before program participation is terminated.

The legal questions that are raised by such community corrections activities are few compared with those of prisoners' rights. Most controversy surrounding community corrections involves community opposition to the location of such facilities.[11] There have been no Supreme Court decisions or significant constitutional rulings on such programs, except the body of probation and parole cases that we discussed earlier in this chapter. Because most kinds of community corrections are tied to sentencing, and because judges have great discretion in sentencing (and also because those who are placed into alternative community sentences are usually so grateful for the opportunity to avoid confinement that they do not raise legal objections), there has been very little litigation involving such programs. The only significant concern would seem to be to ensure that such programs are available to all offenders, without regard to race, gender, disability status, or other unjustifiable distinctions. Otherwise, the guidelines of the probation and parole law discussed earlier are the rules for community placement.

The same concerns apply to prison and jail programs involving community activities: placing inmates in work or study release, on furlough, or on parole is a discretionary function, in which conditions for consideration must be tied to the criminal history and past behavior of the offenders, along with their prospects for successful involvement in community programs or supervision. Apart from impermissible factors of discrimination, the decisions for such releases into the community should be based on eligibility and risk criteria, along with correctional judgment, which are virtually impervious to legal attack. Inmates who are denied community programs are, understandably, unhappy and frequently file administrative grievances about those denials. For a well-managed program (in those places that have community-release or furlough programs), those grievances should be the extent of claims about selections for community releases.

Parole law is a separate and fairly well-defined area, which specifies the legal constraints on parole releases and parole supervision and revocation. In addition to court rulings, specific state and local statutes and policies govern these types of releases into the community, and they provide the answers to most legal questions about community programs for parolees.

Summary

- Probation and parole are similar in that they allow offenders to go into the community, under supervision, rather than be confined. Probationers are under the supervision and control of sentencing judges, and parolees are under the supervision and control of parole boards.

- Persons released on parole are under such restraints on their liberty that they may challenge their custody by using the writ of habeas corpus (*Jones v. Cunningham*).

- When it comes to revoking parole (and the rules for revocation are virtually identical for probationers), there is a liberty interest in remaining on parole. Therefore, a parolee must be given two hearings when his parole is revoked, and he is returned to prison. At the first hearing, near the place of arrest, the parolee must be given notice of the hearing and of the charges; he must be allowed to appear and present evidence; there must be a neutral decision maker; there should ordinarily be opportunity for the questioning of adverse witnesses; and a decision must be made with written reasons for the determination and a statement of evidence relied on. Later, there will be a final hearing, often at the prison where the sentence is to be served, and there are, again, due process steps to be followed. These are similar to the procedural requirements at the first hearing (*Morrissey v. Brewer*).

- The Supreme Court held that probationers who faced revocation of their probation were entitled to the same due process protections the Court had required at a minimum for parole revocations (*Gagnon v. Scarpelli*).

- As to the right to have counsel at revocation hearings, the Supreme Court said that counsel should be provided when the probationer (or parolee) contests the charges or when he contends that there are substantial, complex reasons to support mitigation of the action being considered (*Mempa v. Rhay*).

- Searches of the homes, property, or persons of probationers and parolees may be performed by supervising probation or parole officers without obtaining search warrants (*Griffin v. Wisconsin; United States v. Knights; Samson v. California; Pennsylvania Board of Probation and Parole v. Scott*).

- It is permissible for states to immunize parole board members from liability for their decision making regarding parole release (*Martinez v. California*). In the same case, the Court also held that such decisions do not expose parole board members to liability under 42 U.S.C. § 1983 for mistaken decisions when persons released on parole commit offenses and the victims of those offenses sue. The criminal actions are those of the offender, not of the state. They are not the direct fault of the parole decision makers. The same immunity from liability also applies to probation decision making, because judges are absolutely immune from their judicial actions.

- The decision to place a defendant on probation is part of the sentencing process. Therefore, it is covered by the same due process protections applying to sentencing, which include the right to be present, the right to counsel, and the right to allocution. Sentencing procedures, however, are much more informal, and are not bound by such strict due process protections as the criminal trial itself. The State may choose to permit victim impact evidence as part of the sentencing consideration (*Payne v. Tennessee*).

- The Supreme Court has ruled that the decision to place an inmate on parole is a discretionary one and does not, by the nature of the action itself, require due process protections. No constitutional standards apply to such decision making (*Greenholtz v. Inmates*). State-created liberty interests do not become federally protected liberty interests (*Swarthout v. Cooke*). However, if the state statute for parole requires the release of an inmate if certain conditions are found to exist (mandatory decision making), minimal due process is required. An opportunity for the inmate to appear and be heard at the parole hearing and a notification to the inmate of why parole is denied, if denial occurs, are the only steps required (*Greenholtz v. Inmates; Board of Pardons v. Allen*).

- Where total discretion is given to a board or governor to grant or deny pardons or commutations or clemency (or paroles), no due process hearing is constitutionally required (*Connecticut Board of Pardons v. Dumschat; Ohio Adult Parole Authority v. Woodard*).

- The Supreme Court held that it was constitutionally permissible (causing no ex post facto violation) for the rules of parole to be changed while the offender is confined, awaiting parole (*United States v. Addonizio; California Department of Corrections v. Morales; Garner v. Jones*). However, there is an ex post facto violation when a law is retroactive and disadvantages the affected offender, for example, when an entitlement is taken away that leads to the offender being returned to custody (*Lynce v. Mathis*).

- When a parole board decides to release a parolee, but then changes its mind and says the inmate must stay in prison (rescinding its action), there is no requirement of a hearing before the change is made (*Jago v. Van Curen*).

- It is also permissible, the Supreme Court said, for parole authorities to place a warrant for parole violation (as a "detainer") against a prisoner when he has been imprisoned on a new offense and to hold that warrant against him without any action on it until he completes service of his new sentence (*Moody v. Daggett*).

- In considering whether sex offender registries violate due process or the ex post facto clause, it is necessary to look at the state's statutory scheme. Registries intended to protect the public by providing information about convicted sex offenders have been held not to be punitive and, therefore, not violative of ex post facto or due process limitations (*Smith v. Doe; Connecticut Department of Public Safety v. Doe*).

- "Community corrections" is a broad concept, encompassing all kinds of sanctions and sentencing arrangements that permit offenders to remain principally in the community and not be confined in regular prison facilities. This concept includes probation, parole, prerelease centers, halfway houses, community service, fines, restitution, furloughs, work and study releases, and electronic monitoring.

- Fines (and orders for restitution payments) are frequently used sentences. The Supreme Court held that an indigent defendant cannot be held in jail because of his inability to pay the fine because of lack of funds (*Williams v. Illinois; Tate v. Short*). When an offender's probation was revoked because he did not have the money to continue making payments on his fine (which was one of the conditions of his probation), the Supreme Court said that a revocation action was too hasty. In such a case, the sentencing court would have to make an inquiry into the individual case, and if the probationer had made good-faith efforts to pay but could not, the court should first consider whether alternative methods of punishment would suffice; if they would not, only then could revocation of probation be ordered (*Bearden v. Georgia*).

Thinking About It

Randy Spencer filed a petition for a writ of habeas corpus, seeking to invalidate his September 1992 order revoking parole. Because he had completed the entire term of imprisonment underlying the parole revocation, the court had to decide whether his petition was moot. That is, was there no longer any live issue for the court to consider since his sentence was completely served? From his perspective, Spencer identified four continuing "injuries": the parole revocation could be used to his detriment in a future parole proceeding; the Order of Revocation could be used to increase his sentence in a future sentencing proceeding; the revocation could be used to impeach him should he appear as a witness or litigant in a future judicial proceeding; and the revocation could be used directly against him should he appear as a defendant in a criminal proceeding. What do you think? This case was reported as *Spencer v. Kemna*, 523 U.S. 1 (1998).

Key Terms

allocution
community corrections
commutation
coram nobis
detainer
furlough
suspend

Endnotes

1. Kaeble, D., & Alper, M. *Probation and Parole in the United States, 2018.* Table 1. (Washington, DC: Bureau of Justice Statistics, U.S. Department of Justice, August 2020.) Available: https://www.bjs.gov/content/pub/pdf/ppus16.pdf

2. See endnote 1. Appendix Table 6. The 2001 information came from Glaze, L. *Probation and Parole in the United States, 2001.* Page 6. Washington, DC: Bureau of Justice Statistics, U.S. Department of Justice. August 2002 (revised February 9, 2004).

3. See endnote 1. Appendix Table 6.

4. See endnote 1. Appendix Tables 3, 4, 5 & 7.

5. The Council of State Governments, *National Center for State Compacts.* http://apps.csg.org/ncic/Compact.aspx?id=70. Compacts are laws that are written so that states may cooperate with each other on matters of common interest. The Interstate Compact on Probation and Parole has been superseded by the Interstate Commission for Adult Offender Supervision. https://www.interstatecompact.org/questions-about-interstate-transfers

6. The question before the Supreme Court was "whether the exclusionary rule, which generally prohibits the introduction at criminal trial of evidence obtained in violation of a defendant's Fourth Amendment rights, applies in parole revocation hearings." The Court held that it did not, specifically declining to apply the exclusionary rule to proceedings other than criminal trials. The Court then noted, "Application of the exclusionary rule would both hinder the functioning of state parole systems and alter the traditionally flexible, administrative nature of parole revocation proceedings."

7. This reliance on the mandatory language standard has been called into question by the Supreme Court decision in *Sandin v. Conner*, 515 U.S. 472 (1995). The Court in *Sandin* gave reasons for abandoning the "mandatory language" standard in inmate discipline cases, and it did so, overruling *Hewitt v. Helms.* The *Hewitt* case, like the *Greenholtz* and *Allen* parole cases, was founded on an analysis of due process entitlement generated by a state statute that used mandatory language. This invites states to question and litigate the use of that standard in corrections-related matters such as parole.

8. A commutation is a reduction or melioration of the sentence, meaning either a reduction in the amount of time to be served or a change in some attribute of the sentence, such as making the inmate eligible for parole when he had not been. A pardon is the full-fledged wiping out of the conviction and sentence of the inmate, resulting in his total release, although the pardoning authority typically has the authority to place restrictions, such as supervision requirements, on the releasee. Pardoning power is given by the U.S. Constitution to the president, and most states grant such power to the governor. In Connecticut, a board was established to consider pardon and commutation actions. See U.S. Department of Justice, *Frequently Asked Questions.*

9. *Use of Electronic Offender-Tracking Devices Expands Sharply.* Pew Charitable Trust. September 7, 2016. Available at https://www.pewtrusts.org/en/research-and-analysis/issue-briefs/2016/09/use-of-electronic-offender-tracking-devices-expands-sharply

10. Florida Department of Corrections, *Annual Report 2017-2018.* 14. Available: https://www.justice.gov/archives/dag/page/file/914006/download. Community Re-Entry Centers. These centers house "community custody inmates who are participating in community work release by working at paid employment in the community and minimum custody inmates who are participating in a center work assignment by working in a support capacity for the center (such as food services and laundry).

11. Often, a more significant problem is establishing the location of community facilities and trying to counter the "NIMBY" ("not in my back yard") philosophy of many communities. Opponents use a variety of arguments to oppose the location of community facilities for offenders, raising such issues as proximity to schools, property value effects, and zoning rules. International Community Corrections Association (2018). *ICCA Position on Siting Community Corrections Facilities.* https://www.iccalive.org/icca/icca-policy-position-on-siting-community-corrections-facilities/

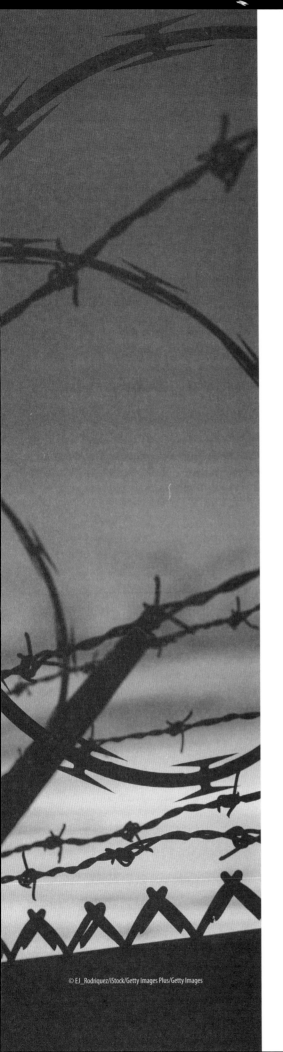

PART 3

Statutory and Administrative Law, Jails, Juveniles, Privatization, and Other Special Issues in Corrections

In Part II, the text examined the constitutional rights of prisoners. The U.S. Constitution is the primary source of prisoners' rights, and, in the past 40 years, most litigation that contested the conditions, programs, and activities in prisons has flowed out of the federal Constitution. Specifically, litigation has been filed by inmates under 42 U.S.C. § 1983 (or with Bivens actions, for federal prisoners), alleging violations of prisoners' constitutional rights and demanding monetary damages or injunctive relief, or both.

But there are other sources of prisoners' rights, and there are other legal issues (besides prisoners' rights) that corrections administrators must be concerned about. In Part III, the text examines some of these other issues and at the sources of law that most affect them.

Note: The information in Part III often covers cases first discussed in Part II, the Constitutional Law of Corrections. Readers may locate these earlier discussions by referring to either the Table of Contents or to the Table of Cases (located at the end of this text).

© EJ_Rodriquez/iStock/Getty Images Plus/Getty Images

CHAPTER 18

Statutory and Administrative Law

This Constitution, and the Laws of the United States which shall be made in Pursuance thereof; and all Treaties made, or which shall be made, under the Authority of the United States, shall be the supreme Law of the Land.

U.S. Constitution, Article VI, Clause 2

CHAPTER OUTLINE

- The Hierarchy of Laws in the United States
- Interstate Compacts and Uniform Laws
  - The Interstate Agreement on Detainers
  - The Uniform Criminal Extradition Act
  - Interstate Compacts for Transfer of Prisoners
  - Interstate Compact for Adult Offender Supervision
  - Interstate Compact for Juveniles
- State and Local Laws; Regulations, Rules, and Policies
- The Federal Bureau of Prisons
- State and Local Corrections
- Accreditation

This chapter examines nonconstitutional sources of law (that is, those outside of the U.S. Constitution) that will be of most concern to corrections workers and to offenders who are in the corrections system.

▶ The Hierarchy of Laws in the United States

The U.S. Constitution is the supreme law of the country. According to the terms of the Constitution (specifically, Article VI, Clause 2), which had to be subscribed to by every state when it joined the Union of states, the Constitution, federal laws, and federal treaties (which can only be made by the federal government) are the "supreme Law of the Land." By that provision, federal laws take precedence over state laws when they conflict with each other.

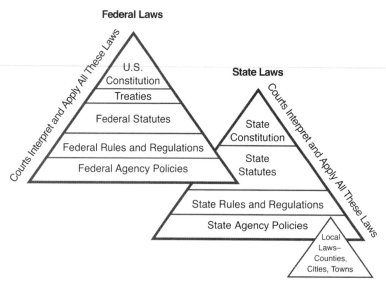

FIGURE 18-1 Hierarchy of Laws in the United States.

FIGURE 18-1 shows the hierarchy of laws in the United States. It depicts the different levels of government and the kinds of laws that are enacted at each level—federal, state, and local.

There are some areas in which the federal and state governments may pass laws governing the same matters, and, therefore, the two kinds of laws may come into conflict. In other areas, such as foreign affairs and treaties, only the federal government has authority to act. Congress has only has the authority to act by powers given to it by the Constitution in Article II. All other matters are left to the authority of the states, as provided by the U.S. Constitution in Amendment 10. For example, see *United States v. Lopez*, 514 U.S. 549 (1995), where a high school student was arrested and charged under the Gun-Free School Zones Act of 1990 (18 U.S.C. § 922(q)) for possession on school premises of a concealed handgun and five bullets. The district court denied the student's motion to dismiss his indictment holding that § 922 fell within Congress' power to "regulate activities in and affecting commerce, and the 'business' of elementary, middle and high schools … affects interstate commerce." Following conviction, the defendant (student) appealed to the Fifth Circuit Court of Appeals. The Fifth Circuit reversed, holding that Congress exceeded its authority to legislate under the Commerce Clause. The Supreme Court agreed, stating that Congress had overstepped its constitutional authority, that the "possession of a gun in a local school zone is in no sense an economic activity that might, through repetition elsewhere, substantially affect any sort of interstate commerce." Texas did have criminal statutes covering the same activity. Legislatures (both the U.S. Congress and state legislatures) have become much more active in the last 100 years, and legislation has come to embrace and affect myriad areas of our lives.

▶ Interstate Compacts and Uniform Laws

The U.S. Constitution specifically forbids states from entering agreements or compacts with other states without the consent of Congress (U.S. Constitution, Article I, Section 10). Congress has given consent for states to enter compacts in certain areas. One of those areas includes a consent to enter compacts between states for cooperative efforts in the prevention of crime and the enforcement of criminal laws and policies (which is authorized under 4 U.S.C. § 112).

> The consent of Congress is hereby given to any two or more States to enter into agreements or compacts for cooperative effort and mutual assistance in the prevention of crime and in the enforcement of their respective criminal laws and policies, and to establish such agencies, joint or otherwise, as they may deem desirable for making effective such agreements and compacts.

With this consent and authority, there have been interstate agreements and compacts drawn up in several areas of criminal justice to allow for such cooperation on criminal matters of mutual concern. Some of those compacts are discussed below.

The Interstate Agreement on Detainers

The provisions of the Interstate Agreement on Detainers (IAD) allow a prosecutor to obtain an individual from another state for prosecution. (The provisions of this agreement are located in Title 18, U.S. Code, Appendix 2, Section 2, Articles I–IX.) The detainer, an official notice to prison authorities that charges are pending elsewhere against an inmate, requests that the custodian notify the requesting state before the inmate is released. Under the terms of this agreement, once the detainer is filed, not only is the holding state (the custodian) obliged to notify the requesting state before the inmate's release but there is also a provision for an inmate to request prompt production for disposition of the pending charges. If such a request is made, the requesting state sends officers to take temporary custody of, and transport the inmate to, the jurisdiction where the charges are pending. Thus, under the agreement, either the prosecutor or the inmate may make a request for transfer to the jurisdiction where charges are pending and from which the detainer has been filed.

The inmate, while being produced on the charges in the receiving state, remains legally in the custody of the original, sending state. A prisoner's sentence continues to run in the sending state, just as if they were still confined there. The inmate must be brought to trial within 180 days of their request; charges are dismissed (by effect of the statute) if the inmate is not tried within that time. There is no hearing required (specifically, no extradition or rendition hearing) before the inmate is transferred to the requesting state. (See the Supreme Court decision in *Cuyler v. Adams*, discussed later in this chapter, for a ruling on that provision of the agreement, which does not provide for a hearing.) At the conclusion of the prosecution (or other disposition of the charges), the inmate must be returned to the state where they were serving their sentence.

These provisions allow for pending charges to be expeditiously disposed of. This may be an advantageous process for the prosecution to use to obtain a defendant who is in custody in another state. But it also may be a definite benefit to inmates, who want to get rid of detainers, which may adversely affect their opportunities for some programs and benefits (such as a reduction in custody, better housing or job assignments, and consideration for community programs). In many cases, the provisions speed up the procedure for trying inmates on charges in different jurisdictions. They may also force a state to drop charges that have been lodged as a detainer, for example, when there is some weakness in a case or in those cases in which prosecution was never fully intended to occur but in which the detainer was lodged merely for notification purposes.

Alabama v. Bozeman, 533 U.S. 146 (2001), is an example of the absolute language of a statute controlling the outcome of a case to the inmate's benefit. Bozeman was in a federal prison on a federal sentence. He also had a nonfederal charge in Alabama. State officials sought state custody of him for the purpose of arraignment and appointment of counsel. Bozeman was transferred to Covington County, Alabama, where he spent the night in the county jail, appeared in local court the next day, and was returned to the federal prison. The following month, he was brought back to Covington County for trial. Bozeman's counsel filed a motion for dismissal based on the IAD, specifically, Article IV(e). This section states that if a trial is not held on any indictment, information, or complaint prior to the inmate returning to the original place of confinement (in this case, to federal custody) the indictment, information, or complaint "shall not be of any further force or effect, and the court shall enter an order dismissing the same with prejudice."

Bozeman was convicted in Covington County, and the court then denied his motion for dismissal of the charges. A state appeals court affirmed. The state supreme court reversed, holding that the language of the statute controlled. The U.S. Supreme Court agreed. It dismissed the state's claim that the statutory violation was "de minimis," that it did not really violate the statutory intent "to protect the prisoner against endless interruption of the rehabilitation programs because of criminal proceedings in other jurisdictions." The Court said the statutory language was absolute; however, even if it were to accept the "de minimis" argument, the Court did not necessarily see the current violation as "trivial."

> [T]o call such a violation "technical," because it means fewer days spent away from the sending State, is to call virtually *every* conceivable anti-shuttling violation "technical"—a circumstance which, like the 13th chime of the clock, shows that Alabama's conception of the provision's purpose is seriously flawed.

Another case, *New York v. Hill*, 528 U.S. 110 (2000), shows that absolute language may be waived. Article III(a) of the IAD provides that an inmate must be brought to trial within 180 days following his request for disposition of the detainer. At a court hearing to set the trial date, Hill's counsel agreed to a trial date outside the 180-day period. Prior to trial and after lapse of the statutory 180-day period, Hill filed for dismissal. The court denied the motion, saying the defense counsel's agreement to the trial date constituted a waiver or abandonment of Hill's rights under the IAD. Hill was convicted. On appeal, he argued that the indictment should have been dismissed. Appeals courts first upheld the conviction and then (in a higher court) reversed it.

The Supreme Court noted that the IAD does not specifically address the effect of a defendant's consent to delay the applicable time limits. The Court had previously recognized that the most basic rights of criminal defendants are subject to waiver.

> **What suffices for waiver depends on the nature of the right at issue …. For certain fundamental rights, the defendant must personally make an informed waiver …. For other rights, however, waiver may be effected by action of counsel. "Although there are basic rights that the attorney cannot waive without the fully informed and publicly acknowledged consent of the client, the lawyer has—and must have—full authority to manage the conduct of the trial."**

Hill's prosecution and conviction beyond the 180-day limit were upheld. In a non-correctional context, there are two other examples of the reading of statutory language. In *Gonzalez v. United States*, 553 U.S. 242 (2008), the Supreme Court, citing *Hill*, held that express consent by counsel, without a specific waiver by the defendant, is sufficient to allow a magistrate judge to preside over jury selection in a felony trial. In *Zedner v. United States*, 547 U.S. 489 (2006), the Supreme Court held that a defendant may not prospectively waive the application of the Speedy Trial Act of 1974, 18 U.S.C. §§ 3161–3174.

The Uniform Criminal Extradition Act

The cooperation required between states is first based on the U.S. Constitution, Article IV, Section 2, Clause 2. This "Extradition Clause" provides that a person who is charged with a crime, and who flees to another state, must, on demand of the executive authority of the state from which he has fled, be delivered to the state having jurisdiction over the crime, which it is alleged he has committed. The federal government further sets rules for extradition in Title 18, U.S. Code, Sections 3181–3196. This law specifies the procedure to be followed when a fugitive's return is sought.

Most states have adopted the Uniform Criminal Extradition Act, which provides for more detailed procedures by states that are parties to the act and that are under the umbrella of the federal constitutional law and statute. Requests for the return of a fugitive who has fled to a foreign country must be handled through the federal government (specifically, the Department of State and the Department of Justice). This is because a sovereign country is under no obligation to surrender a person to another country just because that person is wanted on criminal charges. To accomplish such a transfer (also called a "rendition"), there must be a treaty between the two nations. By such means, through specific diplomatic and legal procedures, a person can be returned from a foreign country for prosecution. (Such a treaty and the corresponding rendition procedures, of course, operate for transfers in both directions, between both countries.)[1]

The Supreme Court considered the somewhat competing provisions of these two compacts—the Interstate Agreement on Detainers and the Uniform Criminal Extradition Act—in the case of *Cuyler v. Adams*, 449 U.S. 433 (1981). Adams was serving a sentence of 30 years in Pennsylvania. A prosecutor in New Jersey lodged a detainer against Adams and moved to bring him to trial on armed robbery charges. This was done pursuant to the IAD. Adams objected to his transfer to New Jersey, claiming that he was entitled to a hearing before his transfer under the provisions of the Extradition Act. (Both states were parties to both compacts.) After examining the provisions and the history of the IAD and the Extradition Act, the Supreme Court held that the rights and protections of the Extradition Act, specifically the right to a hearing before transfer, were reserved for the prisoner.

This was the holding, even though the IAD did not require a hearing by its terms and even though the prosecutor moved to bring the inmate to trial in New Jersey under the IAD. The main difference hinges on who makes the request to be taken to court on the detainer. If the prisoner makes the request, as provided by Article III of the IAD (and, as mentioned previously, there are often reasons why the prisoner wants to request production, such as to get the charges disposed of so they do not remain on file against him for a long period of time), the prisoner is deemed to have waived extradition rights, and there is no need for a hearing. But if the prosecutor requests the transfer, as provided by Article IV of the IAD, the prisoner retains any right that they may have to contest the legality of his transfer to the requesting state. The Supreme Court agreed with lower courts that had held that this provision meant that, upon the prosecutors' requests for transfer, inmates had the rights given them in the Extradition Act to contest the transfers. (If the states are not parties to the Extradition Act, the inmates would have the right to contest the transfers that they would have under existing extradition law in the holding state.)

The case of *New Mexico ex rel. Ortiz v. Reed*, 524 U.S. 151 (1998), involved interstate extradition of a parole violator. In 1993, Ortiz, who had been paroled in 1992, was told by Ohio prison officials that his parole was going to be revoked. Ortiz fled to New Mexico. Ohio sought his extradition, and New Mexico issued the appropriate warrant. After being arrested in 1994, Ortiz sought a writ of habeas corpus from a New Mexico district court. His claim was that he was not a fugitive for purposes of extradition, because he fled under duress. He alleged that Ohio authorities planned to revoke his parole and to "cause him physical harm" if he was returned to an Ohio prison. The New Mexico district court granted the writ, and the state Supreme Court affirmed. In making its determination, the court said the extradition did not comply with one of the four considerations announced by the U.S. Supreme Court in *Michigan v. Doran*, 439 U.S. 282 (1978). Specifically, the New Mexico court held that Ortiz was not a fugitive, instead referring to him as a "refugee from injustice." The court held that he fled to avoid the threat of bodily harm and that this "duress" negated his fugitive status.

The U.S. Supreme Court disagreed. Noting Ohio was not a party to the New Mexico proceeding, the Court rejected the New Mexico court's actions:

> **In case after case we have held that claims relating to what actually happened in the demanding State, the law of the demanding State, and what may be expected to happen in the demanding State when the fugitive returns are issues that must be tried in the courts of that State, and not in those of the asylum State.**

The Court also cited practical reasons for its decision, saying that it would be a great burden on the demanding state (Ohio) to provide witnesses and records in the asylum state (New Mexico) to counter the allegations made. New Mexico had made determinations it was not entitled to make on an extradition matter, the Supreme Court said, and Ortiz would have to be returned to Ohio.

Interstate Compacts for Transfer of Prisoners

Three interstate compacts address the interstate transfer of prison inmates. The national Interstate Compact for Corrections, with 38 states and the District of Columbia as parties, provides for uniform procedures and treatment of prisoners transferred from the supervisory agency of one state to that of a second state. The statutory language, as enacted in most states, covers such areas as purpose, authority, procedures and rights, and choice of law (which state's decisions are conclusive and when).

In addition to the national compact, there is the Western Corrections Compact, with 11 signatory states, providing "for the joint use of corrections facilities in the West." The New England Corrections Compact, adopted by six states, "provides for cooperation in the confinement, treatment, and rehabilitation of offenders." Additional authority for inmate transfers may be found in state statutes, agency policy, judicial action, intergovernmental agreements, memoranda of understanding, and contracts. In 2005, there were 1,587 inmates transferred under interstate compacts, with another 502 inmates transferred through noncompact methods. Transfers to federal prison facilities (345 inmates) and to private prisons (2,466 inmates) were done by means other than interstate compacts. Most inmate transfers were because of facility crowding. Other reasons for transfers were security issues ("poses danger"; "needs protection"), and "other" reasons (special program needs, pending adjudication, and postincident cool down).[2]

Interstate Compact for Adult Offender Supervision

The Interstate Compact for Adult Offender Supervision (ICAOS) became effective in June of 2002, replacing the Interstate Compact for the Supervision of Probation and Parolees. ICAOS, which has been adopted by all 50 states, is a "formal agreement between member states that seeks to promote public safety by systematically controlling the interstate movement of certain adult offenders." (ICAOS addresses the interstate supervision of offenders on some type of community release.) As an example of the purpose of the ICAOS, the Ohio Department of Rehabilitation and Corrections provides the following information:

Purpose

The purpose of the Interstate Commission for Adult Offender Supervision *(ICAOS) is to maximize public safety by addressing the transfer of supervision requirements of the member states and territories. Parole boards, courts and probation agencies are not able to handle the planning for and supervision of probationers and parolees when their residence and family resources exist outside their political boundaries. Most required levels of community-based supervision are available through the cooperation of Interstate Offices in the transfer of supervision.*

Program Overview

Supervision of offenders on community supervision (probation) or parole, who meet specific eligibility criteria, may be transferred to another state under the ICAOS system. All 50 of the United States of America, the District of Columbia, Puerto Rico, and the US Virgin Islands participate as members of the Commission. The Ohio Council and Interstate Commission for Adult Offender Supervision is administered through the Department of Rehabilitation and Correction (Adult Parole Authority).

The Interstate Compact Office facilitates the transfer of supervision services for offenders who are approved to reside and work in a territory other than where they are convicted. The offices enforces policies and procedures to ensure compliance with federal and state law for the transfer of supervision across state lines.

Ohio Department of Rehabilitation and Corrections: *Interstate Compact* - https://drc.ohio.gov/interstate -compact. The ICAOS maintains a website where persons can access the most accurate and updated information about the organization and its function. www.interstatecompact.org

Oregon's Department of Community Corrections states that over 250,000 offenders are being supervised under the ICAOS, with Oregon supervising about 1,300 offenders from other states, and about 1,700 Oregon offenders are being supervised by other states. https://www.oregon.gov/doc/community-corrections/Pages/interstate -compact.aspx. The ICAOS provides additional information on its website: https://www.interstatecompact.org/

Interstate Compact for Juveniles

The Interstate Compact for Juveniles (ICJ) has an interesting developmental background, and serves as a good example of how the news media can effect change. In the early 1950s, *Parade* magazine published a series of articles called "Nobody's Children." These articles showed the plight of runaways in the United States. Inspired by the articles and recognizing the need to do something, a group of organizations met "to develop a uniform set of procedures to facilitate the return of juveniles who ran away to other States and to create a system in which juvenile offenders could be supervised in other States." The involved organizations—the Council of State Governments, National Council on Crime and Delinquency, National Council of Juvenile and Family Court Judges, American Public Welfare Association, National Association of Attorneys General, and Adult Parole and Probation Compact Administrators Association—drafted the Interstate Compact on Juveniles. The compact was approved by these organizations in 1955 and was subsequently ratified by all 50 states, plus the District of Columbia, the Virgin Islands, and Guam.[3]

Based on the successful revision of the Interstate Compact for the Supervision of Probation and Parolees (now ICAOS), the Office of Juvenile Justice and Delinquency Prevention began a similar process for the ICJ. The new compact language was finalized in 2002, became available for introduction to the states in 2003, and became active in 2008. In April 2014, the ICJ completed the ratification of a "new" Compact by all 50 states, plus the District of Columbia, and the US Virgin Islands. Its governing body is the Interstate Commission for Juveniles, whose mission statement provides:

The Interstate Commission for Juveniles, the governing body of the Interstate Compact for Juveniles, through means of joint and cooperative action among the compacting states, preserves child welfare and promotes public safety interests of citizens, including victims of juvenile offenders, by providing enhanced accountability, enforcement, visibility, and communication in the return of juveniles who have left their state of residence without permission and in the cooperative supervision of delinquent juveniles who travel or relocate across state lines.[4]

▶ State and Local Laws; Regulations, Rules, and Policies

In addition to the federal and state governments in the United States there may be several levels of local government such as counties (or parishes in Louisiana), townships, and cities as well as special service entities which cross political boundaries to provide specialized public services such as transportation or natural resource management. The authority of local governments to enact legislation, enforce laws and perform other public functions varies with the authority provided by state law. The most visible aspect of local government with relationships to corrections is a county sheriff who is frequently responsible for operating a county's detention facility.

Besides the laws (usually called **ordinances** in the localities) enacted by the legislature, there are regulations, rules, and policies that are adopted by different levels of government. At the federal level, agencies may be given the authority to adopt rules and regulations. (They cannot do so unless they are given the authority by statute.) The authority to issue rules and regulations may be very broad or specifically limited. Federal agencies, of course, cover an extensive range of affairs. Some regulatory agencies, such as the Federal Communications Commission and the Federal Trade Commission, were established for the primary purpose of issuing rules that regulate their particular area of responsibility. Those regulatory agencies also act to investigate violations of their rules, and they sit in judgment on persons who are accused of violating the rules that they have issued. Congress typically has given each regulatory agency some power of enforcement, including the power to issue penalties (such as revoking a television station's license) for violations. Federal rules are found in a large set of volumes, called the Code of Federal Regulations (CFR). These rules comprise the detailed laws (they are considered to have the authority and effect of the statutory law that authorized the agency to issue them) of most agencies.

Many agencies have internal policies, which govern their day-to-day operations. What is the difference between internal policies and rules? Under the Administrative Procedure Act (this entire area of the law is called "administrative law"), rules should be issued when they affect the conduct of private citizens, when they require certain actions to be taken, or when they incorporate penalties and other enforcement procedures for citizen actions or inactions. If it is a federal rule, it must be published in the Federal Register (a daily compendium of all kinds of new or changed federal rules) for everyone to see. Citizens are invited to comment on the proposed rules. After a period of consideration, the agency may adopt and publish its final rules. Only these final rules are collected in the CFR.

Agencies also need to have rules that govern their internal affairs but that do not directly regulate or affect the private community. These are called policy issuances, and every agency has a set of them. They cover such matters as personnel policies, business operations, transportation, communications (including computers and other recordkeeping systems), and day-to-day operations (such as places and hours of work).

▶ The Federal Bureau of Prisons

The Federal Bureau of Prisons, created by Congress and placed in the Department of Justice (the Director of the Bureau of Prisons is appointed by, and reports to, the U.S. Attorney General), is charged with the "safekeeping, care, and subsistence of all persons charged with or convicted of offenses against the United States, or held as witnesses or otherwise." That mandate is in Title 18, U.S. Code, Section 4042. (The U.S. Marshals Service has the responsibility for holding prisoners awaiting trial; most of these prisoners are held in contract jail facilities—local jails with which the Marshals Service negotiates a contract to hold federal, mainly pretrial, prisoners. The U.S. Probation Service, which is part of the federal court system, is responsible for supervising those offenders who are placed on probation by federal courts, as well as those who are released on parole and supervised release. The U.S. Parole Commission makes parole decisions for federal prisoners; parole was abolished for federal offenses committed on or after November 1, 1987, but parole release and revocation decisions still have to be made for those who committed their offenses before that date and who are still serving those older sentences, for which parole is available.)

In some large cities, especially those with a large number of federal criminal prosecutions, the Bureau of Prisons (BOP) has built detention facilities, primarily to hold pretrial inmates. There are detention centers in Brooklyn, Chicago, Honolulu, Houston, Los Angeles, Miami, New York City, Philadelphia, Puerto Rico, San Diego, and Seattle. These detention centers house both male and female prisoners. The BOP also operates eight exclusively female institutions and an administrative facility at Carswell (Texas) for female offenders. Several of the regular federal prisons have units that are set aside for federal detainees awaiting trial in nearby cities (for example, the Milan, Michigan, Correctional Institution for Detroit and the Englewood, Colorado, Correctional Institution for Denver). Some 122 federal prisons, spread all over the country, hold approximately 170,000 inmates. The institution security level ranges from minimum security in several prison camps to high security in penitentiaries. There are also administrative institutions (such as medical centers), detention facilities (as noted above), and, as it is sometimes called, a "supermax," in Florence, Colorado. The BOP also uses 13 private contracted institutions.

The legal authority of the BOP flows first from its congressional mandate, which established it as a federal agency. That set of laws is contained in Title 18 of the U.S. Code. Congress has also, by statute, provided for the federal sentencing schemes, which authorize federal courts to impose different types of federal sentences. The BOP operates under federal statutes that legislate such matters as good-time allowances for prisoners, parole eligibility, the establishment of prison industries, the provision of medical care (which is accomplished in conjunction with support from the U.S. Public Health Service), and the provision of other programs, such as education, vocational training, and rehabilitative services. Perhaps most important of all, at least as a practical matter, is the appropriation of funds by Congress for the BOP to operate. As in many states, there has been a building program of new prisons, and the money for all of those federal facilities comes from Congress. Just as important, Congress provides for the staffing of those facilities, authorizing each year certain numbers of staff to be employed by the BOP, and appropriating each year the money to pay for those staff members, along with all of the other expenses of running the prisons.

Under that umbrella of legal authority, the BOP issues many regulations and policies. Its regulations are published as federal rules in the Federal Register, allowing the public (including inmates and other interested persons and organizations) to comment on them. After reviewing those comments, final rules are published in the CFR under Title 28.

The Administrative Procedure Act (APA) requires that a reviewing court "hold unlawful and set aside agency action, findings, and conclusions found to be—arbitrary, capricious, an abuse of discretion, or otherwise not in accordance with law." This was the issue in *Arrington v. Daniels*, 516 F.3d 1106 (9th Cir. 2008). Eighteen inmates filed habeas corpus petitions challenging a Bureau of Prisons final rule categorically excluding from early release consideration inmates whose crimes involved the carrying, possession, or use of a firearm or other dangerous weapon or explosives. The lawsuit did not focus on the categorical exclusion; instead, the inmates argued the absence of a rationale for the decision, in violation of the Administrative Procedure Act, Section 706(2)(A). The court agreed.

> Although agencies enjoy wide discretion in fashioning regulations governing the statutes that they are charged with administering, section 706 of the APA requires that they articulate a rationale when they exercise that discretion. This is not an empty requirement. Because we may not substitute our own rationales for those of the agency … when an agency fails to provide an explanation for its actions we are left with no means of reviewing the reasonableness of that action. Here, the Bureau failed to set forth a rationale for its decision to categorically exclude prisoners convicted of offenses involving the carrying, possession, or use of firearms from eligibility for a sentence reduction under § 3621(e). This failure renders the Bureau's final rule invalid under the APA.

The *Arrington* ruling was not based on the agency's decision to exclude a category of inmates, which likely would have withstood judicial scrutiny. It was the agency's lack of an explanation, with this absence rendering the decision arbitrary and capricious. *Arrington* is frequently cited for how a court will review administrative rule making, not necessarily that the outcome is one to which all courts agree. Several federal circuit courts have rejected the reasoning in *Arrington*. See *Gatewood v. Outlaw*, 560 F.3d 843 (8th Cir. 2009), cert. denied 558 U.S. 1139 (2009), declined to follow, finding a public safety rationale despite absence in formal administrative record; *Gardner v. Grandolsky*, 585 F.3d 786 (3rd Cir. 2009); and *Handley v. Chapman*, 587 F.3d 273 (5th Cir. 2009), cert. denied, 562 U.S. 832 (2010). After the court's opinion in *Arrington*, the BOP revised its rule to include a rationale of public safety and the Ninth Circuit upheld the new rule. *Peck v. Thomas*, 697 F.3d 767 (9th Cir. 2012).

BOP rules fill approximately 180 pages of the published CFR. They cover the "core" policies and procedures, those that most directly affect inmates and also persons on the outside. Some key rules deal with inmate classification and transfers, contacts with people in the community (correspondence rules, visiting, telephone contacts, and news media), inmate discipline, medical care, education programs, community programs (furloughs and other releases into the community), inmate property rules, and drug programs.

Beyond these "core" regulations, which are written in very precise terminology, there are implementing policies and background instructions to staff and to others for running the agency. These are called "program statements," and they are all issued out of the headquarters office of the BOP in Washington, DC, where they are signed by the director of the bureau. Most of the program statements are now available on the Internet (http://www.bop.gov). Program statements govern the affairs of the agency nationwide and cover every type of institution in every locality. Locally, wardens and superintendents of institutions are authorized to issue "institution supplements," which establish the local procedures for running the facility. They cannot establish policy or deviate from national policy, but they give necessary local instructions (for example, the details for when telephones

Statutory provision

Title 18, United States Code, Section 4042. Duties of Bureau of Prisons

(1) IN GENERAL.—The Bureau of Prisons, under the direction of the Attorney General, shall—
   (1) have charge of the management and regulation of all Federal penal and correctional institutions;
   (2) … provide for the safekeeping, care, and subsistence of all persons charged with or convicted of offenses against the United States, or held as witnesses or otherwise;

   [Comment: This statute sets the broad framework for the operation of the prison system.]

Statutory provision

Title 18, United States Code, Section 1791. Providing or possessing contraband in prison

(a) OFFENSE.—Whoever—
   (1) in violation of a statute or a rule or order issued under a statute, provides to an inmate of a prison a prohibited object, or attempts to do so; or
   (2) being an inmate of a prison, makes, possesses, or obtains, or attempts to make or obtain, a prohibited object;
   shall be punished as provided in subsection (b) of this section.

   [Comment: This statute recognizes that contraband can endanger institution security and establishes as a criminal act the distribution or possession of contraband.]

Agency rule

Title 28, Code of Federal Regulations, Section 552.10. Purpose and Scope.
In order to further the safe, secure, and orderly running of its institutions, the Bureau of Prisons conducts searches of inmates and of inmate housing and work areas to locate contraband and to deter its introduction and movement. Staff shall employ the least intrusive method of search practicable, as indicated by the type of contraband and the method of suspected introduction.

   [Comment: This rule, adopted by the Bureau of Prisons, is intended to show one of the approaches used by the prison officials to provide for the safekeeping of prisoners and to prevent contraband from being introduced into the prison.]

Agency program statement: internal instructions

Program Statement 5521.06. Searches of Housing Units, Inmates, and Inmate Work Areas.
   Nonintrusive sensors should be used whenever feasible. When searches are required, staff shall avoid unnecessary force and strive to preserve the dignity of the individual being searched.

   [Comment: This program statement language relates to the management of the prison and provides staff with additional guidance on how searches are to be conducted. This represents internal language that is provided to staff and placed in a program statement immediately after Section 552.10.]
   Note: An institution supplement would apply the agency program statement on searches to the individual institution.

   Another example of an agency rule would be a disciplinary act and sanction for possession of contraband. In the event of a legal challenge to the agency rule or policy, a question can arise on the agency's statutory authority to issue its policy. The Supreme Court addressed this in *Chevron U.S.A. v. National Resources Defense Council*, 467 U.S. 837 (1984). In a judicial review of an agency's construction and implementation of a statute, the court is to examine the statute itself to see if Congress has "spoken to" the precise question under focus; if not, the court is to examine whether the agency's action is premised on a permissible construction of that statute.

may be used and how telephone calls are paid for, and the details of the local visiting program, including the days and hours of operation of the visiting room).

   BOX 18-1 shows how law is contained in three levels—statutes, rules, and internal policy (program statements). The specific area addressed in this box is the goal of ensuring safe prisons and ensuring that unauthorized items (contraband) are not introduced into or possessed within the prison.

▶ State and Local Corrections

State and local corrections departments will have the same sort of legal framework, similar to the one just described in some detail for the Bureau of Prisons. They will have (at the state level) a statute (some have authorizing language in the state constitution) that establishes the department, division of corrections, or whatever it is named. Statutes, some in considerable detail but most in general terms, authorize programs, activities, and services in the corrections department. The state legislature must appropriate the money for the operation of the corrections department. A major task for each administrator of a department is to appear before the legislative committee overseeing the corrections area and to answer questions about the goals, plans, and shortcomings of the department. Appropriations committees oversee the department's finances and, in many ways, make its operations effective or not, as they give money to pay for prison necessities (such as food, clothes, and medical care) and staffing. When prison populations swell (usually, in response to get-tough enactments in the legislature on criminal law and sentencing statutes), the legislature is the place where new facilities or the expansion of existing ones are authorized and funded—it is hoped in advance of the population crisis, but in practice it is seldom so. The legislature may also consider, authorize, and provide funding for private companies to provide corrections services for the state. Departments of corrections issue policies for all components of the agency to follow. (Many correctional agencies now place some of their policies on the Internet. See for example, Colorado Department of Corrections https://www.colorado.gov/pacific/cdoc/policies-1) Local administrators usually have the authority to issue local rules to govern local operations.

Some states have adopted uniform rules, regulations and certification programs for the operation of local jails. In 2017 the National Institute of Corrections compiled a collection of sixteen state jail regulations. https://nicic .gov/state-jail-standards. Some states have established commissions to establish rules and regulations for the operations of local jails. One example is Texas which created the Texas Commission on Jail Standards for the purpose of "empower[ing] local government to provide safe, secure, and suitable local jail facilities through proper rules and procedures while promoting innovative programs and ideas. TX Govt Code § 511.009 (2019) and Texas Commission on Jail Standards, *2019 Annual Report (2020).* https://www.tcjs.state.tx.us/wp-content/uploads/2020/07/2019 -TCJS-Annual-Jail-Report.pdf. The Texas state legislature has mandated that local jails comply with the Commission's standards. State Agents of the Commission at least once annually inspect local jails under this jurisdiction to assess compliance with Commission rules and regulations. Facilities that are in compliance receive a certificate attesting to that fact. Non-compliant facilities are advised as to how the facility failed to comply with standards and detailed recommendations on how to correct deficiencies. Special unannounced inspections may be authorized for facilities which are deemed "high risk" or which have previously been found to be non-compliant.

▶ Accreditation

Although, strictly speaking, it is not statute or law, there is another level of authority in corrections that should be mentioned. That is the **accreditation** of corrections facilities and agencies under professional standards. The leading professional association in the corrections field is the American Correctional Association (ACA). Founded in 1870, the association, headquartered in Alexandria, Virginia, serves as an "umbrella" organization for the entire corrections profession, with affiliate organizations serving the many components of corrections, including jails, community corrections, probation and parole authorities, adult corrections administrators, juvenile and youth agencies, and state corrections associations from virtually all of the states. (The ACA also has international affiliations.)

In 1977, the first set of accreditation standards was issued. They were published in the *Manual of Standards for Adult Correctional Institutions.* The standards contained in that volume served as the yardstick for the accreditation procedure, administered by the Commission on Accreditation for Corrections (CAC). The CAC, in partnership with ACA, administers the only national program of accreditation for all components of adult and juvenile corrections. The ACA has recently developed and implemented "performance based standards," which assess "conditions to be achieved and maintained" within the correctional organization. To fully address the variations in the missions of correctional practice, the ACA has developed over 20 different sets of standards ranging from Performance-Based Core Jail Standards—First Edition to Standards for Small Juvenile Detention Facilities.[5]

> The mission of the Commission on Accreditation for Corrections is to upgrade and improve practices and conditions in adult and juvenile correctional facilities and programs through an accreditation process which is founded on a commitment to accountability, professionalism and respect for basic human rights and which recognizes sound and effective correctional practices, while striving towards excellence in the field of corrections.

The movement toward professional accreditation was a gradual one, dating back to the 1960s and even earlier. There were a number of factors that pushed the ACA toward a process of accreditation. These included an understanding that, to be recognized as a profession, corrections needed stronger steps to proclaim and enforce agreed-upon standards; a realization that outside groups were pushing for reforms of all kinds and that corrections itself was the best place for standards to be set; a recognition of the constantly growing involvement (in the 1970s) of the courts in corrections matters, with a corresponding recognition that it was best for corrections to "set its own house in order," and that most courts would appreciate, and perhaps even defer to, those efforts; and a hope that the standards and the auditing process would provide corrections managers with comprehensive and convincing reports and guidelines to inform governmental authorities (legislators and governors, as well as judges) about the needs of the correctional agencies.

It was decided by the ACA that a separate commission was needed to administer the accreditation functions. A process was established to set the standards, and, just as important, a process was also established to modify and amplify them. After the original standards were published and the first institutions pursued them, it was determined that some standards were hard to understand, some were hard to implement, and some were hard to measure. There were also gaps in certain areas. All of these findings pointed to the need for a constant revision process; such a process was adopted and continues today. There is an ACA Standards Committee, which constantly reviews standards alongside the review process of the CAC. Standards are revised based on changing practices, current case law, and agency experiences. The approved standards reflect the views of correctional practitioners, architects, and medical and legal experts. Input and recommendations are sought from agencies that have been through the accreditation process, those who serve on accreditation audit teams, those who work in the field at all levels, and any interested organizations or persons outside of the ACA. The ACA describes its own operation as follows:

> The American Correctional Association and the Commission on Accreditation for Corrections are private, non-profit organizations which administer the only national accreditation program for all components of adult and juvenile corrections. The purpose of these organizations is to promote improvement in the management of correctional agencies through the administration of a voluntary accreditation program and the ongoing development and revision of relevant, useful standards.[6]

Different sets of standards have been established for different types of programs, covering both adults and juveniles. These programs include the administration of correctional agencies and institutions, community residential services, boot camp programs, detention facilities, probation and parole, health care, correctional industries, training, electronic monitoring, day treatment, aftercare services, and food service programs.

In 2010, ACA unveiled Core Jail Standards (CJS) for adult local detention facilities of all sizes. The CJS is a comprehensive set of minimum jail standards. These standards allow jails of all sizes to improve operational effectiveness and efficiency. ACA offers an independent audit of the standards to these facilities, similar to accreditation, although not as rigorous. Successful adherence to the CJS results in certification. More than 1,300 correctional facilities are involved in accreditation.

Early on, most corrections officials realized that legal standards, especially constitutional requirements, were not the same as professional standards. Although it was hoped that accreditation would be helpful in defending against claims of violations of prisoners' rights, it was never (or it should never have been) assured that accreditation would be such a sure defense. What must be emphasized is that the two processes are very different and serve to meet different goals and expectations. Courts review prison (or other agency) conditions to see whether they meet constitutional standards that have been set. If a constitutional standard has not yet been established, the court can address the particular constitutional provision and specify how it should be applied in prison situations. Professional (ACA) standards are based on commonly accepted levels of performance in every area of institutional management and operation. They are not tied to specific constitutional language.

Court rulings may be very instructive to those in the field, especially those who are working constantly on the language of the professional standards. As court standards are set, corrections specialists must make sure that existing ACA standards incorporate the requirements pronounced in court decisions. ACA standards must never fall below the court standards, but, in most areas, they go beyond what the courts have required. As the Supreme Court pointed out in *Rhodes v. Chapman*, 452 U.S. 337 (1981), courts should not rely on the standards for prisons that have been adopted by various organizations (and there are a number of other organizational standards besides the ACAs).[7] In looking at conditions of confinement, the Court said in *Rhodes,* judges are looking at "contemporary standards of decency" as the yardstick to determine violations of the Eighth Amendment. Organization standards set goals adopted or recommended by the organization, but these goals do not tell the courts what the current constitutional "standard of decency" is. According to the Supreme Court, such judgment depends much more on public attitudes than on what organizations publish as their individual and specialized goals.

This is not to say that accreditation is of no legal use to corrections managers. First, if the ACA specialists and experts working on the content of the standards are doing their jobs well, standards will always incorporate at least the minimums set by court rulings. Thus, compliance with the standards should give some assurance that court expectations will be met.

Summary

- The U.S. Constitution is the supreme law of the country. Treaties, which can only be made by the federal government, and federal statutes, are also supreme laws, which take precedence over state laws. Federal powers, however, are limited by the Constitution. Sometimes, federal authorities go beyond the limited powers that are given to them in the Constitution, as Congress did when it made drug activities within local schools a federal crime. Such a matter, the Supreme Court said, should be left to the states to regulate (*United States v. Lopez*).

- Under the Constitution, states may enter into compacts when authorized to do so by Congress. In the criminal justice area, there are several compacts that have been authorized by Congress, which many states have joined. These include compacts on detainers, extradition, transfer of prisoners, adult offender supervision, and juveniles.

- Failure to comply with the literal language of the IAD may bar further criminal proceedings by the requesting state (*Alabama v. Bozeman*). However, the time limits of the IAD may be waived by action of the defendant or his counsel (*New York v. Hill*).

- An inmate has the statutory right to a hearing under Article IV(d) of the IAD before being transferred to another jurisdiction (*Cuyler v. Adams*). Claims relating to conditions in the demanding state are issues that must be tried in the courts of that state (New *Mexico ex rel. Ortiz v. Reed*).

- At all levels of government (federal, state, and local), there are three branches of government (legislative, executive, and judicial). There are also prioritized levels of laws enacted at the different levels of government. At the highest level is a constitution (federal and state); then come the enactments of the legislature (federal, state, and local); next, most levels of government issued published rules and regulations; and most agencies (corrections included) have internal policies governing their operation.

- We looked at one corrections agency, the Federal Bureau of Prisons, to see how these various levels of laws (statutes, rules, and policies) are issued and how they impact the operations of the agency. State and local corrections agencies operate under similar levels of governing laws, but each agency has its own unique set of laws. (And these, of course, at all levels, are impacted by constitutional requirements and the rulings of courts that interpret and apply them.)

- Professional accreditation is a relatively recent development in corrections. The ACA first issued standards for accrediting adult correctional facilities in 1977. Today, all kinds of corrections operations (probation, parole, community corrections, juveniles, and so on) are covered by different sets of accreditation standards. These are administered by the Commission on Accreditation for Corrections (CAC). More than 1,300 correctional facilities and programs are involved in the accreditation process. Accreditation, once achieved, lasts for three years, after which the agency or facility must go through a reaccreditation process.

Thinking About It

Inmate Gibson was serving a prison sentence in the state penitentiary when he committed new criminal conduct using the mail and telephone. Prison officials advised state prosecutors who initiated new criminal charges against Gibson. Gibson was advised of the new charges, and on October 2, executed a request for speedy trial to the State Department of Corrections and Rehabilitation (DOCR). The DOCR sent Gibson's request to the state trial court and state prosecutor on October 13. The court received the request on October 15 and the prosecutor received the request on October 16. Under state law at the time, a person requesting a speedy trial has a right "for the trial to begin within ninety days of the date the party elects this right." The district court set a trial date of January 6, ninety-six days after Gibson delivered his request to prison officials, but eighty-two days after the request was received by the district court. Gibson claimed his speedy trial rights were violated and he was entitled to have the new criminal charges dismissed. How should the court rule? *State v. Gibson*, 889 N.W.2d 852 (ND 2017).

Key Terms

accreditation
ordinance

Endnotes

1. On February 1, 2010, the Office of Public Affairs, U.S. Department of Justice issued a press release announcing the implementation of a new extradition agreement between the European Union and the United States. Negotiations for the agreement began following the September 11, 2001, terrorist attacks in an effort to improve cooperation in criminal matters among the parties. "The agreement on extradition, among other things: replaces lists of offenses that are deemed extraditable with a modern dual criminality standard; contains measures to streamline the exchange of information and transmission of documents; sets rules for determining priority in competing requests for surrender of a fugitive." The agreement has a provision allowing extradition to be conditioned on nonapplication of the death penalty. Available at https://www.justice.gov/opa/pr/useu-agreements-mutual-legal-assistance-and-extradition-enter-force

2. Lis, Inc. *Interstate Transfer of Prison Inmates in the United States.* Longmont, Colorado: National Institute of Corrections Information Center, U.S. Department of Justice, 2006.

3. Holloway, C. *Interstate Compact on Juveniles.* Washington, DC: Office of Justice Programs, Department of Justice, 2000.

4. Interstate Commission for Juveniles. *ICJ Rules—Interstate Commission for Juveniles—Serving Juveniles While Protecting Communities.* March 1, 2020. Available at https://www.juvenilecompact.org/sites/default/files/ICJ%20Rules_Final.pdf. Accessed April 17, 2020.

5. American Correctional Association. Manual of Accreditation Policy and Procedure. March 15, 2017. Available at http://www.aca.org/ACA_Prod_IMIS/docs/standards%20and%20accreditation/ALM-1-3_15_17-Final.pdf

6. Much of the current information for this section comes from publications of the ACA and the CAC, (http://www.aca.org).

7. For example, the National Commission on Correctional Health Care has created standards for different correctional operations: jails, prisons, juvenile facilities, mental health services and opioid treatment programs. https://www.ncchc.org/standards

© EJ_Rodriquez/iStock/Getty Images Plus/Getty Images

CHAPTER 19

Federal Statutes: Equal Employment, Disabilities, and Tort Claims

In enacting Title VII, Congress required the removal of artificial, arbitrary, and unnecessary barriers to employment when the barriers operate invidiously to discriminate on the basis of racial or other impermissible classification.

U.S. Supreme Court, *Dothard v. Rawlinson*

CHAPTER OUTLINE

- Employment Law
  - Failure to Train
  - Standards of Employee Conduct
  - Fair Labor Standards Act, Portal-to-Portal Act
- Equal Employment
- *Dothard v. Rawlinson*
- Title VII and Inmate-Created Hostile Work Environment
- Tort Claims
- The Americans with Disabilities Act (ADA)
  - 2010 ADA Standards for Accessible Design
  - Employment under the ADA
  - Inmate Programs and Services under the ADA
- Other Federal Statutory Laws
  - Prison Rape Elimination Act of 2003
  - Adam Walsh Child Protection and Safety Act of 2006
  - Second Chance Act of 2007
  - First Step Act of 2018

This chapter examines examples of statutory and administrative laws by looking at federal statutes that have a direct impact on prisons and jails at all levels. Please keep in mind that many states and localities have laws on these same topics. The corrections administrator must deal with the complexity of following those statutes and regulations affecting correctional operations, whether their source is federal, state, or local.

In other chapters, the reader was introduced to federal statutes that have a direct and considerable effect on corrections. These include statutes related to constitutional rights. The Civil Rights Act, 42 U.S.C. § 1983, authorizes persons to bring actions in federal courts when they believe their constitutional rights have been denied by state officials (persons acting under color of state law). The federal habeas corpus statute, at 28 U.S.C. § 2254, authorizes the filing of habeas corpus actions by state prisoners in federal courts. In the Religious Freedom Restoration Act, Congress legislatively provided additional protection to religious beliefs and practices above that provided by the First Amendment; because of the Supreme Court's decision in *City of Boerne v. Flores,* 521 U.S. 507 (1997), that act now applies only to federal prisoners' claims of interference with the exercise of religious beliefs. After the *Boerne* decision, Congress passed the Religious Land Use and Institutionalized Persons Act of 2000 (RLUIPA), a renewed effort to achieve the protection of religious activities by institutionalized persons in the states. The Supreme Court upheld RLUIPA in *Cutter v. Wilkinson,* 544 U.S. 709 (2005).

This chapter addresses federal statutes that particularly affect corrections management. The civil rights laws and the Americans with Disabilities Act have a significant impact on the rights of minority groups, including persons with disabilities. Federal laws govern many aspects of these areas, but remember that many states also have laws on the same topics. State, local, and federal laws and regulations can affect employment decisions and, in some cases, also the treatment of offenders. In a similar way, tort claims statutes, at federal and state levels, waive sovereign immunity, allowing persons to bring suits on common law tort injuries against federal, state, and local governments. However, because of the sovereign immunity doctrine, those governments may only be sued to the exact extent allowed by the tort statutes. This chapter will also address recent federal legislation covering such issues as prisoner rape, sex offender registration, and prisoner reentry into the community following incarceration.

▶ Employment Law

In every state, there are laws that govern personnel matters, and the body of these statutes and regulations are called employment law. This body of laws includes employment statutes, the regulations that implement them, and the court decisions that interpret them. In addition to the laws applicable to every employer, state, local, and federal governments have laws specific to the employment of government workers, which sometimes are referred to as civil service laws. These laws set the guidelines, requirements, and standards for the entire range of staffing decisions in a corrections agency. They cover advertising vacancies; eligibility, recruiting, interviewing, testing, and hiring staff members; training the staff; setting standards of job performance, evaluations of work, pay, hours, places of work, and promotions; maintaining relationships with employee bargaining or representation groups (in states in which union activities by state employees are allowed); providing retirement and other special benefits, such as health plans; and handling disciplinary matters, such as demotions, suspensions, and terminations. Typically, a specialist or a separate department (depending on the size of the agency or the facility) handles the details of these employment laws. Each administrator obviously must rely on the expertise and the efficiency of that personnel department or human resources specialist to advise him regarding the intricacies of the employment laws and to keep the agency running as smoothly as possible by adhering to those legal requirements.

It is likely that there is no area of management that is more vital to the smooth operation of the organization than human resource management. The quality of staff is the key to effective operations of corrections or any agency. Dedicated, highly motivated staff members are essential to the professionalism and excellence associated with the prison, jail, probation office, or corrections department. Within the correctional environment, staff—the entire staff—are the critical component.

In many correctional agencies, correctional employees are to be considered "correctional workers" first, and then workers at their specialty. Because a corrections facility is a community composed of many specialized activities, staff represent a wide variety of backgrounds and occupational specialties—plumbers, electricians, landscapers, factory foremen, doctors, teachers, clergy, police officers, private security officers, military personnel, social workers, and many others. Inside the facility in which they all work, they are interdependent. They not only must depend on each other for their safety and the orderly running of the facility but they must be able to work with one another, and with inmates, to achieve what is in the ultimate best interest of all: the security, good order, and discipline of the institution. Two of the more important skills for all correctional workers are the ability to effectively communicate (both among themselves and with inmates) and to show respect for all other persons.

Recruiting and retaining good staff are challenges that involve hard work and creative steps, which are geared to the job market and the employment pool in the particular state or region. Training the staff is of prime importance; more and more resources have been devoted to this area in recent years. At one time, not too long ago, new staff almost exclusively learned on the job. A new recruit was placed in a work area and "learned the ropes" from an experienced worker in that department, who, along the way, was expected to point out the differences between working in a corrections facility and working in the outside community. Security concerns must always be emphasized in corrections work.

Over time, more formal training was developed, including classroom work and even training in a separate "corrections academy" for the state or locality. In addition to initial training, refresher training for all staff, especially in such areas as firearms proficiency; first aid (including CPR and handling injured inmates); self-defense; emergency procedures (hostage-taking, disturbances, etc.); and developments in the law are wise additions to the training schedules at corrections facilities. Virtually all areas of a corrections facility, certainly all areas in which staff work directly with inmates, involve exposure to liability (tort liability and, in some cases, even constitutional liability), particularly if proper training has not been provided. For example, deliberate indifference to an inmate's medical or psychiatric needs (such as when there are indications of suicidal intent, injuries sustained in a fight or work accident, or difficulty in breathing at any time or any place) can be grounds for individual liability under Section 1983 (a violation of the Eighth Amendment, amounting to cruel and unusual punishment).

Failure to Train

Providing good staff training is more than just good management practice. Exposures to legal liability are heightened if staff members are not properly trained in the use of firearms or other use of force, how to behave on escape hunts, how to supervise legal and other visits, and a host of other procedures in the corrections facility. Apart from suits against the individual staff member for shortcomings in their performance, which may have been caused by inadequate or improper training, there have also been suits brought against managers for not providing the proper training for staff members.

A leading case showing the hazards of failure to train is *Davis v. Mason County,* 927 F.2d 1473 (9th Cir. 1991). In Mason County, Washington, there had been four separate incidents in which citizens were arrested by deputies from the sheriff's office. In each incident, there was evidence that the persons arrested were beaten and charged with offenses that were later dropped. In a Section 1983 suit, a jury found the county, the sheriff, and the deputies liable for constitutional violations. The appeals court affirmed the jury verdicts. It found that, in addition to the violations of the constitutional rights of the citizens who were committed by the deputies, the sheriff and the county were properly held liable for failure to provide adequate and proper training to the officers.

The county was liable in *Davis* because it was responsible for setting the policy for the types of action involved. According to the decision in *Monell v. New York City Department of Social Services,* 436 U.S. 658 (1978), a municipality or a county may be held liable under Section 1983, not because of improper actions by its employees, but only when the execution of a government policy established by the municipality or county leads to the injury. In *Davis,* the county's failure to train showed "reckless disregard for," or "deliberate indifference to," the safety of its citizens, the court said. This conclusion was based on the standards set in the Supreme Court decision in *City of Canton v. Harris,* 489 U.S. 378 (1989). In *Harris,* the court held that city or county liability in failure-to-train cases is proper when "the failure to train amounts to deliberate indifference to the rights of persons with whom the police come into contact."[1]

The sheriff was held liable in the *Davis* case because he was a policy-making official, a chief executive officer for the county. He had ultimate authority to train persons in his department, and his actions "constituted county policy" on the matter of training. (This was the holding against the sheriff's argument that the state's civil service commission was responsible for all personnel matters. The court said that the commission was responsible for policy on such matters as hiring, promotions, transfers, and discipline but had no power with respect to law enforcement training.) The court pointed out that the training of deputies in this county was "woefully inadequate." Deputies had not been sent to the State Training Academy, but had received "field training," which the sheriff devised. In fact, most deputies did not even receive that training and were sent out without any training whatsoever. Deputies were not given adequate training on arrest and search procedures. There was no training at all regarding the legal limits to the use of force, and this fact constituted "deliberate indifference" to the rights of citizens, as a matter of law, the court said.

In *Blankenhorn v. City of Orange,* 485 F.3d 463 (9th Cir. 2007), Blankenhorn filed suit to hold the city liable for the arresting officers' alleged use of excessive force. To show that the city had failed to train its officers in the use of excessive force, Blankenhorn focused exclusively on the actions of one officer. The Ninth Circuit ruled that "evidence of the failure to train a single officer is insufficient to establish a municipality's deliberate policy." The court held that absent a showing of a "program-wide inadequacy in training," a shortfall in one officer's training may be considered negligence on the part of the municipality but that this is a much lower fault standard than deliberate indifference.

In *Brumfield v. Hollins,* 551 F.3d 332 (5th Cir. 2008), inmate Smith hanged himself while in a jail "drunk tank" (holding cell). His daughter sued, alleging, in part, that the sheriff had failed to promulgate policies concerning inmate supervision and medical care and that the "Old Jail," as it was known, did not have written policies and procedures to cover such activities, similar to ones existing at a nearby facility (known as the "New Jail"). The court said the validity of prison policies does not depend on whether such policies are written or verbal. Rather, an official policy is "either a policy statement, ordinance, regulation … that has been officially adopted … or a persistent widespread practice of officials or employees, which although not authorized by officially adopted and promulgated policy, is so common and well settled as to constitute a custom that fairly represents the municipality's policy." The court in *Brumfield* ruled that verbal policies did exist for inmate supervision and medical care.

The Supreme Court considered the injurious action of a sheriff's deputy during a traffic stop in the case of *Board of the County Commissioners of Bryan County, Oklahoma v. Brown,* 520 U.S. 397 (1997). Reserve Deputy Burns grabbed passenger Jill Brown's arm and pulled her from her car, severely injuring her knees. She sued Burns, the county sheriff, and the county, claiming, in part that by hiring Burns, the county was liable for what she alleged was his use of excessive force. The district court, following a jury trial, found the county liable based on its "hiring policy" and "training policy" with respect to Burns. The decision was affirmed by the court of appeals on the basis of the hiring claim alone. The Supreme Court said that it did not find the analogy between failure to train and inadequate screening of persons newly hired to be persuasive.

> **Unlike the risk from a particular glaring omission in a training regimen, the risk from a single instance of inadequate screening of an applicant's background is not "obvious" in the abstract; rather, it depends upon the background of the applicant.**

The Court found that what was lacking in the district court's instructions on culpability and, thus, the jury's finding of liability, was a determination on "whether Burns' background made his use of excessive force in making an arrest a plainly obvious consequence of the hiring decision." The lower court's decision was vacated and remanded.

Thus, we have clear word from the courts that government entities and managers can be held liable for failing to set up adequate training programs. At a minimum, to avoid liability for constitutional violations under Section 1983, agencies should be sure that staff are trained in the basics of job performance in any areas where the work they do may implicate constitutional requirements. For example, security personnel must be trained in the proper use of force to subdue or restrain unruly inmates. Mailroom staff must understand the rules for the proper handling of mail, especially the mail sent to and from attorneys and the courts. The implications of constitutional requirements reach into many departments of a prison or jail, and they affect a wide variety of actions by corrections workers. Corrections staff do not have to memorize all kinds of corrections law. What they must know is the policy that affects their work, and managers must make sure that the policy of the agency reflects the constitutional requirements. (It may be helpful for staff to know which policies are based on constitutional mandates so as to be extra careful that there is no deviation below the minimum standards established in those policy areas.)

Standards of Employee Conduct

It is the policy of the Colorado Department of Corrections (DOC) that DOC employees, contract workers, and volunteers are to demonstrate honesty, integrity, and respect for the worth and individuality of human beings as well as a strong commitment to professional and ethical correctional service. DOC employees, contract workers, and volunteers must constantly strive to live up to the highest possible standards of their profession and to incorporate and adhere to the DOC Code of Ethics as its ethical performance standard. [2-CO-1C-04] [5-1C-4069].[2]

All [Minnesota] department employees, when on and off duty, will conduct themselves in a manner that will not bring discredit or criticism to the department. Common sense, good judgment, consistency and the department's mission will be the guiding principles for the expected employee standard of conduct.

Workplace violence is strictly prohibited. The department does not tolerate any form of violence including intimidation, threats of violence (physical or verbal), or violent acts in the workplace. The department promotes, establishes, and maintains a work environment that is free of violence.[3]

Correctional organizations have developed, as represented above, "standards of employee conduct." These standards set out what the employer expects from the employee, and, within the policy, advise the employee of limitations or restrictions in regard to both their on-duty or off-duty behavior. Standards of employee conduct can provide very specific guidance as to prohibited conduct, such as not to give or accept a gift, directly or indirectly, from an inmate or an inmate's family and to prohibit the use, or being under the influence of, alcohol while on duty or immediately prior to reporting for duty. Some prohibitions are less specific, such as "conduct unbecoming," which prohibits on- or off-duty conduct that negatively impacts job performance, not specifically mentioned in administrative regulations: "The act or conduct tends to bring the DOC into disrepute or reflects discredit upon the individual as a DOC employee, contract worker, or volunteer."[4]

The significance of these kinds of standards is so important that agencies often require each employee to receive (and sign for) a copy of the standards upon beginning employment and a new copy any time the standards are modified. In addition to providing guidance on prohibited conduct, agencies may have internal investigatory procedures for determining if prohibited conduct by an employee has occurred. In order to fully carry out this investigatory role, two important rules require employees to report violations of the standards of employee conduct to appropriate officials and that every employee is required to cooperate fully and truthfully in official investigations. Employees have important rights during an investigation, established by law and policy. Some correctional workers have been disciplined, including termination from employment, for not cooperating with these investigations or providing false or misleading statements to investigators. When an employee has been found to have violated the standards, available sanctions can range from an oral reprimand to termination. Some cases of serious misconduct can also result in criminal prosecution.[5]

The U.S. Supreme Court has issued several opinions related to the free speech rights of public employees. The First Amendment protects a public employee's right, under certain circumstances, to speak as a citizen addressing matters of public concern. But when a governmental employee makes "statements pursuant to their official duties, the employees are not speaking as citizens for First Amendment purposes, and the Constitution does not insulate their communications from employer discipline." *Garcetti v. Ceballos,* 547 U.S. 410 (2006). The Supreme Court has recognized that the government has broader powers as an employer than it does as a sovereign and that "[g]overnment employers, like private employers, need a significant degree of control over their employees' words and actions; without it, there would be little chance for the efficient provision of public services." When a public employee speaks on "matters of public concern" as a citizen, a government employer may lawfully restrict the employee's freedom of speech to the extent "necessary for their employers to operate efficiently and effectively." In such cases, courts must "balance the employee's right to engage in speech against the government's interest in promoting the efficiency and effectiveness of the public services it performs through its employees." A public employee's statements in lawsuits and grievances are also protected by the First Amendment's Petition Clause (in addition to the Free Speech clause) provided that such comments are related to a matter of public concern rather than merely private issues. *Borough of Duryea, PA v. Guarnieri*, 564 U.S. 379 (2011).

The case of *City of San Diego v. Roe,* 543 U.S. 77 (2004), concerns a police officer but is informative for its holding regarding a government employee's right of free speech. Roe was a city police officer who sold videotapes of himself engaging in sexually explicit acts. The video was sold in the adults-only section of eBay. Aspects relating to this activity suggested a law enforcement connection (e.g., his code name, clothing clearly identifiable as a police uniform, and a user profile identifying himself as working in law enforcement). After his employer became aware of this conduct, the police department ordered Roe to "cease displaying, manufacturing, distributing, or selling any sexually explicit materials or engaging in any similar behaviors, via the internet, U.S. Mail ... or any other medium available to the public."

Although Roe reduced his activity, he did not stop, nor did he change his seller's profile. Upon discovering this, the police department began termination proceedings, resulting in his dismissal from the department. Roe brought a Section 1983 suit, claiming that the loss of his job violated his First Amendment right to free speech. The district court dismissed the suit, holding that Roe had not shown that his activities qualified as an expression relating to a matter of "public concern" under the Supreme Court's decision in *Connick v. Myers,* 461 U.S. 138 (1983). The appeals court reversed, stating that Roe's conduct did fall within the protected category of citizen commentary on matters of public concern. The appeals court noted that Roe's expression was not an internal workplace grievance, that he was off-duty and away from the worksite during the time, and that his actions were unrelated to his employment.

The Supreme Court reversed, holding that the police department showed "legitimate and substantial interests of its own that were compromised by his [Roe's] speech."

> **The use of the uniform, the law enforcement reference in the Web site, the listing of the speaker as "in the field of law enforcement," and the debased parody of an officer performing indecent acts while in the course of official duties brought the mission of the employer and the professionalism of its officers into serious disrepute.**

Citing its earlier cases, the Court described "public concern" as something that is a subject of legitimate news interest—that is, it is a "subject of general interest and of value and concern to the public at the time of publication." The Court held that Roe's expression did not meet this standard, negating any need to balance his interest against those of the police department.[6]

Fair Labor Standards Act, Portal-to-Portal Act

The Fair Labor Standards Act of 1938, 29 U.S.C. § 201 *et seq.,* was intended to ensure that employees covered by the act were compensated for the work which they performed. The act was amended by the Portal-to-Portal Act of 1947, 29 U.S.C. § 251 *et seq.,* to describe work as compensable if it relates to the principal activity or activities that the employee is expected to perform. Not compensable are activities that are preliminary or postliminary to the principal activity.

IBP, Inc. v. Alvarez, 546 U.S. 21 (2005), is not a prison case but is important in its holding. IBP is a producer of fresh meat and related products. Some IBP employees, for example, those in the slaughter and processing areas, must wear outer garments and protective equipment. Production workers' pay, however, was based on the time spent cutting and bagging meat. IBP employees filed a class action to recover compensation for preproduction and postproduction work, including time spent putting on and taking off protective gear and walking between the locker rooms and the production floor before and after their assigned shifts. The district court held that these activities were unique to the jobs and were compensable, saying that they were "integral and indispensable to the work of the employees who wore such equipment." The court also held that the walking time was compensable as it occurs during the workday. The court of appeals affirmed, although in part for different reasons. IBP did not challenge before the Supreme Court the finding that the putting on and taking off unique protective gear are "principal activities" under the Portal-to-Portal Act. The question that the Court had to decide was whether the walking between the locker rooms and the production areas was compensable. The Court held that it was.

> **[A]ny activity that is "integral and indispensable" to a "principal activity" is itself a "principal activity" under § 4(a) of the Portal-to-Portal Act. Moreover, during a continuous workday, any walking time that occurs after the beginning of the employee's first principal activity and before the end of the employee's last principal activity is … covered by the FLSA.**

Nine years after *IBP, Inc.* the Supreme Court decided another noncorrectional case interpreting the FLSA and Portal to Portal Act. In *Integrity Staffing Solutions Inc, v. Busk,* 574 U.S. 27 (2014) hourly wage workers at a plant in Nevada who fulfilled orders for Amazon sued for compensation when standing in lines to undergo security checks after their shift had ended. The employees claimed the time was solely for the benefit of the employer and sometimes took as long as 25 minutes. The Supreme Court reversed the ruling of the court of appeals and found the time was not compensable.

> **The security screenings at issue here are noncompensable postliminary activities. To begin with, the screenings were not the "principal activity or activities which [the] employee is employed to perform." 29 U.S.C. § 254(a)(1). . . . The security screenings also were not "integral and indispensable" to the employees' duties as warehouse workers. . . . [A]n activity is not integral and indispensable to an employee's principal activities unless it is an intrinsic element of those activities and one with which the employee cannot dispense if he is to perform those activities. The screenings were not an intrinsic element of retrieving products from warehouse shelves or packaging them for shipment. And Integrity Staffing could have eliminated the screenings altogether without impairing the employees' ability to complete their work. . . . We hold that an activity is integral and indispensable to the principal**

activities that an employee is employed to perform—and thus compensable under the FLSA—if it is an intrinsic element of those activities and one with which the employee cannot dispense if he is to perform his principal activities

The nature of prison work requires some staff to perform specific functions prior to reporting to their assigned post. For example, security staff may need to pick up keys or equipment; inmate work supervisors may need to report early to prepare for the arrival of the inmate crews. The issue is whether such activities, and the time it then takes the employees to walk to their duty posts, are compensable. The Supreme Court has not ruled under these facts. However, in 2006, the Federal Labor Relations Authority, in a case involving a prison facility and a local prison union, upheld an arbitrator's ruling that certain employees were entitled to overtime for a specified period.

The Arbitrator … considered each of the departments … concerning which the Union had presented evidence. Beginning with the Custody Department, the Arbitrator found that employees … were entitled to overtime pay because there was "a sufficient showing that staff in this department do work in excess of eight hours and that their excess time worked is more than *de minimis*" …. [T]he Arbitrator found that, although shifts did not officially begin until the time employees reported to their assigned post, a change in shift at the post required an exchange of equipment, an inventory of equipment, and an exchange of information. The Arbitrator found that these activities are "integral to the job[.]" … The Arbitrator concluded that "it still takes at least 15 minutes or more to make a relief at a 24-hour duty post even with the equipment placed at the post." … As to [the Industries] and the Facilities Department, both of which employ inmates, the Arbitrator found that, in order to ensure that equipment and materials were ready for the inmates to begin work when they reported, the staff checks in at the Control Center well before the scheduled beginning of the shift. Based on the evidence presented, the Arbitrator concluded that staff in those departments "have worked more than eight hours with the knowledge of the Agency."[7]

The task for prison officials is to have procedures in place to help ensure that "principal activities" begin and end within the employee's work shift. This could mean that schedules would need to be adjusted and shifts overlap for posts requiring relief (this refers to one staff member replacing another staff member at a specific work position).

A similar issue was raised by federal correctional employees who were required to pass through a metal detector as part of a security screening before reporting for duty. An arbitrator had ruled that the time was compensable because "the security screenings undergone by the [employees] are an intrinsic element of the [employees'] principal activities of providing security to the Agency's facility. Accordingly, the Arbitrator concluded that time the grievants spend undergoing security screenings is compensable under the FLSA and marks the beginning of the compensable, continuous workday." The Agency appealed and the Authority reversed on the grounds the Arbitrator's award was not supported by the factual record and was contrary to the law as announced in *Integrity Staffing Solutions, Inc. v. Busk*.[8]

▶ Equal Employment

In every jurisdiction, there are laws and rules that outlaw discrimination in employment. These laws generally prohibit any kind of decision making (hiring, promotion, conditions of work, disciplining) that is based on race, creed, or color. These are the very broad terms of equal employment law. In practice, and in detail, the laws vary from place to place regarding the exact employment decisions that are covered and the types of discrimination that are banned.

Embracing all discrimination laws in this country is the federal civil rights law, especially the Civil Rights Act of 1964. Title VII of that act (Title 42, U.S. Code, Section 2000e-2) provides the following:

It shall be an unlawful employment practice for an employer—(1) to fail or refuse to hire or to discharge any individual, or otherwise to discriminate against any individual with respect to his compensation, terms, conditions, or privileges of employment, because of such individual's race, color, religion, sex, or national origin; or (2) to limit, segregate, or classify his employees or applicants for employment in any way which would deprive or tend to deprive any individual of employment opportunities or otherwise adversely affect his status as an employee, because of such individual's race, color, religion, sex, or national origin.

In the Equal Employment Opportunity Act of 1972, the coverage of Title VII was extended to state governments. Thus, any state administrator (and any local administrator, by derivation of authority from the state) is considered an employer under the Civil Rights Act and is barred from the discriminatory actions specified in that act.

In an assessment of data from 2017, the Bureau of Labor Statistics reported that 29% (134,000) of persons employed as state bailiffs, correctional officers, and jailers were female.[9] Correctional officers make up the largest number of employees in a correctional facility, and these staff have the most frequent and direct contact with the inmate population. Among 46 states and the Federal Bureau of Prisons, 41,220 female officers were assigned to male institutions on September 30, 2009. Among 45 states and the Federal Bureau of Prisons, 7,499 male officers were assigned to female institutions.[10]

▶ *Dothard v. Rawlinson*

Rawlinson applied to be a correctional counselor (prison guard) in Alabama. She was rejected because she failed to meet the minimum height and weight requirements that had been set for the job: five feet, two inches was the minimum height and 120 pounds was the minimum weight. (An interesting companion plaintiff was Brenda Mieth, who challenged the five feet, nine inches and 160 pounds height and weight requirements for the position of state trooper. The district court upheld her complaint, and Alabama did not appeal the ruling, effectively abandoning those height and weight requirements.) Rawlinson filed a complaint with the Equal Employment Opportunity Commission (EEOC), the agency established to administratively review challenges brought under the federal law, claiming sex discrimination. Besides her complaint based on the discrimination inherent in the height and weight requirements for the job, Rawlinson also complained of the prison rule that barred correctional counselors from working in direct contact with inmates of the opposite sex. The EEOC gave Rawlinson a right-to-sue letter, in effect transferring her case to the federal courts.

A three-judge U.S. district court decided in Rawlinson's favor, finding that the height and weight requirements would exclude more than 40% of the female population but less than 1% of the males who might apply. This was found to show a **prima facie** case of sex discrimination (that is, a claim presumed to be true unless overcome by other evidence), which would be unlawful under Title VII of the 1964 Civil Rights Act. The district court ruled that being male was not a necessary qualification for being a correctional counselor in Alabama, even in the maximum-security penitentiary for which she applied.

The Supreme Court, in *Dothard v. Rawlinson*, 433 U.S. 321 (1977), reversed the judgment of the lower court, at least in part. The Court found and agreed that the facts did show a prima facie case of sex discrimination, because the height and weight requirements served to select applicants in a significantly discriminatory manner. The fact that Rawlinson relied on national statistics to show the pattern of sexual discrimination, rather than statistics of actual applicants in Alabama, was satisfactory, the Court said. However, finding a prima facie pattern of discrimination did not end the matter. The employer could, under employment law and Title VII precedents, show that the discrimination was justified, legally rebutting the sexual discrimination showing. In this case, the Board of Corrections (the agency employer) argued that there was a job-related requirement for the minimum height and weight requirements, because those requirements were necessary to obtain persons who had the strength essential to the performance of the correctional counselor job. This justification was rejected, because Alabama had provided no evidence to support their argument that a certain amount of strength was necessary to perform the job well.

On another basis, however, the Supreme Court decided that Alabama had shown a bona fide occupational qualification (BFOQ) that exempted females from consideration. The evidence showed that the prison system was rife with violent behavior by the inmates; that inmates had frequent contact with the officers in the prison living arrangements (which involved dormitory-style living rather than single cells); that correctional institutions were understaffed; and that a substantial portion of the inmate population (about 20%) was composed of sex offenders, who were mixed in with the general population. Because of these factors, the Court said, the use of female guards in the maximum-security institutions would pose a substantial security problem, directly linked to the sex of the guards. Based on this, the Court found that there was a BFOQ that justified the exclusion of females from the Alabama guard force (at least in the maximum-security facilities).

> **The likelihood that inmates would assault a woman because she was a woman would pose a real threat not only to the victim of the assault but also to the basic control of the penitentiary and protection of its inmates and the other security personnel. The employee's very womanhood would thus directly undermine her capacity to provide the security that is the essence of a correctional counselor's**

responsibility …. On the basis of that evidence, we conclude that the District Court was in error in ruling that being male is not a bona fide occupational qualification for the job of correctional counselor in a "contact" position in an Alabama male maximum security penitentiary.

It was a strange sort of victory for the Alabama corrections system, because the decision was based on a finding that the work environment was "a peculiarly inhospitable one," an environment of violence and disorganization. The decision does shed some light on the nature of the BFOQ, especially in the prison workplace. It is hard to imagine that other correctional agencies would rush to justify male-only hiring of corrections officers on the grounds that their institutions were, in effect, out of control. The decision does, however, show a legal justification for insisting on same-sex job assignments, particularly in positions in which close physical contact is required and where sex offenders are present in the population. (It is unlikely that the presence of sex offenders in the population is a decisive factor, because the Supreme Court itself observed, "There would also be a real risk that other inmates, deprived of a normal heterosexual environment, would assault women guards because they were women." This observation, of course, is relevant whether or not there are many sex offenders in the population.)

There is a statutory exception to facially discriminatory employment practice, such as the sex-based hiring practice of hiring female officers for posts within a female correctional facility, when the sex of the employee is a bona fide occupational qualification or BFOQ. Title 42, U.S. Code § 2000e-2(e)(1)—provides as follows:

> [I]t shall not be an unlawful employment practice for an employer to hire and employ employees … on the basis of… sex … where … sex … is a bona fide occupational qualification reasonably necessary to the normal operation of that particular business or enterprise.

The Supreme Court has noted that "[t]he BFOQ defense is written narrowly, and this Court has read it narrowly." *UAW v. Johnson Controls, Inc.*, 499 U.S. 187 (1999). The "BFOQ defense" applies to "special situations" where employment discrimination is based upon "objective, verifiable requirements" that "concern job-related skills and aptitudes." An "occupational qualification" means a "qualification that affect[s] an employee's ability to do the job."

Since *Dothard v. Rawlinson*, some state and local correctional entities have created sex-specific posts to address issues of sexual abuse and related issues in facilities housing female prisoners. While the Supreme Court has not addressed the BFOQ defense in this context in a correctional setting, several circuit courts of appeal have done so. In *Teamsters Local Union No. 117 v. Washington Department of Corrections*, 789 F.3d 989 (9th Cir. 2015), the Union representing state correctional employees sued the DOC after the DOC designated 110 correctional posts in a state women's prison as female only. The Union sued alleging the decision violated Title VII of the Civil Rights Act by discriminating on the basis of sex. In affirming the district court judgment dismissing the Union's case, the court of appeals noted that the Washington state correctional system:

> [F]aced problems common to a number of states in their women's prisons: sexual abuse and misconduct by prison guards, breaches of inmate privacy, and security gaps. A primary driver, according to prison authorities, was the lack of female correctional officers to oversee female offenders and administer sensitive tasks, such as observing inmates showering and dressing and performing the pat (or "pat-down") and strip searches that are stitched into the fabric of day-to-day prison life.

Washington had difficulties finding females to work correctional posts within female facilities, and beginning in the 1980s, allowed male correctional officers to work female housing units and conduct routine pat searches. The practice of allowing male officers to perform routine pat searches on female inmates was stopped by court decision in *Jordan v. Gardner* (discussed elsewhere, as a violation of the Eighth Amendment) and later in 2012 was prohibited by Washington State law. Following the passage of the Prison Rape Elimination Act of 2003, the state experienced a large increase in substantiated instances of male staff committing sexual misconduct with female inmates, including two highly publicized incidents of female inmates being impregnated by staff. The state's research also revealed that male staff would introduce contraband into the facility as payment for sexual favors. Based on the findings of at least two consultants, the DOC produced a carefully researched request, which included what the duties of each post included and why it was critical to staff that post with a female officer. The DOC believed the facially discriminatory policy was justified because:

> "[i]ncreasing the number of female staff will reduce the risk of sexual misconduct, reduce allegations of sexual misconduct, and protect male staff exposed to vulnerable situations" and unfounded complaints of abuse. The state also emphasized the privacy requirements of female inmates and the operational need

to have female officers on hand to perform necessary searches and other tasks. The requested staffing changes, according to the state, would "ensure the security of the prisons, safety of incarcerated offenders, and protection of the privacy and dignity of female offenders."

In affirming the lower court, and approving the facially discriminatory practice, the court of appeals noted that other courts of appeal had approved similar practices as a means to address the issues of sexual abuse in women's prisons. The state had demonstrated an objective "basis in fact" for "its belief that gender discrimination is `reasonably necessary'—not merely reasonable or convenient—to the normal operation of its business." The DOC presented evidence that there was a "concrete, logical basis for concluding that gender restrictions are reasonably necessary" and that alternatives to sex discrimination have been "reasonably considered and refuted." The DOC's rationale was not just based on reactions to inmate lawsuits but also premised on a need to enhance security (minimizing introduction of contraband) and ensuring the privacy rights of female inmates. The DOC also had carefully limited the discriminatory staffing to certain posts (housing, programs and activities, work crews, and relief posts (officers who fill in for the designated 110 posts upon staff absences)) and presented rational reasons for staffing those posts with female officers.

There is still a difference of opinion among correctional administrators about whether it is best to require corrections officers to be the same sex as the inmate population. Can this not be handled by assigning the opposite sex to noncontact positions—that is, by placing them in work in which they do not come into direct physical contact with inmates? Why is that not a good solution? It is somewhat analogous to the debate about the role of women in combat positions in the military. In most corrections agencies, officers are expected to rotate among the different types of jobs (usually called "posts") in the prisons or jails. In fact, promotion opportunities are often based on the ability to handle well a variety of post assignments. Some places have handled opposite-sex hiring by placing these correctional officers in positions where they do not have contact with inmates, particularly when the inmates are naked, as in the living quarters or during visual (strip) searches. Making the decision more complicated is the fact that some inmates object to being observed without clothes or while scantily clad by a member of the opposite sex. This has been claimed by inmates to be an unwarranted invasion of their privacy. (Cross-gender strip searches present practical problems and raise serious questions about equal employment opportunities under Title VII.)

▶ Title VII and Inmate-Created Hostile Work Environment

The courts have ruled that employers can be liable under Title VII for the third-party harassment of its employees when such conduct creates a hostile work environment. But does this standard apply when the third parties are inmates?

This question was addressed in *Beckford v. Department of Corrections,* 605 F.3d 951 (11th Cir. 2010). In *Beckford,* 14 nonsecurity prison employees sued the Florida Department of Corrections (DOC), claiming the DOC failed to "remedy a sexually hostile work environment" established by male inmates for female employees. The women worked in the prison's "close management" housing dorms, consisting of inmates found unsuitable for the general prison population. These inmates were said to have abused staff, especially female staff, including using gender-specific abusive language and openly masturbating towards female staff (a practice referred to as "gunning"). Suggestions offered by staff to address their concerns were not adopted, nor were complaints to prison management successful. At trial, the DOC's Equal Employment Opportunity investigator said that the department's sexual harassment policy, as explained to the female employees, did not cover harassment by inmates, but if it had, the employees "had fully satisfied the reporting requirements of the policy by complaining to prison management, the Florida Commission on Human Relations, and the Equal Employment Opportunity Commission."

In instructing the jury, the district court asked the jury to decide, after looking at all of the circumstances, whether the "preponderance of the evidence" showed a "hostile or abusive" employment environment. The jury ruled against the department, awarding $45,000 to each employee.

In affirming, the appeals court held that neither inmates nor prisons should be treated differently from other third-party harassers or employers under Title VII. The court recognized that not all harassment by inmates may be reasonably avoided but said the department was required to adopt reasonable measures to curtail inmate harassment. In this instance, the court cited several examples of such reasonable measures, including enforcing the inmate dress policy (inmates were required to wear pants when female staff were in the unit); having male staff accompany female staff while they were in the unit; requiring security staff to write appropriate disciplinary reports; referring for prosecution incidents of masturbation directed toward female staff; and putting in place a specific anti-gunning policy. (Note: the court rejected the DOC's claim that the close management unit inmates were "equal opportunity harassers" and that the women chose to work in that environment. The court held that there was sufficient evidence to show that the harassment was sex-based and that the jury was entitled to find that the DOC made "almost no effort to protect its employees from this sex-based harassment.")

Other circuits have made similar rulings. In *Freitag v. Ayers,* 468 F.3d 528 (9th Cir. 2006), the California Department of Corrections was held liable for its failure to correct a hostile work environment resulting from sexual harassment by male inmates of female staff. Also see *Erickson v. Wisconsin Department of Corrections,* 469 F.3d 600 (7th Cir. 2006). Erickson, a female payroll and benefits specialist at a Wisconsin correctional center, had informed her supervisor and others (including the warden) that she had been "freaked and scared" by the unexpected presence of an inmate in her work area after hours. She was assured that action would be taken to prevent a reoccurrence. It was not, and eight days later, she was raped by the same inmate. Erickson sued under Title VII's hostile work environment provision. The district and appeals court found for Erickson, with the appeals court holding that a reasonable jury could have determined that the department of corrections had sufficient information to recognize the probability that Erickson was being subjected to sexual harassment but "took no remedial action as it was obligated to do under Title VII."

To prevent such holdings based on sexual harassment by inmates, correctional agencies should have clear policy recognizing its obligation to prevent the sexual harassment (and harassment in general) of its employees by inmates, and the steps that are to be taken to prevent this. These steps, at a minimum, should include written policy and directives (covering expectations for both staff and inmate); staff training, including a specific focus on supervisory responsibilities; and taking actions, up to, and referring for, prosecution where warranted, for inmate misconduct in this area.

▸ Tort Claims

When speaking of "torts," there is one type of claim for violations of persons' rights—constitutional torts. These lawsuits involve rights protected under the Constitution and are authorized by federal statute. 42 U.S.C. § 1983. When lawyers talk of tort actions, however, they are usually speaking of common law torts. Common law torts are injuries caused by one person to another, based on some duty owed. They are called "common law" torts because they were developed and defined in English courts and then later adopted by American courts and statutes. One of the most frequently alleged tort at common law is assault and battery. Tort law is used to address a number of injuries to a person or their property, ranging from automobile accidents, to theft or damage to property to fist-fights, to medical malpractice.

Regarding torts, a common defense for tort actions against governments and their agents is the doctrine of sovereign immunity, which applies to all kinds of lawsuits. *Immunity* means protection against being sued or, if sued, against being held liable. *Sovereign* refers to the government (originally, it referred to the king of England; in the United States, it was carried over and refers to the government). So, *sovereign immunity* means that the monarch (or, in the United States, the government) cannot be sued unless the monarch (or government) consents to be sued by waiving sovereign immunity. Therefore, to bring a suit against the government in the United States, the government (usually by legislative action) must have passed a law that says that it consents to allowing persons to sue the government. In such laws, there are usually precise limitations and conditions; the sovereign is allowed to place any restrictions it wants on the authority to sue it—after all, if no law was passed, the sovereign could not be sued at all.

An example is *Ali v. Federal Bureau of Prisons,* 552 U.S. 214 (2008). Ali, a federal inmate, sued the Bureau of Prisons (BOP), claiming that he did not receive all of his personal property following his transfer from one federal institution to another. His administrative tort claim was denied, with prison officials saying that Ali's signature on the receipt form certified the accuracy of the inventory listed, and he had thus relinquished any future claims relating to missing or damaged property. Most governmental agencies, including correctional organizations, prepare a receipt when the agency takes possession of a person's property. Usually, the person is allowed to review the inventory and verify (in writing) its accuracy or note missing items. The person is allowed to review their property when it is returned, and discrepancies are to be noted at that time. Ali sued, alleging violations of the Federal Torts Claims Act, 28 U.S.C. §§ 1346, 2671 et seq. The BOP argued that Ali's claim was barred by the exception in Section 2680(c) for property claims against law enforcement officers. The district court agreed and dismissed

Ali's claim for lack of subject matter jurisdiction. The appeals court affirmed, holding that Section 2680(c)'s statutory language "or any other law enforcement officer" included the Bureau of Prisons. Ali's argument was that this phrase reflects what precedes it, that it includes only law enforcement officers acting in the customs or excise capacity that preceded the language of "any other law enforcement officer."

The Supreme Court affirmed the lower courts, saying that the phrase "any other law enforcement officer" suggests a broad meaning.

> **In the end, we are unpersuaded by petitioner's [the inmate's] attempt to create ambiguity where the statute's text and structure suggest none. Had Congress intended to limit §2680(c)'s reach as petitioner contends, it easily could have written "any other law enforcement officer *acting in a customs or excise capacity.*" Instead, it used the unmodified, all-encompassing phrase "any other law enforcement officer." Nothing in the statutory context requires a narrowing construction—indeed, as we have explained, the statute is most consistent and coherent when "any other law enforcement officer" is read to mean what it literally says.**

Virtually all states and the federal government have laws that allow persons to sue over injuries committed (torts done) by the government or its agents.[11] In any case where a tort has been committed, there are typically administrative procedures established for the victim to use to file a claim against the government. Such claims may involve injuries to the person or to the person's property (such as a negligent government driver hitting a car). Usually, a claim form must be submitted first to allow the government to investigate and consider the claim, before it goes into court. This is true no matter what the size of the claim (whether it concerns a few dollars for property damage or millions of dollars for severe injuries). If the claim is not settled to the claimant's satisfaction, the injured party typically may proceed to court and file a tort suit.

What are the typical kinds of common law torts in prison? Loss of, or damage to, property is probably the most common type of tort claim that is filed. The claim, to be successful, must show that the injury was caused by the negligence of the government official or agent—that is, the official did not exercise the degree of care that is required by the law (or by the government's own policies or regulations) under such circumstances. In *Parratt v. Taylor,* 451 U.S. 527 (1981), an inmate sued for the loss of his hobby materials, which he had ordered by mail and which prison staff had apparently lost. The Supreme Court originally said this was a constitutional tort, stating a "deprivation of property" under the Fourteenth Amendment, but, because the state had a tort claim procedure, the inmate did have process of law to cover his loss. Later, in *Daniels v. Williams,* 474 U.S. 327 (1986), the Supreme Court rejected that analysis, saying that mere negligent action by an official was not enough to trigger the due process clause of the Fourteenth Amendment. States also usually have tort claims procedures available for inmates to use. In any event, for negligent action causing loss of property or minor injury, the remedy for an inmate would be a tort claims procedure, not a claim under the Constitution.

Besides property loss, the most frequently encountered torts in corrections work are assaults (claims against staff members for physical injuries and claims against the government that an inmate was injured in an assault by another inmate, due to the negligence of the staff in not providing proper protection) and medical malpractice. Claims over improper medical care can cover the full range of claims that may be presented in the outside community, and, indeed, the standards used to evaluate tort claims by prisoners are typically the standards of care that prevail in the surrounding community. Medical claims can include allegations of failing to provide care when symptoms or complaints would warrant a certain course of care; taking medical steps against the wishes of the inmate-patient or plain old mistakes in health care, such as amputating the wrong foot, leaving sponges inside the patient during surgery, or making a bad diagnosis.

Tort claims are made against the government. If liability is found (that is, if there was negligence on behalf of the government official or agent), the relief given is money damages, and that money is paid by the government. (This contrasts with constitutional tort claims, where the claims are made against the individual actors, and money damages are typically assessed against the individual officials who are found at fault. Also, injunctive relief is available in constitutional tort actions, but it is not available in common law tort suits or claims.)

Government employees can be subject to constitutional tort liability for conduct, and their employer may be subject to common law tort liability for similar activity. For example, the use of force against a person in custody can generate an "excessive use of force" constitutional claim against the individual officer as well as a common law tort claim for assault and battery against the officer's employer. Although the two types of claims have different elements, different levels of proof, and different remedies, would it be possible for Congress or a state legislature to limit a prisoner's choice as to the type of law suit the prisoner can bring? In some cases, the answer is yes. In *Hui v. Castaneda,* 559 U.S. (2010), a prisoner in federal custody alleged that United States Public Health Service (USPHS) medical staff assigned to provide medical services to inmates in immigration detention were deliberately indifferent to the detainee's serious medical needs. The complaint alleged that following his March 2006 detainment at the San Diego Correctional Facility, the prisoner sought medical care and treatment and that medical staff failed to provide this care in a timely manner. Castaneda was eventually diagnosed with penile cancer and died in 2008.

Prior to his death, Castaneda sued various officials, alleging that they were deliberately indifferent to his serious medical needs. The defendant USPHS officials claimed that a provision of federal law, Title 42 U.S.C. § 233(a), made the Federal Torts Claims Act (FTCA) the exclusive remedy for any personal injury caused by a USPHS officer performing a medical or related function within the scope of his office or employment. After the lower courts denied immunity to the defendant medical officers, they sought review in the U.S. Supreme Court. The Court reversed the lower courts, holding that Congress had intended that the FTCA should be the exclusive remedy for such injuries:

> **Section 233(a) makes the FTCA remedy against the United States "exclusive of any other civil action or proceeding" for any personal injury caused by a PHS officer or employee performing a medical or related function "while acting within the scope of his office or employment." Based on the plain language of § 233(a), we conclude that PHS officers and employees are not personally subject to *Bivens* [constitutional tort] actions for harms arising out of such conduct.**

Thus, in *Hui,* the Supreme Court concluded that Congress could, and did, limit the remedy that persons may seek against particular persons, in this case, USPHS employees who provide medical care and who are acting within the scope of their duties.

Tort claim laws can also create other limitations on a sovereign's waiver of immunity. One such limit in the FTCA is the judgment bar. Under the judgment bar provision (Title 28 U.S. Code § 2676), once a plaintiff receives a judgment, favorable or not, in an FTCA suit, they generally cannot proceed with a suit against an individual employee based on the same underlying facts. Other limitations can include no waiver for intentional torts and no waiver for issues arising from government officials performing "discretionary functions." Two recent Supreme Court cases addressing provisions of the FTCA discuss these exceptions. In *Millbrook v. USA,* 569 U.S. 50 (2013), a federal prisoner sued the United States under the FTCA alleging a federal correctional officer had sexually assaulted him and then threatened him with personal injury if he reported the assault. The district court and court of appeals dismissed the inmate's tort claim law suit because while the FTCA waives the sovereign immunity for certain intentional torts (including assault and battery) committed by federal law enforcement officers (28 U.S. Code§ 2680(h) circuit precedent dictated that the waiver applies only when the actions occur during an arrest, conducting a search and seizing evidence. Since the inmate's allegations of misconduct did not occur during one of the enumerated law enforcement functions, the FTCA did not waive the sovereign immunity of the United States. The Supreme Court reversed, ruling:

> **By its terms, this provision focuses on the *status* of persons whose conduct may be actionable, not the types of activities that may give rise to a tort claim against the United States. The proviso thus distinguishes between the acts for which immunity is waived (*e.g.,* assault and battery), and the class of persons whose acts may give rise to an actionable FTCA claim. The plain text confirms that Congress intended immunity determinations to depend on a federal officer's legal authority, not on a particular exercise of that authority. . . . We hold that the waiver effected by the law enforcement proviso extends to acts or omissions of law enforcement officers that arise within the scope of their employment, regardless of whether the officers are engaged in investigative or law enforcement activity, or are executing a search, seizing evidence, or making an arrest.**

In *Simmons v. Himmelreich,* 578 U.S. ___, 136 S.Ct. 1843 (2016), inmate Himmelreich filed an FTCA lawsuit against the United States alleging that he was seriously injured when prison staff negligently placed him in a cell with an assaultive inmate. The United States moved to dismiss the lawsuit because classification decisions are covered by the discretionary function exception to the FTCA. While the government's motion to dismiss was being decided, Himmelreich sued the individual officers alleging a violation of the Eighth Amendment (under *Bivens*) because staff failed to protect him from attack by another inmate. After the district court dismissed Himmelreich's FTCA claim based on the discretionary function exception, the individual federal officers moved to dismiss the

Bivens action under the judgment bar provision of the FTCA (28 U.S. Code § 2676). The Supreme Court affirmed the judgment of the court of appeals, which ruled that the judgment bar did not apply because by the terms of the FTCA, the bar does not apply when the FTCA action is dismissed on the basis of one of the exceptions listed in 28 U.S. Code § 2680(h) including a discretionary function.

To the extent that a state has a tort claims procedure that covers negligent actions in all kinds of common law tort situations, the individual official of the government should not be individually liable for any loss suffered by the claimant. In most places, the question asked by the government is whether the official was acting "in the course of duty." If so, the official will be covered by the government defending the suit, as a common law tort claim. To be acting within the "course of duty," the employee should be acting in accordance with agency policy, procedures, and training. If this is done, there is some assurance that the actions taken, which may occasionally lead to injuries to inmates or others, will be covered by the government, because the employee will have acted "in the course of his duties." There may be instances when an individual employee is deemed not to have acted within the scope of their official duties. Government officials may purchase individual liability insurance for protection against tort suits. As a matter of extreme caution, some employees (especially doctors and other health care workers) do choose to carry liability (or malpractice) insurance.

In these common law tort situations, when a tort claim or a tort suit is filed against a corrections agency, the case will usually be defended by a government attorney, so it is not necessary for the individual employee to obtain counsel. In those situations in which it is found that the employee was acting outside of the scope of their employment—their instructions or in violation of policy and practice, they may have to obtain their own representation, which will have to be paid for out of their own pocket (or by their insurance company, if they carry liability insurance).

▶ **The Americans with Disabilities Act**

Another federal statute that has considerable impact on corrections is the Americans with Disabilities Act (ADA), which was enacted in 1990. Titles I, II, and III of the Act are codified in Title 42, chapter 126 of the U.S. Code. (A previous law, the Rehabilitation Act of 1973, requires that there be no discrimination against persons with disabilities in federal agencies and programs; the 1973 act also applies to those receiving federal funds or working under federal contracts.) These laws prohibiting discrimination on the basis of disability thus apply to all governmental agencies—federal, state, and local. Attempts to exclude law enforcement and corrections agencies from the ADA's coverage were rejected in Congress. There are three aspects of the law that are of direct importance to corrections: (1) 2010 ADA Standards for Accessible Design, (2) employment, and (3) inmate programs and services.

2010 ADA Standards for Accessible Design

On September 15, 2010, the Department of Justice published revised regulations for Title II (Public Services) of the Americans with Disabilities Act.[12] Among the changes, Subpart D—Program Accessibility added paragraphs (e) and (k) to Title 28, Code of Federal Regulations (CFR) § 35.151 (new construction and alterations) and a new Section 35.152 (Jails, detention and correctional facilities, and community correctional facilities). In Section 35.151, new paragraph (e), *Social service center establishments,* states that halfway houses may fall within the provisions of the 2010 standards relating to residential facilities. New paragraph (k), *Detention and correctional facilities,* discusses the requirements for the new construction of jails, prisons, and other detention and correctional facilities and for alterations to detention and correctional facilities. The Department discussed new paragraph (k) in its comments accompanying publication of the final regulations.

> Based on complaints received by the Department, investigations, and compliance reviews of jails, prisons, and other detention and correctional facilities, the Department has determined that many detention and correctional facilities do not have enough accessible cells, toilets, and shower facilities to meet the needs of their inmates with mobility disabilities and some do not have any at all. Inmates are sometimes housed in medical units or infirmaries separate from the general population simply because there are no accessible cells. In addition, some inmates have alleged that they are housed at a more restrictive classification level simply because no accessible housing exists at the appropriate classification level. The Department's compliance reviews and investigations have substantiated certain of these allegations.
>
> The Department believes that the insufficient number of accessible cells is, in part, due to the fact that most jails and prisons were built long before the ADA became law and, since then, have undergone few

alterations that would trigger the obligation to provide accessible features in accordance with Uniform Federal Accessibility Standards (UFAS) or the 1991 Standards. In addition, the Department has found that even some new correctional facilities lack accessible features. The Department believes that the unmet demand for accessible cells is also due to the changing demographics of the inmate population. With thousands of prisoners serving life sentences without eligibility for parole, prisoners are aging, and the prison population of individuals with disabilities and elderly individuals is growing. A Bureau of Justice Statistics study of State and Federal sentenced inmates (those sentenced to more than one year) shows the total estimated count of State and Federal prisoners aged 55 and older grew by 36,000 inmates from 2000 (44,200) to 2006 (80,200) …. This jump constitutes an increase of 81 percent in prisoners aged 55 and older during this period.

The final rule requires that both the new construction and the alterations of jails, prisons, and other detention and correctional facilities comply with the 2010 ADA Standards for Accessible Design (also issued by the Department September 15, 2010, with an effective date of March 2012), with the objective of making such facilities readily accessible to and usable by persons with disabilities. New Section 35.151, paragraph (k), further specifies that public entities shall provide such accessible mobility features for at least 3%, but no less than one, of the total number of cells being constructed or altered.

Section 35.152, detention and correctional facilities, and the community correctional facilities, is shown in **FIGURE 19-1**. In that figure, paragraph (a), *General*, identifies those areas affected by this section. Paragraph (b), *Discrimination prohibited*, requires public entities (prisons) to ensure that qualified inmates or detainees with disabilities are not excluded from programs, services, or activities of a public entity because a facility is not accessible or usable by a person with disabilities; are housed in the most integrated setting appropriate to the person's needs; and have access to safe and appropriate housing.

---

§ 35.152 Jails, detention and correctional facilities, and community correctional facilities.

(a) *General*. This section applies to public entities that are responsible for the operation or management of adult and juvenile justice jails, detention and correctional facilities, and community correctional facilities, either directly or through contractual, licensing, or other arrangements with public or private entities, in whole or in part, including private correctional facilities.

(b) *Discrimination prohibited*.

(1) Public entities shall ensure that qualified inmates or detainees with disabilities shall not, because a facility is inaccessible to or unusable by individuals with disabilities, be excluded from participation in, or be denied the benefits of, the services, programs, or activities of a public entity, or be subjected to discrimination by any public entity.

(2) Public entities shall ensure that inmates or detainees with disabilities are housed in the most integrated setting appropriate to the needs of the individuals. Unless it is appropriate to make an exception, a public entity—

(i) Shall not place inmates or detainees with disabilities in inappropriate security classifications because no accessible cells or beds are available;

(ii) Shall not place inmates or detainees with disabilities in designated medical areas unless they are actually receiving medical care or treatment;

(iii) Shall not place inmates or detainees with disabilities in facilities that do not offer the same programs as the facilities where they would otherwise be housed; and

(iv) Shall not deprive inmates or detainees with disabilities of visitation with family members by placing them in distant facilities where they would not otherwise be housed.

(3) Public entities shall implement reasonable policies, including physical modifications to additional cells in accordance with the 2010 Standards, so as to ensure that each inmate with a disability is housed in a cell with the accessible elements necessary to afford the inmate access to safe, appropriate housing.

Source: 75 Fed. Reg. 56164 (2010) (codified at 28 CFR 35.152). The quoted material in this section is found on page 56183.

FIGURE 19-1 Jails, Detention and Correctional Facilities, and Community Correctional Facilities, from the 2010 ADA Standards for Accessible Design.

It is anticipated that litigation will arise from these new rules. For example, litigation is likely to occur around the discrimination-prohibited language of Section 35.152, covering such areas as program participation and physical location (the section says inmates or detainees with disabilities shall not be deprived of visitation with family members arising from placement in distant facilities where, except for their disability, they would not otherwise be housed). Correctional personnel should work closely with staff in the appropriate areas to effectively meet the new ADA provisions. Specific attention should be given to the training of program staff to make them familiar with the program and location accessibility requirements.

In *United States v. Georgia,* 546 U.S. 151 (2006), inmate Goodman sued under Title II of the ADA and also 42 U.S.C. § 1983, challenging the conditions of his confinement. He made numerous claims, some of which were described as trivial. The district court, adopting the magistrate judge's recommendation that the complaint allegations were vague and constituted insufficient notice, dismissed the Section 1983 claims, as well as the Title II claims against all individual defendants. Later, the court granted summary judgment to the state defendants on the inmate's Title II claims asking for money damages. The court held that those claims were barred by state sovereign immunity. Goodman appealed.

The appeals court ruled that Goodman's lower court filings alleged sufficient facts to support some Eighth Amendment claims under Section 1983. The appeals court identified three such claims, including one where Goodman "claimed that he was confined for 23-to-24 hours per day in a 12-by-3-foot cell in which he could not turn his wheelchair around." (This, if true, appears to be an example of a cell that is without the mobility features called for in the new ADA regulations discussed above.)

The appeals court returned the case to the district court to allow Goodman to amend his complaint. The appeals court also held that the state's sovereign immunity barred Title II claims for money damages. The Supreme Court agreed to hear only the issue of whether Title II of the ADA nullifies state sovereign immunity. In its opinion, the Court said the inmate's Title II claims for money damages from the state were "evidently based ... on conduct that independently violated ... § 1 of the Fourteenth Amendment." [The alleged denial of the benefits of prison services and programs without due process of law.]

[I]nsofar as Title II creates a private cause of action for damages against the States for conduct that *actually* violates the Fourteenth Amendment, Title II validly abrogates state sovereign immunity.

In *Armstrong v. Schwarzenegger,* 622 F.3d 1058 (9th Cir. 2010), the state of California claimed it was not responsible for providing reasonable accommodations to state prison inmates and parolees with certain disabilities that the state chooses to house in county jails. The inmate-plaintiffs had asked the court to issue "an order requiring Defendants to develop and implement effective policies and procedures ensuring all prisoners and parolees with mobility, vision, hearing, developmental, kidney, and learning disabilities housed in county jails receive the accommodations they need." In denying responsibility, California said that while Title III (on public accommodations and services operated by private entities) barred the affected entities from discriminating either "directly, or through contractual, licensing, or other arrangements," this same language is not in Title II (dealing with public services). According to the State, "Congress unambiguously intended that public entities not be subject to liability for violations of the ADA when they provide programs or services through arrangements with third parties." The district court disagreed and ordered the state to provide the counties housing the affected inmates with a plan to comply with the ADA, to include improving the tracking of inmates (including parolees) in the state houses in county jails; notifying jails when the state sends the county a class member with a disability; and ensuring that an adequate ADA grievance procedure is available to the inmate class members confined in the jails.

The appeals court affirmed, holding that the state was responsible for ensuring reasonable accommodations to disabled prisoners and parolees that the state houses in county jails. Both courts pointed to a regulation promulgated by the U.S. Attorney General, 28 C.F.R. § 35.130(b)(1), that specifically barred discrimination by public entities, either directly or through contractual, licensing, or other arrangements from discriminating against persons with disabilities. The appeals court said that this regulation was developed pursuant to Congressional direction that regulations implementing Title II be consistent with Section 504 of the Rehabilitation Act. The lower courts ruled that although Congress omitted from Title II the language that was used in Title III, this omission did not clearly indicate Congress' intent that public entities would not be liable for violations of the ADA committed by third parties contracting with the public entity. The court noted that Section 504 of the Rehabilitation Act states that a party receiving federal financial aid may not discriminate "directly or through contractual, licensing, or other arrangements, on the basis of handicap."

Another part of *Armstrong* dealt with the Prison Litigation Reform Act (PLRA) and its provision that courts "shall not grant or approve any prospective relief [for prison conditions] unless the court finds that such relief is narrowly drawn, extends no further than necessary to correct the violation of the Federal right, and is the least intrusive means necessary to correct the violation of the Federal right." California argued that this requirement was not met, that the court did not make the requisite findings for correcting ADA violations (on a provision-by-provision basis), and that the plan was not narrowly drawn or minimally intrusive. In rejecting the first argument, the court held that absent a clear statement of Congressional intent for the statutory language, it was appropriate for the court to make a broad (as opposed to provision-by-provision) finding that it found the requisite need, narrowness, and lack of intrusiveness. To do otherwise could lead to unwarranted challenges to the findings and unnecessarily delay resolution.

On the second argument, the court held that the state failed to provide alternatives that were more narrow or less intrusive. "Allowing defendants to develop policies and procedures to meet the ADA's requirements is precisely the type of process that the Supreme Court has indicated is appropriate for devising a suitable remedial plan in a prison litigation case …. A demonstration that an order is burdensome does nothing to prove that it was overly intrusive." The court rejected the state's claim that a more narrowly drawn provision would be for the state to provide information to the county jails to help the counties "enhance" their own ADA compliance. The court saw this suggestion as an effort by the state to pass its responsibility on to the counties; further, that "enhanced" ADA compliance may not be the same as actual compliance. Nor did the court see the state's suggested alternative that the inmate should be allowed to sue for noncompliance as being more narrowly drawn or less intrusive.[13]

Employment under the ADA

The employment section of the law (Title I of the act) bars employment discrimination in hiring and in other employment opportunities against qualified persons with disabilities. The legal definition of a disability is given in Title 42, U.S. Code, Section 12102:

> **The term "disability" means, with respect to an individual—(A) a physical or mental impairment that substantially limits one or more major life activities of such individual; (B) a record of such an impairment; or (C) being regarded as having such an impairment.**

Because the thrust of the act is to provide equal opportunity to disabled persons, the employment section of the law is written to provide an additional type of protection, similar to those protections covered in Title VII of the Civil Rights Act. What kinds of discriminatory actions are prohibited? The law (42 U.S.C. § 12112) says that "no covered entity [defined as an employer, employment agency, labor organization, or joint labor-management committee] shall discriminate against a qualified individual on the basis of disability in regard to job application procedures, the hiring, advancement, or discharge of employees, employee compensation, job training, and other terms, conditions, and privileges of employment." Similar to the protections given in other antidiscrimination laws, some exceptions are allowed. Although an employer is expected to make "reasonable accommodation" for a disabled person to perform a job, in broader terms, the disabled person must be "otherwise qualified" to perform the job.

Looking at the exact language of the law (Section 12113), there is a defense to discrimination charges that is allowed when the employer can show that "qualification standards, tests, or selection criteria that screen out or tend to screen out or otherwise deny a job or benefit to an individual with a disability [have] been shown to be job-related and consistent with business necessity, and such performance cannot be accomplished by reasonable accommodation." This, of course, is similar to the bona fide occupational qualification (BFOQ), which was previously discussed as an exception in the Civil Rights law.

When hiring, the law says that an employer may not make a medical examination or medical inquiries (related to any disability) before the employee is hired. What can be done at the hiring or interview stage is to inquire into the specific ability of the applicant to perform functions that are necessary to the job. After an offer of employment has been made, the employer may condition an offer on the results of a medical exam, but only if all entering employees are subjected to such exams.

Some have heard of the ADA primarily in terms of requiring physical alterations to building entrances, work spaces, or restrooms. But the law has a much broader impact than that. Employers are expected to make efforts to make a job possible for a disabled person to perform, unless doing so will create an "undue hardship." Interpretation of these key terms in the law—"undue hardship," "reasonable accommodation," and "qualified individual"— will, no doubt, be litigated for many years.[14]

It is safe to say that, as in other areas of balancing interests, corrections administrators can most readily show "undue hardship" if an accommodation would adversely affect the security operations of the agency. Accommodations that cost extra money or create some readjustment of duties between jobs will likely have to be made, up to the point that they would be unduly expensive or disruptive. "Undue hardship" is defined in Section 12111 as "an action requiring significant difficulty or expense." In determining whether an accommodation would impose an undue hardship, factors to be considered "include the nature and cost of the accommodation" and such factors as the size, resources, and structure of the employer's operation.

A person who is a "qualified individual with a disability" is a person "who meets legitimate skill, experience, education, or other requirements of an employment position that s/he holds or seeks, and who can perform the essential functions of the position with or without reasonable accommodation …. If the individual is qualified to perform essential job functions except for limitations caused by a disability, the employer must consider whether the individual could perform these functions with a reasonable accommodation."[14] In correctional facilities, just where those boundaries are will have to be explored for different work situations, involving such factors as the degree of contact with inmates, the security levels of different institutions, and the degrees of physical or mental abilities required in specific jobs. In tough cases, or legal challenges by persons with disabilities to the agency's employment practices, the history of the agency in making efforts to accommodate disabled persons in various types of jobs can also become very important.

In *Hennagir v. Utah Department of Corrections* (DOC), 581 F.3d 1256 (10th Cir. 2009), Hennagir had been working for several years as a prison physician assistant (PA) when the DOC made arrangements to enroll its prison medical personnel in the Utah Public Safety Retirement System. This enrollment necessitated that these staff achieve Peace Officer Standards and Training Certification (POST). The certification encompassed an assessment of physical strength, flexibility, and endurance.

Due to her physical disability (which did not appear to be questioned), Hennagir did not complete the training and was determined by the DOC as being unable to meet the new job requirements. She declined several DOC-offered job alternatives, and the DOC notified her that her employment was being terminated. Hennagir sued, alleging, in part, discrimination and denial of reasonable accommodation in violation of the ADA and the Rehabilitation Act.

The district court granted the DOC's motion for summary judgment, finding Hennagir not qualified for the PA position and that her proposed accommodations were not reasonable. The appeals court affirmed, finding that Hennagir did not meet the "qualified individual" standard set forth in the ADA. The court found the safety training requirement an essential job function. In making this determination, the court said it "weigh[s] heavily the employer's judgment regarding whether a job function is essential." The court spoke to the risks involved in "direct inmate contact," noted a prior incident where a DOC medical technician was attacked by an inmate (and the victim's lawsuit), and the subsequent recommendation of the State Risk Management Division that a POST certification requirement be implemented.

The court found insufficient Hennagir's argument that in her work career, prior to the certification requirement, she never had to employ emergency training. The court said that the ADA imposes no limitation on the employer's ability to establish or change aspects of a job and that "We must look instead to whether a job function was essential at the time it was imposed on Hennagir." The court further commented, "Although a deputy [sheriff] may be required physically to restrain inmates only infrequently, the potential for physical confrontation with inmates exists on a daily basis, and the consequence of failing to require a deputy to perform this function when the occasion arises could be a serious threat to security." [citing *Hoskins v. Oakland County Sheriff's Department*, 227 F.3d 719, 727 (6th Cir. 2000)].

With respect to reasonable accommodation, the court held that Hennagir's proposed accommodations—a waiver of the requirement; to "grandfather" her in the position; and a change of job title (without a change in job)—were not reasonable, that each proposal was in effect a request that an essential job function be eliminated.

It is highly desirable, if not essential, for administrators to adopt policies and procedures to show that the administration is aware of the requirements of the ADA and is trying to accommodate them. Personnel policies should be revised to show that the goals of the ADA are understood. For example, statements that the agency does not discriminate in hiring or in other personnel matters should include references to persons with disabilities. Of course, the exceptions allowed by the Act may also be referred to (provided the person does "not pose a direct threat to the health or safety of other individuals in the workplace," or "does not pose a threat to the secure and orderly running of the institution" are phrases that may be considered). Such references are desirable in personnel policies, and they also apply in the area of inmate programs and services.

One goal of the ADA is to integrate persons with disabilities into the mainstream. This should be kept in mind when policies in either area of concern (employment or inmate programs) are considered. To the extent possible, disabled persons should be included in activities along with others. Sometimes, in order to provide access to benefits or services, adaptations may be necessary to accommodate the disabled. A second principle that should be kept in mind in adopting employment policies and procedures is that corrections facilities are not required to accommodate disabled persons if to do so would present a "direct threat." This term is defined in 42 U.S.C. § 12111 as "a significant risk to the health or safety of others that cannot be eliminated by reasonable accommodation." The regulatory definition for "direct threat" is in Title 29, Code of Federal Regulations, Section 1630.2(r). The regulation requires an individualized assessment "of the individual's present ability to safely perform the essential functions of the job." The assessment is to be based on reasonable medical judgment "that relies on the most current medical knowledge and/or the best available objective evidence." The regulation identifies factors to be considered in determining if a person would pose a direct threat. These factors include "(1) The duration of the risk; (2) The nature and severity of the potential harm; (3) The likelihood that the potential harm will occur; and (4) The imminence of the potential harm." The ADA does not confer a right to any particular accommodation.

Inmate Programs and Services under the ADA

[The reader is reminded that new regulations in this area were finalized in September 2010, with some becoming effective in March of 2011 and others (the 2010 Standards for Accessible Design) in March of 2012. Some of the discussion that follows reflects language from earlier editions of this text. While author believe it continues to apply, the true test must await potential litigation challenges.]

Title II of the ADA does require compliance for state and local correctional agencies with respect to programs, services, and activities that are offered to inmates, and also to their visitors, which includes family members, attorneys, religious visitors, and volunteer workers. Not to be forgotten are accommodations for other government workers who may be visiting the facilities, such as parole or probation officers and law enforcement officers (from federal, state, or local levels).

The first, and perhaps most noteworthy, aspect of accommodation is physical access. Correctional activities and services may not be denied to persons with disabilities because the facilities are inaccessible. The ADA does not require, however, that existing facilities be drastically remodeled to meet ADA standards. The requirement for fuller physical accessibility applies to new construction and alterations made to existing structures. Providing program access is not required if it would result in significant difficulty or expense—for example, undue financial or administrative burdens.

Sometimes, ensuring program accessibility may involve changing the location where the activities are conducted rather than making changes to existing physical structures. In making such changes; however, it is important to keep in mind another new provision in Section 35.151, "New construction and alterations," discussed earlier in this chapter. Section 35.151(a)(2)(i) allows for an exception to the design standards for "structural impracticability," but defines this term as applicable "only in those rare circumstances when the unique characteristics of terrain prevent the incorporation of accessibility features." It also is important that corrections officials become familiar with the provisions of new Section 35.152(b), *Discrimination prohibited*, also discussed earlier in this chapter (see Figure 19-1).

Another requirement under the act involves communication. Basically, an agency or facility must make sure that its communications with disabled persons are as effective as its communications with others. As with all other types of accommodation, this requirement does not apply when doing so would require significant difficulty or expense—for example, an undue financial and/or administrative burden. The most obvious example in this area is the use of telecommunication devices for the deaf (TDDs) for persons who are deaf or hard of hearing. Qualified readers or recorded texts are examples of auxiliary aids for persons who are blind or visually impaired. It may be that, in classes or in administrative hearings in prisons (such as disciplinary or parole hearings), sign language interpretation will have to be supplied to deaf prisoners or to those with severe speech impairments. Accommodations must also be sought for inmates who are mentally disabled. It is acceptable to provide special housing units or facilities for inmates with mental disabilities, as long as those inmates are not excluded from the same kinds of programs and services that are available to other inmates. However, they may be excluded when they are not eligible or capable of participating in programs or activities without changing the essential nature of the programs or when including them would pose a threat to the health or safety of others. New Section 35.139, "Direct threat," states that the public entity (prison) is not required to allow a person to take part in, or benefit from the public entity's services, programs, or activities when that person "poses a direct threat to the health or safety of others." Similar to the employment provisions discussed earlier (29 CFR § 1630.2(r)), the determination of a direct threat set out in Section 35.139(b) involves the public entity making an individualized assessment, using current medical knowledge or "the best available" objective evidence to determine "the nature, duration, and severity of the risk; the probability that the potential injury will actually occur; and whether reasonable modifications of policies, practices, or procedures or the provision of auxiliary aids or services will mitigate the risk."

The new ADA provisions set out what are likely to be more stringent requirements with respect to persons with disabilities. This makes it even more important for corrections officials to review their written policies and procedures in all areas in which inmates and visitors to the facility are directly affected. Those policies and procedures should be revised as necessary to show the accommodations that will be made as the need arises. That latter statement points out the critical issue of the classification of inmates (and their visitors): at intake screenings, the needs of any incoming inmate who is disabled must be identified. (With due consideration and sensitivity to privacy issues, it should be remembered that inquiries should be made to the incoming inmate about whether any prospective visitor to that inmate has special needs due to disability.) From this intake assessment, proper classification can be made to accommodate any immediate needs. Such needs may include medical or psychiatric attention, special programming (such as counseling and educational opportunities), special assignment (because the disabled inmate may pose some risk to himself or to others), proper housing and work assignments, and contacts with persons on the outside (by mail, by telephone, or in the visiting room).

During this classification process, and at all times in dealing with the disabled inmate, staff should keep in mind that persons should not be segregated solely on the grounds of their disability; a major goal is to include all disabled persons (mainstreaming) in existing activities. For example, it may be necessary to assign a disabled person to first-floor housing, but that person should be mixed in with other inmates on that floor. To the extent feasible, staff should avoid placing all persons with a particular disability, or all disabled inmates, together in the same housing area. It is important to remember that new Section 35.152(b) establishes an expectation that "inmates or detainees with disabilities are housed in the most integrated setting appropriate to the needs of the individuals." If it becomes necessary to place disabled inmates together in the same housing area, it is important for written documentation, both for setting forth the basis for this approach and to show that it was done with an awareness of the ADA regulations. Failure to do this provides a basis for inmate litigation.

Special program assignments present special challenges. To the extent possible, inmates with disabilities should be assigned to classes, vocational training, drug or alcohol counseling, work programs, work-release programs, and religious programs. Eligibility requirements for such programs are not allowed to exclude disabled inmates unless it can be shown that the requirements are necessary for the service to be provided or for the activity to take place. A program such as a **boot camp** presents a clear dilemma: It is typically for younger offenders with minimal criminal histories, and it offers earlier release than regular incarceration in return for strenuous physical exercise and work. For certain physical disabilities, involvement in the customary military drills, calisthenics, and hard labor would be impossible.

This was the situation facing inmate Ronald Yeskey. His sentencing court imposed a term of 18 to 36 months but recommended he serve the sentence in Pennsylvania's Motivational Boot Camp for first-time offenders. Successful completion of this program could lead to his parole in just six months. Because of Yeskey's hypertension, corrections officials denied him participation in the program. He sued, alleging an ADA violation. The district court dismissed for failure to state a claim; the appeals court reversed. The U.S. Supreme Court reviewed the case.

In *Pennsylvania Department of Corrections v. Yeskey*, 524 U.S. 206 (1998), the Court held that the ADA clearly applies to state prisons. Title II of the ADA provides the following:

> **Subject to the provisions of this subchapter, no qualified individual with a disability shall, by reason of such disability, be excluded from participation in or be denied the benefits of the services, programs, or activities of a public entity, or be subjected to discrimination by any such entity.**

"Public entity" includes "any department, agency, special purpose district, or other instrumentality of a State or States or local government."

The state argued that the ADA language was ambiguous as applied to state prisons and state prisoners. The state claimed that the law was not intended to benefit inmates and the fact that the inmate was held against his will, in effect, removed him from the coverage of the act.

The Supreme Court disagreed. Prisons offer many programs, from recreational to medical to educational, the Court said, all of which are at least "theoretically" beneficial. To bring the point home, the enabling statute in

Pennsylvania calls the Motivational Boot Camp a "program." The Court pointed out that some programs are mandatory for all eligible inmates, giving as an example a drug addict for whom the court orders drug program participation. Also, the Court asserted that even if the words did suggest voluntary participation, all prison programs still would not be excluded: the Court pointed out that participation in the Motivational Boot Camp program and in the services offered by the inmate law library are voluntary.

Yeskey makes it clear that the ADA applies to state prisons. Prison administrators are thus challenged either to adapt existing programs or to create alternatives to provide comparable programs to disabled individuals so that they can obtain the benefits of such programs. This is particularly true where there are reductions in terms to be served (as is typically provided in a boot camp program).

Very similar challenges are presented in prison work programs that may require physical abilities that the disabled do not have but that also offer special benefits for those who participate, such as early release, extra good-time credits, or wages. As time goes by, administrators will continue to be called on to show why inclusion of the disabled in such programs, perhaps with special accommodations, cannot be made without "undue burdens."

Some additional observations about the ADA are as follows:

- Some accommodations would clearly cost too much and would, therefore, be an undue financial burden—for example, providing duplicate law books for blind inmates in braille. However, providing readers for the blind or providing recorded books from the general library for recreational reading may be an effective approach.
- The ADA does not give inmate workers in prison industries the legal status of employees for the benefits of the nondiscrimination portions of the act that protect employees; at least, the regulations implementing the act would indicate this, and no court has yet required such added protection. It remains to be seen how the ADA's new provisions will be interpreted in this area.
- Auxiliary aids of some kind will ordinarily be required to assist disabled inmates so that they can participate in education and special support programs (such as Alcoholics Anonymous). These aids need not be of a particular kind, as long as they are effective. Inmates cannot be required to pay for such special assistance.
- It is permissible at the classification or intake stages of an inmate's incarceration to ask the inmate about his disabilities. Asking about HIV or AIDS status may be permissible, because that status legally qualifies the person as disabled, as long as it is done to ascertain the ability of the individual to participate in regular programs and activities and to determine whether special accommodations will have to be made. Because HIV or AIDS is ordinarily addressed as a medical issue and would be covered in medical screening at intake or classification, it may be best to leave that particular type of disability to the medical staff to review, rather than to handle it by routine classification inquiries (especially because there are special confidentiality concerns that apply).
- The Act applies to all types of state and local facilities, including jails and other short-term institutions. It does not cover the executive branch of the federal government (covered by Title V of the Rehabilitation Act of 1973) but does cover Congress and other entities in the legislative branch of the federal government.

The Supreme Court has not recently issued any correctional opinions relating to the provision of services under the ADA, but many lower courts have. One frequently cited case is *Pierce v. the District of Columbia*, 128 F.Supp.3d 250 (D.D.C 2015). Pierce was a deaf individual who was arrested and confined for 51 days in a D.C. detention facility. He alleged staff never assessed whether, and to what extent, the disability would require accommodation to permit him to communicate with others. Pierce was not provided with a qualified American Sign Language (ASL) interpreter during the entire 51-day period he spent in custody, including the 14-day period that Pierce served in solitary confinement-like conditions. The inmate alleged that his rights under the ADA and the Rehabilitation Act (RA) were violated because of issues related to his hearing disability and: (1) his problems communicating with staff during the facility's medical intake and health services, (2) inmate rehabilitation classes, (3) protective custody procedures that were employed in his case, and (4) the facility's provision of telecommunications, official notifications, and visitation. The District argued that Pierce could communicate effectively and alleged he never advised staff of his need for accommodation.

The court first summarized the elements for a cause of action based on Title II of the ADA and Section 504 of the RA: (1) that the person is a qualified individual with a disability; (2) the person was or is being excluded from participation in; or is being denied benefits, services, programs, or other activities for which a public entity is responsible; or is otherwise being discriminated against by the public entity; and (3) that such exclusion, denial of benefits, or discrimination is by reason of their disability. To prevail on a claim under the RA, a party must also establish that the entity is receiving federal funds. Because it was undisputed that Pierce had never been assessed to determine his needs for accommodation, the district court concluded that the ADA and RA had been violated:

> The record in this matter clearly reveals that, when Pierce arrived at CTF to be taken into custody, prison officials took no steps whatsoever to evaluate his need for accommodation so that he would be able to have meaningful access to prison programs and services within the prison facility. The District's employees and contractors *knew* that Pierce was profoundly deaf, but instead of engaging in an interactive process designed to ascertain what accommodations would be necessary for Pierce to communicate effectively in prison, they merely *assumed* that he could read (and understand) the words they mouthed to him and the notes they wrote to him, even after he told them.

A similar outcome was reached in *Updike v. Multnomah County, Oregon*, 70 F.3d 939 (9th Cir. 2017). Updike was also deaf and after being arrested, he was held in jail for two days. Like Pierce, he was never assessed to determine if his hearing disability required accommodation. Updike's main complaints under the ADA and the RA were: (1) he was denied access to an ASL interpreter during the booking process, (2) he was denied access to a TTD/TTY device to make phone calls; ["*Text telephone (TTY).* A machine that employs graphic communication in the transmission of coded signals through a wire or radio communication system. TTY supersedes the term "TDD" or "telecommunications device for the deaf,"] See 47 C.F.R Section 64.601] (3) staff refused to activate the close captioning on facility televisions; and (4) he was denied access to an ASL interpreter during a medical evaluation. Like the facility in *Pierce*, Multnomah County argued that staff believed Updike was able to communicate effectively, and that while Updike may have preferred to communicate using a TDD/TDY phone and using an ASL interpreter, failure to do so did not violate the federal statutes.

The Ninth Circuit reversed the district court, which had granted summary judgment to the defendants. To establish a claim for violations of the ADA, the person must establish (1) they are a `qualified individual with a disability'; (2) they were or are excluded from participation in or denied the benefits of a public entity's services, programs, or activities, or was otherwise discriminated against by the public entity; and (3) such exclusion, denial of benefits, or discrimination was by reason of their disability. To bring a claim under Section 504 of the RA, the person must establish (1) they are an individual with a disability; (2) they are otherwise qualified to receive the benefit; (3) they were denied the benefits of the program solely by reason of their disability; and (4) the program receives federal financial assistance.

Most courts consider that the relief available under the ADA and Section 504 of the RA are coextensive and consider ADA Title II and Section 504 claims together because "the substantive standards for determining liability are the same." While violations of both statutes are usually pleaded, there is usually only one recovery when a single act is found to violate both statutes.

The court of appeals reversed the district court's dismissal of the ADA and RA claims. Updike had been released from the facility so he could not be given equitable relief. The court of appeals concluded there was still a cause of action for damages from the county if Updike could demonstrate the county, as a public entity, intentionally or with deliberate indifference did not provide a reasonable accommodation to a deaf or hearing-impaired person. The county sought review in the Supreme Court to decide on the question as to when a public entity is liable for money damages, but the Supreme Court denied certiorari. *Multnomah County, Oregon v. Updike*, ___ U.S. ___, 139 S.Ct. 55 (2018).

In *Furgess v. Pennsylvania Department of Corrections*, 933 F.3d 285 (3rd Cir. 2019), the court of appeals addressed the issue of whether a shower for a handicapped inmate was a program, service, or activity as used in the ADA and Section 504 of the RA, and whether the shower was denied as a result of the inmate's disability. Furgess had a disability and needed a wheelchair for mobility, including taking a shower. While initially housed in a unit with a wheelchair-accessible shower stall, he was later moved to the facility's Restrictive Housing Unit (RHU), which did not have a wheelchair-accessible shower. The inmate repeatedly requested access to a wheelchair-accessible shower, and the Superintendent of the facility even directed staff to escort the inmate to a shower location to accommodate his needs. After three months, Furgess was taken to a shower, but one that was not wheelchair accessible. The chair he was provided was inadequate for his movement, and when Furgess tried to leave the stall of his own volition he fell and was knocked unconscious (the shower lacked rails or safety bars). Furgess sued seeking relief, including compensatory damages under the ADA and Section 504 of the RA.

The state argued that a shower was not a program, service, or activity and that the inmate was not denied showers because of his disability but because of his transfer to the RHU. The district court agreed with the DOC and dismissed the claim. The court of appeals reversed.

The court of appeals first noted that Section 504 of the RA defines a "program or activity" quite broadly to include "*all* of the operations of" a state instrumentality. The Third Circuit had interpreted the term broadly and while the ADA did not define "services, programs, or activities," both Congress and Third Circuit had recognized that Title II of the ADA provides at least the same degree of protection as Section 504 of the RA. A prison's provision of showers to inmates fits within this expansive definition of a "service, program, or activity" under Title II, and "program or activity" The court also noted that the Department of Justice guidance on Title II regulations explicitly refers to a prison's provision of hygiene as being covered by the ADA. Corrections systems are unique facilities that inmates cannot leave, so prisons must address the needs of inmates with disabilities by providing "accessible toilet and shower facilities, devices such as a bed transfer or a shower chair, and assistance with hygiene methods for prisoners with physical disabilities." 28 C.F.R. pt. 35, App. A, at 663 (2017).

The court of appeals also found the state's argument that Furgess's inability to shower was because of his misconduct, which justified his placement in the RHU, was unavailing.

> But the reason why Furgess was housed in the RHU is irrelevant. A prisoner's misconduct does not strip him of his right to reasonable accommodations, and a prison's obligation to comply with the ADA and the RA does not disappear when inmates are placed in a segregated housing unit, regardless of the reason for which they are housed there. As the ADA's regulations make clear, the PDOC's failure to equip the RHU with accessible showers does not excuse the prison from its duty to reasonably accommodate prisoners with disabilities.

The court of appeals concluded that Furgess had established that he was denied a shower because of his disability and that the state was "deliberately indifferent" in failing to provide a handicapped-accessible shower.

Title II of the ADA does not apply to private prison corporations. In *Edison v. Douberly*, 604 F.3d 1307(11th Cir. 2010), a Florida state prison inmate (Edison) sued several employees (in their official capacities) of GEO Care Group, Inc. GEO is a private prison corporation. Edison claimed the defendants discriminated against him because of his disabilities, in violation of the ADA, Title II.

Finding that GEO was not a public entity, the district court held the ADA did not apply and granted summary judgment to the defendants. The appeals court affirmed. That court looked at the statutory language (42 U.S.C. § 12131), which defines public entity as "an instrumentality of a State."

> We ... have long recognized that our authority to interpret statutory language is constrained by the plain meaning of the statutory language in the context of the entire statute ... We have affirmed many times that we do not look at one word or term in isolation but rather look to the entire statute and its context .... Our job ... is to interpret the ADA's use of the words "instrumentality of a State" in a manner consistent with their plain meaning and context ... [T]he term "instrumentality of a State" refers to governmental units or units created by them.[15]

On a final note about the ADA and the RA. Courts have held that while a prisoner may seek money damages from a correctional entity, a county, or state, the language of the statutes does not allow for the award of money damages from individual government employees. *Alsbrook v. City of Maumelle*, 184 F.3d 999 (8th Cir. 1999) *en banc*

▶ Other Federal Statutory Laws

This section discusses three recently enacted federal statutes that may have a considerable future impact on corrections. It is important for correctional officials to be aware of the requirements of each statute and to take appropriate action to address those requirements. Whenever possible, it also is valuable for correctional officials to review proposed legislative enactments, both to assess the impact of the legislation on the correctional organization, and, where appropriate, to make recommendations on revising the legislation.

Prison Rape Elimination Act of 2003

Public Law 108-79, the Prison Rape Elimination Act (PREA) of 2003, is codified at 42 U.S.C. §§ 15601-15609. The law's introductory language says the PREA is "[t]o provide for the analysis of the incidence and effects of prison rape in Federal, State, and local institutions and to provide information, resources, recommendations, and funding to protect individuals from prison rape." Among the Act's nine cited purposes are having each prison system make the prevention of prison rape a top priority; putting in place national standards for the detection, prevention, reduction, and punishment of prison rape; and protecting federal, state, and local prisoners' Eighth Amendment rights.

Since 2003, the Bureau of Justice Statistics has collected data on the incidence and prevalence of sexual assault within correctional facilities. The last report, *Sexual Victimization Reported by Adult Correctional Authorities, 2012-15,* was released in 2018.[16] In addition, the National Prison Rape Elimination Commission was established and, as set forth in the public law, given the responsibility to develop national standards. The Commission's approach included public hearings, expert committees, a needs assessment that involved site visits to diverse correctional facilities, and a thorough review of the relevant literature. In 2009, the commission released its report, the "National Prison Rape Elimination Commission Report." On March 10, 2010, the United States Department of Justice published in the Federal Register an advance notice of proposed rulemaking (ANPRM) to invite public comment on the commission's proposed national standards and to solicit information useful to the department in publishing a final rule. On February 3, 2011, the department published its proposed rules on the National Standards to Prevent, Detect, and Respond to Prison Rape. This document proposes a set of national standards and provides responses to the approximately 650 public comments received on the ANPRM.[17] The final rules were published on June 20, 2012.[18]

The commission's 2009 Report refers to the Eighth Amendment's prohibition against cruel and unusual punishment, describing it as "a ban that requires corrections staff to take reasonable steps to protect individuals in their custody from sexual abuse whenever the threat is known or should have been apparent." It may well be that courts, in considering inmate allegations of cruel and unusual punishment under the Eighth Amendment, may look to these standards for guidance on sexual assaults in prison.

Adam Walsh Child Protection and Safety Act of 2006

The introductory language of the Adam Walsh Child Protection and Safety Act of 2006 (AWA, Public Law 109-248) says the Act is "[t]o protect children from sexual exploitation and violent crime, to prevent child abuse and child pornography, to promote Internet safety, and to honor the memory of Adam Walsh and other child victims." Several provisions of the AWA impact on corrections. Title I, codified at 42 U.S.C. 16901 et seq., requires sex offender registration. For the initial registration, a sex offender is required to register "before completing a sentence of imprisonment with respect to the offense giving rise to the registration requirement." An appropriate official is required to notify the sex offender of the registration requirement and to ensure that the registration occurs. The sex offender is expected to provide specific information for inclusion in the registry: name and social security number, residence, employment, school, and vehicle identification, as well as other information required by the U.S. Attorney General. The jurisdiction where the sex offender registers is to provide additional information, for example, a physical description of the offender, current photo, criminal history, and DNA sample. The AWA also amends 18 U.S.C. § 3621, adding a new subsection (f), requiring the Bureau of Prisons to establish sex offender management programs and residential sex offender treatment programs.

The AWA also provides for civil commitment programs for sexually dangerous persons. For example, 42 U.S.C. § 16971 provides for the U.S. Attorney General to make "grants to jurisdictions [defined in the Act to include states, the District of Columbia, Guam, and several other areas] for the purpose of establishing, enhancing, or operating effective civil commitment programs for sexually dangerous persons." The Act also provides, in 18 U.S.C. § 4248, for the civil commitment of a sexually dangerous person in federal custody. The term "sexually dangerous person" is defined in 18 U.S.C. § 4247(a)(5) as "a person who has engaged or attempted to engage in sexually violent conduct or child molestation and who is sexually dangerous to others."[19]

The Supreme Court has upheld the constitutionality of the civil commitment of a sexually dangerous person, most recently in *U.S. v. Comstock,* 560 U.S. (2010), ruling that enactment of 18 U.S.C. § 4248 did not exceed Congress' authority under the necessary and proper clause of the Constitution.

Second Chance Act of 2007

The Second Chance Act of 2007 (Public Law 110-199), codified primarily in 42 U.S.C. §§ 17501-17555, impacts both state and federal governments. The law's introductory language identifies six purposes: (1) to reduce criminal recidivism, to increase public safety, and to help "States, local units of government, and Indian Tribes [to] better address the growing problem of criminal offenders who return to their communities and commit new crimes"; (2) to rebuild offender family ties, with the objective of promoting stable families and communities; (3) to encourage and expand evidence-based programs that strengthen public safety and reduce recidivism; (4) to protect the public and promote law-abiding behavior by providing offenders with necessary services without conferring luxuries or privileges on those offenders; (5) to provide sufficient transitional services to assist offenders in establishing and maintaining a law-abiding life; and (6) to provide confined offenders with educational, literacy, vocational, and job placement services to help in their community reentry. The act provides for grants to be made to various entities, including states and units of local government.

From a specific legislative aspect, the act amends Title 18 U.S.C. Section 4042—Duties of Bureau of Prisons. The amended section specifically requires the Bureau of Prisons to establish both prerelease planning procedures—for example, helping offenders apply for federal and state benefits upon release, and securing such identification and benefits before release—and establishing reentry planning procedures to provide federal inmates with information in seven specific areas: health and nutrition; employment; literacy and education; personal finance and consumer skills; community resources; personal growth and development; and release requirements and procedures. While the act specifically states that none of its provisions are to be taken as creating any right or entitlement to assistance or services, the provisions do formally establish legally mandated requirements.

First Step Act of 2018

The First Step Act of 2018 (P.L. 115-391) was signed into law by President Trump on December 21, 2018. The act has three major components: (1) correctional reform via the establishment of a risk and needs assessment system at the Bureau of Prisons (BOP), (2) sentencing reform via changes to penalties for some federal offenses, and (3) the reauthorization of the Second Chance Act of 2007 (P.L. 110-199).

The Act required the Bureau of Prisons to develop a risk and needs assessment system to assess the recidivism risk of all federal prisoners and to place prisoners in programs and productive activities to reduce the recidivism risk. To encourage participation in risk-reducing programming, offenders who completed recidivism-reducing programs could qualify for additional credits toward release such as home confinement and Residential Reentry Centers. Persons convicted of certain violent offenses were prohibited from receiving such incentives.

The sentencing reform portions addressed issues related to mandatory minimums for some drug offenses and expanded a court's ability to utilize the so-called safety valve provision to sentence low-risk offenders to less-than-mandatory minimum sentences. Certain aspects of the Fair Sentencing Act of 2010, which reduced disparities between sentences for crack and powder cocaine were made retroactive to allow offenders to seek court modification of their pre-Fair Sentencing Act sentences to obtain a new sentence using the provisions of the Fair Sentencing Act.

The Act also reauthorized appropriations for, and expanded the scope of, some grant programs under the Second Chance Act of 2007 (P.L. 110-199), including the Offender Reentry Substance Abuse and Criminal Justice Collaboration Program, the Adult and Juvenile State and Local Offender Demonstration Program, Grants for Family-Based Substance Abuse Treatment, Careers Training Demonstration Grants, and the Community-Based Mentoring and Transitional Service Grants to Nonprofit Organizations Program. Another provision addressed early release for elderly and terminally ill offenders, which is discussed in more detail in Chapter 15 on Inmate Healthcare.

Also included in the First Step Act were other miscellaneous provisions including requiring the BOP to assist inmates when applying for identification documents and other social service programs prior to release; prohibiting, in most cases, shackling of pregnant female offenders; and revising the award of good conduct time (54 days per year) from being calculated on the time served to the time imposed in the sentence.

Summary

- Employment laws for a corrections agency are set by the statutes and policies of the jurisdiction (federal, state, or local) where that agency operates.
- The training of corrections staff is a vital part of maintaining a quality workforce. In addition, there are legal requirements for providing adequate training to staff members in the essentials of their work and especially in those aspects of their jobs directly affecting offenders and their family and friends who have dealings with them while they are in the corrections programs.
- Correctional agencies have standards of employee conduct setting out the expectations for its employees, including the identification of prohibited conduct. An employee may be held accountable, including job

termination, for his off-duty actions that bring the mission of the employer and the professionalism of its staff into serious disrepute (*City of San Diego v. Roe*).

■ Employees whose duties may require them to report to work before the start of their shift are entitled to compensation for walking time that occurs after the beginning of the employee's first principal activity and before the end of the employee's last principal activity (*IBP, Inc. v. Alvarez*).

■ The Federal Civil Rights Act (Title VII) mandates that there be no discrimination in employment practices based on any individual's race, color, religion, sex, or national origin.

■ The Supreme Court, in the case of *Dothard v. Rawlinson,* ruled that the minimum height and weight requirements set for hiring correctional counselors discriminated against female applicants under Title VII. Also, Alabama had not shown that those requirements were necessary for the performance of those jobs, based on strength requirements, which is what state officials had argued. However, the state prevailed because, under Title VII standards, the evidence did show a bona fide occupational qualification, requiring male staff to perform these jobs. This was because the jobs were in a maximum security penitentiary that was understaffed, was beset by violent behavior on the part of inmates, many of whom were sex offenders, all of which justified the males-only hiring policy for the safety of all concerned.

■ Appeals courts have held that correctional agencies may be held liable under Title VII for uncorrected inmate harassment of agency employees when such conduct creates a hostile work environment.

■ Common law tort claims may be brought against governments if there is statutory permission to do so (if the legislature in that jurisdiction has waived its sovereign immunity to be sued). The most frequent tort claims made by inmates are for lost or damaged property, for injuries from assaults, and for medical malpractice. If the government is shown to be liable because of the negligent actions of its employees or agents, payment awards to the injured party are made by the government (not by the individuals who were negligent). This occurs provided that the employee is acting within the scope of her employment.

■ Congress may limit the remedy that persons may seek against particular individuals under certain circumstances. In *Hui v. Castaneda,* the Court held that Congress had made the Federal Tort Claims Act the exclusive remedy to be used for injury caused by the actions of a U.S. Public Health Services officer.

■ The Americans with Disabilities Act of 1990 (ADA) prohibits discrimination against disabled individuals. In 2010, the ADA was revised, including the issuance of the 2010 ADA Standards for Accessible Design, parts of which specifically focus on corrections. The Act prohibits discrimination against disabled persons in employment and inmate programs and services. Regarding employment, reasonable steps must be taken to accommodate an applicant or employee who is a qualified individual with a disability. However, accommodations need not be made if to do so would create an undue hardship. For inmates, corrections officials must similarly take reasonable steps to include persons with disabilities in the programs and services that are provided to other inmates. The goal is always to "mainstream" inmates with disabilities, unless doing so would be significantly difficult or expensive, for example, an undue financial or administrative burden. The Supreme Court, in the case of *Pennsylvania Department of Corrections v. Yeskey,* ruled that the ADA applies to state prisons. In *United States v. Georgia,* the Supreme Court ruled that sovereign immunity does not prevent a state prison inmate from seeking money damages directly from the state for alleged violations of Title II of the ADA.

■ In recent years, several other federal statutes have been enacted with provisions that have, or are likely to have, an effect on correctional administration (Prison Rape Elimination Act of 2003; Adam Walsh Child Protection and Safety Act of 2006; the Second Chance Act of 2007) and the First Step Act of 2018.

Thinking About It

In March 2012, Mathew Neisler was working in a Wisconsin state prison in the prison kitchen. An improperly loaded cart broke his prosthetic leg and caused a cut on the leg above where the prosthetic attached. After trying to work for several weeks, he sought to be relieved from duties due to pain from the injury. He was given an exemption from working. While deemed medically unable to work, he received his usual compensation (forty-two cents an hour) and was not given a different work assignment. In October, after he was still unable to perform his kitchen duties the food service supervisor terminated his employment due to his inability to perform work-related duties. Termination ended his compensation and his ability not to work at another work assignment. The inmate sought administrative relief and he received additional compensation equal to the money he would have received for his kitchen job until he would have been transferred to a new work assignment by DOC policy. Neisler sued the DOC alleging that he had been fired because of a disability in violation of Title II of the ADA. He asked for $50,000 in monetary damages. The state defendants moved for summary judgment, asserting that Neisler is not entitled to pursue an employment-discrimination claim under Title II, that the state's sovereign immunity bars him from suing state officials for monetary damages, and the state had a rational basis for terminating his employment in the kitchen—he was deemed too sick to work.

How should the court rule? *Neisler v. Tuckwell*, 807 F.3d 225 (7th Cir. 2015).

Key Terms

boot camp
prima facie

Endnotes

1. In *Canton,* the Court hypothesized that a single incident, under a few circumstances, could be characterized as "deliberate indifference." As an example, the Court gave a situation where a city fails to train its officers in the constitutional use of deadly force, holding that the "obvious need" to provide such training, and the subsequent failure to do so, could be seen as deliberate indifference. The narrowness of this situation may be illustrated by *Connick v. Thompson,* 563 U.S. 51 (2011). In *Connick,* the Supreme Court considered whether "a district attorney's office may be held liable under § 1983 for failure to train based on a single *Brady* violation." [*Brady* requires the state to provide the defense with information in possession of the state that is favorable to the accused.] Both the district and appeals court found "a pattern of violations is not necessary to prove deliberate indifference when the need for training is 'so obvious.'" In reversing the lower courts, the Supreme Court in *Connick* held that a pattern of violations would need to be shown. In distinguishing a "single incident" from a "pattern," the Court concluded: "Failure to train prosecutors in their *Brady* obligations does not fall within the narrow range of *Canton's* hypothesized single-incident liability. The obvious need for specific legal training that was present in the *Canton* scenario is absent here. Armed police must sometimes make split-second decisions with life-or-death consequences. There is no reason to assume that police academy applicants are familiar with the constitutional constraints on the use of deadly force. And, in the absence of training, there is no way for novice officers to obtain the legal knowledge they require. Under those circumstances, there is an obvious need for some form of training. In stark contrast, "Attorneys are trained in the law and equipped with the tools to interpret and apply legal principles, understand constitutional limits, and exercise legal judgment.'"
2. Administrative Regulation 1450-01. *Code of Conduct.* Colorado Department of Corrections. Effective Date September 1, 2019. Available at https://drive.google.com/file/d/1T3ffeS1gaj-3qrxXACEXMWe7okOCV1qQ/view. Accessed 27 April 2020.
3. Policy 103.220. *Personal Conduct of Employees.* Minnesota Department of Corrections. Effective Date August 21, 2018. Available at http://www.doc.state.mn.us/DocPolicy2/html/DPW_Display_TOC.asp?Opt=103.220.htm. Accessed 27 April 2020.
4. See endnote 3.
5. For example, in December, 2019, a former correctional officer was sentenced to 30 months in federal prison after pleading guilty to charges of conspiracy to permit escape, conspiracy to bribe public officials, permitting escape, and public official accepting a bribe. While employed at the facility, the officer accepted bribes from inmates in the form of cash, prescription medication, and other items. In exchange, the officer allowed inmates to leave the prison grounds without permission from the Warden, to have sexual relations with their girlfriends, wives, and other female acquaintances on prison grounds and at nearby hotels, and to smuggle contraband into the prison, including cellular telephones, controlled substances, and alcohol. In a statement issued by the U.S. Attorney: "Correctional Officers are entrusted to keep the prison and inmates at the facility safe," . . . "[The employee] not only violated the public's trust for his own selfish greed, but also threatened the safety of prison employees, inmates, and the Terre Haute community."
News Release. *Corrupt Terre Haute Federal Correctional Officer Sentenced to 30 Months in Federal Prison.* U.S. Attorney's Office, Southern District of Indiana, December 5, 2019. Available at https://www.justice.gov/usao-sdin/pr/corrupt-terre-haute-federal-correctional-officer-sentenced-30-months-federal-prison. Accessed 27 April 2020.
6. In a prison context, there are occasional news stories about a correctional officer being terminated for posing nude in a magazine. The question that might be litigated in such cases is whether the employee's behavior brings, as stated in *Roe,* the "mission of the employer and the professionalism of its officers into serious disrepute."
7. Federal Labor Relations Authority. *United States Department of Justice, Federal Bureau of Prisons, United States Penitentiary, Marion, Illinois (Agency) and American Federation of Government Employees, Local 2343, Council of Prison Locals, Council 33, (Union).* 61 FLRA 154 September 13, 2006. Available at https://www.flra.gov/decisions/v61/61-154.html. It is worth noting that the arbitrator determined that staff in some departments, for example, food service and unit management, largely adhered to their work shifts and were not entitled to overtime pay.
8. Exceptions to decisions by an arbitrator are submitted to the Federal Labor Relations Authority (the Authority), which is a three-person panel whose primary responsibility under the FLSA is to "resolve exceptions to arbitration awards that arise out of grievances filed by an employee, union, or agency." United States Department of Justice, Federal Bureau of Prisons, Federal Correctional Institution, Bastrop, Texas (Agency) and American Federation of Government Employees, Local 3828 (Union). 70 FLRA No. 119 (2016). Available at https://www.flra.gov/decisions/v70/70-119.html. Accessed April 28, 2020.
9. Bureau of Labor Statistics, *Data USA.* Bailiffs, Correctional Officers and Jailers. Available at https://datausa.io/profile/soc/bailiffs-correctional-officers-jailers. Accessed April 28, 2020. For earlier data on the number of females and males working in opposite gender correctional facilities, see Stephan, J. *Census of State and Federal Correctional Facilities, 2005.* Page 4. (Washington, DC: Bureau of

Justice Statistics, U.S. Department of Justice, 2008). This report states that an estimated 445,000 employees worked in state and federal correctional institutions at the close of 2005.

10. 2010 Directory: Adult and Juvenile Correctional Departments, Institutions, Agencies, and Probation and Parole Authorities. (71st Ed.) *Adult Correctional Security Staff by Gender Supervision, Ratio to Inmates, Turnover Rate, and Vacant Positions on September 30, 2009.* Alexandria, VA: American Correctional Association, 2010.

11. *State Sovereign Immunity and Tort Liability.* National Conference of State Legislatures. August 27, 2010. Available at https://www.ncsl.org/research/transportation/state-sovereign-immunity-and-tort-liability.aspx. Accessed April 28, 2020.

12. Nondiscrimination on the Basis of Disability in State and Local Government Services, 75 Fed. Reg. 56164 (September 15, 2010) (to be codified at 28 CFR Part 35). The quoted material in this section is found on pages 56218–56219. This final rule document is a good resource for those interested in administrative law. Among the areas covered are the department's advance notice of proposed rulemaking; notice of proposed rulemaking; public comments, and the response to these; and the final rule.

13. The *Armstrong* decision also discussed several other areas. For example, the court rejected the state's contention that the state's arrangements were for the incarceration of persons, and not to provide aid, benefit, or service. The court held that the state's arrangements with counties were not only to confine, but to provide such persons with various positive opportunities, citing examples of treatment programs, the use of bathing facilities, and communication. The court also rejected the state's claim that the state was not being given the proper deference (*Turner v. Safley,* 482 U.S. 78 (1987)), that the ordered plan required parolees to be removed from the county jails and sent to California prisons when a jail showed a pattern of non-ADA compliance. The court disagreed, noting that the order does not require placement in a state prison, only that the state either obtain an accommodation within that facility or move the inmate to an appropriate location, which could either be a California facility or a different county jail that can provide the appropriate accommodations.

14. *Americans with Disabilities Act—Questions and Answers.* Washington, DC: U.S. Equal Employment Opportunity Commission and United States Department of Justice, Civil Rights Division. May 2002, last updated November 14, 2008. Accessed November 12, 2020. from https://www.ada.gov/employmt.htm

15. In *Edison,* the appeals court held that Title II (Public Services) of the ADA does not apply to private prison corporations. It is conceivable that, at some future time, an inmate may file similar litigation but claim that the violation occurred under the ADA, Title III (Public Accommodations and Services Operated by Private Entities). Also to be noted is that the language of 28 CFR § 35.152(a), which is effective as of March of 2011, specifically says section 35.152 applies to "public entities that are responsible for the operation or management of adult and juvenile justice jails, detention and correctional facilities, and community correctional facilities, either directly or through contractual, licensing, or other arrangements with public or private entities, in whole or in part, including private correctional facilities." Subpart (b) of this section is the one that covers *"Discrimination prohibited."*

16. *Sexual Victimization Reported by Adult Correctional Authorities, 2012-15.* Bureau of Justice Statistics. Washington, D.C. July 2018. Available at https://www.bjs.gov/content/pub/pdf/svraca1215.pdf . Accessed 01 May 2020.

17. National Standards to Prevent, Detect, and Respond to Prison Rape, 76 Fed. Reg. 6248 (February 3, 2011) (to be codified at 28 CFR Part 115).

18. National Standards to Prevent, Detect, and Respond to Prison Rape; Final Rule. 28 CFR Part 115. Available at https://www.govinfo.gov/content/pkg/CFR-2019-title28-vol2/xml/CFR-2019-title28-vol2-part115.xml

19. The Federal Bureau of Prisons identifies sex offenders as a vulnerable population in a prison setting. Consistent with the Adam Walsh Act, the BOP has a number of Sex Offender Management Programs (SOMPs) located at various institutions. https://www.bop.gov/inmates/custody_and_care/sex_offenders.jsp

20. In an interesting twist to *Yeskey* (boot camp programs), discussed in the ADA section, the Second Chance Act authorizes a pilot program whereby an inmate who meets certain requirements, one of which is being at least age 65, may be released from a Bureau of Prisons facility and placed on home detention until expiration of the inmate's prison term. See 42 U.S.C. § 17541(g).

CHAPTER 20

Jails

Whether it be called a jail, a prison, or a custodial center, the purpose of the facility is to detain. Loss of freedom of choice and privacy are inherent incidents of confinement in such a facility.

U.S. Supreme Court, *Bell v. Wolfish*

CHAPTER OUTLINE

- Constitutional Rights of Jail Inmates: *Bell v. Wolfish*
- Constitutional Issues in Jails
  - Visiting
  - Inmate Suicides
  - Searches
  - Legal Access
  - Personal Injury
- Using Excessive Force
- Conditions of Confinement
- Municipal Liability
- Other Jail Issues and Cases
- Removing the Sheriff from Running the Jail

Jails are designed primarily to function as holding places for those who are held awaiting trial (those who are in custody, not having been released on bail or on recognizance). Because this is the primary function of jails, they are located as close as is feasible to the court(s) where detainees will be taken for trial. (In early days, jails were often built inside the county or city courthouse or just across the street. This is still the case in many jurisdictions, and even new jails are built as close to the courthouse as possible.) Jails also hold some persons who are serving sentences.

The security concerns for jails, because they may be required to hold any level and type of prisoner, are similar to those for prisons. The Supreme Court affirmed this in *Bell v. Wolfish:*

> There must be a "mutual accommodation between institutional needs and objectives and the provisions of the Constitution that are of general application." This principle applies equally to pretrial

detainees and convicted prisoners. A detainee simply does not possess the full range of freedoms of an unincarcerated individual …. [Maintaining institutional security and preserving internal order and discipline are essential goals that may require limitation or retraction of the retained constitutional rights of both convicted prisoners and pretrial detainees … There is no basis for concluding that pretrial detainees pose any lesser security risk than convicted inmates. Indeed, it may be that in certain circumstances they present a greater risk to jail security and order.

Jail administrators must be aware of the court holdings and the constitutional and legal standards for both pretrial detainees and sentenced inmates, because both kinds of inmates are confined in jails. This chapter introduces the reader to the judicial holdings and legal standards that apply to jails, focusing on those that are peculiar to the main jail population: pretrial detainees.

▶ Constitutional Rights of Jail Inmates: *Bell v. Wolfish*

In *Bell v. Wolfish,* 441 U.S. 520 (1979), the Supreme Court provided the constitutional standards that govern the status of pretrial detainees, the major class of prisoners in jails. It is important to distinguish the rights of unconvicted detainees from those of convicted persons. The previous chapters contained discussions related to the legal rights of all prisoners. This chapter will focus on unique legal aspects of the confining persons not yet convicted of criminal offenses.

As first announced in the *Bell* case, it is the Due Process clauses of the Fifth Amendment (for persons in federal custody) and the Fourteenth Amendment (for persons in state custody) that protect the pretrial detainee. Because detainees have not been convicted, they may not be punished. Under due process, detainees may not be deprived of their liberty without due process of law. Therefore, the legal inquiry is whether the detainee has been punished. If there are challenges to conditions in a jail, the question is whether those conditions amount to punishment. The other constitutional protections retained by jail inmates will be examined later. How do courts assess whether the inmate is being punished in the jail? The Supreme Court did not leave it to the lower courts to decide what amounted to punishment; it provided guidance on how to test the conditions in order to determine whether they are punishment. The test is this: Was the action taken, was the restriction imposed, or were the conditions created for the purpose of punishment, or, on the other side, was there a valid governmental purpose that supported the conditions?

[I]f a particular condition or restriction of pretrial detention is reasonably related to a legitimate governmental objective, it does not, without more, amount to "punishment."

The government's objective in running a jail is usually to maintain security and order. If the conditions or restrictions that are complained about are necessary to maintain security and order, there has not been unconstitutional punishment.

Based on these standards and measurements in assessing conditions at the federal jail in New York City, the Supreme Court in *Bell* concluded that crowding, including the double-bunking of inmates in single cells and even the bunking of inmates in recreation areas and corridors, did not amount to punishment.

In addition, as the Supreme Court indicated in *Bell,* factors other than just the number of inmates and the square footage in the cells are important. It also is important to look at such things as how long inmates are held at the jail, how much time they have to spend in their cells each day, whether there are activities for them outside of their cells, and whether the large number of inmates adversely affects the delivery of other important services, such as food, clothing, sanitation, and health care. It is also important to look at whether the crowded conditions are just temporary or long term and, if the latter is true, whether jail authorities (and local legislative and judicial authorities) are making plans to alleviate the crowded conditions.

From *Bell v. Wolfish,* we also know that jail inmates are protected when other rights, protected under specific constitutional provisions, are implicated. For example, inmates in *Bell v. Wolfish* complained of a rule at the jail that specified that they could only order books and magazines from the publisher (books could not be sent in by family or friends). This raised a First Amendment question. The Supreme Court upheld the jail's publisher-only rule, saying that it was reasonably related to a security concern. Thus, the test used to support a restriction on First Amendment activities is virtually the same as that used to show no due process violation: whether the government had a legitimate, reasonable interest in protecting the security and order of the jail.

The same kind of justification for governmental restrictions was found in *Bell* with respect to two search issues: searching the living quarters of inmates (the exact question was whether the inmate had the right to be present during the search of his quarters) and conducting visual strip searches after contact visiting. The Fourth Amendment forbids unreasonable searches. The Supreme Court found that there were valid security reasons for both of these search procedures (not allowing the inmates to be present during the searches of their cells and conducting the body cavity searches after visiting), so they were, in the jail context, reasonable. All issues in *Bell* were decided on the grounds that the government's actions were reasonable and necessary under the circumstances, because they were tied to the maintenance of security and order in the facility. It was the technical, legal analyses under different provisions of the Constitution that differed. The advice to jail administrators is clear: be certain that any regulations and practices used at the jail, particularly when they are in areas where constitutional rights might be claimed, are justifiable under concerns about keeping security and order at the facility.

Jails do not only hold pretrial detainees. The converse is also true—sometimes correctional facilities that mainly house convicted offenders will also house, for a number of reasons, pretrial detainees. The holdings of *Bell v. Wolfish* deal with detainees at the federal jail, those who were not yet convicted. But the jail in *Bell* held other inmates, as most jails do. There are usually persons at a jail who are serving short sentences. It just makes good sense, for economic and practical reasons, to keep short-term prisoners at a jail rather than transport them to a prison or other correctional institution. The length of time for holding those serving short-term sentences differs; in some places, it is all sentences of a year or less, six months or fewer, or some other time frame. But it is virtually a universal rule that jails will keep such short-term prisoners. Exceptions can be made for prisoners who are disruptive, those who pose an escape risk, or those who otherwise need to be moved to a different facility.

Exceptions have also been made in the opposite direction: because of crowding in prisons, prisoners who would otherwise be sent to a prison must be held in the local jails, often as required in court orders, until there is room for them at the prison. Local jails also provide contract boarding for sentenced state prisoners. (At mid-year 2018, local jails housed 248,500 convicted prisoners.)[1] This, of course, has caused jail populations to swell, adding to the existing pressures. Jails also hold other sentenced prisoners—those who have been returned to the local court to be tried on additional charges or to testify in the cases of other persons; those who have challenged their convictions by appeal or by collateral attack and who are ordered back by the local court to consult with counsel or to be present for a hearing; and, those who have been arrested as parole or probation violators and are being held locally, awaiting revocation hearings.

Finally, jail administrators may want to keep a core of sentenced inmates (sometimes called a "cadre") for maintenance and other work at the jail. These inmates may be serving a longer sentence than the ordinary jail term of a year or less; they may have volunteered to stay at the jail, rather than go to a state prison, in order to remain closer to home or, in some cases, even to have better living conditions.

In mid-year 2018, there were 745,200 738,400 inmates confined in local jails. See **FIGURE 20-1**, Jail Population Data. Reflecting the transient nature of jails, this one-day population snapshot was a relatively small percentage of all admissions (an estimated 10.6 million) over the 12-month period ending June 30, 2018. Approximately 34% of those confined were either sentenced offenders, or convicted offenders, awaiting sentencing. At midyear 2018, the jail population was 85% male, 50% white and the average stay for all jail inmates was 25 days (although many people booked into local jails spend less than 24 hours). Jails employ 221,600 employees, with 79% of that number working as correctional officers.[2]

The constitutional rights of those who are convicted and being held in the local jail are the same as those for prisoners held in prisons or correctional institutions. Therefore, the standards discussed elsewhere in the text relating to inmate rights in all kinds of prison situations apply to jails, unless the jailer can show that local conditions (particularly related to security) require different considerations. In *Bell,* the Supreme Court found that the issues of mail (incoming publications and the receipt of packages) and searches (cell searches and strip searches) were all governed by the same concerns of security and order. For this reason, the government's policies and practices regarding convicted and sentenced prisoners were valid, just as they were for the pretrial detainees.

Digitalization and electronic communications are being used in jails to reduce the influx of contraband and to better promote community ties with inmate friends and relatives. The chapter on inmate mail reviewed inmate mail policies, which prohibited letters and approved only postcards.[3] In addition to these changes, some jails have begun offering eMessaging as a way to maintain community connections. In **BOX 20-1**, the Fort Bend County (Texas) Jail eMessaging system is described:

In the last decade, more jails and prisons have implemented postcard only correspondence rules.[4]

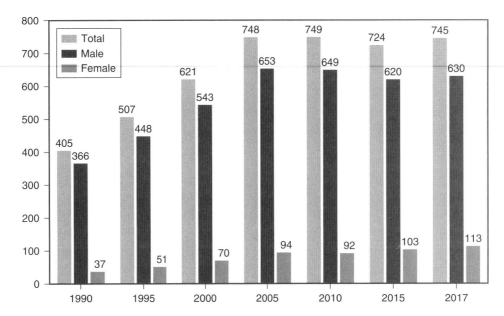

FIGURE 20-1 Jail Population Data (in thousands).

Data from Zeng, Z. Jail Inmates in 2017. (Washington, DC: Bureau of Justice Statistics, U.S. Department of Justice, April 2019, Table 2. Available: https://www.bjs.gov/content/pub/pdf/ji17.pdf. Accessed 11 February 2020.

BOX 20-1   Mail Options and Rules for Inmates at the Fort Bend County Jail

eMessaging is available with inmates at the Fort Bend County Sheriff's Office. eMessaging allows two-way communication with your friend or family member. At this time, the eMessaging service does not allow attachments, so no pictures can be attached to the message. All eMessages sent and received are subject to being read by law enforcement staff. The purchase price for an eMessage includes one free reply from the inmate. After one successful eMessage between an eMessage user and an inmate, the inmate can purchase eMessages from his or her account to initiate messages to the approved eMessage user.

Inmate Mail

All inmate mail must contain the sender's full name and complete return address, the inmate's full name (the name he or she is booked into jail under), and the inmate's jail identification number. If incoming mail does not have this information on it, it will be returned to the sender. Letters with no return address or improper addresses will be sent to the U.S. Post Office for final disposition.

Mailing Address for Standard Inmate Mail:
Fort Bend County Sheriff's Office
Inmate Full Name, Full Jail ID#
1410 Richmond Parkway
Richmond, TX 77469

All inmate mail is inspected upon receipt by the Fort Bend County Sheriff's Office.

Incoming mail with perfume, fluids of any kind (to include lipstick), make-up, and other substances may be returned to the sender.

Fort Bend County Sheriff's Office Inmate Services, run by our Chaplain Ministry, accepts paperback books and magazines as donations. Hardbound books are not permitted. All books and magazines become property of the Fort Bend County Sheriff's Office Inmate Services upon receipt and will be distributed to the intended inmates after being vetted for appropriate images and other content.

Books and magazines must be delivered by the United States Postal Service (USPS) and must be sent to the following address:

Fort Bend County Sheriff's Office
Inmate Full Name, Full Jail ID#
Attn: Inmate Books/Magazines
1410 Richmond Parkway
Richmond, Texas 77469

If mail is sent "Signature Required" or if a signature is required at delivery, the package will be returned to sender.

The Fort Bend County Sheriff's Office is not responsible for any lost, damaged, or destroyed publications.

The following items may NOT be sent to inmates. Unauthorized items received through the mail will be considered contraband and the entire package may be confiscated and disposed or returned to sender. Unauthorized items will not be stored in the facility's property room.

- Musical greeting cards
- Blank envelopes, writing paper, drawing paper, notepads, greeting cards, etc.
- Pens, pencils, markers, other writing instruments
- Obscene pictures (Pictures depicting FULL or PARTIAL nudity)
- Packages
- Stickers
- Cash
- Food or food items
- Contraband
- Stamps
- Computer-generated materials downloaded from the Internet
- Medicine

Photographs will only be accepted if they are deemed not offensive; are not of a sexual nature; do not contain gang references; are completely unaltered; and do not display guns, drugs, or drug paraphernalia. Photographs shall not be larger than 8" x 10."

Legal paperwork from attorneys may be received, but the front of the envelope must be marked "Legal Mail-Open only in the presence of the inmate."

Fort Bend County, Texas Detention Services. Accessed 20 February 2020.
https://www.fortbendcountytx.gov/government/departments/administration-of-justice/sheriff-s-office/bureaus-divisions/detention-division/emessaging-and-inmate-mail.

▶ Constitutional Issues in Jails

This section analyzes other court rulings related to constitutional issues in a jail context.

Visiting

Block v. Rutherford, 468 U.S. 576 (1984), raised the question of whether the sheriff of the Los Angeles County Jail could restrict pretrial detainees to noncontact visiting. The Supreme Court (reversing the lower courts) held that he could. The Court said that, because there was a legitimate government objective that was being pursued (the prevention of the introduction of contraband), the prohibition of contact visits was permissible. The Court specifically held that contact visits were not constitutionally required.

Many jails in the United States have prohibited contact visits and permit only noncontact visiting in glass partitioned areas or using video visiting either from a video visitation station at the correctional facility or from a remote location using a computer. In **BOX 20-2**, the Lake County, Illinois, visitation policy is set forth.[5]

Houchins v. KQED, Inc., 483 U.S. 1 (1978), involved a request by a television station to visit and film an area of the county jail where an inmate had recently committed suicide. The Supreme Court restated its holding in the prison cases in which media representatives had requested individual interviews (*Pell v. Procunier*, 417 U.S. 817 (1974), and *Saxbe v. Washington Post*, 417 U.S. 843 (1974)). The Court held that the media did not have any right of access to the jail under the First Amendment. The sheriff was not required to give the media access to the jail because it was an area that was not generally open to the public, and the media has no more right of access to such areas (to prisons or to jails) than the general public.

Grabowski v. Jackson County Public Defenders Office, 47 F.3d 1386 (5th Cir. 1995), dealt with Grabowski's challenges to his conviction and sentence. A portion of his challenges related to jail conditions. Grabowski claimed that Section 1983 violations occurred when his visiting privileges with his girlfriend were revoked and when he was denied telephone and recreation privileges while he was a pretrial detainee. At the request of the public defender, Grabowski had been granted in-house visits with his girlfriend, who was also an inmate at the jail. His privileges were revoked when Grabowski had a shouting match with a paralegal, to whom he directed a racial

The following provides information to assist you in scheduling noncontact visitation with inmates at the Lake County Adult Correctional Facility. Our goal is to provide family and friends the opportunity to schedule visitation at a time that is convenient to your personal schedule, your family, and lifestyle.

All noncontact visits with inmates will be conducted over a video visitation system. Friends and family may come directly to the visitation center or opt to schedule a remote visit from home on a personal computer or other electronic device. All visits are monitored and recorded.

Terms & Conditions

- Each inmate can receive noncontact, on-site, 30-minute visit per week free of charge. This visit can occur after the inmate has been classified.
- You may visit the same inmate only once per day.
- The inmate must have the visitor on their approved visitors list in order to visit. Additions to the visitor list must be completed prior to scheduling the visit.
- All visits must be scheduled 24 hours in advance. Walk-in visits will not be authorized.
- Visits may be cancelled in the event of a facility emergency.
- All visitors entering the visitation area are subject to search and may be checked for active warrants.
- Visitors are required to show proof of identification using at least one of the following:
  - State driver's license or identification card.
  - Valid military I.D.
  - Student I.D.
  - Mexican Matricula card
  - Passport with attached photo
  - Government I.D. card
  - Illinois Bar association card or Court Services Identification.
- Persons under the age of 18 years are not allowed to visit unless accompanied by a parent or legal guardian. Proof of guardianship, birth certificates, or marriage licenses may be required.
- All visits are monitored and recorded.
- Visits may be cancelled at any time for legal proceedings or because of inmate or visitor misconduct or violation of visitation rules.
- There are no refunds for remote visits that are missed or canceled because of inmate or visitor misconduct.
- All remote visits are subject to charges set by SecurusTech. Charges may fluctuate.

Rules

- No smoking, drinking or eating are allowed in the visitation center.
- Two adults and one child or one adult and two children are allowed to visit at one time. Children must be under close adult supervision.
- Visitors must arrive at the visitation center 15 minutes prior to the visit. Visitors arriving late may only receive the balance of their scheduled visit time. There will be no refunds or credits for late or missed visits.
- No nudity, provocative clothing, tight fitting clothing or sleepwear will be allowed during the visit.
- Visitors or inmates exposing sexual organs will have their visit terminated and their visitation privileges permanently barred.
- The visitor must remain at the visitation booth. If the visitor leaves the booth, the visit will be terminated.
- Visitors appearing to be under the influence of drugs or alcohol, loud or disorderly in the visitation center or disrespectful to staff will be removed from the center and visitation privileges suspended and may be subject to criminal charges.
- No cell phones or other electronic devices are allowed in the visitation center. All personal property must be secured in the lockers provided in the main lobby.
- Damaging or defacing the equipment or any area of the visitation center will lead to a termination of the visit, permanent suspension of visitation privileges, and criminal charges.
- Visitors may not record visitation sessions for any reason.

slur in the presence of other (mostly black) inmates. Jail officials said his conduct was disruptive and certainly not in accord with the special visitation privileges that had been granted to him. The court held that no constitutional rights were violated in the revocation of visiting privileges, because the action was reasonably related to the maintenance of security and order in the jail. Regarding the withdrawal of Grabowski's telephone, recreation, and canteen privileges, the court held that the evidence showed that those actions were taken for his own safety and not for punishment (which would be the impermissible reason for any action taken against a detainee). Following the incident already referred to (with the paralegal), Grabowski was involved in altercations with other inmates (mostly black), a fire was set in his cell, and he was threatened. Officials moved him into protective custody, where the privileges in question were not available. Here too the court found good justification for the officials' actions, based on concerns for institutional security and order, as well as the safety of Grabowski himself.[6]

A jail inmate's loss of telephone privileges was also upheld in *Valdez v. Rosenbaum,* 302 F.3d 1039 (9th Cir. 2002). Valdez had been identified as the leader of a drug smuggling conspiracy. In pretrial detention, he was first housed in the jail's general population, with access to four telephones. In October of 1998, the federal prosecutor asked the U.S. marshal to suspend Valdez's telephone privileges. New indictments were about to be issued; in addition to naming Valdez, five new defendants would be named, who were not yet in custody. The prosecutor wanted to curtail Valdez's ability to communicate with those people. Based on the request, Valdez was placed in administrative segregation, and his telephone contacts were limited to one daily attorney telephone call. His visits were not curtailed. Because there was a delay in arresting the other defendants, Valdez remained under the segregated restrictions for about four and a half months. He was returned to the general population after one of the captured coconspirators was released. The prosecutor saw this release on bail as making Valdez's restricted status unnecessary.

Following his conviction (he received a 30-year sentence), Valdez filed a Section 1983 suit, alleging, in part, that the telephone restrictions violated his constitutional rights to due process and freedom of speech. The trial court held that Valdez's constitutional rights had been violated. The appeals court disagreed, holding that there was no violation of his constitutional rights.

The appeals court held that preventing Valdez from tipping off his coconspirators was a legitimate governmental interest, showing that the restrictions imposed were not for the purpose of punishing him (which, under *Bell,* would be improper). Another sign of reasonableness was shown by the fact that the restrictions were ended once one coconspirator was released on bail. The court (applying *Turner v. Safley,* 482 U.S. 78 (1987), factors) also held that there was no First Amendment violation of Valdez's freedom of speech, as the restriction was rationally related to a legitimate governmental interest. Furthermore, Valdez retained the right of communication through such means as visiting and correspondence; to allow him telephone access would have required prison officials to allocate additional resources for monitoring purposes. Consequently, there was no easy alternative to the restrictions that were used.

Inmate Suicides

The problem of suicides is one that is likely more pressing in jails than in prisons. Many of the reported cases that have dealt with inmate suicides came out of jails. In some circuits the courts will apply an Eighth Amendment standard-were correctional officials deliberately indifferent to the serious medical needs of the offender. In other circuits, the courts have begun to apply an objective reasonableness standard to the actions taken by jail staff to eliminate inmate suicide. Under both standards, the risk of suicide has been determined to be a "serious medical need" by the courts. *Estate of Clark v. Walker,* 865 F.3d 544 (7th Cir. 2017). Before 2015, the legal standard most circuits used followed Eighth Amendment case law: the constitutional standard had an objective component: did the offender have an objectively serious medical condition; and a subjective component: did the official *know of,* and disregard, an excessive risk to inmate health and safety. When applied to a suicide situation, the subjective component was did a corrections official have actual knowledge that the detainee had a substantial risk of suicide; and the objective component was did the corrections official fail to take reasonable steps to prevent the suicide. *Whitney v. City of St. Louis, MO.* 887 F.3d 857 (8th Cir. 2018). Whether in custody of the police, in jail, or in prison, staff must be on the lookout for suicidal tendencies and take steps to prevent suicides when indications of suicidal risk are clear, based on the circumstances of the individual case.

One court, in *Gish v. Thomas,* 516 F.3d 952 (11th Cir. 2008), held that deliberate indifference requires a "strong likelihood" rather than a "mere possibility" that self-inflicted harm will occur. That was the situation in *Heflin v. Stewart County,* 958 F.2d 709 (6th Cir. 1992), where a deputy sheriff failed to cut down an inmate who was hanging himself. His failure to take steps to try to save the inmate (his decision was to wait until emergency medical staff arrived) was found to amount to negligent care and deliberate indifference. However, officers were not held liable in *Freedman v. City of Allentown,* 853 F.2d 1111 (3rd Cir. 1988), (there was no deliberate indifference found) when they did not realize there was a suicidal risk because of scars that were observable on the inmate's wrists and neck.

There was a similar finding in *Brumfield v. Hollins,* 551 F.3d 332 (5th Cir. 2008). This case also involved an inmate (Smith) who hanged himself. Smith, who had been arrested the previous evening for drunk driving, was being housed in the jail's drunk tank. His belt, watch, jacket, and hat were removed from his person. Around 1:30 a.m. the following morning Smith was found lying on the floor in his cell, his shoelaces around his neck. Without removing the shoelaces, three different people felt for a pulse, found none and assumed Smith was dead. It wasn't until the ambulance crew arrived 20 minutes later that the noose was removed, and life-saving techniques began. In considering this information, the appeals court said, "[w]hile the deputies' conclusion that Smith was already dead and their resulting failure to make any attempt to save Smith's life are arguably negligent, negligent conduct alone does not amount to deliberate indifference." In distinguishing *Heflin,* the court said that the Sixth Circuit (in *Heflin*) applied an objective analysis of "deliberate indifference" (what the actor should have known), which was rejected by the Supreme Court in *Farmer v. Brennan,* 511 U.S. 825 (1994). The *Brumfield* court applied the current subjective "deliberate indifference" test (what the actor actually knew), which was established in *Farmer v. Brennan.*

After the Supreme Court decision in *Kingsley v. Hendrickson* (discussed below relating to use of force, and also addressed in the chapter on medical issues) in 2015, federal circuits began reevaluating its suicide jurisprudence. Based on the ruling in *Kingsley,* some lower courts are now distinguishing the legal standard used in Due Process claims filed by unconvicted detainees from the standard used for claims by convicted offenders under the cruel and unusual punishment clause of the Eighth Amendment. In *Kingsley,* the Court explained why the Eighth Amendment standard for excessive use of force did not apply to a similar Fourteenth Amendment claim:

> *"The language of the two Clauses [Eighth and Fourteenth Amendments] differs, and the nature of the claims often differs. And, most importantly, pretrial detainees (unlike convicted prisoners) cannot be punished at all, much less `maliciously and sadistically.'"* . . . *"[A] pretrial detainee can prevail by providing only objective evidence that the challenged governmental action is not rationally related to a legitimate governmental objective or that it is excessive in relation to that purpose."*

Kingsley does not expressly limit the standard to cases of excessive use of force, and some lower federal courts have ruled that Fourteenth Amendment Due Process claims by state detainees should be evaluated under the *Kingsley* standard, including failure to protect. It is an important distinction because the objective reasonableness standard is less demanding to establish than attempting to prove a government actor's subjective state of mind. At the time of publication of this text, at least three circuits have applied the *Kingsley* "objective reasonableness" standard to jail suicides: *Miranda v. County of Lake,* 900 F.3d 335 (7th Cir. 2018); *Gordon v. County of Orange,* 888 F.3d 1118 (9th Cir. 2018); and *Bruno v. City of Schenectady,* 727 F.Appx. 717 (2nd Cir. 2018) while four circuits have declined to extend the ruling in *Kingsley* and continue to use the deliberate indifference analysis: *Whitney v. City of St. Louis,* 887 F.3d 857 (8th Cir. 2018); *Nam Dang v. Sheriff, Seminole County, Fl,* 871 F.3d 1272 (11th Cir. 2017); *Alderson v. Concordia Parish Correctional Facility.* 848 F.3d 415 (5th Cir. 2017) and *Strain v. Regalado,* ___ F.3d ___ Case No. 19-5071 (10th Cir. 2020) decided October 9, 2020.

A Supreme Court case that deals with the suicide of a jail inmate is *Logue v. United States,* 412 U.S. 521 (1973). The decision in that case primarily dealt with whether the federal government could be held liable for the negligence (a common law tort) of local jail officials who were holding a federal prisoner who committed suicide. The Court said the government could not be held liable because the county jail staff were not agents or employees of the federal government. However, the Court said that there could be tort liability attributable to the United States if the federal agent (a deputy U.S. marshal) who placed the inmate in the jail knew that there were suicidal problems and did not alert the jail officials to those problems so that they could take appropriate precautionary, surveillance steps.

Searches

Bell v. Wolfish, as previously noted, dealt with other issues besides the central issue of whether the crowded conditions at the jail were unconstitutional. Two of the issues dealt with searches. The standard for examining searches under the Constitution is determining whether the searches were reasonable. (The Constitution forbids "unreasonable searches and seizures.") The Supreme Court held that the cell searches conducted at that jail were an "appropriate security measure" and were, therefore, reasonable. Inmates claimed that they should be present when their cells were searched, but the Court said that was unnecessary and, indeed, could be contrary to the security needs for conducting effective room searches. (That same issue, the right of an inmate to be present during the search of his cell, was raised again in *Block v. Rutherford*, and the Supreme Court affirmed and repeated its holding in *Bell*: that the inmate does not have a right to be present during the search of his cell.)

Another part of the *Bell* decision dealt with body cavity searches of inmates, which were conducted by jail staff after all contact visits. The Court upheld the necessity of conducting such searches in order to detect contraband. The searches were found to be reasonable under the Constitution. The Court warned, however, that such searches might easily be abused and, therefore, cautioned that they should be conducted professionally and reasonably.

After *Bell v. Wolfish* was decided, ten circuit courts of appeals applied the *Wolfish* balancing test and concluded that an arrestee charged with minor offenses may not be strip searched prior to placement into the general population of a jail consistent with the Fourth Amendment unless the facility had reasonable suspicion that the detainee was concealing a weapon or other contraband. In 2008, the *en banc* Eleventh Circuit Court of Appeals reversed its precedent and ruled that a jail's blanket policy of strip searching all arrestees upon entering the facility was reasonable even in the absence of individualized suspicion. *Powell v. Barrett*, 541 F.3d 1298 (11th Cir. 2008) (en banc). In 2009, the *en banc* Ninth Circuit Court of Appeals also reversed its precedent and upheld a blanket policy of strip searching all arrestees before they entered San Francisco's general jail population. *Bull v. City and County of San Francisco*, 595 F.3d 964 (9th Cir. 2010) (en banc).

In *Florence v. Chosen Board of Freeholders*, 566 U.S. 318 (2012), the Supreme Court resolved a split among the circuit courts of appeals concerning the constitutionality of jails performing visual searches of all persons admitted to the jail's general population, regardless of individualized suspicion of risk to the facility. The precise question the Court addressed was: *Whether the Fourth Amendment permits a jail to conduct a suspicionless strip search of every individual arrested for any minor offense no matter what the circumstances.*

Mr. Florence had failed to make timely installment payments on a fine imposed for two crimes, and a warrant was issued for his arrest. The fine was later paid, but the warrant was never withdrawn. Florence was arrested pursuant to that warrant during a traffic stop and he was transported to jail. The intake processing at the first jail where Mr. Florence was held *"required every arrestee to shower with a delousing agent. Officers would check arrestees for scars, marks, gang tattoos, and contraband as they disrobed. . . . [Florence] claims he was also instructed to open his mouth, lift his tongue, hold out his arms, turn around, and lift his genitals."* When he was transferred to a second jail, he underwent a similar intake screening, although the Court noted that apparently there was no physical contact between staff and Mr. Florence during the process. He was released without charges being filed and then filed a Section 1983 action alleging the searches violated his right to be free from unreasonable searches and seizures. After the court of appeals ruled that the jails' policies on visual searches were constitutionally valid, Mr. Florence sought review in the Supreme Court.

The Court's analysis began with a recitation of the security and safety issues facing jail administrators and staff and then addressing the importance of maintaining security and order within correctional facilities: **"*Maintaining safety and order at these institutions [jails] requires the expertise of correctional officials, who must have substantial discretion to devise reasonable solutions to the problems they face.*"** In noting its earlier decision in *Bell v. Wolfish* that had upheld the Bureau of Prisons' visual search policy despite only one incident of contraband being recovered, the Court stated:

> **The Court nonetheless upheld the search policy. It deferred to the judgment of correctional officials that the inspections served not only to discover but also to deter the smuggling of weapons, drugs, and other prohibited items inside. [citation omitted]. The Court explained that there is no mechanical way to determine whether intrusions on an inmate's privacy are reasonable.[citation omitted] The need for a particular search must be balanced against the resulting invasion of personal rights.**

The importance of the visual searches at issue served a number of important governmental interests in detecting: contraband (weapons, drugs, alcohol, currency, lighters, and matches concealed by new detainees); the presence of wounds, communicable diseases or lice; tattoos or other identifying marking of gangs or other disruptive groups that would pose a threat to the safety of inmates and staff.

The Court then explained the many justifications for having a policy of general application rather than trying to carve out exceptions for certain detainees, which are exacerbated by the large number of detainees processed and the short duration of many detentions. These include: the difficulty of identifying which detainees might pose a risk of violence, escape, or drug smuggling and that the deterrent value of searches for contraband depends on the unpredictability of the searches. The record developed in this case demonstrated that even persons arrested and booked into jail for minor offenses had been found with contraband hidden by their genitals or in their rectal cavities. Persons may be coerced by others to attempt to smuggle contraband into a correctional facility by being arrested for a minor offense.

While acknowledging the burden placed on detainees by the general policy of visual searches for persons entering the general population of a jail, the Court concluded that the balancing between the rights of detainees favored the policy:

> *These cases establish that correctional officials must be permitted to devise reasonable search policies to detect and deter the possession of contraband in their facilities. [citation omitted] ("[M]aintaining institutional security and preserving internal order and discipline are essential goals that may require limitation or retraction of retained constitutional rights of both convicted prisoners and pretrial detainees"). The task of determining whether a policy is reasonably related to legitimate security interests is "peculiarly within the province and professional expertise of corrections officials." [Citation omitted]. This Court has repeated the admonition that, "`in the absence of substantial evidence in the record to indicate that the officials have exaggerated their response to these considerations courts should ordinarily defer to their expert judgment in such matters.'"*

Lanza v. New York, 370 U.S. 139 (1962), dealt with the visit between a jail inmate and his brother. Their conversation during visiting was monitored and recorded. The Supreme Court upheld authorities' use of that taped conversation at hearings. The Court notably pointed out that a jail is not the equivalent of a man's house. Privacy is lost in a jail (or prison) setting, and surveillance throughout a jail (including in visiting areas) must be conducted. A similar case is *United States v. Hearst*, 563 F.2d 1331 (9th Cir. 1977), *cert. denied*, 435 U.S. 1000 (1978), in which a federal court of appeals upheld Hearst's conviction and the use at trial of an intercepted conversation during visiting that Hearst had had at a county jail. The court found that there was a valid governmental purpose (for security reasons) to monitor and record visiting room conversations and that the tapes from such monitoring could be turned over to law enforcement officials for their use.

Legal Access

A state prisoner was being held in a local jail, awaiting transfer to state prison to serve his term of imprisonment. He complained that the jail library holdings were inadequate (not nearly as large as those in the prison libraries) and that one hour per week of access time to the library was also inadequate. The federal court of appeals held, in *Strickler v. Waters*, 989 F.2d 1375 (4th Cir. 1993), that the library had a reasonable collection of law books, including state and federal codes, some reporters of cases, and legal encyclopedia sets, which were sufficient for the time the inmate was held in the jail. Perhaps anticipating *Lewis v. Casey*, 518 U.S. 343 (1996), the court also said that the inmate had not shown that he had suffered any actual prejudice in any pending or contemplated legal action.

A civil rights violation was claimed by a pretrial detainee who said that his incoming legal mail was opened and read in *Walker v. Navarro County Jail*, 4 F.3d 410 (5th Cir. 1993). The court held that opening and checking the incoming mail without censoring it did not amount to a constitutional violation. The claim also failed because the inmate failed to allege he was in any way prejudiced by the jailer's conduct. In *Kane v. Garcia Espitia*, 546 U.S. 9 (2005), a Supreme Court per curiam opinion, Garcia Espitia said he had received no law library access while in jail before trial and only around four hours during the trial (he had chosen not to be represented by an attorney). Garcia Espitia claimed his restricted library access violated his Sixth Amendment rights. Following conviction, he filed for a writ of habeas corpus, with the district court denying relief. The Court of Appeals for the Ninth Circuit reversed, saying that "the lack of any pretrial access to law books violated Garcia Espitia's constitutional right to represent himself." The Supreme Court disagreed, holding there was no clearly established right of law library access to a defendant who was representing himself.

Personal Injury

There are two leading cases that limit the use of the due process clause to pursue injuries (to person or to property) as violations of the Constitution: *Daniels v. Williams*, 474 U.S. 327 (1986) and *Davidson v. Cannon*, 474 U.S. 344 (1986). Of those two cases, *Daniels v. Williams* was a jail case. The inmate, Daniels, sued officials when he was injured in a fall on a stairway at a city jail. He claimed that staff had been negligent in leaving a pillow on the stairs, which caused his fall. The Supreme Court said that such a claim does not amount to a constitutional violation. The Fourteenth Amendment (due process) is intended to apply against much more serious matters—the abuse of power by government officials, not their negligence. Claims like this one, asserting negligence on the part of the jail officials, did not state a claim for violation of due process of law.

Although negligent acts causing personal injury or loss of property did not state constitutional violations (under 42 U.S.C. § 1983), they could (and perhaps even should) be considered under traditional tort law. Most jurisdictions have waived their sovereign immunity and have made their tort claims acts (or the equivalent) available to prisoners, meaning that jail inmates may be able to recover damages in a tort claim or lawsuit for negligent acts of officials. (Remember that these claims would be brought against the state or government entity, not against the individual officials, as in a Section 1983 action.)

▶ Using Excessive Force

The U.S. Constitution has four different provisions that protect persons from the uses of excessive force by government agents: the Fourth Amendment unreasonable search and seizure prohibition when making an arrest or other investigatory stops — *Graham v. Connor, 490 U.S. 386* (1989); the Eighth Amendment's prohibition against "cruel and unusual" punishments for persons convicted of criminal offenses and in the custody of the government — *Hudson v. McMillian*, 503 U.S. 1 (1992); and the Fifth (as applied to the federal government) or Fourteenth Amendments' "Due Process Clause" for pretrial detainees. The U.S. Supreme Court had never expressly identified the source of constitutional protection from excessive force for pretrial detainees but indicated in dicta "*that the Due Process Clause protects a pretrial detainee from the use of excessive force that amounts to punishment.*" *Graham v. Connor*, footnote 10. The courts of appeals, while recognizing that pretrial detainees were entitled to broader protection than sentenced inmates, had generally relied upon analytical frameworks similar to the Eighth Amendment. Excessive use of force claims under the Eighth Amendment have two components, an objective one — was the injury sufficiently serious and a subjective one — what was the state of mind of the actor?

In *Kingsley v. Hendrickson*, 576 U.S. 389 (2015), the Court provided guidance on how claims of excessive use of force arising under the Due Process clause should be analyzed. Michael Kingsley was a detainee in a county jail and alleged that jail officials had used excessive force against him. At trial, the district court directed the jury to consider whether the jail officials had been reckless in their use of force against the detainee. The jury returned a verdict for the jail officials and the inmate appealed. The court of appeals affirmed the verdict, concluding that to prevail on a claim of excessive force, the detainee must demonstrate the officer intended to violate the detainee's rights or acted with reckless disregard of the detainee's rights. The detainee sought review in the U.S. Supreme Court, which granted certiorari to address this issue: *Whether the requirements of a 42 U.S.C. § 1983 excessive force claim brought by a plaintiff who was a pretrial detainee at the time of the incident are satisfied by a showing that the state actor deliberately used force against the pretrial detainee and the use of force was objectively unreasonable.*

The Court noted that circuit courts were split as to whether such claims required an assessment of the state actor's subjective state of mind or whether the conduct should be analyzed under the "objectively reasonable" standard, which required no analysis of the actor's state of mind. The Court reversed the court of appeal's decision and ruled that a detainee alleging an excessive use of force must only prove that the force was objectively unreasonable.

In reaching this conclusion, the Court relied on its previous cases addressing the rights of detainees. In *Bell v. Wolfish*, the Court had ruled that in the absence of an expressed intent to punish, "*a pretrial detainee can prevail by providing only objective evidence that the challenged governmental action is not rationally related to a legitimate governmental objective or that it is excessive in relation to that purpose.*"

This standard also protects government defendants who act in good faith.

[We recognize that "[r]unning a prison is an inordinately difficult undertaking," [citation omitted] and that "safety and order at these institutions requires the expertise of correctional officials, who must have substantial discretion to devise reasonable solutions to the problems they face," [citation omitted]. Officers facing disturbances "are often forced to make split-second judgments—in circumstances that are tense, uncertain, and rapidly evolving." [Citation omitted]. For these reasons, we have stressed that a court must judge the reasonableness of the force used from the perspective and with the knowledge of the defendant officer. We have also explained that a court must take account of the legitimate interests

in managing a jail, acknowledging as part of the objective reasonableness analysis that deference to policies and practices needed to maintain order and institutional security is appropriate.

The Court relied upon its earlier ruling under the Fourth Amendment in *Graham v. Connor* to evaluate the constitutionality of a government actor's conduct. Determining whether a government actor's conduct was objectively unreasonable cannot be done mechanically because this determination *"turns on the facts and circumstances of each case."* Reasonableness must be assessed based on what the officer knew at the time, not *"with the 20/20 vision of hindsight."* Courts must also consider the important governmental interests in maintaining the safety and security of correctional institutions.

In determining reasonableness, courts may consider the following factors:

. . . the relationship between the need for the use of force and the amount of force used; the extent of the plaintiff's injury; any effort made by the officer to temper or to limit the amount of force; the severity of the security problem at issue; the threat reasonably perceived by the officer; and whether the plaintiff was actively resisting. . . . We do not consider this list to be exclusive.

Because it was unclear if the trial court's erroneous jury instruction on the mental standard needed to be proven against an officer in an excessive force case against a pretrial detainee was harmless, the judgments of the lower courts were vacated and remanded.

A significant question left open by *Kingsley* is whether the objective reasonableness standard is applicable to other aspects of a detainee's confinement. The *Kingsley* standard has been applied in failure to protect [inmate assault] cases: *Castro v. County of Los Angeles*, 833 F.3d 1060 (9th Cir. 2016) *en banc, cert. denied* 137 S.Ct. 831(2017); overall conditions of confinement: *Darnell v. Pineiro*, 849 F.3d 17 (2nd Cir. 2017); and [self-harm/denial of medical care] *Miranda v. County of Lake*, 900 F3d 335 (7th Cir. 2018) while other circuits have considered but decided not to extend *Kingsley*. *Whitney v. City of St. Louis*, 887 F.3d 857 (8th Cir. 2018); *Dang by and Through Dang v. Sheriff, Seminole County*, 871 F.3d 1272 (11th Cir. 2017), *Alderson v. Concordia Parish Correctional Facility*, 848 F.3d 415 (5th Cir. 2017), and most recently *Strain v. Regalado*, ___ F.3d ___ Case No. 19-5071 (10th Cir. 2020) decided October 9, 2020.

▶ Conditions of Confinement

Most federal circuits continue to evaluate a detainee's conditions of confinement under a deliberate indifference to serious needs analysis developed in Eighth Amendment cases. After the Supreme Court's decision in *Kingsley v. Hendrickson* discussed above, two circuits have announced changes to the analysis of claims by pretrial detainees alleging unconstitutional conditions of confinement.

In *Darnell v. Pineiro*, 849 F.3d 17 (2nd Cir. 2017), the court of appeals reviewed the grant of summary judgment to New York City corrections officials for conditions at the Brooklyn Central Booking facility. Plaintiffs alleged they were kept for up to 24 hours in unconstitutional conditions including: (1) Overcrowding; (2) Unusable Toilets; (3) Garbage and Inadequate Sanitation; (4) Infestation; (5) Lack of Toiletries and Other Hygienic Items; (6) Inadequate Nutrition; (7) Extreme Temperatures and Poor Ventilation; (8) Deprivation of Sleep; and (9) Crime and Intimidation. There was no factual dispute that any of the plaintiffs were exposed to these conditions for more than 24 hours or suffered any serious injury. The district court evaluated the plaintiffs' claim under the two-pronged deliberate indifference standard. The district court granted summary judgment to the defendants, reasoning that the plaintiffs failed to meet both the objective and subjective requirements for a claim of unconstitutional conditions of confinement based on a theory of deliberate indifference. The district court concluded the plaintiffs could not *"establish an objectively substantial deprivation of any constitutional rights because no plaintiff actually suffered a serious injury, or was "regularly denied his or her basic human needs or was exposed to conditions that posed an unreasonable risk of serious damage to his or her future health" for more than twenty-four hours"* The district court also ruled that none of the plaintiffs could *"establish the "subjective prong" of a deliberate indifference claim by proving that the individual defendants were actually aware of any dangerous conditions, or that the individual defendants acted unreasonably in responding to any such conditions; nor, for similar reasons, could the plaintiffs establish that the individual defendants acted with punitive intent."*

Relying on the Supreme Court's decision in *Kingsley*, the court of appeals reversed. The appeals court noted that a pretrial detainee's claims of unconstitutional conditions of confinement are governed by the Due

Process Clause of the Fourteenth Amendment rather than the Cruel and Unusual Punishments Clause of the Eighth Amendment. To establish a § 1983 claim for allegedly unconstitutional conditions of confinement, a pre-trial detainee may demonstrate that officers acted with deliberate indifference to the challenged conditions. The detainee must satisfy two prongs to prove a claim, an "objective prong" showing that the challenged conditions were sufficiently serious to constitute objective deprivations of the right to due process, and a "subjective prong" showing that the officer acted with at least deliberate indifference to the challenged conditions.

This is a very similar analysis to one used in Eighth Amendment conditions of confinement cases by sentenced offenders. The difference is in what is necessary to establish the subjective component. The appellate court reasoned that the term "subjective" component was misleading because the Supreme Court in *Farmer v. Brennan* equated the term with recklessness. As recognized in *Farmer v. Brennan*, recklessness "can be defined subjectively (what a person actually knew, and disregarded), or objectively (what a reasonable person knew, or should have known)." The appellate court in *Darnell* further reasoned that the Court's decision in *Kingsley* indicated that the Supreme Court's application of the Eighth Amendment "subjective" definition of recklessness should not be applied to claims by pretrial detainees under the Due Process Clause. Instead, courts, in addressing claims under the Due Process clause, should apply the objective definition of recklessness — what a reasonable person knows, or should have known. This eliminates the need for a pretrial plaintiff to prove the defendant's state of mind."

The court of appeals also concluded that the district court's finding on the objective component of the due process deliberate indifference standard was erroneous. In conditions of confinement cases brought under either of the Eighth and Fourteenth Amendments, the plaintiff must establish an objective deprivation, "the inmate must show that the conditions, either alone or in combination, pose an unreasonable risk of serious damage to his health," which includes the risk of serious damage to "physical and mental soundness." The court of appeals disapproved of the district court's conclusion that a prisoner may state a claim for unconstitutional conditions of confinement only when subject to the conditions for longer than 24 hours or which cause some type of serious injury.

The court of appeals summarized the new standard for due process violations this way:

> *Therefore, to establish a claim for deliberate indifference to conditions of confinement under the Due Process Clause of the Fourteenth Amendment, the pretrial detainee must prove that the defendant-official acted intentionally to impose the alleged condition, or recklessly failed to act with reasonable care to mitigate the risk that the condition posed to the pretrial detainee even though the defendant-official knew, or should have known, that the condition posed an excessive risk to health or safety. In other words, the "subjective prong" (or "mens rea prong") of a deliberate indifference claim is defined objectively.*

Readers are reminded that not all of the circuits have adopted this change in analyzing conditions of confinement claims for pretrial detainees. In July of 2020, the 6th Circuit, in the unreported case of *Cameron v. Bouchard*, 6th Cir. Case No. 20-1469 (decided July 9, 2020) noted the split in concerning the application of *Kingsley v. Hendrickson* to issues other than the use of force:

> Since *Kingsley*, the circuits have split on whether deliberate indifference claims arising under the Fourteenth Amendment are still governed by *Farmer* (requiring a subjective inquiry for an officer's state of mind), or instead are governed by *Kingsley* (requiring an objective inquiry for an officer's state of mind). Compare *Castro v. Cty. of Los Angeles,* 833 F.3d 1060, 1070 (9th Cir. 2016) (en banc) (adopting a new objective standard for deliberate indifference claims brought by pretrial detainees); *Darnell v. Pineiro,* 849 F.3d 17, 35 (2d Cir. 2017) (same); *Miranda v. Cty. of Lake,* 900 F.3d 335, 351-52 (7th Cir. 2018) (same) with *Alderson v. Concordia Parish Corr. Facility,* 848 F.3d 415, 419 n. 4 (5th Cir. 2017) (declining to reconsider its earlier precedent treating Eighth and Fourteenth Amendment claims alike); *Whitney v. City of St. Louis,* 887 F.3d 857, 860 n.4 (8th Cir. 2018) (same); *Nam Dang by and through Vina Dang v. Sheriff, Seminole Cty. Florida,* 871 F.3d 1272, 1279 n.2 (11th Cir. 2017) (same).

▸ Municipal Liability

A county or city can be held liable under 42 U.S.C. § 1983 for constitutional violations committed by its employees only when the employees are carrying out policy set by the county or city. However, a county or city may be liable for the unconstitutional conduct of its employee because of a failure to train or supervise an employee. In *Davis v. Mason County,* 927 F.2d 1473 (9th Cir. 1991), the county and the sheriff were held liable for failure to set up a program of adequate training for deputy sheriffs. Whether it occurred on the streets or inside the jail, the deputies themselves would be held liable for the beatings that were administered to persons they had arrested. But because they had had inadequate (virtually no) training regarding the proper use of force, the sheriff himself (who was responsible for setting training policy) and the county (which was ultimately responsible for training policy) were also found liable. In *City of Canton v. Harris*, 489 U.S. 378 (1989), the Supreme Court has set the training requirement standard: a city or county may be held liable if it is shown that its failure to train "amounts to deliberate indifference to the rights of persons" with whom officers come into contact.

Failure to give proper training was also an issue in *Warner v. Grand County*, 57 F.3d 962 (10th Cir. 1995). This Section 1983 action was brought by two female plaintiffs, alleging constitutional violations when they were strip-searched following their arrest for possessing marijuana. The suit was brought against the police officer, a private citizen who assisted the police, the sheriff, and the county. After the arrest, the police officer called for assistance, which was given by the female director of a crisis center; she had assisted in the transfer and searches of female detainees on many occasions. One question was whether Parker (the female private citizen) was entitled to the qualified immunity defense that was available to state employees. The district court gave her such immunity, and the court of appeals agreed, saying that she had served as an officer's agent, carrying out an investigative function of the local government. The courts said that she should be shielded from liability in the same manner as the government employees. The arresting officer in this case was also granted qualified immunity, protecting him from the suit, because he had acted in accordance with the law that was established at the time. The legal standard was that strip searches could be performed (upon transfer of the arrestee to a detention facility soon after arrest) if there was reasonable suspicion that the suspect possessed drugs or other contraband or if the suspect was to be placed in the general jail population. The officer in *Warner* had reasonable suspicion, the courts said, that the two suspects possessed additional drugs (in addition to the marijuana found at the arrest scene); therefore, the strip search that he directed to be performed was in accordance with existing standards (in the 10th Circuit) for such searches.

The sheriff and the county were sued, because it was alleged that they had a policy and custom of not adequately training officers on constitutional arrest and search standards. (The sheriff and the county could not be held liable for the actual conducting of the searches.) The courts said that the plaintiffs might show that the defendants had failed to train officers as a deliberate or conscious choice. If that was the case, it could implicate the sheriff and county on the basis of setting policy (failure to train) that violated constitutional standards (citing *City of Canton*). The court of appeals, however, said that was not the case here. Grand County had a clear policy that there would be no warrantless strip searches of temporary detainees. That policy, conveyed to all officers, barred the conducting of strip searches of female detainees, because all female arrestees who required incarceration were taken to San Juan County Jail and were not kept in Grand County. The evidence showed that no female arrestees had been kept in Grand County Jail since 1989 (more than five years earlier). There was nothing to show that either the sheriff or the county had reason to think there would be any female strip searches, because the policy prohibited female strip searches for temporary detainees and that policy had been consistently followed. Summary judgment for the sheriff and the county was affirmed on the grounds that they had not been shown to be deliberately indifferent to these plaintiffs' rights or to the need for more training for officers.

▶ Other Jail Issues and Cases

In a case that combines elements of our discussion of inmate suicides and the health care that is owed to all inmates, a Louisiana appeals court overturned an award of $100,000 to the family of a detainee who died in jail from an overdose of the "ecstasy" drug in *Brown v. Lee*, 639 So.2d 897 (La. App. 1996). The detainee had been arrested for drunken driving and, when interrogated, had denied any drug use. He was presenting only the symptoms of intoxication. The appeals court refused to hold the sheriff liable, saying that it would be unreasonable to require him to provide medical treatment to every intoxicated person who was in his custody. Finding no such duty, there was no liability for negligent action or failure to act.

The case of *Anderson v. County of Kern*, 45 F.3d 1310 (9th Cir. 1995), presented three major issues about jail conditions and the treatment of detainees. The first issue involved the use of a "safety cell" at the Kern County Jail. One such cell, which was 10 feet by 10 feet, was covered with rubberized foam padding and contained a pit toilet with a grate covering in the floor. There was evidence that violent inmates were sometimes chained to the floor grate. The cell was mostly used for the temporary holding of suicidal and mentally disturbed inmates when they became very disruptive or threatening. When an inmate was placed in the cell, staff were required to check on the inmate's condition and safety every 15 to 30 minutes. In addition, the supervisor in charge reviewed the inmate's placement in the cell (whether it needed to be continued) every four hours.

Inmates challenged the use of this cell, claiming that to use it was a violation of the Eighth and Fourteenth Amendments. The court noted that, because the jail held both pretrial detainees and sentenced prisoners, the questions to be addressed were whether placement in the cell constituted an intentional infliction of pain or a denial of basic human needs (which would show an Eighth Amendment, cruel and unusual punishment violation) and whether officials acted with deliberate indifference to the inmates' needs when they were placed in the cell, showing an intent to punish them (a Fourteenth Amendment violation, for pretrial detainees). The court of appeals affirmed the district court's holding that conditions in the safety cell were not unconstitutional. Even though the evidence showed that the conditions in the cell could be unsanitary and even though the court conceded that it was a very severe environment, the court said that it was needed to deal with very serious safety concerns. It was also noted that placement into the cell was temporary and short in duration.

A second issue in the *Anderson* case involved the conditions in the administrative segregation unit of the jail. Inmates were placed in administrative segregation for different reasons: because they were subject to attacks, they were high security risks, they were former law enforcement officers, or they were notorious criminals. The court noted that it was established in *Hewitt v. Helms,* 459 U.S. 460 (1983), that placement in more restrictive quarters was within the terms of confinement ordinarily contemplated for a prison sentence (and, one may assume from this court's approach, for a jailed inmate). The district court had ordered jail officials to determine whether some of these segregated prisoners could be allowed to exercise together or to use the day room together. (The jail practiced total separation of all segregation inmates. Officials testified that these inmates could never be allowed together, for fear of someone being harmed.) The court of appeals ruled that the district court order went too far. There was no constitutional violation in the use of the segregation unit and no need for any corrective action. Although conditions in isolated segregation confinement were not pleasant, they did not show deliberate indifference to the needs of the inmates, and they were required for safety and security reasons. Finding no constitutional level of violation, the court of appeals asserted that it was improper for the district court to order any corrective action. *Wright v. Rushen,* 642 F.2d 1129 (9th Cir. 1981), was cited to support that proposition.

A third issue in *Anderson* concerned health care. The district court had ordered a translator (an employee, and not an inmate, preferably from the medical staff) to translate, when requested by inmates, during medical and mental health interviews. The court noted that the U.S. Seventh Circuit Court of Appeals, in *Wellman v. Faulkner,* 715 F.2d 269 (7th Cir. 1983), had said that a failure to provide translators could constitute deliberate indifference to the medical needs of non-English speaking inmates. This circuit court agreed with that approach and with the district court, saying that it was necessary during medical interviews to have a translator (who is not an inmate, because inmate translators would be potentially inaccurate or unreliable in their translations).

In *Bryant v. Maffucci,* 923 F.2d 979 (2nd Cir. 1991), a New York detainee claimed a Section 1983 violation because she had not been promptly scheduled for an abortion and also because the physician had made an error in estimating her gestational age. The court of appeals held that these facts only showed negligence, which occurred when jail officials delayed her letter to the physician requesting the abortion appointment. Also, there was no evidence to show that the physician could not rely on the sonogram reading that had been made; at the most, any error in setting the inmate's gestational age was also negligence and not a violation of the inmate's right to privacy or a deliberate indifference to her medical needs (which are the constitutional standards). Thus, there was no showing of constitutional violations of the inmate's rights.

In *Cooper v. Dyke,* 814 F.2d 941 (4th Cir. 1987), a 16-year-old boy was shot during an altercation at a skating rink. The boy and his friends left the rink in a van and were stopped by police. While some in the van fled, Cooper and his friend Hill went towards the police, saying they had both been shot. The friend's injury was visible, Cooper's was not. An ambulance was called, and the arriving paramedics began to examine the two boys. Meanwhile, the police had set up a roadblock and were detaining several busloads of people leaving the skating rink. The conditions became chaotic with disruptions and threats being made both to the boys and to the officers. Cooper's gunshot wound was not discovered at the scene (paramedics were afraid for their safety and were unable to conduct a thorough exam, at one point stopping their exam and going back toward the ambulance while the police regained control). Cooper and two others were taken to the police station where they were handcuffed to a detention rail. Although the three testified that they constantly complained that Cooper had been shot, he was not attended to until one of his friends vomited on Cooper and Cooper failed to respond. Taken by ambulance to the hospital, Cooper was found to be in "profound shock and in need of immediate surgery."

Police officers were found liable under Section 1983 for deliberate indifference to Cooper's repeated pleas for medical attention to his wound. The court of appeals affirmed the jury's verdict. The defense of the police officers had been that they relied on the paramedics' examination, and the fact that there was an examination showed there was no deliberate indifference to the condition of the detainee. The court held, however, that it was permissible for the jury to make its conclusions, in effect finding that the police officers were not justified in relying on the paramedics since the examination had been performed under such chaotic conditions. The repeated complaints of Cooper under these circumstances should not have been ignored.

And, in an unusual kind of medical complaint, in *Frohmader v. Wayne,* 958 F.2d 1024 (10th Cir. 1992), a Colorado inmate alleged constitutional violations because jail officials were deliberately indifferent to his complaints of claustrophobia and agoraphobia (apparently, his fears of being confined in close spaces and with lots of other persons). The court held that, even if it was shown that there was indifference to these complaints, the detainee had not proved that those fears constituted a "serious medical need," which is another aspect of the standard that the inmate must show in order to sustain a claim for Eighth (or Fourteenth) Amendment violations with respect to medical care.

▶ Removing the Sheriff from Running the Jail

A most unusual action with respect to a sheriff and a county jail was the subject of *Beck v. County of Santa Clara,* 204 Cal. App. 3d 789 (6th Dist. CA 1988). In this case, because of dissatisfaction with the repeated problems (including legal problems) at the county jail, the county board of supervisors transferred all duties relating to the jail from the elected sheriff and placed the jail under a nonelected, appointed department head. This matter had been submitted to popular vote and was approved. The court noted that ordinarily it would not be permissible to remove certain duties that were historically performed by an elected public official and place them under a person who was not elected to perform them. However, because the sheriff had no personal right to perform the jail duties (and there was nothing in state law that mandated that those duties be performed by the sheriff only), the court approved the action of the board of supervisors, which had been affirmed by popular vote in the county.

Summary

- The leading case on constitutional requirements for jail conditions is *Bell v. Wolfish.* The Supreme Court ruled in this case that, because of due process clause protections, a pretrial inmate may not be punished. How do we tell if the inmate is being punished? If the condition complained about is reasonably related to a legitimate governmental objective (usually the objective is security or good order), there has been no punishment.

- Other rights, protected by other constitutional provisions, are guaranteed to pretrial detainees, but they may all be limited by security concerns at the jail. In *Bell,* it was permissible for jail officials to limit incoming publications to publisher-only mailings. The Supreme Court also upheld jail practices of conducting cell searches without the inmates being present and the conducting of visual (body cavity) searches after contact visiting. The Supreme Court has recently agreed to consider whether jail officials may have a constitutional policy permitting strip searches of all persons to include misdemeanants booked into the general population of the jail.

- Other Supreme Court cases have dealt with other constitutional claims by jail inmates. In *Block v. Rutherford,* the Court held that it was permissible for a jail to limit visiting to noncontact visiting. The Court also said that a television station did not have to be permitted to come into a jail to film a story on a jail suicide (*Houchins v. KQED, Inc*).

- Prior to 2015, most federal courts applied Eighth Amendment standards to a pretrial detainees Due Process claims under the Fourteenth Amendment. In *Kingsley v. Hendrickson,* the Supreme Court announced that the proper standard for assessing a pretrial detainee's use of excessive force claim is the objective reasonableness of the actor's conduct rather than the subjective mental state (acting with deliberate indifference) of the government actor. While some circuits still retain the subjective mental state component for detainee claims other than excessive use of force, other circuits have begun to extend the *Kingsley* "objective reasonableness" standard to other aspects of a detainee's confinement such as failure to protect and health care.

- Courts have held that no privacy is to be expected in jail visits, so it is permissible for authorities to monitor and tape conversations between inmates and their visitors (*Lanza v. New York; United States v. Hearst*).

- The Supreme Court held that, in a suit based on allegations of government negligence causing an inmate to fall in a stairway, mere negligence did not state a constitutional claim against the jail officials. For a constitutional (Fourteenth Amendment) violation, a more serious action must be shown, amounting to abuse by officials of their governmental powers, to sustain a liability judgment against the officials (*Daniels v. Williams*). Negligence by government officials would support a common law tort claim, if that procedure was available in the jurisdiction where the accident occurred.

- A county, a city, a sheriff, or other supervisory personnel may be held liable for failing to train employees on the basic rights of citizens and on the constitutional requirements of their jobs. Liability has been proved, and affirmed in cases in which arrestees were beaten (where excessive force was used); in cases in which strip searches were performed in inappropriate and unnecessary circumstances; and in cases in which arrests were made improperly.

- A major federal appellate decision (*Anderson v. County of Kern*) held that severely austere conditions in a small padded cell with a pit toilet in the floor did not amount to Fourteenth Amendment violations (or Eighth Amendment violations, for sentenced inmates) when it was used for short-term confinement of severely disturbed inmates. That case also approved the jail's use of administrative segregation cells, where the inmates were not allowed to exercise together, because of the jail's concerns for the inmates' safety. The court did require the jail to employ a staff translator to assist non-English speaking inmates during medical and mental health interviews.

- In *Beck v. County of Santa Clara,* a California court upheld the removal of a sheriff from running the county jail because of repeated difficulties at the jail, including adverse court decisions and other legal problems. The removal was made by action of the county board of supervisors and was approved by county voters in a referendum.

Thinking About It

In May of 2013, McAdoo was housed in the Hot Springs County Detention Center as a pretrial detainee. He was involved in a fight with another inmate. After being told to stop three times by staff, and failing to comply, staff took McAdoo to the floor and restrained him. McAdoo complained to staff of pain in his shoulder and he was taken to a community emergency department at a local hospital. The treating physician diagnosed McAdoo with a dislocated shoulder and prescribed ten hydrocodone tablets for pain, to be taken every four hours, as needed. McAdoo also wore a splint to restrain the shoulder. The jail's policy banned all narcotic drugs, so jail officials refused to fill McAdoo's hydrocodone prescription. Instead, the jail offered McAdoo — free of charge — his choice of non-prescription pain relievers, to be taken every four to six hours, depending on the dose. The inmate was returned to the community healthcare facility two days later and after further diagnostic testing he was diagnosed with a significant injury, which required immediate surgery. Because McAdoo refused to sign an acknowledgment that he would be liable for medical expenses, no follow-up care was provided. The inmate was sentenced to prison and upon arrival at a state correctional facility, he had surgery on the shoulder. McAdoo sued county jail officials alleging (1) excessive use of force, and (2) failure to provide necessary medical treatment by refusing to allow him to have prescription pain medication. How should a court rule? This case was reported as *McAdoo v. Martin*, 899 F.3d 521 (8th Cir. 2018).

Endnotes

1. Zeng, Z. *Jail Inmates in 2018*. U.S. Department of Justice, Bureau of Justice Statistics, March 2020. Washington, D.C. Table 3. https://www.bjs.gov/content/pub/pdf/ji18.pdf Accessed November 10, 2020. Using 2019 data, Louisiana (16,567), Texas (12,055), Kentucky (10,862) and Tennessee (7,048) were the states with the highest number of state prisoners in local jails. Nine states reported housing no state sentenced prisoners, and four states (Connecticut, Delaware, Rhode Island, and Vermont operate an integrated jail and prison system within the state. Carson, E. E. *Prisoners in 2019*. U.S. Department of Justice, Bureau of Justice Statistics, October 2020. Washington, D.C. Table 18. Louisiana may be an outlier as the state's DOC acknowledges that it has too many state prisoners to house in state facilities. *"At present, there are more than 36,000 offenders serving time for state felonies. Louisiana simply doesn't have the capacity to house all of these offenders in state correctional facilities. Capacity at state facilities is just under 19,000. Therefore, the state*

relies upon parish and private facilities throughout Louisiana to house and care for offenders. The state reimburses these entities for housing offenders." Louisiana Department of Public Safety & Corrections, Frequently Asked Questions. Available at https://doc.louisiana.gov/public-programs-resources/frequently-asked-questions/. Accessed February 26, 2020.

2. Zeng, Z. *Jail Inmates in 2018.* Statistical Tables 1, 4, 8, and 10. (Washington, DC: Bureau of Justice Statistics, U.S. Department of Justice, March 2020)

3. In *Covell v. Arpaio,* 662 F.Supp.2d 1146 (D. AZ 2009), the inmate, representing himself, claimed his First Amendment rights were violated by the Maricopa County Lower Buckeye Jail (Phoenix, Arizona) policy of restricting an inmate's incoming nonprivileged mail to metered postcards. The district court, applying the *Turner v. Safley* test, held that there was no violation and granted the defendant's motion for summary judgment. Applying *Turner,* the court held that the jail's policy had a rational connection to a legitimate penological objective—preventing the smuggling of contraband into the jail; that there were alternative means for communication (metered postcards, visiting, and telephone calls); that prison staff had shown that by allowing regular stamped mail there is an increased possibility of contraband (e.g., various drugs were found contained on the back of postage stamps) being smuggled into the prison, with this possibly resulting in conflicts and potential violence between inmates; and that the inmate failed to meet his burden of showing obvious, easy alternatives to the postcard regulation. For an opposite finding, see *Martinez v. Maketa,* where inmates at the El Paso County Jail challenged the jail's policy of requiring that inmates use jail-supplied four-by-six inch postcards for their outgoing correspondence, with some exceptions. On December 20, 2010, the United States District Court for the District of Colorado issued a stipulated order granting a preliminary injunction to stop the postcard-only policy. That same day, the jail dropped its policy of restricting inmate outgoing mail to postcards. *Stipulated Order Granting Preliminary Injunction* (Civil Action No. 10-cv-02242-WYD-KLM). Also see *Jail Drops Postcard-Only Policy Following ACLU Lawsuit.* American Civil Liberties Union. Accessed November 10, 2020 April 17, 2011 from https://aclu-co.org/colorado-springs-jail-drops-postcard-only-policy-following-aclu-lawsuit/. The El Paso County Sheriff's Office's current mail policy may be found using this link. https://www.epcsheriffsoffice.com/sections-detention-bureau/operations-division/inmate-mail. Accessed November 10, 2020.

4. See *Simpson v. County of Cape Girardeau, MO,* 879 F.3d 273 (8th Cir. 2018) in which the Eighth Circuit concluded the postcard-only policy for the county jail did not deny an inmate [and the sender] the right to communicate under the First Amendment.

5. Lake County (Illinois) Sheriff's Office. https://www.lakecountyil.gov/2036/Visitation-Rules
Accessed February 20, 2020.

6. In *Grabowski v. Jackson County Public Defender's Office,* 79 F.3d 478 (5th Cir. 1996), the full court looked at this case en banc, vacating the previous panel opinion. The only defendant in this new consideration was Jackson County, Mississippi, which was being sued for alleged constitutional violations. In ruling against Grabowski, the court stated that on the record before the court, there was no showing of the existence of a policy or custom of the county under which any employee violated the inmate's constitutional rights.

CHAPTER 21

Juveniles and Young Offenders

Under our Constitution, the condition of being a boy does not justify a kangaroo court.

U.S. Supreme Court, *In re Gault*

CHAPTER OUTLINE

This chapter examines the special considerations that are given in the criminal justice system to younger persons. Most of these (from the perspective of different, specialized treatment) are juveniles. In some jurisdictions, young offenders—those in age between juveniles and adults—are given some degree of special attention, both legally and correctionally. We will look at the practical and legal aspects of treating those more youthful offenders.

▶ Juveniles: History and Background

Like so much of the legal system in the United States, including many aspects of the criminal justice area, the juvenile justice system can be traced to laws and practices in the law of England. The basic approach of old English law to the offenses committed by children was based on assumptions about criminal responsibility (whether the individual had the mental capacity to commit crimes). The English, by the 1700s, had established the following principles for dealing with children in the criminal law: (1) Children under seven years old were irrebuttably presumed to be incapable of having criminal intent. Those children, therefore, were never brought to court on criminal charges. (2) Children between 7 and 14 years were rebuttably presumed to be incapable of having criminal intent. That meant that those children were not prosecuted for criminal acts unless the state could prove that they were mentally capable of forming criminal intent. (3) Persons over the age of 14 years were presumed to be able to form criminal intent (that presumption, of course, as for adults, could be rebutted by the defendant, showing that they were not mentally able to understand right from wrong or to conform their behavior to legal requirements) and were prosecuted as adults. These divisions between adults and children carried over to American law. See, for example, *Allen v. United States*, 150 U.S. 551 (1893).

Along with the definitions of criminal responsibility according to age, legal concepts of guardianship were also developed. Early in English history, there was the concept of **parens patriae**, which recognized the king as being the "father of the country." Within this concept, the king (later, more broadly, the government) was responsible for the welfare of children and of others (such as mental incompetents) who were not able to be properly cared for by their families. The persons needing such special care or protection were called **wards** of the state and were placed under the protection of the king *(parens patriae)*. This concept developed into the guardianship of wards of the state. To determine the need for such protection, and to declare the legal status of the wards, the children were taken before chancery courts, not criminal courts. Chancery courts were established to keep the "king's conscience" and to decide on matters based on ideas of fairness and doing the right thing, without strict adherence to established principles of statutory or common law. The rules for conducting proceedings were much more relaxed in these courts. The chancery courts took responsibility for looking out for the welfare of children (and others who needed protection), which, over the centuries, developed into the law of juveniles.

▶ Juvenile Court Concepts

Over time, the age of criminal responsibility was raised from 14 to 16 years and then, in many places, to 18 years. In most states in the United States today, 18 years is the age when children (juveniles) are presumed to become adults and are held responsible for their criminal behavior. Some of the other legal concepts that have historically been applied to juvenile court proceedings follow. Later in this chapter, modifications that are being made to some of these concepts are addressed.[1]

Juveniles are not found "guilty" of "committing crimes," they are adjudicated of committing delinquent acts. Flowing from this concept (which really flows from the old English concept of children not being responsible for their acts) is an avoidance of using terms that connote criminality: Juveniles are not prosecuted, they are "proceeded against." There is not a crime involved; there is an act of delinquency. There is no verdict of guilty; there is a "finding of delinquency." A juvenile is not sentenced; instead, there is a "disposition." The juveniles are not defendants in court, they are juveniles charged with being delinquents, at the worst, "criminal offenders."

The **juvenile court** (which may be a separate court, a separate division of a municipal or county court, or a court of general jurisdiction sitting in special session as a juvenile court) sits in protection of the welfare of the juvenile. These courts may be known by various names, such as district, superior, circuit, county, family, or probate. The court proceedings are much less formal than those for adults. The juvenile court sits in the position of judicial protector (guardian) of the rights, and the best interests, of the juvenile. They are often closed to public attendance to protect the privacy of the juvenile.

While previously many juvenile court proceedings were closed to the public and juvenile records sealed, beginning in the 1990s, states began opening juvenile proceedings to the public and making juvenile records available to victims, schools, law enforcement agencies, and the media.[2] In 1976, an eleven year old boy in Oklahoma was arrested for shooting and killing another person. At a public detention hearing, members of the media learned the juvenile's name and took the juvenile's picture. The state court ordered the media not to publish or otherwise disseminate the name and photo of the juvenile. After the state supreme court affirmed the lower court, the U.S. Supreme Court in *Oklahoma Publishing Co. v. District Court in and for Oklahoma City*, 480 U.S. 308 (1977) reversed, holding that:

> *There is no evidence that [the media] acquired the information unlawfully or even without the State's implicit approval. The name and picture of the juvenile here were "publicly revealed in connection with the prosecution of the crime," . . . . Under these circumstances, the District Court's order abridges the freedom of the press in violation of the First and Fourteenth Amendment.*

Two years later, the Supreme Court decided *Smith v. Daily Mail*, 443 U.S. 97 (1979), which addressed the constitutionality of a state law that imposed criminal sanctions on the publication of the name of a person in juvenile court. In this case, a 14-year-old high school student shot and killed another student at a West Virginia high school in the presence of witnesses. Media outlet reporters obtained the name and photo of the alleged shooter from interviewing the witnesses and from other sources. After one of the media outlets published the juvenile's name and photo, another media outlet published the name. Both outlets were charged with violating the state's juvenile confidentiality law in state court. The Supreme Court affirmed the West Virginia Supreme Court of Appeals that the law abridged the freedom of the press guaranteed by the First Amendment. While recognizing the state's interests in protecting the privacy of juvenile offenders, promoting rehabilitation and protecting the juvenile against future loss of employment opportunities due to notoriety, the Court concluded that *"[t]he asserted state interest cannot justify the statute's imposition of criminal sanctions on this type of publication [the truthful publication of an alleged juvenile delinquent's name lawfully obtained by a newspaper]."*

Confidentiality of juvenile court proceedings varies significantly among the states. Generally, most states protect the confidentiality of juvenile court proceedings while the case is pending.[3] Juvenile records are generally obtainable by law enforcement agencies. Records are generally authorized for release to schools; government agencies typically charged with providing welfare or human services programs, and in some states, to victims of juvenile crimes and the media.[4]

Disposition of the juvenile case is based on the concern for the welfare of the juvenile. They are not sentenced to punishment. The court will order what is needed, in the court's judgment, for the welfare of the child, and this is done in the name of treatment. Cases are disposed of quickly (the average juvenile case takes much less time in court than an adult case). **TABLE 21-1** identifies distinctions between the juvenile and criminal justice systems. For example, one distinction is the intake–prosecution stage. In the juvenile justice system, "[t]he decision to file a petition for court action is based on both social and legal factors"; in the adult criminal justice system, "[t]he prosecution decision is based largely on legal facts." In the juvenile justice system, "[d]isposition decisions are based on individual and social factors, offense severity, and youth's offense history." In the adult criminal justice system, "[s]entencing decisions are bound primarily by the severity of the current offense and by the offender's criminal history." With regard to the concept of guilt, in the juvenile justice system, "[i]f guilt is established, the youth is adjudicated delinquent regardless of offense." In the adult criminal justice system, "[g]uilt must be established on individual offenses charged for conviction."

Depending on state law, records of the court proceedings for juveniles may be sealed. This means that the public (including the media) may not peruse the court records. It also means that, under the historical protection of the juvenile's status, they may not be used in later court proceedings, for example, if the juvenile is prosecuted when he becomes an adult.

Juveniles are not sent to prison. They are placed, if they need institutional care, in facilities that have been called by many titles, including training schools, residential facilities, juvenile homes, shelters, cottages, and boys' (and girls') ranches, farms, and camps. There is some movement toward handling more juveniles in regular adult proceedings, as shown in **TABLE 21-2**. This table indicates that the number of referrals of juveniles to adult or criminal courts increased by over 500% from 1972 to 2000 and by another 25% from 2000 to 2009. The number of juvenile cases that were waived into adult court declined from an estimated 13,100 in 1994 (2.6% of petitioned cases) to 3,800 in 2017 (1.4% of petitioned cases). The decline may be explained in part by the increased number of jurisdictions, which allow certain juveniles to be charged mandatorily or, upon the prosecutor's discretion, directly in adult court.

The length of jurisdiction over a case is indeterminate. The juvenile court may retain jurisdiction in order to modify its orders or to do whatever else is in the best interest of the juvenile, ordinarily until the individual's 21st birthday. (In a few states, once juveniles are brought into juvenile court, they may be kept under the court's jurisdiction for some time past their 21st birthdays.) Commitments to facilities are for shorter periods than for most adults: a juvenile may be committed for a period of months or years (not to exceed his 21st birthday). In addition, a juvenile may be committed for an indeterminate amount of time, with their release to be determined (based on reports of their adjustment and betterment) by the court, juvenile parole or institutional authorities, or, at the maximum, until their 21st birthday.[5] If it is possible, they will be returned at the earliest feasible time to the community, with continued supervision and assistance from juvenile staff (government or private).

There are three ways in which juveniles are brought before juvenile courts. First, there are those who are charged with acts of delinquency, which would be crimes if they were committed by adults. (These are the ones we have mainly considered in the previous discussion—the persons who, but for their young age, would be treated as accused persons and criminals in the criminal justice system.) However, flowing from the concept that the state should look after the welfare of all children who have special needs, there are two other categories of juveniles who may be brought before the courts. The first group includes those juveniles who have violated societal rules that are not criminal for adults. These are called **status offenders**. A status offense (such as failing to attend school,

TABLE 21-1 Distinctions between the Juvenile Justice System and the Criminal Justice System

Although the juvenile and criminal justice systems are more alike in some jurisdictions than in others, generalizations can be made about the distinctions between the two systems and about their common ground

Juvenile Justice System	Common Ground	Criminal Justice System
■ Youth behavior is malleable. ■ Rehabilitation is usually a viable goal. ■ Youth are in families and not independent.	■ Community protection is a primary goal. ■ Law violators must be held accountable. ■ Constitutional rights apply.	■ Sanctions should be proportional to the offense. ■ General deterrence works. ■ Rehabilitation is not a primary goal.
Prevention		
■ Many specific delinquency prevention activities (e.g., school, church, recreation) are used. ■ Prevention is intended to change individual behavior and is often focused on reducing risk factors and increasing protective factors in the individual, family, and community.	■ Educational approaches are taken to specific behaviors (drunk driving, drug use).	■ Prevention activities are generalized and are aimed at deterrence (e.g., Crime Watch).
Law Enforcement		
■ Specialized "juvenile" units are used. ■ Some additional behaviors are prohibited (truancy, running away, curfew violations). ■ Some limitations are placed on public access to information. ■ A significant number of youth are diverted away from the juvenile justice system, often into alternative programs.	■ Jurisdiction involves the full range of criminal behavior. ■ Constitutional and procedural safeguards exist. ■ Both reactive and proactive approaches (targeted at offense types, neighborhoods, etc.) are used. ■ Community policing strategies are employed.	■ Open public access to all information is required. ■ Law enforcement exercises discretion to divert offenders out of the criminal justice system.
Intake—Prosecution		
■ In many instances, juvenile court intake, not the prosecutor, decides what cases to file. ■ The decision to file a petition for court action is based on both social and legal factors. ■ A significant portion of cases are diverted from formal case processing. ■ Intake, or the prosecutor, diverts cases from formal processing to services operated by the juvenile court, prosecutor's office, or outside agencies.	■ Probable cause must be established. ■ The prosecutor acts on behalf of the State.	■ Plea bargaining is common. ■ The prosecution decision is based largely on legal facts. ■ Prosecution is valuable in building history for subsequent offenses. ■ Prosecution exercises discretion to withhold charges or divert offenders out of the criminal justice system.

Juvenile Justice System	Common Ground	Criminal Justice System
Detention Jail/lockup		
▪ Juveniles may be detained for their own protection or the community's protection. ▪ Juveniles may not be confined with adults unless there is "sight and sound separation."	▪ Accused offenders may be held in custody to ensure their appearance in court. ▪ Detention alternatives of home or electronic detention are used.	▪ Accused individuals have the right to apply for bond/bail release.
Adjudication—Conviction		
▪ Juvenile court proceedings are "quasi-civil" (not criminal) and may be confidential. ▪ If guilt is established, the youth is adjudicated delinquent regardless of offense. ▪ Right to jury trial is not afforded in all States.	▪ Standard of "proof beyond a reasonable doubt" is required. ▪ Rights to be represented by an attorney, to confront witnesses, and to remain silent are afforded. ▪ Appeals to a higher court are allowed. ▪ Experimentation with specialized courts (i.e., drug courts, gun courts) is underway.	▪ Defendants have a constitutional right to a jury trial. ▪ Guilt must be established on individual offenses charged for conviction. ▪ All proceedings are open.
Disposition—Sentencing		
▪ Disposition decisions are based on individual and social factors, offense severity, and youth's offense history. ▪ Dispositional philosophy includes a significant rehabilitation component. ▪ Many dispositional alternatives are operated by the juvenile court. ▪ Dispositions cover a wide range of community-based and residential services. ▪ Disposition orders may be directed to people other than the offender (e.g., parents). ▪ Disposition may be indeterminate, based on progress demonstrated by the youth.	▪ Decisions are influenced by current offense, offending history, and social factors. ▪ Decisions hold offenders accountable. ▪ Decisions may give consideration to victims (e.g., restitution and "no contact" orders). ▪ Decisions may not be cruel or unusual.	▪ Sentencing decisions are bound primarily by the severity of the current offense and by the offender's criminal history. ▪ Sentencing philosophy is based largely on proportionality and punishment. ▪ Sentence is often determinate, based on offense.
Aftercare—Parole		
▪ Function combines surveillance and reintegration activities (e.g., family, school, work).	▪ The behavior of individuals released from correctional settings is monitored. ▪ Violation of conditions can result in reincarceration.	▪ Function is primarily surveillance and reporting to monitor illicit behavior.

Snyder, Howard N., and Sickmund, Melissa. (1999). Juvenile Offenders and Victims: 1999 National Report. Pages 94–96. Washington, DC: Office of Juvenile Justice and Delinquency Prevention, U.S. Department of Justice. https://www.ncjrs.gov/html/ojjdp/nationalreport99/chapter4.pdf

TABLE 21-2 Distribution of Juveniles Taken into Police Custody in 1972, 1982, 1992, 2002, 2011 and 2017

Distribution	1972	1982	1992	2002	2011	2017
Referred to juvenile court jurisdiction	50.8%	58.9	62.5	72.8	68.4	68.2
Handled within department and released	45%	32.5	30.1	18.1	22	22
Referred to criminal or adult court	1.3%	5.4	4.7	7.0	7.3	7.6
Referred to other police agency	1.6%	1.5	1.1	1.4	1.9	1.3
Referred to welfare agency	1.3%	1.6	1.7	0.7	0.4	0.8

Data from Maguire, K., ed. Sourcebook of Criminal Justice Statistics, Table 4.26.2009. Available from http://www.albany.edu/sourcebook/pdf/t4262009.pdf. January 3, 2011. Data from 2017 Federal Bureau of Investigation. 2018. *Crime in the United States 2017.* [Uniform Crime Reports online] Table 68. Washington, D.C. Accessed September 16, 2020. Available from https://ucr.fbi .gov/crime-in-the.u.s/2017/crime-in-the.u.s.-2017/topic-pages/tables/table-68

running away from home or violating a curfew for young people) may be grounds for bringing the juvenile before the court on a petition requesting that steps be taken to correct the situation or change the behavior of the child. There is also a group of juveniles who are **dependent children**. In most jurisdictions, these children may also be brought before juvenile courts to verify their dependency status in order for the courts to determine the best steps that can be taken for their welfare. Foster parents or group foster homes may be used for such children. They may be removed from the legal responsibility of their parents (or other relatives) and placed under the guardianship of designated alternative parents.

In juvenile cases, a **petition** is a document filed in juvenile court alleging that a juvenile is a delinquent, a status offender, or a dependent and asking the court to assume jurisdiction over the juvenile or asking that the juvenile be transferred to a criminal court for prosecution as an adult. There has been a significant decline in the number of juvenile cases formally processed in juvenile court and the dispositions given. See Juvenile Justice Data Bullets.

▶ Juvenile Justice System Data Bullets

- In 2017, approximately 818,900 delinquency cases were handled in juvenile courts. This is about one half of the total number of delinquency cases processed in 2005.[i]
- In 2017, juvenile petitions were categorized as: 32% property offenses (e.g., burglary, larceny-theft); 29% offenses against persons (e.g., criminal homicide, forcible rape, simple and aggravated assault); 25% public order offenses (e.g., obstruction of justice, disorderly conduct); and 13% drug law violations.[ii]

	1985	2017
Percentage of delinquency petitions initiated against females.[iii]	19%	27%
Percentage of juveniles adjudicated delinquent who received probation.[iv]	59%	63%
Percentage of juveniles adjudicated delinquent who received residential placement.[v]	31%	28%

i. *Delinquency Cases. OJJDP Statistical Briefing Book.* Online. Available: https://www.ojjdp.gov/ojstatbb/court/qa06201.asp?qaDate=2017. Released on April 23, 2019
ii. Id.
iii. Hockenberry, S. *Juvenile Justice Statistics.* Page 4. U.S. Department of Justice. Office of Justice Programs. October 2019. Available: https://ojjdp.ojp.gov/sites/g/files/xyckuh176/files/media/document/253105.pdf
iv. *Characteristics of delinquency cases handled by juvenile courts, 2017. OJJDP Statistical Briefing Book.* Online. Available: https://www .ojjdp.gov/ojstatbb/court/qa06206.asp?qaDate=2017 . Released on April 23, 2019.
v. *Adjudicated Delinquency Cases. OJJDP Statistical Briefing Book.* Online. Available: https://www.ojjdp.gov/ojstatbb/court/qa06501 .asp?qaDate=2017. Released on April 23, 2019.

- In 2017, juveniles were adjudicated delinquent in 53% (more than 248,000) of the petitioned cases.[vi]
- The estimated number of juveniles in residential placement declined from 105,000 in 1997 to 44,000 in 2017.[vii]
- In 2017, juveniles in residential placement had been adjudicated for person offenses (41%); property offenses (22%); drug offenses (5%); public order offenses (13%); technical violations (15%) [e.g., violations of the conditions of parole, probation, or court orders] and status offenses (4%).[viii]
- Over the last 20 years, females have accounted for an estimated 14% of juveniles in residential placement.[ix]
- In 2017, juveniles aged 16 and 17 years accounted for 55% of those receiving juvenile residential placement.[x]
- The proportion of persons receiving "other" sanctions (other than probation or residential placement) has declined from 11% in 1985 to 9% in 2017.[xi]
- The number of juveniles in state adult correctional facilities has declined by 76% [3,892 to 935] from 2000 to 2017.[xii]
- The number of juvenile cases that were judicially waived into adult court declined from an estimated 13,100 in 1994 (2.6% of petitioned cases) to 3,800 in 2017 (1.4% of petitioned cases). The decline may be explained in part by the increased number of jurisdictions allowing certain juveniles to be charged mandatorily, or upon the prosecutor's discretion, in adult court.[xiii]

The greatest majority of juveniles in residential placement have been adjudicated for a crime against the person, although that placement declined from 31% in 1985 to 25% in 2007 but has increased to 41% in 2017. The proportion of persons receiving other sanctions had declined from 11% in 1985 to 9% in 2017.[6]

In these different kinds of dispositions, the terminology used in courts (and the mechanics of sanctioning, as well as the percentages spread among such dispositions) are very similar to those used for adult offenders. For juvenile delinquents, probation offices screen cases and submit reports to juvenile courts on recommended dispositions; they provide supervision to those placed on probation; and they deliver aftercare services to many juveniles when they are released from residential programs. How these duties are performed, and whether they are even performed by probation officers, varies from one jurisdiction to another. Not all probation officers, for example, provide aftercare services. In some jurisdictions, the prosecutor screens cases and makes recommendations to the court for dispositions. In all jurisdictions, probation officers are responsible for the supervision of probationers when probation is ordered by the juvenile courts. Probation is, by far, the most commonly used sanction for juvenile delinquents and especially so for first offenders.

▶ More Sophisticated Juveniles

You will recall that, under English law, there was a rebuttable presumption that children over the age of 7 years and up to the age of 14 years were not criminally responsible and should not be tried or punished as adult criminals. That concept has been transformed, under the U.S. juvenile law system, into the presumption that juveniles should be processed in juvenile courts. What is the age ceiling for juvenile court jurisdiction? Ordinarily, the term "juvenile" refers to persons under the age of 18 years, although a few states have set a maximum age of juvenile

---

vi. *Adjudicated Delinquency Cases. OJJDP Statistical Briefing Book.* Online. Available: https://www.ojjdp.gov/ojstatbb/court/qa06501.asp?qaDate=2017. Released on April 23, 2019.

vii. *Disposition of Adjudicated Cases. OJJDP Statistical Briefing Book.* Online. Available: https://www.ojjdp.gov/ojstatbb/court/qa06802.asp?qaDate=2017. Released on April 23, 2019. 1985 Data from Knoll, C. & Sickmund, M. *Delinquency Cases in Juvenile Court. (2007).* Pages 1–3. (Washington, DC: Office of Juvenile Justice and Delinquency Prevention, U.S. Department of Justice. 2010.)

viii. *One Day Count of Juveniles in Residential Placement Facilities. OJJDP Statistical Briefing Book.* Online. Available: https://www.ojjdp.gov/ojstatbb/corrections/qa08201.asp?qaDate=2017. Released on April 23, 2019.

ix. *Offense Profile of Juveniles held in Residential Placement. OJJDP Statistical Briefing Book.* Online. Available: https://www.ojjdp.gov/ojstatbb/corrections/qa08301.asp?qaDate=2017. Released on October 31, 2019.

x. *Female Proportion of Juveniles in residential placement. OJJDP Statistical Briefing Book.* Online. Available: https://www.ojjdp.gov/ojstatbb/corrections/qa08202.asp?qaDate=2017. Released on October 31, 2019.

xi. *Age Profile of Juveniles in Residential Placement Facilities. OJJDP Statistical Briefing Book.* Online. Available: https://www.ojjdp.gov/ojstatbb/corrections/qa08204.asp?qaDate=2017. Released on April 23, 2019.

xii. See note v. above

xiii. *Juveniles in State Prisons OJJDP Statistical Briefing Book.* Online. Available: https://www.ojjdp.gov/ojstatbb/corrections/qa08204.asp?qaDate=2017. Released on April 23, 2019.

xiv. Hockenberry, S. & Puzzanchera, C. *Juvenile Court Statistics. (2017).* Pittsburgh, PA. National Center for Juvenile Justice. Available: http://www.ncjj.org/pdf/jcsreports/jcs2017report.pdf

jurisdiction at 17 years (five states have set the age at 16: Georgia, Michigan, Missouri, Texas, and Wisconsin).[7] Exceptions are possible, and it is permissible for a court to find that a juvenile is of sufficient maturity that they should be tried as an adult.

Every state has a means for juveniles to be tried in adult criminal courts under certain circumstances. There are three types of transfer laws. The first is legislative (automatic transfer), which is in effect in 29 states. These cases require the juvenile's transfer if statutory requirements are met. An example is a juvenile, who is 14 years or older, and alleged to have committed a violent felony. In this instance, the case either begins in criminal court or, if it starts in juvenile court, it is transferred to criminal court.

The second type of transfer law is judicial transfer, operating in 45 states and the District of Columbia. A judicial transfer leaves to the juvenile court judge the discretion to decide whether a juvenile should be transferred after the prosecution files a motion to transfer. The third type is prosecutorial direct-file laws, in 14 states and the District of Columbia. In this instance, the discretion rests with the prosecutor, allowing them to decide whether to file charges in the juvenile or criminal court. (Twenty-five states also have reverse waiver laws, giving to the criminal court judge the discretion to transfer the case back to juvenile court, or, for sentencing purposes, to treat the defendant as a juvenile.[8] In 33 states and the District of Columbia, a juvenile who has been convicted of an offense as an adult will always be processed as an adult.

For the traditional juvenile transfer to adult criminal court to occur, usually by motion of the prosecutor (but sometimes on motion of the court itself, or by the probation office, or even by the parents, or by the juvenile themselves), the court hears evidence, reviews reports and recommendations, and considers arguments on the issue of whether the juvenile is of such a degree of maturity or sophistication that their case should be heard in adult court. If the court decides that adult proceedings are appropriate for the individual, the judge enters an order that waives jurisdiction over the juvenile by the juvenile court and transfers the case to the local court of adult criminal prosecution. The number of juvenile cases that were judicially waived into adult court declined from an estimated 13,100 in 1994 (2.6% of petitioned cases) to 3,800 in 2017 (1.4% of petitioned cases).[9]

In the 1980s, there was a public perception that serious juvenile crime was increasing and that the system needed to "get tough." Many states began to pass more punitive laws. In the 1990s, as a result of this effort to crack down on juvenile crime, there were five areas of change:

1. Transfer provisions: Forty-five states passed laws to make it easier to transfer juvenile offenders from the juvenile justice system to the adult criminal justice system.
2. Sentencing authority: Thirty-one states gave criminal and juvenile courts expanded (tougher) sentencing options for juveniles.
3. Confidentiality: Forty-seven states modified their laws to make juvenile records and proceedings more open.
4. Victim rights: Twenty-two states expanded the role of victims of juvenile crime in the juvenile justice process.
5. Correctional programming: Due to new transfer and sentencing laws, adult and juvenile correctional administrators developed new programs for juvenile offenders.

In addition, some states have modified their juvenile code "purpose" clauses not only with respect to the underlying philosophies and assumptions but also in how they approach their task. Most states fall within one of the following five purpose clauses. Components of Balanced and Restorative Justice (BARJ) are the most common in state purpose clauses. Supporters of this concept believe the balanced attention of juvenile courts should focus on three primary interests: public safety, individual accountability to victims and to the community, and the development of skills to help offenders live productive and law-abiding lives.

A second type of purpose clause is modeled on language from the Standard Juvenile Court Act and has more of the *parens patriae* concept: "each child coming within the jurisdiction of the court shall receive … care, guidance, and control that will conduce to his welfare and the best interest of the state, and that when he is removed from the control of his parents the court shall secure for him care as nearly as possible equivalent to that which they should have given him."

A third group of states uses language found in the purpose clause of a 1960s document (Legislative Guide for Drafting Family and Juvenile Court Acts). This document lists four purposes: providing for the care, protection, and the wholesome development of children involved with the juvenile court; removing from children committing delinquent acts the consequences of criminal behavior and substituting supervision, care, and rehabilitation;

removing a child from his home only when necessary for his welfare or for public safety; and assuring that the involved parties have their constitutional and other legal rights.

Purpose clauses in some states focus on being "tough." These stress community protection, offender accountability, deterrence, or outright punishment. A final small group of states has purpose clauses that focus on the welfare and best interests of the child, with this being the primary purpose of the juvenile court system. An example is Massachusetts, which says accused juveniles shall be "treated, not as criminals, but as children in need of aid, encouragement and guidance. Proceedings against children ... shall not be deemed criminal proceedings."[10]

▶ *Kent v. United States*

Compared with adult criminal defendants and prisoners, there has been little attention paid to the rights of juveniles under the Constitution. Most of the decisions that exist are interpretations of requirements of the juvenile statutes in particular states and many deal with the procedures that must be followed in cases of delinquency, status offenses, or dependency. Some have dealt with the programs that are offered to juveniles and the conditions under which juveniles are held when they are detained or committed.

In *Kent* (and *Gault*), the Supreme Court reviewed the rights of juveniles and the constitutional protections to which they are entitled. *Kent v. United States,* 383 U.S. 541 (1966), dealt with a youth of 16 whose case was waived by a juvenile court judge to adult court. Kent broke into an apartment, stole a wallet, and raped the woman who was there. He was interrogated by police (without presence of counsel) and admitted to these offenses, as well as others that he had committed earlier. His mother thereafter retained counsel. The juvenile court held no hearing. The judge did not talk to Kent, his mother, or his counsel. The judge considered reports submitted by court staff, the social service department, and the probation section (Kent was on probation for an offense he had committed when he was 14). Kent's counsel requested that he be allowed to review the file that the judge was considering, but that was denied. The Juvenile Court Act, under which the District of Columbia juvenile judge was acting, stated that the case of a juvenile who was 16 years of age or older and charged with an offense that would be a felony if committed by an adult could be waived to adult court, based on "full investigation" by the juvenile judge. No hearing was mandated by the statute or by court rules, and none was ordinarily conducted. Kent appealed the order waiving his case to adult court. The District of Columbia courts denied his appeals, holding that the juvenile court had complied with the juvenile statute and its purposes.

Kent was indicted in U.S. district court (the adult trial court for felonies in the District of Columbia) on eight counts, covering housebreaking, robbery, and rape. At trial, he was found to be not guilty by reason of insanity on the rape counts. He was convicted on the other counts and received a sentence of 30 to 90 years. (Under District of Columbia law, he was mandatorily committed to St. Elizabeth's Hospital for treatment on the basis of the insanity acquittal.) Kent again appealed his prosecution in adult court and his convictions there. The court of appeals upheld the procedures that had been followed. But the Supreme Court held that the transfer proceedings that had been used to send Kent from juvenile court to adult court were invalid.

> **While there can be no doubt of the original laudable purpose of juvenile courts, studies and critiques in recent years raise serious questions as to whether actual performance measures well enough against theoretical purpose to make tolerable the immunity of the process from the reach of constitutional guarantees applicable to adults.... It is clear beyond dispute that the waiver of jurisdiction is a "critically important" action determining vitally important statutory rights of the juvenile .... [A]s a condition to a valid waiver order, [Kent] was entitled to a hearing, including access by his counsel to the social records and probation or similar reports which presumably are considered by the court, and to a statement of reasons for the Juvenile Court's decision.**

This conclusion was reached based on "constitutional principles relating to due process and the assistance of counsel."

The Supreme Court noted in its review of Kent's case that the theory of the juvenile court statute was rooted in social welfare philosophy rather than in traditional criminal concepts.

> **The Juvenile Court is theoretically engaged in determining the needs of the child and of society rather than adjudicating criminal conduct. The objectives are to provide measures of guidance and**

rehabilitation for the child and protection for society, not to fix criminal responsibility, guilt, and punishment. The State is *parens patriae* rather than prosecuting attorney and judge. But the admonition to function in a "parental" relationship is not an invitation to procedural arbitrariness.

For the first time, the Supreme Court set minimum constitutional (due process) requirements for juvenile waiver proceedings. It said, "Meaningful review [by the juvenile judge] requires that the reviewing court should review. It should not be remitted to assumptions." Furthermore, there had to be a hearing, which could be informal. There was also a right to counsel, which could not be a mere formality; the counsel had to be given access to the records that were considered by the court. (In a strange twist for the disposition of the case, the Supreme Court noted that it ordinarily would have reversed the lower courts' rulings and sent the case back to the juvenile court for a proper determination, with a hearing, on the waiver decision. But Kent had by this time passed the age of 21, so the juvenile court no longer had jurisdiction over him. The Supreme Court resisted the suggestion by Kent that his conviction and sentence be totally vacated as improper and remanded the case to the [adult] district court for a hearing *de novo* (that is, as if there had been no earlier decision) on the waiver, in accord with the new constitutional requirements laid down by the Supreme Court.)

▶ *In re Gault*

Gault, a 15 year old, was taken into custody by a county sheriff in Arizona, without notice to his parents. When he was placed in a detention home, Gault's mother was advised that he was being held there for making an obscene phone call. His hearing in juvenile court was held the next day. The petition that was filed against him did not refer to any facts but only stated that he was a delinquent minor. At the hearing, an officer said that when he was questioned, Gault admitted making lewd remarks on the phone. Neither Gault nor his parents were advised of any right to have counsel. He was committed to the Arizona State Industrial School for the remainder of his minority (until he reached age 21). Gault's parents filed a petition for habeas corpus, which was denied in the Arizona courts (including the Supreme Court of Arizona).

The U.S. Supreme Court reversed in *In re Gault,* 387 U.S. 1 (1967). The Court held that Gault had been denied due process under the Constitution because his juvenile delinquency proceedings did not comply with minimum requirements for fair treatment.

> **Due process of law is the primary and indispensable foundation of individual freedom. It is the basic and essential term in the social compact which defines the rights of the individual and delimits the powers which the state may exercise.**

The Court noted that it was claimed by those arguing in favor of the informal juvenile proceedings that those proceedings were designed to benefit juveniles, not to punish criminal behavior, which is the purpose of criminal proceedings. The Court refused to accept the state's defense of the closed, informal juvenile proceeding. After all, the Court pointed out, this juvenile process resulted in a boy being committed to an institution, where he could be deprived of his liberty for years. Whatever the institution might euphemistically be called, the Court said (in this case, it was called an "Industrial School"), the boy's world became "a building with whitewashed walls, regimented routine, and institutional hours."

> **Under our Constitution, the condition of being a boy does not justify a kangaroo court .... As [other commentators] have put it, "The rhetoric of the juvenile court movement has developed without any necessarily close correspondence to the realities of court and institutional routines."**

The Court also observed that, in *Kent,* it was said (there, with respect to waiver of a juvenile to adult court):

> **[T]here is no place in our system of law for reaching a result of such tremendous consequences ... without hearing, without effective assistance of counsel, without a statement of reasons [for the action taken].**

The Court in *Gault* adopted this same view, with respect to the delinquency hearing for a juvenile.

> **We do not mean … to indicate that the hearing to be held must conform with all of the requirements of a criminal trial or even of the usual administrative hearing; but we do hold that the hearing must measure up to the essentials of due process and fair treatment.**

Well, if a juvenile hearing does not have to match the process of a criminal trial or even an administrative hearing, what due process is required at a juvenile hearing? Fortunately, the Supreme Court gave us the minimum constitutional requirements:

1. There must be advance written notice to the child and to his parents of the specific charges and the factual allegations that support the delinquency petition or charges. These must be provided sufficiently in advance of the hearing to permit preparation for the hearing.
2. There must be notification to the child and to his parents of the child's right to be represented by counsel, either retained by them or, if they cannot afford counsel, appointed by the court.
3. The child must be entitled to the application of the constitutional privilege against self-incrimination.
4. Absent a valid confession, a determination of delinquency and an order of commitment must be based only on sworn testimony, subjected to the opportunity for cross-examination.

(As to another question that had been raised in *Gault,* the Supreme Court avoided the issue of whether there was a constitutional right to appellate review of the delinquency and commitment determination. This avoidance was based on procedural grounds, because the case had not developed in a way that permitted the Court to review that question.)

▶ *In re Winship*

What should be the standard of proof in juvenile proceedings? This was the issue before the Supreme Court in the case of *In re Winship,* 397 U.S. 358 (1970). In this case, a 12-year-old boy was found to have stolen $112 from a woman's purse. The petition charging the boy with delinquency alleged that if the act had been committed by an adult, the crime would have been larceny. The governing New York law stated that "[a]ny determination at the conclusion of [an adjudicatory] hearing that a [juvenile] did an act or acts must be based on a preponderance of the evidence." The youth was subsequently ordered to be placed in a training school for 18 months, subject to possible annual extensions until his 18th birthday, which for Winship would have been six years down the road. The appeals courts affirmed.

In reversing, the Supreme Court noted that, for criminal cases, a guilty finding requires proof to be established beyond a reasonable doubt. The Court observed that the standard is important because the accused is facing a possible loss of liberty, and the defendant will also be stigmatized if convicted.

> **Accordingly, a society that values the good name and freedom of every individual should not condemn a man for commission of a crime when there is reasonable doubt about his guilt.**

Thus, the question before the Court was whether juveniles also are constitutionally entitled to this same standard when charged with the equivalent of a criminal law violation. In answering yes, the Court rejected the contrary conclusions of the New York Court of Appeals. The appeals court had argued against stricter standards on the grounds that the delinquency adjudication was not a conviction; that the juvenile proceedings were designed not to punish, but to "save" the child; that to impose the higher standard (of proof beyond a reasonable doubt) would risk the "destruction" of the beneficial aspects of the juvenile process; that to allow a child to prevail was probably not in his best interest; and that there was only a "tenuous" difference between the two standards. The Supreme Court commented that the trial judge had acknowledged that the proof might not show the boy's guilt beyond a reasonable doubt.

> **In sum, the constitutional safeguard of proof beyond a reasonable doubt is as much required during the adjudicatory stage of a delinquency proceeding as are those constitutional safeguards applied in *Gault*—notice of charges, right to counsel, the rights of confrontation and examination, and the privilege against self incrimination. We therefore hold, in agreement with Chief Judge Fuld in dissent in the Court of Appeals, "that, where a 12-year old child is charged with an act of stealing which renders him liable to confinement for as long as six years, then, as a matter of due process … the case against him must be proved beyond a reasonable doubt."**

▶ *McKeiver v. Pennsylvania; Breed v. Jones; Schall v. Martin*

Other Supreme Court decisions in the 1970s and 1980s addressed whether juveniles appearing before the juvenile court were constitutionally entitled to jury trials; whether an adjudicated delinquent could subsequently be referred to adult criminal court; and whether preventive detention may be used for juveniles.

McKeiver v. Pennsylvania, 403 U.S. 528 (1971), involved two separate lower court cases (McKeiver and Terry), later consolidated. McKeiver, age 16, was charged with robbery, larceny, and receiving stolen goods. At the adjudication hearing, his counsel's request for a jury trial was denied. McKeiver was adjudged a delinquent.

In the companion case, Terry, age 15, was charged with assault and battery on a police officer and conspiracy. His attorney's request for a jury trial was denied, and Terry was adjudged a delinquent. The state supreme court consolidated the two cases. The question considered by the court was "whether there is a constitutional right to a jury trial in juvenile court." The court held there was no such right. The United States Supreme Court affirmed, finding that the due process clause of the Fourteenth Amendment did not require jury trials in the juvenile court.

> All the litigants here agree that the applicable due process standard in juvenile proceedings, as developed by *Gault* and *Winship*, is fundamental fairness. As that standard was applied in those two cases, we have an emphasis on factfinding procedures …. But one cannot say that in our legal system the jury is a necessary component of accurate factfinding ….
>
> The imposition of the jury trial on the juvenile court system would not strengthen greatly, if at all, the factfinding function, and would, contrarily, provide an attrition of the juvenile court's assumed ability to function in a unique manner.

While the Supreme Court held that there is no constitutional right to a jury trial in juvenile court, states do have the option to provide for such trials. For example, Kansas state law (K.S.A. Section 38-2357 provides: *The trial of a felony or misdemeanor case shall be to the court unless the juvenile requests a jury trial in writing within 30 days from the date of the juvenile's entry of a plea of not guilty. . . . .* The Kansas Supreme Court in *In Re LM*, 186 P.3d 164 (Kan. 2008) reversed its earlier precedent and concluded that juveniles had a right to a trial by jury. The court, in making its ruling and over-ruling its precedent, noted that the state had shifted its goal of rehabilitation of juveniles to one of protecting the public: "The primary goals of the juvenile justice code are to promote public safety, hold juvenile offenders accountable for their behavior and improve their ability to live more productively and responsibly in the community."

In *Breed v. Jones*, 421 U.S. 519 (1975), Jones, age 17 years, following a juvenile court adjudicatory hearing, was found to have violated a criminal statute (robbery). Two weeks later, he had a dispositional hearing and was found unfit for treatment as a juvenile. Prosecution as an adult was ordered. He was convicted in adult court of robbery in the first degree and committed to the state youth authority.

Through his mother as **guardian ad litem**, Jones filed a petition for a writ of habeas corpus, alleging his transfer to adult court and subsequent trial constituted double jeopardy. The district court denied the petition, holding that juvenile adjudication is not a trial. The appeals court reversed. In support of its finding that jeopardy attached at the adjudicatory hearing, the appeals court said the juvenile court had the power to "impose severe restrictions upon the juvenile's liberty" and that to hold jeopardy did not attach allows "the prosecution to review in advance the accused's defense and…hear him testify about the crime charged." The court found such a procedure "offensive to [its] concepts of basic, even-handed fairness."

In agreeing to hear the case, the Supreme Court stated that a conflict existed on this issue between courts of appeals and the highest courts of a number of states and also mentioned "the importance of final resolution … to the administration of the juvenile-court system."

The Court found a violation of the double jeopardy clause of the Fifth Amendment, as applied to the states through the Fourteenth Amendment. The Court opinion, which resulted in the vacating of Jones's adult conviction, pointed out that Jones went through two trials for the same offense and twice had to marshal his resources against those of the state. The Court held that juvenile court adjudication with a finding that the juvenile had violated a criminal statute is equivalent to trial in criminal court. The Court said to require transfer hearings prior to adjudicatory hearings does not affect the nature of such hearings or the quality of decision making at the transfer hearings but did express concern when a transfer hearing occurs after the adjudicatory hearing.

Knowledge of the risk of transfer after an adjudicatory hearing can only undermine the potential for informality and cooperation which was intended to be the hallmark of the juvenile-court system. Rather than concerning themselves with the matter at hand, establishing innocence or seeking a disposition best suited to individual correctional needs ... the juvenile and his attorney are pressed into a posture of adversary wariness that is conducive to neither.

In *Schall v. Martin,* 467 U.S. 253 (1984), the Supreme Court examined whether preventive detention of juveniles under New York's Family Court Act (FCA) is compatible with the "fundamental fairness" required by due process. Section 320.5(3)(b) of that Act allowed pretrial detention of an accused juvenile delinquent upon a finding of serious risk that the juvenile "may before the return date commit an act which if committed by an adult would constitute a crime."

Martin, age 14, was arrested and charged with robbery, assault, and possession of a weapon. Finding a serious risk that Martin would commit another crime if released, the Family Court judge ordered Martin detained pending adjudication. While still in preventive detention, Martin filed a habeas corpus action in which he challenged the fundamental fairness of preventive detention. (The filing was done as a class action and the class was later certified by the district court.)

The district court held that pretrial detention under § 320.5(3)(b) violated due process. The court of appeals affirmed, commenting that most juveniles detained under the statute either have their petitions dismissed prior to adjudication or are released after adjudication, concluding that the statute is principally used "not for preventive purposes, but to impose punishment for unadjudicated criminal acts."

The Supreme Court reversed. The Court looked at whether preventive detention of juveniles under the FCA statute is compatible with the "fundamental fairness" required by due process. The Court held it was:

Every state [and the District of Columbia] permits preventive detention of juveniles accused of crime .... In light of the uniform legislative judgment that pretrial detention of juveniles properly promotes the interests of both society and the juvenile, we conclude ... the practice serves a legitimate regulatory purpose compatible with the "fundamental fairness" demanded by the Due Process Clause in juvenile proceedings.

As to the issue of punishment, the Court observed that the statute itself gave no indication that preventive detention is used or intended as punishment. Disagreeing with the lower court, the Supreme Court said pretrial detention did not have to be seen as punitive just because a juvenile was put on probation or subsequently released subject to conditions. The Court saw such actions as reinforcing the original determination of the need for close supervision and as protecting both the juvenile and society from the risks of pretrial crime. The Court found there were sufficient procedures (notice, hearing, and a statement of the facts and reasons) prior to any detention under the statute, with provisions for a formal probable cause hearing shortly thereafter, if the factfinding hearing is not scheduled within three days. The Court opinion also referenced the *parens patriae* state interest in promoting the welfare of children.

Children, by definition, are not assumed to have the capacity to take care of themselves. They are assumed to be subject to the control of their parents, and if parental control falters, the State must play its part as *parens patriae.*

▶ Death Penalty for Juvenile Offenders

This chapter began with the recognition of the special considerations the criminal justice system affords younger persons. A significant part of this chapter has examined Supreme Court decisions that have set the constitutional framework for the functioning of the juvenile court. The next section of this chapter will continue to look at these special considerations, but from a different perspective—that of sentencing.

From 1988 through 2005, the Supreme Court decided three cases dealing with the constitutionality of imposing the death penalty for a capital offense committed by a juvenile. In *Thompson v. Oklahoma,* 487 U.S. 815 (1988), the Court ruled that the death penalty could not be constitutionally imposed on persons for capital offenses committed at age 15 years or younger. One year later, in *Stanford v. Kentucky,* 492 U.S. 361 (1989), the Court ruled that the death penalty could be constitutionally imposed on juveniles who committed capital offenses at age 16 or 17 years. In 2005, in *Roper v. Simmons,* 543 U.S. 551 (2005), the Court reversed *Stanford* and ruled that the Eighth and Fourteenth Amendments are violated when the sentence of death is imposed on a person for a capital offense committed while the person was younger than 18 years. These cases will be analyzed in the order in which each was decided.

In *Thompson v. Oklahoma,* the Court ruled that imposing the death penalty on a juvenile for a capital offense committed when the juvenile was 15 violated the Eighth Amendment. Thompson was one of four persons who had brutally murdered Thompson's former brother-in-law. Each of the four was convicted of murder and sentenced to death. In determining whether the death penalty could be constitutionally imposed on a person for a crime committed at age 15, the Court held that the prohibition against cruel and unusual punishments had to be interpreted "according to its text, by considering history, tradition, and precedent, and with due regard for its purpose and function in the constitutional design." This process involves a consideration of the "evolving standards of decency that mark the progress of a maturing society" to determine those punishments that are so disproportionate as to be cruel and unusual.

The Court next identified a number of areas—for example, death penalty states that set a minimum age (none had set the age lower than 16); the views of respected professional organizations; and jury actions (the last execution of a person who committed their crime while under the age of 16 had been done over 40 years earlier, in 1948)—to determine that current standards of decency did not allow executing a person under age 16 at the time of the crime. The Court further said in *Thompson:*

> **The reasons why juveniles are not trusted with the privileges and responsibilities of an adult also explain why their irresponsible conduct is not as morally reprehensible as that of an adult.**

The Court also concluded that two principal social purposes for imposing the death penalty are retribution and deterrence of capital crimes. It is not inconsistent with society's "respect for the dignity of man" to extract retribution by capital punishment for the moral outrage caused by "particularly offensive conduct." However, the Court ruled:

> **Given the lesser culpability of the juvenile offender, the teenager's capacity for growth, and society's fiduciary obligations to its children, this conclusion is simply inapplicable to the execution of a fifteen year-old offender.**

The Court also ruled that prohibiting the execution of persons who committed capital crimes at an age younger than 16 would not diminish the deterrent value of capital punishment. Because imposing the death penalty on juveniles who committed capital crimes at an age younger than 16 promoted neither of the societal purposes of retribution or deterrence, the offender's execution would be "nothing more than the purposeless and needless imposition of pain and suffering."

The next year, in *Stanford,* the Court held that the Eighth and Fourteenth Amendments did not bar the execution of a person over age 15 and under age 18. Stanford was 17 when he participated in the rape and murder of a gas station attendant, which occurred as part of a robbery. Stanford was waived into adult court pursuant to state law based on the seriousness of the offenses and his past delinquencies. Following a trial, he was convicted and sentenced to death. The state supreme court affirmed the waiver into adult court, the conviction, and sentence. In upholding the constitutionality of the death penalty imposed for offenses committed while the person was 16 or 17, the Court pointed out that 22 of the 37 states that provided for the death penalty allowed the execution of 16 year olds, and 25 states allowed for the execution of 17 year-olds. The Court said this indicated the absence of a national consensus that such executions would be cruel and unusual. The Court also declined the invitation that it bring its own judgment to this issue as to whether the death penalty for juveniles is acceptable or cruel and unusual.

Sixteen years after ruling that the Constitution did not prohibit the execution of persons for crimes committed when they were 16 or 17, the Court reversed its *Stanford* decision in *Roper v. Simmons,* 543 U.S. 551 (2005). In 1993, when Simmons was 17, he and a 15-year-old accomplice kidnapped and murdered a female victim. Prior to the crime, Simmons told his friends that he wanted to kill someone and that because he was a minor he could get away with it. He and the accomplice broke into the victim's home, bound her, took her to a nearby railroad trestle where she was thrown into the river under the trestle. After the crime was committed, Simmons bragged to his friends about killing the woman, leading to his arrest and eventual confession.

At age 17, Simmons was outside the criminal jurisdiction of the juvenile court system in Missouri. Tried as an adult, the jury found him guilty of murder, and he was sentenced to death. His conviction and sentence were affirmed by the state supreme court. After the Supreme Court issued its opinion in *Atkins v. Virginia,* 536 U.S. 304 (2002), barring the execution of a mentally retarded (this is the term used by the courts) person, Simmons filed a new petition for postconviction relief, claiming that the reasoning of *Atkins* bars executing a juvenile who was under the age 18 at the time of the criminal act. The state supreme court agreed, holding that a "national consensus has developed against the execution of juvenile offenders." Simmons' death sentence was set aside, and he was resentenced to "life imprisonment without eligibility for probation, parole, or release except by act of the Governor."

In affirming the lower court, the Supreme Court first restated the principles announced in *Thompson v. Oklahoma* (discussed above)—that the prohibition against cruel and unusual punishments had to be interpreted by considering the history, tradition, and precedent of the Eighth Amendment, and also whether the punishment was so disproportionate to the crime that the "evolving standards of decency" are offended. The Court would do this by looking at the objective indications of consensus and then, in the exercise of its own independent judgment, determine whether the death penalty is a disproportionate punishment for juveniles.

To assess national consensus, the Court used the same process it had used in *Atkins,* looking at where the states stood with regard to the execution of juveniles. The Court concluded that 30 states prohibited the death penalty for juveniles, including 12 states that prohibited the death penalty for all offenses. Even in those states with capital punishment, 18 states prohibited imposing the death sentence for crimes committed by juveniles. Of the 20 states that permitted the use of the death penalty for crimes committed by juveniles, it had been imposed only infrequently. Only six states since the *Stanford* decision had executed prisoners for crimes committed as a juvenile, and only three states had done so in the 10 years before the *Roper* decision.

The Court also looked at what was occurring in society from a broader perspective:

Since *Stanford,* no State that previously prohibited capital punishment for juveniles has reinstated it. This fact, coupled with the trend toward abolition of the juvenile death penalty, carries special force in light of the general popularity of anticrime legislation … and in light of the particular trend in recent years toward cracking down on juvenile crime in other respects ….

As in *Atkins*, the objective indicia of consensus in this case—the rejection of the juvenile death penalty in the majority of States; the infrequency of its use even where it remains on the books; and the consistency in the trend toward abolition of the practice—provide sufficient evidence that today our society views juveniles, in the words *Atkins* used respecting the mentally retarded, as "categorically less culpable than the average criminal."

The Court held that imposing the death penalty on an offender for an offense committed as a juvenile is prohibited by the Eighth Amendment. Because the death penalty is the most severe punishment society can impose, the Court said that its application must be limited to persons committing the most serious crimes and whose "extreme culpability" makes that person the most deserving to be executed. The Court considered three general differences between juveniles and adults, using these differences to support its holding that juveniles cannot with reliability be classified among the worst offenders. First, as put forth by scientific and sociological studies, "[a] lack of maturity and an underdeveloped sense of responsibility are found in youth more often than adults and are more understandable among the young." Second, the Court pointed to juveniles being more vulnerable or susceptible to negative pressures, with this discussed in the context that juveniles have less control, or less experience with control, over their own environment. Third, the juvenile's character is less well formed compared with that of an adult; the personality traits are more transitory and less firmed up.

These differences render suspect any conclusion that a juvenile falls among the worst offenders. The susceptibility of juveniles to immature and irresponsible behavior means "their irresponsible conduct is not as morally reprehensible as that of an adult." … Their own vulnerability and comparative lack of control over their immediate surroundings mean juveniles have a greater claim than adults to be forgiven for failing to escape negative influences in their whole environment …. The reality that juveniles still struggle to define their identity means it is less supportable to conclude that even a heinous crime committed by a juvenile is evidence of irretrievably depraved character. From a moral standpoint it would be misguided to equate the failings of a minor with those of an adult, for a greater possibility exists that a minor's character deficiencies will be reformed.

As it had in *Thompson,* the Court concluded that the two social purposes served by the death penalty—retribution and deterrence of capital crimes by future offenders—were not as strong in cases involving juveniles.

The Court also rejected the argument that the death penalty determination should be made on a case-by-case basis, holding that the differences between juvenile and adult offenders are too significant and too well understood to risk allowing the "brutality or cold-blooded nature" of a particular crime to overpower mitigating arguments.

A final issue in *Roper* concerned the United States being the only country to still give official sanction to the juvenile death penalty. Acknowledging that this information was not controlling, the Court nonetheless saw the practices of other countries as instructive in the Court's interpretation of the Eighth Amendment's prohibition against cruel and unusual punishment.

The opinion of the world community, while not controlling our outcome, does provide respected and significant confirmation for our own conclusions.

▶ *Graham v. Florida*

In *Roper,* the Supreme Court held it was unconstitutional to impose the death penalty on offenders who were under the age of 18 at the time of their homicide crime. *Graham v. Florida*, 560 U.S. 48 (2010), continued the examination of the sentencing of juveniles in adult criminal courts and the "evolving standards of decency" by addressing whether the Eighth Amendment is violated when a juvenile is sentenced to life in prison without parole for a nonhomicide crime?

Terrence Graham, at age 16, was one of four youths who attempted to rob a barbecue restaurant. As allowed by state statute, he was charged as an adult. The specific charges were armed burglary with assault or battery, a first-degree felony carrying a maximum penalty of life in prison with no possibility of parole, and attempted armed robbery, a second-degree felony with a maximum penalty of 15 years.

Under a plea agreement, Graham pleaded guilty to both charges. The plea agreement was accepted by the trial court, and an adjudication of guilt was withheld, with Graham sentenced to concurrent three-year terms of probation. The first 12 months of his probation were served in the county jail.

Less than six months after release, at age 17, Graham was arrested for a home invasion robbery. It also was alleged that he took part in a second robbery later that evening, during which one of his two accomplices (who also were involved in the first robbery) was shot.

The trial court found Graham had violated his probation by committing a home invasion robbery, possessing a firearm, and by associating with persons involved in criminal activities. The court sentenced Graham to the maximum sentence for his crimes, which was life imprisonment in the case of the armed burglary. Because Florida had abolished parole, this meant Graham had no possibility of release, other than executive clemency.

Graham filed a motion in the trial court, saying his sentence violated the Eighth Amendment's bar against cruel and unusual punishment. Not getting a response, the motion was considered denied, and Graham filed with the appeals court. That court affirmed, holding that Graham's sentence "was not grossly disproportionate to his crimes." The court found Graham incapable of rehabilitation. The state Supreme Court denied review. The U.S. Supreme Court granted certiorari, to review the case.

As in *Roper*, the Court said determining whether a punishment was cruel and unusual necessitated looking at the "evolving standards of decency that mark the progress of a maturing society." While the standard remains the same, its applicability changes as the basic mores of society change.

In making its analysis, the Court said, "[t]he present case involves an issue the Court has not considered previously: a categorical challenge to a term-of-years sentence .... This case implicates a particular type of sentence as it applies to an entire class of offenders who have committed a range of crimes."

In looking at objective indicia, the Court found the majority of states (37 plus the District of Columbia) had legislation authorizing life sentences without parole for juvenile nonhomicide offenders under some circumstances. Federal law also allowed the possibility of life without parole for offenders as young as age 13. The state argued that this showed the absence of a national consensus that such sentences are cruel and unusual. The Court disagreed, saying an examination of actual sentencing practice in the authorizing states shows a consensus against its use, that only 109 (later amended to 123) juvenile offenders were serving such sentences. Of these, 77 were in one state, with the remaining offenders (46) confined in just 10 states. Twenty-six states, the District of Columbia, and the federal government had not imposed such sentences, although they had the statutory authorization to do so. Furthermore, the fact that states allow for this sentence, but don't impose it, should not be seen as viewing the sentence as appropriate. The Court said these findings show how rarely such sentences are imposed. The Court concluded that it was fair to say that a national consensus had developed against authorizing life sentences without parole for juvenile nonhomicide offenders.

The Court next considered its responsibility to interpret the Eighth Amendment, looking at how culpable the offenders were with respect to their crimes and characteristics, along with the severity of the punishment. Also involved was a consideration of how the challenged sentencing practice serves legitimate penological goals.

Pointing out juveniles' "lack of maturity and…underdeveloped sense of responsibility," their being "more vulnerable or susceptible to negative influences …" and their characters being "not as well formed," the Court, citing *Roper*, said that "juvenile offenders cannot with reliability be classified among the worst offenders."

Having looked at the status of the offenders, the Court next considered the nature of the offense. While serious nonhomicide crimes can be devastating, such crimes were not seen as comparable to murder in their "severity and irrevocability."

> **[W]hen compared to an adult murderer, a juvenile offender who did not kill or intend to kill has a twice diminished moral culpability. The age of the offender and the nature of the crime each bear on the analysis.**

The sentence of life without parole, the Court said, is "the second most severe penalty permitted by law"—there is an alteration of life that is irrevocable and a deprivation of basic liberties without significant hope of restoration. For a juvenile, because of their age, a sentence of life without parole was seen as especially harsh punishment, since, on average, they would serve more years and a higher percentage of her life in prison than an adult offender.

In looking at the penological justifications, the Court said:

> **A sentence lacking any legitimate penological justification is … disproportionate to the offense. With respect to life without parole for juvenile nonhomicide offenders, none of the goals of penal sanctions that have been recognized as legitimate—retribution, deterrence, incapacitation, and rehabilitation … —provides an adequate justification.**

The Court said retribution is appropriate where the criminal sentence is directly related to the personal culpability of the criminal offender. Because a juvenile is less culpable than an adult, the case for retribution is not as strong with a juvenile. Further weakening the argument for retribution is the fact that the juvenile did not commit a homicide. The Court held that to impose the second most severe penalty (life in prison without parole) on the less culpable juvenile nonhomicide offender is not proportional to the crime.

Deterrence was not seen as viable as the juvenile's lack of maturity and underdeveloped sense of responsibility makes it less likely for them to consider the possible punishments when making decisions. Any limited deterrent effect provided by life without parole was held insufficient to justify that sentence.

Incapacitation of the juvenile nonhomicide offender for life without parole was not viable as it implies a judgment that the juvenile is incorrigible, incapable of change. This is contrary to earlier determinations, with the Court holding, "[a] life without parole sentence improperly denies the juvenile offender a chance to demonstrate growth and maturity."

As to the final rationale, the Court said a life sentence without parole cannot be justified by the goal of rehabilitation. "The penalty forswears altogether the rehabilitative idea" and was inappropriate when considering the "juvenile nonhomicide offender's capacity for change and limited moral culpability."

Based on its finding that penological theory does not justify life without parole for juvenile nonhomicide offenders, the limited culpability of juvenile nonhomicide offenders, and the severity of life without parole sentences, the Court held that life imprisonment without parole for a juvenile nonhomicide offender is unconstitutional under the Eighth Amendment.

> **This clear line is necessary to prevent the possibility that life without parole sentences will be imposed on juvenile nonhomicide offenders who are not sufficiently culpable to merit that punishment. Because "[t]he age of 18 is the point where society draws the line for many purposes between childhood and adulthood," those who were below that age when the offense was committed may not be sentenced to life without parole for a nonhomicide crime.**
>
> **[W]hile the Eighth Amendment forbids a State from imposing a life without parole sentence on a juvenile nonhomicide offender, it does not require the State to release that offender …. Those who commit truly horrifying crimes as juveniles may turn out to be irredeemable, and thus deserving of**

incarceration …. **The Eighth Amendment does not foreclose the possibility that persons convicted of nonhomicide crimes committed before adulthood will remain behind bars for life. It does forbid States from making the judgment at the outset that those offenders never will be fit to reenter society.**

Terrance Graham's sentence guarantees he will die in prison without any meaningful opportunity to obtain release, no matter what he might do [to show otherwise] … The State has denied him any chance to later demonstrate that he is fit to rejoin society based solely on a nonhomicide crime … committed while … a child in the eyes of the law. This the Eighth Amendment does not permit.

As it did in *Roper,* the Court opinion also looked to global practices, finding that only the United States imposes life without parole sentences on juvenile nonhomicide offenders. Saying such findings are not dispositive as to what the Eighth Amendment means, the Court nonetheless found them to be relevant.

The Court has treated the laws and practices of other nations and international agreements as relevant to the Eighth Amendment not because those norms are binding or controlling but because the judgment of the world's nations that a particular sentencing practice is inconsistent with basic principles of decency demonstrates that the Court's rationale has respected reasoning to support it.

The Court briefly considered, and rejected as inadequate, two alternative approaches. The first was the state's argument that state laws consider the juvenile offender's age. This argument was rejected based on the view that subjective judgments could still occur, for example that the crime showed an "irretrievably depraved character." The second approach was for a case-by-case assessment. Citing *Roper,* the Court held that "it does not follow that courts taking a case-by-case proportionality approach could, with sufficient accuracy, distinguish the few incorrigible juvenile offenders from the many that have the capacity for change." Another concern with the case-by-case approach dealt with juveniles having a greater distrust of adults and being less likely than adults to work effectively with their lawyers, thus impairing the quality of representation. The categorical rule avoids the risk that, as a result of such difficulties, a court or jury would erroneously conclude that there was sufficient culpability to deserve life without parole for a nonhomicide offense. The Court also saw the categorical rule as giving "all juvenile nonhomicide offenders a chance to demonstrate maturity and reform."

▶ *Miller v. Alabama*

After *Graham v. Florida,* an unanswered question was whether a juvenile who commits a homicide may be mandatorily sentenced to life without parole (LWOP). In *Miller v. Alabama,* 567 U.S. 460 (2012), the Court consolidated two cases in which juveniles had been subjected to a mandatory LWOP for capital crimes to consider whether such sentences violate the Eighth Amendment.

In the first case, *Jackson v. Norris,* Kuntrell Jackson was 14 years old when he and two other juveniles robbed a video store in November of 1999. During the crime, an accomplice armed with a sawed-off shotgun shot and killed the clerk. Arkansas law allowed prosecutors to charge persons as young as 14 years in adult court for certain serious crimes. Jackson petitioned the court to be transferred to juvenile court, but considering the seriousness of the offense, Jackson's previous record of shoplifting and auto theft, and a psychiatric evaluation, the request was denied. At trial in adult court, the state conceded that Jackson did not pull the trigger and Jackson was convicted of felony murder as an accomplice and aggravated robbery. While Jackson knew his accomplice was carrying a sawed-off shotgun, it was unclear that Jackson knew of his co-defendant's plan to use the weapon or if he intended the clerk to be killed. Jackson was convicted of both charges, and under the state's mandatory sentencing scheme, was sentenced to LWOP. Jackson's conviction was affirmed on direct appeal. After the Supreme Court decided *Roper v. Simmons,* Jackson sought habeas corpus relief arguing that based on the rationale in *Roper,* sentencing a juvenile to LWOP violated the Eighth Amendment. While his habeas appeal case was pending in the state supreme court, *Graham v. Florida* was decided. The Arkansas Supreme Court distinguished the *Graham* decision on the grounds that *Graham* dealt with non-homicide cases and affirmed the denial of the state habeas corpus petition.

Evan Miller was also 14 years old when he and a friend killed a neighbor with whom they had been drinking and using drugs. Miller's mother was addicted to alcohol and drugs, his stepfather abused him, and Miller himself used alcohol and drugs. He had attempted suicide four times, with the first attempt coming at age six. After drinking and smoking marijuana at the neighbor's trailer, the neighbor passed out. Miller took the victim's wallet and split the $300 cash found in the wallet with his friend. The neighbor awoke when Miller attempted to put his wallet back in his pocket, and he grabbed Miller by the throat. Miller struck the neighbor with a baseball bat. The neighbor released Miller, but Miller repeatedly struck the neighbor with the bat. Miller placed a sheet over the neighbor's head, told him "`I am God, I've come to take your life,'" and struck the neighbor one more time with the bat. The trailer was then set on fire and the neighbor died of blunt force injury and smoke inhalation.

Under Alabama law, Miller was first charged in juvenile court, but the prosecutor was allowed to seek transfer to adult court. Based on the seriousness of the charges, Miller's "mental maturity," and his juvenile record (truancy and criminal mischief), he was transferred to adult court. Based in large part on the testimony of his friend who was present, Miller was convicted of murder in the course of arson. Alabama had a similar law to Arkansas, which required persons convicted of certain homicide crimes to be mandatorily sentenced to LWOP, and Miller was so sentenced. His conviction and sentencing were affirmed by the Alabama Court of Criminal Appeals. The Supreme Court granted certiorari in both cases to resolve this question: *Does such a life—without [parole] sentence violate the Eighth and Fourteenth Amendments when it is imposed upon a fourteen-year-old as a result of a mandatory sentencing scheme that categorically precludes consideration of the offender's young age or any other mitigating circumstances?*

Relying upon the concept of proportionality in punishment to both the offense and the offender, the Court found that its proportionality precedents had approved, in some cases, *"categorical bans on sentencing practices based on mismatches between the culpability of a class of offenders and the severity of a penalty."* These bans would include prohibiting capital punishment for non-homicide cases, the death penalty for juveniles, and most recently, mandatory LWOP sentences for non-homicide juvenile cases. The Court also reasoned it had likened a sentence of a mandatory LWOP for a juvenile as a death penalty in *Graham v. Florida*, and that the Court had "prohibited [the] mandatory imposition of capital punishment, requiring that sentencing authorities consider the characteristics of a defendant and the details of his offense before sentencing him to death."

In ruling that the mandatory imposition of LWOP for a capital offense committed by a juvenile violated the Eighth Amendment, the Court reasoned:

> *. . . Roper and Graham establish that children are constitutionally different from adults for purposes of sentencing. Because juveniles have diminished culpability and greater prospects for reform, we explained, "they are less deserving of the most severe punishments." . . .*
>
> *Mandatory life without parole for a juvenile precludes consideration of his chronological age and its hallmark features — among them, immaturity, impetuosity, and failure to appreciate risks and consequences. It prevents taking into account the family and home environment that surrounds him — and from which he cannot usually extricate himself — no matter how brutal or dysfunctional. It neglects the circumstances of the homicide offense, including the extent of his participation in the conduct and the way familial and peer pressures may have affected him. Indeed, it ignores that he might have been charged and convicted of a lesser offense if not for incompetencies associated with youth — for example, his inability to deal with police officers or prosecutors (including on a plea agreement) or his incapacity to assist his own attorneys.*

The Court did not categorically prohibit sentences of LWOP for juveniles convicted of homicide offenses, it only required an individualized consideration of relevant factors including age, maturity, family circumstances and the ability to deal with police, prosecutors and their own attorney.

> *But given all we have said in Roper, Graham, and this decision about children's diminished culpability and heightened capacity for change, we think appropriate occasions for sentencing juveniles to this harshest possible penalty will be uncommon. That is especially so because of the great difficulty we noted in Roper and Graham of distinguishing at this early age between "the juvenile offender whose crime reflects unfortunate yet transient immaturity, and the rare juvenile offender whose crime reflects irreparable corruption."*

The Court's opinion in *Miller v. Alabama* [*Miller*] did not address the issue of whether its ruling applied only to those cases pending trial and on appeal, or if it also applied to convictions that had become final. In *Montgomery v. Louisiana*, 577 U.S. 460, (2016) the Court ruled its decision in *Miller* announced a new substantive rule that the Constitution required to be applied retroactively. Henry Montgomery was 17 years old in 1963 when he shot and killed a police officer. He was initially sentenced to death, but because of errors in his first trial, he was retried, convicted, and mandatorily sentenced to LWOP. After *Miller*, Montgomery sought to be resentenced, but state courts in Louisiana determined that the holding in the *Miller* case was not retroactive. The Supreme Court granted certiorari to answer the following question: *whether Miller [v. Alabama] adopts a new substantive rule that applies retroactively on collateral review to people condemned as juveniles to die in prison?* Substantive rules establish *"categorical constitutional guarantees that place certain criminal laws and punishments altogether beyond the State's power to impose,"* and if a penalty has been imposed in violation of the Constitution, that sentence is unlawful. In holding the state must consider the individualized circumstances of juvenile offenders like Mr. Montgomery, the Court stated:

> ***Miller*, then, did more than require a sentencer to consider a juvenile offender's youth before imposing life without parole; it established that the penological justifications for life without parole collapse in light of "the distinctive attributes of youth." [citation omitted] Even if a court considers a child's age before sentencing him or her to a lifetime in prison, that sentence still violates the Eighth Amendment for a child whose crime reflects "'unfortunate yet transient immaturity.'" [citation omitted]. Because *Miller* determined that sentencing a child to life without parole is excessive for all but "'the rare juvenile offender whose crime reflects irreparable corruption,'" [citation omitted], it rendered life without parole an unconstitutional penalty for "a class of defendants because of their status" — that is, juvenile offenders whose crimes reflect the transient immaturity of youth. [citation omitted]. As a result, *Miller* announced a substantive rule of constitutional law. Like other substantive rules, *Miller* is retroactive because it "'necessarily carr[ies] a significant risk that a defendant'" — here, the vast majority of juvenile offenders — "'faces a punishment that the law cannot impose upon him.'" [citation omitted]

In November of 2020, the Supreme Court heard oral argument in the case of *Jones v Mississippi* to determine if a life without parole sentence imposed for a homicide crime committed by a juvenile requires the sentencing court to determine if the juvenile is "permanently incorrigible" before imposing such a sentence. Jones was convicted of the 2004 murder of his grandfather and was sentenced to life without parole under state law. The conviction and sentence was affirmed on appeal. After the Supreme Court decision in *Miller v. Alabama*, Jones sought to have his LWOP sentence vacated. He was granted a new sentencing hearing and the circuit court, after considering the factors announced in *Miller*, sentenced Jones to LWOP. The trial court's decision was affirmed by the state appellate court. Jones has sought review in the Supreme Court on this question: "Whether the Eighth Amendment requires the sentencing authority to make a finding that a juvenile is permanently incorrigible before imposing a sentence of life without parole."

▶ Boot Camps

Boot camp programs are geared primarily to young offenders. This type of intensive institutional treatment is sometimes called "shock incarceration." It may be included in a special type of sentencing, called "intermediate sanctions" or "alternative sentencing." These terms are imprecise, and they are not clearly defined, but they are mentioned here because they are encountered in discussions about criminal justice, sentencing, and the role of corrections.

Boot camps are facilities that emphasize military drill, physical training, and hard labor. Their name comes from military boot camp training, and many aspects of such programs are patterned on military regimens. They have been geared to young male offenders who are sentenced for nonviolent offenses. The length of stay in a boot camp is intended to be short. Daily life is planned to be long and hard, with heavily structured activity.

Most agencies began operating their camps in the 1980s and 1990s. By 1995, there were 75 boot camps for adults operated by state correctional agencies. Thirty juvenile boot camps were operated by state and local agencies, and 18 boot camps in local jails were operated by larger counties. While the early camps stressed military discipline, physical training, and hard work, later camps added such components as alcohol and drug treatment and problem-solving strategies. Some also added intensive post-release services such as electronic monitoring and home confinement.[11]

In a sense, boot camps replaced the specialized treatment of youth offenders that was favored by many penologists and corrections professionals after World War II. Patterned in the United States on the Borstal system in England, specialized youth facilities and programs were developed for youthful offenders—those in their late teens (older than juvenile offenders) and early twenties. California had a Youth Authority that was a model of this type of sentencing. Many states and the federal government also had special youth offender laws. Offenders in this category were committed, typically for indeterminate terms, for specialized treatment that emphasized education, vocational training, counseling, and work. They were to be released when corrections authorities concluded that they had successfully completed their needed treatment programs. They were released to parole-type supervision in the community. The length of time spent in an institution and under supervision was, in theory, geared to the needs of the offender and not to the seriousness of the offense. The offenders were usually convicted, like adults (and unlike juveniles), but were sometimes given sentences that could be set aside or sealed if the youths were successful in their programming.

As an alternative, boot camps have been supported with the following arguments: they are cheaper to run and thus reduce costs; they help to reduce the crowding in regular prison facilities; they are seen (by judges, legislators, the media, and the public) as being tougher on offenders and thus more fitting as punishment; they help to rehabilitate the offender; and they deter future crime and reduce recidivism. Like the specialized youthful offender programs described previously, the underlying concept is that concentrating on persons of this younger age, who are not criminally sophisticated and not entrenched in criminal careers, will produce good results, because they are still amenable to treatment programs and change. The boot camp programs teach respect for authority, self-discipline skills, accountability, pride in achievements, self-esteem, and good work habits.

For reasons discussed later in this section, the use of boot camps began to drop in the mid-1990s, and by the year 2000, nearly one-third of state prison boot camps had closed, with the average daily population in state boot camps dropping by more than 30%.[12]

In the 1990s, correctional boot camps also became increasingly popular for juvenile delinquents, but, as with adult boot camps, the use of juvenile boot camps also has dropped. In 1996, 27 states were operating 48 residential boot camps for adjudicated juveniles. Offenders often wore military-style uniforms, marched to and from activities, and responded quickly to the orders of the "drill instructors." The daily schedule ordinarily included drills and ceremony practice, physical fitness activities, and challenge programs, as well as academic education. Misbehavior could be handled by summary punishment.[13] In 2007, juvenile boot camps operated in 11 states, with a total population of fewer than 1,400 juveniles.[14]

Evaluation of the arguments for boot camps brings mixed results but seems to suggest that boot camps are not a viable approach, especially for juveniles. Because of the shorter terms served, there are overall cost savings and the demand for regular prison beds is reduced. Obviously, if the program is large, the savings will be greater. (This assumes that those going into boot camps would otherwise be incarcerated. If these are inmates who would otherwise be on probation, the cost savings are negligible.) As to the rehabilitation of inmates and the reduction of recidivism rates due to "shock incarceration" or deterrence, the studies do not show that boot camps are significantly different from traditional prison programs in terms of results. This was found to be true despite the fact that inmates who successfully completed boot camp programs reported that they had developed better attitudes toward authority, better self-esteem, and improved social attitudes.[15] (One aspect must be carefully assessed: because boot camp inmates are a selected group of offenders, they must be compared with offenders of similar backgrounds for valid assessments.)

Juvenile boot camps are also seen as unsuccessful in reducing recidivism. One study found "a preponderance of evidence showing that the boot camp and shock type of deterrence programs either did not affect subsequent offending or actually increased recidivism."[16]

There have been few legal challenges to the conditions of boot camp facilities and programs.[17] Where such programs exist, most offenders probably have been told (by their sentencing judges and probably by their lawyers) that they are fortunate to be given the opportunities afforded by boot camp, so they do not bring lawsuits (after all, their days are so long, and the purpose is to render them so exhausted, that few of them probably have the time or energy to draw up legal papers!). The main legal problems are sentencing ones, involving matters of equal protection or equal opportunity under the criminal law. Because the boot camp sentence is perceived as providing some advantages (including shorter terms, special programming, and early return to homes and family), the main legal questions are ones of parity. Specifically, does the sentencing or the opportunity for the program benefits discriminate against women offenders, against disabled persons, and against older offenders or others who are excluded by the definitions of eligibility for the boot camp program? It seems clear that, on the surface, it does. Government officials considering or operating such programs would probably be well-advised to examine their resources in advance of any legal challenge (because they certainly will be required to provide such evaluations and reports in defense against such a challenge). This examination of boot camp programs should include the following: the numbers of persons who would be included if the programs were expanded to include more offenders; whether the programs could include more offenders; and whether females, disabled offenders, or wider categories of offenders (in age or other criteria) might be included in the programs by special accommodations or other steps.

▶ **Juvenile Justice and Delinquency Prevention Act (JDDPA)**

In 1938, Congress passed its first set of federal laws to address criminal acts committed by juveniles when it promulgated the Federal Juvenile Delinquency Act. That set of laws was significantly modified in 1974 when Congress passed the Juvenile Justice and Delinquency Prevention Act (JDDPA). The stated purpose of the JDDPA was "to provide basic procedural rights for juveniles who came under federal jurisdiction and to bring federal procedures up to the standards set by various model acts, many state codes and court decisions." The JDDPA established a set of specific procedures to by followed by the Attorney General in addressing acts of delinquency including that, except in cases which occur in the special maritime and territorial jurisdiction of the United States,[18] federal crimes of violence or other serious drug offenses, the federal government must make efforts to have juvenile offenses handled by state and local officials rather than the federal government. Title 18, U.S. Code Section 5032. As a result of these limitations, when a juvenile is sentenced to a period of residential placement, the term is usually limited to the individual's 21st birthday or the expiration of the federal maximum sentence for that offense, whichever is shorter, and the juvenile is placed in a state or private contract facility by the Bureau of Prisons. In 2017, there were 27 juveniles (26 males and 1 female) housed in contract facilities by the Bureau of Prisons.[19]

The JDDPA was reauthorized and amended in 2018. The Act has had significant impact on juvenile corrections, including standards related to housing juveniles in adult correctional facilities. The Act addresses four major concerns: (1) keeping status offenders (such as truants) out of secure detention or correctional facilities; (2) prohibiting the housing of juveniles in facilities in which they would have sight or sound contact with adult inmates; (3) when a juvenile is being tried as an adult, the juvenile should not be held in an adult facility, but may be held for up to six hours (forty-eight hours in rural facilities) while they are being processed, waiting to be released, waiting for transfer to a juvenile facility or waiting for a court appearance; and (4) requiring states to demonstrate progress on reducing racial and ethnic disparities which exist in the state's juvenile justice system.

The 1974 JDDPA also created the Office of Juvenile Justice and Delinquency Prevention (OJJDP) "to support local and state efforts to prevent delinquency and improve the juvenile justice system." The OJJDP fulfills its mission by awarding funds to states to support local juvenile justice programs, funding research and training initiatives, and developing priorities and goals for federal juvenile justice programs.[20]

Summary

- Juveniles in the U.S. criminal justice system are treated under special rules that are designed for their protection. These rules derive from concepts in the English legal system, in which children who committed offenses were taken before chancery court judges and were processed under the concept of *parens patriae,* which stipulates that the monarch (the government) is the protector of their rights and welfare.
- Special juvenile courts are the rule in the United States. Proceedings in these courts are usually not public. Juvenile records are sealed or specially protected. Specialized terms used in juvenile court proceedings reflect the ideas of treating juveniles differently from adults: juveniles are "proceeded against," not prosecuted; they are "found to be delinquent," not convicted; they are issued a disposition by the court, not a sentence; they are sent to training schools (or other similarly named facilities), not to prisons.
- Juveniles, especially those in the upper age ranges (although the ages vary from state to state, mostly to 16 and 17 year olds), may be transferred to adult court for prosecution for violent or serious offenses. In recent years, when it has been widely perceived that juveniles are involved in more sophisticated criminal activity at younger ages, there has been a get-tough movement, which has resulted in procedures for the referral of larger numbers of juveniles to adult courts in many states.
- The Supreme Court, in 1966, after decades of deference in all levels of courts to the concepts of juvenile processing in which protective and informal procedures were the rule, said that transfers of juveniles to adult courts (waiver of juvenile court jurisdiction) must be accompanied by some due process protections. These protections include the right to a hearing, access by counsel to the reports used by the juvenile court in making its decision, and a statement of the reasons for the court's decision (*Kent v. United States*).
- In regular juvenile court cases (and not just the transfer cases, which *Kent* dealt with), the Supreme Court said that delinquency proceedings must also include minimal due process protections. Although not as extensive as adult criminal proceedings, these hearings require (at a minimum) the following: advance written notice to the juvenile and his parents; the opportunity to be represented by counsel; the availability

of the privilege against self-incrimination; and a determination by the court of delinquency based on sworn testimony, subject to cross-examination (*In re Gault*).

- Juveniles, like adults, are constitutionally entitled to a standard of proof beyond a reasonable doubt during the adjudicatory stage of the juvenile court process (*In re Winship*).
- During the 1970s and 1980s, the Court held that jury trials were not constitutionally required for juveniles appearing before the juvenile court and that to require such trials could lessen the court's assumed ability to function in a unique manner (*McKeiver v. Pennsylvania*). States may provide jury trials for persons accused of committing juvenile offenses. The Court also held that an adjudicated delinquent could not subsequently be referred to adult criminal court, as this would constitute double jeopardy (*Breed v. Jones*); and that the use of preventive detention for juveniles properly promotes the interests of both society and the juvenile and that the practice serves a legitimate regulatory purpose compatible with the "fundamental fairness" demanded by the Due Process Clause in juvenile proceedings (*Schall v. Martin*).
- From 1988 through 2005, the Supreme Court decided three cases dealing with juvenile offenders and the death penalty. In *Thompson v. Oklahoma,* the Court held that the death penalty could not be imposed on persons for capital offenses committed at age 15 years or younger. A year later, in *Stanford v. Kentucky,* the Court upheld use of the death penalty for persons committing capital offenses at age 16 or 17. In 2005, in *Roper v. Simmons,* this ruling was reversed, with the Court holding that the Eighth and Fourteenth Amendments are violated when the sentence of death is imposed on a person for a capital offense that was committed by a person under the age of 18. A guiding principle in each of these cases was the "evolving standards of decency that mark the progress of a maturing society to determine which punishments are so disproportionate as to be cruel and unusual."
- The "evolving standard of decency" also was used in determining that it is unconstitutional to impose a sentence of life imprisonment without parole on a nonhomicide juvenile offender (*Graham v. Florida*).
- The Supreme Court in *Miller v. Alabama* determined that mandatory sentences of life without parole (LWOP) for juvenile offenders convicted of homicide offenses violated the Eighth Amendment because such sentences failed to consider the individual characteristics of juvenile offenders. Miller did not categorically prohibit LWOP sentences for juveniles who are convicted of murder, but such sentences should be rare and imposed only after an individual assessment of the offender and the offense.
- The rule prohibiting mandatory LWOP sentences for juveniles convicted of homicide offenses was deemed to be retroactive and applicable to sentences that had become final before the *Miller v. Alabama* decision. *Montgomery v Louisiana*.
- Youthful offenders are those who are technically adults (above the age of juveniles in a particular jurisdiction) but who are at the lower range of adulthood (typically, those in their late teens and early twenties). Many states have had specialized programs mandated in corrections facilities for such younger adult offenders, based on the concept that they are usually less sophisticated and more amenable to treatment and rehabilitation programs.
- A special kind of corrections program is the boot camp. Boot camps feature military drills and hard labor. The per-day costs of boot camps may be slightly higher than those for regular corrections institutions, but because stays in boot camps are significantly shorter, the costs per inmate commitment are lower. Claims of higher rehabilitation (and lower recidivism) rates for those sent to boot camps have not been sustained by studies, which so far have shown about the same recidivism rates for both those who were placed in boot camps and those who were sent to traditional prisons. In recent years, the use of such camps has decreased.

Thinking About It

A sixteen-year-old juvenile, A, shot and killed three people in a robbery of a store. Tried as an adult, A was convicted of three counts of first-degree murder and sentenced to three consecutive life terms of imprisonment. Under state law, a person serving a life sentence was eligible for release after serving 30 years. The three sentences effectively established a minimum 90-year sentence. Another juvenile, B, was 17 years old when B and an accomplice went to B's high school and shot at a teenager who had been involved in a dispute with B. In the course of the shooting, four persons were shot, including one who was paralyzed. B was charged with four counts of aggravated attempted murder and four counts of aggravated assault. A jury convicted B of the four counts of aggravated assault and the judge sentenced B to 25 years on each count to be served consecutively (total 100 years). Under state sentence computation and parole rules, B would not be entitled to early release until 50 years of the sentence had been served. Both A and B argued that because their sentences were the "functional equivalents" to death or LWOP sentences, they were entitled to consideration of their special circumstances as juveniles announced in *Roper, Graham, Miller,* and *Montgomery.* Should the Supreme Court's rulings in *Roper, Graham, Miller and Montgomery* apply to long sentences imposed on juveniles, which are not technically LWOP? See *State v. Ali,* 895 N.W. 2d 237 (MN 2017) and *Ali v. Roy,* 950 F.3d 572 (8th Cir. 2020); *McCollough v. Maryland,* 192 A.3d 295 (Md. App. 2018).

Key Terms

dependent children
guardian ad litem
juvenile court
parens patriae
petition (juvenile)
status offender
ward

Endnotes

1. While most states set 17 as the oldest age for original juvenile court jurisdiction, a few states have set ages at 15 or 16. Some states also set a minimum age (from ages 6 to 10) for original juvenile court jurisdiction in delinquency matters. Finally, states have set an upper age over which the juvenile court can retain jurisdiction for the purpose of disposition in delinquency matters. This ranges from ages 18 to 24 or the full term of the disposition order. Office of Justice Programs. Sickmund, M. & Puzzanchera, C. *Juvenile Offenders and Victims: 2014 National Report.* Page 93. (Washington, DC: Office of Juvenile Justice and Delinquency Prevention, U.S. Department of Justice, 2014. Available from: https://www.ojjdp.gov/ojstatbb/nr2014/downloads/NR2014.pdf. Accessed 14 March 2020.

2. See note 1. Pages 97-98.

3. Shah, R. & Fine, L. *Juvenile Records—A National Review of State Laws on Confidentiality, Sealing and Expungement.* 2014. Juvenile Justice Center. Available at: http://njjn.org/uploads/digital-library/Juvenile_Records_A_National_Review_of_State_Laws_on_Confidentiality_Sealing_and_Expungement.pdf. Accessed 16 March 2020.

4. For example, Colorado Revised Statutes 19-1-304, for records related to a juvenile delinquency proceeding are open without a court order to: "(XVI) The principal, or the principal's designee, of a school in which the juvenile is or will be enrolled as a student and, if the student is or will be enrolled in a public school, to the superintendent of the school district in which the student is or will be enrolled, or such superintendent's designee." Juvenile proceedings open to victim—For example, California WIC Section 676.5 giving victims of juvenile offenses the right to be present at court proceedings. Juvenile proceedings open to the general public, including the media: See, for example, Arizona Rule of Procedures for the Juvenile Courts 19: "B. Proceedings. Delinquency, incorrigibility, diversion involving delinquent acts and transfer proceedings shall be open to the public, except upon the court's written finding of a need to protect the best interests of a victim, the juvenile, a witness, the state, or a clear public interest in confidentiality." See also *Access to Juvenile Justice,* Reporters Committee for Freedom of the Press, Spring 2012. Available at: https://www.rcfp.org/wp-content/uploads/imported/SJAJJ.pdf. Accessed 16 March 2020.

5. In some states, the juvenile court, under "blended sentencing" laws, may impose criminal sanctions on certain juvenile offenders. These laws broaden the sanctioning powers of the juvenile court so that certain juvenile offenders can be handled in the same manner as adult offenders, thus exposing these juvenile offenders to harsher penalties. Further information on blended sentencing may be found in Chapter 4: Juvenile justice system structure and process, *Juvenile Offenders and Victims: 2014 National Report* pages 99-100 and 105–106.

6. 1985 Data from Knoll, C. and Sickmund, M. *Delinquency Cases in Juvenile Court, 2007.* Pages 1–3. (Washington, DC: Office of Juvenile Justice and Delinquency Prevention, U.S. Department of Justice. 2010.) 2017 Data from Hockenberry, S. *Delinquency Cases in Juvenile Court, 2017.* pp. 1–3. (Washington, DC: Office of Juvenile Justice and Delinquency Prevention, U.S. Department of Justice. October 2019.) Available at: See endnote 1: *Juvenile Offenders and Victims: 2017 National Report.* https://ojjdp.ojp.gov/sites/g/files/xyckuh176/files/media/document/253105.pdf. Accessed 15 March, 2020.

7. Tiegen, A. *Juvenile Age of Jurisdiction and Transfer Laws to Adult Courts.* April 7, 2020. National Conference of State Legislatures. Available at https://www.ncsl.org/research/civil-and-criminal-justice/juvenile-age-of-jurisdiction-and-transfer-to-adult-court-laws.aspx. Accessed April 8, 2020.

8. Redding, R. *Juvenile Transfer Laws: An Effective Deterrent to Delinquency?* Page 2. (Washington, DC: Office of Juvenile Justice and Delinquency Prevention, U.S. Department of Justice, 2010.)

9. Adams, B. and Addie S. *Delinquency Cases Waived to Criminal Court, 2007.* Page 1. (Washington, DC: Office of Juvenile Justice and Delinquency Prevention, U.S. Department of Justice, 2010.) https://www.ojjdp.gov/ojstatbb/population/index.html And OJJDP Statistical Briefing Book. *Juvenile Court Statistics 2017.* 38. Available- http://www.ncjj.org/pdf/jcsreports/jcs2017report.pdf

10. See endnote 1: *Juvenile Offenders and Victims: 2014 National Report.* pp. 85–88. The quoted material on the Massachusetts law is taken from Mass. Gen. L. ch. 119, §53.

11. *Correctional Boot Camps: Lessons from a Decade of Research.* p. 2. (Washington, DC: Office of Justice Programs, U.S. Department of Justice, 2003.)

12. See endnote 11.

13. MacKenzie, D., Gover, A., Armstrong, G., & Mitchell, O. *A National Study Comparing the Environments of Boot Camps with Traditional Facilities for Juvenile Offenders.* Page 1. (Washington, DC: National Institute of Justice, U.S. Department of Justice, 2001.)

14. Sickmund, M. 2010. *Juvenile boot camps, 1997-2007.* Pittsburgh, PA: National Center for Juvenile Justice.

15. *Correctional Boot Camps: Lessons from a Decade of Research.* See endnote 11. This study found that participants in boot camp programs reported positive short-term changes in attitudes and behaviors and also better problem-solving and coping skills. However, with few exceptions, these changes did not result in reduced recidivism. With respect to the positive change reported by participants, let us share an anecdote that was told by an administrator of a boot camp. This camp had a graduation ceremony, to which family members were invited. An inmate's mother came to his graduation and was so impressed with the program and with her son's improvement that she asked the administrator, "How do I get my other son in?"

16. Austin, A., Johnson, K., & Weitzer, R. *Alternatives to the Secure Detention and Confinement of Juvenile Offenders.* Page 22. (Washington, DC: Office of Justice Programs, Department of Justice, 2005.)

17. *Residential Treatment Programs: Concerns Regarding Abuse and Death in Certain Programs for Troubled Youth.* Available from http://www.gao.gov/new.items/d08146t.pdf. A recent example, while not resulting in convictions, shows the concerns posed by boot camps and supports the need to ensure that staff is sufficiently trained. According to court filings, a 14-year-old boy was committed to the state's department of juvenile justice and placed in a boot camp. Upon arrival, he was given a physical assessment consisting of two minutes of push-ups, two minutes of sit-ups, and a run of about 1.5 miles. Prior to completing the run, the youth fell to the ground. He was said to have been restrained by the guards at the camp and subjected to multiple uses of force. Drill instructors at the boot camp forced the youth to inhale ammonia on several occasions, each time with staff covering his mouth. The youth became unresponsive during the last forced application of ammonia. (The incident was recorded on videotape.) Taken to a medical center, then a hospital, the youth was unable to be revived and died the next day. An autopsy performed first reported a natural death due to complications of a sickle cell trait. A second autopsy, however, found that the victim's death was due to oxygen deprivation. Eight staff were charged with manslaughter. In 2007, they were acquitted. A federal investigation was opened. In an April 16, 2010, press release, the U.S. Department of Justice announced that it would not pursue federal criminal civil rights charges against the eight staff. The press release said that prosecutors, under the applicable federal criminal civil rights laws, "must establish, beyond a reasonable doubt, that an official 'willfully' deprived an individual of a constitutional right, meaning that the official acted with the deliberate and specific intent to do something the law forbids …. Neither accident, mistake, fear, negligence nor bad judgment is sufficient to establish a federal criminal civil rights violation." The evidence was found insufficient to pursue federal charges. For more general information in this area, see the U.S. Government Accountability Office (GAO) 2007 report, The report refers to finding thousands of abuse allegations, covering the years between 1990 and 2007. GAO also looked at 10 closed civil or criminal cases involving the death of a teenager in a private residential treatment program between the years 1990 and 2004. For most of the 10 cases, GAO found there was ineffective management, with the needs of program participants and staff being ignored. The report also refers to the hiring of untrained staff, a lack of adequate nourishment, and reckless or negligent operating practices.

18. Because the creation and enforcement of criminal laws is primarily a state function, federal criminal jurisdiction is more limited. Title 18, U.S. Code, Section 7 defines "special maritime and territorial jurisdiction of the United States" to include: (3) "Any lands reserved or acquired for the use of the United States and under the exclusive or concurrent jurisdiction thereof, or any place purchased or otherwise acquired by the United States by consent of the legislature of the State in which the same shall be, for the erection of a fort, magazine, arsenal, dockyard, or other needful building." This definition includes many military bases, and other federal enclaves having exclusive federal jurisdiction. Title 18, U.S. Code, Section 1153, (The Major Crimes Act) gives the federal government exclusive jurisdiction over enumerated federal offenses, including murder, kidnapping, maiming, and some sexual assaults, committed by Indians (the term used in the statute) in Indian Country as defined in Title 18, U.S. Code, Section 1151. See *United States v. Antelope*, 430 U.S. 631 (1977).

19. Carson, E.A. *Prisoners in 2019.* Table 12. Bureau of Justice Statistics, Washington, D.C. April 2020.

20. *About the Office of Juvenile Justice and Delinquency Prevention.* Available- https://ojjdp.ojp.gov/about. Accessed 13 April 2020.

CHAPTER 22

Privatization Issues in Corrections

Government has the ultimate authority and responsibility for corrections. For its most effective operation, corrections should use all appropriate resources, both public and private.

American Correctional Association,
Public Correctional Policy on Private Sector Involvement in Corrections 1985-7

CHAPTER OUTLINE

- History of Privatization
- Contracting for Services
- Pros and Cons of Privatization
- Legal Issues in Privatization
- *Richardson v. McKnight; Correctional Services Corporation v. Malesko; Minneci v. Pollard*

In recent years, **privatization** has become a pressing issue in corrections. In the United States, and in several other nations, there have been moves toward using private prisons and jails. This chapter examines the background of the privatization movement, the pros and cons in the debate over its use, and the legal implications an administrator may encounter in privatizing.

▶ History of Privatization

Using private facilities for confining offenders is by no means a new concept. In England, jails were run under what was called private enterprise as far back as the Middle Ages, and probably before. There were some efforts (in the 14th to 17th centuries) to set some standards for the jails, but conditions were generally pretty miserable. By the 18th century, jailers in England made their money by charging fees. Fees (set by the individual jailers) were demanded for all sorts of items and services, from food and clothing to certain aspects of special punishments (such as taking irons off) and even release from custody. Those with more money could purchase liquor, tobacco, and special family visits. Very little money was available from public funds. Prisoners without funds got money for jail services by working, begging, or from charities.[1] This system led to many abuses.

There were reformers who proposed changing the conditions, the most notable of whom was probably John Howard. In the late 18th century, Howard proposed ideas for the betterment of English prisons and jails. Some of his ideas were gleaned from his visits to institutions on the European continent. He recommended the classification of prisoners (separating them by age, sex, and seriousness of offenses), work programs for the reformation of prisoners, and religious penitence as an underlying philosophy for running jails. He specifically recommended paying jailers a government salary, rather than operating jails based on fees paid by inmates and their families.

American colonial criminal justice procedures, including the operation of jails, were copied from the English practice without much change. Prisoners were rarely separated by type—women and children were often confined with hardened adult male criminals. Many jails were very crowded; most were unsanitary. Payments were extracted for special services, such as better meals or other privileges. The government gave some money to the jailer (often the sheriff) for basic services, but it was widely accepted that jailers could charge additional money for virtually any type of special benefit. In many places, inmates worked for jailers at their farms or other businesses. In some places, inmates were "rented out" for working for others in the community, with payments going to the jailers, not to the inmates.

In this climate of private exploitation in the jails, reforms came in the United States. These reforms largely flowed from the ideas of John Howard and other reformers in Europe, and the reforms were supported by strong voices within the United States, particularly from religious groups. The Walnut Street Jail in Philadelphia and the Newgate and Auburn Prisons in New York were established as prototypes of the reformed (government-run) prison system. Solitary confinement (for personal reflection) and hard labor (not for wages but for its inherent therapeutic effect) were cornerstones of these new approaches. Thus, correctional theory arrived at the **penitentiary**, a place where prisoners with a strict code of silence (at Auburn) lived in separate cells, worked hard, were disciplined with corporal punishment, and had plenty of time to reflect on their mistaken ways and to repent.

Auburn became the model for prisons throughout the United States. The "silent system," along with a heavy work ethic, became a perfect environment for factories in the prisons, which produced all kinds of products. At some prisons, private companies in the community provided raw materials, and items were produced within the prison that were then sold by the private companies in the community. At other prisons, inmates were delivered to outside factories for work under contract at the private site. Alternatively, a shop area in the prison was rented to the private manufacturer, complete with prison labor, which was furnished at a very cheap rate. Other prisons performed the entire manufacturing process, from raw products through to finished goods and sales, from inside the prisons. Thus, prison industries were born. The industrial revolution meshed with the cheap supply of labor in the prisons. Many private manufacturers made handsome profits from the prison labor pool. Not all prison labor occurred in factories, however. In many states, inmates worked in local stone quarries, in gravel pits, on logging operations, on road-building projects, or—in virtually all of the states—on farms, where goods were produced for prison consumption (to make the institutions self-sufficient to the extent possible) and, sometimes, even for the sale of prison farm products to the outside community.

Besides renting out shop areas inside the prisons, or renting out prisoners (convict leasing) to work in outside factories, there were instances where the operation of an entire prison (primarily to save money) was leased to a private contractor. The first known instance of a completely private, leased institution in the United States was the Frankfort, Kentucky, State Prison. In 1825, a local businessman leased the prison for five years and paid the state $1,000 a year to take over completely the management of the Auburn-style facility (and with it the labor of the 200 inmates who were his to use under rules he set and for production he devised).

In the 1800s, several other states did the same, leasing the prisons to private operators, usually to avoid the financial pressures of the government having to run them. After the Civil War, states in the South used such leases to private firms or individuals for economic savings. Besides leasing the facilities, private companies also rented prison laborers out of regular prisons run by the government. By the late 1800s and early 1900s, the leasing of convicts was generally phased out. But some practices—inmates being used on private projects for the personal benefit of wardens and sheriffs, work on the prison farm being performed for little or no pay, and prison labor being provided for the benefit of private citizens—continued into the 1900s.

This pattern of prisons and jails in Anglo-American history was a shift from largely private control (certainly very little governmental responsibility) in early English jails, through a reform period in the late 1700s and the 1800s when conditions for prisoners were improved in the penitentiary movement, mandated, and financed at government expense. There were some elements of private enterprise pervading prisons in the later 1800s in

America and then a shift to almost total government control and very little private involvement in the 1900s. With this historical perspective, the assumptions that prisons and jails are necessarily governmental in nature are not accurate, and that private involvement in corrections facilities was, in past centuries, a common practice. The history of that fluctuating degree of private involvement is not a particularly positive one. It is rife with abusive treatment of prisoners and corruption, and it is indicative (in many instances) of facilities that were operated for personal gain rather than for any commitment to what we would consider today to be sound penological goals.

▶ Contracting for Services

In recent years, there is one area of privatization that is widely used by corrections agencies. That is the practice of correctional facilities contracting for specific services within the walls of jails and prisons that are built by, and otherwise operated by, government appropriations and staff. Examples of such services are food, health care, mental health, commissary, substance abuse treatment, and education. This list is not all-inclusive, as other services, such as college, vocational, and work training, may also be provided.

As corrections facilities have become presumptively governmental agencies, authorized by statute, staffed by government employees, and funded solely with government monies, the assumption has been that all types of programs and services are provided by the agencies' staff. In the traditional prison or jail—since the 1920s—government officials, under public laws and regulations and at government expense, have managed all functions of the institution. This has come to cover an immense range of activities. The largest function, in numbers of staff and in dollars spent, is the security function—providing custodial staff or guards to keep order and control in the facility. Beyond that, these basic services for inmates are required: providing maintenance of the physical plant and the grounds, food and clothes, safety and sanitation, and health services of all kinds. In addition, there are programs, usually introduced under the umbrella of rehabilitative opportunities, which are so widespread as to be deemed essential in modern corrections. These include recreation and hobbies, religious services, education at many levels, vocational training classes, individual and group counseling, group support services (such as Alcoholics Anonymous and substance abuse programs), and other organization activities (such as Jaycees and Girl Scouts). Also, there are all kinds of work assignments, including those in factory settings (usually called prison industries), in maintenance and upkeep jobs, and on farms and other off-site locations.

The prevailing practice in all American correctional agencies has been to provide all of these corrections services as governmental activities in institutions that are constructed and maintained at government expense. In some program areas, the services provided are augmented by volunteer services. This is especially prevalent in religious and educational programs in many agencies. The traditional practice of funding, staffing, and providing services in all areas exclusively with government resources is currently challenged by the offer of private companies and individuals to perform many, or all, of these functions by means of contracts. As discussed earlier in this chapter, the involvement of the private sector should not be surprising. But it is surprising, largely because we have come to accept the recent pattern in which the government performs virtually all corrections functions.

Corrections agencies have come to accept private performance of specific, isolated services as a matter of necessity. Regarding health services, for example, smaller jails and prisons cannot economically hope to provide the full range of medical care that is expected, both by individual inmates and by legal requirements, while competing for staff with the healthcare marketplace. At a minimum, contracts with medical specialists are entered into to provide specialized care (for eye exams, orthopedics, dentistry, surgery, or whatever is needed). Contracts with local hospitals are usually necessary, unless there is a local, publicly funded hospital that is obligated to take inmate–patients. Even large corrections systems that have tried to maintain a healthcare staff of doctors, nurses, paraprofessionals, and some specialists have encountered staffing difficulties, usually in certain medical specialties. This has led many to contract with companies which provide a full range of health services.

Similarly, prisons and jails traditionally provided their own food services. Institutions built kitchens and dining rooms and staffed these facilities with trained food service personnel. Inmates performed much of the unskilled work in food preparation, such as serving food on cafeteria lines and cleaning duties. Because of difficulties (usually financial) in providing good food service, especially in certain areas of the country, agencies have turned to food service companies to provide all kinds of food service. ("All kinds" includes not only regular food service on the "main line," the main cafeteria line in the prison, but also special food preparation and service, such as for religious and medical diets and for persons who are restricted or segregated and cannot come to the regular dining area.)

Preparing and serving food, and staffing medical examination and treatment rooms, in a prison or jail setting involve special concerns, mainly regarding security and the supervision of inmates, that a typical private company is not trained or equipped to handle. For this reason, the contracts for these services (or for any other contracted services, such as education or counseling) must involve special elements. These include requirements for security precautions, training of the staff who are in contact with, or who may even supervise inmates, and close coordination with other departments in the facility, especially the security department, to ensure proper oversight of the inmates. Such special requirements should be built into the contracts (specifically in the clauses that outline the specifications for the work, when bids are solicited, and the required standards of performance of the contracts). After the contracts are awarded and performance begins, the contracts must be closely monitored to ensure that any aspects of performance which may threaten security concerns, or the orderly running of the institution, are promptly corrected.

A firm that is not able to make such corrections in its performance should be terminated, which is always a special problem in the handling of private contracts for services. If a company is severely deficient in its performance—for example, regarding the quality of personnel who are provided, or in the laxity of its approach to security concerns—what happens to the contract? How quickly can it be terminated? What happens to the parties involved during the termination period? Who will provide the services after the departure of the deficient contractor? These are all questions that, unfortunately, corrections facilities have had to face. If it was difficult to find health coverage in the first place, finding a quick replacement may be even more difficult or impossible. If a food service company is badly deficient, it is not that easy to step back in with agency staff and supplies or to find a good replacement from the private sector. These may be infrequent occurrences, but they are still events that must be anticipated by the agency when entering any service contract. Counsel for the agency must make sure that contracts contain adequate details for ensuring that minimal performance standards are met by the contractor and that a cancellation of the contract is provided for, in the most expedient way possible within the law of the jurisdiction, when performance is seriously deficient.

▶ Pros and Cons of Privatization

The provision of specific services (such as medical or food services) by private contractors has been widely accepted in the corrections field. In some jurisdictions, agencies lack legal authority to contract with private companies for work that is to be done directly with inmates inside prisons or jails. (Virtually all jurisdictions allow for private contracting for construction work for building, renovating, or repairing buildings.) In many places, administrators have become so dependent upon private services that they do not see how they could survive without them.

But the real debate, and the area that still is a concern to many, is whether the operation of entire correctional facilities should be managed by private companies. When we talk about the controversy of privatization in corrections, we are focusing on the building and operation of private prisons and jails. This move (back) to private facilities dates only from the 1980s. In 1986, U.S. Corrections Corporation opened a private prison in Marion, Kentucky, for minimum security inmates. In the 1980s, Corrections Corporation of America (now CoreCivic) operated a jail in Bay County, Florida (holding all levels of security), two detention facilities for the Immigration and Naturalization Service, and a halfway house for the Federal Bureau of Prisons. (Halfway houses and community corrections facilities had, for some time, been an exception to government operation of corrections agencies, because many of them were operated by private organizations. Some of these were for-profit companies, and many were nonprofit organizations, including religious groups. The Dismas Houses, Salvation Army, and Volunteers of America were leaders in the community corrections field. Persons working in corrections do not consider those types of operations as part of the central debate, which concerns the operation of traditional, secure corrections facilities.)

As of December 31, 2018, in the United States, there were more than 118,000 state or federal prisoners in private facilities. This represents 8% of all prisoners. This compares with 87,369 state or federal prisoners in private facilities as of December 31, 2000 (6.3% of all prisoners).[2]

Several factors led to the sudden growth of this industry. There was rapid growth in prison and jail populations and the aging of old prison buildings and jails. In the 1960s, there had been a strong push against traditional institutions and for alternatives to corrections or for nonincarcerative punishments. Prisons in many jurisdictions were scaled down, and legislatures were glad not to have to spend money on keeping up old buildings or building new ones. This trend continued into the 1970s. Then, with constant pressures resulting from increases in the crime rate, and especially increases in drug use and all kinds of drug offenses, tougher and tougher laws were passed to try to cope with the high crime rates. The construction of new prisons and jails became essential. Court decisions criticizing outmoded programs, often because those programs were housed in decrepit buildings, increased the pressure to build. In the 1980s and into the 1990s, new jail and prison construction was going on everywhere. However, simply building new prisons and jails was not sufficient: the new buildings had to be staffed and run from year to year, and those operating expenses were high. The U.S. General Accounting Office (GAO) reported that prison operating costs (state and federal) increased from about $3.1 billion in fiscal year 1980 to over $17 billion in fiscal year 1994, an increase of almost 550%.[3] By 2015, the Vera Institute estimated that the operational costs of prisons in 45 states was almost $43 billion, with 14 states each spending in excess of $1 billion annually on prisons. The 2015 report also indicates that the 45 states were spending an average of over $33,000 per inmate. Since 2010, many states have decreased their prison populations and, subsequently, reduced their expenditures on corrections. Today, state corrections [$63.5 billion] is the fifth-largest category of states' collective spending (behind Medicaid, K-12 education, Higher Education, and Transportation).[4]

In most places in the mid-1990s, a "get-tough-on-crime" sentiment was prevailing in the legislatures. Such legislatures reversed earlier efforts to release more offenders to the streets and demanded that more offenders be locked up, and for longer periods of time. At the same time, inharmoniously, there was a push for greater fiscal economies and a downsizing of government functions. These various political pressures made privatization look appealing in many jurisdictions. The biggest selling point of private companies had been that they could provide a total facility less costly than the government could. Private corrections companies also claimed that they could build and get a facility open and running more quickly than the government could. The latter claim seems to be supported by experience: because private firms are not bound by governmental rules that tend to slow down prison construction, such as political pressures from unhappy neighbors, environmental restraints, and requirements of competitive bidding and construction contracting, private firms have shown an ability to open new facilities more quickly. It is also claimed, by private corrections companies, that they raise the money to build new institutions more quickly from private investors or from lenders, while the government has to work more slowly, getting appropriations from the legislature or going through a bond-issuing process. In addition, working with existing designs ("cookie-cutter" plans), private firms can begin site preparation and construction more quickly.[5] A criticism of privatization is that this aspect allows prisons to be built without public agreement. Public entities may be required to seek voter approval for a construction bond for a publicly operated facility; the needed construction costs for a privately operated prison can be included in the state's prison operating budget.

As with all of these claims and counterclaims, it is hard to establish exact comparisons, because comparable facilities must be used to make these comparisons valid. Nonetheless, it is generally accepted that it takes the government at least two to three years to build a correctional facility, while some private companies claim it can build a facility in 12 to 18 months (and in fact, have done so). Minimum security facilities are built in even less time by private firms (as quickly as six months, in some cases). In order to conserve funds, private facilities are often designed to require the fewest number of staff, and this may make valid comparisons more difficult. Critics wonder if this low staffing level comes at the expense of security. Another concern that has been raised is whether private companies, in a rush to make quick deadlines, cut corners and do not use the same quality materials and construction methods that are present in government construction. This is a valid concern, and it should be met by stringent requirements in the contract with the private firm that will build the facility, just as it is when the government contracts with a private company to build a facility that it plans to operate itself. Writing a contract with strict, thorough specifications and then carefully monitoring it are the essential elements for all private work done for the government through contracting.

Another claimed advantage of privately operated prisons is that, by using private facilities, the government may more effectively and quickly respond to variations in the prison population. As previously noted, private corrections have a faster startup time in building private prisons. On the other hand, if the prison population decreases, the government may choose not to extend the contract. In some jurisdictions, public contracts may only be entered for one, two, or three years. It may be of some assurance to the government to know that it can get out of a situation if it proves to be undesirable. The loss of government contracts can mean financial distress for private companies when contracts are terminated, depriving the company of revenue intended to pay for the construction and staffing. Such contracts also avoid the need for the government to lay off its own staff if downsizing is required.

While private prisons appear beneficial in allowing the government to more efficiently expand and contract the number of prison beds, other privatization claims are more suspect. Privatization supporters have frequently claimed appreciable cost savings in the building of, and, the operation of, private prisons. These claims are extremely hard to evaluate and prove. One reason, which was already referred to, is the "apples and oranges" problem—the difficulty in making sure that comparisons are between facilities of truly comparable features.[6] Another even bigger problem is the hidden nature of many costs of corrections. These cover such things as capital costs (depreciation and amortization methods may be very different), employee benefits packages (particularly retirement plans, bonuses, insurance, and health plans), legal services, insurance, liability costs, staff training, transportation costs, interagency personnel costs (governments can often borrow some personnel, full- or part-time, from other agencies), and the true costs of programs and services, including agency monitoring for contract compliance. An agency would be ill-advised to conclude that it can contract out a jail or prison operation and then walk away and assume that the contracted cost is the end of the matter. Essential to a good contractual operation—and this cannot be overemphasized—is close, careful monitoring of all aspects of the private performance. That monitoring must be conducted by experienced persons; this is not a cheap aspect of privatization.

The experienced monitor is critical; one of their primary and obvious tasks is to ensure that the contract guidelines are followed. The monitor, however, should not do the work or, unless specified in the contract, dictate the approach to be used. For the monitor to do either of these takes away from the purpose and integrity of privatization and skews any assessment of the process.

In 2016, the Department of Justice's Office of Inspector General (OIG) conducted an audit of private correctional facilities contracted by the Federal Bureau of Prisons (BOP). The audit compared 14 private correctional facilities with 14 Bureau operated facilities with comparable inmate populations. The audit concluded: "[I]n most key areas, contract prisons incurred more safety and security incidents per capita than comparable BOP institutions and that the BOP needs to improve how it monitors contract prisons in several areas." The data analyzed was collected from October 1, 2010, through September 30, 2014 (FYs 2011, 2012, 2013 and 2014), in eight key categories: (1) contraband, (2) reports of incidents, (3) lockdowns, (4) inmate discipline, (5) telephone monitoring, (6) selected grievances, (7) urinalysis drug testing, and (8) sexual misconduct. "With the exception of fewer incidents of positive drug tests and sexual misconduct, the contract prisons had more incidents per capita than the BOP institutions in all of the other categories of data we examined. . . . Contract prisons also had higher rates of assaults, both by inmates on other inmates and by inmates on staff."[7] The OIG report noted that the BOP needed to improve its oversight of contract prisons. While agreeing that on-site monitors as used by the BOP were best positioned to ensure contract compliance issues, some procedures used by the BOP were not sufficient to allow efficient oversight of private prisons' compliance with contract requirements and BOP policies in some areas.

Another concern that is present in conducting a cost analysis is the lack of rigorous controls to prevent staff manipulation and to ensure that inmate behavior is measured in a standard manner. In discussing the debate over the cost-efficiency of prisons, a Bureau of Justice Assistance's monograph on privatized prisons stated that many studies had "serious methodological flaws"[8]

How are the claimed savings achieved by private firms? The biggest savings, no doubt, are in personnel costs. The private firms typically employ nonunionized labor and offer the lowest benefits packages and wages that can be negotiated and maintained. Supervision and training are provided by experienced staff members, many of whom are hired from the ranks of state or federal agencies, or from the retirees' ranks of those government agencies. Savings also result from centralized management, which, especially in the large companies, can provide broader programs and services at cost savings, compared with what can be provided by a small jurisdiction, such as a county or a small state. Private companies claim that they are able to save because, unlike the government agencies, they do not have to be involved in political hassling, bureaucratic red tape (personnel requirements and financial accounting procedures, for example), and complex dealings with the legislature. Perhaps the most significant factor is that privatization promotes competition among companies, so minimizing costs is essential to obtaining contracts in the first place and to retaining them in the future.

These facts about the nature of private operations also serve to point out some of the arguments against privatization. For example, private firms are in business to make a profit, and they must do so in order to satisfy investors and to stay in business.[9] Critics of privatization point to the private sector in police protection; how do you compare, in your experience, the quality of staff in "rent-a-cop" operations with those in government police forces? After all, a majority of security personnel [police] in this country are privately employed—at factories, shopping malls, universities, hospitals, and so on.

What of the right to strike? If the staff at a privately run facility want to organize and stage some kind of work action to achieve union goals, what should the position of the government be? Can such a situation be adequately covered by contract terms? If there is a no-strike clause (as there is for most government workers, especially those in law enforcement), how can it be enforced against private workers? The current privatization experience is still too short to make a final, balanced assessment. Again, strict contract requirements and close monitoring are the keys to avoid sad consequences. When it comes to the quality of staff, one must wonder whether it is possible to ensure, by contract, that high standards are met and kept, when it is difficult to do so when a government manager has direct control of hiring, training, promoting, and firing in a traditional government agency.

The following views are presented in the Bureau of Justice Assistance's monograph on privatized prisons:[10]

What seems to have evolved in the United States is a privatization model that essentially mimics the public model but achieves modest cost savings, at least initially, by making modest reductions in staffing patterns, fringe benefits, and other labor-related costs. There is no evidence showing that private prisons will have a dramatic impact on how prisons operate ....

Despite these criticisms, privatization still provides a vital function within the correctional system .... [P]rivatization has forced the public sector to reexamine how it conducts business .... In this sense, privatization has served as a catalyst for change ...

Several recent reports have attempted to quantify the cost-effectiveness of private corrections compared to public corrections. A legislative audit in Georgia indicated that the cost of housing comparable inmates [males and medium security] cost the state of Georgia $44.56 per day compared to $49.07 per day in private correctional facilities and $21.63 per day in county correctional facilities. At the time of the audit, Georgia's total per day inmate cost was $65.58. The cost figures for private correctional facilities may include costs associated with the construction of the facility rather than being limited to current supervision costs.[11] An October 2016 analysis of three states' summary of the cost of private and state corrections concluded that:

Private prisons do not currently offer a clear advantage over their public-sector counterparts in terms of cost or quality. The wide variation across prisons, differences between the public and private sector, and data limitations render a comprehensive, direct comparison of cost and quality across prison sectors infeasible. However, existing studies that attempt to account for differences in the population served show that private prisons do not offer clear cost savings or quality improvements.[12]

In September of 2010, Arizona's Office of the Auditor General conducted a performance audit of the state's department of corrections. With respect to private prisons, the audit "[a]fter adjusting state and private rates to make them more comparable ... found that rates paid to private facilities were higher [than for state-operated facilities] for both minimum and medium custody beds, the two categories of beds for which the Department contracts." The report also noted that the costs were not directly comparable, stating that private prisons "do not have all the same responsibilities and costs as state-operated facilities." One example was that private prisons do not accept inmates with serious medical needs.[13]

The Arizona Auditor's report referred to a 2009 University of Utah article on prison privatization and the cost and quality of confinement indicators. That article reported on 12 studies. Eight of the studies that "met inclusion criteria provided information on cost of confinement." Four of these studies identified private prison cost savings, two studies found no difference in cost savings, and two found that publicly managed prisons cost less.[14]

Perhaps the clearest need for further and improved research on public-private prisons was shown by a 2008 Department of Justice publication reporting on two cost and performance analyses of the same four prisons (one privately operated and three publicly operated). The two analyses showed different cost findings. The two primary reasons for this were the different approaches used for handling the size of the inmate population and what was included in overhead costs. The article points out the need to develop a uniform performance measure.[15]

The VERA Institute for Justice reports that some states in fiscal year 2011 cut back on their use of private prisons. This report said it is a "subject of debate" on whether cost savings may be realized from using privately contracted facilities.[16]

With respect to the decline in the numbers of prisoners held in private correctional facilities, an October 2020 Bureau of Justice Statistics report, *Prisoners in 2019*, indicates that from 2009–2019, state and federal prison populations declined by 11.4% (Table 1). Thirty-six state departments of correction reported a drop in prison population from 2018 to 2019. (Table 2). https://www.bjs.gov/content/pub/pdf/p19.pdf. This same resource indicates that the percentage of prisoners held in private correctional facilities was about 8% in 2019, which is about the same percentage as in 2009 but higher than the 6.3% of state and federal prisoners held in private facilities in 2000. In 2019 five states (Hawaii, Montana, New Mexico, Oklahoma, and Tennessee) housed more than 20% of their inmates in private correctional facilities, and 14 states housed no inmates in private facilities (Table 18).

From a different perspective, one state has proposed selling several of its state prisons to private prison operators and then contracting with those companies to house inmates.[17]

▶ Legal Issues in Privatization

The underlying issue of privatizing prisons, in a sense, is a quasi-legal one, or it may be labeled a philosophical question that is related to the function of government: Is it proper for private entities to exercise the function of confining, of punishing, fellow citizens? Privatization opponents believe it is not:

> In many instances, private prison operators are paid according to the number of inmates housed. Arguably, it is in the operator's financial interests to encourage lengthier sentences for inmates to keep bed spaces filled …. Critics of prison privatization argue that firms will cut corners, from construction materials to hiring inexperienced personnel, forsaking security and quality of service in the process of making a profit.[18]

Providing particular services, such as food service or individual medical care, is one thing, but it is quite a different matter to take over an entire facility, both from the viewpoint of the individual inmates and in consideration of the protection of the public. The most difficult aspects of this issue are the ones involving custody and security. Can, or should, private staff members punish inmates for violations of rules—rules that may differ from those in government-run prisons? Can this be done to the extent that it is done by government staff, such as by placing offending inmates in solitary confinement, taking away all sorts of privileges (including some, such as correspondence and visiting, that affect the families as well as the inmates), and even affecting the length of time served (as in good-time allowances and parole recommendations)? Can, may, or should, private guards use force to control inmates, including deadly force, in cases of attempted escapes or riots? If they cannot do these things, how is the public to be protected? These are the most sensitive questions. The questions become more intense the higher the level of security of the institution and the higher the degree of sophistication or violent behavior that is present in the inmate population. In fact, private companies have so far operated in this country primarily at lower-security-level institutions. A 2005 census of correctional facilities under state or federal authority, by facility security level, identified only eight (from a total of 415 private facilities) that operated at a maximum level of security and 43 that operated at a medium level of security.[19] It is at the maximum type of facility where the security concerns just mentioned would be the most pressing. But those same concerns are present in the lower-level institutions—just to a lesser degree.

Some states have tackled the security issue by placing limits on the actions of private-sector staff: they are (in some places) only allowed to take summary and minor disciplinary actions against inmates; higher levels of disciplinary punishments are considered and imposed by regular government staff. (Some places use government staff for all disciplinary punishments against inmates.) As to the use of force, the private staff on the scene must be allowed to take immediate action in some situations. However, it is generally anticipated and provided for in the arrangements with the private company that, in the case of major disturbances, government staff (police or corrections officers) will be called on to handle the situation. Requirements on the use of deadly force (such as instructions for firing at fleeing prisoners) cannot be avoided, just because the officer with the weapon is a private rather than a government employee. Constitutional limits apply (see especially the discussion on the use of force and the cases of *Tennessee v. Garner*, 471 U.S. 1 (1985), and *Whitley v. Albers*, 475 U.S. 312 (1986)). To the extent that private corrections officers (or private security police in shopping malls, for that matter) are issued weapons and have authority to use them, they must be carefully trained in the standards for using force, especially the limitations on the use of potentially deadly force.

The drafting of a good contract and the careful monitoring of that contract are essential to producing good results in private operations of prisons. They are, to a large degree, legal concerns. It is, of course, necessary to have a lawyer work closely with the appropriate government staff, such as the contract monitors and those working in the program areas, in order to prepare tight legal contracts, under the rules and standards of contracting in the jurisdiction. Ideally, the lawyer should not only be proficient in writing contracts but should also be knowledgeable in criminal justice concerns and the demands of corrections operations. The legal staff should continue to be involved with the team that monitors the performance of a contract. Contract monitors do not have to be attorneys, but they should be trained by attorneys about the details of their jobs, and attorneys should be available to answer questions that arise from the actual monitoring.

In many situations, the corrections agency will assign at least one staff member to the private facility on a full-time basis to act as a monitor. This monitor must have access to the inmates and the staff, to all areas of the institution, and to all records and reports at any time. Periodic (intermittent) inspections of facilities are less costly and cause less friction with private management, but they are less effective in ensuring good contract performance. "Constant monitoring of all aspects of internal performance is essential to a good contractual relationship."[20] A troubling aspect of contract drafting and implementation is providing for the handling of violations of the contract. Isolated, minor problems can, of course, be handled by warnings and negotiations, but there must be provisions in the contract for sanctions for serious abuses. These may be in the form of dollar penalties or withholding of some payment under the contract, which is deemed to be the most effective curative tool for a private corporation. If the violations continue, there must be provisions for additional sanctions, including termination of the contract.

Another significant legal issue is liability. Private companies will usually cover their exposure to liability by taking out liability insurance for all types of claims. As to ordinary, common law tort actions, such as medical malpractice or injuries from faulty equipment, the insurance should cover any losses due to inmate claims (or claims that may be made by visitors or by staff for injuries caused by negligent conditions or staff actions). The government, in the contract, will usually require the private company to be insured and to hold harmless the government for any such legal claims. In this portion of the contract, the language must be broad enough, and specific enough, to cover all types of claims that might be brought in relation to the operations of the private facility. The private company will typically have its own counsel, but property and injury claims will usually be handled by the insurance carrier.

The tougher legal question is the liability of the government or the contractor for constitutional violations. The language of 42 U.S.C. § 1983 allows such suits for claimed violations by any person who was acting under color of state law. It appears that liability cannot be avoided for constitutional violations by contracting the government service to a private entity. The leading case on this is *West v. Atkins,* 487 U.S. 42 (1988), where the Supreme Court said that the claimed violations of constitutional rights (a claim of deliberate indifference to the inmate's medical needs) were valid under Section 1983 because the private physician who was being sued in that case was performing a function for the state. The fact that the physician was under contract to perform medical services did not remove the physician (or the state) from obligations and liability under the civil rights law.

▶ *Richardson v. McKnight; Correctional Services Corporation v. Malesko; Minneci v. Pollard*

In *Richardson v. McKnight,* 521 U.S. 399 (1997), two prison guards who worked for a private firm claimed they were entitled to qualified immunity from inmate lawsuits charging a Section 1983 violation. McKnight, an inmate in a private prison in Tennessee, filed the constitutional tort action, alleging that the officers placed him in "extremely tight physical restraints," causing a deprivation of his constitutional rights. The district court held the officers were not entitled to immunity because they worked for a private company, not the government. The appeals court, primarily for reasons of "public policy," agreed that immunity was inappropriate.

In affirming, the Supreme Court looked at several issues. One was whether there was a "firmly rooted" tradition of immunity for privately employed prison guards. As was discussed earlier, correctional functions have never been the exclusive domain of the government. The Court found "no evidence that the law gave purely private companies or their employees any special immunity from such suits."

The Court also considered whether the purposes of qualified immunity warranted a reversal. The officers correctly noted that state prison guards were entitled to qualified immunity; the officers therefore argued that, since they do the same work as state prison guards, they too should have this entitlement. In addressing the "functional approach" (people who do the same work), the Court acknowledged using the approach in some prior circumstances, but held that its prior applicability was more directed to the type of immunity—qualified or absolute—that the public official should receive. The Court recognized important differences between private and state workers with respect to immunity. The Court reviewed some of these differences and concluded:

> **Our examination of history and purpose thus reveals nothing special enough about the job or about its organizational structure that would warrant providing these private prison guards with a governmental immunity. The job is one that private industry might, or might not, perform; and which history shows private firms did sometimes perform without relevant immunities. The organizational structure is one subject to the ordinary competitive pressures that normally help private firms adjust their behavior in response to the incentives that tort suits provide—pressures not necessarily present in government departments.**

In closing, the Court gave three caveats. First, the Court was not finding there was Section 1983 liability, but only that there was no entitlement to qualified immunity for a private prison guard. Second, the holding was narrowly drawn to apply to a private firm, "systematically organized" to perform a major administrative task, such as managing an institution, that receives limited direct government supervision and which undertakes the task for profit and potentially is in competition with other companies. Excluded from this case's coverage are those activities undertaken by a private person as an adjunct to government or acting under close government supervision (as in *West v. Atkins).* Third, the Court left open the issue of whether the defendants could successfully claim a "good faith" defense in this kind of lawsuit.

After *Richardson,* most lower courts generally adopted a position that prison workers who were employed by a private agency were not entitled to the protections of qualified immunity. However, *Richardson* contained two significant caveats: its holding was narrowly drawn to apply to a private firm, "systematically organized" to perform a major administrative task, such as managing an institution, that receives limited direct government supervision and that undertakes the task for profit and potentially is in competition with other companies. A second caveat was that the *Richardson* decision did not apply to those activities undertaken by a private person as an adjunct to government or acting under close government supervision. Fifteen years after *Richardson,* the Court provided further guidance on the availability of the qualified immunity defense to private persons working to provide governmental services.

In 2006 the city of Rialto, California hired a private attorney (Filarsky) to conduct an investigation into whether a city fire fighter (Delia) was working on home improvement projects while on city paid sick leave. Delia had been observed purchasing building supplies, including large rolls of insulation, at a home improvement store. Filarsky was part of an investigative team which also included two city employed fire officials. As part of the investigation, Filarsky, with the concurrence of the city employed fire fighters and the city fire chief, requested to inspect Delia's home, which on the advice of counsel, Delia declined to permit. Filarsky then asked Delia if he would bring the building materials out of the house so they could be inspected, which Delia also refused to do on advice of counsel. Filarsky advised Delia and Delia's attorney that Filarsky would obtain an order from the fire chief directing Delia to produce the building material for inspection. Delia's counsel repeatedly advised the team that this would be a Fourth Amendment violation and that Delia would sue all those involved. An order was prepared by Filarsky and signed by the fire chief ordering Delia to provide the material for inspection. Delia did comply, bringing out several rolls of insulation for inspection.

Delia then filed a Section 1983 action against the city, the city fire department, the fire chief, and the members of the investigation team including Filarsky, alleging the order violated Delia's rights under the Fourth and Fourteenth Amendments. The district court granted qualified immunity to all of the individual defendants (including Filarsky) and dismissed the lawsuit. The court of appeals affirmed the dismissal except for the claim against Filarsky because "as a private attorney and not a City employee, he was not entitled to seek the protection of qualified immunity." The Supreme Court granted certiorari to address this question: "*whether an individual hired by the government to do its work is prohibited from seeking such immunity, solely because he works for the government on something other than a permanent or full-time basis." Filarsky v. Delia,* 566 U.S. 377 (2012).

In the *Filarsky* decision, the Court noted that its previous decision in *Richardson* was a self-consciously "narrow" decision. [citation omitted] ("[W]e have answered the immunity question narrowly, in the context in which it arose") and that the *Richardson* holding was not meant to foreclose all claims of immunity by private individuals. In deciding the question of qualified immunity, the Court conducted an analysis of common law liability and immunity at the time of the passage of Title 42, U.S. Code, Section 1983 in 1871. Common law recognized that government actors were afforded certain protections from liability because "the public good can best be secured by allowing officers charged with the duty of deciding upon the rights of others, to act upon their own free, unbiased convictions, uninfluenced by any apprehensions." In 1871 until well into the 20th century, much of the work of government was conducted by private persons who provided government services only temporarily or occasionally. As examples, the Court noted that local store owners also served as postmasters, private attorneys conducted criminal prosecutions for the state, and even the Attorney General of the United States was a part time job. The common law did not draw distinctions "between public servants and private individuals engaged in public service in according protection to those carrying out government responsibilities." Examples of private individuals receiving immunity for actions taken while engaged in public service on a temporary or occasional basis included part time justices of the peace who had judicial immunity or private persons assisting public law enforcement officials (a posse) in carrying out public duties.

> **We read § 1983 "in harmony with general principles of tort immunities and defenses." [citation omitted]. And we "proceed on the assumption that common-law principles of. . . immunity were incorporated into our judicial system and that they should not be abrogated absent clear legislative intent to do so." [citation omitted]. Under this assumption, immunity under § 1983 should not vary depending on whether an individual working for the government does so as a full-time employee, or on some other basis.**

The Court then identified the public policy grounds which supported extending qualified immunity to private persons performing public services. "Ensuring that those who serve the government do so "with the decisiveness and the judgment required by the public good," [citation omitted] is of vital importance regardless whether the individual sued as a state actor works full-time or on some other basis. Providing immunity to private persons performing public functions to the same extent as public employees ensures that qualified individuals are not deterred from entering public service.

> **Because government employees will often be protected from suit by some form of immunity, those [private individuals] working alongside them could be left holding the bag—facing full liability for actions taken in conjunction with government employees who enjoy immunity for the same activity. Under such circumstances, any private individual with a choice might think twice before accepting a government assignment.**

One purpose of qualified immunity is to minimize the distractions to the performance of public service created by defending routine lawsuits. If public officials, protected from such distractions by qualified immunity are still required in order to participate, as witnesses, in the lawsuit against the private individual, the public interest is not served. Denying immunity to private persons who perform public services also results in arbitrary line drawing. If a private person works half time for the city, or full time for a year, would that person qualify for immunity? The uncertainty of whether immunity would apply "frustrate[s] the purposes that immunity is meant to serve."

The Court then distinguished its previous decision in *Richardson* because in that case:

> **"[A] private firm, systematically organized to assume a major lengthy administrative task (managing an institution) with limited direct supervision by the government, undertak[ing] that task for profit and potentially in competition with other firms"— combined sufficiently to mitigate the concerns underlying recognition of governmental immunity under § 1983. Nothing of the sort is involved here, or in the typical case of an individual hired by the government to assist in carrying out its work.**

The Court then reversed the court of appeals ruling:

> **Though not a public employee, Filarsky was retained by the City to assist in conducting an official investigation into potential wrongdoing. There is no dispute that government employees performing such work are entitled to seek the protection of qualified immunity. The Court of Appeals rejected Filarsky's claim to the protection accorded Wells, Bekker, and Peel solely because he was not a permanent, full-time employee of the City. The common law, however, did not draw such distinctions, and we see no justification for doing so under § 1983.**

The holding in *Filarsky* instructs that in determining whether qualified immunity is available to private actors performing public functions depends on two factors: (1) the principles of tort immunities and defenses applicable at common law around the time of § 1983's enactment in 1871 and (2) the public purposes served by granting immunity.

The courts of appeal have not been uniform in applying the rules of *Richardson* and *Filarksy* to private persons providing services in state and local correctional facilities. In *McCollum v. Tepe*, 693 F.3d 696 (6th Cir 2012), the Sixth Circuit declined to extend the defense of qualified immunity to a private psychiatrist who worked for a non-profit health care organization providing contract mental health services to a county jail. After a detainee committed suicide in the jail, the decedent's representative sued alleging a violation of the inmate's right to protection from self-harm. The court of appeals considered the ruling of *Filarsky* and *Richardson* and determined that in deciding whether qualified immunity applies to a private person providing public services requires analysis of two elements: "(1) is there was a firmly rooted history of immunity for similarly situated parties at common law; and (2) whether granting immunity would be consistent with the history and purpose of § 1983." After examining case law from the mid to late 1800s, the court of appeals found no common law or statutory basis for immunity to private physicians providing medical services in public institutions at the time of the passage of section 1983. The court also determined that it is odd that a private physician providing the same services as a public employee physician would not be entitled to raise a qualified immunity defense simply because a private entity and not a public entity paid them. However, as noted in *Richardson*, a private firm's ability to "offset any increased employee liability risk with higher pay or extra benefits," the "continual... need for deterring constitutional violations[,] and ... [the] sense that the [private] firm's tasks are not enormously different in respect to their importance from various other publicly important tasks carried out by private firms," dictate that immunity should not be available under these facts. The Seventh Circuit has followed the rationale of *McCollum* in ruling that qualified immunity does not apply to private medical personnel in prisons. See *Estate of Clark v. Walker*, 865 F.3d 544 (7th Cir. 2017).

The Fifth and the Tenth Circuits have extended qualified immunity to private medical personnel working in state prisons. In *Perniciero v. Lea*, 901 F.3d 241 (5th Cir. 2018) the court of appeals ruled that decisions from other circuits denying qualified immunity to private medical personnel in public prisons were distinguishable. Psychiatrists who were on the faculty at Tulane University also provided contract services to the Eastern Louisiana Mental Health System. A patient sued a state employed psychiatrist and the two contractors alleging a failure to protect. The court of appeals noted the split in circuit law on whether private medical personnel providing public services could avail themselves of qualified immunity. The Fifth Circuit focused on the three governmental interests outlined in *Filarsky*: (1) preventing unwarranted timidity in the exercise of official duties; (2) ensuring that highly skilled and qualified candidates are not deterred from public service by the threat of liability; and (3) protecting public employees — and their work — from all of the distraction that litigation entails. In addressing the first interest, the court noted that the relationship between the state and the contract psychiatrists were very different from the situation in *Richardson*. While working at the state hospital, the private psychiatrists were supervised by state employees. Unlike the corporate structure in *Richardson*, Tulane University, which provided the contract psychiatrists operated principally as an educational organization and was not "systematically organized" to perform the "major administrative task" of providing mental-health care at state facilities.

The second factor, deterrence from public service, was also different. The court noted that it is highly specialized private sector professionals "who do not depend on any one stream of work for their livelihoods and who have the freedom to select other opportunities that carry less risk of liability — who are particularly likely to decline public service if not given the same immunity as their public counterparts." Because litigation would be distracting to not only the private health care providers, but the public employees who work with the private providers, the government has an interest in extending the protection of qualified immunity to private persons providing public services within a public facility.

In *Estate of Lockett v. Fallin*, 841 F.3d 1098 (10th Cir. 2016) the Tenth Circuit ruled that the private contract physician who was involved in an Oklahoma execution by lethal injection could raise the defense of qualified immunity. The case involved allegations of cruel and unusual punishment associated with the execution. In affirming the district court's dismissal of the lawsuit, the court of appeals concluded that a physician employed by the state who carried out the same duties in an unquestionably governmental function would have been entitled to raise the qualified immunity defense:

> If participants in an execution could be held liable for problems during the execution, that would necessarily implicate *Filarsky*'s concerns about "[t]he public interest in ensuring performance of government duties free from the distractions that can accompany even routine lawsuits," which the Court noted "is also implicated when individuals other than permanent government employees discharge these duties."

Richardson holds that prison guards employed by a private corporation operating a private correctional facility are not entitled to qualified immunity under 42 U.S.C. § 1983. The federal equivalent to a Section 1983 action is a *Bivens* lawsuit. *Correctional Services Corporation v. Malesko,* 534 U.S. 61 (2001), looks at the question of whether a private firm acting under color of federal law may be held liable under *Bivens.*

Correctional Services Corporation (CSC) contracted with the Federal Bureau of Prisons to house released federal inmates at its New York City halfway house. Malesko was sent to the halfway house to serve out the balance of his sentence. His verified heart condition limited his ability to climb stairs. While at the house, he lived on the fifth floor, taking the elevator to and from his room. In 1994, the facility changed its policy and authorized use of the elevator only for those residents living on the sixth floor or above. Malesko was exempted because of his heart condition. However, on March 28, 1994, CSC employee Urena told Malesko he could not use the elevator, requiring him to climb the stairs. He had a heart attack and fell, injuring his ear.

In 1999, Malesko filed a lawsuit against CSC and CSC employees. The district court considered the complaint under *Bivens* and dismissed it, saying "a *Bivens* action may only be maintained against an individual" and that it did not apply to CSC. The statute of limitations barred suit against the other, individual defendants. The appeals court affirmed with respect to dismissal of the complaint against the individual defendants, but it held that private corporations should be held liable under *Bivens,* thus providing a remedy for constitutional violations. The Supreme Court reversed, holding that the purpose of a *Bivens* action is to deter the officer, not the agency.[21] Whether such liability charges against private prison facilities should exist, as independent legal recovery actions, was seen by the Court as a question for Congress to address. The Court further noted that Malesko had not been without remedies, citing both the Bureau of Prisons' grievance procedure and a possible remedy in tort, allowing Malesko to allege negligence on the part of the CSC staff.

In both *Richardson* and, indirectly, in *Correctional Services Corporation,* the Supreme Court recognized that private prison staff are not immune from litigation alleging constitutional violations. The Court has not addressed whether employees of a private prison operating under contract with a state or federal entity are acting under color of state law (allowing for a Section 1983 action) or federal law (allowing for a *Bivens* action).

In 2012, the Supreme Court refused to extend an implied cause of action for a violation of a federal prisoner's constitutional rights by employees of a private prison under *Bivens.* Inmate Pollard alleged that private prison employees had violated his right to be free from cruel and unusual punishment protected by the Eighth Amendment when prison officials allegedly failed to provide timely and necessary medical and personal care (claiming that the injury rendered him unable to feed or bathe himself). Pollard also claimed that prison officials had forced him to return to his prison work assignment prior to an adequate period of recovery.

A federal Magistrate Judge concluded a *Bivens* cause of action was not available to Pollard, finding that state law provided him with alternative remedies (tort action) and that GEO employees did not act under color of federal law. The district court adopted the Magistrate's recommendation that Pollard's suit be dismissed for failure to state a claim. The appeals court in *Pollard v. GEO Group, Inc.,* 607 F.3d 583 (9th Cir. 2010) reversed, holding that *Bivens* "allows a federal prisoner to recover for violations of his constitutional rights by employees of private corporations operating federal prisons." The court of appeals also ruled that "despite the contrary holding in the Fourth Circuit in *Holly v. Scott,* 484 F.3d 287 (4th Cir. 2006), we conclude that the GEO employees act under color of federal law for purposes of *Bivens* liability."

In May 2011, the United States Supreme Court granted the petition for a writ of certiorari in *Pollard,* to answer the following question: "[w]hether the Court should imply a cause of action under *Bivens*… against individual employees of private companies that contract with the Federal government to provide prison services, where the plaintiff has adequate alternative remedies for the harm alleged and the defendants have no employment or contractual relationship with the government." In *Minneci v. Pollard,* 565 U.S. 118 (2012) the Court held that Pollard could not assert a *Bivens* claim because his "Eighth Amendment claim focuses upon a kind of conduct that typically falls within the scope of traditional state tort law. And in the case of a privately employed defendant, state tort law provides an 'alternative, existing process' capable of protecting the constitutional interests at stake." The Court said, "the prisoner must seek a remedy under state tort law." The Court relied upon its earlier decision in *Wilkie v. Robbins,* 551 U.S. 537 (2007) to determine if a *Bivens* remedy should be implied:

In the first place, there is the question whether any alternative, existing process for protecting the [constitutionally recognized] interest amounts to a convincing reason for the Judicial Branch to refrain from providing a new and freestanding remedy in damages. . . . But even in the absence of an alternative, a *Bivens* remedy is a subject of judgment: `the federal courts must make the kind

of remedial determination that is appropriate for a common-law tribunal, paying particular heed, however, to any special factors counselling hesitation before authorizing a new kind of federal litigation.'" . . . The existence of that alternative here constitutes a "convincing reason for the Judicial Branch to refrain from providing a new and freestanding remedy in damages."

The Court rejected Pollard's claim that extension of *Bivens* was appropriate since his lawsuit was so similar to the case of *Carlson v. Green* where the Supreme Court had extended *Bivens* [both cases arose under the Eighth Amendment]. The Court first concluded that in *Carlson v. Green* the case involved federal prison employees, not private prison employees, and that federal law precluded an injured individual from ordinarily suing the federal government for the state law torts of federal employees. (See 28 U.S.C. §§ 2671, 2679(b)(1) (Westfall Act) (substituting United States as defendant in tort action against federal employee).

Pollard had also argued the Court should find a consistent platform to remedy similar injuries which are not dependent on state law because state law varies. This argument was rejected as "the Court has implied *Bivens* action only where any alternative remedy against individual officers was "nonexistent" or where plaintiff "lacked *any alternative remedy*" at all." [emphasis in original]. Pollard also argued that state tort remedies were not adequate to protect the constitutional interests of injured persons. The Court rejected this argument concluding that even if state tort law remedies may be less generous than remedies under federal constitutional law, state law and constitutional remedies "need not be perfectly congruent."

For these reasons, where, as here, a federal prisoner seeks damages from privately employed personnel working at a privately operated federal prison, where the conduct allegedly amounts to a violation of the Eighth Amendment, and where that conduct is of a kind that typically falls within the scope of traditional state tort law (such as the conduct involving improper medical care at issue here), the prisoner must seek a remedy under state tort law. We cannot imply a *Bivens* remedy in such a case.

In an endnote, the Court noted that the private prison employees had not asked the Supreme Court to review the circuit court of appeals ruling that private prison employees who confine federal prisoners act under color of federal law.

After *Pollard*, the Supreme Court decided *Ziglar v. Abassi* and *Hernandez v. Mesa* [these cases are discussed in detail in other chapters] in which the Supreme Court declined to extend *Bivens* claims against federal employees into new contexts. In *Vega v. United States, et al*, 881 F.3d 1146 (9th Cir. 2018), the Ninth Circuit addressed the issue of whether the Court's rulings in *Pollard* precluded extending *Bivens* liability to private contractors for allegedly violating a federal prisoner's First and Fifth Amendment rights. Vega was a federal prisoner who was transferred to a private residential re-entry center (RRC) to complete the service of his federal sentence. Vega alleged that RRC staff violated his First and Fifth Amendment rights by writing a false incident report and having him transferred back to a secure federal facility. Vega was transferred to a different RRC about 3 months later. The district court dismissed Vega's claim against the private RRC employees based on the *Minneci* ruling that "clarified that private employees acting under color of federal law cannot be held liable under *Bivens*." The Ninth Circuit ruled that *Minneci* did not completely prohibit extending *Bivens* to employees of private companies. Using the Supreme Court's ruling in *Ziglar v. Abassi*, the court of appeals ruled that neither the Supreme Court nor the Ninth Circuit had extended Bivens liability to "a prisoner's First Amendment access to court or Fifth Amendment procedural due process claims arising out of a prison disciplinary process, the circumstances of Vega's case against private defendants plainly present a "new context" under *Abbasi*." The court of appeals affirmed the dismissal of Vega's claims against the private employees because Vega had adequate alternative remedies at his disposal. The court declined to consider whether any special factors counseled hesitation.

With respect to private prisons, there also is one overriding question—does the government have the authority to contract away a government function? The ultimate answer, by U.S. Supreme Court decision, has not yet been given.[22]

Perhaps the most severe critic of privatization on a broad and legal front, Professor Ira Robbins, has concluded that contracting away functions probably can be legally supported on some levels but not on others.[23] The courts (including the Supreme Court) have usually upheld the delegation of authority by executive agencies at the federal and state levels. What is not allowed is the delegation of legislative or judicial functions. The management of individual correctional functions, such as food and health services, has been upheld legally. Some other functions that more directly affect the lives of inmates have also been upheld. States have commonly permitted private parties to perform law enforcement functions, such as in the case of private security police, and those functions have included the right to detain a person suspected of breaking the law (a shoplifter, for example). But then, a private citizen in the United States also has the right to perform a citizen's arrest. Confining persons in a jail or in a prison is a different matter because it has been considered (in recent times, at least) to be a function for the government alone. This is an issue that will have to be litigated in each jurisdiction, but it can best be handled (legally) for now by having the legislature authorize the delegation of the function to private parties.

The delegation of rulemaking and decisions on inmate discipline are seen by Professor Robbins as very different matters, ones where the courts may say private contractors may not take over the government function (because they approach the nature of legislative and adjudicative functions). Private companies must be able to conduct routine activities concerning the management of inmates when they take over the running of an entire facility, such as record keeping, assigning inmates to housing and jobs, and scheduling activities (including visiting, recreation, work, and programs). Such routine functions, which must be done if any management of the inmate population is to be accomplished by the private company, would also have to be accompanied by the issuance of rules to cover them. These kinds of "routine" rules, Robbins predicts, will be upheld as a delegated function. When those rules cross over into the area of outlining the consequences for breaking the rules and exercising disciplinary authority, Robbins sees those as a more essential government function, because they entail adjudication of misconduct, they affect the terms to be served, and they embody strict constitutional standards of process.[24]

This whole area of the legality and constitutionality of private prisons and jails at the federal and the state levels is one that has only begun to be litigated. The provision of specialized services by contract, such as a food service department, does not present significant legal problems, as long as the jurisdiction has the legal authority (specifically found in statutes) to contract for such matters. Further, the contracting for lower security facilities and detention facilities is also defensible, again, as long as there is statutory authority to contract, the contracts are carefully drawn and monitored, and there is provision for disciplinary action to be taken (or at least supervised) by government corrections staff. Finally, some critics of private corrections have serious reservations about the wisdom (although not necessarily the legality) of contracting with a private company to run a maximum-security facility. Privatization should be evaluated carefully and methodically. Starting with an evaluation of the performance of private companies in the lower security institutions should be an initial step. After the assessment of the ability of private corrections to perform at that lower level correctional agencies should move cautiously toward allowing private management of the highest level of institutions. This is necessary for the most important part of the mission of corrections: the protection of the public. Whether the Supreme Court will ultimately uphold the private operation of higher-security prisons remains an open question.

Summary

- Privatization in corrections follows two paths: contracting for special services and programs (such as food services and health services), which is widely practiced and accepted and contracting for the building and operation of an entire correctional facility, which is of more recent vintage (since the 1980s) and is the focus of heated debate among corrections officials and commentators.
- Historically, the running of prisons and jails by private parties is a very old concept. In England, it goes back at least to the Middle Ages. Prison reformers argued for better conditions in jails and prisons in the 18th and 19th centuries, and improvements were achieved largely through legislation and the transition of all types of corrections facilities to management by state and local governments. It was only in the 1900s that we came to assume that corrections are, at all levels, a government function.
- There have always been exceptions to the government-only rule for corrections operations. Prisons and jails have been constructed, renovated, and expanded by private construction contracts. Some inmate services, especially in specialized health care, have been contracted to private organizations in many jurisdictions. Community facilities, especially halfway houses, have also been operated by private organizations.
- The main debate is over the operation, by private companies, of entire corrections facilities, jails, and prisons that confine sophisticated inmates in high-security surroundings. In recent years, a number of corporations have entered the corrections business seeking to build (or remodel) and run jails and prisons.
- The private firms argued that, in a climate of heavy demand for prison and jail beds, they could get a facility running more quickly and at a lower expense than the government could. It is sometimes hard to get exact comparative figures, but studies do seem to support the claims that private companies can act faster than

the government in getting new facilities into operation. What is open to more debate, and what needs more study and hard evidence, is whether the quality of operation provided by private companies is comparable to government operations. The quality of the staff is an extremely important factor and one that must be emphasized during the privatization process. The quality of all services and programs in a facility must be ensured, to the extent possible, by the terms of the private contract and by careful monitoring of the performance of the contract.

■ As private firms move up the ladder into the operation of high-security institutions and the inmates under their supervision become more sophisticated, concerns about the abilities of private employees (and the underlying philosophical questions of what responsibilities in corrections should be turned over to them) increase. Of special concern are the questions of whether private-sector employees should be authorized to use deadly force, to take disciplinary actions that affect the freedom of inmates, and to issue rules for the management of inmates.

■ Persons who provide services to inmates under contract are not immune from suits for constitutional violations (*West v. Atkins*). Officials and staff who run private prisons and jails may be sued for constitutional torts under 42 U.S.C. Section 1983, because they are operating under color of state law. They may also be sued for common law torts for injuries or losses caused by their wrongful actions.

■ The Supreme Court has ruled that prison guards hired by a private firm are not entitled to qualified immunity from inmate suits charging a Section 1983 violation *(Richardson v. McKnight)*. The Court has held that private firms operating under color of federal law are not subject to liability under *Bivens* suits (*Correctional Services Corporation v. Malesko*).

■ The Supreme Court has declined to extend an implied Bivens cause of action for federal prisoners who claim that they were injured by private correctional company employees as such claims are adequately addressed under state law. *Minneci v. Pollard.*

■ What has not been settled in the courts is the propriety of private firms running entire corrections facilities as a broad legal or constitutional question.

Thinking About It

Should a private prison have direct responsibility for those actions that affect a person's loss of life, liberty, or property? For example, an inmate's loss of good time has the impact of extending his prison stay, and an inmate's disciplinary infraction may lead to placement in segregation.

Key Terms

penitentiary
privatization

Endnotes

1. For a full review of the history of private jails and prisons, see *Punishment for Profit,* especially Chapter 2 (pages 19–44), "A Historical Review of Private Prisons." Shichor, D. *Punishment for Profit.* Thousand Oaks, CA: Sage Publications. 1995.
2. Carson, E.A. *Prisoners in 2018.* Table 18. (Washington, DC: Bureau of Justice Statistics, U.S. Department of Justice, April 2020.)
3. Austin, J. and Coventry, G. *Emerging Issues on Privatized Prisons.* Page 1. (Washington, DC: Bureau of Justice Assistance, U.S. Department of Justice, 2001.
4. *The Continuing Fiscal Crisis in Corrections: Setting a New Course.* The Vera Institute of Justice. October 2010. Accessed February 25, 2011 from http://www.vera.org/content/continuing-fiscal-crisis-in-corrections. This report suggests that the fiscal crisis beginning in 2007 has motivated lawmakers to look at who is punished and how this is accomplished. Contributing to this reevaluation are the high recidivism rate, lower crime rates, and research reports examining how corrections may function more effectively at a lower financial cost. As stated in the VERA report (page 5): "State policy makers appear less inclined to be reflexively 'tough on crime.' Indeed, it is becoming more typical—if not expected—that policies are driven by the growing body of evidence about effective responses: a 'smart on crime' approach." In one instance, the report refers (on page 14) to "research and evidence suggesting that mandatory supervision and other prison alternatives are more effective and cost efficient for many lower-risk, nonviolent offenders." See also *The Price of Prisons- Prison Spending in 2015.* The Vera Institute. Available- https://www.vera.org/publications/price-of-prisons-2015 -state-spending-trends/price-of-prisons-2015-state-spending-trends/price-of-prisons-2015-state-spending-trends-prison-spending. This report noted: "Since 2010, nearly half of states have reduced their spending on prisons. Most of these states did so through deliberate choices to reduce the size of their prison populations and downsize their prison staff. These states have fewer people in state

prisons, fewer state resources dedicated to incarceration, and can even boast lower crime rates than five years ago. They demonstrate that a growing prison system is not inevitable, and there are steps that states can take to downsize." See also *State Expenditure Report 2019*, National Association of State Budget Officers. Washington, D.C. Available- https://higherlogicdownload.s3.amazonaws.com/NASBO/9d2d2db1-c943-4f1b-b750-0fca152d64c2/UploadedImages/SER%20Archive/2019_State_Expenditure_Report-S.pdf. Accessed 13 April 2020.

5. See endnote 3, *Emerging Issues on Privatized Prisons,* page 15.

6. In November 2019, the Private Prison Information Act of 2019 [HR 5087 and S. 2773] was introduced into both houses of Congress. The purpose of the legislation was: "To require non-Federal prison, correctional, and detention facilities holding Federal prisoners or detainees under a contract with the Federal Government to make the same information available to the public that Federal prisons and correctional facilities are required to make available." The bill would make records of a non-federal correctional or detention facility, defined as a one privately owned or owned by a state of local government, and holding federal prisoners, records of the federal agency contracting for purposes of the federal Freedom of Information Act. The bills have been referred to committees in each House.

7. U.S. Department of Justice, Office of Inspector General, *Review of the Federal Bureau of Prisons' Monitoring of Contract Prisons.* August 2016. Available- https://oig.justice.gov/reports/2016/e1606.pdf#page=2

8. See endnote 3, page 37.

9. One of the two of largest companies involved in private corrections, CoreCivic (formerly Corrections Corporation of America) (Accessed 13 April 2020 from: http://ir.corecivic.com/. CoreCivic's Mission Statement provides:

    Our Mission We help government better the public good through: CoreCivic Safety — We operate safe, secure facilities that provide high quality services and effective reentry programs that enhance public safety. CoreCivic Community — We deliver proven and innovative practices in settings that help people obtain employment, successfully reintegrate into society, and keep communities safe. CoreCivic Properties — We offer innovative and flexible real estate solutions that provide value to government and the people they serve.

    The website also provides information on the value of the corporation's stock. http://ir.corecivic.com/stock-information/stock-quote-chart

    Another large private corrections corporation is The GEO Group, Inc. Its website provides information on the company's mission:

    GEO's mission is to develop innovative public-private partnerships with government agencies around the globe that deliver high quality, correctional, community reentry, and electronic monitoring services while providing industry leading rehabilitation and community reintegration programs to the men and women entrusted to our care. Available- https://www.geogroup.com/who_we_are. Accessed 13 April 2020. Like CoreCivic, the GEO Group website contains information for investors. http://investors.geogroup.com/

    The reader may wish to compare these statements with those of government agencies (Departments of Corrections).

10. See endnote 3, pages 59–60.

11. *Georgia Department of Corrections-Requested Information on Bed Demand and Agency Strategy.* Report No. 18-12. December 2018. Georgia Department of Audits and Accounts. Available- https://www.audits.ga.gov/rsaAudits/report/index. Accessed 13 April 2020.

12. Mumford, M., Schanzenbach, D.W, & Nunn, R. *The Economics of Private Prisons.* The Brookings Report. October 16, 2016. Available- https://www.brookings.edu/research/the-economics-of-private-prisons/. Accessed 13 April 2020.

13. *Department of Corrections—Prison Population Growth.* Phoenix, Arizona: Office of the Auditor General, State of Arizona. September 2010. Pages 19–21. Available- https://www.azauditor.gov/sites/default/files/10-08_0.pdf. Accessed 13 April 2020. This report notes that Arizona law requires the Department to consider contracting for private prisons. Title 41-1609.02, provides, in part: "A. Before expanding an existing minimum or medium security level prison or before establishing a new minimum or medium security level prison, the director shall give consideration to contracting for private prisons for the incarceration of: [lists five categories, including female inmates and inmates over the age of 55].""B. Before entering into a contract with a private prison facility contractor for the incarceration of prisoners listed in subsection A of this section, the director shall determine that the contractor will provide at least the same quality of services as this state at a lower cost or that the contractor will provide services superior in quality to those provided by this state at essentially the same cost. In making this determination, the director shall consider the following: [lists 9 factors, among these being security, food service, inmate health services, and inmate discipline]." The complete language of § 41-1609.02 is available from https://www.azleg.gov/viewdocument/?docName=https://www.azleg.gov/ars/41/01609-02.htm. Accessed 13 April 2020.

14. Lundahl, B., Kunz, C., Brownell, C., Harris, N., and Van Vleet, R. "Prison Privatization: A Meta-analysis of Cost and Quantity of Confinement Indicators." *Research on Social Work Practice.* 19 (2009): 383–394. The study reported, on page 393, that the data reviewed "do not support a move toward privatization at this time. Similarly, the data do not clearly discourage privatization despite a slight advantage for publicly managed prisons in skills training." With respect to cost savings that may occur from privatizing prisons, the study found such savings were not guaranteed and "appear minimal."

15. Gaes, G. *Cost, Performance Studies Look at Prison Privatization.* (Washington, DC: National Institute of Justice, U.S. Department of Justice, 2008.)

16. See endnote 4. *The Continuing Fiscal Crisis in Corrections: Setting a New Course.* The report notes (on page 12) that as prison populations drop, the factors that make private prisons attractive as a means to solve prison overcrowding become less relevant.

17. *Prisons for Profit—A look at prison privatization.* American Civil Liberties Union of Ohio. April 2011. Available from https://www.acluohio.org/assets/issues/CriminalJustice/PrisonsForProfit2011_04.pdf. Accessed 13 April 2020. The ACLU, which does not support the proposed action to privatize state prisons, says its report "seeks to explore the many problems that plague prisons for profit, in the areas of fiscal efficiency, safety, contributions to the community, accountability and effect on recidivism."

18. See endnote 3, pages 16–17. A leading critic of privatized prisons, Professor Ira Robbins of the Washington College of Law, American University, asserts that "[b]y their very nature, private-incarceration companies are more interested in doing well than doing good." Robbins, I. "The Case Against the Prison-Industrial Complex." *Public Interest Law Reporter* (winter 1997): 44.

19. Stephan, J. *Census of State and Federal Correctional Facilities, 2005.* Appendix table 5. (Washington, DC: Bureau of Justice Statistics, U.S. Department of Justice, 2008.) Among its other findings is the following: about 90% of public correctional facilities and 60% of private correctional facilities offered academic and vocational training programs in 2005, and counseling programs were offered in nearly all public facilities and in about 75% of the private facilities. The inmate per correctional officer ratio was 5 to 1 in public correctional facilities and 6.9 to 1 in the private facilities. Excluded from this report were city, county, and regional jails, and private facilities that did not primarily hold state or federal inmates. Also not included were facilities for the military, U.S. Immigration and Customs Enforcement, Bureau of Indian Affairs, U.S. Marshals Service, and correctional hospital wards not operated by correctional authorities.

20. See endnote 3, page 16.

21. The Court cited *FDIC v. Meyer,* 510 U.S. 471 (1994), where it declined to extend a *Bivens* action to permit suit against a federal agency. The Court said that, if given a choice, a plaintiff would always sue a federal agency instead of a person, who could raise the affirmative defense of qualified immunity. Such a development was seen as resulting in the "evisceration of the *Bivens* remedy, rather than its extension."

22. While the U.S. Supreme Court has yet to rule on this issue, in 2009, Israel's High Court of Justice ruled that privately run prisons are unconstitutional *(Academic Center of Law and Business v. Minister of Finance).* In its opinion, Israel's Supreme Court said (page 78), in part: " When the state transfers the power to imprison someone, with the invasive powers that go with it, to a private corporation that operates on a profit-making basis, this action—both in practice and on an ethical and symbolic level—expresses a divestment of a significant part of the state's responsibility for the fate of the inmates, by exposing them to a violation of their rights by a private profit-making enterprise. This conduct of the state violates the human dignity of the inmates of a privately managed prison, since the public purposes that underlie their imprisonment and give it legitimacy are undermined, and, as described above, their imprisonment becomes a means for a private corporation to make a profit. This symbolic significance derives … from the very existence of a private corporation that has been given powers to keep human beings behind bars while making a financial profit from their imprisonment …"

23. Robbins, I. *The Legal Dimensions of Private Incarceration, Prisoners, and the Law.* New York: Clark Boardman, 1989. I. Robbins, correspondence with author, June 9, 2003.

24. See endnote 23.

CHAPTER 23

Loss of Rights of Convicted Persons

Iowa Constitution, Article II, Section 5.

A person adjudged mentally incompetent to vote or a person convicted of any infamous crime shall not be entitled to the privilege of an elector.

Florida Constitution, Article VI, Section 4

SECTION 4.   Disqualifications.

(a) No person convicted of a felony, or adjudicated in this or any other state to be mentally incompetent, shall be qualified to vote or hold office until restoration of civil rights or removal of disability. Except as provided in subsection (b) of this section, any disqualification from voting arising from a felony conviction shall terminate and voting rights shall be restored upon completion of all terms of sentence including parole or probation.
(b) No person convicted of murder or a felony sexual offense shall be qualified to vote until restoration of civil rights.
(c) No person may appear on the ballot for re-election to any of the following offices:
    (1) Florida representative, (2) Florida senator, (3) Florida Lieutenant governor, (4) any office of the Florida cabinet, (5) U.S. Representative from Florida, or (6) U.S. Senator from Florida.

Idaho Constitution, Article VI, Section 3

No person is permitted to vote, serve as a juror, or hold any civil office who has, at any place, been convicted of a felony, and who has not been restored to the rights of citizenship, or who, at the time of such election, is confined in prison on conviction of a criminal offense.

Wisconsin Constitution, Article XIII, Section 3(2)

No person convicted of a felony, in any court within the United States, no person convicted in federal court of a crime designated, at the time of commission, under federal law as a misdemeanor involving a violation of public trust and no person convicted, in a court of a state, of a crime designated, at the time of commission, under the law of the state as a misdemeanor involving a violation of public trust shall be eligible to any office of trust, profit or honor in this state unless pardoned of the conviction.

Illinois Constitution, Article III, Section 2:

A person convicted of a felony, or otherwise under sentence in a correctional institution or jail, shall lose the right to vote, which right shall be restored not later than upon completion of his sentence.

CHAPTER OUTLINE

- Background
- Bars to Employment and Other Impediments: *DeVeau v. Braisted*
- Voting Rights: *Richardson v. Ramirez; Hunter v. Underwood*
- Restoration of Rights

This chapter examines some of the restrictions that are placed on the rights of released offenders and the efforts that have been made in some places to remove many of those restrictions. Historically, there were times when persons convicted of serious (or "infamous") crimes were assumed to have forfeited all of their civil rights. After all, at one time in English history (particularly in the 17th and 18th centuries), the most serious crimes carried the death penalty, and persons under sentence of death were presumed to have forfeited all of their rights—even to civilized treatment—while they were awaiting execution. The introduction of prisons was considered a highly enlightened advance over the widespread use of capital punishment.

By the 20th century, prison reforms advanced to the point where the principal purpose of incarceration was to rehabilitate the offender, to improve them to the point where they could function as a law-abiding citizen upon release. That penological philosophy, of course, assumed that virtually all offenders would be released from prison and that they would then be expected (from the positive and wonderful programs they had experienced in prison) to be productive citizens, avoiding all temptations to criminal conduct.

One thing that stood in the way of those rehabilitative goals (idealistic as they always were) was the fact that, embedded in the laws of the country (and probably in the attitudes of most of its citizens), there were impediments to reentering society as an equal participant. Employment opportunities were especially challenging, and many other restrictions were also in place.

▶ Background

More than 614,844 sentenced prisoners were released from state and federal jurisdiction during 2018. More than 70% of the inmates released in 2018 were released under some form of supervision; the remainder were released without supervision.[1] For these offenders, adjusting to mainstream American life without committing new crimes is a major challenge. Reducing recidivism is also a major goal of the judiciary, particularly during sentencing, when judges select the appropriate sentence for a convicted offender. It is also a major goal of the corrections professionals, whether they are probation or parole officers, community corrections staff, jail workers, or prison officials.

Many obstacles stand in the way of these offenders while they are adjusting to law-abiding life in the community. Some offenders have little education. Many of them have trouble finding decent jobs. Although, in some jurisdictions, there are resources to help released offenders find jobs (help may be available from probation and parole officers, other community corrections staff, private agencies, or individuals), many receive no help at all. Not only do they lack references of a good work history but their criminal records are also held against them by many employers (even though this may be done very tacitly). Only a minority of offenders have an established home to return to (whether with a spouse, parents, or otherwise), so most must find housing on their own. Again, social service (welfare) agencies or other community organizations, governmental or private, may be of some help. But most offenders have been on their own.

Against these obstacles, which are well known and documented in the criminal justice field, it is not surprising that many offenders are back in prison either serving time for a new prison sentence or for a technical release violation (e.g., failing a drug test; an arrest for a new crime) within three years of their release. In 2018, almost 28% of the 606,000 prison admissions were for violations of release conditions,[2] which could be either new criminal conduct or technical violations.[2] An older study indicated that 45.4% of 1999 prison releasees and 43.3% of 2004 prison releasees were reconfined within three years of their release, either for a new crime or for violating their release conditions. The report states, "[i]f more than 4 out of 10 adult American offenders still return to prison within three years of their release, the system designed to deter them from continued criminal behavior clearly is falling short. That is an unhappy reality, not just for offenders, but for the safety of American communities."[3] Federal offenders had a slightly better recidivism rate with 29% being reincarcerated within 29 months of release, 32% being reconvicted within 30 months of release, and 34% being rearrested with 36 months of release.[4]

Efforts are being made to address these concerns. One significant example is the Second Chance Act of 2007. A stated purpose of this Act is to reduce criminal recidivism. Among the Act's other purposes are providing sufficient transitional services to offenders and providing offenders, while confined, with educational, literacy, vocational, and job placement services to help them upon reentry into the community. Another such program at the federal level is the First Step Act of 2018, which requires the Bureau of Prisons (BOP) to: (1) develop a risk and needs assessment system to be used by the BOP to assess the recidivism risk and criminogenic needs of all federal prisoners and to place prisoners in recidivism-reducing programs and productive activities to address their needs and reduce this risk; (2) assist inmates in applying for federal and state benefits and obtain identification, including a social security card, driver's license or other official photo identification, and birth certificate; and (3) develop guidance for wardens of prisons and community-based facilities to enter into recidivism-reducing partnerships with nonprofit and other private organizations, including faith-based and community-based organizations to deliver recidivism-reduction programming.

A report by the California state auditor demonstrates that the state's recidivism rate, as defined as reincarceration for a subsequent crime within three years of release, has remained at around 50% since 2000. The state had budgeted $234 million for rehabilitation programs in 2013–2014 for expanded programs including cognitive behavioral therapy (CBT), vocational education, and academic education to all of its 36 prisons. The state budget for in-house rehabilitation programs was increased in FY 2018–2019 to $298 million. One conclusion the Auditor made was that the corrections department was not placing inmates in appropriate rehabilitation programs, resulting in inmates being released without their rehabilitation needs being met.[5]

Added to the impediments faced by released offenders are legal ones. This chapter examines some of those legal restrictions on the rights of offenders following their convictions. As a general introduction, in 2000, the Office of the Pardon Attorney, United States Department of Justice, identified a number of the collateral consequences that federal law imposes on persons following a felony conviction.[6] These include the following:

■ Ineligibility to vote in federal elections (determined by state law; for examples, see the opening quotations for this chapter). States may vary in their approach on this issue. The two ends of the spectrum—Vermont allows its prisoners to vote (see Title 17, Chapter 43, sections 2121 and 2122 of the Vermont Statutes), while in Kentucky, a person convicted of a felony is permanently ineligible to vote, unless they receive a pardon (see section 145 of the Kentucky Constitution).

■ Ineligibility to serve on a federal jury; 28 U.S.C. § 1865(b) says "[the chief judge of the district court or other designated person specified in (b)] shall deem any person qualified to serve on … Juries in the district court unless he …. (5) has a charge pending against him for the commission of, or has been convicted in a

State or Federal court of record of, a crime punishable by imprisonment for more than one year and his civil rights have not been restored."

- Possible loss of or ineligibility to hold federal office or employment (can depend on the type of position and the nature of the offender's crime); for example, the sentencing court may order disqualification from the federal office when the person is convicted of bribing a public official or accepting a bribe (see 18 U.S.C. § 201(b)).

- Absent an exception being made, ineligibility to enlist in the military (10 U.S.C. § 504, discussed in the next section); loss of veterans benefits for mutiny, treason, sabotage, or rendering assistance to an enemy of the United States or of its allies (see 38 U.S.C. § 6104).

- Loss of federal firearms privileges; (18 U.S. C. § 922(g)(1) prohibits a person convicted in any court of a crime that has a punishment exceeding one year in prison "to ship or transport in interstate or foreign commerce, or possess in or affecting commerce, any firearm or ammunition; or to receive any firearm or ammunition which has been shipped or transported in interstate or foreign commerce".[7]

- Restrictions on occupation as a condition of probation (requires a "reasonably direct relationship" between a person's occupation, business, or profession, and the offense conduct; see 18 U.S.C. § 3563(b)(5)).

- Possible loss of or ineligibility to acquire a federal license (of different types) for particular convictions; for an example relating to a commercial motor vehicle operator's license, see 49 U.S.C. § 31310(b)(1)(C)—"using a commercial motor vehicle in committing a felony."

- For particular convictions (involving dishonesty, breach of trust, or money laundering), restrictions on being an "institution-affiliated party" (for example, a director, officer, employee, agent, or controlling stockholder) with respect to an insured depository institution (a bank or other financial institution); for an example, with respect to a person convicted of "any criminal offense involving dishonesty or a breach of trust or money laundering ...," see 12 U.S.C. § 1829(a).

- Ineligibility to serve in various capacities relating to a labor organization or an employee benefits plan (for particular convictions); see 29 U.S.C. § 504, "Prohibition against certain persons holding office." Paragraph (a) says "[n]o person ... who has been convicted of, or served any part of a prison term resulting from his conviction of, robbery, bribery, extortion, embezzlement, ... [or] any felony involving abuse or misuse of such person's position or employment in a labor organization or employee benefit plan to seek or obtain an illegal gain at the expense of the members of the labor organization or the beneficiaries of the employee benefit plan, ... shall serve or be permitted to serve—(1) as a consultant or adviser to any labor organization, (2) as an officer, director, trustee, ... or representative in any capacity of any labor organization ... "

- Restrictions on participating in certain federal contracts or programs; see 10 U.S.C. § 2408(a), which states, in part, "(a) PROHIBITION.—(1) An individual who is convicted of fraud or any other felony arising out of a contract with the Department of Defense shall be prohibited from ...: (A) Working in a management or supervisory capacity on any defense contract or any first tier subcontract of a defense contract."

- Sexual offender registration and notification; every state has legislation that requires convicted sex offenders to provide their place(s) of residence to designated authorities.

- Restrictions on certain federal benefits; for example, a person is not eligible for federally assisted housing if subject to a lifetime registration under a state sexual offender registration program (see 42 U.S.C. § 13663). Other examples of federal benefits that may be affected relate to passports (see 22 U.S.C. § 2714) and to eligibility to receive food stamps or temporary assistance to needy families (see 21 U.S.C. § 862a).

- Possible ineligibility to enter the United States (for aliens convicted of crimes involving moral turpitude, see 8 U.S.C. § 1182(a)(2)(A)).

It is worth noting that some of the limitations or ineligibilities may be for a limited time. For example, the prohibitions in 29 U.S.C. § 504, relating to involvement in labor organizations and employee benefit plans, last for up to 13 years after conviction or after the end of such imprisonment. The statute discusses the means by which this period may be further reduced.

Of course, many states have similar types of restrictions on offenders' rights or even some additional ones. In the following sections, we will look at both federal and state law with respect to several types of disabilities.

▶ Bars to Employment and Other Impediments: *DeVeau v. Braisted*

As noted above, there are statutes, federal and state, that bar offenders (usually felons) from holding certain kinds of jobs. Persons with felony records are generally barred from serving in the armed forces of the United States. Title 10, U.S. Code, Section 504, provides:

> **No person who is insane, … or who has been convicted of a felony, may be enlisted in any armed force.**

Exceptions can be made by the secretary (of any of the armed services) in "meritorious cases."

In *DeVeau v. Braisted,* 363 U.S. 144 (1960), the Supreme Court upheld a state law that prohibited a felon from serving as an officer of a waterfront labor union. New York had a statute that barred the collection of union dues from waterfront workers for any union that had an officer or agent who had been convicted of a felony (and had not been pardoned). This law was challenged, mainly on the grounds that it conflicted with a federal law, the Labor–Management Reporting and Disclosure Act of 1959, which provided that no person who had been convicted of certain serious felonies could serve as a union official. The Supreme Court allowed the state law to stand and, in its opinion, noted:

> **Barring convicted felons from certain employments is a familiar legislative device to insure against corruption in specified, vital areas. Federal law has frequently and of old utilized this type of disqualification …. [The Court noted the ban on enlistment into the armed forces.] A citizen is not competent to serve on federal grand or petit juries if he has been "convicted in a State or Federal court of record of a crime punishable by imprisonment for more than one year and his civil rights have not been restored by pardon or amnesty." 28 U.S.C. Sec. 1861. In addition, a large group of federal statutes disqualify persons "from holding any office of honor, trust, or profit under the United States" because of their conviction of certain crimes, generally involving official misconduct. [Citing numerous federal statutes.]**

Some states also have statutory or constitutional provisions that bar felons or persons convicted of certain offenses from holding public offices or from obtaining government jobs.

▶ Voting Rights: *Richardson v. Ramirez; Hunter v. Underwood*

Most of the collateral consequences of a criminal conviction are products of state law, such as limitations on voting and ability to obtain an occupational license. Once again, look carefully at the epigraphs at the beginning of the chapter. These are state constitutional restrictions that may be imposed on persons' voting rights based on criminal convictions. Iowa has one of the most restrictive (the Iowa Supreme Court recently ruled that the term "infamous crime" meant any felony-*Griffin v. Pate*, 884 N.W 3rd 182 (Iowa 2016), while other states have less-extensive restrictions to those states that have no restrictions. The National Conference of State Legislatures have classified the various states' voting restrictions based on a felony conviction into four broad categories: (1) states with no restrictions [2]; (2) states which prohibit voting while incarcerated but then automatically restore the right after release [17]; (3) states which prohibit voting while incarcerated and until completion of release supervision, then automatic restoration of voting rights [21]; and (4) states which prohibit voting during incarceration and release supervision, and possibly an additional period, but also require some additional steps, other than registration, to regain the right to vote [11].[8] Note that Iowa and Florida fit into the 4th category; Idaho and Wisconsin [note Wisconsin also disenfranchises for misdemeanors involving a violation of public trust) in category 3 and Illinois in category 2.

Vermont is one of two states that places no restrictions on voting based on a criminal conviction. Vermont DOC Policy 324.01, Inmate Voting, provides as follows:

> POLICY: Pursuant to Vermont state law, individuals convicted of a crime shall retain their right to vote by absentee ballot in a primary or general election during the term of their confinement, provided the individual meets all other voting requirements. The DOC shall ensure that each correctional facility provides basic information and assistance to inmates qualified to vote. The Volunteer Services Coordinator shall develop any necessary procedures to ensure the right to vote may be carried out.

As you will see in more detail later, the 14th Amendment, passed after the American Civil War, contained this provision in section 2:

… But when the right to vote at any election for the choice of electors for President and Vice President of the United States, Representatives in Congress, the executive and judicial officers of a state, or the members of the legislature thereof, is denied to any of the male inhabitants of such state, being twenty-one years of age, and citizens of the United States, or in any way abridged, **except for participation in rebellion, or other crime**[], the basis of representation therein shall be reduced in the proportion which the number of such male citizens shall bear to the whole number of male citizens twenty-one years of age in such state.

This language has been used to uphold against constitutional challenge state and federal laws which restrict the right to vote for persons convicted of crimes. Some states have begun to roll back the restrictions on voting rights of ex-felons. Florida's Constitution was recently amended to remove its automatic lifetime ban on felon disenfranchisement. In 2018, New York's governor issued an executive order allowing persons on felony parole to vote. Other states have taken steps to be more restrictive.

Three persons completed service of their prison sentences and paroles in California. They claimed that when the state denied them the right to vote because of their status as ex-felons, the state was denying them the equal protection of the laws that they were entitled to under the Fourteenth Amendment. The Supreme Court of California agreed with them and found the ban on voting unconstitutional. The U.S. Supreme Court reversed that ruling in *Richardson v. Ramirez,* 418 U.S. 24 (1974).

The state constitution in California provided that, "[l]aws shall be made to exclude from voting persons convicted of bribery, perjury, forgery, malfeasance in office, or other high crimes." The California Elections Code required that an affidavit made at the time of registering to vote must show whether the prospective voter had been convicted of "a felony which disqualifies [him] from voting." The county clerk was authorized to cancel the registration of any voter who had been convicted of "any infamous crime or of the embezzlement or misappropriation of any public money." Other sections of the law allowed a voter to be challenged on the grounds that they were convicted of a felony or of the embezzlement or misappropriation of public money. State law did allow for the restoration of the right to vote to convicted persons by executive pardon or by judicial review.

The decision by the California Supreme Court, striking down the voting bans in the state laws, was based on other U.S. Supreme Court decisions that had held that there must be a compelling state interest in order to justify exclusion of a particular class from voting. The state supreme court had found no such state interest with regard to ex-felons. The U.S. Supreme Court disagreed. It relied primarily on little-used Section 2 of the Fourteenth Amendment. Section 2 provides that the right to vote for president and vice president, representatives in Congress, and all state officials shall not be abridged (or if it is abridged, there are penalties for doing so), "except for participation in rebellion, or other crime." Of course, the language in that amendment was adopted in the aftermath of the Civil War. Even considering that history, the Supreme Court said, in *Richardson,* that the language means just what it says: that participation in crime is a justifiable ground for denying the franchise (the right to vote). Further, the Court noted that "29 states had provisions in their constitutions which prohibited, or authorized the legislature to prohibit, exercise of the franchise by persons convicted of felonies or infamous crime."

The justices of the U.S. Supreme Court recognized that they had been urged to endorse the more modern view, "that it is essential to the process of rehabilitating the ex-felon that he be returned to his role in society as a fully participating citizen when he has completed the serving of his term." They did not reject that notion. Rather, they pointed out that setting voting requirements, including the standards for registering voters, is the responsibility of the individual states. It is up to California, or any individual state, to decide whether it wants to adopt the "more enlightened" view that ex-felons should be allowed to vote, the Supreme Court said. Until that happened, it was not unconstitutional for a state, by its constitution or its statutes, to bar ex-felons from voting, the Supreme Court ruled.

A different result was reached by the U.S. Supreme Court in the case of *Hunter v. Underwood,* 471 U.S. 222 (1985). That case dealt with an Alabama constitutional provision that barred persons who had been convicted of a crime "involving moral turpitude" from voting. The history of that provision showed that it was adopted in 1901 in order to keep Blacks from voting; it was believed (by the Alabama legislators) that more Blacks than Whites were convicted of such crimes. The Supreme Court struck down that provision in the Alabama constitution, because it was found to be a violation of the Equal Protection Clause of the Fourteenth Amendment. It was the discriminatory intent that was shown in adopting the voting clause, as well as its continuing discriminatory effect of excluding more Blacks than Whites, that led the Court to find it unconstitutional.[9]

Besides revoking voting rights, some states, by statute, bar convicted felons from serving on juries. For example, Chapter 9, Article I, Section 9.3 of the North Carolina General Statutes details such restrictions:

> All persons are qualified to serve as jurors and to be included on the jury list who are citizens of the State and residents of the county … who have not been convicted of a felony or pleaded guilty or nolo contendere to an indictment charging a felony (or if convicted of a felony or having pleaded guilty or nolo contendere to an indictment charging a felony have had their citizenship restored pursuant to law) …. Persons not qualified under this section are subject to challenge for cause.

For a recent description of the 50,000 federal and state statutes and regulations that are impacted by a felony conviction, see *United States v. Nesbeth*, 188 F.Supp. 3d 179 (EDNY 2016).

▶ Restoration of Rights

Under the U.S. Constitution (Article II, Section 2), the president has the power to grant pardons. The power to pardon is a very sweeping power. In the federal government, there is a pardon attorney, located in the Department of Justice, who receives applications for pardons from all over the country. After review, the pardon attorney makes recommendations to the president as to whether a pardon should be granted. A pardon discharges the offender from all aspects of the conviction (unless the pardoning authority places conditions or restrictions on the nature and extent of the pardon; legally, the pardoning authority can place restrictions of any kind on the grant of pardon). A pardon, therefore, usually acts to restore to the offender the right to vote, to serve on juries, and to hold public office.

Applications to the president are made with some frequency, but pardons are granted infrequently. For example, for the fiscal years covering the presidency of George W. Bush (2001–2009), 2,498 petitions for pardon were received, with 189 granted and 1,729 denied. For the 96 months of the presidency of Barack Obama (2009–2017), 3,395 petitions were received, with 212 petitions granted and 1,708 denied. In the first three years (37.5 months) of the Trump administration 1,233 petitions were received, with 25 petitions granted and 82 denied. (These numbers include pardon petitions carried over from the previous administration.) In addition to pardons, the pardoning authority (the president, for the federal government) also can grant commutations of sentences. Commutations are reductions in the terms of the sentence, without wiping out the conviction and sentence (wiping out or vacating the conviction and sentence usually happens with a pardon). During the presidency of George W. Bush, there were 8,576 petitions for commutation received in the Office of the Pardon Attorney, with 11 granted and 7,498 denied. During the presidency of Barack Obama, 33,149 petitions for commutation were received, with 1,715 being granted and 18,749 denied. During President Trumps first 37.5 months in office, 6,722 commutation petitions were received, with 10 being granted and 98 being denied.[10]

In the states, the pardoning authority may be the governor of the state, or it may be a board of pardons or paroles. Alabama utilizes a state Pardons and Parole Board to review and act on pardon and voter restoration petitions for all but capital cases. In 2018, the Board granted 80% of the over 1,000 petitions for parole and 22% of more than 1,600 voter restoration petitions.[11] More recent examples include Minnesota, which granted 0 pardons or commutations in 2019 but did grant 14 of 58 petitions for *pardon extraordinary* [Pardon Extraordinary–a statutorily created relief granted to applicants who have served their sentences. When a pardon extraordinary is granted, the court is directed to issue an order setting aside the conviction and the applicant is no longer required to report the conviction, except under specified circumstances. The original conviction and the pardon extraordinary are recorded on the applicant's criminal record] and Kansas, where the Prisoner Review Board recommended three persons for executive clemency out of 35 applicants.[12] The effect of a pardon varies among the states. Some pardons expunge convictions and in other states a pardon relieves the offender of collateral consequences, but conviction remains. In some states, even when a person has been pardoned, the criminal behavior may still be taken into account in decisions about licensing for some occupations or professions. For example, embezzlement or other financial wrongdoing may be taken into account in deciding on public accountant licensing; likewise, violations of trust or "morally reprehensible" crimes may still be considered in licensing attorneys.

Some states have adopted statutes that operate to automatically restore the rights of convicted persons after they have satisfactorily completed their sentences or after a certain period of time elapses after they are released from their sentences. For example, Indiana Code § 3-7-13-4, *Disfranchisement of prisoners,* says that a person who is convicted of a crime and imprisoned following conviction is "deprived of the right of suffrage [vote]." Section 3-7-13-5, *Restoration of right to vote,* says that a person who is otherwise qualified to register [interestingly, this section doesn't say to vote] is eligible to register once the person is no longer imprisoned or subject to lawful detention. (In addition, section 3-7-13-6, *Disfranchisement of prisoners; exceptions,* provides the right to register and to vote to a person who is on probation, parole, subject to home detention, or in a community corrections program.)

These restoration-of-rights statutes serve to provide much of the same relief that pardons provide. Like pardons, the restoration of rights does not mean that all vestiges of the conviction are removed: licensing authorities for some fields may still consider the criminal record of the offender. It is always a tough, practical question as to how the offender who has been pardoned should answer when they are asked, on employment applications for example, whether they have ever been convicted. In some states, an executive pardon can serve as an expungement of the conviction. In other states, the conviction remains and in some states the record is public. A person whose criminal offense has been pardoned should check for the effect of that pardon in the state in which they are applying for the benefit such as professional license or job.

Other statutes provide that released offenders should not be discriminated against, either in their civil rights (such as voting) or in employment. An employment example is shown by Hawaii Revised Statute § 378-2.5(a), which provides that "(a) Subject to subsection (b), an employer may inquire about and consider an individual's criminal conviction record concerning hiring, termination, or the terms, conditions, or privileges of employment; provided that the conviction record bears a rational relationship to the duties and responsibilities of the position.

Paragraph (b) of § 378-2.5 provides: Inquiry into, and consideration of, conviction records for prospective employees shall take place only after the prospective employee has received a conditional offer of employment which may be withdrawn if the prospective employee has a conviction record that bears a rational relationship to the duties and responsibilities of the position.

Paragraph (c) of § 378-2.5 provides: (c) For purposes of this section, "conviction" means an adjudication by a court of competent jurisdiction that the defendant committed a crime, not including final judgments required to be confidential pursuant to section 571-84; provided that the employer may consider the employee's conviction record falling within a period that shall not exceed the most recent 10 years, excluding periods of incarceration. If the employee or prospective employee claims that the period of incarceration was less than what is shown on the employee's or prospective employee's conviction record, an employer shall provide the employee or prospective employee with an opportunity to present documentary evidence of a date of release to establish a period of incarceration that is shorter than the sentence imposed for the employee's or prospective employee's conviction.

Also, the Supreme Court, in *Schware v. Board of Bar Examiners,* 353 U.S. 232 (1957), has said that government employment for an ex-offender should not be denied unless there is a reasonable connection between the requirements of the job and the concerns over his particular criminal record.

There is a difficult question regarding whether ex-offenders should be employed in corrections agencies. Corrections officials do not agree on the answer. In fact, some agencies have employed ex-offenders in many different kinds of jobs. Probably the strongest concerns about their ability to work successfully would be in high-security facilities, and certainly in those facilities where the ex-offender had been recently confined. Persons convicted of misdemeanor domestic violence offenses, or having had an order for protection, may be deemed disqualified as federal law prohibits such persons from possessing firearms. See Title 18, U.S. Code § 922(g) The nature of the offense, and other information about the individual offender, would enter into the hiring decision, and this would agree with the thinking of the Supreme Court in the *Schware* case. The same would be true with respect to different kinds of licensing: removal of license (or refusal to grant a new license) would be justified, based on the nature of the work covered by the licensure and the criminal history of the offender. The constitutional protection under such circumstances is the due process clause; the equal protection clause may also be implicated.

As we have seen, juvenile records are generally sealed, and, indeed, in many places, they are expunged after release from any juvenile commitment. (If the records are **expunged**, it means they may be sealed or destroyed, and they legally may not be referred to in any situation. If the records are **sealed**, it means that they will remain in existence, but they may not be accessed or referred to for any purpose absent specific authority, such as a court giving permission.) There has been some movement to provide for the sealing or expunging of adult criminal records.

Some states have such provisions. There is a wide variation, however, as to how these provisions are applied. In some states, a deferred imposition of sentence allows a person who successfully completes all of the terms of their probation to have the conviction or guilty plea set aside, the charge dismissed, and the record sealed. See N.D. Rule of Crim. P. 32.1. Some states apply sealing to probation records. An example is in Arkansas, where Ark. Code Ann. Sec. 16-93-303, paragraph (d) states "After successful completion of probation placed on the defendant under this section, a defendant is considered as not having a felony conviction except for ...," listing five areas of exception, including a determination of habitual offender status, and for sentencing. (Ark. Code Ann. Sec. 16-90-902 states that following expungement of the person's record, the individual "shall have all privileges and rights restored" and **(b)** Upon the entry of the uniform order to seal records of an individual, the individual's underlying conduct shall be deemed as a matter of law never to have occurred, and the individual may state that no such conduct ever occurred and that no such records exist.") Some apply sealing only to first-time, nonviolent offenders (for example, RI [Rhode Island] Gen. Laws Sec. 12-1.3-2(a)). Others authorize expunging for a misdemeanor with no other convictions or charges pending (for example, Okla. [Oklahoma] Stat. Ann., Title 22, Sec. 18, A(8) when at least 10 years have passed since the judgment was entered).

Appendix 7 contains a table showing the collateral consequences of a felony conviction in several areas: restoration of voting rights, public employment, jury service, firearm ownership, and parental rights. The table also shows whether there is a registration requirement for convicted sex offenders.

The U.S. Commission on Civil Rights has extensively reviewed the impact of collateral consequences on offenders. The consequences for persons with criminal histories include "barriers to voting, jury service, holding public office, securing employment, obtaining housing, receiving public assistance, owning a firearm, getting a driver's license, qualifying for financial aid and college admission, qualifying for military service, and maintaining legal status as an immigrant." The Commission's key recommendations include: (1) Collateral consequences should be tailored to serve public safety; (2) Policymakers should avoid punitive mandatory consequences that do not serve public safety, bear no rational relationship to the offense committed, and impede people convicted of crimes from safely reentering and becoming contributing members of society; (3) Jurisdictions that impose collateral consequences should periodically review the consequences imposed by law or regulation to evaluate whether they are necessary to protect public safety and if they are related to the underlying offenses.[13]

The area of collateral consequences is receiving increased attention, which is likely to continue. In 2009, the Uniform Law Commission[14] published the "Uniform Collateral Consequences of Conviction Act [UCCCA]."[15] The UCCCA was amended in 2010 and has been enacted in one state.

The UCCCA, among other provisions, calls for the collection of a state's collateral consequences (both automatic bars and discretionary penalties) into a single document. The American Bar Association, by means of a National Institute of Justice grant, is categorizing the collateral consequences laws of each state for dissemination via a publicly accessible website. The ABA's National Inventory of Collateral Consequences of Conviction (NICCC) can be found at https://niccc.nationalreentryresourcecenter.org/. This compilation will mark the first time this information is readily available. A second provision is that the Act, if implemented by the state, helps ensure that the defendant in a criminal case is aware of the collateral consequences, so she is better able to make an informed decision about how to proceed.

The UCCCA also provides a benefit to defense counsel, and, by implication, to a more efficient judicial process. In *Padilla v. Kentucky,* 559 U.S. 336 (2010), Padilla was a legal permanent resident of the United States and had been for more than 40 years. Following his arrest for drug distribution charges, Padilla pleaded guilty, a plea which made his deportation "virtually mandatory." Padilla claimed that his attorney did not advise him that by pleading guilty he faced the possibility of deportation. In fact, Padilla claimed that he was told that based on the period of time he had been in the United States, he did not need to worry about his immigration status. The Supreme Court of Kentucky denied Padilla postconviction relief and held that "the Sixth Amendment's guarantee of effective assistance of counsel does not protect a criminal defendant from erroneous advice about deportation because it is merely a 'collateral' consequence of his conviction." The U.S. Supreme Court agreed with Padilla that constitutionally competent counsel would have advised him of the risk of deportation. The Court, however, said that whether Padilla was entitled to relief depended on whether he has been prejudiced. The Court remanded the case for further proceedings.

The UCCCA addresses two issues raised by *Padilla.* First, the Act helps ensure that counsel have a resource for identifying collateral consequences that may be faced by their clients. Second, although *Padilla* applies only to deportation, it is conceivable that courts in the future may extend the *Padilla* holding to other collateral consequences. This possibility was addressed in the concurring *Padilla* opinion: "criminal convictions can carry a wide variety of consequences other than conviction and sentencing, including … the loss of the right to vote, disqualification from public benefits, … and loss of business or professional licenses …. All of those consequences are 'seriou[s]…'"

Summary

- The millions of offenders who are released into the community each year face many obstacles in reintegrating into mainstream community life. Finding housing and jobs upon release are immediate and universal problems. Discrimination against ex-offenders is prevalent in many areas.

- There are a number of collateral consequences that federal law imposes following a felony conviction. For example, there are laws that bar ex-felons from certain employment, such as in the armed forces or from serving as an officer of a waterfront labor union *(DeVeau v. Braisted)*.

- Voting qualifications are, for the most part, left to the states. The Supreme Court upheld voting bans against ex-felons in California *(Richardson v. Ramirez)*. An Alabama voting ban was disapproved, because the history of its enactment showed that it was used for racial disqualification, an impermissible purpose under the Constitution *(Hunter v. Underwood)*.

- There are provisions in the U.S. Constitution and in the states for the restoration of rights to released offenders. The president (under the Constitution) and the governors (in most states) have the authority to grant pardons or commutations of sentences. Pardons usually act to wipe out all effects of convictions. Many states have also enacted laws that restore rights to many convicted persons, for certain offenses, upon release or after certain periods of time have elapsed without a new offense being committed.

Thinking About It

The federal constitution places no restriction on voting rights of convicted felons, and so restrictions like those discussed in this chapter are the product of state constitutions and statutes. Do you think felons (and serious misdemeanants) should be disenfranchised as a result of a criminal conviction? If so, for how long (while incarcerated, while on community supervision, for a period of time after community supervision is completed, or forever)?

Key Terms

expunged
seal

Endnotes

1. Carson, E.A. *Prisoners in 2018.* Table 8. (Washington, DC: Bureau of Justice Statistics, U.S. Department of Justice, April 2020.)

2. Note 1. Another study of data submitted from 30 states conducted by the Bureau of Justice Statistics indicates that in a cohort of prisoners released in 2005, 68% had been arrested within three years of release. That percentage climbed to 83% by the 9th year following release. Alper, M., Durose, M.R., & Markman, J. *2018 Update on prisoner recidivism: A 9-year follow-up period (2005-2014).* (Washington, DC: Bureau of Justice Statistics, U.S. Department of Justice, May 2018.) Remember that not all arrests end up in conviction or in termination of conditional release.

3. Pew Center on the States. *State of Recidivism: The revolving door of America's prisons.* pp. 1–16. (Washington, DC: The Pew Charitable Trusts, 2011.) In its Executive Summary, the report speaks to economic forces and the other entities that have a role in recidivism: "[A]s the nation's slumping economy continues to force states to do more with less, policymakers are asking tougher questions about corrections outcomes. One key element of that analysis is measuring recidivism, or the rate at which offenders return to prison. Prisons, of course, are not solely responsible for recidivism results. Parole and probation agencies, along with social service providers and community organizations, play a critical role …. This report seeks to elevate the public discussion about recidivism, prompting policy makers and the public to dig more deeply into the factors that impact rates of return to prison, and into effective strategies for reducing them."

4. *Recidivism among federal offenders-a comprehensive overview.* U.S. Sentencing Commission. Washington, D.C. March 2016. This report indicates that persons released at an earlier age had a higher recidivism rate. For example, those released between the ages of 26 and 30 had a 62.2% chance of being rearrested while those released after age 60 had only a 16% chance of being rearrested. Offenders with a more significant criminal history had higher rates of recidivism than those with a less-extensive criminal history. Males had a higher rearrest rate than females, and those with less than a high school diploma (60.4%) were three times more likely to be arrested than those with a college degree (19.1%).

5. California State Auditor Report 2018-113. California Department of Corrections and Rehabilitation. January 2019. Available at https://www.auditor.ca.gov/pdfs/reports/2018-113.pdf

6. *Federal statutes imposing collateral consequences upon conviction.* (Washington, DC: Office of the Pardon Attorney. United States Department of Justice, 2000.) This list is provided to give the reader a general idea of the type of civil disabilities that exist.

7. Title 18 U.S.C. § 922(g)(9) prohibits gun possession if a person has been convicted in any court of a misdemeanor crime of domestic violence. Law enforcement officers are not excluded from this provision, and such a conviction could impact the officer's future employment. Persons have challenged the constitutionality of the firearm prohibition as a violation of their rights under the Second Amendment. Most courts have interpreted the Second Amendment, and the Supreme Court's decisions in *District of Columbia v. Heller*, 554 U.S. 570 (2008) and *McDonald v. City of Chicago*, 561 U.S. 742 (2010) in a manner that upholds the constitutionality of Title 18 U.S. Code Section 922(g)(1). *Kanter v. Barr*, 919 F.3d 437 (7th Cir. 2019) ('[E]very federal court of appeals to address the issue has held that section 922(g)(1) does not violate the Second Amendment on its face.") The *Kanter* opinion further notes that circuits are split as to whether a felon may use an "as applied" argument to challenge the ban on firearm possession.

8. *Felon Voting Rights.* National Conference of State Legislatures. October 14, 2019. Available at https://www.ncsl.org/research/elections-and-campaigns/felon-voting-rights.aspx

9. In *Farrakhan v. Gregoire,* 623 F.3d 990 (9th Cir. 2010) en banc, six minority citizens, including Farrakhan, claimed their loss of voting rights under Washington state's felon disenfranchisement law was a violation of section 2 of the Voting Rights Act (VRA), codified in 42 U.S.C. § 1973(a), resulting in a denial or abridgement of the right to vote based on race. No claim was made that the law was passed specifically to deny minorities the right to vote, nor that their convictions and subsequent disenfranchisement were based on intentional racial discrimination by the state's criminal justice system. Although the district court did find discrimination in the state's criminal justice system based on race, it held that this was only one factor in a section 2 (VRA) "totality of circumstances" analysis, and that other factors counterbalanced this evidence of racial disparities. Affirming the district court grant of summary judgment to the state defendants, the appeals court in its en banc per curiam opinion held that a "section 2 VRA challenge to a felon disenfranchisement law based on the operation of a state's criminal justice system must at least show that the criminal justice system is infected by *intentional* discrimination or that the felon disenfranchisement law was enacted with such intent."

10. *Clemency Statistics.* Washington, DC: Office of the Pardon Attorney, U.S. Department of Justice. Accessed 06 April 2020 from https://www.justice.gov/pardon/clemency-statistics. Clemency petitions may carry over from one administration to the next administration.

11. State of Alabama Board of Parsons and Parole Annual Report. FY 2018, Available at https://paroles.alabama.gov/wp-content/uploads/2017-2018_Annual_Report.pdf. Accessed 07 April 2020. See also Margaret Colgate Love, *50 State comparison pardon policy and practice.* Restoration of Rights Center. Updated March 15, 2020. Available at http://ccresourcecenter.org/state-restoration-profiles/50-state-comparisoncharacteristics-of-pardon-authorities-2/ Accessed 07 April 2020.

12. *Minnesota Board of Pardons—Annual Report to the Legislature—2019 Activity.* (Saint Paul, MN: Minnesota Board of Pardons.) Available at https://mn.gov/doc/assets/2018%20Board%20of%20Pardons%20Report%20to%20Legislature_tcm1089-377834.pdf. In Kansas, the Prisoner Review Board [PRB] reviews applications for clemency and makes recommendations for executive clemency to the governor. In 2018, the PRB received 35 petitions for clemency and favorably approved three. Kansas DOC Clemency-Updated January 2, 2019. Available at https://www.doc.ks.gov/prb/clemency.

13. *Collateral consequences: The crossroads of punishment, redemption, and the effects on communities.* U.S. Commission on Civil Rights. Washington, D.C. June 2019. Available at https://www.usccr.gov/pubs/2019/06-13-Collateral-Consequences.pdf. Accessed 07 April 2020.

14. The Uniform Law Commission (ULC), formerly known as the National Conference of Commissioners on Uniform State Law, has worked to advance uniformity of state law for more than a century. Originally created in 1892, the ULC assesses what areas of the law should be uniform from state to state and drafts statutory text to propose for enactment by state legislatures. Commissioners are appointed from every state, the District of Columbia, the U.S. Virgin Islands, and Puerto Rico. The roster of commissioners includes state legislators, practitioners, judges, and law professors. Commissioners receive no salary or fees for their work with the ULC.

15. *Uniform Collateral Consequences of Conviction Act.* Uniform Law Commission. Accessed 07 April 2020. Available at https://www.uniformlaws.org/HigherLogic/System/DownloadDocumentFile.ashx?DocumentFileKey=4d0b1e62-d93d-d80c-4bea-9158fe10c61a&forceDialog=0 In August 2010, the American Bar Association approved the UCCCA as "an appropriate Act for those states desiring to adopt the specific substantive law suggested therein." As of April 2020, the UCCCA had been enacted in Vermont [Title 13, Chap. 231, Sections 8001-8017] and introduced in four other states.

© EJ_Rodriquez/iStock/Getty Images Plus/Getty Images

CHAPTER 24

In Conclusion: A Postscript

▶ Introduction

The following was written by Clair Cripe, the first author of this text. It is included because I believe his observations: (1) assist readers in understanding the importance and influence of judicial opinions in shaping how correctional agencies function; and (2) are still applicable in the 21st century. Historically, the two cases described in detail, *Jones* and *Morales*, were decided near the end of the rehabilitative era of corrections, and this era was soon replaced by the get tough on crime era of prisons being a place of incarceration and incapacitation with rehabilitation being an afterthought. In fact, Title 18, U.S. Code § 3582 instructs federal judges "that imprisonment is not an appropriate means of promoting correction and rehabilitation."

Introduction by Clair Cripe

It is axiomatic that the law is an evolving, constantly changing set of rules and principles. If the law is obtained from statutes, we know for certain that those laws can be amended, and they do change from one political generation to another. If the law is obtained from the courts—and that is the principal source of the law considered in this book—it too can shift from time to time or from place to place. The Supreme Court gives us most of what we have as a national set of legal rules and principles, but even that court can change its mind, overrule an earlier decision, or give us more "enlightenment" on what the law really is.

As we have seen, it is a basic premise from the Supreme Court that the Eighth Amendment concept of "cruel and unusual punishment" is a shifting standard, evolving along with changing (and presumptively improving) attitudes of the American public. This idea of evolving standards can be applied to other constitutional standards as well, although perhaps not as openly and not with Supreme Court assertion, as in the case of discussions of the Eighth Amendment. But it must be allowed that even the Constitution, our most solid base of legal authority and constancy, is open to different interpretations at different times by the Supreme Court, as the makeup of the Court changes by only a few justices, who bring very different views on some basic concepts and rulings. Or if the Supreme Court has not yet ruled on a question, or if its rulings are not crystal clear and broadly inclusive, the lower courts will give us differing interpretations of clauses in the Constitution. This has to be frustrating and sometimes confusing to many observers; but it does give a lot of work to lawyers!

All of this is done within the context of a legal system that relies heavily on the concept of **stare decisis**. It is the foundation of our common law that we rely on the value of precedent: If a court of controlling jurisdiction has spoken on a legal question and has given us the legal principles that control that question, other courts will use that judicial ruling and will apply it in future cases that raise the same or a similar question. The rest of us, lawyers and nonlawyers alike, should be able to rely on the principle of "stare decisis": the decision has been made, so let it stand! This principle, as you can see, is in constant tension with the idea that the law is evolving and should be allowed to change. This state of tension means that we must turn to lawyers, who are trained to juggle these two concepts and to give us advice about what principles we can rely on, what questions have not been answered, which rulings are open to interpretation, and which law is likely to be changed.

▶ A History: Two Cases

To further explore the idea of these shifting concepts of the law, let us present two court opinions that deal with leading corrections issues. Because they are about 40 years old, they give us some historical perspective of what courts were saying in those "olden times." They were considered, for many years and by many professors, judges, and corrections attorneys, as enlightened, persuasive rulings on difficult questions of prison and jail management. Not until the Supreme Court spoke on these questions, which these lower courts had addressed, did we find out how wrong they were![1]

▶ *Jones v. Wittenberg*

The case of *Jones v. Wittenberg*, 323 F.Supp. 93 (N.D. Ohio 1971), dealt with numerous complaints about the conditions in the Lucas County, Ohio, jail. The lawsuit was brought under Section 1983, alleging constitutional violations, and also under Title 28, U.S. Code, Section 2201, seeking a declaratory judgment (a ruling as to the rights and duties of the parties); it was a class action suit, on behalf of all inmates at the jail. The U.S. district judge, in his published opinion, described many poor conditions and deficiencies at the jail. These included poor sanitary conditions, poor ventilation and lighting, inadequate food and clothing, crowded conditions in cells and in visiting areas, inadequate staff supervision, minimal medical coverage, and inmate discipline without notice or hearings. Expert witnesses presented by the plaintiffs testified that the jail was "outstandingly bad from every standpoint." The court reviewed what case law guidance there was at the time, including references to cases that cautioned that courts should be reluctant to interfere with the administration of detention facilities. (This was a passing reference to the old "hands-off" doctrine, which was virtually abandoned by this time, in 1971.)

The court in *Jones* noted that it would not refrain from dealing with allegations of constitutional violations (that is, it would not keep its hands off "vital issues of civil rights"). The court then observed that there were two classes of inmates at the Lucas County Jail: prisoners serving sentences and pretrial detainees. For the sentenced prisoners, the question was whether their treatment violated the Eighth Amendment—whether it amounted to cruel and unusual punishment. How the court was going to come out on that question was predicted by the (what shall we say?) vigor with which it described the conditions at the jail and by the following paragraph of "legal" discussion:

> "The official policy of the State of Ohio is that the standards of punishment which prevailed in medieval times are to be followed in dealing with those convicted of crimes. Insofar as possible, they are to be removed to remote places and confined in harsh and forbidding prisons. In constructing its newest prison facility, the State selected one of its more sparsely populated areas as a site, and a medieval French prison as the basic model for the building."

(This discussion, in a case involving the Lucas County Jail, was located in downtown Toledo!) With this as a preface, it was no surprise that the court concluded that the sentenced prisoners were being cruelly and unusually punished: "The cruelty is a refined sort, much more comparable to the Chinese water torture than to such crudities as breaking on the wheel."

The case, being a conditions-of-jail case, is better known for its ruling on the second category of inmates, the pretrial detainees. With respect to them, the court said, "they are not to be subjected to any hardship except those absolutely requisite for the purpose of confinement only, and they retain all the rights of an ordinary citizen except the right to go and come as they please." Using that standard, their treatment at the jail denied them the equal protection of the laws. (The court also said they were being punished "without any semblance of due process or fair treatment." That statement correctly anticipated the standard of *Bell v. Wolfish,* 441 U.S. 520 (1979), but this court in *Jones* seemed to rely more on the equal protection clause than the due process clause.) And what was the class of persons to whom the jail detainees were similarly situated for the purposes of "equal protection"? It was "ordinary citizens," the people of the free world, those in the outside community. (It is hard to think of any two classes of persons who are much more dissimilarly situated, for legal and practical analysis.) The court arrived at that conclusion because the jail inmates "are only in jail awaiting trial, and are, according to our law, presumed to be innocent of any wrongdoing."

These conclusions did not just affect the inmates, the staff, and the administrators of the Lucas County Jail. The words of the court in *Jones* were often quoted in articles analyzing the legal rights of jail inmates. In addition, the legal standards of *Jones* were adopted by judges in other parts of the country, who wanted to remedy the bad conditions they found in their local jails.

▶ *Morales v. Schmidt*

The second case is *Morales v. Schmidt,* 340 F.Supp. 544 (W.D. Wis. 1972). The question in *Morales* was a fairly narrow one, although it was one of the first federal rulings on the important First Amendment issue of prisoner mail. Morales was an inmate in the Wisconsin State Prison. His wife's sister was on his mailing list, and he wrote a letter to her. A prison social worker read the outgoing letter and never mailed it. Some time later, the name of the sister-in-law was removed from Morales's list of approved correspondents.

Morales sued, claiming violation of his constitutional right to free speech. (This case was decided, of course, before the Supreme Court's first guidance on inmate correspondence in *Procunier v. Martinez,* 416 U.S. 396 (1974), and long before the further guidance of *Turner v. Safley,* 482 U.S. 78 (1987), and *Thornburgh v. Abbott,* 490 U.S. 401 (1989).) Prison officials justified interference with this correspondence on the grounds that they had discovered, after the disputed letter was read, that Morales was the father of an illegitimate child born to his sister-in-law, that he was then, and he remained, married to his wife Sandra (who was unaware that her husband was the father of her sister's child), and that Morales wanted to continue his illicit relationship with Sandra's sister. The prison authorities removed the sister-in-law from Morales's correspondence list because they believed he should not be permitted to correspond with the woman with whom he had the illicit sexual relationship (which he apparently wished to continue).

The federal district judge in *Morales* noted that there was (by 1972) "a flood of constitutional lawsuits by prisoners." This flood of suits had heavily burdened correctional authorities, as well as the federal courts. The court observed also the language from the Supreme Court decision in *Price v. Johnston,* 334 U.S. 266 (1948), which had been for many years the absolute foundation of many court actions dismissing prisoner suits: "Lawful incarceration brings about the necessary withdrawal or limitation of many privileges and rights, a retraction justified by the considerations underlying our penal system." The court in *Morales* also noted an even more rigid warning from the Supreme Court: "[I]t is not the function of the courts to superintend the treatment and discipline of prisoners in penitentiaries, but only to deliver from imprisonment those who are illegally confined." This statement was made in *Stroud v. Swope,* 187 F.2d 850 (9th Cir. 1951). But why did the court even refer to those cases advising deference to prison administrators and a "hands-off" attitude? This judge was not about to hold back from his review of claims by inmates of constitutional violations. And this was true, even though the court observed that there was virtually no guidance from other courts about what the rights of a prisoner were in this context.

The opinion in *Morales* may be most noteworthy for this language:

"With respect to the intrinsic importance of the challenges, I am persuaded that the institution of prison probably must end. In many respects it is as intolerable within the United States as was the institution of slavery, equally brutalizing to all involved, equally toxic to the social system, equally subversive of the brotherhood of man, even more costly by some standards, and probably less rational."

(Oh my. Well, with that sermon delivered, it may not be hard to guess how this judge decided this case—and, indeed, on which side he came down on most prison cases.)

The district judge's legal analysis of the correspondence rights of Morales was as follows:

"[T]hose convicted of crime should continue to share with the general population the full latent protection of the Fourteenth Amendment." That protection would be equal protection of the laws and due process. But are prisoners to have unfettered access to the mails, under the First Amendment? And what of prison officials' concerns about security or other governmental interests? This court said, "I conclude that freedom to use the mails is a First Amendment freedom …. [A] member of the general population would be free to correspond by mail with his wife's sister [without regard to the 'illicit' circumstances present in this case] …. [E]ach individual's interest in corresponding by mail with another is fairly to be characterized as a 'fundamental' interest. [If the government wants to deny this freedom to an inmate], the burden is upon the defendant [prison official] to show a compelling governmental interest in this differential in treatment."

Applying these standards to this case, the court concluded that the government's interest in banning this correspondence (and thereby "diminishing the likelihood of such future unlawful sexual activity by one convicted of a past crime") was not a compelling one. Denying Morales the opportunity to correspond with his sister-in-law was a deprivation of his rights under the First and the Fourteenth Amendments. Prison officials were enjoined from continuing the ban on that correspondence.[2]

▶ Closing Comments

From these cases, the following points may be made: (1) The cases were well-written and were frequently quoted by others. Their influence was more than that of an ordinary district court ruling, which would be legally conclusive only in that court's home district. (2) The cases are strong examples of the principle, cynical as it may be, that judges decide cases according to their gut reactions to the facts they hear. Sometimes, they do not even hear the facts of the case before them. Sometimes, they have heard of conditions (in the local jail or in a nearby prison) from various sources—the media, attorneys, law clerks, or others around the courthouse, classes or seminars they have attended, or even comments from friends and acquaintances at social gatherings.

The point is, much as we insist on the principle that judges come to cases unbiased and without preconceptions about the outcome, the fact is that that principle is often not true. It especially is not true in many (if not most) prison and jail cases. These two highly influential cases, *Jones* and *Morales,* are very instructive on this point, because the judges said more than they needed to. They showed us quite clearly in their language their bias on the nature of jails and prisons. Of course, judges can be slanted as much to the other (government) side as these two judges seemed to be slanted to the inmates' side.

(3) The district judges in these two cases were not evil men or bad judges. Neither were they saints (as one of the [previous] authors heard some prisoner advocates refer to them) or great judges. Judges are human beings. Federal judges are sometimes considered, on overall assessment, to be the best of the lot. [A previous author of this text] knew the judge on the *Morales* case, Judge Doyle, personally; he was a fine man, a respected jurist, and an extremely careful and sensitive judge (perhaps too sensitive, as seen in the *Morales* case language, to deal realistically with criminal justice matters). Much as we would like to have our cases heard by judges who are absolutely impartial, who come to the case without any preconceptions, such ideal situations are, unfortunately, the exception more often than the rule.

After this discussion of these two corrections decisions, we come back to the point underlying this summary: do not think of "corrections law" as being a set of fixed rules. The Supreme Court gave us, in *Bell v. Wolfish* (for *Jones v. Wittenberg)* and in *Procunier v. Martinez, Turner v. Safley,* and *Thornburgh v. Abbott* (for *Morales v. Schmidt),* principles of constitutional interpretation that totally rejected the legal analyses and conclusions of those two federal district court judges. From *Bell,* we know for certain that jail inmates do not have all the rights of free citizens, except the right to come and go as they please (the concept underlying the *Jones* ruling). In addition, the Supreme Court flatly rejected the idea that the presumption of innocence for detainees had anything at all to do with evaluating the conditions of the jail where they were held. From *Turner* and *Thornburgh* we know that to restrict inmate correspondence there need be only a reasonable relationship to a legitimate government purpose (not a compelling government interest). (Judge Doyle's comparison of "the institution of prison" to slavery and prediction of its necessary end is interesting commentary but hardly sound legal or political principle, at least for the foreseeable future.)

In *Rhodes v. Chapman,* 452 U.S. 337 (1981), the Supreme Court made the optimistic observation that the standards for interpreting the Constitution (in that case, specifically the Eighth Amendment) reflect the progress that is made in a maturing society. If viewed from a broad historical perspective, we can see that conditions in prisons have drastically changed over the decades. To some extent, improvements in prisons and jails can be attributed to the involvement of the courts in constantly assessing the conditions and programs in those facilities, pursuant to constitutional (and American society's) expectations. We have to continue with that optimism—that our society, as it matures, will produce prisons that are more civilized and decent.

Like it or not, the law is in constant flux. What you have in this book are three aspects of the law in its current state: (1) an identification of the issues that, from a legal standpoint, are the most challenging to the field of corrections; (2) a presentation of those legal principles that are the firmest, best guidance we have right now—the decisions of the Supreme Court and some controlling statutes (and even some treaties); and (3) some discussion of the lower court decisions, where the Supreme Court has not yet ruled. With those in mind, you will be equipped, it is hoped, to understand the current status of "corrections law." Just stay tuned for those changes and new rulings, which are sure to come!

Key Terms
stare decisis

Endnotes

1. Clair A. Cripe, the first author of this text has been involved in the development of correctional litigation since the early 1960s. Here is his "confession": It is true that I present these cases with a particular bias—that of a corrections attorney who was dismayed at the time by the mistaken assumptions and the legal approaches of these cases. Every author on corrections matters writes with some bias, based on her experience and the ideas she has about the purposes of corrections, the role of corrections staff, and the inherent status of prisoners. Every corrections lawyer (whether prisoner advocate, law professor, or government attorney) also approaches his work and his writing with bias, although precious few have ever admitted, or tried to describe, that bias in their writing. Here is my bias: I came into the corrections field in 1962, because of my interest in criminal justice matters broadly, and in prisoners' rights (more exactly, just how prisoners were treated) specifically. Over time, I became more and more informed about the demands of good prison management and the very difficult problems of working with prisoners. Of course, I also had some personal ideas about the role of the law: I thought the courts were right to tackle serious questions of constitutional rights, but I was appalled by the readiness of some judges to jump in and manage matters where they had no expert background (and, in my view, no legal business) to be intruding. For a fuller presentation of my view on activist judges, see Cripe, C.(1990). "Court, corrections, and the constitution: A practitioner's view," in *Courts, Corrections, and the Constitution,* ed. J. J. DiIulio, Jr. (New York: Oxford University Press).

2. On appeal, *Morales* was reversed and remanded. The appeals court said the state was not required to show a compelling interest to justify its restriction on correspondence but only had to show a reasonable and necessary relationship toward achieving a justified purpose of confinement. *Morales v. Schmidt,* 494 F.2d 85 (7th Cir. 1974).

Glossary

Listed here are words and terms that are used in this text and that are often encountered in corrections, criminal justice, and the law. Many of the definitions were taken from the Dictionary of Criminal Justice Data Terminology, published by the U.S. Department of Justice, Law Enforcement Assistance Administration (1976, 1981).

A

abscond (corrections) To depart from a geographic area or jurisdiction prescribed by the conditions of one's probation or parole, without authorization. (*Caution:* this term is not to be used as a synonym for escape.)

abscond (court) To intentionally absent or conceal oneself unlawfully in order to avoid a legal proceeding.

accreditation Recognition by an authority that an organization, program, or facility has achieved high professional standards. (In corrections, there is an accreditation program administered by a commission associated with the American Correctional Association.)

acquittal A judgment of a court, based either on the verdict of a jury or a judicial officer, that the defendant is not guilty of the offense(s) for which they has been tried or the finding that the evidence is insufficient to support a conviction.

adjudication (criminal) The judicial decision that terminates a criminal proceeding with a judgment of conviction or acquittal or a dismissal of the case.

adjudication (juvenile) The juvenile court decision that terminates an adjudicatory hearing with a judgment that the juvenile is a delinquent, a status offender, or a dependent, or that the allegations in the petition are not sustained.

administrative law The body of law created by administrative agencies (such as regulatory agencies). These laws are seen in the form of rules, regulations, orders, and interpretive decisions.

adult A person who is within the original jurisdiction of a criminal court rather than a juvenile court because their age at the time of an alleged criminal act was above a statutorily specified limit.

affidavit A written statement of facts, confirmed by oath or affirmation of the person making it (the affiant).

allocution Inquiry made by a judge directly to a defendant who has been convicted as to whether there is any legal reason why judgment should not be rendered. More frequently today, asking the defendant at the sentencing phase of the criminal proceeding for any statement in mitigation of the sentence.

alternative facility An alternative place of confinement (to traditional confinement institutions, such as prisons or jails), with lesser security controls, which may be used as an option in sentencing or in an inmate's placement by corrections authorities.

amicus curiae Latin for "friend of the court." A person or organization who is not a party but who has a strong interest in a legal matter and who asks permission to lodge their views with the court (usually in an appellate court) in an amicus brief.

answer (civil procedure) The pleading filed by the defendant, responding to the plaintiff's allegations in the complaint. It is a written statement that sets out the defendant's factual and legal grounds for his defense.

appeal A request by either party that a case be removed from a lower court to a higher court in order for a trial proceeding to be reviewed by the higher court. It also refers to the review by an appeals court of a lower court's proceedings or outcome.

appellant A person who initiates an appeal (ordinarily, the person who has lost in the lower court).

appellee The opposing party to an appellant (usually, the person who has prevailed in the lower court and who defends in the higher court the results or rulings in that lower court).

arraignment The appearance of a person (soon after arrest or after charges have been lodged) before a court in order that the court may inform them of the accusation(s) against them and in order that they may enter their plea to the charges.

arrest Taking a person into custody by authority of the law for the purpose of charging them with a criminal offense or for the purpose of initiating juvenile proceedings, terminating with the recording of a specific offense.

assault The unlawful intentional infliction, or attempted or threatened infliction, of injury upon another. (Also defined as an unlawful physical attack by one person upon another.)

attorney A person trained in the law, admitted to practice before the bar of a given jurisdiction, and authorized to advise, represent, and act for other persons in legal proceedings. (Used interchangeably with lawyer or counsel.)

B

battery The unlawful use of force against the person of another. Technically, offensive touching or bodily injury to another person.

Bill of Rights A common term for the first 10 Amendments to the U.S. Constitution.

Bivens action An action in federal court, alleging a civil rights violation by federal officials. Named for a Supreme Court opinion (*Bivens v. Six Unknown Narcotics Agents*) that allows a lawsuit for such federal agents' violations equivalent to the lawsuits authorized by 42 U.S.C. § 1983 for violations of civil rights by persons operating under color of state law.

bona fide In good faith. Honestly, openly, without deceit.

bond (appearance bond) A written promise by a financially responsible person to pay the bail sum if the offender does not follow the terms of release. See also release on bail.

booking An action by police that officially records an arrest and identifies the person, the place, the time, the arresting authority, and the reason for the arrest.

boot camp A camp that emphasizes programs of intensive, militaristic regimens. It is used as an alternative to regular imprisonment. It has been used principally for younger offenders, and it requires a shorter term of confinement than ordinarily would be imposed.

brief A written document prepared by counsel that presents facts, discussion of contested issues, legal references, and arguments pertaining to the case before a trial court or an appellate court.

burden of proof The necessity of proving a fact or facts in dispute in a case. The obligation a party has to introduce sufficient evidence to convince the trier of fact that an essential fact or conclusion is true.

C

camp A correctional facility, usually located in a rural setting and usually of a low-security level, for the confinement of adults or juveniles who have been committed after their adjudication.

canon law (church law) The body of law established by religious organizations, administered by religious officials, for the determination of rights and liabilities under matters subject to religious jurisdiction.

capacity (corrections) The number of inmates or residents that a correctional facility can house.

capital punishment The sanction of the death penalty. Now used only with great procedural protections, in cases where it is authorized by criminal statute.

case (criminal court) A single charging document under the jurisdiction of a criminal court. Also used to refer to a single defendant or any individual who is the object of criminal prosecution. (Used in the same sense for a juvenile who is being processed in juvenile court.)

case (legal proceedings) The court proceeding, whether civil or criminal, in all its aspects. Also used to refer to a report of a court decision in legal publications, such as court reporters.

case law The cumulated law, as given in the decisions of courts. The aggregate of reported cases on a particular subject, or from a particular source, or in toto.

caseload (corrections) The total number of clients registered with a corrections agency, or with an individual officer within an agency, during a specified time period. (Usually refers to persons under probation or parole supervision, or those assigned to caseworkers inside a corrections facility.)

caseload (court) The total number of cases filed in a given court, or before a certain judicial officer, during a given period of time.

caveat A warning or notice to beware or to exercise caution or special care.

certiorari A writ issued by a superior court to an inferior court of record, ordering the certification of the records and proceedings in the case, so that the record (the case) may be reviewed for any error and corrected, as needed. A form of appellate review. (Now, used principally to apply to reviews by the U.S. Supreme Court of actions by lower courts. To obtain a Supreme Court review, an applicant files a petition for a writ of certiorari.)

chancery (court of chancery) A court to hear cases in equity (in England and some places in the United States).

charge A formal allegation that a specific person has committed a specific offense. (Inside a corrections facility, used to refer to allegations of misconduct against persons, under the facility's administrative disciplinary code.)

charging document A formal written accusation, filed in a court, alleging that a specified person has committed a specific offense. (Inside a corrections facility, the written accusation alleging that inmates have committed certain acts of misconduct.) In court, there are three kinds of charging documents: complaint, information, and indictment. When the charging document is filed in a court, that initiates criminal proceedings against the accused.

checks and balances Procedures established by constitutional requirements, whereby each of the three branches of government has some constraints on the other two.

citation (criminal court) A written order issued by a law enforcement officer directing an alleged offender to appear in a specific court at a specified time in order to answer a criminal charge.

citation (legal research) The reference to the exact place in legal reference books where a court decision can be found. Usually, a citation (also called a cite) refers to a certain collection of legal books and includes the volume and page numbers where a decision is located.

civil law The body of law that determines private rights and liabilities, as distinguished from criminal law.

civil liberties (civil rights) Personal rights guaranteed by the Constitution. The liberties of any member of society, particularly against government encroachment, but restrained as need be for the protection of the rights of others.

class action An action brought by one (or a few) plaintiff(s) on behalf of a large group of persons, all of whom have similar interests in pursuing the action.

classification (corrections) The systematic arrangement, usually prescribed by written policy, of persons or things into similar groups, based on specified criteria. There are two principal subjects of classification in corrections: (1) correctional facilities, or portions of facilities, usually grouped by security level (such as minimum, medium, maximum, high, or low) or special purpose (such as pretrial status, protective custody, or medical or mental health facilities); (2) inmates, whereby offenders are grouped according to their backgrounds, their special needs, their legal status, and their custody requirements (reflecting any requirements for special security precautions).

clemency An act (usually by the executive) of forgiveness or leniency. The granting of a pardon or a commutation of sentence.

commitment The action of a judicial officer ordering that a convicted adult, or an adjudicated juvenile, be admitted into a correctional facility. (May be used to refer to an order for the admission of a person before final adjudication for a temporary, special purpose, such as a commitment of a criminal defendant to a mental health facility to determine competency to stand trial. May also be used to refer to an order for admission of a patient for mental health observation and treatment, termed a civil commitment.)

common law Those principles and rules, applicable to government and individuals, that do not rest for their original authority on statutes but on statements (rulings) found in decisions of courts. In a broader sense, it is sometimes used to refer to the Anglo-American system of justice and legal concepts.

community corrections All of those organizations, facilities, and programs that operate in a locality outside of traditional confinement facilities.

community facility A correctional facility from which residents are regularly permitted to depart, without escort, for the purpose of using community resources, such as schools or treatment programs, or seeking or holding employment. (May be used during preadjudication or for the commitment of adults or juveniles.)

community service A sentence (or alternative to sentencing) in which the offender performs work benefiting a charity, a government operation, or another organization; the work is approved by the sentencing court as being in the public's (or community's) interest.

commutation The act of clemency, reducing a sentence. Changing a sentence to one that is less severe.

compact An agreement between persons, nations, or states. Often used to describe agreements between states concerning matters of mutual interest and concern (interstate compacts). Compacts between states must receive the approval of Congress, as required by Article I, Section 10 of the U.S. Constitution.

competent With respect to the law, having sufficient ability to act or participate in a legal matter. With respect to court proceedings or administrative hearings, possessing sufficient understanding, especially the mental capacity, to be involved in the proceeding, whether as a party or a witness.

complaint (civil procedure) The initial pleading filed in court, by which a legal action is commenced. This is the pleading that sets out a claim for relief, including the factual and legal grounds for such relief.

complaint (criminal procedure) A formal, written accusation made by any person, often a prosecutor, and filed in a court, alleging that a specified person has committed a specific offense. (Usually used in misdemeanor cases or to initiate probable cause hearings in felony cases.)

concurrent sentences Two or more terms of imprisonment that are served simultaneously, "running together," in whole or in part. (The opposite: consecutive sentences.) Example: Two five-year sentences and one three-year sentence, if served concurrently, result in a maximum of five years imprisonment.

confinement The status of being in secured custody, where the person is not free to come and go, unless escorted.

confinement facility A correctional facility from which the inmates are not permitted to depart unaccompanied. (This is a broad term for detention facilities [jails] and corrections institutions [prisons]. Some community facilities have such restrictions on their inmates, to the degree that they may be considered confinement facilities. Similarly, some jails and prisons allow some inmates to reenter the community unescorted to participate in work-release or other programs. Such jails and prisons are still considered confinement facilities if the majority of the inmates are not regularly released for such unescorted activities in the community.)

conjugal visits Visits with a spouse or other intimate partner which allows the prisoner and their visitor to be together in an area away from the visiting room where they have more privacy and the opportunity for sexual intimacy.

consecutive sentences One term of imprisonment being served following another. (In some places, called "from and after" sentences.) Example: Two five-year sentences and one three-year sentence, if served consecutively, result in a maximum of 13 years imprisonment.

consent Voluntary agreement to the proposal or request of another person.

consent decree A decree (judgment or order of a court) that is agreed to by both parties in a lawsuit and, when approved by the court, is binding on them both.

constitution A statement of the fundamental laws or principles that are agreed on to govern a nation, a state, an organization, or a society.

contraband (corrections) Material that is prohibited, either by law or regulation. It includes material that can reasonably be expected to cause physical injury or to adversely affect the security, safety, or good order of a prison or jail.

contract An agreement, between competent persons, with consideration (that is, a price paid [not always money] for a promise) to do, or refrain from doing, a particular thing.

convict An adult who has been found guilty and sentenced in criminal court and who is confined in a confinement facility. (Virtually a slang term today; inmate and prisoner are the preferred terms.)

conviction A judgment of a court, based either on the verdict of a jury or a judicial officer or on the guilty plea of the defendant, that the defendant is guilty of the offense for which they have been tried.

coram nobis Technically, a writ of error coram nobis. An order at common law to correct a judgment in the same court in which it was entered.

correctional agency A federal, state, or local criminal justice agency, under a single administrative authority, of which the principal functions are the investigation, intake screening, supervision, custody, confinement, or treatment of alleged or adjudicated adult offenders, or juvenile delinquents or status offenders. (This includes probation agencies, parole agencies, juvenile agencies, and agencies that administer correctional facilities.)

correctional facility A building, a set of buildings, or an area enclosing a set of buildings operated by an agency (public or private) for the custody or treatment of adjudicated and committed persons, or persons subject to criminal or juvenile justice proceedings.

correctional institution A generic name for long-term adult confinement facilities (often called prisons, federal or state correctional institutions, or penitentiaries) and juvenile and youth confinement facilities (sometimes called training schools, reformatories, boys' ranches, and the like).

correctional officer An employee of a correctional agency whose duties include one or more of the functions of the agency. Used most often to refer to those employees who are responsible for the security functions of correctional facilities and for the direct supervision of inmates. (A colloquial synonym is guard.)

corrections A generic term that includes all government agencies, facilities, programs, procedures, personnel, and techniques concerned with the investigation, intake, custody, confinement, supervision, or treatment of alleged or adjudicated adult offenders, juvenile delinquents, or status offenders.

counsel See attorney.

count (corrections) The procedure for "taking the roll" of all persons who are present in a correctional facility. Records of the facility show the exact number of persons who should be present at a given time; during regularly scheduled (and sometimes irregular or random) counting times, staff members verify that all persons assigned to the facility are accounted for. When a count is taken, all inmates are required to be and remain at their assigned location for that particular time until the count is "cleared"—that is, the correct count is verified.

count (court) Each separate offense, as listed in a complaint, information, or indictment.

court An agency or individual officer of the judicial branch of government, authorized or established by statute or constitution, which has the authority to decide controversies in law and disputed matters of fact brought before it.

court of appeals A court that does not try cases, but rather hears appeals.

court of general jurisdiction A court that has the legal authority to try all civil cases and criminal offenses, including all felonies.

court of limited jurisdiction A court with authority to try cases, but only cases of certain kinds. Such courts often have no authority to try felony cases, or they have authority that is limited to only certain kinds of felonies.

crime (criminal offense) An act committed or omitted in violation of a law forbidding or commanding it, for which an adult can be punished, upon conviction, by incarceration or other penalties, or for which a juvenile can be brought under the jurisdiction of a juvenile court and adjudicated as a delinquent or transferred to adult court.

criminal justice agency Any court with criminal jurisdiction and any other government agency or subunit that defends indigents or of which the principal functions or activities consist of the prevention, detection, and investigation of crime; the apprehension, detention, and prosecution of alleged offenders; the confinement or official correctional supervision of accused or convicted persons; or the administrative or technical support of these functions.

criminal laws (penal laws) The body of state and federal statutes that impose penalties for offenses against the state. (Criminal law is the entire body of law—statutes, court opinions, rules—that defines offenses against the state, sets rules for their prosecution, and authorizes sanctions for committing offenses.)

criminal proceedings Proceedings in a court of law, undertaken to determine the guilt or innocence of an adult accused of a crime.

cruel and unusual punishment Excessive, inhumane penalties or correctional treatment, prohibited by the Eighth Amendment to the U.S. Constitution.

D

damages Monetary awards in civil cases, given by court order (judgment) to a person who has been harmed by another.

deadly force Force intended or likely to cause death or serious bodily harm.

decision A determination or conclusion reached by a court. Usually used to refer to the written report of a court that states its conclusion or determination of the case. The decision reached by a court is reflected in its opinion. (See that definition.)

declaratory relief (declaratory judgment) A court judgment that sets out conclusively the rights and duties of parties but involves no coercive or monetary relief.

defamation A tort, involving the unprivileged publication of false statements, which result in injury to another. The injury suffered may be contempt, ridicule, hatred, or damage to reputation.

defendant A person against whom a criminal proceeding is undertaken or a person against whom a civil legal action is brought.

defense attorney An attorney who represents the defendant in a legal proceeding.

delinquency Juvenile actions or conduct in violation of criminal law (and sometimes also in committing status offenses).

delinquent A juvenile who has been adjudicated by a judicial officer of a juvenile court as having committed a delinquent act, which is an act for which an adult could be prosecuted in a criminal court.

de novo Anew, afresh, as if there had been no earlier decision.

dependent children Juveniles without family or support, or who have deficient family or support. These children may appear before juvenile courts to verify their dependency status so the courts may determine the best steps that can be taken for their welfare.

deposition The testimony of a witness taken under oath, not in open court, in response to oral questions, pursuant to a rule or order that authorizes such questioning. The testimony is transcribed and is usually intended for use at a later trial.

detainer A notice that informs prison authorities that charges (or sometimes an unserved sentence, as for an escapee) are pending elsewhere against an inmate, and asks that the custodian notify the requesting jurisdiction before the inmate is released.

detention The legally authorized holding in confinement of a person subject to criminal or juvenile court proceedings, until the point of commitment to a correctional facility, release to an alternative facility, or release to the community.

detention center A facility that provides temporary care in a physically restricting environment for juveniles in custody pending court disposition.

detention facility A generic term for all types of facilities that hold adults or juveniles in confinement pending adjudication; such facilities also often hold adults who are sentenced for a year or less of confinement, and, in some instances, postadjudicated juveniles. These facilities may variously be called jails, county farms, work camps, road camps, detention centers, shelters, or juvenile halls.

determinate sentence A sentence, usually to a term of imprisonment, for a period of time that is fixed by statute. (Similar to a mandatory sentence, but not identical.)

deterrence The act, or theory, of stopping action by frightening the potential actor. In penology (sentencing philosophy), deterrence refers to the discouragement of crime because of fear of its consequences (the sanctions that may be imposed). There are two aspects of deterrence: specific (or individual) deterrence—discouragement of the individual offender; and

general deterrence—discouragement of a large number of persons who might consider the criminal conduct but who might be convinced not to engage in that conduct because of its adverse consequences, as shown by the punishment of others.

diagnosis (or classification) center A unit within a correctional institution, or a separate facility, that holds persons in custody for the purpose of determining to which correctional facility or program they should be committed.

dictum (plural, dicta) A statement in a court opinion that is not essential to support the decision. A legal principle or conclusion (in an opinion) that is not necessary to the decision of the case.

disciplinary confinement The act (and the place) of confining inmates separately because of their institutional misconduct. Segregation for disciplinary reasons. (Variously called disciplinary detention, disciplinary segregation, punitive segregation, and isolation.)

discipline (corrections) The program in a corrections agency or facility of punishing inmates who violate the internal code of conduct adopted for that agency or facility.

discovery (court procedure) A procedural tool or remedy used to compel an adverse party or a witness to answer allegations and interrogatories, to disclose facts within their knowledge, or to produce documents or records, all of which are designed to help the requesting party to better prepare and present their case.

dismissal A decision by a judicial officer to terminate a case without a trial or without any further proceedings.

dissent A disagreement with an opinion. Used most often to refer to the refusal of a judge (or judges) to agree with the majority of the court on the case being decided in an appellate court. If an opinion is written by the dissenter(s), it is called a dissenting opinion.

distinguish In the law, used to point out essential differences. To distinguish a case means to show why a particular prior case (decision) is inapplicable to the case now before the court, usually when it would be damaging if the prior case were applicable or controlling.

diversion The official halting or suspension of formal criminal or juvenile justice proceedings against an alleged offender and referral of that person to a treatment or care program administered by a nonjustice or private agency, or to a proceeding with noncriminal consequences.

double jeopardy A prohibition against a person being prosecuted after there was a first trial for the same offense. The Fifth Amendment of the U.S. Constitution provides that no person shall "be subject for the same offence to be twice put in jeopardy of life or limb."

due process (due process of law) Exercise of the powers and authority of government in those ways that are prescribed by settled principles of law. There is a wide range of principles and procedures that may be prescribed (that is, process that may be due) according to the nature of the proceedings. The minimum process (principles and procedures) requires adequate advance notice of the proceeding, an opportunity to be heard and to assert one's rights, and consideration before a person or tribunal that is authorized by law to hear and determine the matter, according to established rules of good order.

due process clause The constitutional statement that protects persons from certain governmental actions unless prescribed rules and procedures are followed. There are two such clauses in the U.S. Constitution; these appear in the Fifth Amendment (for federal government actions) and in the Fourteenth Amendment (for state actions). Almost all state constitutions also have such clauses.

E

electronic law library A method of providing legal materials, such as statutes and court opinions, in an electronic format, rather than in paper volumes.

en banc (courts) A proceeding in which all members of a particular court will participate in hearing and deciding a case.

equal protection of the laws A guarantee in a clause of the Fourteenth Amendment to the U.S. Constitution that persons in like circumstances should be given equal protection in their personal rights.

equity (courts) An alternative, established in English law, to the ordinary forms of civil law and justice. The emphasis in equity is to provide fair and just results in cases in which the common law or ordinary laws do not appear adequate. Equity concentrates on the persons who are present in court without trying to establish rights to govern other cases. (In the United States, in most jurisdictions, equity and law have been combined in courts of general jurisdiction.)

escape The unlawful departure of a lawfully confined person from a confinement facility or from custody while being transported or officially escorted.

evidence Any type of proof that is presented at trial, consisting of witnesses' testimony, records, documents, and other physical objects. Used to prove (or disprove) a fact relevant to the case being tried.

execution The act of carrying out an order or judgment of a court. (Sometimes used in common parlance to refer to carrying out a sentence of death.)

exhaustion A requirement that relief must be pursued in another procedure or place before it can be pursued in a particular court. Used especially for *exhaustion of administrative remedies* (requiring that such remedies be used, where they are available, before a lawsuit is filed) and *exhaustion of state remedies* (requiring that state remedies be pursued before federal actions are undertaken).

ex-offender An offender who is no longer under the jurisdiction of any criminal justice agency.

ex parte Used in the title of a case, or in an application to a court, to indicate that the action is brought on behalf of only one party, without notice to any adverse party.

ex post facto Literally, after the act is committed. Used to signify something done after the fact, which is intended to affect something that was done before. An ex post facto law refers to a law that is enacted to impose a penalty for doing something that was lawful when it was done or to increase the punishment for a crime, making the sanction greater than when the crime was committed.

expunge To seal or purge arrest, criminal, or juvenile record information.

extradition The surrender by the authorities of one state (or country) of an accused or convicted offender to another state (or country), upon demand by authorities of that other state (or country). The surrender is usually made by the governor of the state where the offender is located, and it is initiated after an official request has been made to that governor and following a review of the legitimacy of the request. (Also known as rendition.)

F

facial challenge A claim that a statute is unconstitutional on its face. A facial challenge does not get into the consideration of any specific facts but is limited to the issue of whether the statute itself, as written, is unconstitutional.

false imprisonment A tort, involving the unlawful restraint by one person of the physical liberty of another. (May also be a crime.)

federal Pertaining to the national government of the United States of America. The government of a community of independent states, joined in a union having central and predominate authority.

felony A criminal offense punishable by death or by incarceration in a confinement facility for a period of which the lower limit is prescribed by statute in a given jurisdiction, typically more than one year.

filing In criminal proceedings, the commencement of legal action by entering a charging document into the official record of a court.

finding The official determination of a judicial officer or administrative body regarding a disputed matter of fact or law. (Also called a ruling or a decision.)

fine A penalty imposed on a convicted person by a court that requires payment of a specified sum of money.

forfeiture The loss of something by way of penalty. (An example in corrections is good-time forfeiture. See good time.)

fugitive A person who has concealed themselves or fled a given jurisdiction in order to avoid confinement or prosecution. (Not exactly the same as an escapee—some but not necessarily all escapees may be fugitives.)

furlough A temporary leave of absence, authorizing an inmate to depart from a correctional facility for a specified purpose, to a specific place, and with strict time limitations. These actions must be authorized by statute or, in rare cases, by judicial order.

G

good time An award, authorized by statute, which reduces the length of time an inmate must spend in prison. It is given for satisfactory conduct in prison. There may also be authorization for *extra good time*, an additional award for particularly meritorious or outstanding actions or behavior. Good time does not usually reduce the total length of the sentence. Initially conceived as an incentive for good behavior, it has become virtually an automatic award in most places, lost only when the inmate misbehaves (withholding good time for current awards, forfeiture of good time for accumulated awards). In a few jurisdictions, the good-time allowance may reduce the maximum term of the sentence or even the parole eligibility date (the earliest date the inmate can be considered for parole release).

grand jury A body of persons who have been selected and sworn to investigate criminal activity and the conduct of public officials and who hear evidence and legal advice from a prosecutor against an accused person to determine whether there is sufficient evidence to bring that person to trial. The decision of a grand jury that there is sufficient evidence for trial results in an indictment or "true bill," which is "handed up" by the grand jury. (See jury for a trial jury and petit jury definition.)

grievance (corrections) A complaint filed by an inmate in an informal procedure, which is reviewed in a mechanism established by a corrections agency. Relief may be given for conditions or actions that are found in the review process to have been wrongful.

guardian A person who is given the legal authority to take care of another person.

guardian ad litem An individual appointed by the court to function on behalf of an incompetent or an infant and to represent the interests of that incompetent or infant in a suit to which that person is a party.

guilt Responsibility for wrongdoing. Guilty is used in criminal practice to denote a conclusion (by a defendant's plea or by a finding by a judge or jury) that an accused person is responsible for the crimes or offenses for which he has been charged.

H

habeas corpus A writ (a court process or order) of ancient origin, used to obtain immediate relief by release from illegal confinement or custody. (Technically, this is the writ of *habeas corpus ad subjiciendum.* Other writs of habeas corpus are used to obtain a person in custody before a court, for prosecution [*habeas corpus ad prosequendum*] or for testifying [*habeas corpus ad testificandum*].)

halfway house A residential facility for adjudicated adults or juveniles or those subject to criminal or juvenile proceedings that is intended to provide an alternative to confinement (in less-secure surroundings) for persons not suitable for probation or other supervised release, or for those needing a period of readjustment to the community after confinement. A facility designed to assist a person to readjust to community life. (The same term may also be used for group homes for hospital releasees.) Most often used for those being released from correctional institutions ("halfway-out houses") but may also be used in lieu of placement into secure facilities ("halfway-in houses"). Also called a residential re-entry center.

hearing A proceeding in which arguments, witnesses, or evidence is heard by a judicial officer or by an administrative body.

hearing officer The official who is given authority to conduct a hearing.

hold harmless An agreement in which one party assumes the liability in a situation, relieving the other party of legal responsibility.

holding The legal principle decided by a court's opinion or ruling.

I

immunity Exemption by law. Freedom from a duty, or from liability, because actions are protected by law. Immunity from criminal prosecution may be either transactional immunity or use immunity. Transactional immunity provides immunity from prosecution for an offense to which a witness's compelled testimony relates. Use immunity bars a person's compelled testimony and its fruits from being used in any manner in connection with the criminal prosecution of the person. Qualified immunity protects a governmental official from personal liability for an alleged constitutional violation when the law in the area is not clearly established.

incapacitation The inability to act. In penology (sentencing philosophy), the justification for a term of imprisonment on the grounds that it renders the offender unable to commit offenses during the time of his imprisonment.

incarceration Imprisonment. Confinement in a jail or prison.

indemnification Compensation given to reimburse a person for a loss already sustained by him.

indeterminate sentence A sentence imposed, not for a precise period of time, but often with a minimum and a maximum period of confinement, with the release of the offender usually controlled by correctional authorities, based on the behavior and successful achievement of the offender.

indictment A formal, written accusation made by a grand jury and filed in a court, alleging that a specified person has committed a specific offense.

in forma pauperis Literally, in the nature of a pauper. Indigent; lacking funds to pay certain fees or costs in court.

informant A person, usually undisclosed to the accused, who provides information or accusations against another person. (Also called an informer.)

information A formal, written accusation made by a prosecutor and filed in a court, alleging that a specified person has committed a specific offense.

infraction An offense punishable by fine or other penalty, but not by incarceration. (In some places, this is called a violation.)

injunction (court action) A lawsuit brought, historically in a court of equity, to protect the rights of a plaintiff against the actions (or inactions) of a defendant, to avoid or right a wrong.

injunction (court order) A writ (order) to restrain a person from doing that which he should not do, or requiring him to do that which he should do. (The latter is sometimes called a mandatory injunction or mandamus.) This relief is entered to avoid irreparable injury (under the "rules of conscience" of an equity court) to any individual's person, or property, or other rights.

injury Any wrong or damage done to another's person, rights, reputation, or property.

inmate A person in custody in a confinement facility. (Prisoner is virtually a synonym, but see that definition for the difference.)

in re In the matter of. In the titles of court cases, indicates those unusual actions that are brought without the traditional two opposing parties.

insanity In the law, denotes a degree of mental disease or illness that renders a person not responsible for their conduct. It indicates a state of mental incapacity, which serves as a legal defense to criminal charges.

institutional capacity The officially stated number of inmates or residents that a correctional facility is designed to house, exclusive of extraordinary arrangement to accommodate crowded conditions. (Also called design capacity.)

instructions Rules and directions the trial judge gives to a jury to use in their deliberations on the facts of the case.

interrogatories (court procedure) A method of discovery. Written questions about facts of a case that an attorney submits in advance of trial to persons who are believed to have knowledge about those facts.

J

jail A confinement facility, usually administered by a local law enforcement agency, such as a sheriff's department, which is intended for adults, but may sometimes contain juveniles, which persons are being detained pending adjudication or are committed, after adjudication, for a short period of time (usually a year or less).

jail sentence The penalty of commitment to the jurisdiction of a confinement facility system for adults, where the custodial authority is limited to holding persons sentenced to a year or less of confinement.

judge A judicial officer, either elected or appointed to the office, who presides over a court of law. The position is created by statute or by constitution. The decisions of a judge are final at that level of adjudication and may only be reviewed by a judge (or judges) of a higher court. (Some lower-level judges are called magistrates, justices of the peace, or commissioners. If the decisions of these judicial officers (see that definition) are not subject to de novo review, but are reviewable only on appeal to a higher level court, and if their positions are created by statute or by constitution, they are appropriately called judges under this definition. If any of those attributes of the office are missing, they may be considered subjudicial or subordinate judicial officers, not judges.)

judgment The statement of the decision of a court, amounting to final disposition of the case at that level. It is sometimes made orally in a courtroom, but it is finalized by entry into the records of the court. In a criminal case, it is an official, recorded statement that the defendant is convicted or acquitted of the offense charged.

judicial notice The acknowledgment by a court that certain facts are accepted as true, without the taking of evidence, because of a wide acceptance of their reliability. Examples are the content of statutes and geographic and calendar facts.

judicial officer Any person exercising judicial powers in a court of law.

jurisdiction The precise geographic territory, subject matter, or person(s) over which lawful authority may be exercised, as defined by constitutional provisions or by statute.

jury, trial jury, petit jury A body of persons, the number of which is defined by constitution, by statute, or by court rules, that is selected according to law, sworn to determine certain matters of fact in a criminal action, and sworn to render a verdict of guilty or not guilty (in a criminal case). (In civil cases, a jury, as defined by statute or by court rules, decides certain matters of fact and renders a verdict for either the plaintiff or the defendant, including, in most cases, the amount of damages that are awarded to the prevailing party.)

juvenile A person subject to juvenile court proceedings or to certain other special status or treatment because his age is below the statutorily specified limit of adulthood.

juvenile court The term for courts that have original jurisdiction over persons statutorily defined as juveniles and alleged to be delinquents, status offenders, or dependents. It may be a separate court, established by constitution or by statute, it may be a division of a court, or it may be a court of broader or general jurisdiction sitting in special session on juvenile matters.

juvenile justice agency A government agency, or a subunit of an agency, of which the functions are the investigation, supervision, adjudication, care, or confinement of juveniles whose conduct or condition has brought or could bring them within the jurisdiction of a juvenile court.

L

law enforcement agency A federal, state, or local criminal justice agency of which the principal functions are the prevention, detection, and investigation of crime and the apprehension of offenders.

law enforcement officer An employee of a law enforcement agency who is an officer sworn to carry out law enforcement duties, or a sworn employee of a prosecutorial agency who primarily performs investigative duties. (Also called peace officer or police officer.)

lawyer See attorney.

liability The condition of being legally responsible for damages, or other relief, to the prevailing party in a tort or other civil action. (Also refers to the obligation to perform a contract or to pay indebtedness.)

libel Defamation (see that definition) by means of print, writing, pictures, or signs. A publication that is injurious to the reputation of another.

liberty Freedom from restraints. As provided in the Fifth and Fourteenth Amendments, no person shall be deprived of "life, liberty, or property, without due process of law."

license Permission granted by a government (or other authorized) official to perform some act or to engage in some business activity. The written statement of such official permission.

M

magistrate An official with limited judicial authority. In U.S. practice, an inferior judicial officer.

majority opinion The opinion of an appellate court in which the majority of its participating members join. Therefore, it is the controlling opinion for the case. (See also plurality opinion.)

mandamus A writ (order) requiring a person to do what he should do. Sometimes called a mandatory injunction. See also injunction (court order).

mandatory sentence A sentence requiring, by statute, a defendant to be imprisoned for a period of time, allowing no (or little) discretion to the sentencing court. Often, these statutes provide that sentences may not be suspended and that probation and parole are not available to the offender.

master (court procedure) A person appointed by a court to assist in specified duties in a particular case. The duties to be performed are spelled out in an order and often include the gathering of facts and the taking of testimony. A master will then prepare a report of his actions for the court.

misdemeanor An offense usually punishable by incarceration in a local confinement facility (jail), for a period of which the upper limit is prescribed by statute in a given jurisdiction; the period is less than that of a felony and is typically limited to a year or less.

monitor A person who watches. In court proceedings, it is a type of master (see that definition) who is ordered to observe specified things and then to report those observations to the court.

moot A question that is unsettled, open to argument. In the law, a question not yet settled by judicial decisions. In common legal usage, it means an action or dispute has become uncontroversial, because the controlling issues or facts or questions have disappeared or become academic.

motion An oral or written request made by a party to any action, before, during, or after a trial, that a court issue a ruling or an order on any matter of procedure or substance related to the case.

motion to produce documents (court procedure) A method of discovery. A motion to obtain from the opposing side any documents that may be relevant to the case.

municipality A legally incorporated (or otherwise authorized) body of citizens, defined in a limited geographic area, organized for the purpose of local government. (May be in a particular state, city, town, borough, township, or village.)

N

negligence The failure to use such care as a reasonably prudent person would use under the same or similar circumstances. In the law, it is the doing of something that a prudent person would not have done, or the failure to do something that a prudent person would have done. It is the failure to live up to that standard of conduct that the law expects in order to protect other persons against unreasonable risk of harm.

nolo contendere Literally, no contest. A defendant's formal answer (plea) in court to the charges in a complaint, information, or indictment, in which he states that he does not contest the charges. Although it is not a legal admission of guilt, it subjects the defendant to the same legal consequences as a plea of guilty.

O

offender An adult who has been charged with (strictly, that person is an alleged offender) or convicted of a criminal offense.

officer (corrections) A corrections officer is a staff member in a corrections facility who is responsible for order and security in the facility and for the direct supervision of inmates. All of the corrections officers in the facility constitute the security force or the custody department. (Sometimes referred to as guard, but corrections officer is the preferred name, just as police officer is preferred to cop in law enforcement.)

opinion (court) The statement by a judge or a court of the decision reached in a case. It is usually given in writing and typically sets out the issue(s) presented in the case, the facts of the case, the law that applies, and the reasoning used to reach a conclusion or judgment. (See also dissent.)

order (court) A direction or command by a judge or court. The conclusion of a court on any motion or proceeding.

ordinance Broadly, the same as a law or a statute. Most often used to refer to a municipal statute, the enactment of the legislative body of a municipality.

P

pardon An executive act of grace that exempts an individual from the punishment the law inflicts for a crime he has committed. It may be issued as a full or a partial pardon, because it absolves all or a portion of the legal consequences of the crime. It may be absolute, or conditional, if it imposes a condition on the operation of the exemption.

parens patriae Literally, father (or parent) of the country. The concept that the king (the government) has protective responsibility for those who are not able to care for themselves, particularly children and mentally incompetent individuals.

parole The status of an offender who has been conditionally released from a confinement facility prior to the expiration of his sentence and placed under the supervision of a parole agency. The various aspects of parole—such as which inmates are eligible for parole and when, who is the paroling authority, the setting of parole standards (conditions), and the authority to revoke parole and to terminate parole—are defined by statute.

parole authority A correctional agency or a person who has the authority to release on parole adults or juveniles committed to confinement facilities, to revoke parole, and to discharge from parole. (Usually, the parole authority is a parole board or a parole commission.)

parole violation An act or a failure to act by a parolee that does not conform to the conditions of his parole and that may serve as grounds for the revocation of his parole.

parolee A person who has been conditionally released from a correctional institution prior to the expiration of his sentence and placed under the supervision of a parole agency.

penalty The punishment that is affixed by law or by judicial decision to the commission of a particular offense. It may be death, imprisonment (which may be a prison sentence or a jail sentence), an alternative facility sanction, a fine, restitution, or a loss of civil privileges. (Also called a sanction or punishment.)

penitentiary In the United States, a place of imprisonment (historically, for those sentenced to terms of imprisonment with hard labor; more recently, for adults sentenced for felonies or for long terms). A penitentiary is a type of prison that historically dates back to a time when "penitence" (religious reflection) was the prime element of confinement of adult offenders, which was based on the Auburn, New York, model. The name persists, usually in the titles of large facilities for high-security, long-term adult offenders.

per curiam Literally, by the court. Used to denote an opinion of the whole court, rather than one written (as is usual) by a particular judge. Often used for a brief announcement of the disposition of a case, without a full opinion.

person A human being or a group of human beings considered a legal unit, which has the lawful capacity to defend rights, to incur obligations, to prosecute and defend claims, or which can be prosecuted or adjudicated.

petition (juvenile) A document filed in juvenile court alleging that a juvenile is a delinquent, a status offender, or a dependent and asking that the court assume jurisdiction over the juvenile or asking that the juvenile be transferred to a criminal court for prosecution as an adult.

petition (legal proceeding) A document filed in a court having civil or general jurisdiction, asking that special relief within the jurisdiction of that court be granted. Used in habeas corpus proceedings as the document filed by a person who is in custody, asking for release from custody. Used in the Supreme Court as the document filed by a person requesting that the court issue a writ of certiorari, indicating that the case will be reviewed by that court.

petitioner The party who files a petition.

petty offense A minor criminal offense that is triable by a magistrate or subjudicial officer, without a jury. (The definition of the offenses so triable will be made by statute. In some places, it may include misdemeanors.)

plaintiff The party who initiates a civil action. The person who files a complaint in court. (Technically, also the prosecutor, the state, or the United States in a criminal action, but it is seldom used in that context.)

plea A defendant's formal answer in court to the criminal charges brought against him in a complaint, an information, or an indictment.

plurality opinion An opinion of an appellate court, in which less than a majority of the justices (or judges) join, but in which more join than in any other opinion of the court.

police officer See law enforcement officer.

population The collective group of persons in a given status. A sentenced population is the body of adjudicated persons moving from courts into correctional facilities. The population of a jail or prison is the total number of persons confined at that facility at a given time.

precedent A court decision that provides authoritative guidance or principle for a later case that has a similar question of law. A determination of a point of law made by a court, which is to be followed by a court of the same rank or of lower rank in a subsequent case that presents the same legal problem. (See stare decisis.)

preponderance of evidence Evidence that is of greater weight than that offered on the other side. It is more convincing, or more probable than not, when weighed by the trier of fact.

presentence report The document resulting from an investigation undertaken by a probation agency or other designated authority, at the request of a criminal court, into the past behavior, family circumstances, and personality of an adult who has been convicted of a crime, in order to assist the court in determining the most appropriate sentence. (For a juvenile, the same kind of report is called a predisposition report.)

presumption At law, a rule that certain facts give rise to a conclusion that is assumed to be true unless it is rebutted.

prima facie Literally, at first sight; on the face of it. A fact or matter presumed to be true, unless it is disproved by some evidence to the contrary.

prison A confinement facility having custodial authority over adults sentenced to confinement for more than a year. An adult correctional institution is another name for the same type of facility. See also penitentiary.

prisoner A person (either sentenced or unsentenced) in custody in a confinement facility, or in the personal custody of a criminal justice official while being transported from, to, or between confinement facilities.

prisoners' rights Those privileges and rights that are legally, and especially constitutionally, retained by and guaranteed to inmates of correctional facilities.

privacy (records) The principles and procedures developed to ensure the security and confidentiality of record information relating to individuals, in order to protect the privacy of the persons identified in those records.

privatization The performance of governmental function by private enterprise (a nongovernmental person or corporation). The performance is arranged for by the government through contract or other agreement.

probable cause A set of facts and circumstances that would induce a reasonably intelligent and prudent person to believe that an accused person had committed a specific offense.

probation The conditional freedom granted by a judicial officer to an alleged offender or an adjudicated adult or juvenile, as long as the person meets certain conditions of behavior, for a given period of time. The conditions and period of time are set by the judicial officer. The offender is released into the community, under the supervision of a probation officer.

probation (sentence) Probation given by a sentencing judge, requiring that a defendant fulfill certain conditions of behavior and accept the supervision of a probation agency. It is usually given in lieu of a sentence of confinement (along with a suspension of the execution of a sentence of confinement or with a suspension of the imposition of a sentence of confinement), although sometimes it is used along with (in addition to) a jail sentence. (As a rule, probation is tied to the suspension of a sentence; whenever a sentence is suspended, the defendant should be placed on probation.)

probation agency A correctional agency of which the principal functions are the supervision of adults or juveniles who are placed on probation status and the investigation of adults or juveniles for the purpose of preparing presentence or predisposition reports to assist the court in determining the proper sentence (for adults) or the proper disposition (for juveniles).

probation officer An employee of a probation agency whose primary duties include one or more of the probation agency functions.

probation violation An act or a failure to act by a probationer that does not conform to the conditions of his probation. (It may be a grounds for revocation of probation—see that definition.)

probationer A person required by a court or probation agency to meet certain conditions of behavior as required by a sentence or disposition of probation.

procedural law Methods of proceeding, typically in a court, by which a legal right or duty is enforced. Distinguished from substantive law, which defines the rights, responsibilities, and duties of persons.

process A broad term for any action by a court, usually in writing.

pro se Acting as one's own attorney in legal or administrative proceedings.

prosecutor An attorney employed by a government agency or subunit, whose official duty is to initiate and pursue criminal proceedings on behalf of the government against persons accused of committing criminal offenses.

public defender An attorney employed by a government agency or subunit, whose official duty is to represent criminal defendants who are unable to hire private counsel.

punishment See penalty.

purge The complete removal of arrest, criminal, or juvenile record information from a given records system.

R

reasonable suspicion A set of facts (used as the standard, for example, to stop a suspected offender in a public place) that would lead a prudent person under the circumstances to believe criminal activity is present.

rebut To defeat, refute, or take away the effect of something. To contradict or deny, by facts or argument.

recidivist (recidivism) A repeat offender. One who habitually commits crimes.

reformatory A correctional institution that is intended as a place of confinement for persons convicted of crimes of a less serious nature (and sometimes only for persons of a youthful age), who appear to be amenable to reformation by a course of treatment, education, work, and discipline during their confinement.

regulation An order by competent authority, most often an agency of the executive branch, setting rules for actions that are under the agency's control.

rehabilitation Restoring an offender to a law-abiding lifestyle. In penology (sentencing philosophy), rehabilitation refers to the theory that a purpose of sentencing is to help the offender live a crime-free life in the community. To that end, a corrections agency is expected to have rehabilitation programs, which improve the offender's prospects of being a productive and law-abiding citizen.

release (corrections) The authorized, lawful exit from detention or confinement facilities of persons subject to criminal or juvenile proceedings (detention) or those serving sentences (confinement facilities).

release on bail The release, by a judicial officer, of an accused person who has been taken into custody, upon his promise to pay a certain sum of money if he fails to appear in court as required, the promise of which may or may not be secured by the deposit of an actual sum of money or property.

release on own recognizance The release, by a judicial officer, of an accused person who has been taken into custody, upon his promise to appear in court as required for criminal proceedings. Also known as ROR (Release on Recognizance).

relief (court procedure) A broad term used to describe the assistance, redress, or benefit that a complainant wishes to receive from a court. Examples are orders of injunction, declaratory relief, and money damages.

remand To send back. To return the person or matter to the place from which it came.

requests for admissions (court procedure) A method of discovery. Written statements of facts about a case; these statements are formally sent to the opposing party, who is asked to admit or deny that certain facts are true. Those which are admitted usually will be accepted by the court as having been established and as not requiring proof at trial.

rescission The abrogation, annulment, or cancellation of a contract. Nullifying a contract or an action, to put an end to it, as if it never took place.

residential treatment center An alternative means of disposition or sentencing in a government facility that provides less strict controls than a training school (for juveniles) or a confinement facility (for adults), usually allowing the offenders greater contact with the community.

respondent The party who files a response.

response The pleading filed by the respondent in an equity action. An answer to a petition (such as a petition for a writ of habeas corpus) or other proceeding in equity or to a petition (for writ of certiorari) in the Supreme Court.

restitution Compensation or reparation by one person for loss or injury caused to another. In criminal law, a court sanction requiring restoration by the offender to a person of that of which he has been wrongfully deprived, or payment by the offender of some monetary amount to the wronged person (victim) to compensate for injury or loss caused by criminal conduct.

retained counsel An attorney who is not employed by a government agency for indigents or assigned by the court, but who is privately hired to represent a person in a legal proceeding.

retribution In sentencing philosophy, the theory that every crime deserves a concomitant punishment.

reverse To overturn by contrary judgment or decision. To set aside, repeal, or revoke. A reversal occurs when a superior court sets aside, overturns or reverses the decision of a lower court.

revocation Generally, the recall of some power or the voiding of something that has been granted. An administrative act by a parole authority removing a person from parole, or a judicial order by a court removing a person from probation in response to a violation on the part of the parolee or the probationer.

revocation hearing An administrative (parole) or judicial (probation) hearing on the question of whether a person's probation or parole status should be revoked.

rights of defendants Those powers and privileges that are legally, and especially constitutionally, guaranteed to every criminal defendant.

runaway A juvenile who has committed the status offense of leaving the custody and home of his parents, guardians, or custodians without permission and failing to return within a reasonable length of time.

S

sanction See penalty.

sanity Soundness of mind. In criminal law, the opposite of insanity (see that definition).

scope of employment The boundaries that define the actions that an employee (or agent) is expected to perform and the manner in which those actions are to be performed.

seal (records) The removal, for the benefit of the individual, of arrest, criminal, or juvenile record information from routinely available status to a status requiring special procedures (usually approval by a judicial authority) for access.

search The close examination of a person, their house, or other property for the purpose of discovering any contraband, illicit property, or evidence of criminal activity. The act of looking for anything that offends against the law (by law enforcement officials) or against misconduct codes (by corrections officers).

search warrant A written order, issued by a judicial officer, authorizing the search and seizure of property, for evidence of criminal activity, including illicit goods and the fruits of crime.

security (corrections) The degree of restriction of inmate movement and the degree of custodial controls over inmates within a correctional facility, usually divided into maximum, medium, and minimum levels (of security).

segregation (corrections) The separation of inmates in correctional facilities from the regular population. It is usually done for disciplinary reasons, but it may be done for a variety of other administrative reasons such as awaiting transfer, for protection, or pending investigation. Also used to denote the place (the separate unit) in a facility where inmates are housed separately and under tighter control. This place is known in different facilities as disciplinary detention, administrative detention, punitive detention, segregation, isolation, and (colloquially) the hole.

seizure The act of taking possession of property, usually from the possession of another person.

sentence (criminal law) The penalty (sanction) imposed by a court on a convicted person. This includes a court decision to suspend (defer) the imposition or the execution of a penalty and place the defendant on probation.

sentence, mandatory A statutory requirement that a certain penalty, a certain minimum penalty, or a penalty with severe restrictions (such as no parole eligibility) shall be imposed and executed upon certain convicted offenders.

separation of powers A principle of government that divides powers and responsibilities between separate branches of the government, such as the legislative, executive and judicial branches.

sentence, suspended The court decision of either postponing the pronouncing of sentence upon a convicted person or postponing the execution of a sentence that has been pronounced by the court.

shakedown (corrections) Vernacular in correctional facilities for the search of a person or place.

show cause order An order to appear and to give reasons to the court why a particular order contemplated by or requested from the court should not be entered or executed. An order to explain to the court why a proposed action should not be taken.

slander Defamation (see that definition) by spoken words.

sovereign The person (ruler) or body (government) in which supreme authority is vested. Sovereign immunity is the immunity (see that definition) of the sovereign from liability.

stare decisis Literally, to stand by decisions. This is the legal doctrine that courts will adhere to principles settled by court decisions in other cases in which the facts are substantially the same. It is a strong judicial policy that a point of law that is determined in a court will be followed by that court, or a court of lower rank, in a later case that presents the same legal question.

status offender A juvenile who has been adjudicated by a judicial officer of a juvenile court as having committed a status offense, which is an act or conduct that is an offense only when committed or engaged in by a juvenile (that is, it would not be a crime if committed by an adult).

statute An act of a legislature declaring, commanding, or prohibiting something.

statutory law The body of law created by the acts of the legislatures.

subjudicial officer A judicial officer who is invested with certain limited judicial powers and functions but whose decisions in criminal or other cases are usually subject to de novo review by a judge.

subpoena A written order issued by a judicial officer requiring a specified person to appear in a designated court at a specified time in order to serve as a witness in a case under the jurisdiction of that court or to bring material (documents, etc.) to that court.

substantial evidence Evidence that a reasoning mind would accept as sufficient to support a particular conclusion. (It is more than a *scintilla* of evidence, but it may be less than a *preponderance* of the evidence.)

substantive law The whole area of the law that creates and defines legal rights and obligations. Distinguished from procedural law, which is the methods of proceeding by which a legal right or duty is enforced.

summary judgment The court's disposition of a case summarily—that is, without the need for a trial. Based on the facts shown in the pleadings and by affidavits, a court's determination that judgment can be entered before trial because the facts necessary to decide the case are already clearly presented and are not controverted, so that trial (which is intended to resolve disputed facts) is unnecessary.

summons A written order issued by a judicial officer requiring a person accused of a criminal offense to appear in a designated court at a specified time to answer a charge. Also, an order in a civil case to respond or answer in court.

superintendent In corrections, the person in charge of a correctional facility. In most places, it is used as the title for the manager of a lower security correctional facility. (Similar to warden—see that definition.)

supreme court An appellate court at the highest level in most states and in the federal court system. The court of last resort in the particular jurisdiction. The U.S. Supreme Court is the highest court in the federal court system and the highest court in the nation.

suspect A person considered by a criminal justice agency to be one who may have committed a specific criminal offense but who has not been arrested or charged.

suspend To postpone, delay, or discontinue. A suspended sentence is one that is imposed but not executed.

suspicion The belief that a person has committed a criminal offense, based on facts and circumstances that are insufficient to constitute probable cause.

T

time served The time spent in confinement by a convicted person until a given date or until the date of release. (Sometimes used to refer only to the time spent in a confinement facility after a sentence is imposed.)

toll To suspend or stop the requirements of any law.

tort A wrong. An injury to the person or property of another, outside of any contractual agreement. A breach of duty that the law (by statute or by common law) has said is owed to another person. (Some acts may be either crimes or torts or both—crimes are offenses against the public, whereas torts are injuries to private persons, which may be pursued in civil courts.)

training school A correctional institution for juveniles adjudicated to be delinquents or status offenders and committed to confinement by a judicial officer.

transfer (corrections) The movement of an inmate from one facility to another.

transfer to adult court The decision by a juvenile court, resulting from a transfer hearing, that jurisdiction over an alleged delinquent will be waived by the juvenile court and that the individual should be prosecuted as an adult in a criminal court.

trial The examination of issues of fact and law in a case or controversy, beginning when the jury has been selected in a jury trial, when the first witness is sworn, or when the first evidence is introduced in a court trial, and concluding when a verdict is reached or the case is dismissed.

trial by judge (court trial) A trial in which there is no jury and in which a judicial officer determines the issues of fact as well as the law in the case. Also called a bench trial.

trial by jury (jury trial) A trial in which a jury determines the issues of fact in a case and renders a verdict.

trial court A judicial officer who is authorized to conduct trials. (Usually used to distinguish from appeals courts.)

V

vacate To cancel, set aside, annul (declare of no validity).

venue The geographic area from which the jury is drawn and in which the trial is held in a criminal case. More broadly, the place (county, city, district) where a case is to be tried. Today, the proper venue for an action is set by statute, with the possibility for it to be changed by agreement of the parties or by court order upon application of a party. (Not to be confused with jurisdiction, which may not be changed by consent or waiver.)

verdict In criminal proceedings, the decision made by a jury (in a jury trial) or by a judicial officer (in a court trial) that a defendant is either guilty or not guilty of the offense for which he has been tried. In civil proceedings, the decision made by a jury or by a judicial officer in favor of the claim of the plaintiff or the counterclaim or defense of the defendant.

victim A person who has suffered death, physical or mental suffering, or loss of property as the result of an actual or attempted criminal offense committed by another person.

W

waiver The relinquishing of a known right. The abandonment of a claim, right, or privilege.

waiver of summons A process authorized in federal courts and some state courts allowing a plaintiff to request the defendant to waive service of the summons, eliminating some costs of the litigation. A defendant who waives service of summons is still required to respond or answer to the complaint.

ward A person placed under the care of a guardian as a consequence of being legally unable to manage his own affairs. Used especially in juvenile law, meaning a child who is under special protection of the state or a juvenile court.

warden Historically, a guardian; a keeper of wards. Today, used principally as the title of the person in charge (the chief executive officer) of a correctional facility. (In many jurisdictions, used for the title of such a person in a maximum or medium security facility, whereas superintendent is used for lower security facilities.)

warrant, arrest A document issued by a judicial officer that directs a law enforcement officer to arrest a person who has been accused of an offense.

warrant, bench A document issued by a judicial officer directing that a person (who has failed to obey a notice or a court order to appear in court) be brought before the court.

warrant, search A document issued by a judicial officer that directs a law enforcement officer to conduct a search for specified property or persons at a specific location, to seize the property or persons, if found, and to account for the results of the search to the issuing judicial officer.

withholding (good-time withholding) See good time.

witness A person who directly perceives an event or thing or who has expert knowledge relevant to a case. Also, such a person who is called to testify in a hearing or trial.

work release A correctional program that allows an inmate to leave a facility for the purpose of working in the community during the day but requires him to return to the facility for nights and weekends (for all nonworking hours). Similarly, study release allows the same kind of leave for attendance at educational activities in the community.

writ A written judicial order requiring a specified act to be performed or to be refrained from.

Y

youthful offender A person, adjudicated in criminal court, who is above the statutory age limit for juveniles but is below a specified upper age limit set by statute, for whom special correctional commitments (often indeterminate in nature), release supervision, and record-sealing procedures are made available by statute.

Table of Cases

These are the cases that are discussed and cited in this book. Decisions of the U.S. Supreme Court are in **bold** print. Decisions of all other courts are in regular print. References are to pages in this book. If a case appears at more than one place in the book, the number in **bold** print indicates where a principal discussion of that case is located.

Index